economics: the science of scarcity

THE DRYDEN PRESS, INC.

HINSDALE, ILLINOIS

HEINZ KOHLER AMHERST COLLEGE

economics

the science of scarcity

Copyright © 1970 by The Dryden Press, Inc.
All rights reserved
Library of Congress Catalogue Card Number: 74-96848
SBN: 03-078195-7
Printed in the United States of America
Design by Lynn Braswell
01234   19   987654321

preface

WHY THIS BOOK WAS WRITTEN

I believe economics to be an exciting subject. In the United States hundreds of thousands of students are introduced to it every year. Yet it is my guess that most of them find it boring and dismally complicated. They are glad when it is over. They have not caught a glimpse of the enjoyment they might have had from the study of economics.

This probably happened because they were deluged with a mass of incoherent detail, which was designed to lay the groundwork for the training of professional economists. But most of those taking their first economics course will never take another one. Material that might be useful later on in an advanced course serves no purpose for these students but first to be crammed and then handed back at examinations. No wonder excitement is missing.

To make matters worse, beginners are typically swamped with language which contributes to confusion instead of understanding. At exams, they can hide behind the bulwark of jargon while actually knowing nothing at all.

Ask them, a few weeks after the final exam, about a simple news report on economic events, and they cannot grasp its significance or even understand its meaning. But there is no need for thousands of students to be dismissed from even a brief, single course study of economics, still unable to recognize or analyze some of the most important issues of our time. Some of these issues, after all, involve the peace and welfare of mankind. But students are so dismissed, devoid of lasting knowledge, or unable to communicate to others what they do know. It is hoped that this book will help make an end to this state of affairs.

AN IMPORTANT FIRST LESSON

Some of the trouble cannot be solved except by way of exhortation. It lies in the attitude with which students and teachers approach the study of economics. We are all human. Whether we choose to believe it or not, we are driven more by emotion than by anything else.

This very effectively hinders our understanding of the world we wish to study. We are likely to have formed certain images of the world and are equally likely not to want them disturbed.

Consider how many people, though they have never studied economics, "know" that another stock market crash would usher in another Great Depression, that money must be backed by gold to retain its value, that government deficits cannot help but devalue the dollar, that a perpetually growing national debt must lead to national bankruptcy, that city problems can be solved with more money, or that socialism is bound to be inefficient (and capitalism is not). These are topics discussed in newspapers and magazines, on radio and television, over lunch with one's friends, and even in eloquent speeches by prominent people on the Senate floor.

Yet all these statements are wrong. They are typical of the hearsay and half-truths which dominate our minds as we approach the study of economics; typical of what makes this study so much more difficult. As Will Rogers is said to have put it, "The trouble isn't what people don't know, it's what they do know that isn't so."

This is the first lesson even the occasional student of economics has to learn: we do not know the truth by instinct. What we regard now as fantastic may in fact turn out to be true. What seems natural and obvious, such as the flatness of the earth, can easily be wrong. Unless we are willing to expose ourselves to new points of view, to engage in dialogue rather than to preach and self-justify, we cannot learn anything.

HOW THIS BOOK IS TRYING TO HELP

Unless this first lesson has been learned, this book cannot hope to accomplish anything. But if we approach the study of economics with an open mind, the second major cause of difficulty, the incoherent presentation of the subject and the concentration on jargon and technical details, is much easier to overcome. Textbook and teacher can excite a student in his initial exposure to economics by concentrating on *important matters* and *presenting them clearly and in logical sequence*. This book will try to do just that.

This book has been constructed by taking a series of economic problems, selected from those typically found in any major newspaper within the span of almost any week. These problems have been used as the raw material for the discussion of economics. Note the reports and selections introducing the chapters. These materials certainly deal with the kind of topics that anyone who has ever come in contact with economics should be able to understand and, if the occasion arises, explain to someone else. Thus the kinds of issues habitually treated by the press or government reports have been selected as "important" for purposes of this text.

No attempt was made to include materials just because they have always been included in the textbooks. This book does not aim to give encyclopedic detail or to train professional economists. On the other hand, the "important" materials selected have not been presented in disorderly fashion. They have been put in a certain sequence that facilitates understanding and that brings out clearly the structure of economic science. Since economics deals with the elimination of scarcity, the everyday problems treated in this book have been sorted out and placed under four major headings:

1. How can we reduce scarcity by using resources fully?
2. How can we reduce scarcity by using resources in economically efficient ways?
3. How can we reduce scarcity by enlarging our productive capacity?
4. What can we say about the ways in which we share our output?

All these matters are discussed, furthermore, in language that any person willing to pay attention to can understand. I know from my own students that both concentration on essentials and understandable language are prerequisites for lasting enjoyment and knowledge.

A NOTE OF THANKS

There are many to whom I am greatly indebted. Foremost among these are untold numbers of my students who insisted on getting it right and who forced me to improve upon my presentation. Further, I am particularly grateful to Professors Daniel Feinberg of New York Community College, Bernard J. McCarney of Illinois State University, Daniel Orr of the University of California, John Tower of Oakland University, and Norman Townshend-Zellner of the Center for Education (Director) and California State College, Fullerton, all of whose suggestive and stimulating reviews of the manuscript were immensely helpful in preparing the final draft. They are, of course, in no way responsible for any present shortcomings of the book. There is also the editor, Milton S. Mautner, with whom I worked most closely in drafting this text. Many of his suggestions have proved very valuable, indeed. I feel very grateful toward him. I am also indebted in many small ways to my colleagues at Amherst College, and to Amherst College for providing me with a most congenial atmosphere in which to learn, teach, and write.

Most of all, I must thank Mrs. Eleanor Starzyk who did the lion's share of typing and retyping what must have seemed like interminable drafts.

HEINZ KOHLER

Amherst, Massachusetts
December 1969

a note to the teacher

Although authors have a certain self-interest in making this claim, this book really *is* different from all others presently available in the field of introductory economics. It is different, furthermore, not just for the sake of being different, but in order to bring about a genuine improvement in the teaching of elementary economics.

There are three things new about this book. First, this book concentrates on major problems. Second, this book has a theme. Third, this book looks at the whole world.

THIS BOOK CONCENTRATES ON MAJOR PROBLEMS

The audience for which this book is mainly written are the great numbers of students who take one and only one course in economics. As has been pointed out in the Preface, it would be a pity if this one exposure to our subject failed to make any significant and favorable impact. We cannot reasonably hope to raise the degree of economic literacy attained if we act in the introductory course as if we were teaching future professionals. Mostly we are not. What most students need is a view of the general outlines of economic science. They do not need to know about the intricacies. If this one exposure to economics is to serve any useful function at all, students must be given the ability to discern and confront the major economic issues, and only the major ones. As was also pointed out in the Preface, what are "important" issues has mostly been decided on the basis of the issues typically covered in the recent past in the press or government reports. About these, and only these issues, our students will continue to read in the newspapers and magazines of the future. These are the issues that they will want to discuss with others even after this course has come and gone. These are the issues on which they will have to act as voting citizens. Scan through the book and look at the various selections introducing the chapters. Few will fail to agree that these are indeed the major economic issues of the 1970's. By the same token, most will agree that the issues not found in the daily press and the deliberations of governments and therefore not found in this book—however much room is devoted to them in traditional texts—are not the important ones.

THIS BOOK HAS A THEME

It is, of course, the privilege of every author to order the material at hand. This has been done here. Rather than present problem after problem without showing whether and how things hang together, the selected materials have been ordered under the main theme of our discipline, the theme of *overcoming scarcity*. By picking up this theme in the very beginning and never letting it out of sight, the chances of student comprehension are further enhanced. Not only are the issues discussed the major economic issues of our day, but they are also placed into an easily remembered logical framework. Chapters 1 and 2 are introductory. They illustrate the nature of the economic problem and of our kind of economic system. This is followed by a division of the text into four major parts.

We can try to meet the challenge of scarcity, argues Part 1, by using given resources fully. Part 2 shows the additional possibilities inherent in paying attention to economic efficiency. Part 3 explores the issue of economic growth, of breaking out of the limitations imposed by *given* resources. Finally, Part 4 reminds us of the importance of sharing wisely whatever output we have managed to produce.

Within each of these major parts, great emphasis is placed on logical coherence. Chapter 3, which introduces Part 1, brings to life the nature of the unemployment problem. It looks back into our history, but it also looks at the lives of the unemployed in our midst today. If we do not like what we see, continues the chapter, we must agree on the meaning of certain terms. This enables us to gather data and study the facts about unemployment. It also makes us aware of different types of unemployment.

Not any less serious to our economic well-being, continues Chapter 4, is the problem of inflation. Again, as would-be policy makers, who want to put an end to this unwelcome erosion of the value of the dollar, we must know the facts. As a preliminary to policy, we must be able to measure changes in the price level. We must distinguish different types of inflation.

Almost inadvertently, Chapters 3 and 4 have set the stage for dealing with the problems discussed. The concepts of aggregate supply and aggregate demand have crept into the discussion. They are developed more fully in Chapters 5 and 6, respectively. As a natural sequel, in Chapter 7, the classical and Keynesian explanations of the actual levels of output, employment, and prices are contrasted and the latter is fully developed.

Chapter 8 is optional. It is somewhat unorthodox for the elementary level. It describes and analyzes business cycles and forecasting with the help of an accelerator-multiplier model, presented with a simple numerical example. I have found that students can gain a great deal by being made aware of the dynamic questions usually ignored in the Keynesian comparative static approach. Their interest also is likely to pick up greatly when the question of forecasting is discussed. Since we always draw policy conclusions from the Keynesian analysis, I think we owe it to our students (time permitting) to make them see that, quite apart from repeated autonomous changes in the real world, there may also be other reasons that prevent the economy from reaching, in reality, a new equilibrium GNP. This is shown with the use of period analysis which, although not true dynamics, is a step beyond comparative statics that elementary students are quite capable of taking. Being so prepared, they will have a much more realistic view of the possibilities of economic policy, and they will not be surprised that in reality things do not work out as easily as in the textbook. Teachers will note that the "dynamic" discussion of Chapter 8 is fully integrated with the comparative static discussion of Chapter 7. They will also note, however, that Chapter 8 can be omitted without any difficulty.

Having thus been prepared, through Chapter 7 or, more elaborately, through Chapters 7 and 8, policy conclusions are presented to the student: monetary policy in Chapter 10, following a general introduction to money and banking in Chapter 9; and fiscal policy in Chapter 12, following a similar general treatment of government spending and taxing in Chapter 11. Teachers who are so inclined may terminate the discussion of full employment at this point. All of the remaining Chapters of Part 1 (Chapters 13 through 17) are optional.

Chapter 13 on the national debt is an elaboration on fiscal policy. Therefore, it can be omitted easily. Again, however, inclusion of the subject is likely to enhance student interest.

Chapter 14 is optional also, because it further elaborates on the possible effects of policy. Having been shown how fiscal-monetary policies may attempt to reach full employment without demand inflation, students are now already aware of some of their limitations: The public may resist such policies, policy makers may make mistakes, the dynamics of the situation may preclude victory. Worse yet, states Chapter 14, there are other obstacles: chronic unemployment as well as cost-push inflation may not be responsive to such policies *at all*. We have to face the trade-off along the Phillips curve. Optional Chapter 15 delves even more deeply into the problem: balance of payments considerations may circumscribe the freedom of policy makers. Hence there is, in these two chapters, a discussion of federal programs to increase labor mobility, of wage-price guideposts, of exchange rates, and the international monetary mechanism. By presenting these problems in this way, students will see their relevance to the main issue of fighting scarcity.

Optional Chapters 16 and 17 talk about full employment in the Soviet economy. They are commented upon in the next section.

Chapter 18, in Part 2, takes up the issue of "big" business and antitrust laws. As such, it is an example of the relevance of microeconomics to the main issue of overcoming scarcity. With the simplest of examples it is shown how scarcity might be decreased still further, without the use of additional resources, after full employment has been reached. Without burdening the student at all with the morass of technical detail that is usually presented at this point, a clear idea is given of the concept of economic efficiency. This general idea is reinforced three times: in Chapter 19 through a discussion of agriculture, in optional Chapter 20 through a discussion of labor unions, and in Chapter 21 through a discussion of the free trade argument. Chapter 22, finally draws the policy conclusions for the United States economy. Although highly recommended, it may be omitted. An honest answer is given. Economists do not know how to measure the degree of economic efficiency prevailing. They do not know what difference antitrust and similar policies make in the fight against scarcity. Students, however, know why economists are interested in these matters, why they continue to be front-page news.

Chapter 23, also optional, deals with economic efficiency in the socialist economy. It is commented on below.

Part 3 continues the theme of the book. It examines the importance of economic growth. The possibilities involved here are brought out clearly in Chapter 24 which deals with United States economic growth only. Very valuable extensions of this theme are made in the following two chapters on economic growth in the Soviet Union (Chapter 25) and in the underdeveloped countries (Chapter 26). But the latter two chapters are optional. Those pressed for time may omit them.

Part 4 addresses itself to the burning question of how we should share our output. All students should read the two chapters given here. Although GNP may be higher than ever due to our full and efficient use of our growing productive capacity, argues Part 4, we may be in serious trouble. Income inequality and poverty may tear the nation apart, Chapter 27 shows. The relentless pursuit of private satisfaction may starve the public sector of the means to deal with the side effects of these private actions. As Chapter 28 attempts to show, this is nowhere more obvious than in the current crisis of this urban society. Ultimately, slums, traffic congestion, and the pollution of our environment are nothing else but the consequence of our unwillingness to share our output wisely.

THIS BOOK LOOKS AT THE WHOLE WORLD

Comparative economic systems has traditionally been treated as a sort of appendix. Although the material remains optional here, it is fully integrated with the theme.

This book is not content with a final chapter on the socialist economy. To show students that the *same* economic problem haunts the whole of mankind and that there are *many* ways of dealing with it, there is not only discussion of underdeveloped countries (Chapter 26), but there are also four chapters on the Soviet-type economy. They form an integral part of this book. This has been done because such a study can immeasurably increase the understanding of the economic issues facing the *United States* type economy. It has also been done because students are extremely interested in the subject, being quite aware that the United States-Soviet confrontation is likely to be a major issue for many years to come.

Chapter 16, for example, introduces the nature of central planning. The discussion of input-output analysis in this chapter is ideally suited to review the discussion in previous chapters of the nature of the price system, of intermediate versus final goods, of the two ways of measuring GNP, and so on. The material can also be used later, in the discussion of economic development, to show why central planning does not have to be synonymous with government ownership of resources and physical commands. This chapter allows a much deeper understanding of the magnificent work of a price system, since it emphasizes the enormous interdependence of an economy and the difficulties of dealing with it centrally.

Chapter 17 presents a discussion of actual Soviet planning, of Soviet GSP (gross social product), and of the Soviet experience with unemployment and inflation. All this can be used for review of similar earlier discussions of the United States. In this way, students can become increasingly aware of the importance of definitions, why they are all arbitrary, yet not unreasonable, and why they may differ over space and time. (This theme is continued throughout the book, covering such subjects as unemployment, money supply, balance of payments deficit, underdevelopment, poverty, and so on.) Students will be much less tempted to make unjustifiable international comparisons in the later discussion of Soviet versus United States growth or of underdevelopment.

Chapter 23, superficially, does nothing more than develop the Lange model of competitive socialism and relate to it present Soviet decentralization reforms. Naturally, these are of great interest to students. On a deeper level, the chapter does much more. It reinforces the understanding of perfect competition and its efficiency. It teaches the important distinction between market prices and prices in the generic sense and why the latter are essential guides in practice for efficient resource use anywhere. And such treatment seems eminently preferable to that obscure confusing appendix on "do we need interest and rent in socialism?"

Finally, Chapter 25 discusses the fascinating Soviet example of achieving rapid growth. (This is reinforced by a Chinese-Indian case study in Chapter 26.) However, those who have neither time nor desire to use the four "Soviet" chapters can easily omit them. The remainder of the text is still an integrated whole.

SUPPORTING MATERIALS

As a quick look at the Table of Contents will show, this book has cut out a great many topics found in other introductory texts. As was noted above, this has been deliberate. The idea has been to aim the book at the student, not the teacher, and to leave out everything not relevant to the major economic issues of our day. Alternative ways of saying the same thing have also been omitted.

The accompanying *Instructor's Manual,* however, points out when and where teachers might introduce additional materials if they feel this is desirable. It also shows which sections *within* nonoptional chapters may be omitted. The Manual also contains detailed comments on each chapter and the likely pedagogical problems encountered, as well as many test items (True-False, Multiple Choice, and Discussion Questions). There are also answers to all of the text questions for review and discussion.

My *Readings in Economics,* 2nd edition (New York: Holt, Rinehart, and Winston, 1969) also brings together a great deal of material which can be used, as the teacher wishes, to supplement or expand upon the text.

Finally, note the availability of a *programmed Study Guide* which is a self-help device for students. It warns of the major difficulties likely to be encountered. It takes students through the entire text in easy step-by-step fashion, allowing them to test themselves.

ALTERNATIVE PRESENTATIONS

Some teachers undoubtedly will prefer to change the sequence in which the material is presented here. Others may want to shorten the course. Both of these options are available. The following table outlines some of the possibilities.

BASIC COURSE	EXPANDED COURSE
1. Chapters 1 and 2 for introduction	The basic course, but:
2. Chapters 3–7, 9–12 and 24 for "macro"	add any of these: 8, 13–17, 25, 26
3. Chapters 18, 19, 21, 27, and 28 for "micro"	add any of these: 20, 22, 23

NOTE: The "macro-micro" sequence, whether basic or expanded, is interchangeable.

Recommended for a *one-semester course:* the basic course plus those optional chapters found suitable by the instructor.

Recommended for a *two-semester course:* the expanded course minus those optional chapters not found suitable by the instructor.

Recommended for a *quarter course:* chapters 1 and 2, plus the basic macro sequence *or* chapters 1 and 2, plus the basic micro sequence.

a guide to the student

Some students may be unfamiliar with the use of graphs which are most useful in a study of economics. Their meaning and use is described in this section.

There is nothing difficult about graphs. They are only shorthand ways of presenting information which could be described more laboriously in words or in tabular form. Graphs are drawn on squared paper, as in Figure A THE SYSTEM OF COORDINATES. The paper is divided by a horizontal axis, such as line *xx′* (also called the *abscissa*), and a vertical axis, such as line *yy′* (also called the *ordinate*) into four "quadrants," labeled I through IV. Note that the two axes intersect at right angles at a point called the *origin*, and always labeled 0. Each axis has a scale of numerical values. On the vertical scale, or ordinate, all values above 0 are positive, those below 0 are negative. On the horizontal scale, or abscissa, all values to the right of 0 are positive, those to the left are negative. The origin thus counts as zero.

The whole of Figure A is called the *system of coordinates*.

We have drawn Figure A so that equal distances from 0 on both the horizontal and vertical axes represent equal units (each small square both horizontally and vertically equals one unit). But it does not have to be this way. In fact, the horizontal and vertical axes often use different units of measurement (see Figure B). The important thing is that once the unit of measurement has been chosen for either the horizontal or vertical axis, it must remain consistent for that axis. We may label the fifth unit toward x′ on the horizontal axis 3,000 if we like, but then the tenth unit must be 6,000 (instead of 10), the fifteenth 9,000 (instead of 15).

In this book we will mostly be concerned with relationships among variables which lie in the first quadrant (I). On rare occasions we make use also of the fourth quadrant (IV). That is, one of the variables will always be positive (measured from 0 toward x′), while the other may be positive (0 toward y′) or occasionally negative (0 toward y). Thus you will never find any graphs containing quadrants II and III. Most of them, in fact, will only contain quadrant I.

Let us be specific. Suppose we want to graph the information found in Table A THE SUPPLY OF APPLES.

We proceed by putting the two column headings on the axes of a graph. It is perfectly arbitrary which column heading goes on which axis. However, let us follow tradition and put price on the vertical axis. Then we choose any convenient units of measurement for the axes. Since all data in Table A are positive, we only need to draw the first quadrant. This has been done in Figure B PREPARING THE GRAPH.

The next step involves locating the five sets of price-quantity data given in the table. This is akin to finding the location of a geographic point on a map from given longitude and lati-

Figure A   THE SYSTEM OF COORDINATES

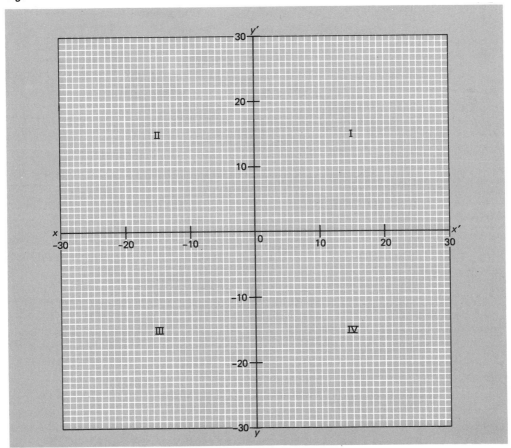

a guide to the student

Table A   THE SUPPLY OF APPLES

PRICE (CENTS PER POUND)	QUANTITY OF APPLES OFFERED FOR SALE (POUNDS PER DAY)
10	5
20	10
30	15
40	20
50	25

Figure B   PREPARING THE GRAPH

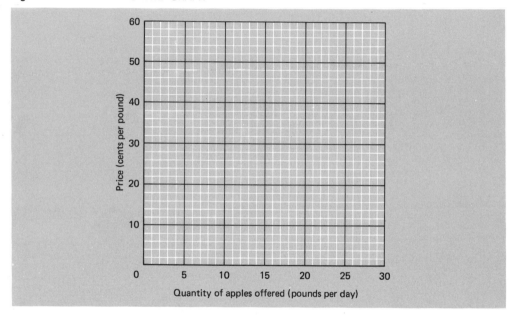

Quantity of apples offered (pounds per day)

tude information. As in Figure C FINDING POINTS IN A GRAPH we can draw perpendiculars from the relevant points on the two axes; their meeting point is a point on our graph. For example, to graph the 10 cent–5 lb. combination, we draw a perpendicular across the vertical axis at 10 cents and across the horizontal axis at 5 lb. They meet at P. We proceed in the same way for all other points for which we have specific information.

If we can be sure that the same relationship between price and quantity offered also holds between those points (that, numerically, price *always* equals double quantity as it does in Table A), we can connect all points in Figure C by a straight line and conclude, for instance, that 12.5 lb. would be offered at a price of 25 cents. (Can you locate the point?) The finished graph is shown below as Figure D THE FINISHED GRAPH—APPLE SUPPLY.

Figure C FINDING POINTS IN A GRAPH

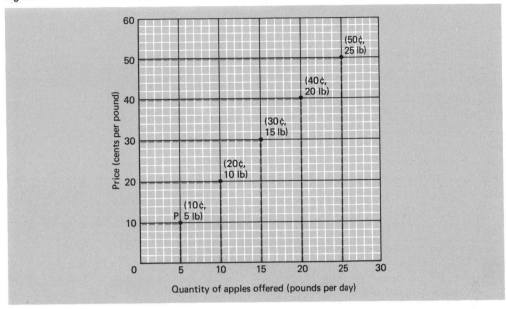

Figure D THE FINISHED GRAPH—APPLE SUPPLY

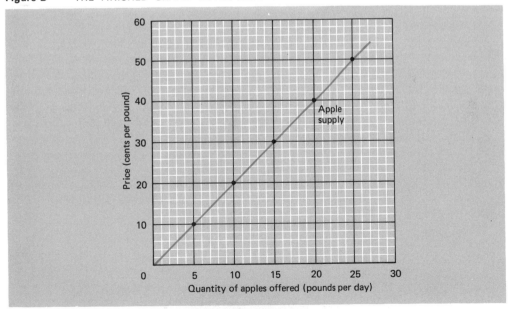

All graphs in this book are representations, as is Figure D, of numerical data, as in Table A. Just look at the labels on the axes (and if you ever graph anything, do not forget to put in the labels), and you will know what the column headings of the corresponding table must have been.

SIMPLE TIME SERIES GRAPHS

Many graphs encountered in this book are so-called time series graphs. They only differ from the above example in that one of the sets of data graphed represents time, that is, days, or weeks, or years. Consider Table B UNITED STATES POPULATION.

Table B   UNITED STATES POPULATION (MID-YEAR ESTIMATES)

YEAR	MILLIONS OF PERSONS
1960	180.7
1962	186.7
1964	192.1
1966	196.9
1968	201.1

This information is graphed in Figure E. The graphing procedure used was exactly as noted above:

1.   One prepares the graph by choosing the quadrant or quadrants required, labeling the axes with the column headings of the table, and putting units on the axes.

Figure E   UNITED STATES POPULATION

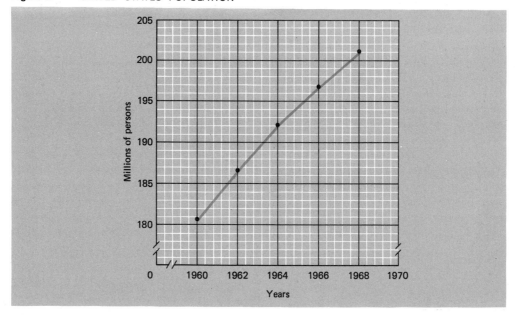

2. One finds the points in the graph corresponding to the combinations shown in each row of the table.

3. One connects the points by drawing straight lines between them.

Note how in Figure E both the horizontal and vertical axes have been interrupted between the origin and the first unit shown. In this way we avoid having to make space for all the years since Christ's birth and for all the population sizes below 180 million for which we have no entries.

COMPLEX TIME SERIES GRAPHS

On occasion, it is useful to graph a more complex set of data, involving two variables (as in Table A) *in addition to* time. Table C A PERSON'S INCOME AND SPENDING is an example.

Table C shows a hypothetical person's annual income and spending over a period of five years. It is obvious how this person's spending has varied with the size of his income. If we graph the data in the two dollar columns of Table C by the now familiar procedure we get the dots in Figure F INCOME VERSUS SPENDING. Were we to connect the dots by straight lines,

Table C   A PERSON'S INCOME AND SPENDING

YEAR	INCOME	SPENDING
1965	$5,000	$4,000
1966	6,000	4,800
1967	8,000	6,400
1968	7,500	6,000
1969	4,000	4,000

Figure F   INCOME VERSUS SPENDING

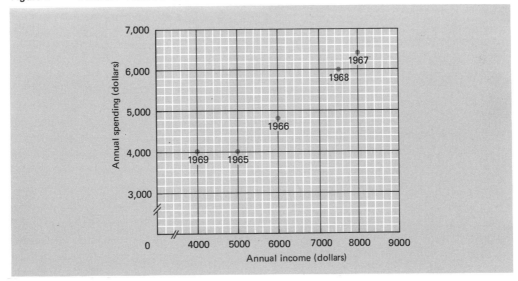

the observed "correlation" between income and spending would show up clearly by the fact of an upward sloping line.

In this case the dots have not been connected by lines, however, because it does not make any particular sense. The dots have rather been labeled in accordance with the year to which they belong. Thus all the information contained in Table C is also shown in Figure F which is a graph of it.

SUPERIMPOSING GRAPHS

The above types of graphs are the basic types encountered in this book. On occasion, however, different graphs are superimposed on each other or added together. These, too, are simple procedures.

Suppose we find the demand for apples to vary with their price as shown in Table D THE DEMAND FOR APPLES.

Table D   THE DEMAND FOR APPLES

PRICE (CENTS PER POUND)	QUANTITY OF APPLES DEMANDED (POUNDS PER DAY)
10	25
20	20
30	15
40	10
50	5

Just as Table A THE SUPPLY OF APPLES was graphed in Figure D THE FINISHED GRAPH—APPLE SUPPLY, the above data of Table D THE DEMAND FOR APPLES have been graphed in Figure G APPLE DEMAND.

Notice how Figures D and G have a common labeling of the axes. Hence we can *superimpose* the two graphs on each other. We can place both the data of Table A and those of Table D in the same graph. Figure H APPLE SUPPLY AND DEMAND does just that.

Note how we can see with one glance that only at a price of 30 cents are demand and supply equal! This then is the type of superimposed graph you may find on occasion in this book. Not very difficult at all, is it?

ADDING GRAPHS TOGETHER

Finally, we will on rare occasions add different graphs together. This makes sense only if it is possible to add the underlying tabular data together. Consider once more Table A. Suppose it describes the behavior of the owner of a roadside stand in the countryside. Let us

Figure G APPLE DEMAND

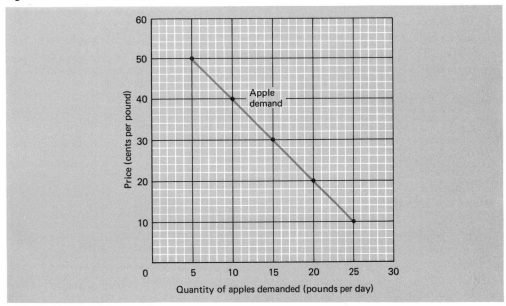

Figure H APPLE SUPPLY AND DEMAND

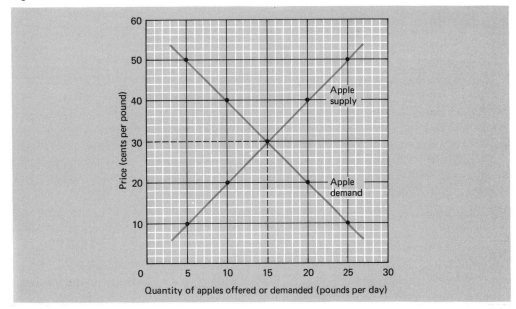

call him Mr. Green. Now suppose Mr. Brown, two miles down the same road, thinks about matters differently, as shown in Table E BROWN'S SUPPLY OF APPLES.

Table E   BROWN'S SUPPLY OF APPLES

PRICE (CENTS PER POUND)	QUANTITY OF APPLES OFFERED FOR SALE (POUNDS PER DAY)
10	20
20	25
30	30
40	35
50	40

Naturally, Mr. Brown's potential offers can be graphed as Mr. Green's were graphed earlier in Figure D. This is shown in Figure I BROWN'S APPLE SUPPLY.

Figure I   BROWN'S APPLE SUPPLY

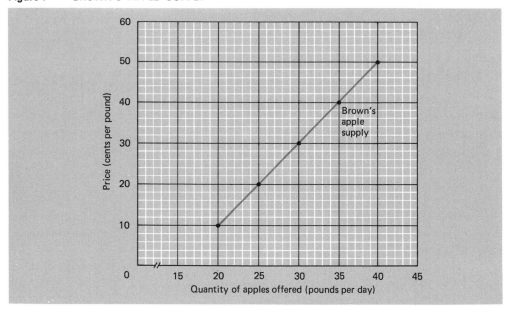

But now suppose we are neither interested in Green's, nor in Brown's individual offers. Suppose we only care to know how much they supply *together*. Naturally, we can just add together at each price the quantities offered by them. By looking at Tables A *and* E, we note that $5 + 20 = 25$ pounds are offered at 10 cents, that $10 + 25 = 35$ pounds are offered at 20 cents, and so on. If we graph this information, we get the heavy line of Figure J GREEN'S AND BROWN'S COMBINED APPLE SUPPLY.

Figure J GREEN'S AND BROWN'S COMBINED APPLE SUPPLY

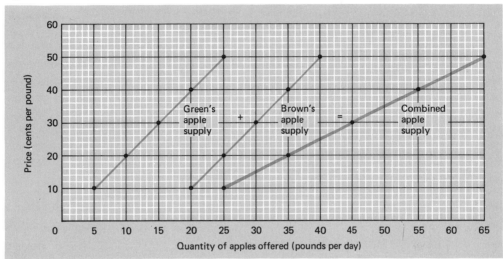

For comparison, the thin lines in Figure J repeat Figures D and I. The heavy line is the (horizontal) *addition* of the thin ones. Note how, at each price, the horizontal difference between the combined supply and Green's supply equals Brown's supply. Similarly, the horizontal distance between the combined supply and Brown's supply measures Green's supply.

A TEST

The above types of graphs are virtually the only ones found in this book. (You will not have any trouble with the exceptions. They are a map and a variety of pictorial representations, as of blocks, silver dollars, and even a bathtub!)

You now may want to test your understanding of graphs by looking at a few of those found in the text. A simple graphing of two variables can be found, for instance, in Figures 2.2 (p. 27), 14.3 (p. 320), 24.3 (p. 566), or 27.1 (p. 641). Simple time series graphs can be found in Figures 3.2 (p. 59), 4.1 (p. 79), 11.3 (p. 243), or 27.2 (p. 647). More complex time series graphs are represented by Figures 6.5 (p. 131) and 14.1 (p. 306). Finally, for superimposed graphs look at Figures 3.4 (p. 64), 7.1 (p. 155), 10.1 (p. 225), 14.2 (p. 309), 18.2 (p. 411), or 28.1 (p. 685), and for graphs added together, at Figure 6.9 (p. 141).

A FINAL NOTE

Some students may become particularly interested in some subject and wish to explore it further, or they may wish to know how to improve the effectiveness of their studies. For this purpose you may wish to use the *programmed Study Guide* which is a self-contained self-help device for students. It is keyed to the text and contains a chapter by chapter guide to references as well as to problems likely encountered by beginners. There are many questions (with answers) for self-examination.

Finally, note the Glossary and the list of symbols at the end of this book. They will help in the study of the new TERMS listed at the end of each chapter, and in clearing up any problems encountered with the notation.

contents

1

the economic problem

SUPPOSE YOU WERE PRESENTED with a magic wand that could grant all your wishes. Chances are that it would not take you long to prepare a most impressive list of wants you would like to have satisfied.

At first you might ask for material things. If you just happen to be hungry, you might call for nothing more complicated than a meal, although you might include better and more varied foods than you usually get. Having satisfied this most immediate want, you might wish for new clothes, more of them and more beautiful ones than you ever thought of owning before. Surely though, your appetite would just have begun to be aroused. You might as well wish for that flashy sports car you admired so last week, and for that fancy telescope or camera you could never quite afford. And just to make things perfect, why not look ahead and plan for the future? Why not add a house at the edge of town, with a breath-taking view and lovely gardens and a pool in their midst? But why stop here? More likely than not, your mind would wander on restlessly, as you would contemplate your life, present and future. You would think of that cottage by the sea (and a yacht to go with it), and maybe even of a private plane to get you there fast. The more you wished for, the more would open before your mind a vast panorama of things to make life more comfortable, enjoyable, and beautiful.

Nor would your wishing be confined to material objects, or *commodities*. You would note how *services*, or the use of other people's labor and of their property, could brighten your days just as much. After all, by now you would already "need" a gardener and a house-keeper just to take care of your newly won properties! You certainly would be foolish to forgo adequate medical care and, if the thought pleased you, nights on the town and trips to the far corners of the world.

Of course, you might also come to wish for more intimate things, personal and intangible, yet so important for the quality of life: wisdom, courage, and the experience of love.

We need not belabor the point. What is true for you is probably typical for the majority of mankind: there is virtually no limit to the variety and number of human wants. If we asked everyone in the human family to list what he wished to have or do or be, the ingredients of human welfare so defined would defy anyone's ability to count. The size of that list would be beyond comprehension. It would, furthermore, grow every day. There are at least three reasons for this. Even those wants that are satisfied often tend to recur (for example, your need to eat and to have your hair cut). New wants are created by new inventions (40 years ago, there were no television sets, jet planes, or ballpoint pens, so you probably would not have asked for them). In addition, the number of people is growing. Thus, it is hardly exaggerated to say that *human wants are virtually infinite.*

GOODS—THE MEANS TO SATISFY WANTS

However, as we all know too well, not all wants can be satisfied. There are no magic wands. For us as individuals, the closest substitute would be a big pile of money in our hands. With its help, we could fulfill many of our wants. But, as you well know, we never seem to have enough money. Thus, many of our wants remain unfulfilled. Why is this so? Is it really because there is not enough money to go around? Because it would be easy enough for our government to print more money and give it to us, we may suspect that the problem lies deeper than that. What are the real reasons we often have to go without? And is there anything we can do about them?

These questions are central to the study of economics. In a very general way, we can define the study of economics as a study of how human wants can be satisfied as much as possible. As a result, we shall concern ourselves with the process by which goods are provided to people, *a good being any commodity or service capable of satisfying human wants.* By studying this process, we can find out why not all wants can be satisfied fully.

Goods That Cannot Be Produced

This is not to say, however, that we shall be concerned with the satisfaction of *all* types of wants. The satisfaction of some human wants lies beyond the skills of even the professional economist.

If people lack food, they can be given bread. If people lack health, they can be helped by a doctor's skill and equipment and be given drugs. But what if they lack wisdom, courage, or love? There is no commodity they can own, there is no service on which they can draw that would unquestionably satisfy such wants. Like the Wizard of Oz, we are at a loss. Wisdom, courage, and love—peace, justice, and freedom—these we can recognize as ingredients of welfare, perhaps even the most important ones. Yet, no one can produce goods capable of stilling a man's thirst for these imponderables. Such goods are "priceless." They cannot be bought anywhere on earth, and many a man, throughout a long life, searches in vain for a substitute. When we do not deal with these matters here, we are not denying their importance. We are only placing the satisfaction of this group of wants beyond economics. The skill of economists is not sufficient to deal with wants of this kind.

Goods That Are Free

On the other hand, there are a few wants that can be satisfied by the provision of clearly identifiable goods, but that will likewise remain beyond our concern. These are wants that are already fully satisfied for all people at the same time, without anyone having to do anything about it. Take man's desire to breathe. This requires nothing more than the provision of a certain commodity—air. As it happens, air on earth is plentiful enough for everyone. In fact, on the surface of the earth, it is provided by nature when and where needed in quantities greater than desired by all people. As a result, air need not be bought anywhere on earth, and it has no price. Such goods, which need not be provided by man, are called *free goods.* We shall not be concerned with human wants that can be satisfied with free goods.[1]

---

[1] It is getting increasingly difficult to find examples of free goods. Note, therefore, that the above paragraph is carefully written to avoid the term *pure* air. Increasingly, only polluted air is free, and we may be paying for pure air, as we are paying for pure water, in a variety of indirect ways. We may have higher medical costs; anti-smog devices on power-plant smoke stacks may raise our electric bills; our cars may cost more as similar devices are installed; and so on.

Wants that can be satisfied with goods that *cannot* be made or with goods that *need not* be made are called *noneconomic wants*.

Economic Goods

This leaves us to deal with the fulfillment of those human wants, still virtually infinite, that can be satisfied by goods that are not free, but that man is capable of providing. Such wants are called *economic wants*. Such goods are called *economic goods*. They are all the goods you can buy at a price, if only you have the money.

At first glance, it seems easy enough to provide economic goods. Consider again the list above. If people want to own material objects, or *commodities,* such as food, clothing, cars, houses, yachts, and airplanes, we do not really need a magic wand at all. All we have to do is arrange for their production by setting aside the necessary ingredients used in the productive process.

Similarly, if people want the use of someone else's labor or property, or *services*, be they those of gardeners, housekeepers, doctors, musicians, trans-Atlantic jets, or hotel rooms, all we have to do is arrange for their production by setting aside the necessary personnel and commodities capable of performing such services.

At least, so it seems.

SCARCITY—THE CENTRAL CONCERN OF ECONOMICS

Reflection will show, however, that our problems are not over even when we confine our task to the study of how *economic* wants can be satisfied. True enough, we are not concerned with the mysterious creation of wisdom, courage, or love, but with clear-cut technical matters, such as the provision of houses and the treatment of pneumonia. All we have to do, we said above, is to set aside the necessary ingredients used in the productive process. Get qualified carpenters, the right kind of wood and tools, and we shall have houses in no time. Get qualified doctors, the right kind of instruments and drugs, and we shall cure pneumonia. It is as easy as that!

Except for one thing. Although it is easy enough to find the ingredients needed for the production of a limited quantity on any *one* economic good, we shall not find enough to produce *all* the economic goods all people want. This *scarcity of productive ingredients* in relation to virtually infinite human wants is the real reason why we often have to go without. It is not scarcity of money at all!

Let us review. Human wants are virtually infinite. Some of them are noneconomic wants, either because we cannot produce goods to satisfy them (there is no recipe) or because we need not do so (the required goods are free). The remaining *economic* wants are practically infinite, too. To satisfy them all, we would require an infinitely large array of economic goods. In turn, this would require an infinitely large set of ingredients capable of making goods. Such an infinite quantity of ingredients is not available. This is the "economic problem," the challenge man must face in every country, even the richest in the world. This book will show you how man, in turn, is challenging this inescapable fact of scarcity.

RESOURCES AND THE PROCESS OF PRODUCTION

Let us take a closer look at the process of production. The *productive process covers any activity that helps make economic goods available to people where and when they are wanted.* Sowing wheat is part of the productive process. So is harvesting wheat. So is turning it into flour. So is baking cake from flour. So is transporting cake. So is storing and selling cake. Only when the cake is finally bought by a household shall we consider the process of production to have ended. At the moment the cake, or any good, enters the possession of a household, it becomes a *consumer good.* Then the process of consumption, or direct-want satisfaction, begins. Thus, the *process of production,* as we shall use the term, quite sensibly goes beyond the point of physical manufacture and includes all activities required to bring a good to its ultimate user.

The process of production, like the baking of a cake, involves the use of ingredients. We shall call them *resources,* or *factors of production.* We classify them into three major groups: labor, land, and capital.

Labor

The good sense of this three-group classification will, perhaps, be most easily perceived if we engage, as scientists are fond of doing, in a "thought experiment." Imagine yourself being stranded on a deserted island, somewhat of a modern-day Robinson Crusoe. To what extent would you be able to satisfy your wants? On what would the availability of goods to you depend?

Certainly not on the money in your pocket! Clearly, more than ever before in your life, you would have to rely on your own *efforts.* Unless you thought and planned and worked, you would have nothing, and very shortly you would die of hunger and exposure. Human labor is thus seen to be a crucial ingredient for the process of production; money is not. We shall include in labor *all types of human effort,* mental or physical, put forth in the process of production. It is important to notice how very comprehensive this classification is. Although the term *labor* often brings to mind the man engaged in muscular effort, working by the sweat of his brow, our categorization goes further than that. It includes not only the farmer plowing his field behind a pair of oxen in some faraway land, but also his lucky American counterpart running a diesel tractor. And it includes the work of the engineer who designed the tractor, as well as the work of the executive who is in charge of the tractor-making enterprise.

Just as Robinson Crusoe would need a minimum of rest to survive and would thus have a maximum of, perhaps, 16 hours a day in which to work, it is clear that no society has an infinite amount of labor.

The size of the population sets an upper limit to its quantity. But the actual limit is far below this. The very young, the very old, and the very sick cannot possibly aid in the production of economic goods, however many of them they might need to consume. How about the others? Are they part of the labor force or not? The answer will depend on the values of our society. If it is decided that all who can work must work, the answer is yes. If, as in the United States, people may voluntarily refrain from working, the answer is no.

Even after we have established the number of people to be counted in the labor force, we still do not know the quantity of labor available for the process of production. How many hours in a day can we reasonably expect people to work, how many days in a year? Different societies will make different decisions, and these decisions will change over time. In the United States, people worked 11 hours a day, including Sundays, as recently as 100 years ago. Now we are close to the 35-hour week.

Nor is this the end of the story. Even a labor force defined in "man-hours available per year" is only vaguely defined. The quality of labor is important too. We all know that two people working 8 hours each are not necessarily equally productive. People who are well fed and healthy, both physically and mentally, who are educated and happy, who consider work honorable and enjoyable, will be much more productive than others who are working equally long, but for whom the opposites hold. A sick and desperate Robinson Crusoe will produce much less than a healthy and hopeful one. Similarly, a labor force that has a core of entrepreneurs, people with a spirit of inquiry and innovation, filled with organizing and operating energy, is worth infinitely more than one poorly blessed in this regard. An ingenious and energetic Robinson Crusoe will do a lot better than a stupid and lazy one.

For any given country, the quality and size of its labor force can change dramatically over time. At any given time, the quality and size of the labor force differs among countries. But at any given moment, the total quantity of the resource called labor is limited.

Land

Let us return to our island. The nature of the island itself is extremely important, too. All by yourself in isolation, surrounded by thin air, you would produce nothing. And so it takes little imagination to see how you would start exploring your new home as soon as you could gather your wits. What kind of plant and animal life is there? Is there fresh water? How about caves and building stones and timber? Is there arable land? These and many other questions would come into your mind. Your life would depend on answers to them as much as on your willingness and ability to put in a good day's work.

Thus, we must come to recognize a second group of resources to which we shall refer simply as *land*. This will be our shorthand way of describing all natural resources or *gifts of nature*, productive ingredients that no man has made and that are as yet untouched by human hands.

The soil of the earth in its virgin state is obviously part of this grouping. It varies widely in usefulness over the face of the earth. Topography, fertility, temperature, and humidity differ from place to place. As a result, soil can mean all sorts of things to all kinds of people.

To some it will be ocean shores lashed by floods; to others, intensely cold tundras battered by icy winds. Some live on mountains subject to earthquakes, erosion, and volcanic eruptions, whereas others till small oases, threatened by drifting sands and suffering from relentless heat. A few lucky ones inherit fertile plains of grass and woods and frequent rain, together with great reservoirs of plant and animal life.

In the same way, the oceans of the earth belong to this category. They provide not only fish, but also a multitude of other things, such as algae, magnesium salts, petroleum, gold, and cheap routes of transport.

In fact, the whole of nature, the energy of the sun, of winds, of the tides, the gravity of the earth, is used in man's quest to make economic goods. The Industrial Revolution over the past 200 years would be unthinkable without nature's plentiful provision of minerals and fuels. Their usefulness varies greatly, depending on such factors as the ease of extraction, refining, and transportation. As with labor, the quantity of natural resources, or land, is limited, even for the richest of nations.

_____

Capital

Quite possibly, you could survive on our island, and a nation might survive, with nothing but labor and land to assist in the making of economic goods. You might sleep in a suitable cave, drink fresh water from a spring out of your hollowed hands, gather bananas and coconuts from the trees around you, and occasionally even catch a fish with your bare hands or a stick. Undoubtedly, however, life would be somewhat less than luxurious.

Like the real Robinson Crusoe, you can be expected to set your goals higher than that. One of the first things you might do after your shipwreck, having reassuringly found all your limbs present and in working order, may in fact not be an exploration of the island, but a careful investigation of the wreck. You might find and ax or a box of nails, a net or a pail, a knife or a dozen planks. Somewhat intuitively you would grasp their enormous significance. These man-made things could make your life immeasurably easier when applied, together with your muscle and brain, to the gifts of nature around you.

Even if you are not so lucky and inherit no set of tools from the past, you would certainly think about making some before long. You would realize, as primitive man did, that it is often worthwhile to forgo immediate satisfaction of wants in order to accumulate a set of tools that will vastly increase your productivity. Instead of spending 8 hours to catch half a dozen small fish, you may go hungry for two days, while building a canoe and making a net. In days to come, you will more than make up for the dozen fish lost. Again, instead of walking half a mile to the spring four times a day to drink from your hollowed hands, you may find it worthwhile going hungry and thirsty long enough to make a pail or even build an aqueduct from hollowed trees right to the mouth of your cave. Such roundabout methods of production, where you sacrifice immediate-want satisfaction for the sake of accumulating tools and equipment, will turn out to increase greatly the quantity of output in the long run. The tools and equipment will make life a good deal more pleasant (before the aqueduct, you never could have taken a bath at your cave). They will give you some things you otherwise could never have had at all (you can go on the ocean to catch larger fish in the canoe, you can get enough food in half the time and have time to relax).

This *total of man-made resources* is what we shall call *capital*. It includes all *buildings*, all types of *equipment*, and all producers' *inventories*. In one way or another, all these are used in the process of production. These three terms, furthermore, will be used by us in the widest sense possible. Buildings may be factory buildings or schools or airport control towers. Equipment may be complicated machines or simple tools; a system of roads and bridges or the trucks driving on them; the latest computer or a simple typewriter. Equipment may even include domesticated animals, which are clearly not a gift of nature (and therefore *land*, as we have defined it) as wild animals are. By having been tamed and bred, they are in a sense man-made and so may be treated as capital. In the same way, a field created by man through clearing land, irrigating, fertilizing, and so forth would be equipment and thus be called capital. Finally, inventories include goods partially or completely finished, as well as raw materials. For example, shoes at your home would be called consumer goods, having been bought by a household. But identical shoes on the store's shelf would be called capital, because they are still being used in the process of production. An inventory of iron ore in the yard of a steel mill would be capital, too, whereas identical unmined ore in the earth would be classified as land. Clearly, ore in the yard is not a gift of nature, having been brought there with considerable human effort and having thus become man-made. It is extremely important that you remember this definition of capital: man-made buildings, equipment, inventories.

When laymen talk about their capital, they are often thinking of quite different things, such as money, stocks, deeds, and bonds. These should be referred to as *financial* capital. To an individual in modern society, such items are equivalent to wealth. However, they are, in fact, not wealth itself but claims against it. They tell us who owns the real capital they represent. A society could easily increase such paper claims a millionfold. Yet, if no corresponding increase in the form of real buildings, equipment, and inventories occurred, it would not be richer at all. It could not produce more on that account, just as Robinson Crusoe could not do a thing with money and bonds. One cannot produce goods with money, stocks, or bonds. For such production, one ultimately needs labor and material objects, such as land and tools.

Throughout this book, we are interested in *real* capital, physical things, such as factory buildings, machines, roads, piles of iron ore in the yard, and boxes of shoes in the store, all of which are used in the process of production.

Of course, no one who has grown up in the twentieth century needs to have pointed out to him the enormous importance capital plays in the process of production. Without it, all societies would produce much less than they are producing. Yet, no matter how much capital we have, no matter how its quality and quantity may change over time or differ over space, no society has an infinite amount of it.

Labor, land, capital—these, then, are the types of resources used in the process of production. These resources are scarce compared to the quantities we need to satisfy everyone's economic wants. Therefore, we must use these resources ever so carefully, ever so frugally, so as to make the best of a bad situation. Indeed, it is from the need to *economize* scarce resources that economics gets its name.

THE ENVIRONMENT AND THE PROCESS OF PRODUCTION

Let us recall that we have defined the process of production as any activity that helps make available to people economic goods where and when they are wanted. We have seen that this involves the use of labor, land, and capital. We have noted in passing that the process of production may well involve several stages. The making of a cake involves, long before your purchase, the use of labor (a farmer's toil), land (a virgin pasture, sunshine, rain), and capital (a barn, chickens, cows, a field, machinery, seed) to produce wheat, milk, and eggs. It involves, again, labor (the trucker's, the miller's, the dairyman's) and capital (trucks, roads, buildings, equipment, wheat, milk) to make flour and process the milk. It involves, once more, labor (the trucker's, the baker's) and capital (trucks, roads, flour, processed milk, eggs, buildings, equipment) to make a cake. And it involves, finally, labor (the trucker's, the wholesaler's, the retailer's) and capital (trucks, roads, refrigerators, shelves, packages, cakes) to make an economic good, the cake, available to you. Only then has the process of production ended. If this sounds complicated, consider that we are here looking at a relatively simple good and have simplified even this account greatly.

We shall return to this little story later on. Right now, however, it helps us to see one more thing: how much can be produced from given resources depends on more than the mere quantities and qualities of the resources that are available. It depends also on the environment in which they are used, on matters of technology, division of labor, and economic institutions.

Technical Knowledge

Just as the baking of a cake requires a recipe, the production of all economic goods requires technical knowledge. Someone must get the idea that he can make fire, build shelter, till land, raise animals in captivity, make flour, refrigerators, and trucks. The kinds of knowledge available and used in the productive process are of enormous importance in determining how much output we can get out of given resources. After someone has discovered how to improve plants and animals through selective breeding, how to eliminate impurities from ores, how to harness vast amounts of electric or nuclear power, any given set of resources will produce much more than before.

This seems obvious, yet is often forgotten. The ancient Romans or the American Indians could have used many of the resources modern Italians or Americans are using, yet they did not recognize their importance. In fact, to them these were not resources at all, because they were not transformable into goods to satisfy wants.

To put it another way, suppose for a moment that you lived in a society that had lost all the technical knowledge presently available. Even if the same amounts of labor, land, and capital existed, you would be in great trouble. Could you, without a technical handbook, without expert help, without previous training, produce a single pair of shoes of the type you are now wearing? You might work for years before producing anything half as good. And the same would be true of the many other goods you enjoy. How about producing a single page of paper?

Assuming the necessary ingredients were available on the island, how many of the goods you now enjoy could you *not* produce if you were put in Crusoe's place, just because of lack of knowledge? This is the importance of technical knowledge, of the recipe of production. Unlike most things, it can be given away and yet retained by the giver, enriching all who come in contact with it.

Specialization and Exchange

Another important environmental factor is the degree to which the process of production is organized on the basis of specialization and exchange, rather than the self-sufficiency of every person or region. This again influences the output producible from a given set of resources. Just imagine how few goods we would enjoy if we insisted on making all of them ourselves. Or if, like Crusoe, we had to do so? There is no doubt that even with the same resources we now have at our disposal, and the same technical knowledge we now hold, we would be incredibly poor without specialization. Goods available would be fewer and of lower quality.

This would be so for a number of reasons. For one thing, different people have different inherent talents and should concentrate on what they can do best. Even where this is not so already, skills can be created, for a division of labor among people reduces each person's work to a simple operation and increases the dexterity with which each participant produces his portion of society's output. "Practice makes perfect." This advantage is lost to the Jack-of-all-trades. The division of labor also saves time, which is lost in passing between two operations, possibly in two places, with two different sets of tools.

Adam Smith enunciated the advantages of the division of labor 200 years ago, when he pointed out that a pinmaker could not produce twenty pins a day if he himself had to do everything that was required—drawing out the wire, straightening it, cutting it, pointing it, grinding it for receiving the head, making the head, and so on. Yet, Adam Smith observed that ten people, only poorly equipped with machinery but with the proper division of labor among them, were able to make 48,000 pins in one day.

Further, specialization stimulates the invention of machines and makes their use possible. If we all made our own cars, none of us would install an assembly line! As each person specializes in the production of one good or part thereof, exchanging most or all of it with others who also specialize, total output from given resources is greatly increased. At the same time, of course, our dependence on other individuals also is greatly increased. You might think about the effect the appearance of Friday would have on Crusoe's island economy. Not only would it increase the quantity of labor available, and possibly the total of technical knowledge, but it would also open up possibilities for a division of labor for the reasons given above. As a result, output may be higher in this economy than it would be if Crusoe and Friday resided on two different islands and we added together their products.

Similar advantages, of course, accrue to regions within a country and nations that may specialize in producing goods they are particularly suited to make in light of their current endowment with resources. It would be manifestly absurd to grow bananas in New England, although it could be done in hothouses, just as it would be unwise (under present circumstances) to have our cars produced in Idaho and our potatoes around Detroit.

Institutional Framework

Finally, the institutional framework within which economic activity is carried out helps to determine what given resources are capable of producing. This includes such matters as who owns the resources and who puts them to use on the basis of what kinds of incentives. In purely *capitalist societies*, all resources are privately owned and are used by their owners as they see fit. In purely *socialist societies*, land and capital are owned by all people together (collectively), and they are put to use by the government, acting for the people as a whole. In the real world, all societies are mixed in this regard, although most countries are closer to one extreme or the other. The United States, for example, is a predominantly capitalist society with some public ownership and use of resources, whereas the Soviet Union is a predominantly socialist society with some private ownership and use of resources.

The use of resources is also arranged differently in different societies. It may be arranged in capitalism or socialism through a system of markets, that is, through the sale and purchase of resource services for money, as is predominantly the case in the United States. Or it may be arranged through command, that is, by allocation without the intervention of money, as it is in some societies whose economies are centrally planned or guided by tradition. The type of framework within which resources are put to use will affect how productive they are, but there is no way to tell the ideal framework beforehand for all times and all places.

WEAPONS AGAINST SCARCITY

We have seen that the amount we can produce depends on the quantity and quality of resources available, as well as on the environment in which they are used. At any given moment, these factors are fixed. How then do we go about our task of overcoming scarcity? Economists everywhere agree on a number of ways to fight scarcity, although they do not by any means agree on which is most important. The general usefulness of these weapons against scarcity, however, cannot be questioned.

Full Employment

First, we should *utilize all resources fully*. This is only common sense. If our problem is scarcity, if even full use of resources cannot produce enough economic goods to satisfy everyone's economic wants, then not using resources fully would amount to madness. We would be leaving scarcity more intense than it would have to be. We would be like a starving man with mountains of food in the pantry who, though able, refuses to prepare a meal.

Full employment of resources is thus a major weapon in the attack on scarcity. Part 1 of this book discusses what full employment means, and whether and how it can be achieved.

Efficiency

Second, we should *utilize all resources efficiently*. This means not wasting them during their use and, also, putting them to the best possible use.

If we have full employment, but some resources are wasted, we still have fewer goods than we might have had without waste. This would be akin to our starving man using all the food he has, but dropping half of it on the floor as he eats. Or we may use all our resources, but not for the best possible purpose; a different use might improve our well-being and reduce scarcity still further. This would be akin to letting our man use all his food, but providing it in the wrong proportions, or in such a way (as by overcooking it) that its nutritive value is less than it might have been.

Efficient employment of resources thus becomes the second major weapon in the assault on scarcity. Part 2 discusses what efficient employment of resources means, and whether and how it can be brought about.

Growth

Third, we might try to *increase the quantity and quality of resources* at our disposal, or *change the environment* in which they are used. Output, as a result, could be made to grow just as surely as by the elimination of unemployment and inefficiencies. This assumes that the new resources are also fully and efficiently put to use. In the case of our hungry friend, there may be a way to increase the amount or quality of food in the pantry, or to use a better recipe.

Growth of resources and changes in the productive environment are thus the third weapon in the economist's arsenal. They will be discussed in Part 3.

An Alternative?

A fourth possible weapon in the struggle against scarcity lies in the possibility of reducing wants rather than satisfying them. All of the above, full and efficient use of growing resources, are directed at providing more goods to satisfy wants. The neglect of the fourth possibility shows a typical bias of the Western world. In some parts of the world freedom from desire for economic goods is held by some people to be the route to happiness. Perfect happiness is rejection of all economic wants. We can, however, ignore this approach. We can do so because, first, it belongs to the realm of religion or philosophy and, second, we can reasonably suspect that the Western materialistic approach, which is to try to satisfy rather than suppress wants, has infected the rest of the world rather thoroughly! This is not to deny, of course, that even in the West all of us at some time prefer more leisure to material goods (as when we decide not to work that extra hour or not to take that other job). Nevertheless, it seems fair to infer that people in general are more eager to satisfy than ready to forgo the satisfaction of their economic wants.

SHARING THE OUTPUT

Finally, and this will be the topic of the concluding Part 4, we must pay attention to how we share the nation's output among ourselves. In our enthusiasm, we may bring about full and efficient utilization of a growing quantity of resources, though noticing somewhat belatedly that we have traded serious noneconomic troubles for the overall reduction in scarcity. The quality of life depends on more than the quantities of economic goods we manage to produce. It also depends on what kinds of goods these are and in whose hands they are placed. We have already noted how the production of goods for individual households may have repercussions on society at large. If we fulfill people's desire to have cars, but their production and use poisons the air we breathe, we may endanger man's very survival in the long run. Thus, we must forgo at least some present satisfaction (producing less of some goods) to produce antipollution devices to prevent or offset the bad side effects of our use of other goods.

The battle against scarcity has many such side effects, most of which cannot be traced to the production and use of any one particular good. What, for instance, causes urban blight and city riots? What is responsible for the social tensions of our time? There are many answers, but certainly not least among these in importance is the way we *distribute* our national output among ourselves. We may produce the highest output imaginable, but as long as it is shared so unequally that a significant minority of Americans remain desperately poor, our society will have major problems. This question of justice, which we take up in Part 4, takes us in part beyond objective scientific inquiry. It moves us from the realm of asking what is and might be done into the realm of saying what ought to be done. Sooner or later, every man of science must step beyond the conventional boundaries of his subject matter. Such boundaries have their uses, but they should not be used in the name of scientific "detachment" as an excuse to exclude the important.

SUMMARY

1   In this chapter, we have seen that the primary concern of economics is overcoming scarcity. Scarcity arises from the fact that human wants are virtually infinite, whereas goods, or means to satisfy them, are not.

Very few goods are free, that is, are provided by nature when and where needed in quantities greater than those desired. Certain goods man cannot produce. Those that are not free, but which man can produce, are called economic goods. Although man can probably, if he chooses to do so, produce enough of any one economic good to satisfy a particular want completely (at least for a while), he cannot produce enough of all economic goods to satisfy all economic wants simultaneously.

In other words, *the* economic problem is scarcity, and the scarcity referred to is that of economic goods. It is a problem common to all countries.

2 Economic goods are scarce because we have only limited quantities of the productive resources needed to produce them. These resources are classified as labor, land, and capital. The total of economic goods producible from these resources is also influenced strongly by such factors as technical knowledge, the degree of specialization and exchange prevalent in the particular society, and the institutional framework within which production is carried out.

3 Economists study the productive process by which scarcity is decreased or by which the availability of economic goods is increased. Their particular concern is with (a) using given resources fully and (b) efficiently, while (c) increasing the quantity and improving the quality of resources or improving the environment in which they are used.

4 Yet, we must never forget that the production of economic goods is just one part of the solution of the economic problem. The correct distribution of economic goods among the people is an equally important aspect of the battle against scarcity.

TERMS[2]

capital	labor
capitalism	land
commodity	noneconomic wants
consumer good	process of consumption
economic good	process of production
economic wants	resource
free good	scarcity
good	service
infinity of wants	socialism

QUESTIONS FOR REVIEW AND DISCUSSION

1 What is the primary concern of economics? Which are the three major weapons economists propose to use in dealing with the central problem they face?

2 Make a list of wants that recur after being satisfied. Does it include all wants?

3 Make a list of wants that have been created by new inventions in this century. Think of private goods (for example, antibiotics or cars bought privately) and social goods (for example, hydrogen bombs or antipollution devices bought by the government in the name of all citizens).

4 "The existence of agricultural surpluses in the United States proves that many agricultural goods are free goods." Do you agree? (Hint: Human want is not the same as ability to buy.)

[2] Terms are defined in the Glossary at the end of the book.

5   Can you think of goods that were once free, but are not free now?

6   Free public education is not a free good. Why?

7   "Coal deposits may be a free gift of nature, but they are not a free good." Discuss.

8   When men live on the moon, will water be a free good? Is it free on earth?

9   Would you classify the following as free goods: air, sunshine, rain, water, sand at the beach, privacy, a date with a girl, a conversation? Why or why not?

10 Which of the following are capital: an automobile assembly plant, a toy truck, an acre of land, 100 cubic feet of coal, a natural waterfall, a highway, a can of peas, a passenger automobile, a cow, a truck driver, a college building? Why or why not? (Hint: in six cases, the answer will be "It depends." It depends on what?)

11 The production of capital goods has been called a roundabout way of making consumer goods. Explain. Why do something in roundabout fashion when one could do it more directly?

12 Explain how technical knowledge influences the quantity of economic goods produced. Give a specific example.

13 Cite a case from your own experience of how specialization and exchange influence the quantity of economic goods produced. (By the way, do you know of any case in which a person or a region does *not* specialize?)

14 "There are a number of distinct factors responsible for the increase in output per man under the division of labor." Explain.

15 Both capital accumulation and specialization cannot be carried on without limit. Can you figure out why?

16 The text says that the institutional framework of society may influence how much is produced. It specifically mentions the matter of "who owns the resources and who puts them to use on the basis of what kinds of incentives." Can you think of specific examples?

17 "The United States, producing roughly $1,000 billion of commodities and services annually, is best described as an economy of abundance. Clearly, there is enough for all. However, output is incorrectly distributed and that is why some of us are left with unsatisfied wants." Discuss.

18 The "unproductive" middleman (wholesaler, retailer, insurance agent, and so forth) is not unproductive at all. Discuss.

19 "Scarcity would persist even with unlimited resources. This is so because life is not endless, hence our ability to satisfy our wants would still be limited by the scarcity of time." Discuss.

20 It has been argued, for example by Harvard Professor John Kenneth Galbraith, that wants are not really insatiable. Gailbraith pictures the natural tendency of man as working for a minimum level of food and shelter, keeping the remainder of his time for relaxation and fun. Yet, somehow in the United States, he argues, leisure is regarded with misgiving. An increase in output *beyond* the necessary minimum is regarded as the prime test of social achievement. Instead of trying to achieve a fixed minimum of goods with a minimum of effort, we are forever asking for more. But, argues Galbraith, these wants are artificially created in us by advertising, holding before us novelty after novelty and appealing to our vanity and our sense of competitive adornment. Economists who talk of infinite wants are talking nonsense. In fact, economics, forever trying to satisfy these artificial wants is missing the whole point of man's existence. Discuss.

THE INVISIBLE HAND

On coming to Paris for a visit, I said to myself: Here are a million human beings who would all die in a few days if supplies of all sorts did not flow into this great metropolis. It staggers the imagination to try to comprehend the vast multiplicity of objects that mus pass through its gates tomorrow, if its inhabitants are to be preserved from the horrors of famine, insurrection, and pillage. And yet all are sleeping peacefully at this moment, without being disturbed for a single instant by the idea of so frightful a prospect. . . .

How does each succeeding day manage to bring to this gigantic market just what is necessary—neither too much nor too little? What, then, is the resourceful and secret power that governs the amazing regularity of such complicated movements, a regularity in which everyone has such implicit faith, although his prosperity and his very life depend upon it? That power is . . . the principle of free exchange. We put our faith in that inner light which Providence has placed in the hearts of all men, and to which has been entrusted the preservation and the unlimited improvement of our species, a light we term *self-interest*, which is so illuminating, so constant, and so penetrating, when it is left free of every hindrance. Where would you be, inhabitants of Paris, if some cabinet minister decided to substitute for that power contrivances of his own invention, however superior we might suppose them to be: if he proposed to subject this prodigious mechanism to his supreme direction, to take control of all of it into his own hands, to determine by whom, where, how, and under what conditions everything should be produced, transported, exchanged, and consumed? Although there may be much suffering within your walls, although misery, despair, and perhaps starvation, cause more tears to flow than your warm-hearted charity can wipe away, it is probable. I dare say it is certain, that the arbitrary intervention of the government would infinitely multiply this suffering and spread among all of you the ills that now affect only a small number of your fellow citizens.

Frédéric Bastiat (1845)

2

the nature of the market economy

EVERY ECONOMY, THAT of a Robinson Crusoe as well as that of the United States, must deal with the identical problem. It must find a way of rationally "allocating" its limited resources in the face of virtually unlimited human wants. That means it must choose which wants are to be satisfied and then assign resources to the production of specific goods. If it wants to satisfy people's wants as much as possible, furthermore, it must certainly use its resources to the fullest. This seemed easy enough for a Robinson Crusoe. He only needed the will to do so. Then, he could plan all his economic activities in his mind, and he needed never once lose sight of the whole as he made his plan a reality. Yet, who plans, oversees, and guides economic activity in the United States? Who, if anyone, makes sure that we do not waste resources in involuntary idleness or in less urgent pursuits while crying needs remain unfulfilled? In this chapter, we shall give a preliminary answer to at least the first of these questions. Parts 1 and 2 will build on that foundation in search for an answer to the second.

THE INCREDIBLE PRICE SYSTEM

Imagine what it would be like to plan the economic activity not just of a small island as Robinson Crusoe did, but of the entire United States. Imagine you were this country's complete economic dictator, and nothing could happen without your direction. How would you go about deciding what to produce, and how, and when, and where, and for whom? How could you prevent enormous waste by making mistakes in all these decisions? On what basis would you conclude that John Doe should mine iron ore to be made into steel to be made into machines to make plows to prepare a field to grow red cabbages? Wouldn't it be better, if he taught logic and mathematics at a college, in order to train young minds to build eventually better computers to diagnose and cure disease? And if we do need red cabbages, how many are needed and where exactly should they be sent, and when?

Consider that there are hundreds of thousands of goods. In fact, there are equally as many resources, once we stop to consider the different qualities contained in each of the three broad classes discussed in Chapter 1. Thus, your chances of making a complete mess of things are excellent, indeed. Neither you nor any other human being could possibly avoid them.

Now consider another story. Think of New York City, Chicago, or Los Angeles. There are millions of people living in these cities. In a matter of days, they would all starve without the continual flow of goods into the cities. And what variety and quantity of goods these are! Thousands of tons of bread and fruit, trainloads of milk and coal, furniture and shirts, hairspray and bobby pins! These goods come not only from the surrounding countryside, but from all the states of the union—indeed, from the farthest corners of the globe. And they have been traveling, and are now traveling, for days and months with New York, Chicago, or Los Angeles as their destination. The same, of course, is true, on a smaller scale, for every city, town, and village in this country. And so it happens that you and I, and 200 million people like us, sleep easily each night, without the slightest fear of breakdown of the complicated machinery that supports our lives. How come we do not live in mortal terror that this elaborate economic machinery, on which our existence depends, will suddenly grind to a halt? How can we comfortably sit in our warm houses, trustingly believing that we will find in a nearby store any one of hundreds of thousands of items to eat, drink, wear, and play with? What makes us so sure that any and all these can be picked up, or even delivered to our doorstep in response to a telephone call?

If you have considered seriously how hard—how impossible—it would be for *you* to plan for all this, you will admit that all this is a most remarkable achievement. So accustomed are we to this smoothly running machinery, the economic machinery of our land, that we are not even aware of it! Yet, who or what is this machinery? It is not any private individual or organization. It is not any local, state, or federal government. It is not any conscious body of men at all! The remarkable order that we perceive in our economic affairs is not the order of conscious planning by a central intelligence; it is the order of the *price system*, something that was designed by nobody, evolved by itself, and, ever-changing, survives!

The Circular Flow

We know that the economic actions of millions of diverse individuals in the United States are in fact unconsciously coordinated. And it is not a matter of chaos and anarchy, but of order. It works. Let us try to see how.

First of all, our economy is a *capitalist economy*. That means our resources, be they labor, land, or capital, are for the most part privately owned.

Our economy is also a *money and exchange economy*. The services of these resources— the use of someone's labor, land, or capital—can be had in exchange for money, or the payment of wages, profits, rents, and interest. The goods that are produced with these resources can be had for money, too. In fact, all resources and all economic goods have a price indicating the terms at which exchange is possible. A loaf of bread can be had for 23 cents, a washing machine for $123. A truck can be rented for $9 per hour, and a gardener be hired for half that amount.

Finally, our economy is a *free-enterprise economy*. That means everyone is free (within limits we can ignore for the moment) to engage in any economic activity he likes. If you want to sell your labor services as a gardener, you may. If you rather go to college to become a teacher, you may. If you are lucky enough to have inherited lots of land and capital, you may allow them to be used for any purpose you like, and you may completely withhold your labor from *any* use. However you derive your money income, you may spend most of it as you like. If you hate onions, you don't have to buy any. If you love ice cream, you can buy all you can afford. If you are enterprising enough to gather together lots of labor, land, and capital under your control, you may use them to produce cars. Or hairnets. Or red cabbages. Or almost anything. Again, once you have decided to produce red cabbages, you may do so by utilizing lots of land and machinery and little labor. Or you may instead use relatively little land, but lots of fertilizer and tender loving care. If you make a profit in your business, you can for the most part decide what to do with it. You may buy onions or ice cream to take home, or another sack of fertilizer to grow more and better cabbages.

In short, everybody in our free-enterprise, capitalist, money-and-exchange economy is free to seek his own economic gain by selling the goods and resources he privately owns for

money and buying with money whatever goods and resources he wishes. Figure 2.1 THE CIR-
CULAR FLOW gives a simplified picture of this economy. It shows the flow of goods and resources and their monetary counterflows.

On the left-hand side of Figure 2.1, we find the households of which there are some 60
million in the United States. Each household contains one or more persons, in the latter case,
usually under one roof and making joint financial decisions with the aim of maximizing the
well-being of its members. Toward the outside, households typically act as a single unit. It is

Figure 2.1   THE CIRCULAR FLOW

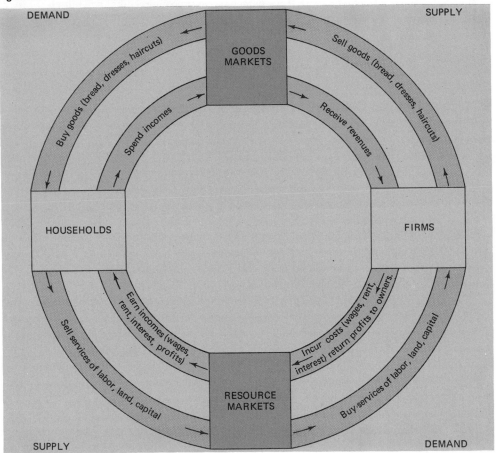

*This circular-flow diagram is a simplified picture of the capitalist economy. Households as owners of
resources supply resource services to firms, which demand them to produce goods. Goods are in turn
supplied to and demanded by households (outer circle of real goods and resources). Put differently, firms
incur costs, which (together with profits) become the incomes of households, which are spent on goods
bought from firms (inner circle of dollars).*

for our purposes of no interest how households are organized internally to arrive at decisions about selling resources and buying goods. Households face some 12 million business firms, pictured on the right. Each firm is run by one or more entrepreneurs, people providing a special kind of labor that organizes the production of goods by combining labor, land, and capital. For their organizing, innovating, and risk-taking activities, entrepreneurs hope to make as large a profit as possible. Toward the outside, each firm, too, acts as a unit. Again, for our purposes it is of no interest how firms are organized internally to arrive at decisions about buying resouces and selling goods.

It is now clear that households face firms on two fronts, so to speak, with two kinds of markets intervening. There are, pictured on top, the markets for goods, or the outputs of the economy. There are, pictured at the bottom, the markets for resources, or the economy's inputs. A market, it should be noted, embraces all contact points, of whatever kind, between buyers and sellers of a given good or resource. As the economist uses the term, it is not confined to one location and time, as old-fashioned open-air markets might have been confined to the town square every Monday, Wednesday, and Friday. The markets we are talking about are invisible.

It is now easy to picture households as owners of resources trying to sell the services of their resources for as much as they will bring. Someone who has only his labor to offer will naturally try to get the highest wage possible (lower left corner of Figure 2.1). Someone with entrepreneurial ability will try for the highest possible profit income. Someone who owns property will similarly strive for the highest possible rent and interest return for its use. Firms, on the other hand, will find it in their self-interest to buy nonentrepreneurial resource services at the lowest possible prices (lower right corner). In this way, they minimize costs and hence maximize profits for their household owners. Thus, the interplay between the two parties will come to establish prices for the resources traded in the resource markets. We shall investigate this process in more detail shortly.

Similarly, households, as earners of money incomes, will try to buy goods they desire (and can afford) at the lowest possible prices in the many markets where goods are traded (upper left corner of Figure 2.1). This is, in fact, what you are doing every time you shop around for the "best buy," regardless of whether you walk from store to store, scan through a mail-order catalogue, or "let your fingers do the walking through the yellow pages" of your local telephone directory. On the other hand, business firms naturally will not maximize profits unless they sell their goods for as much as they can get. This is, indeed, what they will attempt to do (upper right corner). The interaction of buyers and sellers in the goods markets will establish prices for all goods. This, too, we shall study in more detail shortly.

Notice how the diagram brings out the circularity of economic activity. There is the *real* (outer) flow of resources and goods. It shows how human sweat and thought and nature's gifts and man-made tools are turned into bread, dresses, haircuts, and all the other goods people want. Then there is the *monetary* (inner) flow of dollars of cost and income, expenditures, and revenues that simply *reflects* the more basic, real forces at work. Theoretically, these money flows are not necessary. We can imagine households and firms *bartering* resources for goods. In fact, however, given the degree of specialization prevailing in our multimillion households-firms-products economy, we would be in trouble without money to help us carry out the myriad of required exchanges.

Because all relationships between households and firms take the form of competition for the best "deal" in either of the two markets pictured, you can easily see why our economy is also often referred to as a *market*, or *competitive*, economy. These terms are usually used in contrast to *command* economy in which economic transactions are guided by a central human authority, a possibility we shall investigate further in Chapter 16. Notice also that the competition of the market economy is peaceful. The inevitable conflicts of interest that arise in a world of scarcity, wherein not everyone can have everything, are in effect solved by saying: "You have something I want. Would you give it to me if I give you something you want, and at better terms than anyone else?"

The Governor

The maket economy has, as we noted, no central *human* authority at all, but it has a central authority, nevertheless. We might say that the market economy is governed by the *price system*, by the totality of interdependent prices in goods and resource markets to which self-seeking households and businessmen respond and which, in turn, continually respond to their actions. Just suppose most households suddenly decided to buy more steak and fewer pork chops. What would happen? First, the markets for steaks and pork chops would undergo a significant change. In the former, sellers would notice an unusually brisk demand. They would find their inventories disappearing at an alarming rate. They would increase orders to their suppliers, and, quite likely, the price of steak would rise. Pork, on the other hand, would accumulate at the supermarkets in ever-increasing quantities, tending to choke storage facilities. Retailers would quickly reduce orders, and, quite possibly, the price of pork would fall. If the change in household demand were to persist, these price changes would become the *signals* transmitting the need for further change throughout the economy. It is exactly this kind of information that any human central planner simply could not get nor digest, but that, through price changes, is transmitted to all those of whom further action is required. Those who raise cattle, for instance, would find their profits rise. The pig-raising business would be in the doldrums. Reduced profits and increasing losses would discourage people from this line of activity. Unusually high profits would coax more people to raise cattle and encourage existing ranchers to expand their operations. All the owners of resources in the cattle business would find their incomes rising. Resources would be attracted into this line, just when enterprising men would have the incentive to expand it. All the owners of resources in pig raising would find their incomes stagnant or falling. Labor, land, and capital would be taken out of this line by their owners, just when businessmen have the urge to contract it.

Price change is the signal, profit the carrot, and loss the stick needed to bring about the adjustments required by the households' change of mind. Households, like kings, decide ultimately what gets produced! By spending their money on steak, rather than pork, they are in effect "voting" to have scarce resources used to make steak and not pork. They could have instead voted to shift resources to the production of bicycles. Or concert halls. Or red cabbages. It all depends on how they are casting their "dollar votes." Ours is essentially a system of *consumer sovereignty*. As people go out shopping every day, they are in effect engaged in a continuous referendum telling producers what they must produce. Businessmen who follow the signals of the price system are rewarded with profit. Those who refuse to follow are eliminated by losses. The price system is the invisible mysterious *governor* that guides us all by disseminating information to just those parties of whom action is required.

In fact, as you might have experienced yourself, it is thrilling to recognize how such order can prevail in a complex economic system without a human hand to guide it. Adam Smith, whose *The Wealth of Nations* (1776) makes him the founder of modern economics, described the price system in these words:

> Every individual endeavors to employ his [resources] so that [their] produce may be of greatest value. He generally neither intends to promote the public interest, nor knows how much he is promoting it. He intends only his own security, only his own gain. And he is in this led by an *Invisible Hand* to promote an end which was no part of his intention. By pursuing his own interest he frequently promotes that of society more effectually than when he really intends to promote it.

A Word of Caution

Adam Smith concluded that any interference with the free-enterprise system by the government is almost certain to be harmful. From this developed a trend, during the last century, toward less and less government control of economic activities. The proponents of *laissez-faire* (complete governmental noninterference with the economy) argued that government's role was complete if it restricted itself to protecting life, liberty, and property, and upholding the sanctity of contracts by providing judicial redress. No one could possibly improve on the "invisible hand."

The important thing for us to see at the moment, however, is only the *possibility* of an economic order without central human direction. Whether it is perfection itself, as proponents of laissez-faire have claimed, is a matter taken up again in Part 2. We might, however, note three points right now.

First, a price system will bring about order, but not necessarily justice. It is hard-boiled and impersonal. If you are born rich, with lots of land and capital to sell, you will get a lot of money income and you can cast a lot of dollar votes in the market for goods, possibly without the slightest need to work. If your neighbor is poor, owning no land and capital, and if he is also unlucky, having been born with low intelligence or been prevented from acquiring a skill that sells for much in the labor market, he will get little money income. He will have few dollar votes to cast in the goods market, possibly while having to work 50 hours a week. Businessmen, however, will employ resources to make a profit; they will follow the path where dollar votes are heaviest. Thus, your demand for vitamins for your dog and a Cadillac for yourself may be satisfied before your neighbor's for vitamins and toys for his child. We shall return to this matter of justice in Part 4.

Second, although complete laissez-faire was never reached, the tide has turned. The economic role of government has been steadily expanding since the end of the last century. Hard as it may be to comprehend the magnificent work of the price system as the governor of our economy, it is easy enough to notice the variety of governmental economic activities. They sometimes aid, but often restrict, the free operation of the price system. Consider tariffs, the regulation of public utilities (broadcasting, television, telephones, electric power, water, gas, and so on), minimum wages, agricultural price floors, rent and interest-rate ceilings, zoning ordinances, pure food and drug laws, fair labor practice acts, social security, police protection, national defense, local-state-federal taxation. And so on. In fact, the various levels of government in the United States are now buying close to a quarter of national output. No wonder it is difficult to realize how much economic life still proceeds *without* direct government intervention. Clearly, though, at least some of this governmental economic activity is absolutely necessary to sustain our kind of community life. Thus, our economy now is certainly a *mixed* one, with private enterprise and public institutions sharing in the decision-making process that guides the use of resources. We shall continue to discuss this subject throughout the book.

Third, economists who followed Adam Smith have refined his notions about the price system considerably. In brief, they have noted that all the virtues claimed for the market economy hold only if competition is *perfect*: if no buyer or seller is a big enough part of the market to have a personal influence on price, if traded goods and resources are standardized, if people are well informed about the market, and if they are free to enter and leave it at will. Yet, this is often not true in the United States. Many of us sing the praises of competition in general, but we don't like the impersonal verdict of the price system when it hits too close to home. Price changes, for instance, can "make or break" us, so we try to gain at least some control over them. Many groups in our economy have succeeded in doing so, the most notable exception being millions of farmers who are individually producing a negligible fraction of the total crop (and all of whom have not yet succeeded in getting the government on their side establishing price supports). Take unions. Their main purpose is to control wages by group action. Thus, they interfere with the price system that may dictate, as in the case of our pig farmers above, a *fall* in wages. Or take some of the industrial giants. They have grown to such size that they supply a significant percentage of the market of a given product. It is naïve to think that the automaker or steelmaker is as helpless when it comes to price as is farmer Brown who raises one millionth of our annual crop of onions. Thus, competition is in many ways greatly restricted. We shall evaluate the consequences of this at great length in Part 2. There we shall look at perfect competition as a standard with which we can compare the actual economy.

A CLOSER LOOK AT SUPPLY AND DEMAND

We have noted that our economy is not one of *perfect* competition, owing to the significant economic power of government, unions, and large business, and that the price system does not automatically solve all questions of justice. We return in the remainder of this chapter to a closer look at free enterprise. We shall investigate exactly how market prices are established in perfect competition, thereby enabling the price system to do the remarkable job of guiding economic activity. What follows is thus only an elaboration on the circular flow section above. It is also a rough sketch of U.S. reality, somewhat of a tool for interpreting its broad features. As such, the material to be developed now helps us to understand our economy better and enables us to make a number of useful predictions in the real world of less than perfect competition.

Demand

You will notice the word "demand" appearing in the upper left and lower right corners of Figure 2.1 THE CIRCULAR FLOW. This illustrates that in any market, be it for a good or a resource, there must be some party willing and able to buy or the market will not function. *Demand* is, in fact, the economist's term for willingness and ability to buy. Note the careful wording, for demand is not the same as desire or want. You may want new shoes, but you are not demanding them unless you are also able and willing to pay for them. *Demand is want backed by purchasing power.*

Thus, unlike want, demand is limited. What is your demand for shoes? You will immediately notice that one cannot answer such a question, except by mumbling, "It all depends." For one thing, a time interval has to be specified. You will certainly give a different answer, depending on whether the questioner refers to this day, this week, this year, or your lifetime.

Well then, what is your demand for shoes this year? Again, you might well be perplexed. It still depends—on your income, for instance (as Figure 2.1 shows so clearly). If your income is $600 this year, you may buy a different quantity of everything than if it were $10,000.

O.K. What is your demand for shoes this year, if your income is $10,000 this year? One pair? Two? Five? But wait! What do shoes sell for? Suppose they are $500 a pair. Won't that change your answer? Of course, it will, and so will many other factors. Not only are you likely to vary your purchases with your income and the price of the good in question, but also with *all other factors* influencing your economic well-being. Your answer would differ, would it not, if you had to spend 90 percent, rather than 10 percent, of your $10,000 income on food. It would depend on your personal tastes in matters of dress, on the number of shoes you already owned, and so on. Thus, asking a question about demand is a lot easier than getting an answer. But we might proceed as follows.

Because your demand for shoes apparently depends on many things (your income, the price of shoes, the prices of other goods, your tastes, number of shoes already owned, and so on), why not specify all but one of these factors, possibly all but the most significant, *as fixed.* Then we can show how the quantity you demand varies with variation in the one factor only. Economists call this invoking the *ceteris paribus* clause, the Latin equivalent for "everything else being held equal." Suppose we do just that. And suppose, being interested at present in explaining how market prices are set, we allow only the price of shoes to vary. That is, throughout our considerations we hold everything else equal: your income does not change, nor do other prices, nor your tastes, and so on. All these, we assume, are constant at some (unspecified) levels. We might come up with something like Table 2.1, which shows how, every-

Table 2.1   THE DEMAND SCHEDULE

	PRICE ($ PER PAIR OF SHOES) P	QUANTITY OF SHOES DEMANDED (PAIRS PER YEAR) Q
A	32	2
B	16	4
C	8	6
D	4	8
E	2	10

A demand schedule *is a list that shows how—given everything else—quantity demanded varies with price. At lower price, P, quantity demanded, Q, is higher. Thus, demand is a whole series of price-quantity combinations.*

thing else being held equal, the quantity of shoes you are willing and able to buy per year varies with price. The lower the price, the greater the quantity. This makes a lot of sense. At a very high price, you are likely to satisfy only your very urgent wants. At lower ones, you can afford to gratify your less important ones. In this case, you may decide to buy many different pairs for different occasions or purposes.

This kind of demand schedule can, of course, be shown graphically, as in Figure 2.2 THE DEMAND CURVE. Note how each pair of numbers from Table 2.1 has been transferred to Figure 2.2, the points being located from the axes very much as you can locate a point on a map, if given latitude and longitude.[1] The smooth curve drawn through the dots is a *demand curve.* It shows that, everything else being held equal, only a lower price will coax out a larger quantity demanded. This is true for almost all goods, as well as resources, be they corn or cotton, gasoline or ice cream, plane rides or movie tickets, doctors' services or rental cars. It is referred to as the *law of downward-sloping demand.*

One final point. What if we relax the everything-else-being-equal clause and allow a change in one of the "givens"? Clearly, we would have to derive a completely new Table 2.1. If your income doubled or you developed a taste for fancy dress, you might buy twice as many shoes at *any* of the prices shown there. If food prices doubled, or you decided that going barefoot summers is good for your health, you might buy half as many shoes at any price. Thus, we could draw an entirely new demand curve in Figure 2.2. It would lie completely to the right of the curve shown there, indicating the effect on your demand for shoes of the doubling of income or greater taste for fancy dress. It would lie completely to the left of the curve shown, if food prices doubled or taste turned you away from wearing shoes. Such a *shift* of the entire demand curve is called a *change in demand.* This is always the result of a change in one of the factors not explicitly shown on the axes of the graph (and conveniently tucked away with the everything-else-being-held-equal clause). On the other hand, a *movement along* a given demand curve is called a *change in quantity demanded.* It is always the result of a

---

[1] Those not familiar with the technique of graphing are also referred to A Guide to the Student.

Figure 2.2   THE DEMAND CURVE

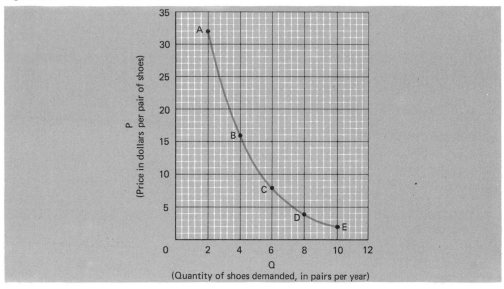

Price is plotted on the vertical axis, quantity demanded horizontally. Each pair of data from Table 2.1 is plotted as a heavy dot (A through E). A smooth curve, the demand curve, has been drawn through the dots. This illustrates the law of downward-sloping demand: when price is lower, quantity demanded is higher, everything else being held equal.

Figure 2.3   MOVEMENT ALONG VS. SHIFT OF THE DEMAND CURVE

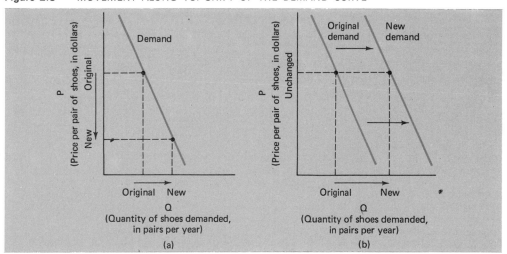

Part (a) shows a change in quantity demanded. It is owing to a fall in price, given everything else. Demand (the curve) has not changed. Part (b) shows a change in demand. It is owing to a change in one of the factors previously taken as fixed. The shift to the right pictured here may be owing to a rise in income, a fall in the prices of complementary goods (such as dresses or suits), and so on. Whatever price is, more shoes will be bought at the price now than before. All this can, of course, work in the opposite direction as well.

change in the variable depicted on one of the axes of the graph (here, price on the vertical axis).

You absolutely must understand this distinction. Reread the above. Then study Figure 2.3 MOVEMENT ALONG VS. SHIFT OF THE DEMAND CURVE. It is self-explanatory.

_____

Supply

Note the word "supply" in the upper right and lower left corners of Figure 2.1 THE CIRCULAR FLOW. This supplements the demand sides of the two markets. Just as a market cannot function without buyers, it is dead without people able and willing to sell. *Supply* is the economist's term for this ability and willingness.

Just as we derived a hypothetical demand schedule, we can derive a hypothetical schedule of a supplier, as in Table 2.2. Table 2.2 shows how, everything else being held equal, the quantity of shoes someone is able and willing to sell per year varies with price. The lower the price, the lower the quantity. This, too, makes a lot of sense. At a very low price, one is less likely to profit by acquiring the necessary resources and producing the good than at a higher price. Possibly, production of another, higher-priced product will be preferred. At a higher price prospects are brighter. One can afford to buy resources previously too expensive; one possibly can bid them away from someone else; it may pay to press into service otherwise

Table 2.2   THE SUPPLY SCHEDULE

	PRICE (DOLLARS PER PAIR OF SHOES) P	QUANTITY OF SHOES SUPPLIED (PAIRS PER YEAR) Q
A	32	10
B	16	8
C	8	6
D	4	4
E	2	2

A supply schedule is a list that shows how—given everything else—quantity supplied varies with price. At lower price, P, quantity supplied, Q, is lower also. Thus, supply, as demand, is a whole series of price-quantity combinations.

uneconomical standby equipment, to produce less of something else, and so on. Thus, quantity supplied goes up.

This kind of supply schedule can again be graphed, as in Figure 2.4 THE SUPPLY CURVE, and by the same method. The smooth curve drawn through the dots is called a *supply curve*. It shows that, everything else being held equal, only a higher price will coax out a larger quantity supplied. It is referred to as the *law of upward-sloping supply*.

Here, as earlier in the case of demand, the everything-else-being-held-equal assumption is crucial. If we allow any other relevant factor to change (resource prices fall, prices of other goods produced by the firm rise, technical know-how changes, and so on), we must again derive a completely new Table 2.2. Then our firm can be expected to supply more (or less) of the good in question at *any* price shown here. This would again show up graphically as a *shift* of the supply curve (and be called a *change in supply*). As in the case of demand, note how this

Figure 2.4   THE SUPPLY CURVE

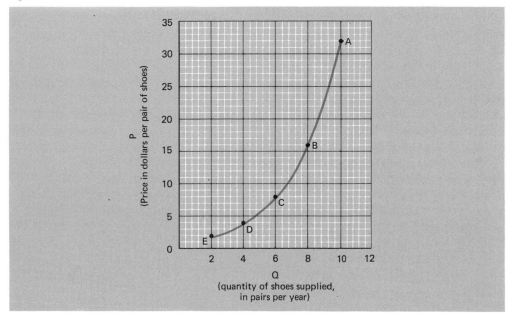

With price on the vertical and quantity supplied on the horizontal axis, each pair of data from Table 2.2 THE SUPPLY SCHEDULE *is plotted as a heavy dot (A through E). A smooth curve, the* supply curve, *has been drawn through the dots. This illustrates the law of upward-sloping supply: when price is higher, quantity supplied is higher, everything else being held equal.*

would result from a change in one of the factors not explicitly shown on the axes of the graph (and instead included in the everything-else-being-held-equal assumption). Correspondingly, a *movement along* a given supply curve is called a *change in quantity supplied*. It is always the result of a change in the variable depicted on one of the axes of the graph (here price on the vertical axis).

Market Equilibrium

What has been said for one buyer and one seller can be said about others. Their individual demand curves (or supply curves) can be added together. If, at $8 per pair, you demand six pairs of shoes per year and I demand twelve, we together demand eighteen. This can be continued for all demanders and all potential prices. It can be repeated for all suppliers. Thus, we derive *market* demand and *market* supply curves. They would look exactly like Figures 2.2 and 2.4, except that the quantities on the horizontal axes would be larger. Possibly, Q would now represent million pairs of shoes per year, rather than just pairs of shoes.

In this aggregate case, we can also add another reason for the law of downward-sloping demand: the lower the price, the more buyers are likely to enter the market. Quantity demanded rises not only because given buyers buy more. Similarly, the law of upward-sloping supply is reinforced: the higher the price, the more sellers are likely to appear. Quantity supplied rises not only because given sellers offer more.

So far, we have only been speculating. "If price is this," we said, "quantity demanded (or supplied) would be that." Now we can find what price and quantity *actually* would be. Suppose the market demand and supply schedules were those of Table 2.3. What would happen in a perfectly competitive market? Clearly, price could not stay for long at $32 per pair of shoes. Sellers would then find it profitable to offer 10 million pairs per year, but buyers would take only 2 million pairs. Like it or not, 8 million pairs of unwanted shoes would accumulate on the shelves. Unhappy sellers, bidding against one another, would tend to depress the price. As it falls, quantity demanded goes up (existing buyers buy more, new buyers come into the market). Quantity supplied goes down (existing firms supply less, possibly get out of this business altogether).

Similarly, price could not for long remain at $2 per pair. Few sellers would find it worthwhile being in the business. They would offer only 2 million pairs per year, but buyers would be ready to buy 10 million pairs. The shortage would be keenly felt. Many potential buyers would go without. Trying to get shoes that do not exist, they would, competing against one

Table 2.3   DEMAND AND SUPPLY SCHEDULES COMPARED

	PRICE PER PAIR OF SHOES (DOLLARS)	QUANTITY DEMANDED	QUANTITY SUPPLIED	SURPLUS (+) OR SHORTAGE (−)	EFFECT ON PRICE
		(MILLION PAIRS OF SHOES PER YEAR)			
	P		Q		
A	32	2	10	+8	pressure to fall
B	16	4	8	+4	pressure to fall
C	8	6	6	0	neutral
D	4	8	4	−4	pressure to rise
E	2	10	2	−8	pressure to rise

Combining market demand and market supply schedules, we find only one price at which quantity demanded equals quantity supplied. This is the equilibrium price, here $8, toward which the market will tend.

another, pull up price. As it rises, quantity supplied goes up (existing sellers produce more, new sellers enter the field). Quantity demanded goes down (existing buyers buy fewer shoes, some buy none at all).

In the long run, there is thus only one price and quantity that brings *equilibrium,* eliminates any innate tendency to change. Price will tend to become $8, quantity traded 6 million pairs of shoes per year. These are the equilibrium price and equilibrium quantity. At that price, buyers in the aggregate go on willingly buying 6 million pairs, sellers go on happily offering the same amount. Only a change in demand or supply (that is, a change in the quantity columns of Table 2.3) can upset the equilibrium.

Figure 2.5   DEMAND AND SUPPLY CURVES SUPERIMPOSED

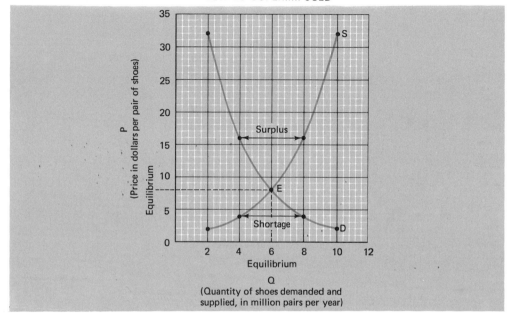

This graph of Table 2.3 illustrates the establishment of equilibrium price and quantity in the perfectly competitive market. These are found at intersection E, of the demand and supply curves, which are labeled D and S, respectively. At any higher price, there are surpluses, tending to depress price. At any lower ones, there are shortages, tending to raise price.

This same story can be told graphically. Consider Figure 2.5 DEMAND AND SUPPLY CURVES SUPERIMPOSED. It is a graph of Table 2.3 DEMAND AND SUPPLY SCHEDULES COMPARED. It is immediately obvious that there is only one possible equilibrium position in this market: the point of intersection, E, of the demand and supply curves. At that price, and at no other price, are buyers willing and able to take exactly what sellers are willing and able to bring to market (6 million pairs of shoes per year).

At *any* higher price we would find surpluses. Graphically, they can be measured by the horizontal distance between the two curves at a given price, say $16. In this case, quantity supplied would be eight, quantity demanded only four. Thus, *actual* trade (were a $16 price ever to prevail) could only involve four, whereas 4 million other pairs accumulate on the shelves. Hence, price tends to fall toward E through competition among sellers.

At *any* lower price, say $4, we would find shortages. They are also read off horizontally, because quantity is graphed on the horizontal axis. In this case, quantity supplied would be only four, quantity demanded eight. Thus, *actual* trade could only involve four, whereas potential demanders of another 4 million pairs go without. This time it is unhappy buyers who will pull the price *up* toward E as they compete with one another.

Watch out. The price change does not cause any change in demand or supply (that refers to the entire curves and they have not changed); it causes changes in quantities demanded and in quantities supplied, as buyers and sellers *move along* given curves toward equilibrium point E.

From Partial to General Equilibrium

What we have said about the market for shoes can, of course, be said about all other markets, including the markets for all other goods as well as those for resources, such as labor. By trial and error, as in this case, the actions of millions of households and firms will tend to establish, through the forces of demand and supply, equilibrium prices and quantities in all markets. They will thus come to create more than only a *partial* equilibrium (in one market), but a *general* equilibrium throughout the economy. Thus, Figure 2.5 DEMAND AND SUPPLY CURVES SUPERIMPOSED, is sort of a microscopic view into the markets depicted at the top and bottom of Figure 2.1 THE CIRCULAR FLOW. What we have seen here in detail, must be imagined to happen there a hundred thousand times. Moreover, matters there are greatly more com-

Figure 2.6   RISE IN THE DEMAND FOR STEAK

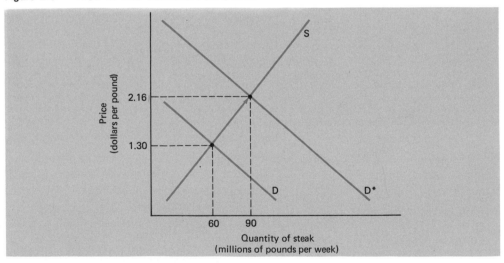

A rise in the demand for steak, caused by a change in consumer taste, leads to higher price and higher quantity traded in a perfectly competitive market. Although supply (the entire curve) has not changed, the higher price coaxes out a higher quantity supplied. It causes sellers to move to a different point on the curve, as by stepping up production. The arrow shows the movement of the equilibrium point.

plicated. It is the privilege of the partial analyst to ignore repercussions on other markets. By tucking away, in the everything-else-being-held-equal clause, all the complicating material, we have been able to keep things nice and simple.

When we look back at the whole economy of Figure 2.1, however, we cannot do this. Reality does not hold everything else constant for us. We must realize, like it or not, that everything does depend on everything else and that any change in one market will have inevitable repercussions in all other markets. This interdependence of markets is somewhat sketchily illustrated in Figures 2.6 to 2.11.

Consider our earlier example. If households' tastes change and they buy more steak and fewer pork chops, we noted earlier that the price of steak is likely to go up, that of pork chops likely to go down. This can now be shown graphically with the type of diagram just used in Figure 2.5 DEMAND AND SUPPLY CURVES SUPERIMPOSED. The demand for steak having risen (people are able and willing to buy more at *any* price), demand curve D in Figure 2.6 shifts to D*. You must imagine that demand curve D has completely disappeared and is replaced by D*. The equilibrium moves along the unchanged supply curve S from the DS intersection to the D*S intersection. New equilibrium price and quantity are higher than before, as you can read off on the axes. Price rises from $1.30 to $2.16 per pound. Quantity traded rises from 60 million to 90 million pounds per week. (Can you show how a failure of price to rise above its old level would cause shortages at that old level?)

Figure 2.7   FALL IN THE DEMAND FOR PORK

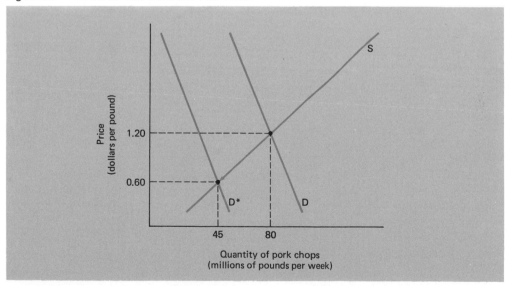

A fall in the demand for pork, caused by a change in consumer taste, leads to a lower price and lower quantity traded in a perfectly competitive market. Although supply (the entire curve) has not changed, the lower price results in lower quantity supplied. It causes sellers to move to a different point on the curve, as by decreasing their rate of production. The arrow shows the movement of the equilibrium point.

Figure 2.8   RISE IN THE DEMAND FOR PASTURE LAND

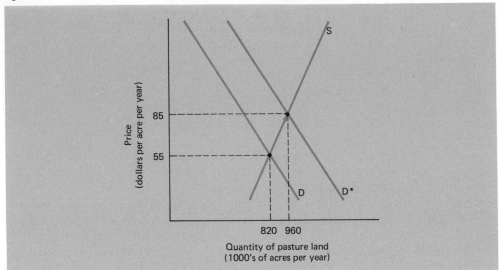

A rise in the demand for pasture land, caused by a rise in the demand for steak, leads to a higher price and higher quantity traded in a perfectly competitive market. Although supply (the entire curve) has not changed, the higher price coaxes out a higher quantity supplied. It causes sellers to move to a different point on the curve, for example, by taking land out of other uses. The arrow shows the movement of the equilibrium point.

Figure 2.9   RISE IN THE DEMAND FOR YACHTS

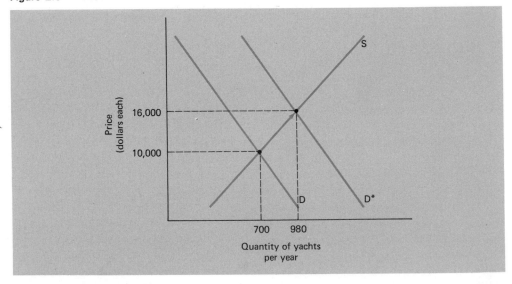

A rise in the demand for yachts, caused by a rise in the income of pasture land owners, leads to a higher price and higher quantity traded in a perfectly competitive market. Although supply (the entire curve) has not changed, the higher price coaxes out a higher quantity supplied. It causes sellers to move to a different point on the curve, as by stepping up production. The arrow shows the movement of the equilibrium point.

Similarly, the fall in the demand for pork can be illustrated by a shift of demand curve D left to D* in Figure 2.7. Equilibrium price and quantity fall. Price falls from $1.20 to $0.60 per pound. Quantity traded drops from 80 million to 45 million pounds per week.

There will be thousands of other effects, however. For instance, we already noted how the demand for resources will rise with the demand for the product they help produce. Thus, the demand for pasture land may rise as the cattle business expands because steaks sell so well. This is shown in Figure 2.8, which shows the rent on pasture land to rise and the quantity used with it. Rent rises from $55 per year on the acre to $85; the acreage used for pastures rises from 820,000 to 960,000.

The higher incomes of pasture land owners may enable them to live more luxuriously in turn. Among other things, they may buy more yachts. As shown in Figure 2.9, the demand for yachts rises and with it their price and the quantity traded. Price rises from $10,000 per yacht to $16,000. Quantity traded goes from 700 to 980 yachts per year.

On the other hand, farmers who raise fewer pigs will now buy less corn to feed pigs. Thus, the demand for corn falls, as is shown in Figure 2.10. With this fall in demand, we find lower price and lower quantity traded in the corn market. Price falls from $1.70 per bushel to $0.90 per bushel. Quantity traded falls from 120 million bushels per year to 80 million. But note how pig-raisers reduced demand for corn by the horizontal distance between D and D*, or by 70 million bushels per year at the old price. Yet, quantity traded fell eventually by much less,

Figure 2.10   FALL IN THE DEMAND FOR CORN

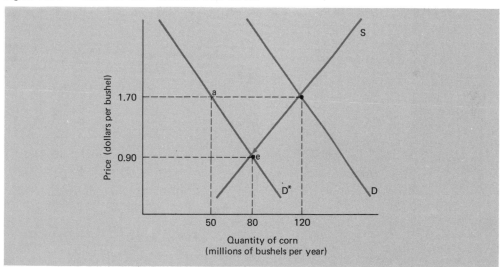

A fall in the demand for corn, caused by decreased needs for feed by pig raising farmers, leads to a lower price and lower quantity traded in a perfectly competitive market. Although supply (the entire curve) has not changed, the lower price results in lower quantity supplied. It causes sellers to move to a different point on the curve, for example, by decreasing their rate of production. The arrow shows the movement of the equilibrium point.

by 40 million bushels only. This happened because the lower price induced someone to buy more corn. Someone moved *along* the new demand curve from a to e, as price fell from its old level of $1.70 to its new level of $0.90 per bushel. Suppose these mysterious buyers are producers of cornflakes. Having bought cheaper corn, they may now offer any given quantity of cornflakes for less, or, what is the same thing, supply a greater quantity of cornflakes at any given price. In Figure 2.11, therefore, supply of cornflakes rises from S to S*. (Yes, it *rises*, although it may first appear as if the new supply curve is *below* the old one. But remember: quantity is not measured vertically, but horizontally. Thus, at any price the new curve S* shows a larger quantity than the old one.) With the rise in supply of cornflakes, equilibrium price falls and quantity rises. Corn being cheaper, cornflakes now sell for 30 cents a package, rather than for 58 cents. As a result, 170 million packages are sold per week, rather than 88 million.

Clearly, we could continue our story endlessly. All the people who directly or indirectly contribute labor, land, or capital to the production of steak will find their fortunes rising, as our owners of pasture land did. Their good luck will, in turn spread to others, as to the makers of yachts. All the people who contribute labor, land, or capital to the production of pork will find their livelihood threatened, as our corn producers did. This will, of course, affect others, too. Farmers growing corn may buy fewer plows and refrigerators, for instance. Finally, there will be a myriad of seemingly unrelated effects. As we just saw, your breakfast cereal may suddenly be cheaper.

Figure 2.11   RISE IN THE SUPPLY OF CORNFLAKES

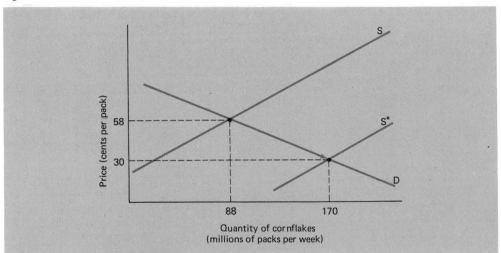

A rise in the supply of cornflakes, caused by their producers' ability to buy corn for less, leads to a lower price, but higher quantity traded in a perfectly competitive market. Although demand (the entire curve) has not changed, the lower price results in higher quantity demanded. It causes buyers to move to a different point on the curve, for example, by increasing their rate of consumption. The arrow shows the movement of the equilibrium point.

You can easily imagine how the repercussions of any other change in demand or supply will be similarly spread, in ever-widening circles, but also in ever-weakening ones, throughout the economy. This is akin to the wave effect of a stone that is thrown into a pond.

If you understand the above, you have a pretty good picture, although a highly idealized one, of the behavior of a market economy. It is not run by one man or a committee of men. Rather, the interaction of millions of them, in hundreds of thousands of interdependent markets, simultaneously operating and chasing after ever-changing equilibria, solves the complex problem of allocating our resources. Note how beautifully and simply price changes in the cases just studied tell land owners to put more land into cattle grazing and less into growing corn, tell yacht producers to step up production and tell households to eat more cornflakes (now that corn is less scarce because pigs eat less). No human brain, no computer even in sight, could so quickly transmit all this relevant information to just the right parties at just the right time. As we shall see, there are many things wrong with the actual market economy in which we live, but this should not keep us from admiring its accomplishments.

SUMMARY

1 Although every economy faces the identical problem of scarcity, there are alternative ways of allocating resources among their possible uses. One would be through central human direction. Another is the unconscious, and often unnoticed, resource allocation through a price system.

2 A price system is utilized by the United States, which has a capitalist, money-and-exchange, free-enterprise economy. Private owners of goods and resources essentially are free to buy and sell them for money as they please, seeking only their self-interest.

3 In so doing, they compete against one another in goods and resource markets. Hence the name market, or competitive, economy. Forces of demand and supply establish market prices that become the signals guiding and coordinating the actions of self-seeking buyers and sellers.

4 The market economy permits a substantial degree of consumer sovereignty. Resources will be channeled in directions desired most by households, as indicated by their dollar votes in the markets. This is so because businesses that follow the guidance of the price system will make profits and prosper; those that do not, suffer losses and are eliminated. Thus, it appears that the economy is guided by an invisible hand.

5 It must be noted that the U.S. market economy is far from *perfectly* competitive. This requires, among other things, that no single market participant has any appreciable personal influence on any price. Governments, unions, and large businesses, however, possess significant economic power. Thus, the economy is a mixed one, standing between unconscious market control and conscious human control. It must also be noted that even a perfectly competitive economy would not address itself satisfactorily to some questions, such as the question of justice in the distribution of goods among persons.

6 The perfectly competitive model of an economy is, nevertheless, very useful in that it allows us to study the possibility of an unconsciously directed economic order in all its purity. This enables us to understand the broad features of the U.S. economy better.

7   The perfectly competitive model can be illustrated with the help of demand and supply curves. The forces of demand and supply tend to establish equilibrium market prices. Any change in one market has, however, repercussions on practically all others, because markets are interdependent. It is in this way that information, which no single individual could possibly possess, is put together, weighted, and transmitted in understandable form to all. Because every change, from changing relative scarcities of resources to changes in technology and tastes, will be reflected in appropriate price changes, the price system can properly become the governor of the economy. Everyone looks to prices for information he could neither get nor understand in any other form, and he acts on that basis.

TERMS[2]

ceteris paribus clause	"law of supply"
circular flow	market
command economy	market economy
competitive economy	mixed economy
consumer sovereignty	partial vs. general equilibrium
demand	perfect competition
demand curve	price system
demand schedule	profit
dollar votes	quantity demanded
entrepreneur	quantity supplied
equilibrium	rent
firm	resource market
free-enterprise economy	shortage
goods market	supply
household	supply curve
interest	supply schedule
invisible hand	surplus
laissez-faire	wage
"law of demand"	

SYMBOLS

P

Q

QUESTIONS FOR REVIEW AND DISCUSSION

1   Why would it be so difficult for any man or committee or computer even to plan economic activity centrally?

[2] Terms and symbols are defined in the Glossary at the end of the book.

2 The price system has been described as "simply marvelous." What is so marvelous about the price system?

3 Explain the meaning of the "circular flow."

4 Evaluate the importance of money in our economy. How would we fare without it?

5 "Private vice is public virtue." Evaluate in light of what you have read about self-seeking households and firms and the "invisible hand."

6 The text says "ours is essentially a system of consumer sovereignty." Can you think of exceptions?

7 "Government should keep hands off the economy." Discuss, bringing out arguments in favor and against.

8 Explain the importance of distinguishing between economic order and economic justice. Do you think this has any relevance to the United States today? How about *political* order and justice?

9 "Ours is not a price system, it's a profit-and-loss system." Discuss, trying to make sense of the statement.

10 When a demand curve shifts, we experience all of these: a change in demand, a change in quantity demanded, and a change in quantity supplied. Explain.

11 "An increase in supply and a simultaneous increase in demand could well lead to a rise in price with quantity traded unchanged." Evaluate. Is it true? Is it false? Why?

12 "What one person buys is always what another sells. Look at any book of statistics! Supply and demand can never differ. It's illogical." Discuss. Is it true? Is it false? Why? (The Glossary might help.)

13 The price of carpenter services may well depend on oil land royalties. Explain. (Remember the interdependence of markets.)

14 "To live, people need water, but not diamonds. Yet the former costs almost nothing, and the latter command an enormous price. This proves that demand has nothing to do with price." Evaluate. (Look at each sentence: Is it true? Is it false? Why?)

15 Write down a scale of hypothetical prices for movie tickets, cigarettes, and restaurant meals. Estimate your own demand schedules for these items and graph each. What kind of factors may change your *demand?* Make a list. Show the graphical effects of each possible demand change.

16 What kind of factors may shift a household's supply curve of labor? A firm's demand curve for labor?

17 "Although we should all like to escape the hardship implied by higher market price, show that rising market prices may perform some useful functions in time of scarcity." Evaluate this quotation. Aren't all things *always* scarce?

18 What effects would the invention and production of mechanical cotton pickers have on a plantation economy based on manual labor? (Remember the interdependence of markets.)

19 "If price rises, demand falls, but a fall in demand lowers price, so we end up where we started." Evaluate. (Look at each part of the sentence: Is it true? Is it false? Why?)

20 Spell out the process by which price must settle down at the intersection of supply and demand curves. (Ask yourself what would happen if price were higher. What if it were lower?)

In this part of the book, we shall discuss whether the full utilization of resources can be brought about in the modern economy. Although we shall refer mostly to data and institutions in the United States, the economic analysis presented here can be regarded as applicable to most developed capitalist countries in the world. By making only appropriate changes in the descriptive material, we could just as well be telling the story of Australia, Canada, Japan, New Zealand, or the countries of Western Europe. Two final chapters, however, look at the same problem in the very different context of the centrally planned, socialist economy.

full employment of resources

Manpower Message of the President

The question of our day is this: In an economy capable of sustaining high employment, how can we assure every American who is willing to work the right to earn a living?

We have always paid lipservice to that right.

But there are many Americans for whom the right has never been real:

> —The boy who becomes a man without developing the ability to earn a living.
>
> —The citizen who is barred from a job because of other men's prejudices.
>
> —The worker who loses his job to a machine and is told he is too old for anything else.
>
> —The boy or girl from the slums whose summers are empty because there is nothing to do.
>
> —The man and the woman blocked from productive employment by barriers rooted in poverty: lack of health, lack of education, lack of training, lack of motivation.

Their idleness is a tragic waste both of the human spirit and of the economic resources of a great Nation.

It is a waste that an enlightened Nation should not tolerate.

It is a waste that a Nation concerned by disorders in its city streets *cannot* tolerate.

Lyndon B. Johnson (1968)

3

A T THIS POINT, we have become aware of two things. First, we realize that it would be utter folly to leave resources unused at a time when many people want many goods they cannot have. Thus, it is only sensible to employ our resources fully. Second, we have had at least a glimpse of the nature of the mechanism by which resources are being put to work in the United States. We saw that this mechanism, which is the price system, steers resources in the directions most urgently desired by those people who can back up their wants with purchasing power. This is so because people are free to follow their self-interest, and private businesses, out to make profits, would go bankrupt if they did not heed the advice transmitted to them by rising and falling prices. In this chapter, we go a step further by describing the nature of one of two persistent problems of the modern market economy: unemployment. We consider how unemployment is measured and what its historical incidence has been in the U.S. economy. In the next chapter, we shall look at unemployment's twin, inflation, and thereafter at both their causes and cures.

THE COSTS OF UNEMPLOYMENT

Open your daily newspaper, or study American history, and stories about unemployment of men and machines abound. In our newspapers and magazines these are the kind of headlines we see: "Idle Rate Rises for 2nd Month. Unemployment at Highest Level for 2 Years." "GE Slashes Syracuse Work Force 20 Per Cent. Third Round of Cutbacks in 90 days. Similar Throughout U.S." "National Unemployment Rate Steady at 4.1 Per Cent, Government Says."

Clearly, such headlines herald important costs to society.

The most obvious cost, of course, is the loss of goods that might have been produced with the unemployed resources. The enforced idleness of resources is equivalent to the unused medicine a sick man refuses to take; he remains sick. Society has to contend with more scarcity than necessary. Yet, in the case of labor, the costs of unemployment go far beyond the loss of goods that might have been. Unemployment can inflict wounds that tear apart civilized society.

The most dramatic instance of this is the Great Depression of the 1930s. This is a period with which most readers of this book will be only faintly familiar, for fewer than 14 percent of today's population were adults in 1930. But try to imagine what it must have been like living in a country in which millions, many millions, were unemployed for years on end. To be sure, initially their unemployment may almost have seemed a welcome vacation. Hopefully and vigorously went the search for a new job. But when it did not come soon, the vacation-type atmosphere quickly vanished. Job-hunting turned desperate. Week after week, month after month, there was no luck. Then the clothes wore out, the few valuables were sold to feed the family, the food became less, and worse. Despair began to move in, followed by stark poverty. By the thousands, people were evicted from their apartments, lost their houses, were pushed off their farms. Think how they must have felt, living with friends, making a few rooms serve a dozen people, shivering through a winter, listening to their children cry for bread.

Think of the mental anguish of a man in this position, unable to look at his family because he feels so guilty, frightened at his own inability to help them, irritable because he dislikes the stigma of charity, angry because society denies him the opportunity to earn his own living. There just was no place for him and those he loved! No wonder the parks and streets were filled with men in shabby clothes, refusing to even move. No wonder others, by the thousands, wandered through the countryside, aimlessly, scraping by on almost nothing, pursued by the police and "respectable" citizens who wanted nothing to do with them. Witness the testimony given in 1932 before a Senate subcommittee by Mr. De Schweinitz:[1]

"When I appeared before the Subcommittee . . . last December, I stated that there were 238,000 persons out of work in Philadelphia. . . . There are now 298,000 persons out of work. . . .

In December I told you that 43,000 families were receiving relief. Today 55,000 families are receiving relief.

In December, our per family grant was $4.39 per week per family. It is now $4.23 per family. Of this $4.23 per family, about $3.93 is an allowance for food. This is about two-thirds of the amount needed to provide a health-maintaining diet. . . . I want to tell you about an experience we had in Philadelphia when our private funds were exhausted and before public funds became available. . . .

There was a period of about 11 days when many families received nothing. We have received reports from workers as to how these families managed. The material I am about to give you is typical, although it is based on a small sample. . . .

· · ·

One woman said she borrowed 50 cents from a friend and bought stale bread for 3½ cents per loaf, and that is all they had for eleven days except for one or two meals.

· · ·

Here is a family of a pregnant mother and three children. They had only two meals a day and managed by having breakfast about 11 o'clock in the morning and then advancing the time of their evening meal. Breakfast consisted of cocoa, and bread and butter; the evening meal of canned soup.

One woman went along the docks and picked up vegetables that fell from the wagons. Sometimes the fish vendors gave her fish at the end of the day. On two different occasions this family was without food for a day and a half. . . .

Another family . . . for two days had nothing to eat but bread, and during most of the rest of the time they had only two meals a day. Their meals consisted of bread and coffee for breakfast, and bread and raw or cooked carrots for dinner.

The gas company was careful not to turn off gas in a great many of these families, so in some instances food could be cooked.

Another family did not have food for two days. Then the husband went out and gathered dandelions and the family lived on them. . . . Still another family thinking to get as much as possible with their last food order bought potatoes and for 11 days lived only on them. . . .

I should also like to say that when we talk to people who ask about unemployment they say, "Well, people manage to get along somehow or other, don't they? You do not have very many people who really drop dead of starvation." That is perfectly true. Actually, death from starvation is not a frequent occurrence. . . . They live on inadequacies, and because they

---

[1] *Federal Cooperation in Unemployment Relief,* Hearings Before Senate Subcommittee on Manufactures, 72d Congress, 1st Session, 1932, pp. 20–26. The testimony was given in May 1932.

live on inadequacies the thing does not become dramatic and we do not hear about it. Yet the cost in human suffering is just as great as if they starved to death overnight.

Another witness, Mr. Ameringer, had this to say:[2]

In the State of Washington I was told that the forest fires raging in that region all summer and fall were caused by unemployed timber workers and bankrupt farmers in an endeavor to earn a few honest dollars as fire fighters. The last thing I saw on the night I left Seattle was numbers of women searching for scraps of food in the refuse piles of the principal market of that city. A number of Montana citizens told me of thousands of bushels of wheat left in the fields uncut on account of its low price that hardly paid for the harvesting. In Oregon I saw thousands of bushels of apples rotting in the orchards. Only absolute flawless apples were still salable, at from 40 to 50 cents a box containing 200 apples. At the same time, there are millions of children who, on account of the poverty of their parents, will not eat one apple this winter.

While I was in Oregon the Portland Oregonian bemoaned the fact that thousands of ewes were killed by the sheep raisers because they did not bring enough in the market to pay the freight on them. And while Oregon sheep raisers fed mutton to the buzzards, I saw men picking for meat scraps in the garbage cans in the cities of New York and Chicago. I talked to one man in a restaurant in Chicago. He told me of his experience in raising sheep. He said that he had killed 3,000 sheep this fall and thrown them down the canyon, because it cost $1.10 to ship a sheep, and then he would get less than a dollar for it. He said he could not afford to feed the sheep, and he would not let them starve, so he just cut their throats and threw them down the canyon.

The roads of the West and Southwest teem with hungry hitchhikers. The camp fires of the homeless are seen along every railroad track. I saw men, women, and children walking over the hard roads. Most of them were tenant farmers who had lost their all in the late slump in wheat and cotton. Between Clarksville and Russelville, Ark., I picked up a family. The woman was hugging a dead chicken under a ragged coat. When I asked her where she had procured the fowl, first she told me she had found it dead in the road, and then added in grim humor, "They promised me a chicken in the pot, and now I got mine."

Yet we need not dwell in the 1930's. What may seem like ancient history to you, can be found in the midst of contemporary society. To be sure, some things have improved. No depressions of like scope and intensity as that of the 1930's have been experienced since. We now talk of recession to indicate the milder nature of economic downturns. They involve considerably fewer people. Even of these, some are not in desperate straits. Old attitudes and institutions have changed and for the better. Unlike the 1930's there is now widespread unemployment insurance, providing temporary financial support for regular workers laid off. There are now unions providing private unemployment compensation to supplement governmental benefits. But such schemes, though helpful, are hardly enough. They only provide a fraction of regular income. They expire after a number of weeks. And many people fail to qualify for assistance at all, not having held regular jobs for a long enough time. They must rely on inadequate government relief, very much as was done during the 1930's. And

[2] *Unemployment in the United States,* Hearings Before House Committee on Labor, 72d Congress, 1st Session, 1933, pp. 98–99. The testimony was given in February 1932.

to these people the relative mildness of unemployment in the overall economy is of little solace.

Consider the following report on America in the 1960's:[3]

In New York City, some of my friends call 80 Warren Street "the slave market."

It is a big building in downtown Manhattan. Its corridors have the littered, trampled air of a courthouse. They are lined with employment-agency offices. Some of these places list good-paying and highly skilled jobs. But many of them provide the work force for the economic underworld in the big city: the dishwashers and day workers, the fly-by-night jobs.

Early every morning, there is a great press of human beings in 80 Warren Street. It is made up of Puerto Ricans and Negroes, alcoholics, drifters, and disturbed people. Some of them will pay a flat fee (usually around 10 per cent) for a day's work. They pay $0.50 for a $5.00 job and they are given the address of a luncheonette. If all goes well, they will make their wage. If not, they have a legal right to come back and get their half-dollar. But many of them don't know that, for they are people that are not familiar with laws and rights.

But perhaps the most depressing time at 80 Warren Street is in the afternoon. The jobs have all been handed out, yet the people still mill around. Some of them sit on benches in the larger offices. There is no real point to their waiting, yet they have nothing else to do. For some, it is probably a point of pride to be there, a feeling that they are somehow still looking for a job even if they know that there is no chance to get one until early in the morning.

Most of the people at 80 Warren Street were born poor. . . . They are incompetent as far as American society is concerned, lacking the education and the skills to get decent work. If they find steady employment, it will be in a sweatshop or a kitchen. . . .

These people are the rejects of the affluent society. They never had the right skills in the first place, or they lost them when the rest of the economy advanced. They are the ones who make up a huge portion of the culture of poverty in the cities of America. They are to be counted in the millions.

Each big city in the United States has an economic underworld. And often enough this phrase is a literal description: it refers to the kitchens and furnace rooms that are under the city; it tells of the place where tens of thousands of hidden people labor at impossible wages. Like the underworld of crime, the economic underworld is out of sight, clandestine. . . .

Yet the workers in the sweatshops [can] consider themselves lucky. They [may be] making $1 an hour, which [is] something. Two men I talked to were in a different classification: they had passed the line of human obsolescence in this industrial society. They were over forty years of age. They had been laid off at Armour in the summer of 1959. Eighteen months later, neither of them had found a steady job of any kind. "When I come to the hiring window," one of them said, "the man just looks at me; he doesn't even ask questions; he says, 'You're too old.' " . . .

What happens to the man who goes eighteen months without a steady job? The men told me. First, the "luxuries" go: the car, the house, everything that has been purchased on installment but yet not paid for. Then comes doubling up with relatives (and one of the persistent problems in becoming poor is that marriages are often wrecked in the process). Finally—and this is particularly true of the "older" worker—there is relief, formal admission into the other America . . .

In the thirties . . . unemployment was a general problem of the society. A quarter of the work force was in the streets, and everyone was affected. . . . White-collar workers were laid

[3] Michael Harrington, *The Other America* (Baltimore, Md.: Penguin Books, 1963), pp. 25, 26, 31–32, and 35. Reprinted with permission of the Macmillan Company. Copyright © 1962 by Michael Harrington.

off like everyone else. From out of this experience, there came a definition of "good times": if the statistics announced that more people were working than ever before, that was prosperity; if there was a dip in employment, with 4,000,000 to 6,000,000 temporarily laid off, that was a recession.

But the definitions of the thirties blind us to a new reality. It is now possible (or rather it is the reality) to have an increase in the number of employed, an expansion of consumption, a boom in production and, at the same time, localized depressions. In the midst of general prosperity, there will be types of jobs, entire areas, and huge industries in which misery is on the increase. The familiar America of high living standards moves upward; the other America of poverty continues to move downward. . . .

In the thirties . . . there was mass unemployment; in the postwar period there has been class unemployment. Special groups will be singled out by the working of the economy to suffer, while all others will experience prosperity.

The latter point has been corroborated by many others. Consider this report on the Bronx in New York City:[4]

[In the Bronx] live more than 100,000 Puerto Ricans and 100,000 Negroes with their ranks growing, and fewer than 60,000 Irish, Italians, Germans and Jews, with their numbers declining. The area's housing is old and falling apart, with more than 68 per cent of its 84,677 dwelling units in various stages of decay and more than 81 per cent 40 years old or older. Since 1950, when the older ethnic groups began moving out and large numbers of Puerto Ricans and Negroes began moving in, private building has ceased, and the only new construction has been public housing.

More than 70 per cent of those who hold jobs do the kind of semi-skilled or unskilled work that pays the least. The unemployment rate is about 9 per cent, almost double the city-wide rate.

For this and . . . Manhattan's Harlem and Brooklyn's Brownsville the city has found that 28 per cent of the residents have less than $3,000 a year to live on, that 33.9 per cent of the children under 18 are on welfare, that 38.9 per cent of the adults 25 years old or older have less than eight years of schooling, that the juvenile arrest rate is almost double the city's rate, that narcotics addiction and all its attendant problems of muggings and burglaries is epidemic.

Neither these nor other figures, however, quite suggest the quality of life under these conditions.

If, by some misadventure, a tourist wandered into the South Bronx, he would find few residential blocks without one or two empty, windowless, fire-blackened buildings. He would see curbsides ankle-deep in refuse except where the space was taken by the stripped hulks of abandoned autos; streets almost empty of life by day and by night and tenements noisome with the stench of urine and decay.

"You get used to it, baby, but you never like it," said a black youth sitting last week on a stoop on 140th Street near St. Anne's Place.

Again, consider the *Report of the National Advisory Commission on Civil Disorders:*[5]

Despite sustained general economic prosperity and growing skill demands of automated industry, the goal of full employment has become increasingly hard to attain.

[4] *The New York Times,* December 1, 1968, pp. 1, 78. © 1968 by *The New York Times Company.* Reprinted by permission.
[5] Washington, D.C.: Government Printing Office, March 1, 1968, pp. 231–232.

Today there are about two million unemployed, and about ten million underemployed, 6.5 million of whom work full time and earn less than the annual poverty wage.

The most compelling and difficult challenge is presented by some 500,000 "hard-core" unemployed who live within the central cities, lack a basic education, work not at all or only from time to time and are unable to cope with the problems of holding and performing a job. A substantial part of this group is Negro, male, and between the ages of approximately 18 and 25. Members of this group are often among the initial participants in civil disorders. . . .

In the riot cities which we surveyed, Negroes were three times as likely as whites to hold unskilled jobs, which are often part time, seasonal, low-paying, and "dead-end"—a fact that creates a problem for Negroes as significant as unemployment.

Thus, it is not overly difficult to see the parallels to the 1930's. Forty years later, there still are groups of people steeped in human misery, brought up in degrading deprivation, deeply wounded by the lack of opportunity to stand on their own two feet. And there are others, so much better off, with nice full-time jobs, who cannot understand, or will not understand, and who trust that the police can keep the ghettos quiet!

Consider these statistics. In 1967, the United States had on the average 3 million unemployed. This was, by the way, the lowest unemployment figure in 15 years. Of these unemployed, 2.3 million were white, the rest nonwhite; 1.5 million each were male and female; 1.6 million were teenagers or persons over 45 years of age, the rest were of "prime" working age. Throughout the year, one could find 1.6 million persons who were unemployed, but who found a new job within 5 weeks. (That is, although there were always 1.6 million unemployed persons in this category, they were not always the same individuals.) On the other hand, an average of .5 million persons was unemployed for at least 15 weeks, and often substantially longer, during that year.

But percentages tell even more. Absolute numbers as above tell little of the impact on particular groups of people, unless we know the size of the groups. If there were only 2.3 million white people in this country, but 70 million nonwhites, the above figures would imply something quite different from when the group sizes were interchanged. Thus, it is important to relate the numbers of unemployed in a particular group to the size of that group itself. When we do that, we find that the unemployed in 1967 included 3.8 percent of all workers in the United States. They included 3.4 percent of all white workers (2.7 percent of males and 4.6 percent of females), but 7.4 percent of nonwhite workers (6 percent of males and 9.1 percent of females). Similarly, it included 12.9 percent of all, but 26.4 percent of nonwhite, teenagers who were in the labor force.

In addition to the unemployed, there were maybe 2.2 million persons working part time, but wanting full-time jobs. And there were maybe 5 million others who had completely despaired of ever finding work. They were not even looking any more and, therefore, not officially counted as involuntarily unemployed. For all these, the horrors of the Great Depression were a reality, not ancient history. Remember, numbers may be bloodless things, but behind them stand human lives—lives devastated by long-continued and undeserved failure that wipes out self-respect and the will to try or that kindles the fires of resentment and rage. As our flaming cities attest, we neglect the problem of unemployment at our peril. Civilized society that denies a place of dignity to some of its members cannot long survive.

THE MEASUREMENT OF UNEMPLOYMENT

It is, of course, very tempting to dispense a great deal of gratuitous advice. Some people will eagerly tell you that they know exactly what to do about the problem we have just described. But we shall not follow their example, not yet. Instead, before going on to pursue the causes and cures of unemployment, we shall pause to examine the meaning of some of the concepts we have used. We must do this because careless use of vaguely defined layman's terms quickly stifles any intelligent discussion. We must do it also because no discussion can be pursued long in a vacuum. Sooner or later, we will have to look at the facts. Yet, no one can gather the facts for us until we spell out what we mean by the concepts we wish to measure. This always involves making some arbitrary decisions. Not everyone will agree with them, but there is no way to avoid this dilemma.

What, precisely, do we mean when talking about our labor force being employed or unemployed? When are you "in the labor force"? What makes you "employed"? When are you "unemployed"?

Population and Potential Labor Force

There were 199 million people living in the United States on August 1, 1967. No reasonable man can expect all these to be employed in the process of production. Small children do not work for pay. Older ones go to school, often until age 17 at least. On August 1, 1967, there were 71 million Americans below age 18. This leaves at most 128 million people who, given American conditions, were potential members of the labor force. Yet, there must be many persons above age 17, and especially above 65, who, for either physical or mental reasons, are not able to work. These should be excluded from such a figure. Thus, we might want to estimate the potential labor force by excluding from the population all those considered too young to work and those older ones who are physically and mentally unable to work.

The historical record on population and potential labor force for the United States since 1900 is given in the top two lines of Figure 3.1 POPULATION, LABOR FORCE, AND UNEMPLOYMENT.[6] These data are estimates of the U.S. Department of Commerce, which has selected age 16, rather than 18, as the lower limit of the potential labor force. The vertical distance a between the population line and the estimate of the potential labor force in Figure 3.1 represents the segment of the population under age 16, as well as those physically or mentally unable to work and living in institutions (hospitals, prisons, and so on).

Voluntary Unemployment

Given the circumstances of present American society, we can further guess that many even of these aged 16 and above who are officially classified as part of the *potential* labor force are neither actually working for pay nor looking for such work. We expect that most young

---

[6] In the Study Guide, you are given directions on how to find the sources of the data referred to in the text.

Figure 3.1   POPULATION, LABOR FORCE, AND UNEMPLOYMENT

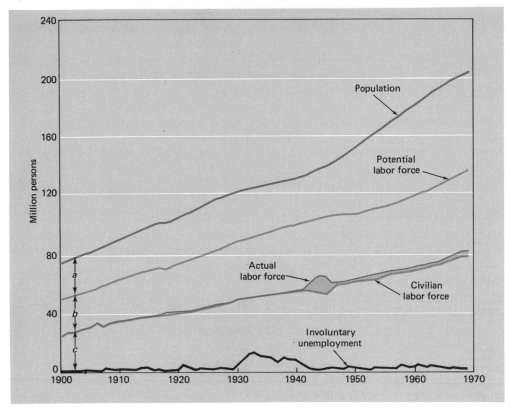

During the twentieth century, the U.S. population has grown without interruption. Excluding persons under age 16 and those institutionalized for physical or mental impairments (distance a), we derive the potential labor force. Excluding the voluntarily unemployed (distance b), we derive the actual labor force. A portion of the actual labor force has always been absorbed by the armed forces (shaded here), leaving a smaller number available for civilian uses. Notice the impact of the two world wars and of the Cold War on the disposition of the actual labor force between military and civilian uses. Distance c shows all persons employed, including those working part time or away from their regular job or business because of illness, vacation, labor-management dispute, bad weather, or personal reasons. Also included are unpaid family members working at least 15 hours a week in a family enterprise. This leaves us with the bottom line, the involuntarily unemployed. Source: U.S. Department of Commerce.

people go to school through age 17. Of course, there are exceptions to this. Some youngsters do not have the chance, ability, or will to go to high school; however, most do. In 1967, there were over 7 million persons aged 16 or 17, and 6 million of them went to high school. It is only reasonable to classify these as "voluntarily unemployed." Many others who are also quite able to work for pay, such as housewives, college students, and people of retirement age, make a similar voluntary decision not to work for pay. To be sure, this means that we now have fewer economic goods than we would if we forced these people to go to work. Americans, however, are willing to make this sacrifice of potential goods, because they could only be obtained by restricting freedom. Forcing people to work would involve trading greater current satisfaction of economic wants for lesser satisfaction of noneconomic wants. Value judgments would have to be made. Would it, for example, be worthwhile to trade more television sets for the care the housewife can give her children? Let us accept prevailing value judgments and not worry about voluntary unemployment at all, provided it is truly voluntary. Furthermore, to the extent that this voluntary unemployment allows people to be educated, it is really a sort of investment, raising the quality of our future labor force and quite possibly allowing us to get more goods in the future than we are forgoing now.

Actual Labor Force

The actual labor force, finally, consists of *all people in the potential labor force who are willing to work at the wage presently paid for the skill and experience they have to offer.*

This definition may seem unnecessarily cumbersome, but reflection will show every word in it to be necessary. As we have seen, some people, such as children and the sick, may not be able to work for pay. If we deduct them from the total population, we are left with the potential labor force. We must reduce this figure further by the amount of voluntary unemployment. This term, however, is not always as clear-cut as we might think. Sure enough, our housewife, *able* to make television sets in the factory, is voluntarily unemployed if she tells us that she does not *wish* to do it. Others, however, may be able *and* willing to work, but under impossible conditions only. What of the college dropout who refuses to do anything but work as a surgeon? He may be able and willing to work, but he is not skilled to work as a surgeon, and we can reasonably classify him with the voluntarily unemployed. The same goes for a surgeon who insists on either getting $10 million for each appendectomy or doing nothing. If this is out of line with the wage presently offered in society for this service, we can doubt his willingness to work at all. No matter how able and "willing" to work, no matter how skilled, he is voluntarily unemployed. Reducing the potential labor force by the number of voluntarily unemployed (anyone 16 or above who, though able, is not looking for work at the going wage for his skill), we arrive at the size of the actual labor force.

It is estimated that the American actual labor force on August 1, 1967, consisted of 83 million people. Thus, roughly 51 million people were voluntarily unemployed (arrived at by subtracting the actual labor force from the potential labor force—official definition—of 134 million). It is hard to enumerate precisely who these voluntarily unemployed are, but we know that there were 36 million housewives in the country at that time, 6 million high school students over age 16, 5 million college students, and 18 million people over 65. Some of those over 65 were housewives (thus already counted), some were working for pay or looking for work (hence in the actual labor force), some were physically or mentally unable to work (therefore, not even in the potential labor force), but there were undoubtedly many others who were voluntarily unemployed.

It is because of the existence of the voluntarily unemployed that the size of the actual labor force at any given time is flexible. In time of war, for example, many countries, either by force, appeals to patriotism, or monetary incentives, get the voluntarily unemployed to work. This augmentation of labor resources makes it possible to produce more goods with which to fight the war. It also cushions a decline in the civilian labor force, as civilian workers go into the armed forces. (The above figure of 83 million includes more than 3 million in the armed forces.)

The size of the actual labor force during the twentieth century is also shown in Figure 3.1. The vertical distance b between this line and the potential labor force represents the voluntarily unemployed. The shaded area on the graph represents the members of the armed forces. Thus, we can calculate the size of the *civilian* labor force as that portion of the actual labor force outside the armed forces.

Involuntary Unemployment—A Definition

Now we can turn to the problem we are really after. What do we mean by full employment or unemployment of labor? At first, this may seem a foolish question. Obviously, you will say, if everyone in the civilian labor force is actually employed, we have full employment. If some people over 16, able to work, willing to work, and not in the armed forces, cannot find jobs at their skills at the going wage, we have involuntary unemployment.

Is this, however, a reasonable approach? Could a government worker, charged with gathering statistics, classify people unambiguously? He probably would return quickly asking for more instructions, and reflection will show that the question was not so foolish after all.

What about the man who works 10 hours a week, but wants to work 40? Is he employed or unemployed? What about the farmer who works 10 days a month because the rain keeps him indoors the rest of the time? What about the engineer who works as a typist, because he cannot find another job? What about the man in Detroit who has just quit his job for another one in San Francisco, which he will take up in three weeks?

bureau of the census definition   Labor force, employment, and unemployment statistics are in fact obtained by the Bureau of the Census through a monthly sample survey of 33,000 households. These persons are interviewed, and interviewers use the following guideline: The bureau considers anyone 16 or above not working *at all* during the week in which statistics are gathered as involuntarily unemployed if he is currently available for work (even if, perhaps, temporarily ill) and if he (1) has looked for work in the preceding 4 weeks or (2) has not looked for work because he is (a) temporarily laid off subject to recall or (b) scheduled to begin a new job within 30 days. "Looking for work," furthermore, can take many forms, such as going to the employment service, applying to an employer in person, answering a want ad, being registered on a union or professional listing, and so on. A person 16 or above who has worked even 1 hour for pay or profit during the survey week is regarded as *employed*. So is a person who has a job or business but is not working because of illness, vacation, labor-management dispute, bad weather, or personal reasons (such as hunting for another job). And so is a family member who has worked at least 15 hours a week in a family enterprise without pay. A person who wants a job, but has stopped looking because he considers it hopeless, is thus not even considered as part of the actual labor force. He is "voluntarily" unemployed! A 1966 study by the Department of Labor revealed that over 5 million of our voluntarily unemployed, or 1 in 10 of their number, were not so "voluntarily" unemployed at all. They were youths in the slums who had no education. Some had prison records. They just knew that they would not get a job, even if it required no skills. So they did not even look. They were old people or blacks or partially disabled persons who had experienced so much rejection that they refused even to search for work. And they were young mothers, eager for work, but who could not work for lack of child-care or transportation facilities. Thus, you see how important it is to understand the meaning of our statistics. Even when the official tally of involuntary unemployment reads zero, we may still have a great problem if many "discouraged" workers are hidden among the genuinely voluntarily unemployed, or if many of the "employed" are only working part time, although against their will.

TYPES OF INVOLUNTARY UNEMPLOYMENT

We have to consider one more thing, however. Think of a man who has been laid off for a week because materials are lacking and of a man who quit his job in Detroit to take up another in San Francisco 3 weeks later. Both are classified with the involuntarily unemployed. Now think of a farmer not working this week because of the weather and of a factory worker away from his regular job because of illness. They are classified with the employed. Such things are bound to happen when we make arbitrary decisions to arrive at a clear-cut definition of a concept. It may not seem right that a man away from work because materials are lacking should be called unemployed, while a farmer away from work because the right weather is lacking should be called employed. Yet, the definition having been made and generally accepted, we had better stick to it or we shall cause even more confusion.

However, acceptance of a definition does not mean blind acceptance, and we can see that our four friends above have a lot in common. As *they* see it, none of them is presently working. One of them would like to, but there are no materials, the other would like to, but having decided to leave Michigan for California, he just cannot arrange the move overnight. The third man would like to work, but he cannot do a thing about the weather, and the last has to wait for his illness to subside. They have more in common than that! All know that they will be back to work soon. The materials are promised for next Tuesday, moving to California does not take forever, weather does change, and illnesses go away. Thus, we can probably conclude that none of our four friends will worry about his employment status very much, regardless of whether he is officially classified one way or another. As they see it, they are out of work now, but they will be back at work soon.

Now think instead of a man who has been working for 5 hours a week for a long time, while all along looking for a 40-hour-a-week job. Or think of the West Virginia coal miner who has been out of work for years, looking and hoping for a job that never materializes. Or think of the carpenter in the midst of a general depression, out of work for almost a decade, with no hope of finding a job because of the general unemployment. Finally, consider a black youth in a city ghetto who has experienced so much rejection that he will not even look for a job. Don't you think these, too, have a lot in common? Official statistics classify the first man as employed, the next two as involuntarily unemployed, and the last one as voluntarily unemployed. But won't they regard themselves as desperately unemployed? Even more important for our purpose, don't these four have very little in common with our four friends above? For practical purposes, these four considered last are out of work now, and they probably will not be back to it soon.

In short, we must recognize, when interpreting official statistics, that there are different types of employment and unemployment. We might have a problem even after we have reached what is officially called full employment, if a great many people have opted out of the labor force, are working only part time, are ill, are out on strike, or are sitting around waiting for a change in the weather. The size of their output, and thus the degree to which we can conquer scarcity, is obviously different from what it would be if everyone worked full-time and were healthy. In the same way, we must recognize that a lot of unemployed, all subject to recall within a week or moving to another state where a job is waiting, means a different thing than the same number of unemployed out of work for years and with little reason to believe that their current search for work will be successful. There are even different kinds of involuntary unemployment, some less serious than others!

Frictional Unemployment

Whenever jobs and men are mismatched, even though the total number of job openings and job seekers roughly coincides, we talk of *frictional unemployment*. In a large and growing economy, such as that of the United States, such unemployment is ever present and largely unavoidable. The unemployed may be in one place, jobs in another. The unemployed may offer one skill, jobs require another. Hence, adjustments are needed. All adjustments take time, so we talk of *frictions* in the economy. We should try (if we want to minimize scarcity) to keep frictional unemployment as low as possible. In some cases, this is easier than in others.

short-run frictional unemployment   The problem most easily solved, or least serious even if not solved, is short-run frictional unemployment.

Think of all the people entering the labor force for the first time. Even if there are jobs for their skills somewhere, it takes time to bring the people and jobs together. In recent years, 2.5 percent of the labor force has consisted of new entrants, and delays between school and the first job have often been lengthy. This is not only owing to lack of information about jobs available, but also to the fact that required skills are lacking. The problem is aggravated for the young by union contracts that protect older workers with seniority, making it harder for young people to get hired. They have to hunt for their jobs longer than most people. This is shown by the fact that the unemployment rate for teenagers (16 to 19) has recently been about three times the average rate for all workers. Even for those in their early twenties (20 to 24), the unemployment rate has still exceeded the average significantly. About 20 percent of total unemployment consists of new entrants (and re-entrants, such as married women, entering the labor force after a period of absence) looking for work.

Now think of the people laid off annually owing to seasonal factors; think of people who quit because they want to improve their status; think of those who are discharged because their employer is going out of business or moving away. Even if they have another job to go to, they will be unemployed for a period lasting from a few days to a few months. These people account for another significant percentage of all unemployed. In fact, in 1966, 58 percent of all involuntary unemployment in the United States was connected with new entry, re-entry, and voluntary job changes alone.

Measured against the civilian labor force, one can safely postulate that such people will always account for at least 1 percent involuntary unemployment of the civilian labor force. (They accounted for 2.2 percent in 1966.) Yet, there is hardly anything we can do about it. We might disseminate more information to help people find jobs faster. We might help them financially, if they cannot afford to move to a new location where they can work. We might eliminate such other barriers to mobility as pension accumulations that cannot be transferred, or artificial restrictions on entering into some occupations. But we can hardly forbid people to quit, nor can we legislate away people's rights to buy this good rather than that one, and so cause temporary layoffs and business failures. Thus, many people argue that short-run frictional unemployment, like genuine voluntary unemployment, is little to worry about. If we could reach, say, 99 percent employment of our civilian labor force, we could be proud of our record. The remaining 1 percent is unavoidable if we want to maintain the individual's right to move in and out of the labor force, or move among occupations, or move geographically. There will always be, it is argued, one man involuntarily unemployed out of a hundred, but it will not always be the same man!

Different people make different estimates of this harmless amount of short-run frictional unemployment. So do not be surprised if someone puts the level at 2 percent or even 4 percent of the civilian labor force, considering a 98 or 96 percent level of employment a sufficiently desirable goal. These things are hard to estimate and, to some degree, a matter of opinion, but the idea that some unemployment is unavoidable and even desirable (in that it maintains freedom) is clear enough.

chronic unemployment   Other types of unemployment are not so easily disposed of, however. What about the mismatching of men and jobs, which cannot be expected to be taken care of soon? Such long-run frictional, or *chronic,* unemployment is a good deal more serious.

One such persistent friction is the existence of discrimination in hiring. Even if jobs are available and men able and willing to perform them, jobs and men may not get together if employers also consider the color of the prospective worker's skin, his sex, age, or religion. If employers would rather hire no one than hire a black man, a Puerto Rican, a woman, a man over 60, or a Jew, we cannot expect things to take care of themselves in a few weeks. These people may remain unemployed for that reason alone. What is needed is a fundamental change in attitudes, and this does not happen overnight. As we already have seen above, in recent years, the rate of unemployment for nonwhites and women, for example, has been substantially higher than for whites and men, no matter which occupation or region of the country we consider.

Another persistent friction is caused by fundamental changes in the structure of the economy. As must happen in a dynamic economy, as time passes, people's tastes and technology change. Some occupations, industries, and geographic areas become increasingly important; some completely new industries appear, whereas other industries live a long life of attrition and finally die out. As a result, the man trained for shoveling coal into locomotives, or running a steam engine, or posting business accounts finds himself outmoded. Time has passed him by. If only he knew how to pilot a jet, to handle a nuclear reactor, or to program a computer!

Here, too, men and jobs are mismatched and may remain so for years. This time, however, it is not because of creed, sex, age, or color of skin, but for a very good reason: the skill offered is not the skill required, and retraining is difficult. Such *structural unemployment* cannot be cured fast, if at all. It requires long periods of retraining at the very least. This is again reflected in our statistics. Certain regions, such as the textile towns of Massachusetts and the isolated coal towns of Appalachia, are suffering from above-average rates of unemployment. And retraining is no more easily achieved than is the elimination of widespread discrimination. Not all workers are, in fact, movable between regions or retrainable for new occupations. Some will not, others cannot, change. Some are too old and lack the psychological requirements for change, some lack education or health (possibly because they were victims of discrimination in the past), and some lack the native intelligence to acquire a new skill.

The last point is especially serious. Take any representative sample of a thousand Americans and you will probably find a distribution of developed intelligence something like the following. Half may be "normal," with an I.Q. somewhere between 90 and 109. A quarter will range from "not so bright" (I.Q. of 70 to 89) for most to "very dull" (I.Q. below 70) for a few. Another quarter will be "very bright" (I.Q. of 110 to 139) for most to "brilliant" (I.Q. above 140) for a few.

Some have argued (although many disagree) that the distribution of brains provided by nature and developed by our school system is becoming more and more unsuited to the assortment of jobs in the American economy. If we needed, say, 70 percent of the labor force to be very bright or brilliant, we would find a constant shortage of such workers. At the same time, there would be a surplus of people able to do the 30 percent of jobs requiring normal or lower intelligence. To the extent that I.Q. scores reflect differences in genetic potential, attempts at retraining would be nothing more than an exercise in futility.

One standard argument in discussing chronic unemployment caused by the upgrading of required skills is that eventually as many high-skill jobs open up as low-skill jobs disappear. This may not, however, be so. Some experts on automation (the automatic handling of the entire production process by self-regulating equipment, not reliant on human strength or guidance), in fact, claim that the jobs created for the production, maintenance, and operation of automated equipment are substantially fewer than the ones eliminated. To the extent that this is true, retraining, even if it were always possible, would not be enough.

General Unemployment

Not all unemployment that we have experienced in the United States in this century can be explained by frictions in the economy. It is not true that there are always the same number of job openings as job seekers, that all we have to do is match the latter with the former by moving people as quickly as we can from school to job, from one job or skill to another, or from one town to the next. There are times of *general* unemployment when many people of all skills, all ages, all races, all creeds, both sexes, and in all places, are unemployed *at the same time*. Increasing their mobility will not help, for there is no better place to go. Such was the case in the 1930's. No one could escape the impact of the Great Depression, and no one could possibly combat it on his own. Employers would not hire, because it made no sense to produce at a time when so little was bought. Human wants were as infinite as ever, resources were crying to be used, yet they lay idle year after year. As we noted above, the loss of self-respect of the unemployed head of a household, his sense of personal failure, the loss of freedom and security of his family, and the gradual decay of his skills were additional costs, however impossible to measure.

Such general unemployment, caused by a general lack of demand (not wants), has existed in most years of this century. In fact, its solution is the key to the full utilization of labor resources. If we could succeed in eliminating all frictional unemployment, we might still have to face the curse of general unemployment. If people do not demand enough output to make employers hire all the labor offered for use, it helps little to make it easier for the unemployed to relocate where they would be needed if people did demand more. It helps little, under these conditions, to persuade employers to give up their racial bias, for even if they become willing to hire a black man in principle, they will hire neither him nor anyone else if the output of his work cannot be sold. It helps little to retrain a coal miner to program a computer or give the ghetto youth a college education if the need for their services depended on people demanding more than they are demanding. In short, measures to curve frictional unemployment will be partially wasted unless they are accompanied by measures to cure general unemployment.

THE HISTORICAL RECORD

Now let us look at the statistical record. The lowest line in Figure 3.1 POPULATION, LABOR FORCE, AND UNEMPLOYMENT shows that involuntary unemployment, as defined above, has existed in the United States for as long as we know. Its extent, however, has varied greatly over time. There were about 1 million involuntarily unemployed from 1900 to 1907, but the total was 3 million in 1908. The number fluctuated from 2 million to 3 million until 1914, then jumped to 4 million in 1915. Unemployment fell below the 2 million mark during the war years, but it was up again to 5 million by 1921. Through the rest of the 1920's, however, it remained much lower. Then came the Great Depression. Unemployment rose from over 4 million in 1930 to about 13 million in 1933. It slowly fell to under 8 million by 1937, only to rise again to over 10 million in the following year. From then on it declined, to under 1 million by

1944. Unemployment has fluctuated, in the postwar era, never falling much below 2 million and at times rising to almost 5 million people.

The same story is told more dramatically by Figure 3.2 THE SERIOUSNESS OF INVOLUNTARY UNEMPLOYMENT. It is particularly helpful because it puts the absolute data in perspective. Five million involuntarily unemployed may sound like a great many, but it clearly means a different thing in a civilian labor force of 20 million people than in a labor force of 1 billion people. Percentage figures often tell a great deal more than absolute ones, as they relate one

Figure 3.2   THE SERIOUSNESS OF INVOLUNTARY UNEMPLOYMENT

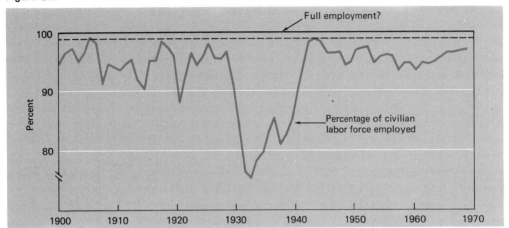

Not once during this century was 100 percent of the American civilian labor force employed. The degree of utilization of the labor force has fluctuated widely, dipping to a low of 75 percent in 1933. On the average, over the years, 93 percent of it was utilized. It is highly questionable whether 100 percent employment is a reasonable goal for which to strive. Given the inevitability of some types of frictional unemployment, the goal should probably be set at 99 percent (the broken line) or even lower. Source: U.S. Department of Commerce.

magnitude (here, involuntary unemployment) to another (here, the civilian labor force). In Figure 3.2, the percentage of involuntary unemployment is represented by the vertical distances *above* the jagged line—by the difference between the percentage of civilian labor force employed and the 100 percent line. In this case, we see that the U.S. record in percentage terms, too, is nothing to be proud of so far as the maintenance of full employment of labor is concerned. (And remember: totally discouraged workers, who are not even looking for jobs, are not in the picture at all.)

Over the long haul from 1900 to the present, more than 7 percent of the civilian labor force has been, on the average, involuntarily unemployed. This comes to about one man out of fifteen. Fluctuations around this average have been marked. Eight or more percent of the civilian labor force was involuntarily unemployed in 1908, 1914, and 1915. The unemployment rate went to 12 percent in 1921. In 1930, it was again above 8 percent, climbing steadily to 25 percent in 1933. Thus, in the depth of the Great Depression, one man in four who wanted to work at the going wage, was able to work, and was looking for work, could not find a job. As Figure 3.2 shows, the unemployment rate never went below 14 percent between 1931 and 1940.

Involuntary unemployment has at times been very low, too. It was about 1 percent in 1906, and again during war years 1918 and 1944. Between 1958 and 1964, it was distressingly high, between 5 percent and 6 percent of the civilian labor force. Yet, in 1968, it was the lowest in 15 years.

Even interpreting this information with care, and realizing that statistics are subject to error and cannot be more than good estimates, this is a sad record for a world of scarcity. It would be even sadder if we converted involuntary *partial* unemployment, officially counted as employment, into its full-time equivalents. A Senate subcommittee has estimated that if we counted every two persons working half time, but wanting to work full time, as one unemployed and one employed, instead of both employed as we do now, it would raise the recorded unemployment estimate by at least 1 percent.[7] Others would add at least another percentage point to count in all those considered voluntarily unemployed who have even given up looking for work.

The American record during the nineteenth century, for which only rough estimates are available, seems not to have been any better than the record in the twentieth century. It is estimated that perhaps 5 percent of the labor force was involuntarily unemployed in 1819, possibly 8 percent in 1838, 1858, and 1885, as many as 14 percent in 1876, and more than 11 percent (at times more than 18 percent) from 1893 to 1898.[8]

UNEMPLOYMENT OF LAND AND CAPITAL

Much of what has been said about labor can also be said about land and capital, although we cannot be equally specific. There are no systematic, reliable statistics on the size of our stock of land and capital (as we defined them in Chapter 1). If we had them, we could presumably show that these resources, too, have increased greatly during the course of this century. We could presumably also show, as we show for labor in Figure 3.1, that there is a difference between the population of land or capital and the potential stocks of land and capital that are usable in the process of production. At any given moment, some land may be unusable (such as flooded soil, a dried-out river, or oil deposits made inaccessible by the ravages of a hurricane). The same is true of capital—a half-burned factory, a washed-out road, or a machine in need of lubricants that are not available.

In addition, owners of land and capital may wish to keep some of these resources unemployed, for whatever reasons. Thus, the stocks available for use in the productive process may be below the potential, just as the civilian labor force is below what it might be. A re-

---

[7] This is discussed in detail in Subcommittee on Economic Statistics of the Joint Economic Committee, U.S. Congress, *Unemployment: Terminology, Measurement, and Analysis* (Washington, D.C.: Government Printing Office. 1961).

[8] See Stanley Lebergott, *Manpower in Economic Growth: The American Record since 1800* (New York: McGraw-Hill, 1964).

cent study by the President's Council of Economic Advisers indicates, for example, that the desired rate at which owners wanted to use capacity in U.S. manufacturing in December 1966 was only 93 percent on the average. The actual figures ranged from a low of 90 percent (in industries as diverse as electrical machinery, chemicals, and food and beverages) to a high of 99 percent (autos).[9] This voluntary unemployment of land and capital explains why in times of war the land and capital used, just as the labor used, can be increased. Minerals are mined at a faster rate, equipment is used for more hours a day, and standby equipment is pressed into service.

There is no doubt, however, that there has also been involuntary unemployment of land and capital, that is, that actual utilization frequently has been below the quantities offered by their owners.

Figure 3.3   LABOR AND CAPITAL UTILIZATION COMPARED

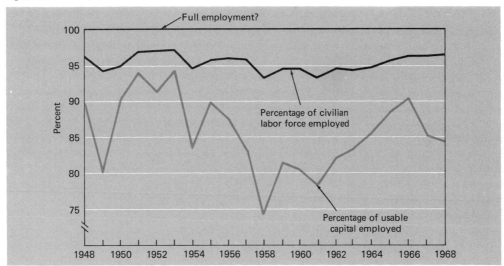

The employment of usable capital in U.S. manufacturing has been well below potential in recent years, the fluctuations in the rate of utilization closely paralleling those in the percentage of the civilian labor force employed. Should we regard the heavy horizontal line as a goal for which to strive, or would a lower one be more desirable? Source: Figure 3.2 and Economic Report of the President (*Washington, D.C.: Government Printing Office, 1969*), p. 270.

The President's Council of Economic Advisers has published data on the actual rate of utilization of American manufacturing capacity in recent years. These data are the basis for Figure 3.3 LABOR AND CAPITAL UTILIZATION COMPARED. The solid line shows the estimated use of the capital stock as a percent of the total available; the broken line repeats, for comparison, the analogous information with respect to labor contained in Figure 3.2. With minor

[9] *Economic Report of the President, 1967* (Washington, D.C.: Government Printing Office, 1967), p. 91.

exceptions, the direction of movement of the two has gone hand in hand, that is, the employment rate of capital increased or decreased at the same time as did that of labor. Both were often substantially below 100 percent utilization.

This must have happened, furthermore, in the case of land and capital for reasons analogous to the ones discussed above with respect to labor. There must exist, at any given moment, short-run frictional unemployment, that is, the temporary kind that occurs when land and capital available and offered for use are mismatched with the places where they are wanted. An idle machine in Pittsburgh may be needed in Los Angeles, a newly produced one cannot instantly be installed, equipment may be temporarily idle for lack of materials or be homeless as a firm goes into bankruptcy. These events are unavoidable, as are short-run frictions in the labor market, and can be expected to be short-lived.

Chronic unemployment can similarly be expected for land and capital. With changes in technical know-how, or permanent shifts of demand among goods, some land and capital becomes unemployed. What is one to do with land ideal for growing rice when the demand for rice disappears? What is one to do with specialized equipment for making propeller-driven aircraft once the jet age arrives? Shipping capital to another firm or town will not solve the problem, for just as in the case of the West Virginia coal miner, there is *no* place where it is wanted. The land suited for rice-growing may have to be "retrained," that is, drained, fertilized, and planted to grow oranges. This takes a long time. Many capital goods that have become obsolete may simply have to be scrapped. Others can possibly be retooled; they may be overhauled to fit the new demands made on them.

Discrimination can also cause chronic unemployment. Union members may refuse to install equipment made by a firm they have decided to boycott.

Finally, just as in the case of labor, we can expect general unemployment of land and capital. This occurs for all types at the same time, because people's spending is insufficient to justify a level of output that would use all the available land and capital.

Unemployment of land and capital may not always lead to direct misery, as in the case of labor, but it does imply the loss of potential goods. Thus, it also stands in direct opposition to the task of fighting scarcity to the limit.

THE UNEMPLOYMENT PARADOX

We have noted that there are many types of unemployment. We have also noted that all these have persisted in our economy for as long as we can look back into our history. Yet, if you have carefully pondered the lessons of the previous chapter, the existence of unemployment in a market economy, *except as a temporary phenomenon*, might strike you as somewhat of a paradox. Consider the market for any type of labor, say, high school social science teachers.

Imagine we made a survey of all school boards in the country and asked each how many high school social science teachers they planned to employ next year. Obviously, this would depend on many things, but given all other factors, the answers we receive will undoubtedly vary with the salary that we assumed to exist. The salary is the price that has to be paid to get this type of labor. Suppose we find that at a price of $12,000 per year, school boards decide not to offer any positions to social science teachers at all, but at correspondingly lower salaries more and more decide to add the subject to their curriculum. If they could get away with paying no more than $2,000 a year, they would hire 600,000 teachers.

We can similarly imagine interviewing all potential teachers. We could ask them under what circumstances they would teach social science in high school next year. Again, this would depend on many things. Let us assume most of those things as fixed. In fact, let us only vary the potential salary paid. We would undoubtedly find that the number of people willing to teach in high school can vary. This will be so even though the number trained to teach social science may be rather fixed in any one year. At $2,000 a year, these people may prefer to do nothing or to offer themselves for other jobs. Quantity supplied is zero. At $12,-000, there may be 600,000 people looking for this kind of job. At $20,000, even college professors will become available for high school jobs.

The information so gathered would look very much like Tables 2.1 and 2.2, which showed the demand for and supply of shoes. In fact, our interviews would have yielded the demand schedule and supply schedule for high school social science teachers. The answers given by school boards would be the demand schedule. The answers given by potential teachers would represent the supply schedule. By graphing these two, we could derive Figure 3.4 THE MARKET FOR HIGH SCHOOL SOCIAL SCIENCE TEACHERS. The information gathered from school boards would appear as the demand curve D. The information gathered from their potential employees would show up as supply curve S. Thus, as in any competitive market, demand and supply are each represented by a schedule and curve rather than by a single number and dot.

We can now use the graphical illustration of the market for this type of labor to predict what would happen next year, given perfect competition among all market participants. (True enough, real world markets for high school teachers may not be perfectly competitive, but let us assume for a moment that they are.) We can predict that such a competitive market would tend to establish a $7,000 salary figure and that 300,000 people would be employed. Only at intersection c do we find equilibrium. There would be no unemployment, because all who want to work in this occupation at this wage would be employed.

At any higher annual wage, there would be a surplus, that is, unemployment. For example, at $10,000 only 120,000 people would be hired (point a), but 480,000 seek employment (point b). The horizontal difference of 360,000 would represent unemployment (ab). A fall in the wage to $7,000 would eliminate it, and for two reasons. First, quantity demanded would rise by 180,000 along ac. Second, quantity supplied would fall by 180,000 along bc. As school boards become readier to hire (because of the lower salary), some potential teachers decide not to work at all or to work at other jobs (also because of the lower salary).

At a lower than equilibrium wage, there would be a shortage. At $2,000, as we noted, nobody could be had. But the shortage (of de) could be eliminated by a rise in pay to the $7,000 equilibrium. Again the reason is twofold: quantity demanded would fall by 300,000 along ec; quantity supplied would rise by 300,000 along dc. As more and more school boards decide to forgo the luxury of social science instruction, more and more potential teachers offer themselves for the job, leaving voluntary unemployment or other jobs behind.

Now we come to the main point. What has been said about social science teachers could

full employment of resources

Figure 3.4   THE MARKET FOR HIGH SCHOOL SOCIAL SCIENCE TEACHERS

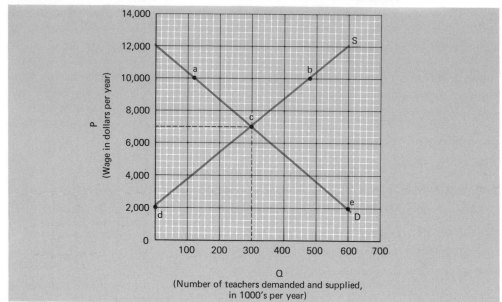

In a perfectly competitive market, demand and supply would establish equilibrium price and quantity for any resource, even the services of high school social science teachers. In this example, their annual salary would be $7,000, and 300,000 of them would be employed. There would be no unemployment. At any higher wage, there would be a surplus of teachers, at a lower one a shortage. At $10,000, for instance, only 120,000 would be hired (point a), but 480,000 would seek employment (point b). The surplus 360,000 would be unemployed. At $2,000, on the other hand, nobody would willingly work (point d). School boards would in vain try to hire 600,000 teachers (point e).

have been said about labor in general. In a perfectly competitive market economy, movements in prices eliminate surpluses and shortages. Thus, they can also be expected to eliminate the particular surplus, commonly called unemployment. Our analysis leads us to expect that unemployment in a market economy, if it exists at all, will be rather short-lived, being eliminated through the price system!

But this is hardly what we have seen to be true earlier in this chapter. Why this paradox? What has gone wrong with the market economy? We cannot fully answer at this point, but we can remind ourselves of an assumption we made in Chapter 2 and again when discussing Figure 3.4 THE MARKET FOR HIGH SCHOOL SOCIAL SCIENCE TEACHERS. We assumed a market economy that was *perfectly* competitive. This allowed us in Chapter 2 to study the principle of the invisible hand in all its purity, without being detracted from the main idea. But clearly, in the real world, which we have been studying in this chapter, competition is not always perfect. If teachers band together in unions, or if school boards act in collusion with one another, it would be wrong to assume that individual buyers or sellers of labor cannot influence the price at which a sale takes place. Nor are all potential high school social science teachers alike and thus akin to the standardized commodity of the perfectly competitive market. Nor does everyone have an equal opportunity to become such a teacher, thereby making the free entry into the market assumption of perfect competition a realistic one. Nor are all market participants fully informed about the market and freely mobile from one place to another. The same, of course, is true in the markets for many other types of labor as well as other resources. In addition, government often intervenes in markets, for example, by setting minimum wages.

Now imagine a labor market with unemployment wherein institutional factors (such as the existence of labor unions or minimum wage laws) *prevent* a decline in wages. In terms of Figure 3.4 THE MARKET FOR HIGH SCHOOL SOCIAL SCIENCE TEACHERS, the salary is at $10,000 per year and is *not allowed* to fall. Should you be surprised if unemployment persists?

Thus, you see why it may be useful at times to make very unrealistic assumptions as we analyze economic problems. If the assumption of a perfectly competitive labor market teaches us that unemployment would be eliminated (by a fall in wages), whereas unemployment is in fact not eliminated in an imperfectly competitive market, we may blame the persistence of unemployment on the observed imperfections in the market. This, in turn, may give us clues for a policy designed to eliminate unemployment: either get rid of market imperfections or counter their effects. We shall turn to these matters in later chapters.

SUMMARY

1   This chapter studies the impact of unemployment on society, both in human terms and in cold statistics. In the case of labor unemployment, the costs of enforced idleness go far beyond potential goods forgone. They involve noneconomic aspects of human welfare as well. The Great Depression of the 1930's is a dramatic case in point, but the plight of the present-day unemployed has equally destructive consequences for society at large.

2   As a preliminary to finding the causes and cures of unemployment, we must agree on exact definitions of relevant terms. This alone makes possible intelligent discussion and the gathering of statistical data. Most important are definitions of labor force, employment, and unemployment.

3   Only a portion of a country's population is available for use in the productive process. The potential labor force (U.S. definition) excludes those too young (under 16) or too sick (living in institutions) to work for pay. The actual labor force excludes, in addition, the voluntarily unemployed. These are all the members of the potential labor force who are unwilling to work at the wage presently paid for the skill and experience they have to offer (as shown by their unwillingness to look for work). The civilian labor force, finally, includes all members of the actual labor force not in the armed forces.

4   According to the U.S. Bureau of the Census, involuntary unemployment consists of all members of the civilian labor force not working at all during the survey week (the week in which statistics are gathered) if they are currently available for work (although, perhaps, temporarily ill) and if they (1) have looked for work in the preceding 4 weeks or (2) have not looked for work because they are (a) temporarily laid off subject to recall or (b) scheduled to begin a new job within 30 days.

5   This implies that anyone working even 1 hour for pay or profit during the survey week is regarded as employed, as are people having a job or business but not working because of illness, vacation, labor-management dispute, bad weather, or personal reasons. A family member working at least 15 hours a week in a family enterprise without pay is also regarded as employed. A person not looking for work, perhaps because he considers it hopeless, is not even counted in the actual labor force. He is voluntarily unemployed.

6   There are several types of involuntary unemployment, which vary in seriousness. Such distinctions are also crucial because different types of unemployment may require different types of remedies. Frictional unemployment exists when jobs and men are mismatched, yet the number of job openings and job seekers roughly coincides. General unemployment exists when the number of job seekers in all or most fields exceeds that of job openings. Short-run frictional unemployment, which might be caused by new entry into the labor force, by seasonal factors, or by regular labor turnover (a cherished American right) is much less serious than chronic unemployment, in which men and jobs fail to get matched because of discrimination or the difficulties of retraining necessitated by changes in demand and technology.

7   There has been involuntary unemployment of labor throughout U.S. history, although it has varied widely in intensity. On the average, 7 percent of the civilian labor force has been involuntarily unemployed since 1900.

8   There is good reason to believe that land and capital have been subject to the same kinds of involuntary unemployment, with similar fluctuations in intensity.

9   The existence of unemployment in a market economy may at first glance appear as somewhat of a paradox. One would expect forces of supply and demand to equilibrate the resource markets, thereby eliminating unemployment, which would appear as surpluses in these markets. Clearly, this is not happening in reality. The reason is simple to comprehend: our market economy is not perfectly competitive.

TERMS[10]

actual labor force	full employment
automation	general unemployment
chronic unemployment	involuntary unemployment
civilian employment	long-run frictional unemployment
civilian labor force	potential labor force
depression	recession
employment	short-run frictional unemployment
frictional unemployment	structural unemployment
voluntary unemployment	

[10] Terms are defined in the Glossary at the end of the book.

QUESTIONS FOR REVIEW AND DISCUSSION

1 The first section of this chapter talks of the great costs of unemployment to society. What are these costs? How serious are they? (Think of an unemployed person you know.)

2 Until quite recently, the Commerce Department set the lower age limit of the potential labor force at 14. Then it raised it to 16. Why do you think it did so? Do you think it should raise the limit further, to say 18?

3 According to the official Commerce Department definition, which of the following are victims of involuntary unemployment? Who in the list is employed? Who is voluntarily unemployed?

a. A man earning $10,000 a year who has been employed for 30 years by a company. Suddenly the boss lowers his (and nobody else's) salary to $5,000. He quits, stays home for a week in anger, then looks for another job.

b. A mother who is taking care of her five children, although she would much rather be teaching school.

c. A student who leaves his summer job to return to college, although he hates college and loved the summer job.

d. A man who just retired, moved to Florida, and works 8 hours a day planting flowers in his own garden (he receives a pension of $500 a month).

e. The pensioner's wife who is willing to give zither lessons for $50 an hour. So far she has not found a student.

f. A man making toothbrushes who has been fired 2 weeks ago because of falling sales, but whose skills are in great demand almost everywhere else. He just started looking for a new job.

g. A high school student who has just been promised a summer job scheduled to start in 2 weeks, when school lets out.

h. A volunteer nurse in a hospital who is working 10 hours a day and not looking for any other activity.

i. A soldier who has been drafted against his will.

j. A married woman who has just decided to look for a job tomorrow.

k. An engineer, laid off when sales fell, who is not being recalled. The story is the same everywhere he looks for work. He is looking very hard; he has even offered to work as a typist, but all he has been offered is a job cutting someone's lawn at 40 cents an hour. He refused that one.

l. A college student who is working 1 hour a day as a taxi driver.

m. A man on strike.

n. A man who is working 2 hours a week in his brother's store without pay. He wants to work and is able to work, for pay, but he will not move to the town where the job is being offered.

o. A teenage black high school dropout who is just sitting around and has given up looking for a job.

p. A black college graduate in accounting who registered with the employment service, but is not getting any offers.

4 "If we eliminated all types of involuntary unemployment, we would reach Utopia." Discuss.

5 "Full employment is 97 percent employment." Do you agree? Why or why not?

6   "If all Americans suddenly decided to buy Fords and no other type of car, it might only lead to short-run frictional unemployment." Discuss.

7   "If all Americans suddenly decided to buy books instead of cars, we might have chronic unemployment." Discuss.

8   "If we stopped automation, job openings would sprout like dandelions." Discuss.

9   In the mid-1700's, a mob of worried English spinners smashed James Hargreave's first workable multispindle frames. Similar labor resistance to the adoption of new techniques has been chronicled in the histories of most developed economies. Why do people's fears of mass unemployment owing to new machines never materialize?

10   "If there is general unemployment, it does not help to cure the causes of frictional unemployment." Discuss.

11   "Everyone in the actual labor force must be either employed or unemployed, but there are also unemployed outside the actual labor force." Comment.

12   "The fact that the unemployment rate for teenagers is significantly above the national average proves that people hiring workers discriminate against teenagers." Do you agree? (Hint: What if teenagers enter and leave the actual labor force more often than other people because they only desire to work intermittently? What if young people in general have a healthy propensity to change jobs voluntarily to test their aptitudes and opportunities?)

13   "The fact that the unemployment rate among blacks is significantly above the national average proves that people hiring workers discriminate against blacks." Discuss. (Hint: what if blacks are presently less skilled than others, have a harder time getting transportation out of inner-city ghettos, and have a different age composition than the population on the average?)

14   Do your answers to questions 12 and 13 prove that people hiring workers do *not* discriminate against teenagers and blacks?

15   Why are some types of unemployment less serious than others?

16   In Figure 3.3 LABOR AND CAPITAL UTILIZATION COMPARED, the labor and capital utilization curves are not strictly comparable because no account is taken of the fact that owners of capital may not wish to use capital 100 percent. To make them comparable, we would have to express the labor employment as a percentage of which? (a) population, (b) potential labor force, (c) actual labor force?

17   By checking in your library's latest *Statistical Abstract of the United States* find out exactly how the Department of Commerce gathers unemployment statistics. How accurate do you think the statistics are? (Hint: ask someone who knows about sampling procedures.)

18   From the same source find out exactly who the unemployed are. Are they city people or rural residents, white or black, male or female, young or old?

19   The text discusses an apparent unemployment paradox. Can you explain in your own words what this is all about?

20   Without reading ahead, how do you think one could cure the various type of unemployment? Write down your answers and compare them to what you think about it at the conclusion of Part 1.

PRICE RISE OF 4.7% IN YEAR IS BIGGEST SINCE KOREAN WAR

December Increase of 0.2%, Low for Recent Months, Puts Index at 123.7

By EDWIN L. DALE Jr.
Special to The New York Times

WASHINGTON, Jan. 29 — The Nixon Administration found itself confronted today with Government reports showing the worst inflation since 1951, the lowest export surplus since the Depression and the highest interest rate on a Government security since the Civil War.

None of the reports were unexpected, and they showed little or no worsening of a well-known situation in the economy in the last month. But they illustrated why President Nixon in his news conference two days ago put economic problems among his most "urgent."

The Labor Department reported that the Consumer Price Index rose two-tenths of 1 per cent in December, less than in most recent months, bringing the increase from a year earlier to 4.7 per cent. The last time inflation was as large was 1951, the first full year of the Korean War, when consumer prices rose by 5.8 per cent.

Index Stands at 123.7

The index last month was 123.7, compared with 100 in the base period 1957-59. Thus, it cost $12.37 to buy the same goods and services that cost $10 a decade ago. . . .

Today's report on prices said the increase in the consumer index was 4.7 per cent from December to December. Taking average prices in the year 1968 as a whole in comparison to 1967 as a whole, the rise was 4.2 per cent, also the largest since 1951.

The wholesale price increase, December to December, was less, at 2.8 per cent. But today's report contained an ominous note.

The index of wholesale prices for all "industrials"—leaving out farm and food products—rose three-tenths of 1 per cent in December and, on a preliminary basis, five-tenths of 1 per cent in January. This is regarded by many economists as perhaps the single most sensitive indicator of inflation.

The December Consumer Price Index of 123.7 compares with a November index of 123.4. The change amounted to a rise of two-tenths of 1 per cent, the smallest increase since September.

Compared with the previous December, those parts of the index showing the sharpest increases last year were medical care, mortgage interest rates, apparel, shoes, public transit and restaurant meals. These increases ranged between 6 and 7 per cent.

Area Prices Up 0.2%

The smallest monthly increase in the New York area's Consumer Price Index in 11 months—0.2 per cent—was recorded in December, Herbert Bienstock, regional director of the United States Bureau of Labor Statistics, announced yesterday.

The increase, the 20th consecutive monthly rise, advanced the index to 127.2.

While the November to December change was small, the total change for the year, 5.3 per cent, was substantially more than the 2.6 per cent change for 1967. Not since 1951 has there been such an increase, Mr. Bienstock said.

All types of goods and services rose in this area in December except transportation, which registered a decline of 0.9 per cent. Leading the increases were housing, up 0.6 per cent, and food, 0.4 per cent.

The biggest advances in the 12-month period were in mortgage interest, up 9 per cent; fresh fruits and vegetables, 8 per cent, and medical care, 7 per cent.

4

the problem
of inflation

OUR DISCUSSION OF the market economy should lead us to expect frequent changes in the prices of all goods and resources. After all, it is through changes in prices that any adjustments in the use of resources are set into motion. As we illustrated in Chapter 2, when households change their tastes and buy steak instead of pork, the prices of steak, pasture land, and yachts may rise, while those of pork, corn, and cornflakes may fall. Similar consequences should follow any other changes in tastes, technology, or resource availability.

Yet look around you, and you will again perceive a strange paradox. Our actual economy seems to behave differently, in a way we are not yet prepared to explain. As newspaper headlines underscore so frequently, we do not find the prices of *some* goods and resources rising (and those of others falling), but we often find prices of *all* or most goods and resources rising at the same time (and few, if any, falling). This pronounced tendency for most or all prices in the economy to rise is called *inflation*. Like unemployment, it is no laughing matter. This chapter considers the nature of inflation and its measurement and historical incidence in the U.S. economy.

THE COSTS OF INFLATION

Inflation is at best an unmitigated nuisance. At worst, it can destroy a society. Consider the impact of inflation.

Redistribution of Real Income

First, inflation brings about a capricious redistribution of the real income of people. Suppose you live on a fixed money income of $100 a week. If the prices of all the things you buy double during a year, you will be able to buy only half as much at the end of the year as at the beginning. You will still spend 100 green dollar bills, but the collection of goods you bring home will be half its original size. Half your *real* income (the goods you actually get for your money) has been taken away. The same principle applies if your money income rises at a slower pace than the prices of goods you buy. If prices double, but your money income rises by only 50 percent, you will find that your real income has fallen to three quarters its original size (you will spend $150, but at doubled prices this only buys what $75 bought previously).

There are many people who live on fixed money incomes or slowly rising ones (relative to the price level rise). People with relatively or even absolutely fixed money incomes include retired people living on pensions or interest income, disabled persons living on social security benefits, those living on unemployment benefits or welfare payments, and widows and orphans living on the proceeds of life insurance policies. People with slowly rising money incomes often also include government employees at all levels of government, from schoolteachers to state troopers and federal judges.

On the other hand, there are groups in the community that manage to make their money incomes rise as fast or faster than the prices of the things they buy. If you get $200, instead of $100, a week, your real income is at least not changed when prices double. If you get $300 instead, your real income has risen by 50 percent (you will spend $300, but at doubled prices this only buys what $150 bought previously).

Many of the younger, actively working people in the community are in this position. They may be factory workers, relying on strong unions to keep wages moving up with the cost of living, or they may be professional people and businessmen in a position to raise their fees and selling prices to cover, or more than cover, any increases in costs.

Thus, the inflationary economy is like a speeding car. Some of us, passengers inside, have a reasonable chance of keeping up with it. Others, standing outside or running alongside, will fall by the wayside. Through no fault of their own, they will get a smaller and smaller portion of the collection of goods the economy produces. Irrespective of their virtue or diligence, people with rapidly rising money incomes will be the happy recipients of the larger share of real income.

Redistribution of Wealth

Second, inflation redistributes existing *wealth* in an equally arbitrary manner. Suppose you go out tomorrow and buy a house, receiving a mortgage for the entire price, $25,000. You effectively own no part of the house. Now imagine all prices to double overnight. Your house can now be sold for $50,000. The bank can be paid off with half that amount. This leaves you with another $25,000, enough to buy half a house at current prices. But you need not actually sell. Through the very fact of inflation, you in effect own half the house, although you have not raised a finger to achieve this. In real terms, your wealth, which was zero, now equals half a house.

Your gain is someone else's loss. Suppose the shoe is on the other foot. Someone else owns $25,000 and, being conservative, places it in a savings account. Although prices double, the savings bank still only owes $25,000 to the saver, just as you only owe that much to the bank. The saver can buy only half as much when the money is returned as before. It is as if half his wealth has been taken from him and given to you.

In this way, inflation redistributes real wealth from creditors to debtors. Persons who (not having foreseen the inflation) have saved cash or are owed fixed amounts of money (savings accounts, mortgages, endowment insurance, bonds, and so on) find their real wealth declining as the purchasing power of each dollar shrinks with the general price rise. Persons who owe fixed money amounts find their real indebtedness continually shrinking. Just as the redistribution of real income from the inactive and economically weak to the active and economically strong, this is a serious injustice. It is why inflation has been labeled the *cruelest tax*. The effect is the same as if, in a period of constant prices, for no reason at all and at random, some people's wealth or income were taxed and others' were subsidized.

Economic and Social Collapse

The severity of these effects will depend, of course, on the severity of the inflation. Inflation can proceed at an extremely slow pace, with prices rising at 1 percent a year. Then we talk of creeping inflation. Its redistributional effects will be mild. But inflation can also walk or run or gallop! When prices rise very fast, we speak of *hyperinflation.* In this case, the entire economy could grind to a standstill, and beyond that the existing social order might well collapse.

Consider how economic behavior is likely to be distorted away from the normal. Businessmen holding inventories of unsold goods will find their value increasing continually and rapidly. They will tend to become speculators and hoarders of existing goods rather than installers of factories and machines and makers of new goods. They will try to buy cheap goods abroad, rather than produce goods at home. Workers, too, will lose all incentive to work for money that is certain to shrink in value on the way home from work. Thus, the productive process will break down.

The use of money will break down, too. People will shun it like the plague. Exchange will degenerate into a complex and clumsy system of bartering goods for goods. All the while, some of the rich (being creditors) will become poor and some of the poor (being debtors) will become rich. Society will be set against itself. The political institutions will be placed under an intolerable strain.

There can be no doubt that hyperinflation is a disaster second to none. Both Europe and Asia have provided examples following the two world wars. The German case of 1921–1923 is classic. Its speed and extent was fantastic. In 1923, a box of matches cost more than the entire German money supply at the start of World War I. Restaurant patrons paid in advance; if they waited until they had finished their meals, the price might double. A formerly huge life insurance policy could not even buy a single loaf of bread. Many beneficiaries did not bother to collect. The proceeds were worth less than the postage needed to notify the company. Conversely, the man owing a mortgage on a house could pay it off with money not sufficient to buy a handkerchief. In fact, at the peak of the inflation in 1923, one American cent could have paid off all mortgages in existence in Germany 10 years earlier! In the 3 years prior to December 1923, wholesale prices rose a trillionfold.

The former German middle class, living on fixed-income securities, were turned into paupers. Their property and influence were wiped out. Beggars, who speculated skillfully, accumulated fabulous wealth. This occurred on a large scale and completely uprooted all social relationships. It undoubtedly contributed greatly to the rise of Hitler.

The Chinese hyperinflation after World War II provided similar spectacular results. In its wake, Mao Tse-tung came to power, and this completely changed the character of that society.

When discussing inflation in the United States, people often implicitly assume that it is of this type. Obviously, this is nonsense. The nearest the United States ever came to hyperinflation was during the Revolutionary War, from 1775 to 1781, when prices rose 165-fold, but they also fell precipitously thereafter. As we shall see shortly, in recent U.S. history, prices have risen very slowly and money incomes often faster. This should not make us complacent, however, when faced with inflation. The magnitude of the stakes involved should now be clear.

THE MEASUREMENT OF INFLATION

As with unemployment, any attempt at curing the disease requires an accurate and dispassionate analysis of the facts. We must be able to measure the extent of inflation. If we cannot do that, we cannot possibly agree on the dose and type of medicine to be prescribed or on the degree of improvement following its application.

We have already implicitly assumed that it makes sense to talk about changes in the price level *in general*. We must now take a closer look at the meaning of the general price level. It is easy enough to see how the price of apples can go up or down, but what has happened to the price *level*, if the prices of apples and shoes go down, new cars and bus rides stay the same, and doctors' and beauty parlor services go up? Here we must agree on a measure of relative importance, and this is again a matter of *arbitrary decision*. The U.S. government prepares a number of price level statistics. The most commonly known is the *consumer price index*. It is constructed by the Bureau of Labor Statistics, a division of the U.S. Department of Labor.

The Consumer Price Index

Let us consider in some detail the precedure followed in putting together the consumer price index. This is not to say that you should learn the following material by heart. The purpose is simply to give you a general appreciation of the need for and meaning of index numbers. Why do we need an index? Even when confining ourselves to prices of consumer goods, it is clearly impossible to measure all changes of all prices of all goods bought by all people in all places. We have no choice but to be content with a complex series of samples.

First, the Bureau of Labor Statistics made a survey in 1960–1961 of some 4,350 urban wage-earners' and clerical workers' families to find out what kinds and quantities of goods they typically bought. It was found that, on the average, 18.2 percent of their spending went for food eaten at home (and another 4.7 percent for restaurant meals), 32.9 percent went for housing (including hotel charges, utilities, furniture), 10.5 percent for apparel and upkeep, 13.7 percent for transportation, and 19.6 percent for health and recreation. On this basis, the bureau established a "market basket" of the *quantities* of 400 commodities and services typically bought by this type of family. They made sure not to fill it all with food, but to include different types of goods in accordance with their importance in the typical family's budget. This market basket has been used since 1964. Statistics for earlier years are based on similar studies of people's spending habits in earlier periods. Also, since 1964, the "family" has been defined to include single persons living alone, but they were excluded prior to that.

Second, the bureau conducts periodic surveys of prices of the goods contained in the basket. It employs 40 full-time and 200 part-time "shoppers" who make personal visits to some 1,750 food and 17,000 other stores in a sample of fifty-six areas, ranging from New York City (1960 population 7.8 million) to Mangum, Oklahoma (1960 population 3,950). Price data obtained from these areas are weighted in accordance with the wage-earner and clerical-worker population in each. Clearly, a price change in Mangum should not count as much as one in New York. The latter affects many more people.

Food, fuels, and a few other items are priced monthly in all areas. Prices of most other goods are obtained monthly in the five largest areas and every 3 months in other areas. They are estimated in-between.

The stores to be included are determined every 3 years, and price data obtained from them are weighted in accordance with their annual sales volume. Again, a price change in a popular New York store should count much more than in one with few customers.

Bureau shoppers are instructed to price the *same* items at the *same* stores at each visit. This is done to ensure that the market basket remains unchanged and only price changes are measured. Shoppers are given detailed training and instructions for this purpose. A dress may be described not only by size, but also by width in hem and seams, seams pressed open, taping on inside of hem, and thread belt loops! Its quality has to be judged by the type of stitching, the number of loose threads, and so on.

Using the price data so obtained, the bureau evaluates the market basket at the prices of each month or year. The value of any one year, the base year, is arbitrarily given an index of 100. Because quantities are always held constant, any subsequent change in the value of the basket must be owing to changes in prices. The price level index is then assumed to have moved as the value of the fixed quantities of goods in the basket.

an illustration   We can show this easily with the help of Table 4.1 CONSTRUCTION OF THE CONSUMER PRICE INDEX. Column (1) of Table 4.1 shows hypothetical quantities of the kind of goods actually bought by the average urban wage-earner's and clerical worker's family in 1960–1961. This would contain in reality 400 entries. (Note that the average purchase of ⅓ new automobile means that every third family bought a new car.) All these entries would be subject to *sampling error*, that is, be correct only within a range of, say, ±20 percent of the figure given and that for only nine out of ten families.

Next imagine that price data for 1957 and 1970 are collected as in columns (2) and (4), again subject to sampling error. Prices for identical goods vary from store to store and day to day, so it is hard to say for sure that the average apple price in 1970 was 27 cents a pound.

Now we can evaluate our market basket as in columns (3) or (5), subject, of course, to any errors that might have crept into our data. The sum of column (3) tells us that the typical urban wage- and clerical-workers' family would have had to spend $2,485 in 1957 to buy the goods it typically bought in 1960–1961. In 1970, it could have only bought the *same* quantities for $3,476.50. Hence, 1970 prices, compared to 1957 (arbitrarily set equal to 100 percent), were higher *in general* by 39.9 percent (all subject to sampling error and our arbitrary choice of families, market basket, and cities).

problems of interpretation   Criticizing the consumer price index is child's play. You may argue that the 1960–1961 survey, which established the proportions in which different types of goods went into the market basket, has been outdated even before it came into use. People may buy different types of goods or goods in different proportions now than they

Table 4.1   CONSTRUCTION OF THE CONSUMER PRICE INDEX (HYPOTHETICAL FIGURES)

MARKET BASKET (QUANTITIES BOUGHT BY AVERAGE FAMILY IN 1960–1961) (1)	1957 PRICES (2)	VALUE AT 1957 PRICES (3) = (1) × (2)	1970 PRICES (4)	VALUE AT 1970 PRICES (5) = (1) × (4)
50 pounds of apples	30¢/lb	$15	27¢/lb	$13.50
3 pairs of leather shoes	$14/pair	$42	$13/pair	$39.00
1 house rental	$1,200/year	$1,200	$2,000/year	$2,000.00
$\frac{1}{3}$ automobile (new)	$2,700/car	$900	$2,700/car	$900.00
960 city bus rides	$0.15 each	$144	$0.15 each	$144.00
21 office visits to doctor	$4 each	$84	$10 each	$210.00
10 permanents	$10 each	$100	$17 each	$170.00
Total		$2,485		$3,476.50
Index		100		139.9

used to. They may buy different *qualities* of goods, or even buy goods that did not exist previously.

You may argue that the index should include more urban areas than it does, or that people other than urban wage-earners and clerical workers should be included. After all, this way we only cover about 56 percent of the urban and about 40 percent of total population. What about professional people, retired people, and rural people? What does the index mean for them? (The answer: very little, unless they buy the kinds and quantities of goods contained in the basket at the places where and times when price data are collected!)

You may argue that the index is biased on the high side. Bureau shoppers, for instance, visit food stores on the first Tuesday, Wednesday, and Thursday of each month. But people buy 75 percent of all food on Thursdays, Fridays, and Saturdays, often taking advantage of weekend specials. The index misses this entirely. President Johnson's National Commission on Food Marketing recommended that different weights be assigned to early-week and late-week food prices to reflect the volumes of food normally purchased in each half week.) There are other problems. Are the prices gathered true prices, or are there secret kickbacks, side payments, quantity discounts, and the like?

Shoppers are likely to miss many quality improvements. A steady or higher price, together with such an improvement, is not the same as a steady or higher price for an unchanged item. Is it possible to judge accurately the introduction of new automobile safety features, as well as maybe better or worse servicing, delivery time, places of delivery? How does one account for city bus rides that are now dirtier, slower, and more cramped than ever? What to do about doctors who can now heal or prevent diseases previously incurable (a new vaccine, new drugs, new techniques)? What about the tire manufacturer who claims his tires now give more mileage? The bureau gives one simple answer: it considers a quality improvement to have taken place only if there was also an objectively measurable increase in cost. This is hardly satisfactory.

Finally, consider the fixed sample of stores. What if people desert the stores in the sample for others with lower prices? The index-maker will not pick this up until the sample is changed, maybe a few years hence.

conclusions   The above may sound overly critical. In a way it is, for the index is the best we can produce. And having such a measure is a lot better than having to guess about the strength of inflation in our economy. Being aware of the shortcomings of price level statistics (as with unemployment statistics) helps us being cautious in their use. Some people are not. Politicians base some of their most vehement oratory on the consumer price index. If it rises by .2 percent a month, they rejoice, if it rises by .4 percent a month, they see disaster ahead. The contracts of millions of union members call for periodic changes in pay depending on movements of the index. Divorce settlements often contain escalator clauses, providing for increases in alimony whenever the index rises minutely. Even some long-term leases on commercial land and buildings have rentals tied to the index. Equally tied are leases on a group of Chicago penthouse apartments. And so are pensions of over a million retired military and civil service employees. Yet, we must realize that we are continuously led astray when seriously watching quivers of a decimal point of the consumer price index. These may well be false soundings, for all the reasons given above. The index can only be expected to give a *very rough* idea of the movements of the price level in the short run. Its construction involves too many compromises and arbitrary decisions to result in anything more than a rough guide. If prices change drastically year by year, as in a hyperinflation, things are different. The index would then be much more reliable, just as it is now a fairly good indicator of the long-term trend when viewed over several years. Given the nature of index numbers, a small change in the index cannot possibly be an exact measure of real change. And one more thing: this problem cannot be avoided by making *other* arbitrary decisions.

What has been said about the consumer price index is true for all other price indexes as well. The government constructs a number of special purpose indexes designed to fit the needs of different users. The *wholesale price index*, for instance, measures price movements of goods bought by firms (ranging from livestock and industrial chemicals to fuels, machinery, hides, and steel scrap). Such an index would clearly be useless for comparing the cost of living of households.

THE HISTORICAL RECORD

Now let us look at the statistical record. The black line in Figure 4.1 MONEY INCOME AND PRICE LEVEL COMPARED shows the movement of the consumer price index in the United States since 1913. Always comparing to the level of consumer prices in 1929 (arbitrarily set equal to 100), these prices have gradually crept up from 58 percent of the 1929 level in 1913 to 203 percent in 1968. Notice the effect on the price level of the two world wars (shaded). However imperfect the data, the long-run inflationary trend is undeniable. So far as consumers are concerned, the value of each dollar has roughly halved since 1929, because the prices paid by consumers have almost exactly doubled.

Figure 4.1   MONEY INCOME AND PRICE LEVEL COMPARED

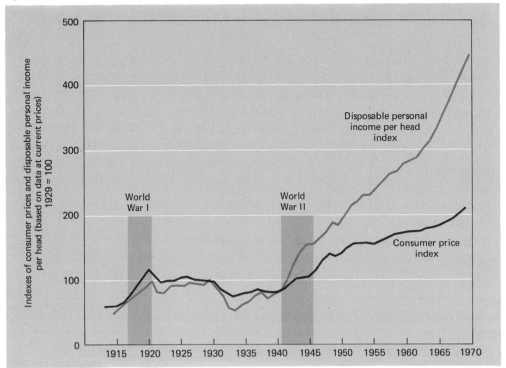

The consumer price index in the United States during the twentieth century has exhibited a steady upward creep. Yet, this inflation has not prevented real income from rising. As is also shown here, the average American's disposable personal money income since the depth of the Great Depression has risen much faster than have consumer prices. Source: Adapted from U.S. Departments of Commerce and Labor.

But notice something else. People in the United States always complain that "things get worse all the time because of inflation." For judging the truth or falsity of such claims, price indexes, however rough, are quite useful. On the one hand, Figure 4.1 confirms the trend the American public so frequently deplores when complaining about the "cheapening of the dollar." Yet Figure 4.1 shows something else, too, just as frequently forgotten by the American public. It shows the behavior of the average American's money income from all sources, after taxes. It is called disposable personal income *per head*. Although being fairly steady during the 1920's, this income fell to almost half the 1929 level by 1933, then has risen continuously (except for 1938–1939 and 1949). From 1940 on, it has been higher than consumer prices relative to 1929. In fact, the disposable money income of the average American has risen *considerably* faster than consumer prices; hence his real income has *risen* despite continuous creeping inflation since 1940. During the 1930's, when consumer prices were *falling*, real incomes fell, because money incomes fell faster than prices! If anything, official data show the average American to have become better off during inflation, not dur-

Figure 4.2   HISTORY OF U.S. WHOLESALE PRICES

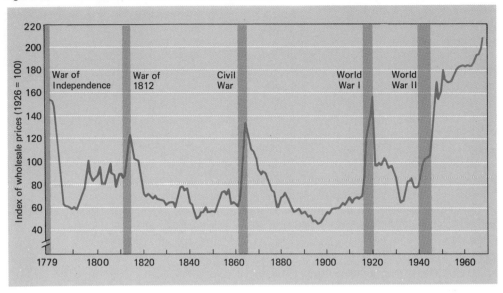

Throughout U.S. history, price levels have moved up and down, similar to a dizzy roller coaster ride. Here we observe the movements of wholesale prices. Note the impact of the five major wars. Note also how, unlike in the four earlier wars, prices did not fall after World War II. Source: U.S. Departments of Commerce and Labor.

ing its absence. This is not to say that he has become better off *because* of inflation (for he would have been better off by more without it). Nor is this to say that *every* American has historically become better off during inflation. This depends on how each individual's disposable money income has changed relative to the consumer price index. Thus the old joke that "inflation is a time when your money won't buy as much as it would have during the depression when you didn't have any" hints at an important truth. The loss of purchasing power of each dollar may be more than made up for by an increased number of dollars available to you. (What has happened to your parents' money income from 1960 to 1968? During that time, the consumer price index rose by almost 12 percent.)

Figure 4.2 takes a similar look at the history of U.S. wholesale prices. As with the consumer price index (Figure 4.1), the inflationary trend since the Great Depression is unmistakable. Wars brought the greatest price increases, but unlike previous postwar periods, prices did not fall after the end of World War II. Given the Cold War, the Korean War, and the Vietnam War, we could argue, of course, that we have not had peace since 1940.

TYPES OF INFLATION

Just as we discovered different types of unemployment, there are at least two types of inflation. One of these has been called *demand-pull inflation*, the other *cost-push inflation*.

Although we shall discuss these at length in later chapters, it will be useful to take a brief look now at the nature of this distinction.

Demand-Pull Inflation

We noticed above how particularly strong increases in the level of prices seem to be associated with wars. (See Figures 4.1 and 4.2.) War is a time when the government must necessarily make large demands on the economy. It must see to it that resources get used to make guns, shells, and army trucks. This would be easy enough, if sufficient quantities of involuntarily idle resources were available. They could simply be drawn out of their unemployment and put to work for these purposes. To some extent, this has happened in many countries. Wars or preparations for war always put a quick end to depression. Usually, however, the governmental demand for war goods is very large relative to the economy's productive capacity. Then idle resources, if any, are not available in sufficient quantities to satisfy this demand. Employed resources must be *diverted* from civilian to public uses. We must *cut down* the production of refrigerators and private houses and cars to *release* resources. They must then be switched to make the higher priority goods demanded by government.

There are several ways of doing this. One of them, alone of interest here, would be for government to simply create whatever money it needed and go out and buy. In this case, possibly all producers experience an increase in demand *at the same time.* Car manufacturers are faced with big government orders and no decline in private purchases. Steel makers find no reduction in the demand for steel to make refrigerators and private houses and cars, but an increase in steel demand to make ammunition and army equipment. So it goes throughout the economy. As in the cases of steaks, pasture land, and yachts in Chapter 2, demand rises and prices rise. Unlike the cases of pork and corn, there is no decline in demand and prices anywhere else. Demand is *pulling prices up* everywhere. Government statisticians would find *all* entries in column (4) of Table 4.1 CONSTRUCTION OF THE CONSUMER PRICE INDEX are bigger than in column (2). Price indexes are going up. We have demand-pull inflation.

Notice something else. Many private households will find their money incomes lagging behind the rising prices. Thus, they will spend as much money as before or even more, yet get *fewer* refrigerators, houses, and cars. Inflation is imposing a "tax" on them. It reduces their power to commandeer resources for private uses. It releases resources for the purposes demanded by government. The steel that some households cannot get (in the form of refrigerators, houses, and cars, which cost more now) is used to make guns, shells, and army trucks.

In the same way, demand-pull inflation can be caused by any other group in the economy that is enabled, in one way or another, to inject a massive dose of demand.

Cost-Push Inflation

During the post-World War II period, economists isolated another form of inflationary virus. They found the price level rising even in periods without excessive overall demand. This is ultimately owing to the kinds of imperfections in the market economy already alluded to in previous chapters. Just as some sellers of goods and resources (large businesses, powerful labor unions) can resist declines in prices of goods and resources in the face of surpluses, they may have the power to *push them up*, regardless of demand or supply. A powerful steel workers' union, for instance, may insist on higher wages. Unless output per man is correspondingly higher, this raises the labor cost per ton of steel. It also reduces the profit of steel makers. Yet, the company may give in to the union and maintain its profit by passing higher costs along to customers in higher prices of steel. Conversely, a giant steel producer may arbitrarily increase his mark-up over costs (although costs have not risen), hoping to raise profits. Again steel prices go up. Typically, one party blames the other for having "started it first," but that is, like the chicken-egg controversy, a fruitless game of mutual recrimination. Any output price increase can be shown to have been preceded at some time in the past by an increase in costs. Any increase in costs is preceded by an increase in output prices somewhere.

Conclusion

Demand-pull inflation is a general rise in prices caused by demanders (say, government and households) trying to buy more than 100 percent of the economy's maximum output. Buyers have enough money to buy (at current prices) more output than can possibly be produced. Thus, prices rise until the excessive claim on real output is cancelled by making each dollar worth less. If we can make only ten cars (presently priced at $2,000 each), but people insist on spending $30,000 on cars, they will not get fifteen cars, or 150 percent of maximum output. Instead, each car will come to sell for $3,000.

Cost-push inflation is a general rise in prices caused by sellers of resources (say, workers and owners of land and capital) trying as a group to get more than 100 percent of the economy's maximum real income. This maximum real income people can get is, of course, equivalent to the maximum output the economy can produce. Cost-push inflation means that those who produce output want to make sure to get a certain percentage of it, but their claims are inconsistent with each other. Prices rise until the inconsistency is removed. If we are producing ten cars (presently priced at $2,000 each), all those contributing to the production must somehow share the ten cars (real income) or the revenue derived from their sale (money income). As a group, they cannot get more. If workers want to get paid $18,000, they are in fact demanding nine cars. Then, at present prices, those who own the factory and make the materials can only get $2,000, or the equivalent of one car. What if they want $12,000, or another six cars? It is clearly impossible to divide up in this way fifteen cars where only ten exist. It is possible, however, for management to pay $18,000 to workers and then to raise the price of each car to $3,000. As a result, everyone's claim on real output is reduced below what it was. Workers get $18,000. Yet at the *new* prices, this is purchasing power over six cars only, not over nine. Others get $12,000, or the equivalent of four cars only, not of six.

In practice, of course, it is next to impossible to distinguish demand-pull from cost-push inflation. A general rise in prices is a general rise in prices. Who can tell with certainty whether they went up because all buyers offered to pay more, hoping to get more goods (and sellers were glad to take more money without delivering more goods), or because all buyers had to pay more because sellers insisted on it (and buyers had to give in)?

For the moment, it is sufficient to have mentioned the possibility of two different types of inflation. Later, when we discuss their cures, we shall have to return to this distinction.

SUMMARY

1   Inflation is a situation in which most or all prices in the economy are rising. It is a serious problem because it leads to a capricious redistribution of real income and wealth.

2   The severity of these effects depends on whether inflation is *creeping* or a *hyperinflation*. The latter can easily cause economic collapse and serious social upheaval. The German case after World War I and the Chinese one after World II provide examples.

3   The extent of inflation can be measured through the construction of price indexes. The construction of the consumer price index is discussed in detail. It shows changes in the value of a fixed typical market basket of goods bought by urban wage-earners' and clerical workers' families.

4   Finding deficiencies in the consumer price index, or any index, is child's play. This is so because in the process of compressing a complex social phenomenon, like the movement of all prices, into one single number many compromises and arbitrary decisions must be made. Those who dislike any one decision cannot escape the problem by making other, equally arbitrary ones.

5   Because of its (unavoidable) deficiencies, we should not overly rely on quivers of a decimal point of the consumer price index. Like any price index, it only gives a very rough idea of price movements in the short run. It is fairly reliable as an indicator of very violent price movements or of long-run changes. And knowing this is better than knowing nothing at all.

6   The historical record of the United States reveals that consumer prices have crept up during this century from 58 percent of their 1929 level in 1913 to 203 percent in 1968. However, since the depth of the Great Depression, disposable personal money income per head has risen faster than consumer prices. The average American's *real* income has risen in spite of inflation.

7   U.S. wholesale prices, though exhibiting great movements up and down until the Great Depression, have steadily crept upward since. Though prices have fallen precipitously after earlier wars, they have not after World War II.

8   Analysis reveals that there are at least two types of inflation, demand-pull and cost-push. Demand-pull inflation is a case of "too much money chasing too few goods." More wants are backed up with purchasing power than can be satisfied by even a fully employed economy. Cost-push inflation denotes a situation in which powerful sellers of goods or resources force higher prices on buyers, regardless of demand or supply.

TERMS[1]

base year	general price level
consumer price index	hyperinflation
cost-push inflation	inflation
creeping inflation	market basket
demand-pull inflation	money vs. real income
disposable personal income	sampling error
escalator clause	wholesale price index

QUESTIONS FOR REVIEW AND DISCUSSION

1 "Inflation may redistribute real income from older to younger generations." Explain.

2 Deflation is a general *fall* in prices. What do you think are its effects?

3 "Inflation is equivalent to imposing a tax." Discuss. (Think of how taxes and inflation would affect you when earning money.)

4 "Inflation might cause serious foreign trade problems." Can you guess why and how?

5 "The best way to save in times of inflation is to buy stock and real estate." Comment. (Imagine yourself doing it.)

6 "If inflation is anticipated, it may not have bad effects." Discuss. (Again, imagine you are involved.)

7 Explain the difficulties of interpreting the meaning of the consumer price index. Do you think it is applicable to *you*?

8 "It is silly to say that the value of money depends on the price index. Does one's weight depend on the scale?" Discuss.

9 "The prices of things I buy rose by 10 percent in the last 5 years. My money income fell by 10 percent. This hurts." Can you figure out how much it hurts by calculating this person's change in real income? (Hint: set up a 5-year price index and money income index by calling the original quantities 100. Then divide the money income index by the price index to get a real income index.)

10 Suppose you were a patriotic citizen who bought a U.S. government bond in 1942 for $18.75 and received back $25 10 years later. How much would you have gained in real purchasing power? (Hint: the consumer price index rose by 63 percent in that period.)

11 Many economists assert that a *constant* consumer price index really indicates a *fall* in prices. Explain.

12 In 1966, the consumer price index (base 1957–1959 = 100) for Boston was 117.0, for San Diego 102.7. This does *not* necessarily mean that consumer goods were cheaper in San Diego. What does it mean?

[1] Terms are defined in the Glossary at the end of the book.

13   In 1967, the consumer price index (compared to 1957–1959=100) stood at 116.3. Yet the price behavior for different groups of goods contained in this overall index was quite different. The component index for medical services stood at 145.6, that for personal care at 136.7, that for transport services at 128.4, that for household services at 127.0. On the other hand, the index for used cars stood at 98.1, for household furnishings at 100.8, for many food items (such as eggs, fats, sugar) at 101.9, and for durable commodities at 104.3. What is the meaning of these component indexes? Can you explain their differences?

14   "Stop complaining about higher prices! Would you really prefer 1953 goods at 1953 prices to 1970 goods at 1970 prices?" Well, would you? (Additional comment: there was no Salk vaccine in 1953.)

15   The text says: "Wars always put a quick end to depression." Explain. Is that the reason for wars?

16   During the Vietnam War, as indicated by the news story introducing this chapter, the United States experienced increasingly serious inflation. Can you explain it?

17   There is a long tradition associating rising money supply with inflation. This is supported by spectacular examples from wars. Do you think this is a logically necessary association, that is, do you think only more money can cause inflation, or could we have inflation even without any increase in the supply of money in the economy? (Write down your answer and reread it after Chapter 10, on monetary policy.)

18   The caption to Figure 4.2 notes "how, unlike in the four earlier wars, prices did not fall after World War II." How do you account for this?

19   MR. A: "Insistence by unions to get higher wages may not raise output prices at all." MR. B: "On the contrary, it will raise output prices and, therefore, fail to raise the workers' real income."
Evaluate. Who is right? Could both be right?

20   Without reading ahead, how do you think one could cure the two types of inflation? Write down your answers and compare them to what you think about it at the conclusion of Part 1.

Advance of GNP Continued Strong In 4th Quarter

Gain, at $16.8 Billion Annual Rate, Trailed Third Period, But Exceeded Year Earlier

Business Outlays Speeded Up

By a WALL STREET JOURNAL *Staff Reporter*

WASHINGTON—The gross national product advanced robustly again in the fourth quarter, the Commerce Department announced.

The gain, at a $16.8 billion annual rate, was only slightly below the $18.1 billion third quarter increase, as consumer spending slowed substantially while total private investment accelerated.

The increase put total Government and private output of goods and services at a record $887.8 billion seasonally adjusted annual rate. While the fourth quarter rise exceeded the $15.7 billion advance of 1967's final period, it was well below the $21.7 billion gain of last year's second quarter and the 20.2 billion first quarter advance.

The 2% advance from the September quarter was made up of a 1% gain in real or physical output, the department said, with price increases accounting for the other 1%.

Smallest Since 1967's 3rd Period

In a speech here just after the GNP figures were released, William H. Chartener, Assistant Commerce Secretary for economic affairs, noted that although the size of the fourth quarter rise was "roughly the same" as that of the third quarter, the composition was "very different." Consumer spending, the biggest single component, rose by only $5.2 billion to a $546.3 billion yearly pace, after a $13.2 billion surge in the September quarter. In contrast, the rise in business and residential fixed investment accelerated by a sharp $6.4 billion to an annual rate of $126 billion after a much slower $3.1 billion rise the previous quarter.

The consumer spending rise was the smallest since a similar gain in the third quarter of 1967. In his speech to the American Mining Congress, however, Mr. Chartener noted that such spending last year moved on an "erratic

zig-zig path," advancing sharply one quarter, then slowing the next. Thus, he said, "I am inclined to view the small fourth quarter advance as having some of this character, not as an indicator of a new and more sluggish trend."

Altogether, the increase in final sales, which with inventory investments make up the total GNP, slowed to a $14.25 billion annual rate in the December quarter from a $21.5 billion rate the quarter before.

Consumer spending on durable goods slipped $300 million to an adjusted annual rate of $84.8 billion, the first decline in five quarters. At $233.5 billion, spending on nondurables was up only $800 million. Outlays on services rose $4.6 billion to an annual rate of $228 billion.

Offsetting the weakness in consumer spending, the total of all forms of private domestic investment ran at an annual rate of $136.1 billion, up $9 billion after declining by $200 million in the September quarter. Spending on private housing construction spurted by $2.3 billion to a $31.8 billion rate from the $29.5 billion posted for both the third and second quarters. Outlays for nonresidential building rose $1 billion to a $29.8 billion rate.

Manufacturers Equipment Investment

Investment in manufacturers equipment advanced by $3.1 billion to a $64.4 billion yearly pace after a $2.8 billion gain the previous quarter. The rate of business inventory accumulation climbed $2.5 billion from the September quarter's $7.5 billion pace; the report noted, however, that data for this volatile component was available only for October and November.

Mr. Chartener said this rate "cannot be sustained very long without efforts to slow down further accumulation—namely through reduced orders or curtailed production schedules." He noted, however, that "we are still far short" of the $15 billion rate of inventory buildup in 1966, which set off the "mini-recession" of early 1967. . . .

Military Spending Rose

Government purchases, at a $101.6 billion annual rate, were $400 million above the September quarter, when they rose $1.2 billion. At an $80 million annual rate, military spending was up $400 million, a slightly slower increase than the $600 million third quarter gain.

Spending by state and local governments rose $2.4 billion to a $100.8 billion annual rate. The increase was a bit slimmer than the $2.8 billion gain of the third quarter.

Based on figures for October and November, the nation's trade surplus in the quarter fell to a $3 billion annual rate, from the $3.3 billion third quarter pace. This surplus, which reflects some service transactions in addition to the net excess of merchandise exports over imports, was slightly under the $3.4 billion level of a year earlier.

In all 1968, the department said, the GNP rose $71 billion, or 9%, to $861 billion.

The Wall Street Journal, January 15, 1969

5

aggregate supply: the gross national product

W E HAVE NOW become acquainted with two major problems of the modern capitalist economy—unemployment and inflation. Do we have to live with them, like inevitable plagues, or can we build a defense against them? To answer this question, we have to learn a great deal more about our economy. In this process, we will gain an understanding of the mechanism that creates unemployment and inflation. Some clues to its nature have already come our way.

We have noted in Chapter 3 how businessmen at times find themselves in a situation in which they could easily produce more, given the resources available in the economy, but demand for goods is insufficient to take all of this potential output. If this situation is typical and experienced by all or most businessmen at the same time, it naturally leads them as a group to employ fewer resources than are available for use. We have *general* unemployment.

We have noted in Chapter 4 how businessmen at other times cannot possibly produce more, given the resources available in the economy, yet people's demand for goods is excessive. People have the money to buy more than can possibly be produced, even at full employment. If this situation is typical and experienced by all or most businessmen at the same time, it leads them as a group to produce the highest possible output and to sell it at increased prices. We have *demand-pull* inflation.

Suppose we call the total amount of money people are both able and willing to spend on newly produced goods during a given period *aggregate demand*. And let us call the value (at current prices) of the maximum quantity of goods that can be newly produced by fully employing our resources during that period *potential aggregate supply*. Then, the two large problems we have dealt with so far can be simply put this way:

General unemployment occurs whenever aggregate demand is smaller than potential aggregate supply. Demand-pull inflation occurs whenever aggregate demand exceeds potential aggregate supply. When we put it this way, it is clear that the concepts of aggregate supply and aggregate demand are crucial for our purposes. We must, indeed, study them in detail. As with unemployment and inflation themselves, it is by no means obvious how aggregate supply and aggregate demand can be measured. In this chapter, we deal with aggregate supply; in the next one, with aggregate demand. Then, by putting them together in Chapter 7, we are ready for the first time to understand fully the mechanism that creates unemployment and inflation in our economy. That understanding, in turn, will show us how to undertake the cure.

There is another reason, however, why the measurement of aggregate supply is important. We might want to know the actual or potential quantity of goods we can produce for purposes other than our concern with unemployment and inflation. By comparing, for instance, particular types of outputs with the nation's total, we can judge whether we like the way in which we have allocated our resources. If we found that half our national output consisted of military hardware, we might want to take corrective measures. This would be akin to a family spending half its income on firearms. Most likely, it could improve its well-being by buying fewer of them and more of other goods. Similarly, we might want to compare the output going to particular groups of people with the nation's total. Just as a family might be unhappy if father took nine tenths of family income for himself, a nation that gives too large or too small a portion of its output to particular groups might find itself in trouble. Again, by comparing their outputs with the nation's total, we can gain an understanding of the relative importance of particular types of producers. And we can gain a better feeling for the economic importance of particular regions in the country. For these reasons, the measurement of aggregate supply takes on added importance.

THE GROSS NATIONAL PRODUCT DEFINED

When you stop to consider the millions of goods that make up the output of a nation—from milk to coal, from bobby pins to steam rollers, from courthouses to appendectomies—you realize what a monumental piece of work it must be to compress all this into a single number. It is a piece of work no less exacting than measuring the nation's general level of prices, a matter we discussed in the previous chapter. Measuring national output, or the *gross national product* (GNP), as it is called officially, also involves a great many arbitrary decisions and, unavoidably, can also yield no more than a rough estimate at the end.

As the concept is used in the United States, GNP is defined as *the sum of the market values of all final goods produced from U.S.-owned resources during a period.* This is quite a mouthful, and it takes some explaining.

A Measure of Production

First, note that the definition calls for "goods produced during a period." Thus, the object is to measure newly created commodities and services, or the increase, usually during a year, of want-satisfying goods to the nation. This increase, furthermore, to be counted in the GNP, must have come from new production, not from stockpiles of goods made in the past nor from imports from abroad.

A Measure of Production from U.S. Resources

Second, the definition calls for production "from U.S.-owned resources." We only intend to measure what U.S. labor, land, and capital have created, wherever these resources were employed. Thus, the output of U.S. resources in Mexico would be part of U.S. GNP; the output of Canadian ones in Detroit would not. This makes sense, because we want to measure the availability of new goods to Americans. Presumably, the portion of output produced by U.S. resources in Mexico belongs to us, that made by Canadian ones in Detroit belongs to Canadians.

Dollars as Measuring Rod

Third, the definition calls for "the sum of the market values of all . . . goods." This is easily understood. Because we cannot meaningfully add *gallons* of milk to *tons* of coal to *numbers* of bobby pins, and so on, we must agree on some kind of common denominator. The dollar values of the items involved—the actual prices paid for them in the markets—are the only common measuring rod available. We add *dollars* of milk to *dollars* of coal to *dollars* of bobby pins, and so on to derive a GNP total in dollars. Using this procedure may, however, cause trouble if the market values refer to values at *current* prices. During inflation, these prices rise. Hence, even if all the *quantities* going into the GNP are constant (that is, the gallons, tons, and numbers don't change), the GNP figure will rise. This is a purely spurious and misleading rise. A given output sells for more. There is no more output than before. The measuring rod of money is flexible. Imagine what it would do to measurements if the length of the inch were to change from year to year!

To avoid this effect, economists also measure the GNP of all years at *constant* prices, or at the prices actually prevailing in any *one* (arbitrarily chosen) year, say 1958. If we measure the outputs of every year—of 1958, 1965, 1970, and (retroactively) 1950—at the prices of 1958, we avoid the distortion resulting from changes in prices. Then, any change in the dollar figure must result from a change in some actual output quantity. Thus, you will find GNP statistics "at current prices" and "at constant prices." For most purposes, the latter are more meaningful, and we shall use them frequently. The actual base year, by whose prices the outputs of all years are measured, can, of course, be any year. Just as the length of an inch could be any length! It is perfectly arbitrary. But once we have chosen such a length, once we have agreed on a base year, we must stick to it, at least throughout the example under discussion.

You will recall our discussion of the consumer price index in the last chapter. For want of any better information, such an index could be used to separate the physical output change from the effect of higher prices when comparing GNP figures. This method of changing GNP data at current prices into GNP data at constant prices is called *deflating the GNP*.

Suppose that the GNP at current prices is $800 billion in 1968, but $900 billion in 1969. And suppose consumer prices, as measured by the consumer price index, changed from 100 in the first to 110 in the second year. (That is, consumer prices rose 10 percent.) Then, we can easily calculate by how much GNP had changed if prices had not changed. (That is, we can calculate the change in "real" GNP.) We simply divide each year's GNP figure at current prices by the price index of the same year and multiply by 100. In our case, we get for 1968:

$$\frac{\text{1968 GNP at current prices}}{\text{1968 price index}} \times 100 = \frac{\$800 \text{ billion}}{100} \times 100 = \$800 \text{ billion.}$$

This only says that the GNP of 1968, at 1968 prices, would have sold for $800 billion, a fact we knew all along. But now we turn to 1969 and get:

$$\frac{\text{1969 GNP at current prices}}{\text{1969 price index}} \times 100 = \frac{\$900 \text{ billion}}{110} \times 100 = \$818.2 \text{ billion.}$$

This tells us something we did not know before, that at constant 1968 prices the 1969 GNP would have sold for only $818.2 billion. Thus, in real terms, we only got $18.2 billion more goods. It just so happened that everything also sold for 10 percent more, and a 10 percent price hike on a $818.2 billion collection of goods yields $900 billion! If we wanted to, we could now report that of the observed 12.5 percent rise in current dollar GNP (from $800 billion to $900 billion) only 2.3 percent was a real increase in physical quantities of goods (from $800 billion to $818.2 billion). The rest, or 10.2 percent increase, only reflected higher prices (from $818.2 billion to $900 billion).

Actually, as you might expect, the government does not use the consumer price index to deflate the entire current dollar GNP, but only the portion of total output consisting of consumer goods. It uses other price indexes for the rest of output and then adds the deflated components together. But the method used is exactly as described here. Now we must return to our discussion of the definition of GNP.

Final Goods Only

Lastly note that the definition calls for the inclusion of *final* goods only. This is also best explained by an example. Most goods go through a great number of production stages. Recall from Chapter 1 the story of baking a cake. We traced one of the ingredients, wheat, from the farmer to the miller to the baker to the retailer to a household. Suppose the relevant statistics are as follows:

STAGE 1: Farmer Black incurs the following costs producing a certain small quantity of wheat (some costs, such as purchases of seed and fertilizer from other firms, are neglected for simplicity):

wages (for his own and hired labor)	$0.60
rent (for land)	0.05
interest (for borrowed money embodied in barn and equipment)	0.05
depreciation (for the wear and tear of capital goods)	0.02
property taxes	0.08
total	$0.80

He sells the wheat to the miller for $1.00. Hence, he made a profit of 20 cents.

STAGE 2: Miller White incurs the following costs producing a certain small quantity of flour:

raw material purchased (wheat)	$1.00
wages (for his own and hired labor)	0.10
interest (for borrowed money embodied in mill and truck)	0.10
depreciation (for the wear and tear of capital goods)	0.02
property and sales taxes	0.03
total	$1.25

He sells the flour to a bakery for $1.50. Hence, he made a profit of 25 cents.

STAGE 3: Baker Brown incurs the following costs producing a cake:

raw materials purchased (flour; others, such as eggs and milk, neglected for simplicity)	$1.50
wages (for his own and hired labor)	0.70
interest (for borrowed money embodied in building and equipment)	0.01
depreciation (for the wear and tear of capital goods)	0.09
property and sales taxes	0.10
total	$2.40

He sells the cake to a retailer for $2.00. Hence, he made a loss, or *negative* profit, of 40 cents.

STAGE 4:   Retailer Green incurs the following costs storing and selling a cake:

raw materials purchased (cake $2.00; others, such as wrappings, neglected for simplicity)	$2.00
wages (for his own and hired labor)	0.05
interest (for borrowed money embodied in store, truck, and other equipment)	0.02
depreciation (for the wear and tear of capital goods)	0.07
property and sales taxes	0.08
total	$2.22

He sells the cake to a household for $2.50. Hence, he made a profit of 28 cents.

Suppose now that all this occurred between March and November of the same year. At market prices, farmer Black produced wheat worth $1, miller White produced flour worth $1.50, baker Brown produced cake in the bakery on November 1 worth $2, and retailer Green produced cake in the hands of the household on November 16 worth $2.50. If you were to measure their *aggregate* output, would you say it was $1 + $1.50 + $2 + $2.50, or a total of $7?

Probably you would hesitate. The only production you could actually find, if you looked around, would be a single cake, worth $2.50. What has gone wrong?

The answer is, of course, that the wheat and the flour and the cake in the bakery on November 1 were *intermediate* goods, goods produced earlier in the year, but *completely used up* in the making of other goods into which their value was incorporated. The cake in the hands of the household on November 16 was a *final* good, a good not resold to another producer during the year. It makes a lot of sense to count national production in terms of final goods only. That is what GNP statisticians do. This avoids the multiple counting of intermediate goods that occurs if everyone's output is added together indiscriminately. Note, however, that in principle any good could be a final good, because a final good is any newly produced good not resold to another producer during the year (and in that sense used up). Suppose our farmer had sold the wheat to the miller who had kept it till the end of the year. Looking at the year as a whole, stages 4, 3, and most of 2 would never have occurred. Hence, wheat worth $1 (in the miller's hand) would have been that year's final output. Thus, you must not get the idea that cake is a final good, but wheat never can be. What is final depends simply on the circumstances. Just ask yourself whether the good, newly produced in this period, was resold to another producer during the period under study. If the answer is yes, it was an intermediate good. If the answer is no, it was a final good. Depending on the circumstances, any particular good may be classed one way at one time, another way at another time.

Final Goods Versus Value-Added Approach

Note that the statistician could eliminate the multiple counting in two ways. The one illustrated here, the *final goods approach*, simply added the output that was not resold to other producers during the year (here the retailer's), forgetting about the other activities (here the farmer's, miller's, and baker's). Another approach, the *value-added approach*, would ask each producer how much value he has *added to* the output taken over from others, and would then add these pieces together. In our case, we would find farmer Black adding $1 to nothing, because we assumed for the sake of simplicity that he bought nothing from any

Figure 5.1   MEASURING OUTPUT: VALUE THE FINAL GOOD OR SUM VALUE ADDED

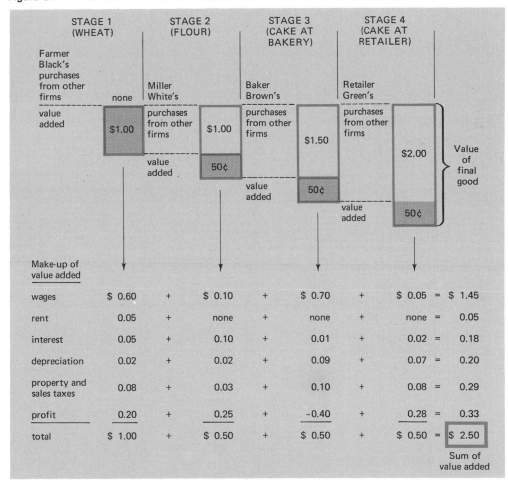

Make-up of value added								
wages	$ 0.60	+	$ 0.10	+	$ 0.70	+	$ 0.05	= $ 1.45
rent	0.05	+	none	+	none	+	none	= 0.05
interest	0.05	+	0.10	+	0.01	+	0.02	= 0.18
depreciation	0.02	+	0.02	+	0.09	+	0.07	= 0.20
property and sales taxes	0.08	+	0.03	+	0.10	+	0.08	= 0.29
profit	0.20	+	0.25	+	−0.40	+	0.28	= 0.33
total	$ 1.00	+	$ 0.50	+	$ 0.50	+	$ 0.50	= $ 2.50

Most goods go through many stages of production. Typically, at each stage a good's value increases until its final value is established at the last stage reached. The value of the final good is by necessity always equal to the sum of the values added at each stage of production. Note how the shaded boxes of value added add up to the colored box denoting value of final good (top). Note also how these identical figures of value of final good and sum of value added equal the total of six types of payments made during the process of production (bottom).

other producer. So $1 is his value added. Miller White, however, *adds* only 50 cents to the value of output by grinding wheat into flour. His value added is 50 cents. Baker Brown buys $1.50 of raw materials from others and sells cakes for $2. His value added is 50 cents. Retailer Green buys $2 of raw materials and sells cake for $2.50. His value added is also 50 cents. The *sum* of value added is $2.50. It is equal to the value of final output! In this way, the final goods approach and the value-added approach always yield the same unduplicated output total.

All this is summarized in Figure 5.1 MEASURING OUTPUT: VALUE THE FINAL GOOD OR SUM VALUE ADDED. The figure is self-explanatory.

THE GROSS NATIONAL PRODUCT COMPILED

Defining a concept such as the GNP is one thing. Actually going out and measuring it is quite another. Some economists concerned themselves with the concept and measurement of a nation's aggregate output as early as the seventeenth century. The comprehensive data now available to us are, however, of much more recent origin. As with the consumer price index, actual systematic attempts at estimation of the national output in the United States go back to the time of World War I. Such work was then undertaken by a private research organization, the National Bureau of Economic Research. The first government-sponsored estimates only appeared in the 1930's. Such official data are now collected by the Office of Business Economics of the U.S. Department of Commerce. They are available for all years since 1929. Earlier data exist, but are even rougher estimates than the official data collected by the government.

The Commerce Department measures the GNP in both of the ways suggested above.

Summing Expenditures

First, the Commerce Department takes the final goods approach, asking who in the economy received final goods produced with American resources, or what is the same thing, who spent how much money buying such final goods. Four broad classes of buyers are distinguished: American households, American private businesses, American governments (all levels), and foreigners.

consumption   The purchases of goods by American households are called *personal consumption expenditures* and are usually shown symbolically by C. These include, first, purchases of commodities typically used up within a year, such as our cake above; these range from food and clothing to drugs and gasoline. In 1969, Americans bought a total of $238.1 billion of such nondurable goods. Consumers also buy services, goods by necessity used up at the moment of purchase, ranging from haircuts and airplane rides to insurance and television repairs. In 1969, they spent another $232.5 billion on services. Finally, households buy commodities that typically last longer than a year, such as automobiles, beds, television sets, and washing machines. In 1969, they spent $86.8 billion on such durables. As is shown in column

(1) of Table 5.1 MEASURING THE GNP, total personal consumption expenditures amounted to $557.4 billion.

investment   The purchases by private American businesses are called *investment expenditures*, and are usually symbolized by I. These include, first, all structures: business plant and residential houses, the latter being included here by tradition and thus excluded from consumer durables. In 1969, such expenditures equaled $64.7 billion. Investment also includes all business purchases of durable equipment, from trucks to assembly lines, from computers to milling machines. A total of $67.4 billion was spent for such purposes in 1969. Finally, included here are *changes* in business inventories, in 1969 of +$6.9 billion. This requires a note of explanation.

Table 5.1   MEASURING THE GNP

(1)		(2)	
Personal consumption expenditures, C	557.4	Wages	545.2
Investment expenditures, I	139.0	Rents	21.4
Government expenditures on goods, G	206.9	Interest	28.4
Net exports, NX	.0	Depreciation	77.5
		Indirect business taxes	76.6
		Profits	154.2
Gross national expenditure, Y	903.3	Gross national income, Y	903.3

This table shows two ways of measuring the GNP. The left-hand column adds the expenditures on final goods, yielding the gross national expenditure. The right-hand column utilizes the value-added approach, summing the gross incomes earned in the process of production, yielding the gross national income. Both totals are identically equal to the GNP. Data refer to the United States in 1969 and are in billions of current dollars. They are seasonally adjusted first quarter data at annual rates. Source: U.S. Department of Commerce.

Consider once more our above story. Suppose the miller had *not* sold the flour this year. He would have had increased inventories of, say, one pound of wheat flour. Surely, it would have been part of our production and a final good at that, not having been sold to another producer during the year and not having been used up in the making of other goods. The miller has invested $1.25 (his cost) in flour in the hope of a profitable future sale. Hence, any increased inventory must be counted in GNP, as the +$6.9 billion above. It is usually evaluated at cost, because profit is not known until the sale has been made.

This figure could, however, also be negative. Suppose next year the story continues via stages 3 and 4: the flour is sold, the cake is baked, the cake is sold to a household. Counting consumer expenditures of $2.50 would leave the impression that next year output of $2.50 was produced *in addition to* this year's flour. We would be double counting again. Hence, the miller's loss of flour inventories would be recorded as a negative number next year (I = −$1.25) together with the household purchase (C = $2.50). This would make it quite clear that half the cake was produced this year (up to the point of having flour of $1.25) and the other half was produced next year (C of $2.50 plus I of $-\$1.25$ also equaling 1.25).

In short, the inventory change figure makes sure that output that has not quite gotten to the last stage in the productive process is counted in the year in which it is produced (positive entry under I) and that output that is sold in one year but was made earlier is not counted in that year (negative entry under I to offset any exaggerated positive entry, as above under C). Positive and negative entries are, of course, netted out. The $+\$6.9$ billion entry in 1969 indicates that, *net*, our inventories went up, although many firms will have experienced decreases and others increases. Adding the three components—structures, equipment, and inventory change—we get total investment expenditures in 1969 of $139.0 billion, also shown in Table 5.1 MEASURING THE GNP.

government   Another large group of purchasers of our output are the various levels of government. *Government expenditures on goods* are symbolized by G. The notation "on goods" may seem redundant at this point, in that all the expenditures listed in column (1) of Table 5.1 are for goods (commodities and services). However, it is useful to point this out here, because we will later be concerned with another type of government expenditure that is not on goods. Government spending shown here includes everything from paper clips and mailmen services to jet fighters and highways. In 1969, the federal government bought $102.4 billion of goods, state and local governments, $104.5 billion. Table 5.1 indicates the total of $206.9 billion.

net exports   This leaves us with foreign purchases of our output. Such exports of commodities and services symbolized by X, amounted to $46.6 billion in 1969. Yet we cannot stop here. One further adjustment is needed.

Just as we had to deduct negative inventory change as part of I (in case any of the spending on our output by households, businesses, governments, and foreigners was on goods produced *in the past*), we must make another deduction. Possibly, some of the same spending— now measured in C, I, G, and X—was on goods produced *abroad*. Households buy Japanese binoculars, businesses buy German machines, the federal government buys Korean food for our soldiers there, and Canadians may buy Volkswagens from us! To the extent that this is true, our measurement of C, I, G, and X overstates *American* production, just as failure to exclude inventory declines would lead to an overstatement of *this year's* American production. We must, therefore, deduct all imports of goods.

This is as good a place as any to do it. Deducting imports from exports we get *net exports*, NX. Because exports were $46.6 billion and imports by coincidence were also $46.6 billion in 1969, net exports were zero. See Table 5.1.

gross national expenditure   Summing the components just discussed, we get the gross national expenditure. In 1969, it was $903.3 billion. It is identically equal to GNP. This is so because measuring who spends how much on final goods is just one way of measuring the GNP. Often the GNP is symbolized by Y. Then, economists say that $C + I + G + NX = Y$.

We now turn to the alternative approach of summing the value added by each producer. Remember, this is just another way of measuring the same total GNP. But it serves as a convenient check on the accuracy of the procedure.

If you were to reread our earlier discussion of value added (in particular look again at Figure 5.1 MEASURING OUTPUT: VALUE THE FINAL GOOD OR SUM VALUE ADDED), you would notice one interesting and useful thing: the value added of a producer *always* equals the sum of incomes earned there if incomes include wages, rents, interest, depreciation, certain taxes, and profits. Take Stage 1. Farmer Black's value added was $1. What were the incomes earned owing to his activity? Some people, including the farmer himself, earned 60 cents in wages (before taxes). Some landlord (possibly farmer Black himself) earned 5 cents in rent (before taxes). Somebody earned 5 cents in interest (before taxes). The local government earned 8 cents in taxes. Farmer Black made a profit of 20 cents. This leaves us with 2 miserable cents, called *depreciation.*

Depreciation is a bookkeeping charge measuring the wear and tear on his capital goods. These 2 cents are not paid out to anyone else. Farmer Black still has them. He might accumulate them in cash to replace the equipment and buildings when they wear out, but he need not. Whatever he does, these 2 cents are part of his *gross* income. The reason is simple.

By neglecting to charge himself depreciation, farmer Black's profit would have been 22 cents. Being a good accountant, however, he realized that this would be an illusion. Though he gained 22 cents (after getting $1 from the miller and paying wages, rent, interest, and property taxes), he also lost 2 cents of equipment. Its life is shorter. He is ahead by only 20 cents. It is just that 2 cents of equipment, used to make wheat that was sold, turned into cash when he got paid! Indeed, the tax laws would agree with him, taxing him only on the 20 cents.

Thus, value added equals the sum of incomes. You may repeat the same for stages 2 through 4. It is always true. (Note how in all three cases the sum of incomes equals 50 cents.)

Table 5.1, column (2), shows the data derived for the United States by this approach in 1969. They are largely self-explanatory. *Indirect business taxes* refer to taxes not levied on income, such as property and sales taxes shown in our examples. They are taxes counted as a cost of doing business. In addition, of course, governments levy so-called direct or income taxes on the wages, rent, interest, and profit incomes shown in the table.

Concluding Comments

Table 5.1 is presented in exactly the form in which the U.S. government publishes GNP statistics. There are two things worth noting about the accounts.

gross versus net investment   In column (1) we observe a $139.0 billion item, *investment expenditures*. This is equal to the production by the private sector of the economy of new capital goods. They are the man-made productive inputs we described in Chapter 1 as being so crucial to the nation's productivity. Without our willingness to forgo some possible immediate satisfaction each year to build capital, our labor and land resources would yield significantly fewer goods in the long run. The item mentioned is, therefore, what you should look for if you want to know the size of any year's *gross addition* to the nation's *privately owned* stock of business capital. It is also referred to as "gross private domestic investment." The italicized words are important. The $139.0 billion item did not measure the *total size* of our 1969 business capital stock, but only the *addition to it* from new production. Further, it only measured the *gross* addition, because our existing business capital stock was partly used up in producing the 1969 GNP. The $77.5 billion depreciation item in column (2) is a rough estimate of this. Deducting it from gross private investment, we get a *net* private investment of $61.5 billion. Only by this amount was our private business capital stock larger at the close of 1969 relative to its beginning.

You may visualize the process with the example of a bathtub. The stock of water in it represents the size of the privately owned capital stock. The water flowing into it represents the amount of gross private investment. The water draining out of it stands for depreciation, the wear and tear of the existing capital stock as it is put to work, together with labor and land, to produce each year's GNP. Clearly, the level of water in the tub depends on the sizes of the in and out flows. If the inflow exceeds the outflow (as in 1969 in the United States), the level of water rises (but only by the difference). If the outflow exceeds the inflow, the level falls (again, by the difference). In the worst case, if we produce no new capital goods, our existing capital goods will slowly disappear (down the drain!) as they wear out. This would be equivalent to a family never repairing its house, never replacing its furniture, car, clothing, and so on. Eventually, it would own nothing.

Also important is the above stress on *privately owned*. In addition to the private creation and use of capital, there is a publicly owned capital stock. In a sense, there is a second compartment in our bathtub! It contains our government buildings and airports, our highways and mail trucks, our aircraft carriers and schools. Clearly, these also contribute to production. These also increase through investment. Yet, this amount is not measured under I, but included in G. These items are treated by the national accountants as if they were used up at the moment of purchase, just like the cake bought by a household or the milk bought by an army base. For this reason, no depreciation estimate is made in future years for publicly owned capital. The entry for depreciation in column (2) of Table 5.1 refers to private capital. Nevertheless, it will serve us well to remember that the nation's *total* stock of capital goes beyond privately owned business facilities. Our annual gross addition to that stock goes beyond what is measured in I and includes part of G. All this is summarized in Figure 5.2 THE CAPITAL STOCK.

income equals output   There is one other matter we should notice. For any period we consider, the value of that period's output (the GNP) is *necessarily* equal to the total of incomes earned in that period (the gross national income). This would also be true if we produced full employment GNP. Hence, we can anticipate one explanation, frequently given by laymen, that we will *not* give for unemployment: "There just isn't enough income to go

Figure 5.2   THE CAPITAL STOCK

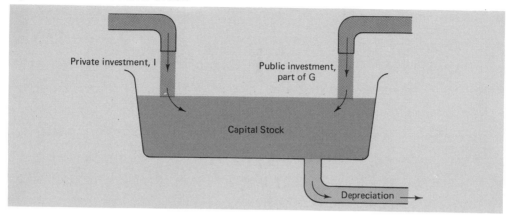

The nation's capital stock includes all man-made productive resources—buildings, equipment, inventories. They are partly owned by private businesses and partly by various levels of government. This stock of capital could be represented by the stock of water in a tub. Through private investment expenditures, I, and through part of government expenditures, part of G, the size of the capital stock is augmented. These two flows tend to raise the water level in the tub. But the very use of capital for production also uses it up. Wear and tear reduces the capital stock. This flow of depreciation, represented by the drain, tends to reduce the level of water in the tub. (Caution: the depreciation figure in Table 5.1 only measures the wear and tear of private capital, that is, only part of the drain shown here.)

around. People in the aggregate just don't earn enough to buy what has been produced. No wonder demand is insufficient and people are laid off." This is simply wrong.

THE HISTORICAL RECORD

Now we are ready to look at the historical record. Figure 5.3 THE HISTORY OF U.S. GNP shows the development of U.S. GNP in constant 1958 dollars since 1900. As we noted above, economists distinguish between current and constant dollars to eliminate the undesirable effects of price changes on the measurement of output.

In Figure 5.3, then, the GNP's of all years since 1900 have been evaluated at the prices prevailing in 1958. As has been mentioned, GNP data prior to 1929 are extremely rough estimates of the magnitudes involved. Figure 5.3 shows that real GNP has grown tremendously during this century, but at a very uneven rate. This reflects the uneven utilization of resources observed in Chapter 3. If we confine our observations to the period since 1929, when estimates are fairly good, we see a continuous fall in the nation's real output of goods (at 1958 prices) from $204 billion in 1929 to $142 billion in 1933. Figure 3.2. THE SERIOUSNESS OF INVOLUNTARY UNEMPLOYMENT showed us the corresponding rise in involuntary labor unemployment to its 1933 peak. The rise in real GNP from 1933 to 1937, and its fall in 1938, are similarly reflected by a corresponding decline and subsequent rise in labor unemployment.

So the story goes. The war years rapidly reduced labor unemployment to the low of 1944, and real GNP rose steadily to a high of $361 billion. Between 1944 and 1947, real GNP declined to $310 billion, and the rate of unemployment of labor rose. Thereafter, real GNP rose in every year except 1954 and 1958, and unemployment of labor showed its largest increases in those same two years. Utilization of capacity (Figure 3.3 LABOR AND CAPITAL UTILIZATION COMPARED) also showed remarkable low points in 1954 and 1958.

THE COST OF UNEMPLOYMENT

A comparison of real GNP with its potential, with what it might have been had all resources been fully used, is even more dramatic. Such a comparison is also provided in Figure 5.3 THE HISTORY OF U.S. GNP.

The potential cannot be anything but a guess. In this case, it has been assumed that real GNP after 1929, a year of substantial full employment, could have grown at a steady rate of 3.2 percent per year. This (conservative) assumption was made because, over the long haul, from 1900 to 1929, it did, in fact, grow at an average rate of 3.5 percent per year.

Such a comparison shows the staggering cost of unemployment in the form of potential goods forgone. In 1933, in the depth of the Great Depression, we probably could have produced $90 billion of additional goods (measured in 1958 prices). Taking the 1930's as a whole,

Figure 5.3   THE HISTORY OF U.S. GNP

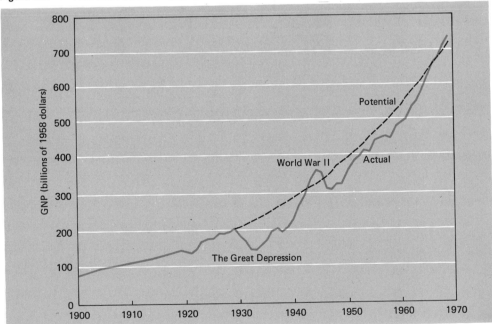

The U.S. GNP (at constant 1958 prices) has grown significantly during this century. Yet, it has grown unevenly, reflecting the uneven utilization of our resources. The broken line shows what might have happened if resources had been fully used. Source: U.S. Department of Commerce.

we failed to produce $670 billion of goods in 1958 prices. This amounts to over $5,000, at 1958 prices, for every single person then living in the United States! In short, the Great Depression cost a family of four during the 1930's an average of $20,000 of goods in terms of 1958 purchasing power. These goods—food, clothing, houses, cars, refrigerators, and so on—could have been produced. They were wanted desperately, but somehow they were not made. In addition to the great psychological costs referred to in Chapter 3, this was the tangible cost of the depression.

Figure 5.3 THE HISTORY OF U.S. GNP shows that U.S. GNP during the peak war years (1943–1945) was above the level one would expect under normal circumstances. This is not surprising. It does not mean that we produced more than we could produce. It does mean that both voluntary and involuntary unemployment were reduced so drastically as to increase our potential above the peacetime trend. Not only did many people work who had no desire to work earlier, but many others, previously employed, worked overtime or more efficiently. As a result, the average American family during the war, despite wartime suppression of consumption, was better fed and clothed than prior to the war.

In the postwar period, since 1946 (except for the very recent years of the Vietnam War), we have returned to the old pattern. Given my estimate of the potential, we might have produced between 1946 and 1965 an annual average of $33 billion more (in 1958 prices) than we did. It means that in these years every person in the United States could have received (in 1958 prices) almost $200 more of goods than he did receive. His wants could have been better satisfied to that degree. They were not, because we left resources involuntarily idle. Or, put more dramatically, it means that we *could* afford the war on poverty and rebuild our cities in a few years—without sacrifice on the part of anyone! Except in years of war, we annually waste in unemployment many times the amounts we claim to be unable to afford for eradicating poverty at home.

OTHER USES OF GNP STATISTICS

As we already noted, statistics on GNP are extremely useful. Although the data are rough, they can effectively dispel some of the odd notions about our economy that people are likely to have. Is it true that government is taking a larger and larger bite out of our GNP? That labor is getting a larger and larger share of it? In which parts of the country is most of our GNP produced? Which are the important industries? The declining ones? What type of producer is most significant? These are questions asked every day. Correct answers to them are of great significance to businessmen, labor leaders, government officials, voters, and many others. In this section, we shall look at some ways in which GNP data can be broken down to give us a picture of the "structure" of our economy.

GNP by Expenditure Components

The left-hand column of Table 5.1 MEASURING THE GNP already told us something about the nature of our economy that is by no means self-evident. Measured at current prices, in 1969, households in the United States only received for personal consumption 61.7 percent of our output. The big hand of government snatched away another 22.9 percent. Businesses got hold of another 15.4 percent, more than half of which replaced capital used up in that year. As we already noted, net exports were zero. The moment we look at it this way, we realize that real GNP (and increases in it) is not necessarily a good measure of household welfare (or changes therein). Yet, this is exactly what is being assumed thousands of times each day. It is an American article of faith. The belief that nobody in the world has it so good, because our GNP is highest, is nearly absolute. So is the belief that we are better off when GNP is up. The GNP is a household word; it is truly worthy of headlines! But is it?

Consider what might happen if the composition of GNP changes. The consumption component might fall (fewer private cars, fewer cigarettes); the other components might rise (more machines, more rockets). Or the composition of any given component might change (fewer schools, more rockets). This may or may not be for the good. Fewer cars and cigarettes and more machines may be desirable. Fewer cars mean fewer accidents, less maiming and death, less pre-emption of space for highways and parking, less pollution of the air. Fewer cigarettes may mean less cancer. More machines may mean more dresses and toys for little girls and boys tomorrow.

A change such as this may also be for the worse. Take fewer schools and more rockets. Are we really better off, if at a moment of national embarrassment (the Bay of Pigs fiasco of 1961) our President promises to land an American on the moon by 1970, ahead of the Russians? What if this means postponement of school construction in the city ghettos? Which is more essential to our welfare? Could the price of glory be too high? There is no simple answer to such questions.

Figure 5.4 THE COMPONENTS OF GNP shows what has happened since 1929 to the percentage of real GNP held by each of the three major components. Even without looking at *their* composition, it is clear from the three totals in Figure 5.4 that movements of the GNP total may well give a false indication of the movement of human welfare. A much better indication of welfare would be what happens to real *consumption* over time. But even that would be imperfect. What if population grows faster than this total? Each person's welfare may be *down!* Thus, measuring real consumption *per head* would be better. Even an increase in this figure would fail to account for possible offsets, however, such as changes in the work week, in the length of vacations, in the conditions of work, in the freedom to change jobs, in the quality of goods, and so on. *Real* GNP data are at best a rough approximation of national welfare. All we can say is that, *given everything else*, any increase in real GNP that can be achieved by putting involuntarily idle resources to work is desirable. Before assessing any real situation, though, we had better look at everything else.

GNP by Income Components

The right-hand column of Table 5.1 MEASURING THE GNP tells us something about the *functional* distribution of income, that is, how much of gross national income is payment for labor,

Figure 5.4   THE COMPONENTS OF GNP

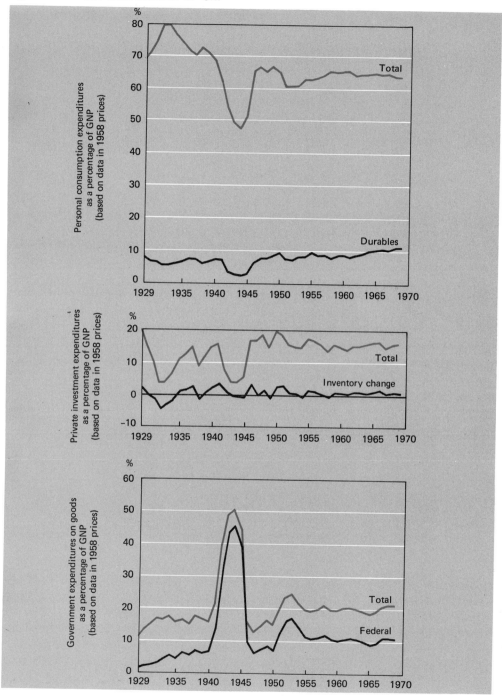

The shares of the various types of goods in the real U.S. GNP (here measured in 1958 dollars) change greatly over time. At times (1933), almost 80 percent of GNP consisted of personal consumption goods; at other times (1944), only 47 percent. At one point (1950), almost 20 percent of our GNP went for private investment; at another (1932), just over 3 percent. At times (1929), governments have taken as little as 11 percent of the GNP for public uses; at other times (1944), over 50 percent. Note also the particular volatility of consumer durable purchases, business inventory change, and federal government spending. Source: U.S. Department of Commerce.

how much payment for capital and land. This kind of information economists in past centuries were most eager to get. They thought that most people had only one type of income. Either you get nothing but labor income, nothing but rental income from land ownership, or nothing but interest and profit income from the ownership of capital and the running of businesses. If this were true, the functional distribution of income would tell us how GNP is divided among "classes" in society. Much of the work of Karl Marx was based on reasoning along this line. He saw GNP divided among masses of poor proletarians on the one hand and a handful of rich landowners and capitalists on the other. Eventually, conditions for the poor would become unbearable and the struggle among the classes would end in revolution, the expropriation of the rich, and a socialist society in which all would share equally the income from land and capital.

As the data stand there, measured at current prices, it appears that in 1969 labor received in the United States just about 60 percent of the total (before income taxes), whereas property (land and capital) received 31 percent (before income taxes) and the rest went to governments as indirect taxes.

This is easily misleading. First, *labor*, as used here, includes payments to all types of human effort, not only to the ditchdigger and assembly-line worker, but also to the corporation executive and the President of the United States. Thus, one can hardly draw any conclusions about returns to various economic classes from this aggregate figure. We would have to look at further detail.

Second, some labor income is hidden in the returns to property. The incomes of a grocer or doctor or farmer appear under *profit*, yet much of this is not what people usually mean when they ask how much profit has been made by the business world. Here, too, much detail is needed. But there can be no doubt that detailed GNP statistics, which are available, can be the starting point for some interesting studies into the distribution of income. Labor and management wrestle constantly over the division of national income "between wages and profits." The argument comes to the fore in each industry every few years as big-union contracts come up for renewal. Thus, the facts, as shown in our statistics, come in handy. Yet, they hold a great surprise when studied carefully: the major income shares have exhibited great stability in the long run. Labor's share has persistently remained between 60 and 70 percent, perhaps with a slight upward drift from 60 to 70 in the last 40 years. In the long run, and looking at the big picture, labor unions have made hardly a dent!

If we look at the return *per unit* of labor and capital since 1900, we find real wages per hour five times as high, the return per dollar of capital about the same. Why are their shares in GNP the same? Because, since the turn of the century, the total capital stock has grown much faster than the labor force. This, together with improved technology, has raised real GNP even faster than the quantities of resources have risen. And it has tended to offset any tendency for the "functional" shares in GNP to change in favor of labor.

In chapter 27 of this book, we shall go further into the question of income distribution. There we shall look at the much more interesting question of *personal* distribution, asking not how much laborers or profit-makers get, but how much income (of whatever name) goes to different persons.

GNP by Origin (Regional and by Industries)

Another fascinating aspect of GNP statistics is finding the origin of our GNP. This may refer to the geographic origin, industry, or type of producer. By pursuing such questions, one can gain a good understanding of what our economy is like.

Did you know, for instance, that 40 percent of 1965 GNP was produced in just five states —California, Illinois, New York, Pennsylvania, and Texas? Does it surprise you to learn that just eleven other states—Florida, Indiana, Maryland, Massachusetts, Michigan, Missouri, New Jersey, North Carolina, Ohio, Virginia, and Wisconsin—produced another 33 percent? That California alone contributed as much to GNP as twenty-four states? These were Alaska, Arizona, Arkansas, Colorado, Delaware, Hawaii, Idaho, Maine, Mississippi, Montana, Nebraska, Nevada, New Hampshire, New Mexico, North Dakota, Oklahoma, Oregon, Rhode Island, South Carolina, South Dakota, Utah, Vermont, West Virginia, and Wyoming.

What is your knowledge of the importance of various industries? Did you know that manufacturing, usually thought of as the backbone of the modern economy, contributed less than 30 percent to our GNP in the mid-1960's? That agriculture contributed less than 4 percent? We will return to this in a later chapter.

GNP by Origin (Legal Type of Producer)

Perhaps the most significant breakdown of the GNP is by type of producer. How much of the GNP is being produced by the small, insignificant firm usually idolized by the advocates of a laissez-faire economy? How much is being produced by mammoth corporate business enterprises? Let us first describe some types of private producers and then look at their significance as suppliers of our GNP.

Single Proprietorships

Single proprietorships—businesses owned by a single person—account for only one seventh of private business sales in the United States. So far as their *numbers* go, they are the most prevalent form of business organization in the United States. There are over 9 million single proprietorships: over 3 million in agriculture, forestry, and fishing; about 2 million in wholesale and retail trade; another 2 million in personal services (barbers, lawyers, doctors). We can easily understand why this is the most numerous form of business organization. It is easy to establish. Anyone who has some money, or can borrow it, has only to decide to be in business for himself, and he is. He needs no one's permission; he is not accountable to anyone. Thus, many people succumb to the desire to be their own bosses. They start and run the business, they alone keep the profits or suffer the losses.

There are disadvantages. First, the single proprietor is liable without limit for business debts. They are regarded as his personal debts. If the business fails, and its debts are greater than the things of value left in the business, a creditor (to whom debts are owed) can take nearly all the proprietor's personal property (house, car, furniture) to satisfy his claims.

Second, a single proprietorship is likely to be perpetually short of money. Ironically, this is likely to get worse if the business is a success. Huge expenditures become necessary to pay for tools, materials, and labor, but the revenues from selling the completed product will not come in until later. What is the owner to do? If he delays paying his bills, he will lose the usual 2 percent discount for bills paid in 30 days. Thus, he ends up paying up to 24 percent interest a year, in effect borrowing money from his suppliers. He probably cannot borrow much from a bank. Bankers know too well that most single proprietorships are destined for failure. Lending much money to them, at any reasonable interest rate, is too risky.

Partly as a result of these disadvantages, most single proprietorships do not last long. Yet, faster than old ones die, new ones come to life. Of those that die, only 5 percent end in bankruptcy. The rest end with the death or illness of the owner or are voluntarily brought to a close because the owner has been disillusioned, lost his money, or has found a good, steady job working for someone else. Being so easy to establish, and often requiring little money initially, new ventures are born, always with the hope that "mine will be different." Frequently, the fields into which single proprietors are apt to go are already overcrowded. Profits are low (over 80 percent have an annual net profit under $5,000, only 7 percent one over $10,000), and the inevitable occurs after a few years at most.

Partnerships

There are almost 1 million partnerships in the United States, half of them in wholesale and retail trade, finance, insurance, and real estate. Partnerships account for only about 5 percent of private business sales in the United States. They differ from the single proprietorship only insofar as there are two or more co-owners. They may start the business as informally as the single proprietor, making only an oral agreement. They may, in a more businesslike fashion, draw up a written agreement dealing with their responsibilities in running the firm, their contributions of money and real property establishing it, and the division of profits or losses among them. The obvious advantage of the partnership is the possibility of getting hold of more money than a single owner may be able to provide. But the main disadvantage of the single proprietorship, *unlimited liability,* remains.

All partners are subject to unlimited liability. Even though a partner may contribute only 1 percent of the funds to establish the business, he may still be called on to pay 100 percent of its debts. Worse still, the *doctrine of mutual agency* in the law of partnerships gives each partner broad powers to act as an agent to commit the whole partnership. Hence, any one partner can, by his actions, put in jeopardy the personal fortunes of any other partner.

Further, the life of the partnership is tenuous. Whenever one partner dies or withdraws, the business ceases to exist. The remaining partners can, of course, draw up a new partnership agreement. For all these reasons, again, borrowing from outside sources is severely hampered. Few partnerships grow to be large.

Corporations

Many Americans believe that corporations are the most important type of business. In a way they are, for they account for 80 percent of private business sales in the United States. It is also true that there are considerably fewer than 1.5 million corporations, and relatively few of them are large. Any business can adopt this legal form of organization. Corporations do not have to be giants, like General Motors, Standard Oil of New Jersey, and American Telephone and Telegraph. Many are of the type we meet daily in our lives—the local grocery, laundry, hardware store, or construction firm. The owners have only to obtain a corporate charter from the government (usually that of a state). This establishes the corporation as a legal entity separate from its owners. In the eyes of the law, the corporation is a *fictitious person*. This artificial being can enter into contracts; buy, hold, and sell property; incur debts, sue and be sued; and be taxed. This is different from any other form of business. Single proprietorships and partnerships have no legal existence distinct from their owners. It is the owners, as real persons, who own property, incur debts, can sue and be sued, and are taxed.

limited liability   Corporations have a number of distinct advantages. First, owners enjoy limited liability. As evidence of ownership, owners receive stock certificates. Every corporation issues on its creation, and possibly from time to time later on, shares of *common stock*. Say 1,000 shares are issued. Anyone holding one share owns 1/1000 of the corporation, anyone owning ten shares owns 10/1000, or 1/100, and so on. Yet, remember the legal fiction: the corporation is a person separate from the owners. The corporation, not the owners, incurs debt. If it goes bankrupt, the corporation, not any owner, is held responsible. Creditors, to satisfy their claims, may take away whatever there is of value that the corporation owns, but they cannot touch the personal property of the stockholders. Whatever their corporation may owe, the stockholders, as real persons, legally owe nothing. In case of bankruptcy, when creditors take away all things of value held by the corporation, the corporation ceases to exist, and the paper shares of stock are worthless. But the most a stockholder can lose is the amount he paid when purchasing the stock. In Britain, the fact of limited liability is indicated in the firm's name by "Ltd.," the abbreviation for "limited," as in "Wilson, Ltd." In the United States, the fact is indicated by "Inc.," the abbreviation for "incorporated," as in "Benway, Inc."

separation of ownership and management   Second, the corporation's ownership can be separated from its management. Given limited liability, owners do not feel that they have to watch, as single proprietors or partners must, everything that goes on in the business. Their personal fortunes are not put in jeopardy every time anyone makes a false move. Usually, each share of stock carries one vote, and stockholders elect a board of directors to represent their interests. The board, in turn, appoints officers who actually manage the business. Thus, the most capable men and administrators can run the firm, without being owners at all. In fact, this is one of the troubles with the single proprietorship and partnership.

Owner and manager must be the same. Hence, success is likely to depend on chance: does the man who has the money to start a business also happen to have the brains to run it?

On the other hand, some people argue that the separation of corporate ownership and management may have drawbacks, especially if the board of directors and officers come to establish a close-knit relationship. Then, they are said to forget all about the true interests of the stockholders. After all, goes the argument, people become part owners (stockholders) of corporations not merely to cast a vote in the election of the board of directors. (In fact, few stockholders bother to vote, so that a voting minority can easily control the corporation.) Stockholders are primarily interested in *earning something* on the money spent on stock. Because they are owners, the corporation's profits, if any, belong to them. But the annual profit can be divided among and paid out to the stockholders as dividends, or it can be retained as undistributed profits.

The corporation has no obligation to pay any dividends. Retained earnings can become an important source of funds for corporate expansion. (Eastman Kodak and Ford have grown this way almost entirely.) Usually, the mass of stockholders are interested in large dividends, whereas the small controlling group (which decides on the disposition of profit) is said to favor retention of earnings. This group, it is claimed, is apt to identify itself more and more with that intangible being—the corporation—and less and less with the unseen numbers of real beings—the stockholders. The controlling group may come to favor growth of the corporation at the expense of most of the stockholders. Worse still, the controlling group may vote itself huge salaries, thus reducing the amount of corporate profits available either for distribution or expansion.

The controlling group may even favor corporate expansion at a point at which the corporation should really be liquidated altogether to avoid either bankruptcy or perpetually low earnings. It is a rare board of directors that will vote itself out of power and a job. In this sense, too, stockholders pay a price for the separation of ownership and control. Thus, at least, some people argue. They view the displacement of the stockholder's entrepreneurial role with alarm. They find the exercise of economic power in his stead by management impertinent and of questionable legitimacy. It is doubtful, however, that the stockholder should be pitied. He is sharing, through dividends, in tremendous economic gain and without effort at that. And often with little risk. He could never do so well by himself. Even when corporate profits are not paid out and are retained, this will show up in the price of his stock. He can sell it with "capital gain" to someone else, thereby cashing in on the successes of "his" firm. In general, it would be a mistake to argue that the professional, salaried "insiders" are using their operating control to the disadvantage of stockholders.

immortality   Third, we come to a point closely related to the one just discussed. The corporation is in principle immortal. Unlike a single proprietorship or a partnership, which cannot outlive their founders, the corporation, as a legal fiction, continues to live no matter what happens to its owners. To the extent that this avoids a liquidation that would be in the best interests of the owners this is bad. In other respects it is good. The firm has continuity, and managers can safely engage in very long-range planning. For example, they can afford to put resources into research and development projects that may not bear fruit for decades, but that eventually may affect profoundly and beneficially not only the corporation profits, but also the economy of the entire nation. What single proprietorship or partnership can possibly take such a long-run view?

access to funds   Fourth, in part because of the above, a corporation can raise large amounts of money. It may come, as we saw, from common stockholders. Anyone, anywhere in the world, can become a stockholder for the relatively small amount required to buy a single share. If a corporation sells 1 million shares for $100 each, it has $100 million, an amount no single proprietorship or partnership can ever hope to raise.

Many people buy common stock precisely because they usually do not need much money to buy a single share. Also, they do not have to worry about unlimited liability, and they do not have to run the business. And they can, at any time, sell their share of stock to someone else. (If a partner decides to get out, the parnership dies; if a stockholder gets out by selling his share to someone else, the corporation lives happily on.) A number of the larger corporations have their stock "listed" at organized trading places, such as the New York Stock Exchange. At such places occur daily exchanges of corporate ownership as shares are bought and sold. However, the stock so traded is typically only a small fraction of the total outstanding. Most corporations, especially the smaller ones, are, in fact, private in the sense that their stock is neither listed nor widely distributed. Frequently, all the stock is held by members of a single family and never changes hands at all.

A corporation can also obtain money through the issue of *preferred stock*. This may be more to the liking of certain potential owners. A holder of preferred stock gets preferred treatment in the payment of dividends. He receives dividends before common stockholders do, but in return for this privilege he normally receives annually *at most* a fixed percentage of the face value of the stock, no matter how profitable the corporation becomes.

Another favorite source of funds, especially for well-known corporations, is the sale of *bonds*. These are corporate promissory notes, or IOU's, nicely printed on gilt paper. They are issued in various denominations, are readily marketable, and promise to the holder payment of so many dollars at regular intervals plus the stated face value at maturity (a stated date). A $1,000 bond promising $60 every year has a *coupon interest rate* of 6 percent. It is called this because the bondholder cuts off a corner of the bond certificate at regular intervals and receives the interest after mailing in the coupon. Note that bondholders are not owners, as are all stockholders. Bondholders are creditors. They *must* be paid interest and principal when due or they can sue the corporation and possibly force it into bankruptcy. In such a case, they would have claim prior to the stockholders on anything of value the corporation owns. In contrast, let us remember, stockholders are owners, and they *may* be paid dividends (if the board of directors so votes). They, as a group, will probably never be repaid the money originally paid in.

double taxation   We should note one major disadvantage. The corporation, as a legal person, has to pay corporate income tax on its profit. The amount left after it pays corporate income tax is either paid out in dividends or retained. Dividends paid to and received by real persons are then taxed again by the personal income tax. Only retained earnings, as long as they remain retained, escape this *double* taxation. Many people, especially small businesses, find this a high price to pay for the corporate advantages of limited liability, separation of ownership and management (when this is a good thing), immortality, and the ease of raising money.

Other Private Producers

Our GNP statistics tell us that the three types of producers discussed above supply about 80 percent of GNP, corporations alone 57 percent. Another 9 percent of GNP comes from private households and private nonprofit organizations serving them (ranging from athletic clubs and labor unions to schools, colleges, hospitals, and a host of religious, charitable, and welfare organizations), as well as various types of cooperatives and nonprofit organizations serving business, such as trade associations.

Government as Producer

Government, as we saw in Table 5.1 MEASURING THE GNP, buys a large portion of GNP, 23 percent in 1969. A lot of this, however, is privately supplied. Only about 11 percent of GNP is *produced* by government. Sometimes it is sold to private parties, often it is not.

government enterprises   Consider your local government's water department, a state turnpike authority, or the federal post office. Here we have publicly owned land and capital, such as reservoirs, pipes, roads, parks, trucks, and office buildings. This land and capital is combined with labor hired by government to provide you with services: to have clean water in your home, roads for your travels, and letters transported wherever you say. For these governmental services, you pay fees designed to cover costs at least roughly (water bills, tolls, and postage), and, whenever you do that, production is deemed to have originated in *government enterprises*. These produce only about 1 percent of GNP.

general government   Certain commodities or services are provided by government "free," that is, they are paid for not by specific fees levied on the recipient of such commodities or services, but by other methods, such as general taxation. These are referred to as production by *general government*. Consider the services provided to all Americans by the police, the courts, the public schools, or the armed forces. The protection of life and property from internal or external enemies and the education of children are certainly among the most urgent wants. Therefore, the provision of services satisfying these wants constitutes making economic goods available. Such services are part of production, and to make them available is to be engaged in the productive process. General government provides about 10 percent of GNP.

Conclusion

Table 5.2 THE SOURCES OF U.S. GNP summarizes our findings with respect to the relative roles of different types of producers as they are revealed by our GNP statistics.

Table 5.2   THE SOURCES OF U.S. GNP[a]

Single proprietorships and partnerships	23%
Corporations	57%
Other private producers	9%
Government enterprises	1%
General government	10%
Total	100%

[a] 1967 data.
Source: U.S. Department of Commerce.

Having looked at our GNP in this way, there can remain little doubt about the mixed nature of our economy. Between them private corporations and governments supply close to 70 percent of our GNP! This is not really surprising. For purposes of production, the corporation is far superior to the individual. With limited liability, immortality, and the comparative ease of raising funds, it avoids the drawbacks of other forms of business. Moreover, although some are apt to stress the bad aspects of ownership separate from management, it is, on balance, probably a blessing.

This enables the corporation to undertake tasks beyond the reach of any individual producer. This is not only true because of the sheer mass of capital required to undertake production of technically advanced products. It is also a matter of *organization.* Corporate propaganda and the vanity of some executives notwithstanding, no significant corporation is run by a single man, or even a small group of men. No single man, or small group of men, can know all that is required to produce even such simple products as steel or gasoline, not to mention television sets and space rockets. It would take a genius to comprehend the principles of metallurgy, chemistry, engineering, procurement, production management, quality control, labor relations, styling, and merchandising. And this is where the modern corporation comes to the rescue. It dispenses with the need for genius. It takes *many* men, informs each deeply and narrowly in a limited area and then provides the mechanism to pool their specialized knowledge, talents, and experience. Modern technology simply requires for many products that producers draw widely on specialized scientific technical knowledge. They cannot get it unless they draw on the expertise of a large group. They provide a mechanism for appraising their information and forcing a decision based on knowledge that goes beyond a few. The modern corporation is admirably suited for this.

Notice something else. Exercise of group power can be rendered unreliable and ineffective by external interference. If any one individual, not being omniscient, tries to gain personal control over decision-making, the quality of the decision is bound to be impaired. The organized intelligence of the group simply cannot be capriciously overruled without adverse effects on the organization. That is why managements of any corporation of size *must* divorce owners from control. That is why stockholders, unless they are already lethargic, must be reduced to passive, functionless figures. That is why management must assure itself a place as a self-perpetuating, autonomous body, either by scheduling annual meetings in obscure and faraway hamlets (thereby discouraging stockholders from attending) or by asking their permissions to vote for them (getting to be their "proxies"). Many of those who have succeeded have grown to giant size. (American Telephone and Telegraph, the world's largest business, has assets of over $35 billion and over 3 million stockholders, no one of whom owns as much as 1 percent of the stock.)

Corporations in the mid-1960s, as we noted, held more than 80 percent of total private business sales; the 100 largest alone accounted for over 14 percent. The 500 largest had over 22 percent. Just 2,000 firms like them could have supplied everything *all* private American businesses are now supplying!

Corporations, large and small, employ over 60 percent of our labor force, produce roughly an equal share of GNP. They have practically all the business (sales) in mining, manufacturing, transport and communications, finance, and insurance. They have almost three quarters of it in trade, two thirds in construction, almost half even in services. The sales of just three corporations (General Motors, Standard Oil of New Jersey, and Ford) in 1965 exceeded those of all farms in the United States. The sales of *each* far exceeded the revenues of any single state. General Motors' revenues were eight times the revenues of the State of New York; they exceeded the entire GNP of most of the world's nations!

Thus we conclude: though the number of corporations is relatively small, and though even most corporations are relatively small, *a small number of corporations are of overwhelming importance in our economy.* By the same token, the small entrepreneur is of secondary importance in our economy. So is the corporate stockholder. The corporate management, a collective entity hard to define, has taken their place.[1] It is a pale image, indeed, of the competitive enterpriser usually envisaged by the exponents of the perfectly competitive market economy.

What has been said of the corporation can in many ways be repeated for government. It also undertakes tasks that are beyond any individual. Think of national defense, space exploration, or justice and order at home. In fact, in many cases, the government allies itself with the corporation, be it in the production of nuclear submarines, supersonic jets, or space rockets. As the large corporation, the government is run by groups, not by individuals. (Notice

---

[1] This group has been called the *technostructure* by John Kenneth Galbraith in his fascinating book, *The New Industrial State* (Boston: Houghton Mifflin, 1967). You might wish to look at it. Much of this last section of the book reflects Galbraith's writing.

the ease with which large business executives can switch from corporate executive suites to the Cabinet room or the governor's mansion.) As with the large corporations, we would be naïve to assume that governments, as either buyers or suppliers of output, would refrain, as the competitive market model would have it, from bending the forces of supply and demand to their needs. These are matters to which we shall return in later chapters.

SUMMARY

1   Aggregate demand is the total amount of money people are both able and willing to spend in a period on newly produced goods. Aggregate supply is the value of goods newly produced in a period. It is usually referred to as the *gross national product* (GNP).

2   The concepts of aggregate demand and aggregate supply appear to be crucial in a study of general unemployment and demand-pull inflation. Relative to potential aggregate supply (the amount we get when using resources fully), aggregate demand is too small when general unemployment occurs, too large where there is demand-pull inflation.

3   The measurement and study of aggregate supply has uses other than those arising from our concern with unemployment and inflation. It helps us answer a variety of questions about the structure of our economy: what types of goods do we produce, how is output distributed, where is it produced, and by whom?

4   GNP is the sum of the market values of all final goods produced from U.S.-owned resources during a period. Each of these words in the definition has special significance and must be understood.

5   The GNP can be evaluated at current prices, or, to avoid the effects of price level changes, at constant prices. Then we talk of *real* GNP.

6   Very important is the fact that the GNP measure includes only *final* goods, goods not resold to another producer during the accounting period. This avoids multiple counting of *intermediate* goods, goods produced earlier in the accounting period and then completely used up in the making of other goods into which their value was incorporated.

7   GNP can be measured by the final goods approach or the value-added (sum of gross incomes) approach. Both yield the identical unduplicated output total. The U.S. Department of Commerce utilizes both approaches. The former approach adds personal consumption expenditures, C, and investment expenditures, I, and government expenditures on goods, G, and net exports, NX, to yield gross national expenditure, Y. The latter approach adds wages, rents, interest, depreciation, indirect business taxes, and profits, yielding gross national income, Y. Gross national income always equals gross national expenditure. Both are measures of GNP.

8   Because in any period the sum of incomes earned equals the value of output produced, unemployment cannot be explained by insufficient purchasing power in the economy if potential GNP were produced.

9   Investment expenditures, I, measure the annual gross addition to the privately owned capital stock. The net addition is smaller, owing to depreciation. The nation's total capital stock also includes publicly owned capital goods.

10   Turning to actual data, we find that U.S. GNP (at constant prices) has grown significantly since the beginning of this century. Yet, it has grown unevenly, reflecting the uneven utilization of resources. The costs in terms of goods forgone have at times been incredibly high; in the 1930's they amounted to $5,000 (at 1958 prices) of economic goods for every single person in the United States. Such waste, on a smaller scale, continues today.

11 Statistics on the GNP by type of producer are particularly important for assessing the degree of economic power held by individual decision-makers in the economy, and hence the likelihood of a perfectly functioning competitive market economy. The various suppliers of the GNP are, therefore, studied in some detail.

12 Single proprietorships and partnerships supply about 23 percent of GNP. Partnerships and single proprietorships have no legal existence separate from their owners. They cease to exist when their owners die or change. Owners are burdened with unlimited liability and often find it difficult to raise funds.

13 Corporations, supplying 57 percent of the GNP, are legal entities separate from their owners. Owners enjoy limited liability. Corporate management can be separated from ownership. Corporations are, in principle, immortal and can, in principle, raise very large sums of money by a variety of means, such as the issue of common stock, preferred stock, and bonds. Being fictitious persons, corporations are subjected to taxation on income.

14 Other private producers, such as households, nonprofit organizations, and cooperatives, supply about 9 percent of GNP.

15 Government, either in genuine government enterprises (charging customers directly for output and attempting to cover costs) or as *general* government (providing output "free"), supplies some 11 percent of GNP.

16 There can be little doubt about the mixed nature of our economy. Private corporations and government supply together about 70 percent of our GNP. And the big corporation is dominant. In the 1960's, the 500 largest accounted for 22 percent of all private business sales.

As government, the big corporation can undertake tasks beyond the reach of any individual or any small firm. Its size and power often exceed that of governmental units. Both government and large corporations can be expected to exert tremendous economic power and to modify greatly the working of our price system away from perfectly competitive standards.

TERMS[2]

aggregate demand	deflating GNP
aggregate supply	depreciation
board of directors	direct tax
bond	dividend
common stock	doctrine of mutual agency
corporation	final goods
coupon interest rate	functional vs. personal income
creditor	distribution

general government vs. government enterprise	partnership
government expenditures on goods	personal consumption expenditures
gross national expenditure	potential GNP
gross national income	preferred stock
gross national product	proxy
gross private domestic investment	raw material
gross vs. net investment	real GNP
indirect business tax	single proprietorship
intermediate goods	stock exchange
investment expenditures	technostructure
limited liability	unlimited liability
net exports	value added
nonprofit organizations	

SYMBOLS

C   NX
G   X
GNP   Y
I $C + I + G + NX = Y$

QUESTIONS FOR REVIEW AND DISCUSSION

1 It is important to distinguish actual from potential aggregate supply, or actual from potential GNP. Explain. What is the GNP?

2 Show how the final goods approach and the value-added approach always yield the same GNP total.

[2] The terms and symbols are defined in the Glossary at the end of the book.

3 Which are the four major components of gross national expenditure? Give examples of what each might include.

4 When a shoeshine boy shines your shoes for 25 cents, a 25-cent service becomes part of the nation's production. Show how this could be measured either by adding the incomes earned in the productive process or by measuring the expenditure on production. Where in the GNP statement (Table 5.1 MEASURING THE GNP) would you make the necessary entries? Can you think of other examples?

5 If GNP rises from $100 billion to $200 billion from one year to the next, while all prices double, what has happened to *real* GNP? What if all prices halved? What if they tripled?

6 MR. X: "Personal consumption expenditures, C, by Americans are a bad measure of *American* output of a *given* period going to households for three reasons:
  a. they include expenditures on foreign goods
  b. they exclude purchases of new residences
  c. they include expenditures on goods produced in past periods.
Thus GNP can never pretend to measure a *given* period's *U.S.* output."
   MR. Y: "You just don't understand. Before GNP is computed your item a is excluded as part of imports. Your item b is included as part of I. Your item c is. . . . By golly, you do have a point."
   MR. Z: "No, he doesn't: c is excluded, too, as part of I, or maybe G."
   Can you show why Z is right? (Hint: think of what happens to private or public enterprise inventories when households buy final goods of past periods.)

7 In the GNP accounts, inventory change may enter as a negative number, imports always do. Explain.

8 MR. A: "Because services produced by a firm cannot be stored and later used up, such services can never be intermediate goods."
   MR. B: "On the contrary, since services produced by a firm must be used up the very moment they are produced, services can never be final goods."
   Comment.

9 Explain the nature of depreciation.

10 "The nation's capital stock is wrongly defined to include only the durable goods held by private business and government. It should also include household durables." Comment.

11 Can net investment ever be negative? Can gross investment? Can the GNP? Explain.

12 "The movements of real GNP alone are no accurate measure of changing welfare." Discuss.

13 What types of producers are found in the U.S. economy? Given the relative importance of the various types of producers, how socialistic is the U.S. economy? (See Chapter 1 or the Glossary for a definition of socialism.)

14 What type of producers are the following? What is each of them producing?
  a. a municipal garbage collector
  b. General Motors
  c. a piano teacher
  d. the nearest brokerage firm you can find
  e. the Federal Aviation Administration
  f. the Tennessee Valley Authority
  g. your local dry cleaner

     h. the National Park Service
     i. the United Auto Workers
     j. the Supreme Court of the United States
     k. a shoeshine boy
     l. a symphony orchestra

15   What are all the advantages and disadvantages of a single proprietorship? Of a partnership? Of a corporation? Make a list of each.

16   "A person may hesitate to become a partner in a great number of partnerships but many people gladly become stockholders of a great number of corporations." Explain.

17   Corporations have a variety of means to obtain funds from internal and external sources, that is, from owners and nonowners. Describe four of them.

18   "Modern corporations are governed undemocratically." Discuss. Does it matter?

19   It is said that widows prefer preferred stock over common stock, and that insurance companies prefer corporate bonds over *any* kind of stock. Can you think of the reasons?

20   "Retained corporate earnings escape double taxation. Yet when they are eventually paid out, they are hit by the personal income tax. Hence, there is no gain in retaining earnings." Do you agree? Explain your answer.

1969 Business Investment Programs and Sales—Strong Advances Expected

After 2 years of little change in fixed investment, businessmen have scheduled a substantial advance in capital expenditures for 1969. According to the latest OBE-SEC survey conducted in late January and February, businessmen plan to spend $73 billion on new plant and equipment in 1969, 14 percent or $9 billion more than in 1968. Investment, which began to move up in the third quarter of last year after a slight pause in the spring, is scheduled to rise considerably in the current quarter and then to ease a little next quarter. However, the survey points to a substantial pickup in the second half.

This year's investment anticipations are accompanied by expectations of good-sized sales gains. Manufacturing and trade firms look forward to 8 percent advances over 1968, while public utilities are projecting a 7 percent rise. The anticipated increases for trade firms and public utilities are the same as those actually experienced in 1968. Manufacturers' sales last year rose by a very sharp 10 percent over 1967, when manufacturing activity was relatively sluggish.

Relative changes in anticipated capital expenditures for 1969 are larger in manufacturing—16 percent—than in nonmanufacturing—12 percent. Except for steel, the various manufacturing industries are all programing substantial increases. Last year, reductions in capital spending were common, and investment for manufacturing as a whole declined 1 percent.

Within nonmanufacturing, all component industries have scheduled higher investment. Public utilities, communications, and railroads are programing the largest relative increases (14 to 30 percent) and commercial firms the smallest (7 percent). For public utilities, the expected rise is about the same as last year's, but for other nonmanufacturing groups, current programs are more expansive.

Final figures for 1968 plant and equipment expenditures place the total at $64.1 billion. The 4 percent increase over 1967 was little different from last August's anticipation but was 2 percentage points less than had been anticipated by businessmen 1 year ago. When the rise in the cost of capital goods is taken into account, it appears that 1968 outlays barely exceeded those in 1967. . . .

Factors in investment plans

Given the pervasiveness of expansion plans among the major industries and the extensive commitments already made in the form of orders for equipment and construction, there can be little question as to the strength of capital goods demand. The extent to which the investment programs revealed in this survey will actually be carried out is problematical. The latest plans come at a time of virtually full employment, and bring into question the adequacy of productive resources, particularly for meeting the extraordinarily large first quarter 1969 programs. Attempts by businessmen to realize programs of the magnitude reported for 1969 would put considerable pressure on available resources and prices.

The climate for new investment was apparently improved last year by the persistent strength in final demand. Sales continued strong; before-tax profits set new records in each quarter, and after-tax profits, despite the surtax, reached a new peak in the fourth quarter. Also, expectations of further increases in capital goods costs probably tended to stimulate orders for capital goods. The tightness in the labor market and the resultant increase in unit labor costs undoubtedly prompted decisions to install more labor-saving equipment.

Although the recent level of overall capacity utilization appears relatively low in historical terms, an increasing number of companies doubt the adequacy of their existing facilities to meet future production needs.

Survey of Current Business, March 1969

6

aggregate demand

In THE PREVIOUS CHAPTER, we have studied the definition and measurement of the economy's aggregate supply of newly produced goods, GNP. Now we turn to aggregate demand, or the total amount of money people are able and willing to spend on such goods.

You will recall why we are pursuing this particular line of inquiry. We had noted that general unemployment seemed to occur whenever aggregate demand was below maximum possible or potential aggregate supply. Demand-pull inflation seemed to occur whenever aggregate demand was above the economy's potential aggregate supply. Thus, we set out to clarify the concepts of aggregate supply and aggregate demand. We hoped that study of their interaction eventually will give us the key to a control of unemployment and inflation. Having discussed aggregate supply, or the GNP, in the last chapter, we now turn to the forces that make people buy the GNP. The purchasers of our GNP could, of course, be classified in many ways, but it is most convenient to follow the division already made by the GNP accountants when measuring expenditures (column (1), Table 5.1 MEASURING THE GNP). Those expenditure statistics show us what people *actually* spent on new goods. We will now consider what determines the amount they are *able and willing* to spend.

CONSUMPTION DEMAND

What best explains the fact that personal consumption expenditures in 1969 were $557.4 billion?

Think of yourself. What determines the amount spent by you or your parents this year on commodites and services? Why don't you or they spend ten times as much because your or their wants are surely that large?

Even the smallest amount of reflection will reveal a familiar dilemma: there are many possible answers. It makes no sense to answer a question about a family's spending on consumer goods with a single dollar figure *unless* we specify the circumstances on which the answer is based. When they change, the answer will change, too. We are asking here a question very much similar to another one asked when we discussed the demand for shoes in Chapter 2 or the demand for high school social science teachers in Chapter 3. And the answer is similar, too: the demand for consumer goods in general, as the demand for one good or resource, depends on almost everything! To reduce the problem to manageable proportion, we must again invoke the everything-else-being-held-equal clause. We must tuck away, for the time being, all but the most important influence by assuming that all other factors are not changing. This makes things a lot easier. Almost everyone will agree that, whatever else may influence household spending on new goods, the *income* available for spending by a household, more than anything else, limits such spending. Just as the demand for *one* good can be shown to be dependent on the price of that good, given everything else, the demands for goods *in general* can be shown dependent on income, given a host of other factors that might also have an influence. In the case of a single good, the importance of price dwarfs all other factors as an explanation of spending. In the case of all goods, the importance of income plays the same role. Just as we derived a whole *schedule* for the demand for shoes with reference to their price, we can derive an entire *schedule* for the demand for consumer goods in general with reference to the consumer's spendable income. This would show for each conceivable income level in a given period alternative amounts the consumer would be able and willing to spend on new goods.

Moreover, not only can we derive such a schedule, but we must. We have no alternative. Someone who tells us that his spending on consumer goods next week may be $98, and tells us nothing else, tells us very little, indeed. Someone who tells us that he will spend $98, provided his income is $110 and all other circumstances of his life are unchanged, tells us a great deal more. And someone who gives us a whole set of answers, for all conceivable levels of incomes and circumstances, tells us more still. If we want to do more than measure what people actually spent (which we already did in the previous chapter), if we want to figure out why they spent what they spent or if we want to predict their behavior, we must insist on such an elaborate answer.

We shall call this answer the *schedule of consumption demand*. We shall denote consumer spendable income, which must clearly be income after taxes, by *disposable personal income*.

Hypothetical Schedule of Consumption Demand

How is consumption demand likely to vary with disposable personal income? Can we be more precise? Even armchair theorizing can give us a possible answer. Imagine you were the head of a household with a certain income. If you had a higher income, you would probably spend more. If you had a lower income, you would probably spend less. What would you be likely to do if your present disposable income were higher by a dollar? Isn't it quite possible that you would spend more, *although not the full dollar*, and increase your saving by the difference? What if your present income were lower by a dollar? Isn't it quite possible that you would spend less, *although not the full dollar*, and decrease your saving by the difference? What if your present income were zero? Isn't it quite possible that you would, nevertheless, spend some positive amount, by borrowing or using up past savings? If you did that you would be *dissaving*, or negatively saving, the difference.

Table 6.1 AN INDIVIDUAL'S CONSUMPTION DEMAND SCHEDULE illustrates such a *possible* relationship for a hypothetical person.

This schedule illustrates the potential behavior of the kind of person we have just discussed. It is, if you wish, a "reading" of his mind. If he had a zero income, he would nevertheless eke out a miserable existence by dissaving $10 per week and spending it on the barest necessities.

If, instead of being zero, his income was $10 a week, he would spend more than otherwise, but he would also save more. In our example, he would increase his standard of living by spending $18, instead of the alternative $10, thus dissaving only $8, instead of $10 as before. (Dissaving 2 less is the same thing as saving 2 more, just as moving from 10 feet below sea level to 8 feet below sea level means coming up, although you remain below!)

If the income of our hypothetical person were not zero, but $120 a week, he would spend only $96 more than if his income were zero. (His actual spending would be $106, but we

Table 6.1   AN INDIVIDUAL'S CONSUMPTION DEMAND SCHEDULE

DISPOSABLE PERSONAL INCOME (1)	CONSUMPTION DEMAND (2)	PERSONAL SAVING (3) = (1) − (2)
$ 0	$ 10	$−10
10	18	− 8
20	26	− 6
30	34	− 4
40	42	− 2
50	50	0
60	58	2
70	66	4
80	74	6
90	82	8
100	90	10
110	98	12
120	106	14

Hypothetical schedule of an individual's weekly disposable income, consumption demand, and saving.

figure that he would spend $10 at zero income, so he would only be spending $96 more.) At the same time that he would spend more, he would also save more. He would save $14 ($120 minus $106) instead of dissaving $10. Thus, he would actually save $24 more than if his income were zero. (Going from 10 feet below sea level to 14 feet above means climbing 24 feet, even though you end up only 14 feet above.)

The same would be true if he moved in the opposite direction. If he started with an income of $70 a week, and imagined that it were $60, our friend would spend not $10 less, but only $8 less, reducing his saving as well by $2.

Schedule of Consumption Demand Graphed

This hypothetical schedule, illustrating this person's behavior in a given period under alternative circumstances, can also be shown graphically. We will call it the consumption demand line.

Figure 6.1 AN INDIVIDUAL'S CONSUMPTION DEMAND AND SAVING is simply an alternative way of showing the same information that is contained in Table 6.1. Measuring weekly disposable personal income from the origin, 0, toward the right along the horizontal axis, and weekly consumption demand and saving upward (or downward) along the vertical axis, we show what this person would spend and save at each income level. Note how the graph shows what Table 6.1 showed earlier:

At zero income his spending this week would be $10, his saving − $10 (he would draw down past savings or borrow that much). At an income of $50, his spending this week would be $50 instead, his saving zero, and so on. We can also read off intermediate positions not con-

Figure 6.1   AN INDIVIDUAL'S CONSUMPTION DEMAND AND SAVING

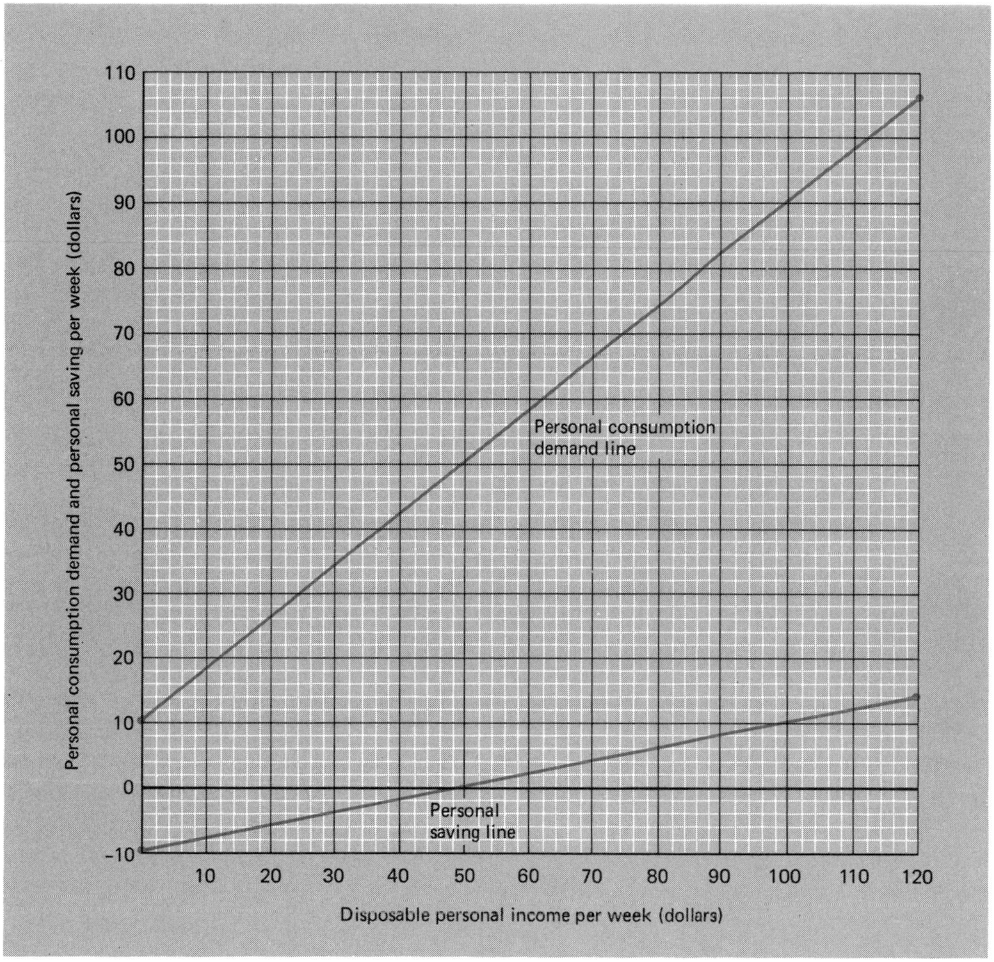

If a person's income were larger, he would probably spend more as well as save more. Thus both the consumption demand and the saving lines are rising to the right. At low incomes, spending may exceed income, so saving is negative. At high incomes, spending may stop short of income, therefore, saving is positive. In all cases, personal consumption demand and personal saving will exactly add up to disposable personal income.

tained in Table 6.1. At an income of $35, for example, our friend this week would spend $38, dissaving $3.

Shifts of the Consumption Demand Line

We have now derived a hypothetical consumption schedule for a hypothetical person and graphed it. Given all other factors that influence his spending, Figure 6.1 shows us how much he would spend each week at alternative weekly income levels. It is, so to speak, a snapshot of a person's mind! What if other factors were different? Then we would have to expect that his consumption schedule would look different. In other words, it should then not surprise us if he changed his mind and gave us different answers than before.

If he were wealthier (inherited a fat bank account and a bundle of government bonds), for example, he might spend $50 more per week at *any* level of income. If he had a great deal of wealth, it would be easier to dissave at low income levels, less necessary to save at high ones. Or, if he had more children, he might spend more at any level of income because he had to. The cost and availability of credit may also affect his spending. If he can borrow easily and cheaply, he may spend more out of a given income than if the opposite holds. His age and marital status may affect his spending. If he is young or newly married, he may spend more out of a given income than if he is old or single. As a result, whenever one of the other factors (besides income) affecting consumption demand changes, we can expect a *shift* of the consumption demand line. The entire line in Figure 6.1 will move up or down, reflecting a change in the person's mind owing to a change in the circumstances of his life. This is summarized in Figure 6.2, which is self-explanatory.

Figure 6.2   MOVEMENT ALONG VERSUS SHIFT OF THE CONSUMPTION DEMAND LINE

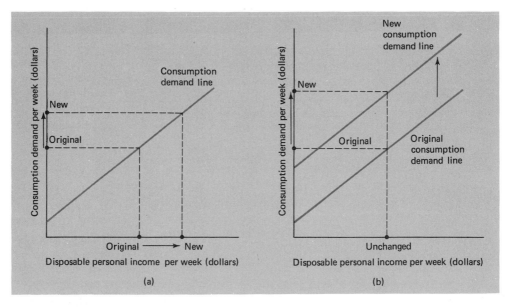

Part (a) shows a change in consumption demand. *It results from a rise in disposable personal income, given everything else. The consumption demand line has not changed. Part (b) shows a* change in the consumption demand line. *It results from a change in one of the factors previously taken as fixed. The upward shift pictured here may be owing to an increase in wealth or in family size, or the result of easier access to credit. Whatever income is, more will be consumed now than before. All this can, of course, work in the opposite direction as well.*

Aggregate Consumption Demand Schedule

Now let us go a step further. We have just talked about one hypothetical person's possible behavior. Other people may behave differently. Someone else may spend $10 more as his income rises by $1. He may spend $10 less as his income falls by $1. Someone may even spend more as his income falls and less as it rises. We have to admit that this is a possibility. Economists postulate that this would be much less likely than the previous example and that if we could look at the behavior of *all* American households spending their *aggregate* disposable income, we would find a consumption demand line of the general type shown in Figure 6.1. This is so because the atypical behavior of some gets lost in the typical behavior of the mass. The behavior of large groups of people follows the laws of probability. And it is highly probable that, no matter what proportion of income different individuals consume, as a group they will ordinarily consume less than the total. No matter how different individuals change consumption demand with a change in income, the group's consumption demand is likely to move up or down with income.

This, therefore, is the economists' hypothesis: *aggregate consumption demand depends on aggregate disposable personal income in the way described by Table 6.1 and Figure 6.1.* These might be reinterpreted to mean that aggregate consumption demand would be (hypothetical figures) always at least $10 billion, even at zero aggregate disposable income. Out of every $1 billion of additional aggregate disposable income, consumers *as a group* would spend $800 million. Given the schedule, we can *predict* the level of consumption demand for any level of aggregate disposable income. Note that economists in making this hypothesis about the mass of consumers are utilizing the *law of large numbers*, which allows us to predict for the whole what may not be predictable for the part. It is because of this law of large numbers, for example, that the National Safety Council can predict with incredible accuracy the number of Americans who are going to be killed over Thanksgiving weekend in highway accidents, although it would be unable to make such a prediction for any particular family. Insurance companies base their calculations on the same law. The life expectancy of a single individual may be uncertain, that of a large group is not.

However, we expect other factors to influence consumption demand in the aggregate, just as they influence it for the individual. If consumers as a group become wealthier, if their age composition changes, credit conditions change, the distribution of income among them changes, or they are swept by sudden new fashions and trends, they may well, as a group, spend more or less of a given aggregate disposable income. In that case, their aggregate consumption line would also shift. Consumers as a group can change their mind, too.

The Meaning of Disposable Personal Income

We have used the concept of aggregate disposable personal income. We had better make sure we understand what it means. This concept can be derived from an earlier acquaintance, gross national income, which we discussed in the previous chapter. *Consumers* (that is, households) clearly do not get all the gross national income. The official statistics for 1969

Figure 6.3   INCOME CONCEPTS

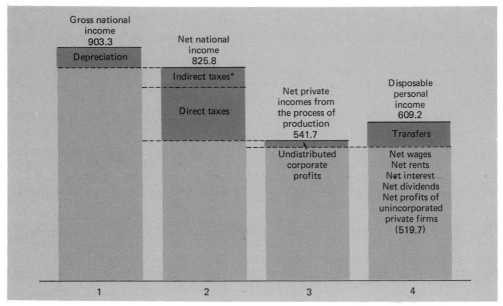

^a Minus losses of government enterprises.

As illustrated by U.S. data from 1969 (in billion dollars), part of national production (depreciation) is retained by producers to make up for the wear and tear of capital used up in the process of production. Another part cannot be bought by households because the corresponding income has been taken away by government through indirect and direct taxes. Still another part cannot be bought by households because the corresponding income has been earned and retained by corporations. Yet government transfers some of its purchasing power back to households, making their disposable income larger than the net income received by them for participating in the process of production. (Can you figure out how much output the government could buy from its net tax revenues?) Source: U.S. Department of Commerce. (Data are seasonally adjusted first quarter data at annual rates.)

show us why. Look at Figure 6.3 INCOME CONCEPTS. The height of column (1) represents the gross national income of $903.3 billion. Its composition was shown earlier in column (2), Table 5.1 MEASURING THE GNP. In 1969, $77.5 billion represented depreciation, the estimate of the wear and tear of the original capital stock that helped to make the $903.3 billion of final goods that year. Firms earned the amount of depreciation as (gross) income, but they also lost an equal amount of buildings and equipment. They certainly did not hand the total over to households, who owned the firms involved, because this represented, as we saw, no profit at all.

Actually, $903.3 billion of goods were produced, and $77.5 billion of others were destroyed. The *net national product,* or the *net national income,* was only $825.8 billion. This is shown in column (2) of Figure 6.3.

The government, by collecting indirect taxes (as property and sales taxes discussed in the previous chapter) of $77.5 billion, acquired during the process of production the purchasing power to buy some of this net output. It was pure coincidence that indirect tax collections equalled the amount of depreciation. However, these tax receipts were partly offset by the losses of government enterprises (or subsidies to private enterprises) of $0.9 billion. On the private incomes earned in the process of production (wages, rents, interest, profits of private businesses), the government levied additional direct (or income) taxes: $51.8 billion of social security taxes, $112.5 billion of personal income taxes, and $43.2 billion of corporate income taxes. This left only $541.7 billion of net income from the process of production for the private sector.

However, as we saw before, some of this was received by corporations, which are fictitious persons. Not only can they be taxed, they can and do also *retain* some of their net income, withholding it from the natural persons who own the corporations. Such undistributed corporate profits amounted to $22.0 billion in 1969, leaving only $519.7 billion of income for natural persons (made up of net wages, net rents, net interest, net profits of unincorporated enterprises, and distributed net corporate profits minus personal taxes thereon, called net dividends). This is shown in column (3).

Finally, in column (4), we reach total disposable personal income, the income figure really available for household spending. It is greater than the $519.7 billion just mentioned, because households receive incomes for other reasons than having currently contributed labor, land, and capital to the process of production. Such other incomes are called *transfers* and amounted to $89.5 billion in 1969 in the form of pensions, social security benefits, government bond interest, and so on. Out of this total disposable personal income of $609.2 billion at current prices, households made personal consumption expenditures of $557.4 billion, as we noted above.

Relation of Aggregate Consumption Demand to GNP

We have postulated so far that aggregate consumption demand is primarily dependent on aggregate disposable personal income. Now we can go a step further. We just saw, with the help of Figure 6.3 INCOME CONCEPTS, that in the United States in 1969 disposable personal income was a fraction of gross national income (67 percent of it). As you can see, only if transfer payments were equal to the sum of depreciation, all tax collections, and undistributed profits (which has never been the case) could disposable personal income equal gross national income. Historically, disposable personal income has always been a fraction of gross national income. It has always, however, been a *large* fraction of it. It follows that consumption demand, being dependent on disposable personal income, is dependent on gross national income. This is sort of like saying that if your purchases of movie tickets depend on the size of your allowance, and your allowance in turn depends on your father's income, then your purchases of movie tickets also depend on your father's income. The *general* nature of the relationship will be the same: your purchases go up or down if your allowance goes up and down, or your purchases go up or down if your father's income goes up or down (because your allowance is a fraction of it). But the *specifics* will differ. Your purchases may be 10 percent of your allowance, but only 1 percent of your father's income (assuming your allowance is, in turn, 10 percent of his income). The same principle can be applied to the consumption demand schedule of Table 6.1 and the line in Figure 6.1. The data in the first two columns of Table 6.1 AN INDIVIDUAL'S CONSUMPTION DEMAND SCHEDULE have been reproduced as the first two columns of Table 6.2 AN AGGREGATE CONSUMPTION DEMAND SCHEDULE. It is now assumed, however, that the data are expressed in billions of dollars per year and refer to all consumers.

Now suppose the values of depreciation, all taxes, undistributed corporate profits and transfer payments to be such that disposable personal income always equals half of GNP, rather than 67 percent as in 1969. We can then derive the third column of Table 6.2. All entries are simply double those of column (1). It is immediately obvious that consumption demand, column (2), bears the same general relationship to either disposable personal income, column (1), or gross national income, column (3). It goes up and down with one as well as the other.

Table 6.2   AN AGGREGATE CONSUMPTION DEMAND SCHEDULE

DISPOSABLE PERSONAL INCOME = $\frac{1}{2}$ Y (1)	CONSUMPTION DEMAND (2)	GROSS NATIONAL INCOME = Y (3)
$ 0	$ 10	$ 0
10	18	20
20	26	40
30	34	60
40	42	80
50	50	100
60	58	120
70	66	140
80	74	160
90	82	180
100	90	200
110	98	220
120	106	240

Hypothetical schedule of aggregate consumption demand as related to aggregate disposable personal income and gross national income, annual data (billions).

How the specifics differ can be perceived visually from Figure 6.4 TWO PICTURES OF AGGREGATE CONSUMPTION DEMAND, a graph of Table 6.2. Whereas the vertical axis measures consumption demand, the horizontal one can be used to measure either disposable personal income or gross national income. If we graph column (2) against column (1) of Table 6.2, we get the steeper line. Except for the fact that we now deal with billions, it is identical with the consumption demand line of Figure 6.1 AN INDIVIDUAL'S CONSUMPTION DEMAND AND SAV-

Figure 6.4   TWO PICTURES OF AGGREGATE CONSUMPTION DEMAND

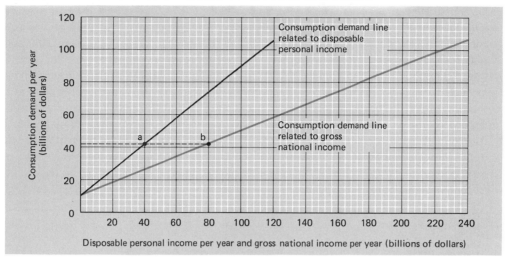

When related to gross national income rather than disposable personal income, a consumption demand line appears to tilt to the right. Here it was assumed that disposable personal income equals half of gross national income. If disposable personal income were a larger fraction of gross national income (or a smaller one), the consumption demand-gross national income line would tilt left of its present position (or right), because point b would be further left (or right).

ING. If we graph column (2) against column (3), we get the flatter line. Measured against gross national income, rather than disposable personal income, the consumption demand line appears to *tilt* to the right.

In fact, this makes good sense, although both lines give the *identical* information, still assuming, of course, that disposable personal income is a constant half of gross national income. Take any level of consumption demand, say $42 billion per year. Go to the right along the dotted line. You will find associated with it a disposable personal income of $40 billion (point a). Hence, by our assumption, what must gross national income be? Of course, $80 billion, and it is (point b). Just as any given level of movie ticket purchases on your part was associated with a higher parental income (point b) than personal allowance (point a).

Alternatively, pick *any* level of gross national income, and find the corresponding level of consumption demand on the flatter line. Then check whether the same level of consumption demand on the steeper line goes with a disposable personal income exactly half the figure you started out with. It will always be true. We will henceforth always work with a consumption demand line like the flatter line in Figure 6.4, relating consumption demand to gross national income. Remember this is perfectly legitimate. Although we recognize that consumption demand depends *directly* on disposable personal income, we know that *indirectly* it depends on GNP as well.

And note something else. This aggregate consumption demand line will *shift*—as will that of a single person—Figure 6.2(b)—whenever there is a change in one of the factors assumed fixed when first deriving the schedule and graphing the line. When consumers as a group become wealthier or when there are more of them, when consumers as a group find it easier to borrow or when income is shared differently among them, then we can expect them to spend different amounts even when GNP has not changed at all.

Furthermore, the aggregate consumption demand line will also *tilt* whenever there is a change in one of the factors intervening between gross national income and disposable personal income. (See again Figure 6.3 INCOME CONCEPTS.) That is, should there be a change in the importance of depreciation allowances made by firms, in the size of taxes people have to pay, in the amount of corporate profit withheld by corporations, or in the amount of transfer payments made to people by government, households may spend more or less even though GNP has not changed at all. Disposable personal income would then be a different fraction of GNP. Therefore, the flatter line in Figure 6.4 would take on a different position, as is described in the caption of that figure.

The Historical Record: C versus Y

Figure 6.5 CONSUMPTION VS. GNP STATISTICS shows all annual combinations of personal consumption expenditures, C, and gross national income, Y, in the United States since 1929. All data are expressed in 1958 prices. They reflect, therefore, the quantities of real output supplied by the economy (aggregate supply, Y, on the horizontal axis) and the quantities households actually consumed (personal consumption expenditures, C, on the vertical axis). As the legend indicates, the consumption-income combinations for different decades are shown by different symbols. The broken line is then drawn through the scatter of these points.

Figure 6.5 shows clearly the substantial increase over time of both real GNP and consumption in the aggregate. No one can fail to notice the strong positive correlation between these two variables. As real GNP changed, so did real consumption, and in the same direction. For example, real GNP was $204 billion in 1929 and consumption was $140 billion. By 1933, GNP had fallen to $142 billion. So had consumption, to $113 billion. Or, again, GNP rose to 203 billion by 1937, whereas consumption went back up to $143 billion. The next year, GNP fell to $193 billion, and consumption, to $140 billion. The broken line indicates this close correlation between the two variables. Except for the plots indicating the years of World War II, when consumption was depressed below normal (because output consisted of tanks rather than private cars, and people were asked in the name of patriotism to save more and spend less), almost all plots are practically on the broken line.

A Historical Consumption Line?

Given these observations, one is tempted to argue that the broken line represents the historically observed American aggregate consumption line corresponding to the flatter line of

Figure 6.5   CONSUMPTION VERSUS GNP STATISTICS

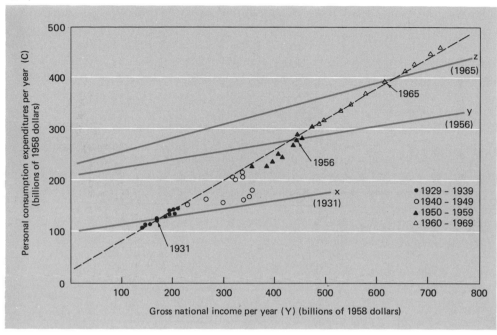

Although, historically, combinations of real GNP and personal consumption spending in the United States have been closely correlated along the broken line, we cannot be sure that this line gives the U.S. consumption demand line. More likely than not, such a line has looked like lines x, y and z, having tilted or shifted upward over time in response to changes in factors other than income. Source: U.S. Department of Commerce.

Figure 6.4 TWO PICTURES OF AGGREGATE CONSUMPTION DEMAND. When yearly income was $169 billion (as it was in 1931), yearly consumption spending was $126 billion. When, instead, yearly income was $446 billion (as it was in 1956), consumption was $281 billion. And when, instead, yearly income was $617 billion (as it was in 1965), consumption was $398 billion (all at 1958 prices, let us remember). See the three labeled dots.

If the broken line were the national consumption line, we could conclude that consumption would have been $126 billion also in 1956 and 1965 (or any other year) had GNP been $169 billion in those years (as it was in 1931). Or that consumption would have been $281 billion also in 1931 and 1965 (or any other year) had GNP been $446 billion in those years (as it was in 1956). Or that consumption would have been $398 billion also in 1931 and 1956 (or any other year) had GNP been $617 billion in those years (as it was in 1965).

But can we really come to these conclusions? The answer is decidedly no. The historical data of Figure 6.5 cannot be used in this way to derive the type of theoretical consumption demand line pictured in Figure 6.4. The theoretical consumption line we have been talking about was something like a snapshot of the (collective) mind of consumers. It was derived by imagining us to ask all consumers how much they would spend on new output this year at alternative imaginary levels of gross national income. All this assumed, of course, all other factors besides income to be constant: consumers' wealth, their tax burden, and so on. Of course, we can expect consumers to actually spend only one of the different amounts shown at different hypothetical incomes along the line of Figure 6.4. Obviously, only one of the many hypothetical income levels for a given year will actually materialize. By the next year, income will be different and if, in addition, other factors affecting spending should change, we must expect consumers to change their minds, that is, we must expect the entire line to shift or tilt and a new spending-income combination be selected *on this new line.*

Clearly, from 1929 to the present, consumers' wealth, access to credit, taxes, and so on must have changed. Hence, it would be inadmissible to connect by a line such as the broken one all consumption-income combinations of that period and assume them to lie on the *same* aggregate consumption demand line. In that period, consumers' minds must have changed many times, as did their living circumstances.

Hence, we can only speculate about the nature of the consumption demand line in any one year. In 1931, it may, for example, have looked like line x in Figure 6.5 CONSUMPTION vs. GNP STATISTICS. This is a line with a completely hypothetical slope, which we have drawn through the one point that plots the actual level of consumption and GNP for that year. ($C = \$126$ billion, $Y = \$169$ billion.) According to line x, if, in 1931, GNP had been \$200 billion, consumption would have been \$130 billion. Had GNP been \$400 billion, consumption would have been \$162 billion. And so on.

But line x is hypothetical; the only thing we actually know is that, in 1931, GNP was \$169 billion, and consumption was \$126 billion. This is the only point of the 1931 consumption line we will ever know. It is the only income-consumption combination in the consumers' mind that was realized through consumers' action. It is the only part of our "snapshot" we can actually verify with statistics.

After 1931, other factors may have changed. By 1956, the invisible consumption line may have moved upward to a position such as line y (perhaps because consumers as a group became wealthier and spent more at any income). According to line y, if 1956 GNP had been \$200 billion, consumption would have been \$242 billion. Had GNP been \$400 billion, consumption would have been \$275 billion. And so on. But the only thing we actually know is that in 1956 GNP was \$446 billion, and consumption was \$281 billion. This is the only point of the 1956 consumption line we will ever know. Whatever the alternatives consumers had in mind for 1956, all the other points on line y, will forever remain a mystery.

After 1956 other factors may have changed again. By 1965, the invisible national consumption demand line (with increased wealth, easier credit, different attitudes toward thrift, different tax laws, and so on) may have been like line z in Figure 6.5. Now people would have spent \$285 billion or \$339 billion, if they had had a GNP of \$200 billion or \$400 billion, respectively. They actually had a GNP of \$618 billion, and consumed \$398 billion in that year. This is the only point of the 1965 consumption demand line we will ever know.

This kind of speculation, furthermore, is fairly well substantiated by economic research.

During World War II, for instance, households accumulated some $250 billion of government securities as well as large bank accounts. They also accumulated a strong pent-up demand for such "hard" goods as cars and refrigerators, which were all but unavailable during the war. At the end of the war, their increased liquidity burned holes in their pockets, and they rushed out to satisfy their long-frustrated demands. Regardless of income, they consumed more. The postwar trends toward buying on credit as well as a general desire "to live it up" probably also contributed to the upward movement of the invisible consumption demand line (as from position *x* to *y* to *z*). For instance, in 1945, only $5.7 billion of consumer credit had been extended (loans for consumer durables, repair and modernization loans, charge accounts, personal loans, and so on). In 1968, the figure had become $97.9 billion. Thus consumers were able to spend some $92 billion during this period unrelated to income. Residential mortgage debt climbed from $24.3 billion to $278.7 billion during the same time. Although such spending is counted under investment, this must have freed funds for consumer spending. (There is, however, a counterforce: by 1967, some 15 percent of disposable personal income was tied up in interest and principal payments.)

Consumer expectations also have played a role in the probable upward move of the consumption demand line. If consumers believe prices are going to rise or goods to become unavailable, they may go out and buy now, saving hardly at all. Something like that happened immediately after the opening of the Korean War in 1950, which woke up memories of World War II shortages.

The main point to remember is this: the consumption demand schedule, like our earlier demand schedule for shoes, shows simultaneously available alternatives—how much people would be willing and able to spend on consumer goods in a given year at all conceivable levels of that year's GNP. This schedule, graphed as a line, is known to us only by speculation and is referred to as the consumption demand schedule or line. In any one year, there is only *one* actual GNP. Hence, only one of these many alternatives will become reality. Only one actual quantity is bought. It is labeled C. It corresponds to one point on the line. It is called that year's personal consumption expenditures, or consumption demand. It is the figure, and the only figure, that statisticians will record in the GNP accounts (as in Table 5.1 MEASURING THE GNP). What has been said for one year, is true for all years. Hence, unless the national consumption demand line never shifts and never tilts (a most unlikely case), our statistics, which record each year only *one* point on the line, each year record a point on a *different* line.

If you understand this point, you have taken a giant step toward understanding the modern theory of consumption demand. This theory, in turn, will help you understand the mechanism that creates unemployment and inflation. Remember: *no one* has ever seen the hypothetical consumption demand line of Figure 6.4. Its existence is a *hypothesis*. If working with this hypothesis helps us explain reality, so much the better. If not, we shall discard it. Such is the nature of scientific inquiry.

INVESTMENT DEMAND

Table 5.1 MEASURING THE GNP also showed the importance of investment expenditures, or of private business spending on new buildings, equipment, and inventories, including the spending on new residences by households. In 1969, such expenditures amounted to $139.0 billion.

We must note one extremely important fact in discussing these expenditures: it is probably correct to argue that *actual* consumer spending, C, equals what consumers *are able and willing* to spend at the prevailing GNP. Similar statements can be made about spending by government or foreigners. There is no one to force them to spend an actual amount different from what they are able and willing to spend. Yet, this is exactly what may happen to business! Business is a gamble. Businesses continually spend money on goods they want to resell; households or government (with the negligible exception of government enterprises) have no such intention. A private business may want to invest $1,000 in a given year (to buy new machinery, say, for $2,000, reduce inventories by $1,000, and so increase capital held by $1,000). But it may actually find it has invested $4,000 instead. It may have bought the machinery and incurred further costs of $2,000 to make goods for sale. If these goods were not sold, but had to be added to inventories, inventories would be up instead of down. Businesses can have *unwanted* changes in inventories they have bought (either outright from other firms, or by incurring costs for their manufacture) and then had to keep. This is properly counted in the statistics of GNP, as in I = $139.0 billion, which contains *all* inventory changes, wanted or not. But we cannot be sure that this is the amount private businessmen were able *and willing* to invest. The amount of *desired* additions to buildings and equipment plus *desired* inventory change (desired in the sense that the businessmen were able and willing to make the investment), we shall denote by investment *demand*. This is the subject of this section.

Determinants of Investment Demand

What makes businessmen able and willing to invest? In the American environment, it is clearly the lure of profit together with the availability of funds. If an automobile manufacturer has experienced unusually brisk sales, made unusually high profits, has large amounts of cash on hand, can easily borrow, and expects demand to continue to grow, he may well decide to add to his capacity and to demand new buildings and equipment from those who produce them. Similarly, a car dealer who is selling cars faster than he can get them from the factory may want to invest, that is, add to his inventory of new cars in order to replenish a dwindling stock, as well as to increase it beyond its previous size so as not to miss an opportunity for profit in a booming market.

On the other hand, when profit expectations are bleak, businessmen may well be discouraged from investing any positive amount. In fact, they may wish to reduce their capital stock by not replacing what wears out, by letting inventories fall through selling without manufacturing. In such a situation, actual investment, I, may be very low or even be negative and investment demand may be even lower. In terms of 1958 prices, for example, actual investment in buildings and equipment fell from $36.9 billion in 1929 to $10.9 billion in 1932, whereas actual inventory change was +$3.5 billion in 1929 and −$6.2 billion in 1932. This is a fall in I from over $40 billion to below $5 billion. Quite possibly, investment demand fell even more than that in 1932.

It is doubtful that there is any one easily quantifiable factor that can help explain investment demand, as disposable personal income (or gross national income) helped explain consumption demand.

Investment is a gamble. Whoever invests by buying buildings, equipment, and inventories gives up something of value now in the hope of getting back more in the future. Investment must pay for itself. Of course, the investor knows today's costs and whether he can get the necessary funds, but he must still guess about the future. And a wrong guess may well mean bankruptcy. And how much there is to guess about! Even purely technical matters may be in doubt. How well will the new machine perform? Will it break down a great deal? When will it be installed and ready for use? When will output be ready for sale? Will strikes interrupt the process of production? Will new technical breakthroughs be likely?

Then there are economic matters. What will happen to costs in the future, to demand for the output, in 1, 5, even 10 years from now? Whoever invests must answer such questions for himself. He must also guess about his competitors: whether they are likely to produce more or less, better goods, or revolutionary substitutes or to come up with new techniques of production or more efficient methods of organization. He must guess about politics, the likelihood of more taxes, easier credit, new laws or court decisions concerning labor and business, the effects of international tensions, wars, and disarmament conferences. Whatever the "climate" in which he makes his decision, he knows that it is going to change and that this change will affect the outcome of his gamble.

Some businessmen anxiously watch prices on the stock market for signs that others are optimistic about the future of business. They invest in buildings, machines, and inventories because others are "investing" in pieces of paper giving them ownership of business. Other businessmen ignore the speculative ups and downs of the stock exchanges. They are spurred on to invest by success in the past, because high profits are both an incentive and a means for further investment. Still others hold back in spite of their own success, in spite of general optimism, as mounting international tensions make them think of war and how it will surely change the business climate.

And this is just the trouble. There are not only so *many* things that influence investment demand, but two different investors may react differently to the same set of circumstances! When profits are large, one may invest (because he expects even larger ones), the other may not (because he expects no improvement in the future, and present capacity is adequate). If future costs are expected to rise, one may invest (because he is sure that this will keep competitors out), the other may not (because this makes his investment unprofitable). If customers' demand rises, one may invest (to meet the demand), another may not (to "work down" excessive inventories or because he considers the rise in demand too slow).

The investment decision involves not only guesswork, but the natural optimism or pessimism of the relatively few important decision-makers in this field. These are so few that we cannot avail ourselves of the law of large numbers. Like epidemics that upset the mortality tables, sudden waves of optimism or pessimism sweep through the business world and upset all probability calculations. Although investment demand greatly influences the course of events, economists have found it to be essentially unpredictable.

There being no neat formula to explain investment demand, for the time being we shall say that investment demand is *autonomously determined*. This is a fancy way of saying that we accept its magnitude as determined by forces other than GNP that we neither fully understand nor are able to control fully. Just as a *part* of consumption demand is determined by a multitude of factors other than income (which explains most consumption spending), so *all* of investment demand is held to be determined by a multitude of variables. Change any one of them, and it will change. There seems to be no single factor that explains most of investment demand. Investment demand is whatever it is!

This is not to say, of course, that we cannot go out and *ask* businessmen what they intend to spend on new capital goods. This is exactly what is being done. But there is no satisfactory way of predicting beforehand what the result of such a survey will be. With households it is different. If we can guess at next year's likely GNP, we can pretty much guess at household spending, even without asking them. Their behavior follows the predictable paths suggested by the consumption schedule.

If we were to graph a schedule of investment demand with respect to gross national income, as we did the consumption schedule, we would get a picture as in Figure 6.6 INVESTMENT DEMAND. This would indicate that in the given year, for a multitude of reasons, investors have decided to demand $80 billion of new capital goods. This they will demand, furthermore, no matter what that year's GNP turns out to be. Hence, the line has a zero slope. In another year, however, the line may be found at a higher or lower level (parallel shift of line). This line, too, can be regarded as a picture of what businessmen have in mind. It is a snapshot of their intentions.

But remember: unlike in the case of consumption demand, actual statistics on investment do not even reveal a single point on this investment demand line. They include undesired investment as well. Thus, the investment demand line also cannot easily be derived from past statistics. A survey of the investment intentions of businessmen would be much more likely to yield such information.

GOVERNMENT DEMAND

In 1969, purchases of commodities and services by all types of government in the United States amounted to $206.9 billion, constituting the second largest category of spending for new output. As in the case of consumer spending, we shall assume that actual government spending, G, and government demand coincide. After all, governments, like private consumers, do not engage in business ventures that are a gamble. (We can ignore the relatively unimportant government enterprises.) On the other hand, our explanation of the *size* of government demand has to be very similar to that for investment demand and dissimilar to that for consumption demand. Although governments may finance a large portion of their spending from tax revenues, and they usually do, the federal government, at least, does not have to do this. Shocking as it may be to the mind accustomed to living in a private household and thinking as people in a family do, the federal government does not have to have any tax revenue at all! It could easily finance any amount of demand through borrowing or the creation of new money. We shall talk about this in detail later on, but at this time we must realize that it would be futile to assume that the federal government demand is in any way limited by income received, as is consumption demand. This, of course, makes it very hard to predict. Like a household, the federal government may borrow; unlike a household, it may borrow without limit (Congress can always change the legal debt ceiling and often does). It can also make its own money. Neither of these statements can necessarily be made about state and local governments.

What then does determine government demand? The answer, unfortunately, is as conplicated as it was for investment demand. In this case, spending depends on a great many

Figure 6.6   INVESTMENT DEMAND

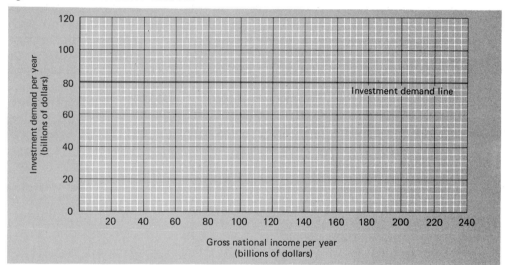

Investment demand is held to be independent of gross national income. From one year to the next, the line is likely to shift up or down in response to businessmen's changed evaluations of the profitability of investment.

political decisions, and these can be just as fickle and unpredictable as those of private businesses concerning investment. The massive purchases by governments in the United States (mainly of privately produced output) are made to satisfy "collective" wants, to give people things that a majority desires but that cannot privately either be bought at all or bought very easily. Things that cannot privately be bought at all, either because the expenditure would be too large or risky or the product could not be appropriated by the buyer all for himself, are by majority vote bought by all and made available to all. National defense, the administration of justice, space exploration, social security, control of floods and air pollution come under this heading.

One can argue endlessly (and voters always do) *how much* of these things governments should buy. One can also argue whether certain other goods should be bought by governments at all, because they could also conceivably be bought privately. It may not always be easy, but we can conceive of the private purchase from private producers of the services of roads, parks, bridges, airfields, ports, education, and so on. It is possible for a private producer to exclude someone from a park unless he pays, but privately produced national defense could not be withheld from anyone. In town meetings, state legislatures, and the Congress of the United States, voters must continually decide whether and how much of what kinds of goods governments should demand. This decision is made every year, and there is no easy way to predict its outcome.

In 1969, for example, the federal government spent $102.4 billion on commodities and services, $80.2 billion of which went for national defense. State and local governments spent another $104.5 billion on commodities and services, the largest portion going for education and health and welfare. There certainly will never be an end to the discussion among citizens of the adequacy or inadequacy of governmental spending. Some will be shocked by such staggering figures and work for a reduction in government demand. Others will point out scornfully that governmental nondefense spending takes but a small percentage of GNP and should be considerably enlarged. They work and vote for an extension of government demand, arguing that government spending on "important" things, such as the fine arts, education for all who are able, medical research, hospitals, and other aspects of civilization, should replace private consumer spending on mouthwashes, comic books, and dogs. Economists know of no scientific law to help predict the annual outcome of this struggle among citizens. Therefore, they consider government demand also to be *autonomously determined.*

This simply indicates that the level of government demand, too, is determined by forces, other than GNP, that we neither fully understand nor control (as is also true of investment demand).

As in the case of intended investment outlays, we can, of course, ask all government agencies about their spending plans. But here, too, is no satisfactory way of predicting beforehand what such a survey will show. Unlike in the case of households, we cannot predict that a higher or lower GNP will "naturally" induce higher or lower government spending and by how much.

Figure 6.7 GOVERNMENT DEMAND is a graph of a government demand schedule for a hypothetical year. It indicates that in the given year, for a multitude of reasons, governments have decided to demand $100 billion of new goods. This they will demand, furthermore, no matter what that year's GNP turns out to be. Hence, the line has a zero slope. In another year, however, it may be found at a higher or lower level (parallel shift of line). This line is analogous to the consumption and investment demand lines. It shows what governments have "in mind," what their spending intentions are.

NET EXPORT DEMAND

In 1969, the purchases of U.S. commodities and services by foreigners were $46.6 billion, U.S. purchases abroad were the same. The zero difference represents net exports. As in

Figure 6.7 GOVERNMENT DEMAND

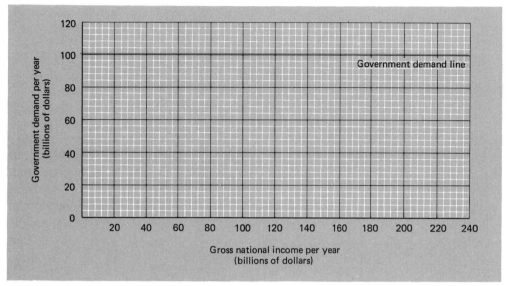

Government demand is held to be independent of gross national income. From one year to the next, the line is likely to shift up or down in response to various governments' decisions to spend more or less.

the case of consumer expenditures, C, and government expenditures on commodities and services, G, we can assume that actual net exports equal net export demand. No one forces foreigners to buy what they do not want from us. Our explanation for the magnitude involved follows the reasoning of the last two sections. Foreign gross purchases here, or our exports, X, depend on a multitude of factors, such as foreign income levels, price levels here and abroad, tastes, tariffs, and politics. Our purchases abroad are similarly determined by households' incomes, relative prices, matters of taste, governmental policies on tariffs and quotas, as well as all the factors that determine investment and government demand. All these elements continually change; all exert a changing impact on net export demand. Economists also postulate net export demand to be *autonomously determined*.

Figure 6.8 NET EXPORT DEMAND is a graph of a net export demand schedule for a hypothetical year. It indicates that in the given year, for a multitude of reasons, the forces that determine exports and imports have set our level of net exports at $12 billion. This came about, furthermore, without any simple dependence on the level of GNP. Hence, the demand line has a zero slope. In another year, it may well come to lie at a higher or lower level (parallel shift of line). Note that this type of demand, unlike the others discussed so far, can also be negative as it in fact was in 1935–1937 and again in 1942–1945. This means that in those years Americans bought more goods abroad than foreigners bought here. Therefore,

Figure 6.8   NET EXPORT DEMAND

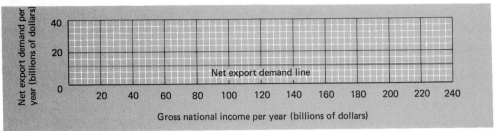

Net export demand is held to be independent of gross national income. From one year to the next, the line is likely to shift up or down in response to the multitude of factors determining foreign trade.

when calculating GNP as the sum of all expenditures, as in Table 5.1 MEASURING THE GNP, we might find that GNP is actually less than the sum of C, I, and G if imports (included in C, I, and G) are greater than exports in any year.

AGGREGATE DEMAND: AD

We have now become acquainted with the components of aggregate demand. It is time to look at the total. How much money are Americans and foreigners able and willing to spend on goods newly produced by us at each conceivable level of GNP? The answer can be easily had. We only have to add together the schedules of consumption, investment, government, and net export demand (Figure 6.4, flatter line, plus Figure 6.6 plus Figure 6.7 plus Figure 6.8). Figure 6.9 AGGREGATE DEMAND does just that.

The lowest line of Figure 6.9 is identical with the flatter line in Figure 6.4. It shows a year's level of consumption demand at each potential level of that year's GNP. If GNP were zero, consumers would, nevertheless, demand $10 billion of goods (point a). If GNP were $240 billion instead, they would demand $106 billion (point e). And so on. This, by the way, is exactly the information found in columns (2) and (3) of Table 6.2 AN AGGREGATE CONSUMPTION DEMAND SCHEDULE. It is a picture of the "mind" of consumers.

Now consider Figure 6.6 INVESTMENT DEMAND. It tells us that at *any* level of GNP, investors would demand the identical $80 billion of capital goods in this year. It follows that *combined* consumption and investment demand must be at each level of GNP exactly $80 billion higher than consumption demand by itself: If GNP is zero, consumption demand is $10 billion (point a), hence consumption plus investment demand is $10 billion + $80 billion, or $90 billion (point b). Similarly, if GNP is $240 billion, consumption demand is $106 billion, hence consumption plus investment demand is $106 billion + $80 billion, or $186 billion (point f).

Draw a line between b and f, and you get all intermediate points. It is the line of com-

Figure 6.9 AGGREGATE DEMAND

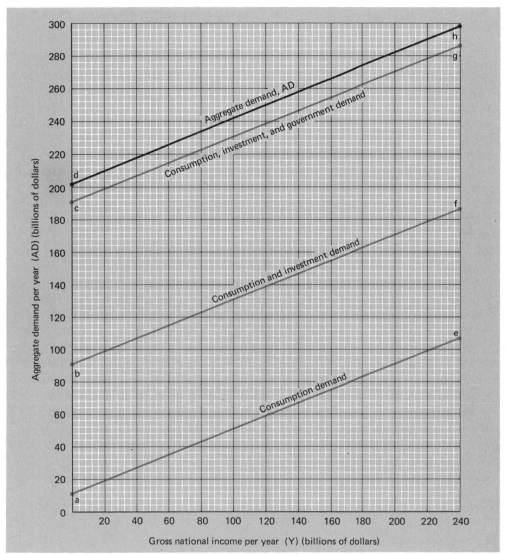

By vertically adding the lines of consumption, investment, government, and net export demand, we derive the line of aggregate demand. It shows, for a number of conceivable levels of GNP in a hypothetical year, how much money consumers, investors, governments, and foreigners combined are able and willing to spend on our new output.

bined consumption and investment demand. Naturally, it lies parallel and above the consumption demand line by exactly $80 billion at each conceivable level of GNP. It shows us the combined spending plans of consumers and businesses, or what the two groups of spenders have in mind.

In the same way, we can now add government demand. It adds, as Figure 6.7 GOVERNMENT DEMAND tells us, another $100 billion to demand at all levels of GNP. At a zero GNP, consumption plus investment plus government demand would be $190 billion (point c lies above b by $100 billion), whereas at a $240 billion GNP, the total would read $286 billion (point g lies above f by $100 billion, too). Hence, the line connecting c and g shows the combined levels of consumption, investment, and government demand. It is a snapshot of the combined minds of households, businesses, and governments.

This leaves us with net export demand. It adds, as Figure 6.8 NET EXPORT DEMAND assumes, another $12 billion to the total. Hence, d is above c and h is above g by that much. Connecting points d and h, we get the *line of aggregate demand*, AD. It shows, for a number of conceivable levels of GNP in a hypothetical year, how much combined money consumers, investors, governments, and foreigners are able and willing to spend on our newly produced output. As if we could read the minds of all potential buyers of new output, the aggregate demand line tells us exactly what they are likely to buy under a great variety of circumstances. As you can read off on the top schedule, if we produced a GNP of $100 billion, people would try to buy a GNP of $242 billion. If we produced a GNP of $150 billion, they would try to buy one of $262 billion. And so on. Naturally, only one of these many alternatives will come true.

In the following chapters, we shall work frequently with the aggregate demand concept and line. Remember, therefore, that it is simply the sum of the four demand components discussed in this chapter. Anything that would change one of the demand schedules and lines will naturally change the aggregate demand schedule and line, too, and in exactly the same fashion. Given everything else, if consumers buy more at each GNP, all people together buy more. Given everything else, if investors demand less at each GNP, all people together demand less. As one schedule changes, so does the schedule of aggregate demand. As one line shifts or tilts, so does the aggregate demand line.

SUMMARY

1 Statistics on the expenditure components of GNP show us what people actually spent on new output given the actual level of GNP. The concept of aggregate demand tries to measure what people are both able and willing to spend at alternative hypothetical levels of GNP. Though the question about actual spending has only one answer (which can be statistically measured), a question about demand has many answers. Demand varies with the circumstances of the demander. It must be described with the help of a schedule, allowing for alternative circumstances.

2 Consumption demand is found to be dependent on a multitude of factors, but primarily on income. A consumption demand schedule shows how consumers would in a given period spend alternative amounts for each conceivable level of that period's spendable income (disposable personal income).

3   It is postulated that the typical person's consumption demand schedule shows some positive level of consumption even at zero income, then rises with income, but with changes in consumption being smaller than changes in income. Graphically, a change in consumption owing to a change in income would be shown by a movement along the consumption demand line, but a change in any other factor affecting consumption by a shift of the entire line. This is certainly also true for the aggregate of consumers.

4   Aggregate disposable personal income is a fraction of GNP. It equals gross national income minus depreciation, all taxes, and undistributed corporate profits, plus transfers. Being dependent in this way on a fraction of GNP, aggregate consumption demand can also be shown to be dependent on GNP.

5   Plotting historically observed data of personal consumption expenditures against GNP, we observe a strong correlation between the two variables. However, we *cannot* take this to be a picture of the aggregate consumption demand line.

6   This is so because over time other factors affecting consumption demand besides GNP must have changed. Hence, the line must have shifted or tilted up or down. Hence, each year's historical data only give us one point on that year's line.

7   As consumption demand, investment demand (which must be carefully distinguished from actual investment expenditures) depends on a great multitude of factors. But unlike in the former case, no one of these is dominant. We assume investment demand to be autonomously determined, which is a fancy way of saying that its magnitude is determined by forces other than GNP that we neither fully understand nor are able to control fully.

8   In the same way, government demand and net export demand are held to be independent of the level of GNP.

9   The schedule of aggregate demand can be derived by adding the component four demand schedules. It shows for a hypothetical year how much money consumers, investors, governments, and foreigners (combined) are able and willing to spend on newly produced output at each conceivable output level. The aggregate demand line is a graph of it.

TERMS[1]

aggregate demand (schedule)	government demand (schedule)
consumer credit	investment demand (schedule)
consumption demand (schedule)	net export demand (schedule)
disposable personal income	net national income or product
dissaving	personal saving (schedule)
	transfers

[1] Terms and symbols are defined in the Glossary at the end of the book.

SYMBOLS

AD

QUESTIONS FOR REVIEW AND DISCUSSION

1 Distinguish the demand line from statistically observed spending data. Distinguish it from wants.

2 Go back to Figure 3.4 THE MARKET FOR HIGH SCHOOL SOCIAL SCIENCE TEACHERS. At a wage of $2,000, distinguish quantity demanded from the quantity a statistician would record. Do you see the connection with question 1?

3 What determines your consumption demand?

4 What factors could make your consumption demand line shift? What additional ones could make the national consumption demand line shift (or tilt)?

5 How do you expect the consumption behavior of different families to differ with age of the adults, assuming they all have the same disposable income?

6 The text talks of *real* consumption. What is the meaning of this? (Hint: remember the discussion of real GNP.)

7 "If my income is zero I spend nothing. If my income rises, I spend 90 cents of every dollar on consumption." Can you draw this person's consumption demand line? How about his saving line?

8 Under what circumstances could aggregate disposable personal income equal GNP?

9 "The text supposes, with reference to Table 6.2 AN AGGREGATE CONSUMPTION SCHEDULE that 'disposable personal income always equals half of *GNP*,' but the table itself shows it to be half of gross national *income*. I am confused." Are you?

10 Calculate the level of net exports from the following data (in billion dollars):
disposable personal income   557
investment expenditures   100
transfers   7
personal consumption expenditures   500
undistributed corporate profits   50
indirect business taxes   20
government expenditures on goods   150
direct taxes   80
depreciation   50

11 The text points out that net export demand has historically been negative at times.
a. What does that mean?
b. *Could* any of the other components of aggregate demand ever be negative?

12 Suppose you are a businessman with a new idea for a product. How would you decide whether to invest money in it?

13 If you invest $100 in a machine and, after a year, get a net return of $103, your investment may well have been unprofitable. Explain.

14 Investment demand, like the demand for consumer durables, fluctuates a great deal. Why do you think this is so?

15 It has been said that investment demand may completely collapse (fall to zero), but consumption demand never will. Evaluate. Could it be true?

16 Look through a few issues of *The Wall Street Journal*. What determinants of investment demand can you detect?

17 Could aggregate demand ever be below the combined level of consumption and government demand? Explain.

18 What effect, if any, do you think the stock market has on the various components of aggregate demand? Why?

19 "Investment is present sacrifice for future benefit. It is also certain sacrifice for uncertain benefit." Relate this quote to the difficulties inherent in trying to "read" the mind of potential investors.

20 There is a certain analogy between the shifting of a consumption demand line, such as Figure 6.1, and the shifting of a demand curve for a single good, such as Figure 2.3(b). What is the analogy?

Chrysler Slashes Auto Output Set For February 20%

Action Is First Big Move of U.S. Car Makers to Curb Rising Dealer Inventories

By a WALL STREET JOURNAL
Staff Reporter

DETROIT—Chrysler Corp. slashed its February car production schedule by about 20%, making the first major move by any U.S. auto maker to curb the sharp rise in inventories of cars in the hands of dealers or en route to them.

In a minor inventory balancing move, Ford Motor Co. plans to put its Wixom, Mich., assembly plant on four-day workweeks in February. Chrysler's far more sweeping move will close five of its seven U.S. auto assembly plants for one or two weeks in February. Its Windsor, Ontario, assembly plant also will be closed for two weeks.

Auto analysts here observed that the Chrysler move, which will knock about 25,000 cars out of the industry's February program, will put only a modest dent in the total inventory. They expect further production cutbacks unless the pace of sales picks up dramatically.

So far, however, there aren't any signs of further major production cuts at General Motors Corp., Ford or American Motors Corp., nor are there any signs of an upturn in sales.

Chrysler said its move is aimed at bringing "car assemblies in line with projected sales." This was interpreted as meaning that Chrysler wants to slow its inventory buildup and not that the company has dropped its estimate of sales. . . .

Chrysler dealers have been carrying a higher inventory than their rivals. On Jan. 1, they had enough cars to cover 78 selling days, while the industry average was only 53 days. Dealers of AMC had 67 days, Ford 58 days and GM 43 days.

Industry inventories have soared faster this month than is normal for this time of year. Dealers had a stock-pile of 1,435,000 cars on Jan. 1, a record for that date, and it's estimated that the total will be about 200,000 cars higher by Feb. 1.

Inventories will climb to about 1,735,000 on March 1, a record for any date, if current production schedules hold at GM, Ford and AMC, and sales are in the area of 625,000 units next month.

The industry rate of sales has slowed gradually since last October, when volume set a record for the sixth consecutive month.

Chrysler's production cuts appear to be aimed mainly at slowing up inventory increases on its full-sized Plymouth Fury and Dodge Polara models and its Chrysler line. Chrysler will close for the two weeks, starting Feb. 3 and Feb. 24, its assembly plants in Windsor, Ontario, and Belvedere, Ill., both of which make Furies and Polaras.

For one week starting Feb. 10, it will close its Jefferson Avenue plant here, which makes Chryslers, and its Newark, Del., plant, which assembles Furies and Chryslers. In the week starting Feb. 17, the company will close its Lynch Road facility here, which makes intermediate-sized Belvedere and Coronet models, and its St. Louis, Mo., plant, which makes Chargers, Coronets and Belvederes.

Unaffected by the production cut will be Chrysler's assembly plants in Hamtramck, Mich., and Los Angeles, which turn out Chrysler's compact and sporty cars. A Chrysler spokesman said none of the company's parts manufacturing plants will be affected by the production cut.

Chrysler originally planned to build about 125,000 cars at its U.S. plants next month. The current target is about 100,000. Its Windsor production target of an estimated 20,000 was cut in half. The furloughs will affect 32,000 workers in the U.S. and Canada.

Ford's short workweeks at its Wixom plant, one of 16 in the U.S., is apparently aimed at slowing production of Thunderbirds, whose sales have slumped lately. Ford also makes Continental and Mark IIIs there. It isn't clear whether Ford took the Wixom short workweeks into account when production of 180,000 in February was targeted. In any case, the effect on Ford's total schedule will be slight.

The Wall Street Journal, January 28, 1969

Steel Makers, Noting Improved Order Rate, See Robust Operations in '69 First Quarter

By a WALL STREET JOURNAL
Staff Reporter

PITTSBURGH—The steel industry is back on the path to recovery it set for itself early this year, mills say, and appears headed for a robust operating rate in the first quarter of 1969.

"The order picture is moving ahead very decently," says a market researcher for a major Eastern mill. "It appeared during the August-September doldrums, and for a while beyond, that we might have to push back our earlier recovery projections." . . .

Mills say that one sign of the return to the projected rate of recovery is the settling down to about 1.5 million tons a month of inventory runoff. . . .

The steel committee of the National Association of Purchasing Management says that "most" of its members report inventories still greater than normal, but "the majority" believe the excess will be consumed by the end of this year. . . .

Reflecting the continued strengthening, mills report orders up "significantly" or "considerably" from the month-earlier period. One mid-Western mill says its orders this week are up 20% to 30% from the month-earlier week while orders for the month to date are 10% to 15% ahead of the comparable October period. Other mills say their order pictures are similar.

The Wall Street Journal, November 25, 1968

7

equilibrium
gnp

W̲E̲ ̲N̲O̲T̲E̲D̲ ̲E̲A̲R̲L̲I̲E̲R̲ how the concepts of aggregate supply and aggregate demand seem to play a crucial role in the explanation of general unemployment as well as of demand-pull inflation. General unemployment occurred whenever aggregate demand was less than the economy's maximum or potential GNP. Demand-pull inflation occurred when aggregate demand exceeded the GNP potential. Now that we have studied the concepts of GNP and aggregate demand in some detail, we can answer the crucial question about the mechanism that determines the actual level of GNP. The description of that mechanism is often referred to as the *theory of income*, or *output determination*, or the *theory of employment*. All these terms mean the same thing. As we have seen, gross national *income* and GNP, or *output*, are identical. Naturally, anything that explains the level of GNP indirectly explains the degree of resource utilization, or of *employment*, too. And anyone who knows that explanation will also know how to influence the levels of output, employment, and prices.

THE CLASSICAL VIEW

The history of economic thought on matters of unemployment and inflation can be divided into two distinct periods. One is called the period of the "classical" economists. It covers roughly from 1776 to 1936. These two dates signify the appearance of two of the greatest books in economics. The first of these was *The Wealth of Nations* by Adam Smith. As we noted earlier, his vision of the "invisible hand" laid the foundation for our understanding of the market economy. His work was expanded and popularized by many economists for a century and a half. Most notable among these exponents were David Ricardo (1772–1823), John Stuart Mill (1806–1873), and Alfred Marshall (1842–1924) in England and Jean Baptiste Say (1767–1832) in France. Eventually, even the public at large came to understand and accept their doctrines about the laissez-faire economy.

At the heart of these teachings, as you might expect, was the "invisible hand." Not only would the price system assure, as we saw in Chapter 2, that the right kinds of goods are produced, but it would also assure full employment. There was, argued these economists, *an automatic tendency in the economy for real GNP to change until it was equal to its potential and then to remain at that level or grow with it.* No one's help would be needed. The economy would "manage itself." What was this benevolent force that would always give us full employment?

Aggregate Output Would Equal Potential Output

Suppose, argued the classical economists, real GNP ever were below the potential. Suppose only some of our resources were used, whereas others were involuntarily idle. What would happen?

Because they were eager to sell the services of their labor and property, private owners of unemployed resources would compete with one another and offer to sell resource services for a lower price. In a manner described in Figure 3.4 THE MARKET FOR HIGH SCHOOL SOCIAL

SCIENCE TEACHERS, wages, for example, would fall. The same would happen to the prices of unemployed land and capital. Rents and interest would fall, too. And private firms, eager to make profits, would respond. They would hire more inputs of labor, land, and capital at lower prices. Unemployment would go down, real output would rise. And as long as *general* involuntary unemployment persisted, resource prices would continue to fall, additional resources would continue to be hired, real GNP would continue to rise. This kind of unemployment *automatically* would take care of itself, because prices of inputs would fall whenever necessary to eliminate unemployment. But, you might say, after having produced it, would the producers of the full employment GNP be able to sell it? Might there not be insufficient purchasing power to take the largest possible GNP off the market? For that, too, the classical economists had a ready answer. It was in two parts: income would equal output; demand would equal income.

Aggregate Income Would Equal Aggregate Output

As we have seen in Chapter 5, what are costs to producers are incomes to someone else. Viewed from the national standpoint, profits are also a "cost" of producing GNP. Without profits, the entrepreneurs in charge of private firms would have no incentive to do their share in the process of production. Hence, the value of output for any given period (free of multiple counting) is identical with the total of incomes earned in the production of that output. GNP and gross national income, as we saw, are always the same. Classical economists argued, therefore, that there was always enough income to buy whatever output had been produced. They were right. The very act of producing goods always generates incomes equal to the value of output. If we produce the maximum possible GNP, we simultaneously and inevitably create enough income to buy it.

Aggregate Demand Would Equal Aggregate Income

Would maximum aggregate output be bought? The classical answer was a decided yes. Income receivers *as a group* would voluntarily spend their *entire* incomes. The amount they *could* spend (gross national income) and the amount they would *want* to spend on output (aggregate demand) would be the same. Those who decided not to spend part of their income on output, those who decided to save, would lend the amount involved at interest and *someone else would spend it for them.* Dollar for dollar, argued the classical economists, unspent income or saving would equal lending would equal borrowing would equal spending by someone else. Only an insane miser would hold income idle if he could earn even .1 percent interest by lending. Only an idiot would borrow at interest and then not spend. Therefore, if maximum full employment GNP was produced, amounting to, say, $70 billion, a gross national income of $70 billion was earned, and aggregate demand would also be $70 billion. In the aggregate, the dollar value of goods supplied would always equal the dollar value of goods demanded. *Supply,* said the classical economists, *creates its own demand.* This is often referred to as *Say's Law,* named after the famous French popularizer of classical doctrines.

To be sure, said the classical economist, Say's Law might not be true for individual goods. The compositions of supply and demand might not match. If $50 billion of wheat and $20 billion of wine were produced, incomes of $70 billion would be earned. Seventy billion dollars would be spent by income recipients themselves or by those to whom they lend their saving. Yet, spenders might well demand $20 billion of wheat and $50 billion of wine! There would be an excess supply of wheat and an excess demand for wine, although the *aggregates* were equal.

In this case, argued the classical economists, the price of wheat would be lowered by anxious sellers faced with a surplus. Resources used in wheat production would receive lower prices or become unemployed as this line of activity became more and more unprofitable. Just as surely, the price of wine would be bid up by anxious buyers faced with a shortage. More resources would be demanded for wine production, and their prices would rise as this line of activity became increasingly attractive to businessmen. For a while, there might be *frictional* unemployment, but it would be only a matter of shifting resources from the wheat industry to the wine industry. As the composition of output shifted toward the composition demanded by spenders (because it would be in the self-interest of profit-seeking firms and rational resource owners to shift them), frictional unemployment would *automatically* disappear, as would general unemployment.

The Role of Government

Involuntary unemployment, of whatever type, would be a temporary phenomenon. Its elimination, argued the classicists, certainly requires *no* action on the part of government. The avoidance of demand-pull inflation, on the other hand, requires nothing more than *responsible* action on the part of government. Because any modern economy would be seriously hampered without the existence of money to facilitate the exchange of output produced in specialized fashion, it is admitted that government must provide us with money. But there is only one correct quantity, and that quantity must be provided. Each unit of money, each green dollar bill, changes hands several times a year to buy new output (and hence create income). If this *income velocity* of money, the number of times it changes hands to buy new output, is seven per year on the average, every single dollar can buy $7 of output. Hence, $10 billion of money can buy $70 billion of output. And if full employment GNP at existing prices sold for $70 billion, the government should supply exactly $10 billion of money to the economy. There its role ends. Naturally, if it supplied more, people would find that, as a group, they are enabled to spend *more* than their income. Then, aggregate demand could exceed aggregate supply, could exceed GNP at current prices. In that case, we would have demand-pull inflation.

Full employment output may be worth $70 billion at current prices. If the government supplies $12 billion of money to the economy, and people spend, on the average, each dollar seven times on output, their aggregate demand will be 7 × $12 billion, or $84 billion. Then, all firms would feel excess demand at the same time. All prices would rise, and the same output would be sold for more. What used to sell for $70 billion will sell for $84 billion, with all the evil consequences of inflation. This would be entirely the government's fault. If the government supplies the right amount of money, and otherwise keeps human hands off the economy, the invisible hand will eliminate both unemployment and inflation.

THE MODERN VIEW—SUMMARY

Whatever the merits of the classical theory may have been in the past, the theory does not fit the modern world. The classical theory is a map of a different world, and it cannot possibly guide us through ours.

Downward Price Inflexibility

Consider the above discussion of our mixed economy (Chapter 5). Owing to the considerable economic power possessed by many, in our world *downward* flexibility of prices of inputs and outputs is practically nonexistent. This can result from union power resisting lower wages, business power resisting lower output prices, government interference legislating minimum wages and prices, or many other factors. At this point, we are only interested in the fact of downward inflexibility, not its cause. Hence, we can doubt that the classic mechanism to get us to full employment can be relied on. It required, as we saw, resource prices, such as wages, to fall in the face of unemployment. This does not always happen nowadays. Therefore, *modern economists deny that any level of output below the potential calls forth an automatic tendency to move toward the potential.*

The Income-Demand Link

Modern economists agree, however, with the classical insight that for any given period the sum of incomes earned equals the value of output produced. But most *modern economists deny that aggregate demand always equals aggregate income* or that any rate of output once reached can be maintained. For instance, they do not go along with their classical predecessors who believed that the saving of some is exactly offset by the borrowing and spending of others.

saving is not lending   Some income recipients at some time keep some of their saving in cash. Whenever a household, for instance, does not turn its entire disposable income into consumption demand, it saves. This amount may well neither be lent to other households (becoming consumption demand), nor to government (becoming government demand for goods there), nor to private businesses (becoming investment demand there). It may be held in cash, thus breaking the link of saving with borrowing and voluntary spending.

Or take the government. Whenever the government does not turn its entire net income from taxes (all taxes minus transfers) into government demand, it also saves. It also may hold cash or repay debt, breaking the link between saving and demand.

Now take a business that, in effect, forces saving on its owner by withholding income from him (depreciation, retained profits). Such a business may decide to hold the saving in cash, or it may use the saving to pay off debt, neither lending nor spending.

lending is not demand   Now suppose all private business saving were automatically and voluntarily invested (in the last examples, the business replaces worn-out machinery or increases its equipment and inventories). Even suppose the exact amount of all other saving was lent. The link between saving and demand would still be imperfect.

How can one lend? The lender can hand over cash to a savings bank. But a savings bank is required by law to *keep* some of this cash as "reserves." Even if it lends the maximum legal amount, and this is used completely to buy new output, demand from borrowed funds will still be smaller than saving.

A business may borrow from a savings bank in order to increase its permanent cash balance rather than to buy a new machine. As we noted in Chapter 5, an expanding business needs an expanding permanent cash balance to carry out its daily transactions. The corner grocery store may be able to get away with never holding more than $1,000 in cash, but General Motors Corporation could not possibly carry on its vast transactions with such a small balance. In short, business borrowing does not necessarily spring from the desire to demand new output.

The same goes for a saver's purchase of stocks or bonds. Even if they are being newly issued, the issuing firm may use the proceeds for a variety of things, which may not necessarily add to the demand for new buildings, equipment, and inventories. It always comes down to the same point: whoever receives the income saved, it may be held in cash by someone somewhere along the line. Hence, demand from borrowed funds may be smaller than saving.

demand from borrowed funds does not require saving   However, demand from borrowed funds may also be larger than saving. As we shall see in a later chapter, modern American banks can and do continuously *create new money*. This may be lent to private businesses, households, or governments desiring to buy new outputs beyond their incomes. Thus, even if saving were zero, we might find demand from borrowed funds of billions of dollars. The classical link up of saving with demand, though possible, is unlikely to occur. Demand from borrowed funds may occur even if nothing is saved. It may be zero, even if saving is huge.

The modern theory of income determination, therefore, denies that there is any invisible hand to assure full employment. It also denies that aggregate demand is necessarily equal to income earned, or to the value of output actually produced. What then does determine the level of our GNP? The modern answer is largely the work of one man, John Maynard Keynes. His book, *The General Theory of Employment, Interest, and Money* (1936), revolutionized economic analysis.

In summary, the modern view is this: Because of the downward inflexibility of prices of resources and goods in our mixed economy, there is no automatic tendency to move the economy to full employment. Because aggregate demand can differ from aggregate income, or the GNP, there is also no tendency for any given GNP to be maintained. Instead, *the GNP, or aggregate supply, will change until it is equal to aggregate demand.* Thus, aggregate demand determines an *equilibrium* level of output and, indirectly, of resource use. Once GNP has changed to equal aggregate demand, there will be no tendency for GNP (and employment) to change further, even if they are below full employment.

If aggregate demand falls, starting at or below full employment, real output and resource use will fall. Prices won't. If aggregate demand rises, and we do not have full employment, real output and resource use will rise. Prices won't. Thus, until we reach full employment, modern economists are standing Say's Law on its head. Demand creates its own supply! Once we have full employment, a further rise in aggregate demand will cause a rise in prices, as everyone tries to buy what neither exists nor can possibly be produced. In this case of demand-pull inflation, a fall in aggregate demand just reduces the tendency for prices to rise and does so without reducing output.

FINDING EQUILIBRIUM GNP

Consider the example used in last chapter's Figure 6.9 AGGREGATE DEMAND. There we imagined to have asked all potential buyers of new output how much they would demand at alternative levels of GNP. Suppose we pick one of those alternatives and assume that an actual GNP of $150 billion is produced. Would that be an equilibrium level of output? Clearly, as we learned in Chapter 5, people would then also earn a gross national income of $150 billion. On this and this only classical and modern economists readily agree.

But people may spend, modern economists argue, more or less than their aggregate income. As this particular "snap-shot" of people's intentions showed, people would try to buy $262 billion of goods at the $150 billion level of GNP. By drawing down past savings or by borrowing, for instance, people in the aggregate would spend $112 billion in excess of their income! Households would demand $70 billion of our new output, private businesses $80 billion, governments $100 billion, and foreigners $12 billion. Clearly, demand and output are not equal. We do not have equilibrium. What will happen?

It all depends on the level of employment of our resources. One thing is for sure. As in the story on steel introducing this chapter, businessmen will find orders going up and inventories going down. They may satisfy demand momentarily by drawing down inventories of goods produced in the past or by importing goods from abroad. At the same time, however, they will try to produce more. If they can (if unemployed resources are available), real GNP and employment will rise. If they cannot (because $150 billion is the maximum possible GNP utilizing all resources fully), they will be sorely tempted to raise prices. We will then have demand-pull inflation. And if real GNP can and does rise, where will it go? Will it go all the way to its maximum, full employment level?

Suppose at full employment, we could produce a GNP of $450 billion. Will output rise that much? Let us try to reason it out. Aggregate demand being $262 billion, we can easily see output rising to that level. And we can see something else: aggregate demand will then be different! Even though (we assumed) businesses, governments, and foreigners continue to spend at an annual rate of $80 billion, $100 billion, and $12 billion, respectively, *regardless* of the level of GNP, households will "change their minds." As the consumption demand schedule illustrates (Table 6.2), they spend more at higher GNP. This is also readily observable from Figure 6.9. Its consumption demand line, you will recall, was a graph of columns (2) and (3) of Table 6.2. As we assumed in that table, every extra dollar of GNP means another 50 cents of household disposable income and 40 cents more consumption spending. Thus, a rise in consumption demand, as GNP rises from $150 billion to $262 billion, should not surprise us. After all, some people who owned resources previously unemployed (when GNP was $150 billion a year) now are getting income from their use (which has lifted GNP to $262 billion a year). We should expect them to want to spend some or most of it. Following our earlier assumption, the extra $112 billion of gross national income brings with it 40 cents times that, or $44.8 billion, of extra household spending. But this makes aggregate demand, at a $262 billion a year GNP level, equal to $262 billion + $44.8 billion, or $306.8 billion. (Can you read this off on Figure 6.9?)

Following our earlier reasoning, output can be expected to rise further to that level—at least. Again, businessmen find inventories disappearing at a fast clip and orders for goods mounting. Again, they go out and hire unemployed resources to produce more to meet that demand. And again, the newly employed will want to spend some or most of their extra income, raising aggregate demand further still.

Where will GNP finally come to rest? Will it ever catch up with aggregate demand? And when it does, will we still have unemployed resources? Questions such as these can most easily be answered by putting to work the tools of analysis acquired in the previous two chapters.

A Graphical Exposition

Consider the situation depicted in Figure 7.1 GNP IN EQUILIBRIUM. Line AD shows what aggregate demand would be at each one of this year's hypothetical GNP's, measured along the horizontal axis. At a zero GNP, aggregate demand would equal $202 billion. At a $200 billion GNP, it would equal $282 billion. At a $450 billion GNP, aggregate demand would equal $382 billion. Note that this is exactly the same aggregate demand schedule we illustrated in Figure 6.9 (the axes of the graph in Figure 7.1 are extended further out, however).

The line labeled AS shows what aggregate supply *of newly produced output* would be at each one of this year's hypothetical GNP's. Because we have defined aggregate supply as the GNP, the interpretation of this line is child's play. If GNP were zero, the amount of GNP available for sale (aggregate supply) would be zero. (We are at point 0.) If GNP were $200 billion, the amount of GNP available for sale would be $200 billion. (We are at point a.) If GNP were $450 billion, the amount of GNP available for sale would be $450 billion. (We are at point b.) In short, the aggregate supply line measures the same thing vertically as horizontally. Distance 0c equals distance ca. Distance 0d equals db, and so on.

This neat little trick allows us to compare directly (in the vertical direction), at each

Figure 7.1   GNP IN EQUILIBRIUM

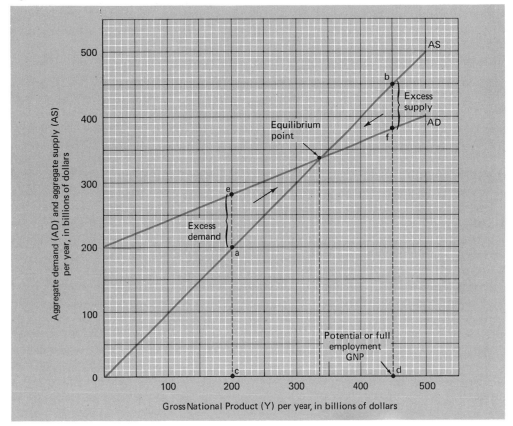

Aggregate demand and aggregate supply establish the equilibrium level of GNP, here at $336⅔ billion, although potential or full employment GNP is at $450 billion. At any GNP below equilibrium, there would be excess demand; at any higher GNP, excess supply. Excess demand causes real GNP to rise toward the equilibrium; excess supply causes it to fall to equilibrium.

conceivable GNP, aggregate demand for and aggregate supply of new output. If GNP actually were $200 billion, aggregate demand would exceed aggregate supply (ce exceeds ca). There would be shortages of many or even all goods, yet assuming potential or full employment GNP to be much larger ($450 billion), there would be lots of idle resources to make them. Quite possibly, the demand by households and governments and foreigners would be temporarily satisfied from previously produced inventories. But businesses as a group would find their demand unsatisfied. Some may buy $80 billion of new buildings and equipment and inventories as planned, but others would lose $82 billion of inventories (distance ae) as not planned. Thus their *actual* investment (measured as I in the GNP accounts) would fall short of their investment *demand*. In this case, actual investment would be $-\$2$ billion, instead of $+\$80$ billion of investment demand. Business would boom. Faster than it is produced, output is sold. Naturally, businessmen would go out and hire idle resources and step up production. Now we can see where all this would lead.

This would continue until a GNP of \$336⅔ billion is reached. At that point, and at that point only, would the community's output equal its aggregate demand. We would have GNP *equilibrium*. This, however, does not denote anything "good," as some people are apt to think. It only means that GNP here would have no further innate tendency to change. Only a change in people's desire to buy, which is unrelated to GNP, that is, graphically a shift or tilt in the AD line, could do that.

unemployment equilibrium

Notice in particular how there would be no tendency whatsoever for GNP to rise further to the assumed full employment level of \$450 billion. If by accident this output ever were produced, aggregate demand would fall short of aggregate supply (df falls short of db). There would be surpluses of many or all goods. Because GNP is \$450 billion and aggregate demand only \$382 billion, businesses as a group will be left with \$68 billion of unwanted inventory increases. Not only do they get their desired \$80 billion of new buildings and equipment and inventories, but a bonus of \$68 billion of undesired goods on top! Their actual investment (measured as I in the GNP accounts) would far exceed their investment demand. Business would be in the doldrums. Naturally, businessmen would cut production and lay off men to "work off" the inventories accumulating against their will. (Notice this sort of reaction in the news story on autos introducing this chapter.) This would continue until equilibrium GNP of \$336⅔ billion is reached. In our example, we would end up with an *unemployment equilibrium,* producing only three quarters of potential GNP. We would have a severe depression, indeed. Yet, the same principle would hold if the AD line intersected the AS line closer to full employment. As long as the intersection point is to the left of the full employment point (here b), we have general unemployment and *no* tendency for it to disappear.

Only if the AD line were to shift or tilt upward to go through b, would we have full employment. This is possible, of course, but without government intervention it would be a matter of pure chance.

demand-pull inflation

Equally likely would be the case where the AD line crosses the AS line *beyond* full employment, to the right of b. (If you cannot visualize it, you might want to draw in such a new aggregate demand line in Figure 7.1, above and parallel to the present one.) In that case, a hypothetical equilibrium point exists to the right of b, but our analysis would have to differ. There would then be excess *demand* at full employment. Business would boom all right, but businessmen could *not* go out and hire idle resources. There would not be any. In this case, they would raise prices. We would have demand-pull inflation. A constant (full employment) real GNP would sell for more and more money. The economy would move toward its hypothetical equilibrium. But all the gains in GNP would be paper gains of higher prices, not real gains of more commodities and services. As long as this situation of excess demand at full employment persisted, we would continue to have demand-pull inflation and no tendency for it to disappear.

Only if the AD line were to shift or tilt *down* to go through b, would we have full employment without demand-pull inflation. This, too, would be a matter of chance. Thus, the modern economy faces a dilemma much like the one Ulysses found when he had to sail through a narrow strait where a man-eating monster dwelt on the one side and a huge whirlpool boiled on the other. Just change the names of the two hazards from the mythological Scylla and Charybdis to general unemployment and demand-pull inflation. If aggregate demand is small enough to avoid plunging us into the whirlpool of inflation, the economy has an excellent chance of running into the monster of unemployment!

An Alternative Exposition

What can be shown in graphs can also be said in words and with a minimum of arithmetic. We have seen how equilibrium occurs where aggregate demand equals aggregate supply. (And we have seen that by chance only this equilibrium coincides with full employment.)

Let us take a closer look at aggregate demand. Still using the example underlying Figure 6.9 and used in Figure 7.1, we can divide aggregate demand into two parts. First, there are "autonomous" demands, demands that do not vary with the level of GNP. This includes investment demand of $80 billion, government demand of $100 billion, and net export demand of $12 billion. It also includes a *portion* of consumption demand, because even at a zero GNP, consumption demand would equal $10 billion. Thus, the total of autonomous aggregate demand equals $202 billion. (It can, by the way, always be read off on the aggregate demand line by asking what aggregate demand would be at a zero GNP.) From here on, things get a little more complicated. There is one component of the total, another *portion* of consumption demand, which also varies with GNP. Any demand that varies with GNP is called "induced" demand. Consider Table 6.2 AN AGGREGATE CONSUMPTION DEMAND SCHEDULE or Figure 6.3 TWO PICTURES OF AGGREGATE CONSUMPTION DEMAND, which is based on it. There we see that a change in GNP from 0 to $240 billion changes consumption demand from $10 billion (the autonomous portion) to $106 billion. Thus,

$$\frac{\text{change in induced consumption demand}}{\text{change in GNP causing it}} = \frac{\$96 \text{ billion}}{\$240 \text{ billion}} = 0.4$$

Economists call this ratio—of change in induced consumption demand to change in GNP causing it—the *marginal propensity to consume GNP,* or mpc for short. It is an extremely important concept. It measures the tendency of households (their "propensity") to spend on consumer goods (to "consume") any extra ("marginal") income. In this case, an extra $240 billion of GNP brings about an extra $96 billion of consumption expenditures. Or each extra dollar of GNP results in 40 cents extra of *induced* consumer spending.

This brings us to a very easy way of measuring induced consumption demand: just multiply the mpc by the GNP. Try it on Table 6.2 or Figure 6.3. It always works.

If GNP is zero, induced consumption demand is $0.4 \times 0 = 0$. If GNP is $100 billion, induced consumption demand is 0.4 × $100 billion, or $40 billion. Add autonomous consumption demand of $10 billion, and you get the total of $50 billion at that level of GNP.

Now we can find the equilibrium level of GNP in six easy steps. To have equilibrium,

(1) aggregate demand must equal aggregate supply, or equal GNP.

But aggregate demand equals autonomous and induced demands. Therefore, in equilibrium

(2) autonomous demands + induced demand must equal GNP.

But induced demand equals, as we just saw, the mpc multiplied by the GNP. Therefore, in equilibrium

(3) autonomous demands + (mpc × GNP) must equal GNP.

This can be rewritten to state that in equilibrium

(4) autonomous demands must equal GNP minus (mpc × GNP).

This can, in turn, be simplified to state that in equilibrium

(5) autonomous demands must equal GNP multiplied by (1 − mpc).

Which, finally, reduces to

$$(6) \quad \frac{\text{autonomous demands}}{1 - \text{mpc}} = \text{equilibrium GNP}$$

This is an extremely important formula. It will be well worth it to memorize it. (But remember: it holds only for our *model* of the economy. A more advanced analysis may yield a different result.)

We can put our formula to the test quickly. In our example, autonomous demands equaled $202 billion. Because the mpc equaled 0.4, the left-hand side of the formula becomes

$$\frac{\$202 \text{ billion}}{1 - 0.4} = \frac{\$202 \text{ billion}}{0.6} = 336\tfrac{2}{3} \text{ billion.}$$

This is exactly the same answer our graphic analysis gave us. It is, of course, also the answer to which our earlier verbal analysis would have led us eventually. We can now, in addition, easily determine the composition of this GNP. By assumption, investment demand would be $80 billion, government demand $100 billion, net export demand $12 billion no matter what GNP is. Autonomous consumption demand would be $10 billion no matter what GNP is. Induced consumption demand would have to equal the mpc times GNP: 0.4 × $336⅔ billion, or $134⅔ billion. Thus, total consumption demand would be $144⅔ billion. Add this up, and you get aggregate demand of $336⅔ billion, which is exactly equal to the value of GNP. If this level of GNP ever were produced, therefore, businessmen would experience no surprises. Inventories would neither rise nor fall against their wishes. They would keep on producing just as much as before.

HOW EQUILIBRIUM GNP CHANGES

Our formula also tells us how equilibrium GNP can change. There are only two possibilities: the level of autonomous demands must change (the AD line *shift*) or the size of the marginal propensity to consume must change (the AD line *tilt*). The former means that someone must want to spend more or less in spite of the fact that gross and net income has not changed. The latter means, for example, that someone must want to spend more or less because his net income has changed, even though gross income has not.

Examples can easily be found. Suppose consumers as a group suddenly decided to become thriftier. No matter what their incomes, they decide to spend less and save more. Autonomous consumption demand may drop from our assumed $10 billion a year to $2 billion a year. Businessmen may be influenced by this, too. Noting the change in consumer attitudes, they may decide that this is a bad time to invest. Why make bulldozers to level driveways if people don't built houses? Why build factories to make television sets if people won't buy them? Investment demand may drop from our assumed $80 billion to $40 billion a year. What will be the result? Our formula provides a quick answer. Autonomous demands have fallen from the earlier $202 billion to $154 billion, reflecting the $48 billion drop in household and business demand. Hence, equilibrium GNP will become

$$\frac{\$202 - \$48 \text{ billion}}{0.6} = \frac{\$154 \text{ billion}}{0.6} = \$256\frac{2}{3} \text{ billion}$$

GNP and with it the level of employment falls by almost 24 percent.

Or take another case, the rapid rise in federal government demand for goods at the start of World War II or during the Vietnam buildup. Say government demand rises from our assumed $100 billion to $160 billion. Immediately, we can tell what will happen to GNP. It will change to become

$$\frac{\$202 \text{ billion} + \$60 \text{ billion}}{0.6} = \frac{\$262 \text{ billion}}{0.6} = \$436\frac{2}{3} \text{ billion}.$$

This will be a rise in *real* GNP, because we assumed the potential at $450 billion. You can see now why wars always put a quick end to depression. You can also see why they easily push us into demand-pull inflation. Had government demand risen by more, say to $180 billion, equilibrium GNP would have become $470 billion, impossible to produce. (Can you figure out how this result was gotten?) In real terms, output could only have risen to $450 billion with inflation setting in at the same time.

The Multiplier

Notice something else. A $48 billion cut in autonomous demand cuts GNP by $80 billion. A $60 billion increase raises it by $100 billion. Any change in autonomous demands gets *multiplied* into a larger change in GNP!

We can easily see the process at work. As households and businessmen spend $48 billion less, businesses produce $48 billion less. Incomes earned by the resources now idle fall by $48 billion. By assumption, it does not affect autonomous demands, but it does affect induced ones! Our mpc tells us that consumers as a group change consumption demand by 40 cents for every $1 change in GNP. Hence, a $48 billion cut in GNP will lead to a further cut in consumption demand of 0.4 × $48 billion, or $19.2 billion. The people who got laid off because of falling demand now in turn demand less. This induces businessmen to cut output by *another* $19.2 billion, because they could not sell as much. As a result, more people are laid off. They lose $19.2 billion in incomes, and they, in turn, will consume 0.4 × $19.2 billion, or $7.68 billion less. And so it goes, in an ever-dwindling chain.

Some people decided to save more. They bought fewer cars and refrigerators. This caused unemployment at Ford and General Electric. This caused people to buy fewer television sets and picnic tables. This caused people to get laid off at Sylvania and Picnic Tables Unlimited. And so on.

If you add it all up, you find the original cut in autonomous demand (of $48 billion) enlarged by cuts in induced demands of $19.2 billion and another $7.68 billion and another $3.072 billion, and so on. It all comes to the grand total of $80 billion, as we observed. (Try to tell a similar "story" about the case of increased government spending getting multiplied into a larger rise in GNP. Don't ever apply a formula thoughtlessly.)

The figure by which any change in autonomous demands must be multiplied to get the eventual change in equilibrium GNP is called the *multiplier*. You can easily see its size in our above formula as

$$\frac{1}{1 - \text{mpc}},$$

or in this case

$$\frac{1}{0.6} = 1\tfrac{2}{3}.$$

Just as in our examples − $48 billion × $1\tfrac{2}{3}$ = − $80 billion, and + $60 billion × $1\tfrac{2}{3}$ = + $100 billion, it is always true that the

> change in autonomous demands × multiplier = change in equilibrium GNP.

The nature of the multiplier, however, is not always what it was here. That depends on how complicated the economy is. If there are other types of induced demands besides consumption, for instance, the multiplier will look different. That is, it will have to be calculated by a more complicated formula.

The size of the multiplier can, of course, also change. We noted in our discussion of Figure 6.3 TWO PICTURES OF AGGREGATE CONSUMPTION DEMAND, for example, how the consumption demand schedule, relating consumption demand to GNP, would *tilt* with a change in the factors intervening between GNP and disposable personal income (that is, with a change in depreciation, taxes, undistributed corporate profits, transfers). Now suppose corporations were to change their profit-withholding policy. Suddenly, they withhold none. For any given GNP above zero, we could expect a larger disposable personal income, hence higher consumption demand. Possibly, induced consumption demand would become not 40 percent of GNP, as we assumed so far, but 43 percent. Thus, the mpc would become 0.43 instead of 0.4.

As a result, equilibrium GNP, given the autonomous demands assumed in Figure 7.1, would become

$$\frac{\$202 \text{ billion}}{1 - 0.43} = \frac{\$202 \text{ billion}}{0.57} = \$354.39 \text{ billion.}$$

Note how this is larger than the \$336.67 billion equilibrium depicted in the earlier figure. This would be the ultimate effect of stockholders' increased receipt and spending of dividend checks, assuming no change in autonomous demands.

Superimpose a \$60 billion increase in government spending on this and you find a new GNP of \$459.65 billion, a \$105.26 billion rise. Compared to the earlier \$100 billion rise, the multiplier has clearly risen. So it has, being now

$$\frac{1}{0.57} = 1.754.$$

A Graphical Exposition of Change

If you like to work with graphs, Figure 7.2 TWO CHANGES IN AGGREGATE DEMAND summarizes our discussion. Consider part (a). Suppose we start at an original GNP equilibrium of \$300 billion at the intersection (at a) of the AD and AS lines. Suddenly any one or all of the autonomous components of aggregate demand rise, that is, demand goes up unrelated to income. The extent of this increase is shown by the upward *shift* of line AD to AD*. At the present GNP, there suddenly opens up a gap of excess demand (ab). GNP will start to rise to the new intersection at c, or from \$300 billion to \$400 billion. If full employment GNP is at or above \$400 billion, this will be a rise in *real* GNP. (If full employment GNP is above \$300 billion and below \$400 billion, this will also involve demand-pull inflation.) Notice how the original

Figure 7.2   TWO CHANGES IN AGGREGATE DEMAND

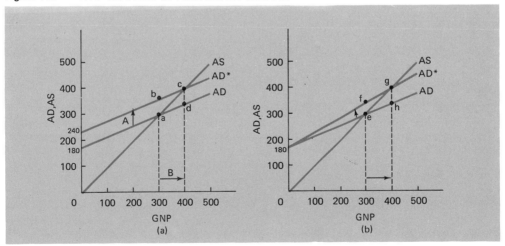

A change in autonomous demands, showing as a shift of the aggregate demand line, will displace a given equilibrium GNP, part (a). So will a change in the size of the multiplier, showing as a tilt of the aggregate demand line, part (b).

increase in autonomous demand (arrow A) has been multiplied, through the addition of induced demand, into a larger increase in real GNP (arrow B). This corresponds exactly to the above example of increased government spending on war.

The same can be worked in reverse. Suppose the original equilibrium is shown by the intersection (at c) of the AD* and AS lines. A fall in autonomous demands now shifts aggregate demand *down* to AD. At the present equilibrium GNP of $400, appears a gap of excess supply (cd). GNP will start to fall to the new intersection at a. If full employment GNP is at or above $400 billion, this amounts to a fall in real GNP. (If full employment GNP is between $300 and $400 billion, this may also involve the elimination of demand-pull inflation.)

As before, the original fall in autonomous demand (arrow A reversed) is multiplied into a larger fall in real GNP (arrow B reversed). This is analogous to the earlier case of increased household thriftiness and decreased desire by business to invest.

Now consider part (b). Starting at the intersection (at e) of the AD and AS lines, we assume an original equilibrium GNP of $300 billion. A change in the multiplier, for reasons discussed above, may displace the aggregate demand line to AD*. Immediately an excess-demand gap opens up at the original GNP (of ef) and pushes the economy, if idle resources permit, to a higher real GNP equilibrium at g. This case would correspond to the just discussed example of corporations withholding less of their earnings, that is, paying out larger dividends.

Conversely, starting at g with the AD* and AS lines, a fall in the multiplier will swing the aggregate demand line down to AD. At $400 billion, an excess-supply gap opens (gh). It pushes the economy to the lower, $300 billion, equilibrium.

SUMMARY

1   The classical economists believed in an *automatic* tendency of the economy to produce a real GNP equal to its potential. They argued that prices of resource services would fall in the face of involuntary unemployment and that firms would, under such circumstances, hire more resources and produce more output. This would continue until full employment was reached. They argued further (correctly) that income equal to the value of output would be generated in the process of production, and (on doubtful grounds) that all of this income and no more would be voluntarily spent on output. Thus, supply (output produced) would create its own demand (voluntary spending). In the aggregate (though not for particular goods), *any* level of output, once reached, can be maintained (Say's Law). As the classical economists saw it, the level of full employment output would be the one reached and maintained. Unless government misbehaved, furthermore, there would be no inflation.

2   Modern economists deny that there exists any automatic tendency to get to full employment. This is blamed, among other things, on the downward inflexibility of prices in our mixed economy. They also deny that aggregate demand always equals aggregate income, or that any rate of output once reached will be maintained. The income not spent on output by some (saving), rather than being lent and spent by someone else, may be held in cash or used to pay off debt. Even if lent, there may be a cash drain into savings bank reserves or borrowing may occur to hold cash. In addition, demand from borrowed funds may be fed through the creation of new money, irrespective of saving.

3   Modern economists argue, rather, that real GNP will come to rest (be in equilibrium, have no innate tendency to change) at that level at which it is equal to aggregate demand. Aggregate demand does not have to equal income, and GNP will change until it does. It can come into equilibrium anywhere at or below potential.

4   The determination of equilibrium GNP can be illustrated graphically with aggregate demand and aggregate supply lines. At the GNP corresponding to their intersection, the amounts produced and demanded (voluntarily bought) are equal. GNP will remain there, regardless of the size of full employment GNP. At any GNP below equilibrium, we have excess demand. At any GNP above equilibrium, we have excess supply. Excess demand leads to a rise in GNP, excess supply to a fall. This is so because they give rise to undesired decreases or increases, respectively, in business inventories. Unless all resources are fully employed, the rise in GNP referred to here is a rise in real GNP, rather than prices. Unless we already have demand-pull inflation, the fall in GNP referred to here is a fall in real GNP, rather than prices.

5   Aggregate demand can be split into autonomous demand, independent of GNP, and induced demand, dependent on GNP. We define the change in induced consumption demand, divided by the change in GNP causing it, as the marginal propensity to consume GNP, or the mpc. The level of induced consumption demand equals, therefore, the mpc multiplied by the GNP. The level of equilibrium GNP equals autonomous plus induced demands, or equals

$$\frac{\text{autonomous demands}}{1 - \text{mpc}}.$$

(This may be different in more complicated models of the economy, however.)

6   Given our model, equilibrium GNP can change only if autonomous demand changes (the AD line shifts) or the mpc changes (the AD line tilts). Any change in autonomous demands leads to a larger change in equilibrium GNP. This reflects the working of the "multiplier," the fact that any original change in autonomous demand leads to further changes in induced demand. The size of the multiplier in our examples equals

$$\frac{1}{1 - \text{mpc}}.$$

TERMS[1]

aggregate supply (line)	marginal propensity to consume GNP
autonomous vs. induced demands	
classical economics	multiplier
equilibrium GNP	saving
excess demand (or supply)	Say's Law
income velocity of money	theory of income (or output) determination
	unemployment equilibrium

[1] Terms and symbols are defined in the Glossary at the end of the book.

SYMBOLS

AS
mpc

QUESTIONS FOR REVIEW AND DISCUSSION

1 The theory of income determination is also a theory of output determination. It is also a theory of employment. Explain.

2 The history of economic thought on matters of unemployment can be divided into two distinct periods. Explain.

3 "Aggregate income always equals aggregate output." Explain.

4 "Aggregate demand always equals aggregate income." Discuss.

5 What is Say's Law?

6 A: "Say's Law does not apply to *individual* goods."
B: "It does not apply *at all*."
    Who is right?

7 What is the role of government envisaged by the classical economists?

8 Summarize in as few words as possible the Keynesian explanation of the level of GNP.

9 Explain what happens to output, employment, and prices if GNP equals $150 billion, but aggregate demand equals $262 billion. Use words only, no graphs, no mathematics.
    a Assume maximum real GNP equals $450 billion.
    b Assume maximum real GNP equals $150 billion.

10 Explain the meaning of the AS line in Figure 7.1 GNP IN EQUILIBRIUM.

11 What is the difference between actual investment expenditures (as measured by the national income accounts and symbolized by I) and investment demand? Why is this difference *the* key to the explanation of actual output and employment? Relate your answer to the two news stories introducing this chapter.

12 What happens if aggregate demand falls short of the value of full employment GNP? Why and how?

13 Tell *in words* what it would mean for "the AD line to shift or tilt upward."

14 Calculate the equilibrium level of GNP, if the mpc equals 0.1 and autonomous consumption, investment, government, and net export demands equal (in billions) $100, 20, 100, and −10, respectively.

15 Redo question 14, assuming the mpc to be zero. To be unity. Can you *explain* your results?

16 Give a *verbal* explanation of the multiplier process.

17 Make a list of events that could change the mpc.

18 It has been said that in a period of depression, if we export more goods abroad (or import fewer), we will end up having more goods at home. Does that make any sense? Could it?

19 It has been said that an attempt by all households to save more may only lead to a fall in GNP and the same aggregate saving as before or even less. Can you explain this?

20   "Graphically, a change in autonomous consumption demand shows as a shifting or tilting of the consumption demand line, a change in induced consumption demand as a movement along it." Evaluate. Is this true? What does it *mean*, in plain English?

The Junior Econometrician's Work Kit.

Predict the U.S. Economy for 1956.
Build Your Own Forecasting Model.

DIRECTIONS:

1. Make up a theory. You might theorize, for instance, that (1) next year's consumption will depend on next year's national income; (2) next year's investment will depend on this year's profits; (3) tax receipts will depend on future Gross National Product. (4) GNP is the sum of consumption, investment, and government expenditures. (5) National income equals GNP minus taxes.

2. Use symbols for words. Call consumption, C; national income, Y; investment, I; preceding year's profits, P_{-1} tax receipts, T; Gross National Product, G; government expenditures, E.

3. Translate your theories into mathematical equations:

(1) $C = aY + b$ (4) $G = C + I + E$
(2) $I = cP_{-1} + d$ (5) $Y = G - T$
(3) $T = eG$

This is your forecasting model. The small letters, a, b, c, d, e, are the constants that make things come out even. For instance, if horses (H) have four legs (L), then $H = aL$; or $H = 4L$. This can be important in the blacksmith business.

4. Calculate the constants. Look up past years' statistics on consumption, income, and so on. From these find values for a, b, c, d, and e that make your equation come out fairly correct.

5. Now you're ready to forecast. Start by forecasting investment from this year's profits. Look up the current rate of corporate profits—it's around $42-billion. The model won't tell what federal, state, and local governments will spend next year—that's politics. But we can estimate it from present budget information—it looks like around $75-billion.

6. Put all available figures into your model. (We've put in the constants for you.)

(1) $C = .7Y + 40$ (4) $G = C + I + 75$
(2) $I = .9 \times 42 + 20$ (5) $Y = G - T$
(3) $T = .2G$

7. Solve the equations. You want values of C, I, T, G, Y. Hints: Do them in this order—(2), (1), (4), (3), (5). In solving (1), remember that I and E are both part of G, $Y = G - T$, and $T = .2G$.

8. Results. (See if yours are the same.) For 1956, consumption will be $260.0-billion; investment, $57.8-billion; GNP, $392.8-billion; tax receipts, $78.6-billion; national income, $314.2-billion. These results are guaranteed—provided that the theories on which they're based are valid.

Business Week, September 24, 1955. Reprinted by permission.

8

business cycles
and
forecasting

W E HAVE SEEN how it is possible for real GNP to settle at a level that leaves the economy well below the full utilization of resources. If aggregate demand is insufficient to justify production of the potential real GNP, less than the potential will be produced; there is then no innate tendency for this undesirable state of affairs to change.

We have also had a glimpse of something else. If there should be a change in one of the autonomous factors (factors other than income influencing aggregate demand) or in the marginal propensity to consume gross national income, equilibrium real GNP will change.

In this chapter, we go a step further, asking *how long* it takes to get from one level of equilibrium GNP to another and what the *path* is that is taken by the actual GNP before any disturbance of an original equilibrium has been taken account of in a new equilibrium. The reason for such questioning goes beyond intellectual curiosity, beyond the desire to explore *imaginary* situations in depth. Indeed, it is prompted, as have been all our efforts so far, by a desire to explain reality. Historically, real GNP has not rested forever in a situation of equilibrium, either at or below full employment, but has fluctuated substantially from year to year, usually around a long-run upward trend and below the levels of its potential.

In this chapter, we shall discuss the reasons for such *business cycles* and how they may be predicted. The purpose of such prediction, naturally, is to help us formulate courses of action that will push GNP and employment to the levels desired by us. Such *economic policy* will be discussed in the next chapters.

THE MEANING OF THE TERM *BUSINESS CYCLE*

Figure 5.3 THE HISTORY OF U.S. GNP showed vividly how real GNP, although growing over the long run, has been almost continually below its potential, *but not always to an equal degree*. Given our particular estimate of the potential, actual real GNP since 1929 has been, on the average, about 12 percent below the potential. If we interpret this average as the long-term trend, we can plot the deviations of actual real GNP from the trend (see Figure 8.1 U.S. GNP: ACTUAL VS. TREND). Note, however, that the trend is only a figment of the imagination. It is a purely mathematical construct and does not have, nor has it ever had, a life of its own. Actual real GNP has moved as the actual line indicates, and very seldom has actual GNP been below the potential by exactly the 12 percent that constitutes the long-run average, indicated by the trend line. Furthermore, as we said in connection with Figure 5.3, the data for 1943–1945, as well as the most recent years, do not say that real GNP was above the potential, but rather indicate that, owing to circumstances of war, the potential, together with the actual real GNP, was raised above the level one could have expected in peace time.

The picture in Figure 8.1 U.S. GNP: ACTUAL VS. TREND of the movements of real GNP around its trend very faintly resembles a never-ending cycle of ups and down. Economists call this observed movement of real GNP, with its concomitant phenomena of changing levels of employment and prices, the *business cycle*. The image typically conjured up by the word *cycle* is that of a regular repetitive movement, over time, of a variable swinging symmetrically around an intermediate position (see Figure 8.2 AN IDEALIZED CYCLE). It hardly

Figure 8.1   U.S. GNP: ACTUAL VS. TREND

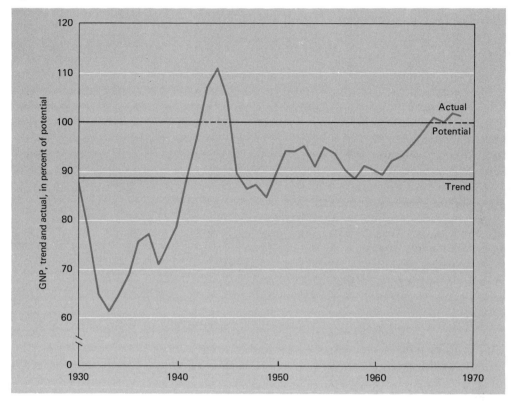

Measured in dollars of 1958 purchasing power, actual GNP in the United States has been, on the average, 12 percent below potential since 1929. In addition, actual GNP has fluctuated widely around this trend. This is a picture of the business cycle in the United States. Source: Figure 5.3 THE HISTORY OF U.S. GNP.

needs emphasizing, in the light of Figure 8.1 U.S. GNP: ACTUAL VS. TREND, that this image is not applicable to the observed movements of real GNP. The real cycles plotted in Figure 8.1 have differed in length, amplitude, and regularity considerably from the ideal in Figure 8.2.[1] Therefore, as we continue to use the term *cycle*, let us keep in mind that reality is not correctly described by Figure 8.2 and that we are referring to the erratic course of real GNP depicted in Figure 8.1 (and Figure 5.3).

---

[1] The length of a single cycle refers to the time elapsed between analogous positions of the variable. For example, we can measure the cycle from the moment it rises above the trend once (point a, Figure 8.2) until it does so again (point b, Figure 8.2). Amplitude refers to the maximum deviations above or below the trend or, in Figure 8.2, distances c and d, which measure the extent of boom and depression, respectively. Regularity refers to smoothness of the movement of the variable in general.

Figure 8.2   AN IDEALIZED CYCLE

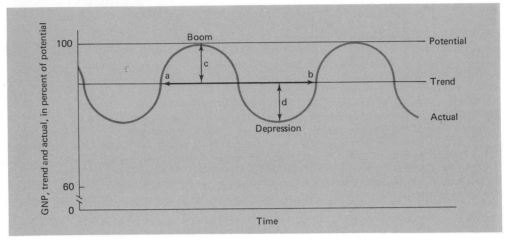

In this idealized version of the business cycle, real GNP swings symmetrically around the trend. Each cycle (distance a to b) is of equal length, each amplitude (distances c or d) is the same, and the movement of the variable is smooth.

THEORIES OF THE CYCLE

Economists have been studying the business cycle intensively for more than a century. In earlier periods they observed that there were such things as "good times" and "bad times." But the more the self-sufficient, agricultural, and precommercial society came to be replaced by an elaborately interdependent, industrialized money economy, the more the evidence grew for a *rhythmical* alternation of boom and bust, one following the other as surely as night follows day! All over the world, in the advanced capitalist countries, economists thought they had discovered a striking phenomenon of a repeating *pattern*, the *business cycle.*

The Russian economist Nikolai D. Kondratieff (1892–ca. 1935), for example, believed he had shown the existence of "long waves" of economic activity, lasting about 60 years, from a point such as a in Figure 8.2 to a point such as b. The French scholar Clement Juglar (1819–1905) found widespread evidence for major cycles of roughly 10 years' duration, evidently superimposed on the Kondratieff waves. The American Wesley C. Mitchell (1874–1948) supported the Juglar thesis by a systematic study of the U.S. experience and reported the onsets of serious economic depressions for the years 1812, 1818, 1825, 1837, 1847, 1857, 1873, 1884, 1890, 1893, 1903, 1907, 1910, 1913, and 1920. To this list we can now add 1929 and 1938. Finally, a British scholar, Joseph Kitchin (writing in the 1920's), has proposed that we recognize the existence of minor cycles of roughly 4 years' duration, which are in turn superimposed on the Juglar cycles. In this way, Kitchin would presumably explain the less serious, but more frequent, economic downturns that have occurred in the United States in 1949, 1954, 1958, and

1961 (see Figure 8.1 U.S. GNP: ACTUAL VS. TREND). The National Bureau of Economic Research, the leading private research organization on cycles in the United States, has plotted hundreds of individual economic data series, ranging from unemployment and the GNP to new machinery orders, housing starts, consumer durable purchases, and the length of the average work week. Such series show a wide spectrum of movements. At any one time, some are rising, others falling. The bureau considers a boom ended when more than half are falling, a depression ended when more than half are rising. On that basis, we had twenty-six expansions since 1854 with an *average* length of 2.5 years. Each ended in a recession.

At the same time that many economists have described the erratic course of real GNP around a long-run upward trend by postulating the existence of a variety of cycles, they and many others have been busy looking for the causes of this type of economic behavior. Many have singled out different causative factors. Yet, one can put these manifold explanations quite easily into two categories—exogenous and endogenous theories.

Exogenous, or External, Theories

The *exogenous* explanations of business cycles have in common that they postulate cycles to be caused by some force outside the economy, beyond the control or predictive power of the economist. Depending on the investigator concerned and the particular data he worked with, different emphasis has been put on different kinds of exogenous forces. Among the many factors that have been suggested as likely exogenous causes of a rise or fall in production and employment are changes in the composition or rate of growth of population, interregional migrations of population, natural catastrophes (floods, earthquakes), political upheavals (revolutions, wars, new laws of significant impact), innovations (new products, new production methods, new forms of business organization, new markets, new sources of supply), the weather, business psychology, and the behavior of central bankers (following the "rules of the gold standard").

In Chapter 6, we have, in fact, developed the tools needed to understand this particular approach to the explanation of business cycles. The exogenous forces talked about here are the same ones that forced us to classify certain categories of aggregate demand as autonomously determined. What is likely to happen if there is a sudden rapid increase or fall in population growth? More likely than not, people in the aggregate would consume more or less out of *any* aggregate income. This is exactly the kind of thing that would make us expect the aggregate consumption demand line to shift up or down. In the same way, governmental demand can be expected to change in the face of natural catastrophe, revolution, or war, whereas net foreign demand certainly will be affected by new laws concerning exports or imports.

Investment demand can be expected to change for all these reasons, as well as the others given above. Think of the effect on investment demand of the invention of the railroad, automobile, space ship, electric power, assembly line, or electronic control machine. Reflect on the effects on investment demand of the introduction of the corporate form of business, the discovery or settling of new territories, or a major discovery of oil deposits.

Imagine the American economy 100 years ago, when agriculture was extremely important (today only 5 percent of those employed work in agriculture). The weather, by affecting agricultural output, could easily influence economic activity in general. A bumper crop, for example, would make increased demands on industry for equipment to harvest, store, and transport what nature had provided, thereby also initiating a boom in that sector of the economy. Although it strikes us as odd today, a competent economist, W. Stanley Jevons, writing in 1875, thought he had established a link between periodic sunspots and the business cycle via the weather, agricultural output, and the demand for industrial goods. H. L. Moore, as late as 1914, linked the cycle to a particular recurring position of the planet Venus, which was thought to influence rainfall on earth.

We have also noted in our discussion of investment demand how waves of optimism and pessimism seem to infect the business world. The psychological explanations of business cycles stressed just this. For some reason, at some time, some influential businessmen *feel* it a good time to invest. The President announces that "prosperity is just around the corner." For some reason, everyone believes it, and investment demand goes up. GNP rises. After a while, however, come the prophets of doom, seeing bad times for business in the offing. An influential business leader announces cuts in investment spending and talks of imminent adjustments in the economy. "The bigger the boom, the bigger the bust," he warns. For some reason, the majority of businessmen follow in his footsteps. No matter how weak the logic, alliteration is a powerful force! At that point, the President announces that "the boom is here to stay," but everyone interprets this as a sure sign that the opposite is going to happen. Present equipment is made to last a while longer. Businessmen wait and see. Aggregate investment demand drops, so do GNP and employment.

Other economists maintained that the business cycle was set off not because businessmen periodically started to feel good or bad, but because *they were enabled to follow their feelings* as central bankers periodically provided them with new money to finance their dreams. At other times, bankers forced them to reduce their indebtedness to the bank. This was caused, it was argued, by the fact that the total amount of money in existence was closely linked to the total amount of gold held by a country and that the supply of gold was periodically increased by new discoveries or imports and decreased by exports of gold. Hence, again, the cycle was linked to a shift in investment demand.

In summary, all the exogenous theories are saying that for some reason, beyond prediction and control, autonomous demands have changed and that such changes just happen to have occurred at intervals regular enough—and even in alternating directions—to bring about the business *cycle.*

Endogenous, or Internal, Theories

The *endogenous* explanations of business cycles do not deny the above possibilities. But they make internal forces in the economy primarily responsible for the course of real GNP. The economy is of such a nature, they argue, that even the slightest disturbance of a given equilibrium GNP by an exogenous force breeds cumulative further change.

the accelerator   The accelerator theory provides an excellent example. It focuses on the relationship between output and the capital stock needed to make it. For many cases, although not always, this relationship is rather fixed. As demand for output rises (for example, as government demand rises owing to war), it may be temporarily possible to satisfy the increased demand either by drawing down inventories of goods made in the past or by increasing the rate of production by putting idle buildings and machines to work, pressing standby equipment into service, or making fully used equipment work overtime. After some time, however, if the increase in demand persists, inventories will be used up, there will be no idle equipment left, and all possibilities for raising output through the use of standby equipment or overtime work of the present capital stock will be exhausted. From this point on, increased demand can be satisfied only from *increased output produced by new capital*. This means that investment demand will arise, be it for new buildings, new machines, or new inventories. The original increase in aggregate demand (caused by the rise in government demand owing to war) eventually has been *accelerated* into a larger increase, having *induced* an increase in investment demand also.

Clearly, the size of this effect will differ from product to product, and the lag involved between increased demand and the occurrence of investment will similarly differ among industries and the circumstances of time. To illustrate the principle, let us assume that in a particular industry $5 million of new capital (buildings, equipment, inventories) is needed after a lag of 1 year for every $10 million of additional output contributed to GNP. We can say that a *change* in GNP requires, 1 year later, a *change* in the capital stock. Note that this change in the capital stock may be called *induced* investment demand. After all, if the assumed government demand of $10 million of output (to fight a war) eventually requires new capital of $5 million, producers will have to demand $5 million of capital goods, that is, their investment demand (induced by the change in output caused by the original government demand) must be of the same magnitude. The ratio of induced investment demand to extra output, or the ratio of extra capital needed for extra output produced, is called the *marginal capital to output ratio,* or the *accelerator*. In our example, this equals $5 million/ $10 million, or 0.5. If we wish, we can recognize explicitly the assumed time lag involved, that is, the fact that a change in output in the *previous* period causes a change in the capital stock or creates induced investment demand in *this* period. We just have to interpret our accelerator to mean that any period's induced investment demand equals 0.5 times the *previous* period's output change. The accelerator theory states that at least a *portion* of aggregate investment demand—the portion we have named *induced investment demand*— depends on prior changes in output. Thus, *total* investment demand can be thought to consist of an autonomous portion (which alone was recognized in the previous chapter) plus an induced portion.

Note that this is similar to our theory about consumption demand. There it was argued that a portion of consumer demand depended on the *level* of income (or output). Here, a portion of investment demand is related to *changes* of income (or output).

the accelerator illustrated   Table 8.1 THE ACCELERATOR ILLUSTRATED illustrates this relationship in detail. Column (2) contains assumed data on an industry's annual contribution to GNP. Column (3) is derived from column (2). It shows the absolute change in output in any year, or, what is the same thing, the output of a given year minus the output of the previous year. For instance, as output rises from $100 million in year 3 to $110 million in year 4, output change in year 4 is given as +$10 million. Looking at the column as a whole, we see that in years 2 and 3, output did not change at all. From years 4 through 11, output rose. From years 12 through 19, it fell.

Table 8.1   THE ACCELERATOR ILLUSTRATED

YEAR	OUTPUT[a]	OUTPUT CHANGE[a]	REQUIRED CHANGE IN CAPITAL STOCK OR INDUCED INVESTMENT DEMAND[a]
(1)	(2)	(3)	(4)
1	100	No data	No data
2	100	0	No data
3	100	0	0
4	110	+10	0
5	130	+20	+ 5
6	170	+40	+10
7	210	+40	+20
8	250	+40	+20
9	280	+30	+20
10	290	+10	+15
11	295	+ 5	+ 5
12	260	−35	+ 2.5
13	220	−40	−17.5
14	175	−45	−20
15	130	−45	−22.5
16	85	−45	−22.5
17	55	−30	−22.5
18	35	−20	−15
19	25	−10	−10
20	No data	No data	− 5

[a] All data in million dollars of constant purchasing power.
When each $1 change in output requires a 50 cent change in the capital stock (or induces 50 cents worth of investment demand), the accelerator equals 50 cents/ $1, or 0.5. In this table, it is assumed that prices do not change over time; thus, all dollars have constant purchasing power. It is also assumed that induced investment demand follows output change with a 1 year lag.

By assumption, any change in output induces a change in the capital stock *1 year later* and *of one half its size.* For example, the output change of year 4, which was +$10 million, leads in year 5 to induced investment demand of +$5 million. Thus, we derive column (4) from column (3).

the accelerator summarized   Immediately, we perceive the following: (1) When output is not changing (years 2 and 3), investment demand induced by it is zero (following with a lag of 1 year in years 3 and 4). (2) When output is rising (years 4 through 11), investment demand induced by it is positive (years 5 through 12). (3) When output is falling (years 12 through 19), investment demand induced by it is negative (years 13 through 20). This means that businessmen reduce their capital stock, possibly by reducing inventories or letting buildings and equipment depreciate faster than they are replaced.

In addition, as long as output is rising at an increasing rate (by 10, then 20, then 40, as it does from years 4 through 6), investment demand induced by it is not only positive, but increasing (years 5 through 7). When output rises at a constant rate (by 40 each in years 6 through 8), investment demand induced by it is not only positive, but constant (years 7 through 9). When output rises at a falling rate (by 40, then 30, then 10, then 5, as it does from years 8 through 11), investment demand induced by it is not only positive, but falling (years 9 through 12). Similarly, output falling at an increasing rate (years 12 through 14), constant rate (years 14 through 16), and falling rate (years 16 through 19) induces negative investment demand that is falling (years 13 through 15), constant (years 15 through 17), and rising (years 17 through 20), respectively.

This is the basis for a typical endogenous theory of the business cycle. Although output is rising or falling (for whatever reason), depending on the *rate* at which it rises or falls, investment demand may be rising or falling in either case, thereby strengthening or reversing the prevailing trend in the movement of output itself.

A Simple Multiplier-Accelerator Model of the Business Cycle

Although any one scholar, insisting that his explanation of the business cycle is the only correct one, can probably be shown to be wrong, the explanations surveyed in the previous section, as a group, are not so bad. To show this, let us perform an intellectual experiment, using the tools developed so far. Let us postulate that the broad features of the U.S. economy, and its behavior can be described as follows:

1. Consumption demand consists of two parts: an autonomous portion (independent of GNP) of originally $10 billion per period, plus an induced portion equal to 0.4 times the *level* of the *previous* GNP.

2. Investment demand consists of an autonomous portion of originally $80 billion per year, plus an induced portion equal to one half the *change* of GNP in the previous period.

3. Government demand and net export demand are both autonomous, equaling $100 billion and $12 billion per period, respectively.

4. Actual GNP in each period adjusts to aggregate demand. The economy is operating well below its productive capacity. Hence, any change in aggregate demand leads to a change in real GNP and employment, not to a change in the level of prices.

All the above are, of course, assumptions, and their validity would have to be investigated thoroughly were we to attempt to say something definite about reality. Yet, the assumptions are not unreasonable. When discussing the consumption demand schedule, we so far have avoided the question of timing entirely. We only postulated that (using the earlier example) with each $1 increase in gross national income, aggregate consumption demand would rise by 40 cents. We did not ask about the time lag between the income increase and the additional consumer demand. It is at least conceivable that the income earned in one period is not disposed of (as spending or saving) until the next period. Think of people earning income throughout May, getting paid on May 31, and spending or saving their May income in June. Or think of a family getting $20,000 a year of income from 1960 through 1969, but only $10,000 from 1970 on. Might they not out of sheer habit spend in 1970 as if they still enjoyed the higher income of 1969, only adjusting their spending in 1971 to the new lower level required by the sad facts of 1970? In these cases, consumption spending of one period (June or 1970 or 1971) depended on income of a previous period (May or 1969 or 1970).

Something like this has now been assumed to hold for consumers as a group. Now suppose we start out observing our hypothetical economy at an original equilibrium as depicted earlier in Figure 7.1 GNP IN EQUILIBRIUM. For simplicity, let us assume the economy has been at this same equilibrium for years. GNP was and is $336⅔ billion. Aggregate demand is the same: autonomous consumption demand is $10 billion; induced consumption demand is 0.4 times last year's GNP, or $134⅔ billion; autonomous investment demand is $80 billion; induced investment demand is 0.5 times last year's GNP change (which was zero), or zero; government demand is $100 billion; and net export demand is $12 billion. This is shown by the year 1 column of Figure 8.3 MULTIPLIER AND ACCELERATOR AT WORK.

Now suppose, as we did earlier, in Chapter 7, that autonomous consumption demand falls permanently by $8 billion and autonomous investment demand falls permanently by $40 billion. That is, starting in year 2, autonomous consumer spending is only $2 billion a year. Autonomous investment spending is only $40 billion. As we calculated earlier (page 159), the ultimate result (at least in the absence of an accelerator) was for GNP to drop to $256⅔ billion. Now we can watch how long it takes and how (if ever) we get there. The immediate result in year 2 is only for aggregate demand and GNP to fall by $48 billion to $288⅔ billion (see column (2)).

In year 3, further effects set in. Induced consumption now drops from its year 2 level of $134⅔ billion to 0.4 times previous GNP, or to 0.4 × $288⅔ billion = $115.47 billion. Add autonomous consumption of $2 billion to this, and you get the total shown in the figure under C. Induced investment appears on the scene equal to 0.5 times previous GNP change, or 0.5 × −$48 billion = −$24 billion. Watch the minus signs: Businessmen *reduce* inventories or *fail to replace* buildings and equipment to this extent. Add autonomous investment of $40 billion to this, and you get the total shown for I in the figure. GNP drops further. See column 3. And note something else: GNP has dropped *below* the figure previously calculated when we only considered the multiplier. (That figure was $256⅔ billion.) The accelerator has accelerated the movement of GNP! This is only common sense. If the original spending cut by some households and businesses leads not only to further cuts in the spending of households thrown into unemployment (negative induced consumption), but also to cuts in their employers' demand for equipment (negative induced investment), the effect must be greater.

Figure 8.3 MULTIPLIER AND ACCELERATOR AT WORK

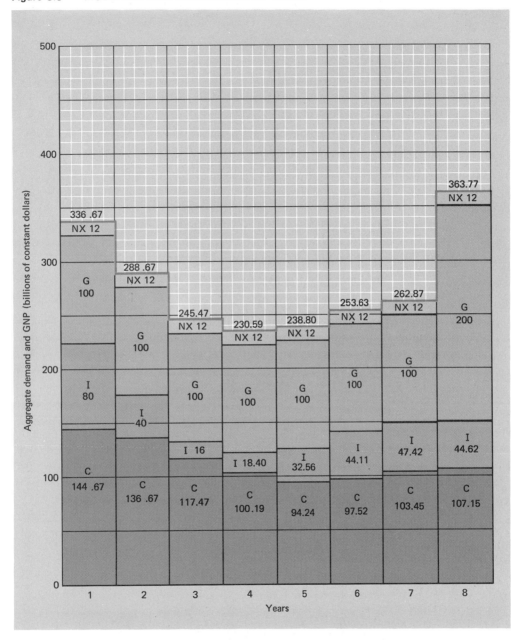

A multiplier-accelerator model of the business cycle shows how exogenous and endogenous forces combine to create an erratic course of GNP (top line of blocks). Note that the consumption and investment expenditure components shown represent the sum of autonomous and induced spending.
Assumptions:

Autonomous consumption demand = $10 billion year 1 and earlier, $2 billion year 2 and later.
Induced consumption demand = 0.4 times previous year's GNP.
Autonomous investment demand = $80 billion year 1 and earlier, $40 billion year 2 and later.
Induced investment demand = 0.5 times previous year's GNP change.
Autonomous government demand = $100 billion all years through 7, then $200 billion.
Autonomous net export demand = $12 billion all years.
GNP in any one year equals the sum of the above six demands in that year.

Nor have we seen the end of it. Watch column (4). Induced consumption in year 4 becomes 0.4 × \$245.47 billion, or \$98.19 billion. Thus, total consumption is \$100.19 billion. Induced investment becomes 0.5 × −\$43.20 billion, or −\$21.60 billion. It is less negative than before because the GNP decline has slowed down. As a result, total investment demand (including the remaining \$40 billion of autonomous demand) is now up.

Again, look at column (5). Induced consumption in year 5 falls to \$92.24 billion, because the previous year's GNP continued to fall. (As always, total consumption is \$2 billion above the induced portion.) Induced investment demand continues to rise to a less negative number, because the GNP decline continued to decelerate. It becomes half the previous GNP change, or −\$7.44 billion. Hence, total investment continues to rise also, and, lo and behold, GNP itself is up.

This is, indeed, a most remarkable result. Although there has not been a single autonomous change since year 1, the decline in GNP induced by these changes contained the very seeds of revival! The data for years 6 and 7 show how the revival continues.

In year 6, both induced consumption and induced investment rise, to \$95.52 billion (0.4 × \$238.80 billion) and \$4.11 billion (0.5 × +\$8.21 billion), respectively. In year 7, they rise further, to \$101.45 billion and \$7.42 billion, respectively. (Can you tell why?)

There is no need to go further. You undoubtedly see the point. We saw in the previous chapter how GNP has a tendency to settle at a level of equilibrium, where aggregate demand for and aggregate supply of new output are equal. We saw how any change in autonomous demand or in the marginal propensity to consume will cause a displacement of GNP to a new equilibrium. Now we have seen how the reaching of a new equilibrium may take years and involve cyclical movements of the GNP on the way. If you ignored for the moment the year 8 data shown in Figure 8.3 and pursued our example further, you would find GNP eventually reaching and maintaining the previously calculated new equilibrium of \$256⅔ billion. But there is no reason to believe that only one disturbance can occur at a time or that no disturbance can occur unless we are in a position of equilibrium. It may well happen that one or more new disturbances will arise before the new equilibrium is reached. Suppose that in year 8 government demand shoots up to \$200 billion because of a war. Immediately, GNP would spurt ahead (as shown in Figure 8.3), with all kinds of consequences in future years.

As a result of all these changes being *superimposed* on the late effects of the disturbance in year 1, actual GNP in year 8 rises way beyond the previously pursued equilibrium. In fact, the equilibrium is now different. Quite probably, however, before it is ever reached, a new disturbance will have led the economy into chasing after still another equilibrium.

An Evaluation of Cycle Theories

Now you can see why the theories of the business cycle *as a group* have some validity. Although we cannot say that business cycles are always caused by households becoming thriftier, businessmen becoming pessimistic, wars starting, or any one of the factors mentioned earlier, we can say that all these may well contribute to the erratic course of GNP observed in reality. It takes little imagination to perceive in the top line of Figure 8.3 MULTIPLIER AND

ACCELERATOR AT WORK a business cycle such as we saw in Figure 8.1 U.S. GNP: ACTUAL VS. TREND or in the actual U.S. data of Figure 5.3 THE HISTORY OF U.S. GNP. In reality, of course, a multitude of disturbances such as we have postulated here occur every year. To the extent that disturbances that tend to raise GNP are more numerous or more powerful than disturbances that tend to lower GNP, the long-run trend is upward. Even the unsophisticated model we have discussed would predict, as a result of exogenous forces, strengthened by endogenous ones, an erratic course of actual GNP, as businessmen continually adjust the level of output to ever-changing levels of aggregate demand. Thus, the degree of resource utilization varies over time, as does the level of real GNP.

At times, real GNP may be very close to its potential. If aggregate demand rises in such a situation of full employment, businessmen will try to hire idle resources that do not exist, bidding up resource prices in general. Higher money incomes will in turn raise aggregate demand further, therefore also bidding up the prices of outputs. We will have a classic case of *demand-pull inflation*. At first in some industries, then in others, and then in most, aggregate demand will come to exceed the value, at current prices, of potential GNP, causing a rise not in real output but in most prices instead. The price rise will be checked when aggregate demand, driven hither and yon by ever-changing exogenous forces and multiplied by rounds of respending, finally falls. As aggregate demand continues to fall, real GNP and employment will fall again below their potentials.

FORECASTING THE BUSINESS CYCLE

For anyone interested in eliminating the business cycle, that is, in eliminating unemployment and inflation, it is tempting to *forecast* the business cycle of the real world. If we had a workable model of our economy, such as the one we have been using, we could predict the result of any autonomous change. Then we could *engineer* changes such that the GNP moves in the direction we approve! If the assumed data in column (1) of Figure 8.3 MULTIPLIER AND ACCELERATOR AT WORK corresponded to U.S. reality, if the U.S. economy were correctly described by the four behavioral assumptions made earlier, and if a change occurred as in year 2, then we could predict that U.S. GNP in year 6, *in the absence of further autonomous changes*, would be $253.63 billion, and so on. If that implied widespread unemployment, we could take measures in advance to prevent this from happening. Like a driver whose eyes tell him that his car is heading for the ditch, we might turn the steering wheel and change course. To "see" where the economy is going, we must learn as much as possible about it and try to predict where it is headed.

Economists have tried to do just that. They have used a great variety of methods, one of which is the *econometric model*. This is a set of equations describing, in as simple terms as possible, the behavior of an economic system with the help of variables that actually have been *measured* (hence econo*metric*). Forecasts of up to 1 year have in fact been very successful. Table 8.2 FORECASTING SUCCESSES, for instance, shows the forecasting record of the model used by the University of Michigan's Research Seminar in Quantitative Economics. The data are arranged in the same form as the official statistics in Chapter 5. Note that the

Table 8.2   FORECASTING SUCCESSES

YEAR		GNP	PERSONAL CONSUMPTION EXPENDITURES	GROSS PRIVATE DOMESTIC INVESTMENT	GOVERNMENT PURCHASES OF COMMODITIES AND SERVICES		NET EXPORTS
		Y	C	I	G		NX
1952	Actual	395.1	239.4	60.5	92.1		3.0
1953	Forecast	409.9	246.7	55.6		107.6	
1953	Actual	412.8	250.8	61.2	99.8	100.9	1.1
1954	Forecast	408.4	260.4	57.9		90.1	
1954	Actual	407.0	255.7	59.4	88.9	91.9	3.0
1955	Forecast	411.6	260.8	73.5		77.3	
1955	Actual	438.0	274.2	75.4	85.2	88.4	3.2
1956	Forecast	446.9	279.5	82.0		85.4	
1956	Actual	446.1	281.4	74.3	85.3	90.3	5.0
1957	Forecast	453.7	288.3	74.5		90.9	
1957	Actual	452.5	288.2	68.8	89.3	95.5	6.2
1958	Forecast	450.4	289.6	66.0		94.8	
1958	Actual	447.3	290.1	60.9	94.2	96.4	2.2
1959	Forecast	456.7	296.0	58.3	97.8		4.6
1959	Actual	475.9	307.3	73.6	94.7		0.3
1960	Forecast	484.8	312.6	74.9	96.5		0.8
1960	Actual	487.7	316.1	72.4	94.9		4.3
1961	Forecast	496.7	323.2	69.4	100.0		4.1
1961	Actual	497.2	322.5	69.0	100.5		5.1
1962	Forecast	530.3	342.0	74.9	109.8		3.6
1962	Actual	529.8	338.4	79.4	107.5		4.5
1963	Forecast	548.6	354.5	79.4	110.1		4.6
1963	Actual	551.0	353.3	82.5	109.6		5.6
1964	Forecast	581.0	371.1	89.7	113.3		6.9
1964	Actual	581.1	373.7	87.8	111.2		8.3
1965	Forecast	605.4	385.3	98.9	118.6		2.6
1965	Actual	617.8	397.7	99.2	114.7		6.2
1966	Forecast[a]	653.5	413.2	109.6	126.8		3.9
1966	Actual	657.1	417.8	108.8	126.5		4.0
1967	Forecast	683.7	435.4	110.6	136.0		1.7
1967	Actual	673.1	430.5	99.5	140.7		2.4
1968	Forecast	703.8	448.6	105.6	148.2		1.4
1968	Actual	706.7	450.9	106.9	149.2		−0.3
1969[b]	Forecast	713.1	453.1	104.4	152.7		2.9

[a] As of April 1966.

[b] Students eager to judge the accuracy of the 1969 forecast should be sure to use preliminary actual data, in 1958 dollars.

Forecasting record of the Michigan econometric model in billions of 1958 dollars. Source: Forecasts calculated from data supplied by the Department of Economics, The University of Michigan. These forecasts were made by Professor Daniel B. Suits and the staff of the Research Seminar in Quantitative Economics at The University of Michigan. Each forecast was prepared and publicly presented during November preceding the year forecast. For purposes of this table, however, forecast and actual values have been converted to 1958 dollars for uniformity of comparison.

symbol I refers to *actual* investment, wanted or not, and is not necessarily identical with investment demand. All forecasts were made in early November preceding the year to which they apply, for example, the 1953 forecast in November 1952. The accuracy of the record speaks for itself. Of particular importance were the correct forecasts of a decline in real GNP in 1954 and 1958.

The model used in 1969 consisted of about sixty statistical equations. Personal consumption expenditures were explained by four separate equations. We have assumed that consumer demand is partly dependent on previous income, partly on other factors that we called autonomous. In fact, a similar road was taken by the Michigan forecasters who explained C by a *single* equation until the 1955 forecast. As you can see from Table 8.2, the 1955 forecast is one of two that were wide off the mark; also, it was the C component of GNP that was so badly predicted. In 1955, consumer demand for new automobiles was unusually strong, and failure to predict this accounted for much of the error. As a result, various types of consumer spending (on autos, other durables, nondurables, and services) have since been forecast separately; different kinds of consumer spending may well depend on different factors, even if all are strongly influenced by disposable personal income and hence GNP. The 1969 model, for instance, made a separate estimate for consumer expenditures on automobiles (which was one of several C equations). It has been found to depend on only *part* of total disposable personal income, namely that part *not* received in kind, or as unemployment insurance, old age annuity, or other transfer payments. This makes good sense, because he who receives income in kind, as "free room and board," for example, automatically "spends" it on room and board. He cannot demand automobiles with that income. The unemployed, the aged, and the indigent may receive money income, but also do not exercise appreciable influence on automobile demand.

Consumer demand for automobiles was also found dependent on the number of cars recently purchased and put on the road. The bigger this number in any one year, the smaller the demand for new cars in the next year.

On the other hand, it was also found that the demand for automobiles rose the larger the number of cars ready to be scrapped, and that it fell with any increase in the unemployment rate of males over 25.

Finally the automobile equation has at times linked demand to consumers' ownership of liquid assets, such as money, savings accounts, and government bonds. Again, this is not surprising. We have argued above, when deriving our hypothetical consumption demand schedule, that spending in any period is likely to be higher the higher income is. Here, we see that some forms of income are less likely than others to be used for the purchase of particular goods. We also argued that *given* income, autonomous forces (such as changes in wealth and age distribution) may change consumer spending and hence shift the consumption demand line. We can now see the truth of this with respect to purchases of automobiles: *given* income, spending is encouraged if there are few new cars on the road, if there are many old ones, if consumers hold large liquid assets, and if few men are unemployed.

The Michigan model explains all other types of expenditures in similar detail. The 1959 forecast, which was the second one to be rather wide off the mark, induced the forecasters to find a more detailed explanation of investment expenditures. In particular, separate explanations of inventory change for durable and nondurable goods were introduced, because a major source of error in 1959 was the neglect of the effects of government defense orders on durable inventories.

THE POSSIBILITY OF ECONOMIC POLICY

The Michigan model is a continually evolving one, mistakes of the past being taken as an incentive and pointer to do better in the future. There are good reasons for this, for, as we have noted, forecasting is not just undertaken for "the fun of it." Its real purpose is to help us formulate an intelligent *economic policy*, measures by government to *eliminate* the business cycle. After all, to know that something *is* does not mean that it has to be. People may have smallpox, but it may be possible to prevent this. We may have a business cycle, but it is not necessary to have it. Actually, we understand the mechanism of business cycles fairly well, just as doctors understand the causes of smallpox. This enables us, if we choose, to anticipate and prevent the undesirable from happening. Here, forecasting of economic activity is most useful. Yet, we should notice that we could do without it, acting after the fact, just as a doctor can help a man even *after* he has contracted a disease. Often there are cures for ills when we understand neither the causes of the disease nor exactly how the medicine effects the cure. Economic policy, therefore, does not depend on forecasting nor on the fullest possible understanding of business cycles. *Anticipatory* economic policy (like preventive medicine) does, but there is still room for reacting after the fact (like treating a disease in progress).

The U.S. Congress has recognized officially that the swings of GNP, which we have called the *business cycle*, are not an immutable fact of nature. In 1946, Congress passed the so-called *Employment Act*, stating:

The Congress declares that it is the continuing policy and responsibility of the Federal Government to use all practicable means . . . for the purpose of creating and maintaining . . . conditions under which there will be afforded useful employment opportunities, including self-employment, for those able, willing, and seeking to work, and to promote maximum employment, production, and purchasing power.

The same act provided that each January the President submit to Congress an *Economic Report* setting forth the levels of employment and production obtained, their trends, a review of government policies during the past year, and a program of such policies for the next one. The President was to be advised in the preparation of the report and on all matters it deals with by a *Council of Economic Advisers* created in the Executive Office of the President and composed of three members and a staff of experts. These have usually consisted of professors on leave of absence from colleges and universities. Finally, the act established a *Joint Economic Committee*, composed of seven members of the Senate and seven of the House, to make a continuing study of matters relating to the report and, by March 1 of each year, to issue a report containing its findings with respect to the recommendations of the President's report.

In short, Congress has recognized that our economic ills will not cure themselves, that there are drugs to cure them, and that no one but the federal government can administer those drugs. It is also true that many Americans do not agree. To paraphrase President Kennedy, many Americans hold fast to the clichés of their forebears, subjecting all facts to a prefabricated set of interpretations, enjoying the comfort of opinion without the discomfort of thought. As a result, they try to solve the problems of the business cycle by incantations from the forgotten past. Being distracted by their own emotions, they sink in a bog of sterile acrimony, refusing to believe that "government hands off" will not cure our economic ills. "The great enemy of the truth," argued the President, "is very often not the lie, deliberate, contrived, and dishonest, but the *myth*, persistent, persuasive, and unrealistic."[2] It divides our efforts and keeps us from doing what we might.

The least we can do, therefore, is to hold in abeyance our emotional response, to take a long, hard look, with an open mind, at the possibility and consequences of governmental policy, deliberately designed to raise the GNP permanently to its potential. This is the subject matter of the following chapters.

SUMMARY

1. The theory of income determination developed in Chapter 7 can be expanded to incorporate dynamic considerations. If we consider matters of timing (which variable *when* affects what other variable *when*), we can develop models of an economy that simulate the business cycle. The irregular movements of real GNP around its trend, together with the concomitant phenomena of changing levels of employment and prices, are referred to as the *business cycle*. The business cycle certainly does not exhibit anything like the definite periodicities found in astronomy.

2. The exogenous theories of the business cycle postulate that cycles are caused by forces outside the economy, beyond the control or predictive power of the economist. Among others, such forces may involve natural catastrophes, political upheavals, great innovations, and the changing moods of large masses of people.

3. The endogenous theories of the business cycle make internal forces in the economy primarily responsible for the course of real GNP. The accelerator theory is an example.

4. The accelerator theory relates at least a portion of investment demand to *changes* in other variables, for instance in GNP. A study of this theory shows that it is possible for the level of investment demand to rise or fall just because the rate at which GNP rises or falls changes. Thus, a change in the rate at which GNP rises may turn this rise into a fall by affecting the level of investment demand. Similarly, a change in the rate at which GNP falls may turn this fall into a rise by affecting the level of investment demand.

5. A combined multiplier-accelerator model of the economy shows that even a single exogenous change, carried on by the accelerator, may create cyclical fluctuations of the GNP.

6. There is no single best theory to explain the business cycle. The economy is built in a certain way (incorporating such internal mechanisms as the multiplier and the accel-

---

[2] From the President's commencement address, Yale University, June 11, 1962. Italics added.

erator), and any one of many possible exogenous forces may set off the business cycle. It is like a pendulum that is built to swing and that will swing no matter who or what pushes it.

7   However, we cannot say that swings of GNP are inevitable. Economists who are aware of the structure of economic relationships may be able to predict and prevent the business cycle. Indeed, this is why we study it. One way of prediction is made possible by the econometric model.

8   On the basis of such prediction, economic policy may be pursued, that is, measures may be undertaken to prevent undesirable fluctuations of GNP. These measures also may be undertaken without forecasts, after the fact. To use the above image, if you push the pendulum, I know that it will swing, and if I want to prevent that, I can. If I know when you will do what, I can push in exactly the opposite way so as to nullify your attempts. The pendulum never gets to swing. However, I can still stop it from swinging once it has started.

9   Economics has made great strides in the past 30 years. This involved, as we saw in the previous chapter, the Keynesian breakthrough in theory. It involved, as we saw in earlier chapters, a vast increase in factual knowledge (the development after World War I of price level and GNP data, after World War II of labor force, employment, and unemployment data). It also involved, with the advance of computer technology, the ability to process vast masses of data and to construct elaborate econometric models used in analysis and forecasting. Finally, it has led economists, through the Employment Act of 1946, from academia to the world of practical affairs.

TERMS[3]

accelerator	Employment Act of 1946
accelerator theory	endogenous theory
boom	exogenous theory
business cycle	Joint Economic Committee
Council of Economic Advisers	Juglar cycle
cycle amplitude	Kitchin cycle
cycle length	Kondratieff wave
econometric model	marginal capital-output ratio
	trend

QUESTIONS FOR REVIEW AND DISCUSSION

1   Why study business cycles?

2   "The business cycle is not a cycle at all." Discuss.

3   Make a list of events that might be classified as exogenous causes of business cycles. How exactly might each affect aggregate demand to start the cycle?

[3] Terms are defined in the Glossary at the end of the book.

4   "The accelerator theory teaches us that investment demand may fall or rise, regardless of whether income is falling or rising. In short, anything goes, and it is a nebulous theory at best." Discuss.

5   The accelerator theory used in this chapter assumes that investment demand may follow a change in GNP with a lag. What accounts for the lag? How can one possibly produce *first* and then demand and make the capital stock necessary for that production *later*?

6   "The accelerator theory is confusing. According to it, a decrease in the capital stock may become desirable at times. But how can the capital stock possibly decrease? If one firm sells a machine, another firm has it!" Comment.

7   The text says (on page 173) that under certain circumstances "investment demand will arise." Why did it not say "investment demand will *rise?*"

8   Give a *verbal* explanation of how multiplier and accelerator may interact with each other.

9   Investment spending in year 8 (Figure 8.3 MULTIPLIER AND ACCELERATOR AT WORK) is falling; it had been rising before. Explain.

10   Could you draw a column for year 9 in Figure 8.3 MULTIPLIER AND ACCELERATOR AT WORK, predicting, in effect, that year's GNP and its components? (Assume there are no further autonomous changes in demand.)

11   Suppose your prediction (previous question) were accurate. Suppose also that economists have estimated that the resources available in year 9 could, if fully employed, produce at most a real GNP of $480 billion. How would you characterize the economic outlook for that year?

12   Answer question 11 on the assumption that maximum real GNP is $400 billion.

13   If you were a member of the President's Council of Economic Advisers, what policy action on the part of government would you propose, if any, to deal with the economic outlook predicted? (Refer to questions 11 and 12.)

14   "During the course of the business cycle the production of durable goods (such as houses, machines, and refrigerators) fluctuates more than that of nondurable goods (such as food)." Why do you think this is so?

15   "We can talk ourselves into a depression." Illustrate this with a numerical example, using column (8), Figure 8.3 MULTIPLIER AND ACCELERATOR AT WORK, as a starting point.

16   "What goes up must come down." Does this apply to GNP? Couldn't a boom go on forever?

17   In plain English, what does it mean when autonomous investment demand is positive and induced investment demand is negative?

18   Write to the Research Seminar in Quantitative Economics, Department of Economics, The University of Michigan, Ann Arbor, Michigan, and ask for their economic forecast for this year. Study it.

19   Try building your own econometric model. (You may derive inspiration from the material obtained in question 18 or from the work kit introducing the chapter.)

20   "One cannot pursue economic policy unless one knows how to forecast economic change." Evaluate. Is it true? Why or why not?

Passing the Buck: Counterfeiters Find Anything Will Work

More Bogus Bills Palmed Off Despite Decline in Quality; Underworld Heavies Join In

By Kenneth G. Slocum
Staff Reporter of The Wall Street Journal

It's the same old story. Some craftsmen build an art into an industry. Then someone figures out how to make a machine do the work. Then the craftsmen can't compete against the machines, so they die out. Then the public is left with mass-produced, but often shoddy, goods.

Now it's happening once again. In the counterfeiting business.

"We used to examine an expert, hand-engraved counterfeit and say, 'Aha! This obviously is the hand of old J. Q. Muggs—he always made that little mistake'," says a white-haired Secret Service agent. "Today it can be any bum with an offset press."

A successful counterfeiter today needn't even have an offset press. Indeed, some authorities claim a Xerox machine will do. Just Xerox a five or a ten on plain white paper, wrinkle the copy, put some coffee stains on it to add color and a worn look and hand it to the nearest cashier. Incredible as it may seem, the chances are fairly good that it will be accepted, even though one side is blank.

If it isn't accepted, of course, there could be a bit of a problem. Counterfeiting is a Federal crime punishable by 15 years in prison for each phony bill produced.

But plenty of people apparently think the risk is worth it. There's no indication how much bogus money is floating around, but the amount that people are getting stuck with is rising sharply. (The person possessing the phony bill when it's discovered is the loser, unless he can prove who gave it to him.)

In the year ended last June 30, the loss to citizens totaled $2.9 million, up nearly 75% from a year earlier and 11 times the loss in 1960. The 1968 figure was the highest since the Treasury Department started keeping records 28 years ago.

The increase is not the result of a new vigilance on the part of bank tellers and cashiers. If anything, these people are becoming more lax, Secret Service men say. Bank tellers used to be experienced money handlers, says one agent, "but today, more often than not, they're kids who have just started to work."

The Big Guy & the Little Guy

In the past, most counterfeiting operations consisted of a skilled engraver and a few people who passed the money for him. But now, say Secret Service agents, the lucrative field is being entered by two new types of criminals: The big-time gangster and the ordinary guy who runs a little short of cash.

"We're seeing more of the underworld heavy in counterfeiting," says one official of the Secret Service, which is charged with catching counterfeiters as well as with protecting Presidents. "He's often the guy who already has a big distribution system for moonshine, narcotics or pornography, and he simply introduces counterfeit money into it."

As an example of how extensive a ring can be, Federal officials cite one they broke up last year in Birmingham, Ala. It was distributing phony bills in nearly every state in the union, the authorities say. So far, they have made 233 arrests in connection with the operation. Some 45 arrests have been made in connection with a ring passing $20 bills in the Cleveland area, but the printing operation still hasn't been found and there are indications the surface has only been scratched.

"Famous counterfeiting operations of the past were nickel and dime operations compared with those of today," says a Secret Service official in Washington.

On the other hand, there still are a lot of counterfeiters who almost literally run nickel and dime operations. These are people who need a few bucks to weather some crisis, and who have access to a printing press or, perhaps, a Xerox machine. A Kentucky newspaper reporter blamed his counterfeiting on heavy losses at the races. An Atlanta executive explained to authorities: "A man can keep his wife with little difficulty—it's the second woman that gets expensive."

Anything Goes

These amateurs are discovering that the gullible public will accept almost anything as legal tender. A few weeks ago an enterprising person in Richmond, Va., simply inked an extra zero on one corner of a $10 bill, submitted it for a minor purchase in a department store and got change for $100.

Some stores also give change for phony money that people get as ads. This money is close enough to real money to catch the consumer's eye but different enough to comply with laws forbidding duplication of currency. Sometimes it says "United States of Arenica." One $10 bill recently accepted as real said: "The Unique Skates of America will pay to any sucker."

Recently, a public-spirited newspaper, eager to help its city curb a counterfeiting wave, printed a picture of a fake $10 bill on the front page. One reader clipped it out, pasted it on light cardboard, wrinkled it a bit and passed it successfully at a local store.

Moans a Secret Service agent: "Nobody looks at his money anymore."

The Wall Street Journal, March 18, 1969

9

money and banking

ONE WAY GOVERNMENT can influence the course of the business cycle is through general monetary policy, the exercise of its power to *create and destroy money*. We have already had a glimpse of this possibility when we noted how consumption or investment demands may vary with the availability of credit to households or businesses, respectively, and how the classical economists feared that government might "misbehave" and cause an economy to be ravaged by inflation. In fact, the lessons taught for so long by the classical economists have been somewhat imperfectly understood, yet all too well accepted by the general public. The very thought of deliberately creating and destroying money immediately induces horror in many people and brings out a strong irrational resistance to any kind of monetary policy. Money is almost regarded as too holy to be tampered with by mere human beings. Certainly, argues the public, dire consequences shall befall the man who violates its intrinsic "soundness" by creating or destroying it for "mere" expediency's sake. Strong are the emotions, but weak is the logic, for the classical doctrines apply to a world of full employment that is not the world in which we always live. In this chapter, we shall study the meaning of money and the nature of banking; in the next, how monetary policy works.

THE IMPORTANCE OF MONEY

We take money for granted. We hardly ever look at it. (Consider the news story introducing this chapter.) Yet money is one of the most remarkable of human inventions. It is at least as old as the written language. All but the most primitive societies have used it. It seems to be an essential tool of civilization. Indeed, it is difficult to imagine life without it. Consider how difficult it would be to carry on the many trillion dollars' worth of transactions we annually handle in the United States. If we had to rely on barter, our economy would collapse. If you could do nothing but paint houses and wanted bread, red cabbage, and a haircut, you would have a hard time finding a baker, farmer, and barber who just required a loaf of bread's worth of painting, a cabbage head's worth, or a haircut's worth. Even indirect barter would be next to impossible. You might take a pig in return for painting another farmer's house, but how could you convert such an indivisible good into bread, cabbage, and a haircut? How could you store it if you did not care to spend your income just yet? And notice how a price system to guide the allocation of resources would be impossible. We would have to express the terms of exchange of every good and resource in terms of every other good and resource. Take the above example, where we trade labor for bread, cabbages, and haircuts. We would have to know the price of labor in terms of the three goods, plus the price of bread in terms of cabbage and haircuts, plus the price of cabbage in terms of haircuts—a total of six prices. Each time we add a good or resource, we add as many prices as there were previous goods or resources (one for the new item in terms of each old one). If we had 3,650 items, there would be 6,659,425 prices among them. If each of us make ten transactions per day, there would have to be 3,650 calculations per year per person. Given a population of 200 million, people in the United States would have to figure out prices 1.3 quadrillion times a year. Taking just 10 seconds each time, this would take 462.5 billion man-days of work. This is over six times as many as we would have available if every man, woman, and child worked 8 hours a day every day of the year!

Thus, money is seen to be absolutely essential. It enables us to have a *unit of account,* a common language with which to express the value of everything, and a *medium of exchange,* a common means by which to exchange the millions of goods and resources that change hands every year. Realizing its enormous importance, let us look more closely at what this thing we call money is.

THE MEANING OF MONEY

Does not every first grader know the meaning of money? To some extent yes, but this will not do for us. Just as in the cases of unemployment, the price level, or the GNP, we must clearly define this important term before we can use it. As before, this involves arbitrary decisions. At different times and in different places, these decisions may be made differently. We know in fact that money has not always meant the same thing to all people. The first money used may well have been *full-bodied money.* Something that had an intrinsic value, a usefulness quite separate from its role as money, was worth *as a good* just as much as it was *as money.* Cattle have been used in this way. (Hence, the term *pecuniary* from the Latin *pecus* meaning cattle.) A cow might be held for its own sake, to give milk, butter, and cheese, and eventually meat and hide, or it might be used as an intermediary, having been received for a chariot today, only to be given up for twelve geese tomorrow. In the history of man, all kinds of economic goods have in this way served as full-bodied money. The lists includes, besides animals, slaves, wool, wine, salt (hence "salary" and "being worth one's salt"), cheese, hard candy, pepper, cocoa beans, tea, tobacco, nails, pots, boats, shells, feathers, sharks' teeth, cigarettes, wampum beads, and precious metals. Many of these have been used and are being used in this century. (This author used cigarettes for all economic transactions throughout most of 1945 in Germany.) It happened that precious metals gained especially wide acceptance, and there are, of course, good reasons for this. Gold and silver, unlike cows, are durable, easily divisible into homogeneous units, and easily transportable. Hence, they have been widely used (as early as 2000 B.C.) as a medium of exchanging or valuing the wide variety of assets that exist. This historical accident has nothing to do with the *logic* of money, and it is certainly not true that money *must* be identical with gold or silver. As we have seen, many other goods have served and are serving this function.

Nor must money be full-bodied. Men found out very quickly, for instance, that there is an even easier way to carry on transactions than carrying around gold or any other kind of full-bodied money. These goods could be left behind in a special place (a bank?) with a trusted person (a banker?) in return for paper receipts acknowledging the fact (of deposit?). And these paper receipts could be used much more easily than cows or gold to carry on transactions. These receipts were, in fact, *representative of full-bodied money.* Whoever held them could, if he chose, redeem them in full-bodied money; but there was little need for it because he could just as easily go out and "redeem" them for other goods by passing on the receipt to someone else. Why bother to get gold or a cow from the "bank" for a gold receipt or a cow receipt if I really want bread and can easily get it by passing on the receipt to the baker. If he wants gold or a cow, he can redeem the receipt, but he will probably just pass it along. As we shall see, such gold receipts (called *gold certificates*) still exist in U.S. banks today, but they have not legally been held by the general public since 1934.

We can now go a step further. Not only does money *not* have to be *identical with* gold or any other economic good, it also does not have to be *redeemable at the place of issue in gold*, or any other economic good. This is not very satisfying emotionally to most people, but it is the only logical conclusion to be derived from the facts. Unromantic as it may sound, money derives its value not from any one particular good we can exchange it for (gold or cows), but from its exchangeability for economic goods in general. Even if a country has no precious metals at all, as long as other commodities and services can be bought with its money, that money has value. This is why everyone would accept it. This is why all kinds of things, worthless or of little usefulness in and of themselves, have been used successfully as money, by exchanging for economic goods that everybody considers of vastly greater value than whatever it is that serves as money. This is why men have used giant stones, porpoise teeth, leather tokens, cartridge shells, and woodpecker scalps as money—why they are now, in the United States, using *nothing but IOU's!* This may come as another shock, but we can easily see how IOU's *could* provide an ideal medium of exchange.

IOU's as Money

Suppose John Doe bought a car, but instead of paying for it he handed to the car dealer an IOU stating "I owe to Mr. Jones $2,000 and promise to pay that amount to him or whoever presents this certificate whenever it is demanded. New York, this 1st day of January, 1970. Signed John Doe." Clearly, Mr. Jones could demand *something* worth $2,000 from John Doe at any time. But why bother? He wants something from Mr. Smith; so why not get $2,000 worth of another good from Mr. Smith, handing *him* the IOU of John Doe? If Mr. Smith knows John Doe, there should be no problem. Mr. Smith gladly hands to Mr. Jones $2,000 of goods because he knows that at any time he could get $2,000 of *something* from John Doe. But why should *he* bother? Mr. Smith probably wants something from Mr. Brown. So why not get $2,000 worth of another good from Mr. Brown, handing *him* the IOU of John Doe? If Mr. Brown knows John Doe, there should be no problem either. Mr. Brown gladly hands Mr. Smith $2,000 of goods because he knows that at anytime he could get $2,000 of *something* from John Doe! And so it could go on forever. John Doe's IOU is being used as *money*. When he signed it, he *created* money, getting something (the car) for nothing (a scrap of paper). As long as no one asks *him* for $2,000 worth of goods, he is richer by that amount just as a successful counterfeiter would be! If anyone ever did ask him to hand over $2,000 worth of goods (say, a piece of land), he would be neither richer nor poorer, having bartered in the end the land for the car. Taking back his IOU, he would tear it to shreds, thereby *destroying* what was used as money. But the IOU *could* circulate forever. John Doe would be richer, no one would be any poorer (we shall note an exception to this in due course), because Mr. Jones got from Mr. Smith what he gave to John Doe, Mr. Smith retrieved from Mr. Brown what he gave to Mr. Jones, and Mr. Brown will similarly spend the "money" (Doe's IOU) whenever he pleases.

An unlikely story? It could not happen to you and me? True enough, for you and I are not very well known nor are we endowed by the Constitution with the right to make money. But now substitute the "U.S. government" for "John Doe," and our story will take on life!

Token Coins

The U.S. government makes money in just this way. It stamps some IOU's on metal, which *as metal* is worth a lot less than *as money,* just as John Doe's IOU *as paper* was hardly worth 1 cent but *as money* it bought goods of $2,000 value. These IOU's are issued by the U.S. Treasury. We call them *token coins.* They are gladly passed along forever, from the Treasury via a bank to Mr. Jones, from Mr. Jones to Mr. Smith, from Mr. Smith to Mr. Brown, and so on. *Never* are they redeemed at the Treasury, nor are they redeemable *there* in anything—not gold, cows, or anything else. Nor are they worth as metal what they are worth as money![1] Then why do we take coins? Of course, because everyone takes them; hence we can use them to get economic goods; everywhere, ironically, except at the U.S. Treasury.

Paper Bills

The Treasury also has in the past printed IOU's on paper, giving us the familiar *paper bills,* in particular, the U.S. Notes (greenbacks) and Silver Certificates. In addition, Federal Reserve Notes are issued by the Federal Reserve System (which is discussed below). All these paper bills, in denominations ranging from $1 to $10,000, are identical with John Doe's IOU— they are IOU's of the U.S. Treasury or the Federal Reserve Banks, forever circulating and noninterest bearing. (In the past, private banks also issued such paper money, but this has been illegal for some time.) Of course, on occasion such paper money does fall into the hands of the Treasury or the Federal Reserve Bank of issue, in which case the money has been "destroyed." The government has, in addition, made paper bills *legal tender.* This makes them by law (because the government says so) acceptable for all private or public debts. We can pay our taxes with them (Then money is "destroyed," as when John Doe would tear up his IOU if he did get it back.) We can pay any private debt with them, and a creditor who refuses to accept them cannot sue us for nonpayment of debt nor charge interest on debts outstanding.

---

[1] There was a point in 1963 when strong industrial demand for silver in the United States (for such things as electronics, photography, dentistry) raised the price of the metal almost to the point where it would become profitable to melt down silver coins. Suppose a quarter contained one-quarter ounce of silver and the market price of silver were $1.60 per ounce. You could melt down the quarter and sell the silver for 40 cents. To avoid that kind of situation, the U.S. government in 1963 promptly began using cheaper copper-nickel materials in the making of dimes and quarters.

Although there was a fine legal distinction prior to 1934, since that time coins also have played the role of legal tender. But this is not inscribed on coins as it is on paper bills. (Look at one.) Analogous to the case of coins, paper bills as paper are obviously worth much less than as money and are not redeemable in anything except economic goods you can buy *in the markets.*

The inscriptions on some paper bills seem to contradict this fact. The Silver Certificates are "redeemable in silver on demand" at the U.S. Treasury, but this does *not* mean that they are representatives of full-bodied money that, like warehouse receipts, would bring you for the asking one dollar's worth of the metal silver for a one dollar Silver Certificate. Instead, the Treasury will redeem them only in one dollar's worth of "silver" coins, which in turn contain a lot less metal than what would cost a dollar. This is, in fact, a remnant of an earlier age, and we should not confuse historical fact with logical necessity. At the moment, the U.S. government is in the process of destroying all Treasury paper bills, and we will eventually be left with nothing but Federal Reserve Notes—plain IOU's redeemable only in all the places where economic goods are sold. This is quite obvious when we read the inscriptions on the latest paper bills. Many earlier Federal Reserve Notes state that they are "redeemable in lawful money at the U.S. Treasury or at any Federal Reserve Bank." Similarly, the Treasury's old U.S. Notes state that "The United States of America will pay to the bearer on demand x dollars," x representing the denomination of the bill. Yet these are nonsensical inscriptions, for the only thing you can redeem a five dollar bill in (at the place of issue) is five one dollar bills or any other combination of smaller denomination coins and bills you like. It is as if John Doe will only redeem an IOU for other IOU's! These inscriptions are also in the process of being changed. The latest one dollar Federal Reserve Notes are inscribed "The United States of America—One Dollar." This does not make them anything else but IOU's. However, it acknowledges the fact that this IOU is neither interest bearing, nor redeemable in anything at the place of issue, nor worth anything in and of itself. But it does buy one dollar's worth of goods anywhere in the United States.

Demand Deposits

Finally, as you well know, there is a third type of money other than coins and paper bills. These are checking accounts or *demand deposits.* They are created and destroyed (quite legally) by private banks, called *commercial banks.* We shall discuss this process below. For the moment it is well to realize that demand deposits, also, are nothing but IOU's, in this case of a private bank, and not even stamped on metal (as in the case of coins) or printed on paper (as in the case of paper bills). Demand *deposits* is actually a bad choice of words, for it gives the impression that the bank has something *on deposit,* such as a pile of coins or paper bills or even gold, in its vault. Nothing is further from the truth. The bank has nothing at all except an *entry in one of its own books* noting the fact that the bank owes you *something* worth a certain amount. (If you have a checking account, you will regularly receive a copy of the bank's books so far as it concerns you. It is called your *bank statement.*)

This again is likely to be a shocking realization for many. There are no paper bills, no coins, no precious metals "backing up" your account. Your account is only a little number on a book, nothing else. Yet somehow it is functional, and we can easily perceive how. Let us go back to John Doe and his car purchase from Mr. Jones. What if he had not given Mr. Jones a *written* IOU corresponding to a paper bill? Imagine John Doe had just said: "I know I owe you *something* worth $2,000, and anytime you ask for it you shall get it. In the meantime, I shall make a note of it in a little black book on my desk." Mr. Jones, all-trusting, agrees. Then Mr. Jones wants to buy something from Mr. Smith and it happens to cost $2,000. He writes a letter to John Doe, asking him to stop owing $2,000 of something to Jones and to please owe it to Smith instead. Jones hands the letter to Smith who agrees and sends it to Doe. What does Doe do now? He takes out his book, crosses out the name "Jones" and puts in its place "Smith." To Smith he now owes something worth $2,000. Yet Smith wants nothing from Doe at all. He buys something from Brown. And Smith, in turn, writes a letter to Doe, asking him to stop owing $2,000 to Smith and to please owe it to Brown instead. He hands the letter to Brown, and the deal goes through. Brown promptly sends it to Doe who, of course, just changes names again in his book. So it can go on forever, unless someday someone wants something from Doe. Then he must deliver *goods* worth $2,000, and he can throw his book away.

Now substitute the name of any commercial bank for John Doe and the word "check" for "letter," and you will see the point. Demand deposits are entries in the bank's books; they are a kind of "ghost money," disembodied coins and paper bills, IOU's that *could* have been stamped on metal or *could* have been printed on paper. They are potential coins, potential paper money; they are oral IOU's if you wish, but nonetheless, they are IOU's. And they are "handed" from person to person via check. As with coins and paper money, they are accepted not because they are redeemable in full-bodied money at the bank, but because they are redeemable in goods wherever goods are for sale. This kind of money, furthermore, cannot be lost or stolen, is more easily portable than coins and paper bills, and provides an easy receipt of payment made via the canceled check (just as Jones's letter to Doe, handed to Smith and by Smith to Doe, is returned by Doe to Jones with the note "paid as requested"). Demand deposits are not legal tender, but they can be freely converted into coin and paper money. This corresponds to the goods Doe might have been ultimately asked to give to someone. (How this is possible, despite the fact that banks do *not* hold a dollar in coins or paper bills for every dollar of demand deposits, we shall see shortly.) Americans in fact make no distinction between coins, paper bills, and demand deposits. Someone who holds $11 of coins, $9 of paper bills, and a demand deposit of $100 can at any time simultaneously spend $120 on commodities and services, but he cannot get goods from the Treasury or the banks.

Defining Money by Its Functions

It is clear at this point that we cannot define money by its *substance,* for that can differ all the way from cows to cowry shells, from woodpecker scalps to IOU's. The best general definition seems to be one describing the *functions* of money, describing what it *does,* rather than what it *is*. These functions have been the same throughout history. They include, as we already noted, the use of money as a *medium of exchange* (and hence as a store of generalized purchasing power) and as a *unit of account* (and hence as a standard to evaluate all assets and liabilities, even if they are not presently being exchanged at all). In the United States, at this moment, dollars in the form of coins, paper bills, and demand deposits alone fulfill *both* these functions. Real estate, buildings, and corporate stock do not; nor do endowment life insurance policies, short-term government bonds, and savings accounts. Yet the latter three, although not accepted in payment for a grocery bill, can quite easily be exchanged for money. For this reason, they are called *near-money,* but are excluded from the official definition of money. Also excluded from that definition are coins, paper bills, and demand deposits as long as they are held by Federal Reserve and commercial banks or the U.S. government. This seems only reasonable, for we recognize in our example above that the return of an IOU to the issuer (John Doe), after having been used as money, amounts to destroying money. Even if John Doe did not tear up his own IOU but kept it, contemplating giving it to Mr. Black for a $2,000 boat, we might not want to call it money in the same sense as it was for Mr. Jones, Mr. Smith, and Mr. Brown. This *is* an arbitrary decision, but it has been made in the same way for coins and paper bills owned by any institution that creates any kind of money at all.

Similarly, John Doe may not throw away his little black book after he finally has delivered $2,000 of goods to someone. He may keep it contemplating to incur a new debt for buying a boat from Mr. Black and to record this fact in the book. In the meantime, however, he owes something only to himself. We might not want to call this money. This, too, is an arbitrary decision, but not an unreasonable one. In the same way, demand deposits owned rather than owed by any institution that creates any kind of money at all are not officially counted in the money supply.

The U.S. money supply is, therefore, defined as *the total of coins, paper bills, and demand deposits owned by the public,* which means by anyone except the U.S. Treasury, the Federal Reserve System, or the domestic commercial banks. Obviously, the latter three, the issuers of IOU's used as money, are the equivalent of our friend John Doe. Table 9.1 shows the U.S. money supply at a recent date. In addition to the figure listed there, $6.1 billion of coins and paper bills were held by domestic commercial banks. The total of coins and paper bills outside the Treasury and the Federal Reserve System included $5.7 billion of coins, $221 million of Silver Certificates, $300 million of U.S. Notes, and $43.3 billion of Federal Reserve Notes. There is also a small amount of other Treasury coin and paper money circulating that is being "retired."

Table 9.1   U.S. MONEY SUPPLY (APRIL 30, 1968)

Coins and paper bills	$43.5 billion
Demand deposits	149.5 billion
Total money supply	$193.0 billion

Source: Federal Reserve Bulletin.

The supply of near money was even larger than the money supply. The cash surrender value of life insurance policies, the value of savings deposits and savings and loan shares, and that of marketable U.S. government securities totaled to a figure several times larger than the money supply. Only a thin line separates money from these near-monies. They must be converted into money before they can be spent. But usually the inconvenience and delay involved is slight. Savings banks, although they may force depositors to wait 30 to 60 days for withdrawal, ordinarily convert at once ("on demand"). Even *certificates of deposit,* which cannot be cashed for a stated time, usually 6 months (after which interest is paid), can be sold by one holder to another in the intervening period. The same is true of short- and medium-term government IOU's, called *Treasury bills, certificates,* and *notes.* These securities mature in periods ranging from 90 days to 5 years, but any holder can easily sell them at once. It is easy to see why people store so much potential purchasing power in the form of near-money: the holder receives interest, whereas he does not if he holds money.

THE CIRCULATION OF MONEY

Now that we know the meaning of money, let us take a closer look at the way in which it circulates. This will become the basis for the discussion of how money is created and destroyed. There is nothing we have to say about the circulation of coins and paper bills. Every reader of this book is thoroughly familiar with the ways in which *cash* (that is, coins and paper bills) gets into his hands and is passed on to others. The circulation of demand deposits, however, is a much more mysterious process. What does happen between the time you write a check (asking your bank to reduce your account in favor of someone else) and the time you get it back in the monthly statement of your account? To understand this, we must look at the balance sheet of a commercial bank, and to do that we must first understand the concept of the balance sheet itself.

The Concept of a Balance Sheet

A balance sheet shows the size and composition of a firm's (or anybody's) wealth at a moment of time. The firm's wealth (net worth) consists of all the things of value it holds (assets) minus all the things of value it owes (liabilities). Thus, net worth = assets minus liabilities. Because net worth is defined as the residual, it must also be true that at any given moment, the assets are exactly balanced by liabilities plus the net worth. This is not as profound a statement as it seems, for it only says that the things of value held by the firm (assets) must be either owed to others (liabilities) or owned by the firm itself (net worth). A typical balance sheet looks like this:

BALANCE SHEET, WONDERFUL TOY CORPORATION, JANUARY 1, 1970, 8 A.M.

ASSETS		LIABILITIES AND NET WORTH	
1. Cash	$ 11,000	7. Accounts payable	$ 24,000
2. Bank deposits	2,500	8. Bonds payable	50,000
3. U.S. government bonds	500		
4. Inventories	10,000		
5. Equipment	50,000		
6. Buildings	100,000	9. Net worth	100,000
	$174,000		$174,000

It is interpreted easily enough. On January 1, 1970 (at 8 A.M.), the Wonderful Toy Corporation held (1) $11,000 of cash, in coins and paper money. It had (2) checking or savings accounts containing $2,500, as well as (3) U.S. government bonds (IOU's of the U.S. government promising repayment at a certain date of a fixed sum with interest) of $500. Its total inventories (4) of raw materials, semifinished, and finished goods were valued at $10,000; all its equipment (5), from chairs and typewriters to complex production machinery, at $50,000. Finally, (6) it held buildings of all sorts valued at $100,000.

Most of these figures were estimates, although they were the best estimates the accountant could make. It was easy enough to make exact entries for (1) and (2), but in all other cases human judgment was involved. Bonds fluctuate in value and could be listed at either cost or market price. The accountant could have evaluated inventories at cost, that is, at the amount paid to other firms to purchase them or the amount spent by the firm to manufacture them. Or, instead, he could have evaluated inventories at their current market prices. The same is true of equipment and buildings; $150,000 was probably the accountant's estimate of the minimum amount the firm could get if it sold the items in their current state. This may well be below actual market price.

In short, the accountant estimated that the firm, were it to "liquidate" itself (turn all its assets into cash), could have gotten *at least* $174,000. Could the owners have kept it all? The answer is no, as the right-hand side of our balance sheet tells us. The firm had (7) a number of unpaid bills, possibly for wages, raw materials, taxes, or fees, amounting to $24,000. It also (8) had borrowed in the past and issued its own IOU's. Such bonds of $50,000 would have had to be repaid in case of liquidation. As a result, the owners would have been left with only $100,000. This is what the firm was really worth to them. Because this is a corporation, a more detailed balance sheet would show the net worth reflecting (a) stock issued (say, $80,000 originally contributed by the stockholders) and (b) all the profits retained since the birth of the firm (say, $20,000).

Note, however, that the above was only a hypothetical argument. Probably the firm will not liquidate itself, but go on in its regular business of buying, manufacturing, selling, borrowing, and paying its bills as time goes by. Although each of such transactions will affect the balance sheet in a particular way, it will not affect its general form. Assets are always balanced by liabilities and net worth, for the latter are nothing but the claims of creditors and owners, respectively, on the corporation's assets in general. Our owners do not own $100,000 (net worth) in addition to the assets, but of the assets. Our creditors have a legal (and prior) claim against the rest of the assets.

To test our understanding, let us follow a number of such transactions and their effect on the balance sheet. Suppose, on January 2, 1970, the Wonderful Toy Corporation borrowed $100,000 cash by issuing more bonds: that is, by selling IOU's signed by the firm promising to repay a certain sum at interest at a certain date. If we were now to draw up a new balance sheet, the required *changes* would have to be:

ASSETS		LIABILITIES AND NET WORTH	
1. Cash	+$100,000	8. Bonds payable	+$100,000

Nothing else except the sum on both sides would be affected. Net worth would be the same, for although the firm would hold $100,000 of additional assets, it would also have $100,000 of additional liabilities.

Now suppose the firm bought machinery worth $100,000 for cash on January 3. Again only two changes would occur on the balance sheet, this time both on the asset side.

ASSETS		LIABILITIES AND NET WORTH
1. Cash	− $100,000	
5. Equipment	+ $100,000	

The total of assets is the same. Only its composition has changed, leaving liabilities and net worth completely unaffected. This reminds us that owners and creditors have claims on the assets in general, rather than on any particular ones. The composition of assets is likely to change all the time.

Finally, let us suppose that, on January 4, all inventories, valued at $10,000 (because, say, they were produced in December at this cost), are sold for $15,000. The inventories are sold on credit. Now the required changes would be:

ASSETS		LIABILITIES AND NET WORTH	
1a. Accounts receivable	+ $15,000		
4. Inventories	− $10,000	9. Net worth	+ $5,000

This time a profit clearly was made, although it has not yet been collected in cash. Hence, the firm's net worth has increased.

Now to look at the balance sheet on the evening of January 4, we would find the following:

BALANCE SHEET, WONDERFUL TOY CORPORATION, JANUARY 4, 1970, 6 P.M.

ASSETS		LIABILITIES AND NET WORTH	
1. Cash	$ 11,000	7. Accounts payable	$ 24,000
1a. Accounts receivable	15,000	8. Bonds payable	150,000
2. Bank deposits	2,500		
3. U.S. government bonds	500		
5. Equipment	150,000		
6. Buildings	100,000	9. Net worth	105,000
	$279,000		$279,000

This statement shows the condition of the firm at that moment in time. It is a still picture of its wealth.

A Commercial Bank's Balance Sheet

A commercial bank is just a special type of corporate business, and its balance sheet may look like this:

A HYPOTHETICAL BALANCE SHEET OF A COMMERCIAL BANK (IN MILLION DOLLARS), SECOND NATIONAL BANK OF AMHERST, MASSACHUSETTS, JANUARY 1, 1970

ASSETS		LIABILITIES AND NET WORTH	
1. Cash	$ 20	7. Demand deposits	
2. Deposit at Federal Reserve Bank		(a) of U.S. government	$ 10
of Boston	20	(b) of other U.S. commercial banks	50
3. Deposits at other U.S.		(c) all others	240
commercial banks	1	8. Time deposits	50
4. U.S. government securities	108	9. Borrowings from Federal Reserve	
5. Loans	250	Bank of Boston	10
6. Other assets	1	10. Net worth	40
	$400		$400

This particular bank holds in its vault coins and paper bills (1). It has a checking account of its own (2) at *its* bank, the Federal Reserve Bank of Boston (to be discussed below). It has checking accounts at other commercial banks like itself (3). It holds U.S. government securities (4), that is, IOU's that *are* interest bearing and do *not* circulate as money. They are popularly called *bonds*, but are officially called *bills, certificates, notes,* or *bonds,* depending on when they are due for repayment (in the form of *other* IOU's that are noninterest bearing and that we call money). The bank also holds IOU's *of its customers,* for personal loans or automobile loans or business loans, and so forth (5). Finally, the bank owns some equipment, a building, and the like, which is listed under "other assets" (6). Note that compared to a nonbank business enterprise, this last item is relatively very small. Under (7), (8), and (9) are listed the bank's own debts, which compared to an ordinary business are huge relative to net worth. The bank owes certain amounts to the government (7a), to other banks like itself (7b), and to the general public, households, and businesses (7c). These debts are noninterest bearing, transferable by check on demand, and evidenced *by nothing else* but entry (7) on the bank's balance sheet. These are the checking accounts we know, and they correspond exactly to our friend John Doe's little black book. In fact, a commercial bank is *defined* as one which has checking accounts. (Note how the bank has $300 million of checking accounts, but only $20 million of coins and paper bills in its vaults. Note also that only item (7c) is by our definition part of the money supply, not (7a), (7b), (1), (2), or (3). Our bank also has other (interest-bearing) debt, namely savings accounts (8) and evidence of its own IOU's, handed over to the Federal Reserve (9). Note that, unlike demand deposits, savings deposits are not transferable by check. They are, like demand deposits, evidenced by *nothing* but an entry in the bank's books. They are called time deposits because they may not be redeemable in money until after a certain time has elapsed. Note also that our bank, although it has issued $50 million of savings account books and $10 million of its own IOU's, and has presumably at the time received something for this, does not now have that much cash on hand. But it could, as the Wonderful Toy Corporation above, sell all its assets for cash, pay off all its debts in cash, and have something remaining, which is the equity of its owners in the business (10).

Check Clearing within a Single Bank

What happens if Mr. Black writes a check for $1,000 and gives it to Mr. Green? If Green deposits the check in the same bank in which Black has an account, it is as simple as John Doe's erasing the name of "Jones" and substituting that of "Smith" in his book. The *changes* in the balance sheet would be:

SECOND NATIONAL BANK OF AMHERST, MASSACHUSETTS

ASSETS	LIABILITIES AND NET WORTH	
	7(c). Demand deposit (Black)	− $1,000
	Demand deposit (Green)	+ $1,000

Many transactions every day are indeed this simple. The bank owes as much as before, but to a different person. Making the entries in its books to transfer demand deposits is called *check clearing*. At the end of the month, Green finds in his statement an entry of + $1,000, and Black a corresponding reduction in his account and his canceled check as evidence for his authorization of this act.

The Federal Reserve System

What if the banks were not the same? Suppose Green deposits Black's check in his bank in Springfield, Massachusetts. Clearly the Springfield bank would not be willing to simply add $1,000 to Green's account, leaving it at that. This would add to its liabilities and, without any compensating entry, it would reduce automatically the net worth of the Springfield bank. It is here that we meet for the first time the role of the *Federal Reserve System*.

It is the American equivalent of a *central bank*, a bank for commercial banks as well as foreign central banks and the U.S. government. It was established in 1914. The United States was divided into twelve districts, each of which has a Federal Reserve Bank, which serves and supervises the commercial member banks in that district and is nominally owned by them. (See Figure 9.1 THE TWELVE FEDERAL RESERVE DISTRICTS.) Each of the twelve Federal Reserve Banks is a dividend-paying corporation owned by the commercial banks of the district that cared to join (such as the state-chartered banks) or had to join by law (such as the nationally chartered banks). Dividends are limited to 6 percent of the stock value issued. The remainder of profits goes mostly to the U.S. Treasury. Similarly, the board of directors of each Federal Reserve Bank is only partly elected by the member banks, who choose six directors, partly appointed by the Washington Board of Governors of the Federal Reserve System, who choose three directors. Because the governors exercise many other supervisory and appointive powers, each Federal Reserve Bank is much more a public than a private institution.

The banks are located in Boston, New York, Philadelphia, Cleveland, Richmond,

Figure 9.1   THE TWELVE FEDERAL RESERVE DISTRICTS

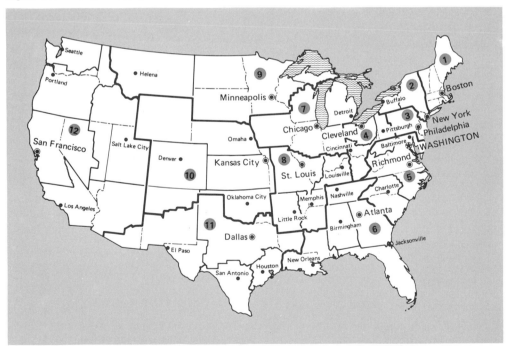

This map shows the location of the twelve Federal Reserve Banks and their branches. Alaska and Hawaii are part of the twelfth district. Source: Federal Reserve Bulletin.

Atlanta, Chicago, St. Louis, Minneapolis, Kansas City, Dallas, and San Francisco. Not all commercial banks have to be members of the system. Only about 6,000 of 14,000 commercial banks in the United States are members, but 70 percent of all deposits are with member banks. The major responsibility for monetary policy lies with the Federal Reserve System. It is run by a Board of Governors in Washington, D.C., composed of seven persons appointed for 14-year terms by the President, confirmed by the Senate and responsible to Congress.

A Federal Reserve Bank's Balance Sheet

A typical balance sheet of a Federal Reserve Bank will help us evaluate the role of the *Fed*, as it is called. We have met item (1) before when we discussed representative full-bodied money. It consists of warehouse receipts of gold issued by the U.S. Treasury. In this example, the Federal Reserve Bank concerned owns $1.7 billion of them. Hence, it can at any time take physical possession of an amount of gold (possibly in Fort Knox) valued at this amount. (Congress has legislated that an ounce of gold is worth $35.) Further, the bank holds IOU's of member banks, called *discounts and advances* (2). This entry reflects (9) on the commercial banks' balance sheets. It is called *discounts* if a member bank borrows (shown by item 9 on the above balance sheet), while pledging as collateral its own customers' IOU's (those listed as item 5 on the commercial banks' balance sheet), just as you might pledge a car when getting an automobile loan. It is called *advances* if a member bank borrows while pledging as collateral other assets, notably government securities (listed under 4 on the commercial banks' balance sheet).

A HYPOTHETICAL BALANCE SHEET OF A FEDERAL RESERVE BANK (IN MILLION DOLLARS)
JANUARY 1, 1970

ASSETS		LIABILITIES AND NET WORTH	
1. Gold certificates	$1,700	5. Federal Reserve Notes	$3,700
2. Discounts and advances	38	6. Demand deposits	
3. U.S. government securities	4,100	(a) of U.S. government	75
4. Other assets	762	(b) of member banks	1,800
		(c) all others, mostly of foreigners	25
		7. Other liabilities	800
		8. Net worth	200
	$6,600		$6,600

In addition, Federal Reserve Banks hold large amounts of government securities (3) and small amounts of other assets (4), such as foreign currencies or bank premises. Item (5) are the noninterest-bearing IOU's issued by the Fed which make up the bulk of paper bills. They correspond exactly to John Doe's IOU while it was circulating. Item (6) is similar to (7) on the commercial banks' balance sheet, but the debts here are owed not to the general public but to the U.S. Treasury (a), member commercial banks (b)—reflecting item (2) on the commercial banks' balance sheets—and chiefly to foreigners (c). The net worth (8) is owned by the member banks and listed in *their* balance sheets under (6). Yet, as we said above, member banks are only owners in name; the Fed is really a public corporation, subject to Congress. What on the Fed's balance sheet is part of the money supply, as we defined it? Item (5), if *not* held by the Treasury or in the vaults of commercial banks, plus item (6c), but not (6a) and (6b).

Check Clearing within a Single Federal Reserve District

We are ready now to proceed with the process of check clearing. The Fed acts for its member banks, all of which have an account with their district bank, as a *check clearing agent*. The Springfield bank *would* add $1,000 to Green's account (only an entry in the book) and send the check on to the Fed at Boston. A member bank almost always sends a check on to the Fed for "clearing" if it is addressed to another bank. The Fed would in turn add $1,000 to the Springfield bank's account. Thus:

NINTH NATIONAL BANK OF SPRINGFIELD, MASSACHUSETTS

ASSETS		LIABILITIES AND NET WORTH	
2. Deposit at Federal Reserve Bank of Boston	+$1,000	7(c). Demand deposit (Green)	+$1,000

The Springfield bank is owed another $1,000 by the Fed; it also owes another $1,000 to a customer (Green). At the same time, the Boston Fed would see that the check had been drawn upon the Amherst bank, and it would reduce the Amherst bank's account at the Fed by $1,000.

FEDERAL RESERVE BANK OF BOSTON, MASSACHUSETTS

ASSETS	LIABILITIES AND NET WORTH	
	6(b). Demand deposit (Springfield bank)	+$1,000
	Demand deposit (Amherst bank)	—$1,000

As a justification for its action, the Fed would send the check to the Amherst bank which would quickly reduce Black's account in turn:

SECOND NATIONAL BANK OF AMHERST, MASSACHUSETTS

ASSETS		LIABILITIES AND NET WORTH	
2. Deposit at Federal Reserve Bank of Boston	—$1,000	7(c). Demand deposit (Black)	—$1,000

The Amherst bank is owed $1,000 less by the Fed, but it also owes $1,000 less to a customer. As a result, the net worth of none of the three banks involved has been affected, and Mr. Black's deposit has been "handed over" to Mr. Green.[2]

Check Clearing Involving Two Federal Reserve Districts

The forgoing procedure can be even more complicated than this. Perhaps Green decides to deposit Mr. Black's check in his bank at Sacramento, California. The Sacramento bank would do just what the Springfield bank did: credit the account of Green, send the check to *its* Federal Reserve Bank (of San Francisco), and have the amount credited to its deposit there:

OLD COUNTRY BANK, SACRAMENTO, CALIFORNIA

ASSETS		LIABILITIES AND NET WORTH	
2. Deposit at Federal Reserve Bank of San Francisco	+$1,000	7(c). Demand deposit (Green)	+$1,000

The San Francisco Fed would indeed credit the account of its Sacramento member, but it could not, as did its Boston counterpart, reduce the account of the Amherst bank. The Amherst bank has *its* account in Boston. As a result, the procedure is the following. Whenever a Federal Reserve Bank receives from a member bank a check for clearing drawn upon a bank *outside* its district, it sends the check to the other district Fed involved (in this case Boston) and receives gold certificates from the other district:

FEDERAL RESERVE BANK OF SAN FRANCISCO, CALIFORNIA

ASSETS		LIABILITIES AND NET WORTH	
1. Gold certificates (from Boston)	+$1,000	6(b). Demand deposit (Sacramento bank)	+$1,000

[2] What if Black had written a check without having an account at all? The Amherst bank would have rejected the check, returning it to the Fed and making no entries on its balance sheet. The Fed would reverse the entries made earlier and send the check to the Springfield bank (interchange plus and minus signs to find new entries). The Springfield bank would similarly reverse the entries made and notify Green that the check had "bounced" and that his account had not gone up by $1,000 after all.

It exchanges increased indebtedness to the member bank for a claim on gold. In the same way, whenever a Federal Reserve Bank receives from another Federal Reserve Bank a check for clearing drawn on one of its members, it reduces the member's account and pays out gold certificates to the other district. Thus we have:

FEDERAL RESERVE BANK OF BOSTON, MASSACHUSETTS

ASSETS		LIABILITIES AND NET WORTH	
1. Gold certificates (to San Francisco)	—$1,000	6(b). Demand deposit (Amherst bank)	—$1,000

It has given up a claim on gold for decreased indebtedness to a member bank. The Amherst bank's entries, finally, are exactly as on page 203 above.

To give you an idea of the magnitude of the check clearing function of the Fed: in 1966, it handled 6 billion checks, with a value exceeding $2 trillion. This total included checks on nonmember banks that are allowed to use the system's facilities.

THE CREATION AND DESTRUCTION OF MONEY

Whenever the money supply, as we have defined it, goes up, new money has been created. When it falls, it has been destroyed. We can now understand how this may happen.

Treasury Cash

The Treasury can at any time physically mint coins or print paper bills (although the latter is now being discontinued). By our definition, however, as long as the Treasury holds on to these, the money supply is unaffected. How does the public first receive these coins and bills? The Treasury could, of course, physically spend them, for example by purchasing army trucks or paying government employees. In reality it does not. It hands over, say, $100 of newly minted coins and newly printed bills to the Fed in return for a deposit. Thus, the entries would be:

FEDERAL RESERVE BANK OF NEW YORK, NEW YORK

ASSETS		LIABILITIES AND NET WORTH	
1(a). Treasury cash	+$100	6(a). Demand deposit (U.S. Government)	+$100

By our definition, *no* money has been created. The Treasury now spends its deposit by writing a check on it, to U.S. Steel, which promptly deposits it in its bank. The entries, similar to our case on pages 202–203, may be as follows, as the check is sent to the Fed for "collection":

FIRST NATIONAL CITY BANK OF NEW YORK, NEW YORK

ASSETS		LIABILITIES AND NET WORTH	
2. Deposit at the Federal Reserve Bank of New York	+$100	7(c). Demand deposit (U.S. Steel)	+$100

FEDERAL RESERVE BANK OF NEW YORK, NEW YORK

ASSETS		LIABILITIES AND NET WORTH	
		6. Demand deposits	
		(a) U.S. government	—$100
		(b) First National City Bank	+$100

In the end, the Fed still holds the Treasury cash, owes an equal amount to the First National City Bank, which in turn owes an equal amount to U.S. Steel. And the latter 7(c) *is* an increase in the money supply. The First National City Bank has *created* money in the form of *demand deposits* (like John Doe's entry in his little black book). Conceivably, if U.S. Steel writes a check on its account which is deposited somewhere (as by Mr. Green above), on which account another check is written and deposited somewhere, and so on, this new money can circulate forever as in the three types of check clearing cases above. The Treasury cash would never get into circulation at all. But suppose U.S. Steel demands to cash its account. In anticipation of this, the First National City Bank may ask the Fed to give it cash for *its* account, then hand over the cash to U.S. Steel for *its* account. The entries are as follows:

FEDERAL RESERVE BANK OF NEW YORK, NEW YORK

ASSETS		LIABILITIES AND NET WORTH	
1(a). Treasury cash	—$100	6(b). Demand deposit (First National City Bank)	—$100

FIRST NATIONAL CITY BANK OF NEW YORK, NEW YORK

ASSETS		LIABILITIES AND NET WORTH	
1. Cash	+$100		
2. Deposit at the Federal Reserve Bank of New York	—$100		
1. Cash	—$100	7(c). Demand deposit (U.S. Steel)	—$100

At this moment, the demand deposit money created by First National City has been destroyed, but the public (in this case U.S. Steel) holds an equal amount of Treasury cash. The money supply is still up by $100, which now circulates from hand to hand in the way familiar to us all. The end effect is exactly as if the Treasury had spent its coins and bills directly by handing them to U.S. Steel. All other entries have exactly been canceled. (Try and see!)

Federal Reserve Notes

The Federal Reserve Banks can at any time physically print their own paper bills. As long as they hold on to them, however, the money supply is unaffected and nothing shows in their balance sheet. (Would you list an IOU of yourself in your balance sheet as long as you had the IOU in hand?) How does the public first get hold of these bills? In more or less the same fashion. As the public hands IOU's to banks and gets checking accounts and then demands to cash its checking accounts, commercial banks, in turn, ask the Fed to cash *their* accounts at the Fed. The Fed, in fact, exchanges one kind of IOU (entries on its books, called demand deposits of member banks) for another kind (paper certificates of indebtedness called Federal Reserve Notes handed to the member banks), and the commercial banks hand them to the public. For instance:

FEDERAL RESERVE BANK OF NEW YORK, NEW YORK

ASSETS	LIABILITIES AND NET WORTH	
	5. Federal Reserve Notes	+$75
	6(b). Demand deposit	
	(First National City Bank)	—$75

FIRST NATIONAL CITY BANK OF NEW YORK, NEW YORK

ASSETS		LIABILITIES AND NET WORTH	
1. Cash	+$75		
2. Deposit at the Federal Reserve Bank of New York	— $75		
*5. Loans	+$75	7(c). Demand deposits (public)	+$75*
1. Cash	—$75	7(c). Demand deposits (public)	—$75

Note that in this example, the money supply has not changed at all until banks made loans, creating demand deposits (7c). As these were cashed, the money supply went up by as much as it went down, as the composition of the supply changed from checking accounts toward more paper bills in the hands of the public. The Fed has created money via the commercial banks which created a deposit, then destroyed it by circulating Federal Reserve Notes.

The destruction of Treasury or Federal Reserve cash, furthermore, follows analogous routes. The public may pay cash *into* banks to pay off its debts. Then the banks would return the public's IOU's to the public and have cash in its vaults (not counted in the money supply). The entries:

FIRST NATIONAL CITY BANK OF NEW YORK, NEW YORK

ASSETS		LIABILITIES AND NET WORTH
1. Cash	+ $75	
5. Loans	− $75	

Regardless of what the banks do with the cash, whether they hold it or return it to the Fed for deposits there, the money supply is down.

Demand Deposits

We have in fact just noted how demand deposits may be created (see the starred items in the statement on page 206). Banks accept, for instance, IOU's from you or me and add an equal dollar amount to our accounts. Hence, the money supply is up. As long as no one cashes the new account but only transfers it via check, the demand deposit portion of the money supply remains up. It can be destroyed by simply reversing the entries in the starred row above. (Change plus signs to minus signs, indicating that the bank returns your IOU, reducing equally the number on your account.)

However, what if the account is cashed? Then the money supply still remains up. Only its composition changes, as the bank simply pays cash out of its vault, reducing its demand deposit liabilities by an equal amount. Well, you will say, if you have been reading carefully, what if *everyone* wants to cash his demand deposits and maybe even his time deposits *at the same time*? Isn't our typical bank on page 198 going to be in deep trouble, having $350 million of deposit liabilities and only $20 million of cash? Aren't all banks going to be in trouble, holding, as we saw above, $6.1 billion of cash, but owing $149.5 billion to the public in demand deposits alone? It may seem troublesome, but it is not.

Another function of the Federal Reserve System (together with certain other agencies) is to *supervise commercial banks* to ensure that banks only hold "sound" assets—IOU's of people likely to repay in full and promptly, and securities that do not fluctuate widely in value (hence no common stock). Banks must be always "solvent," that is, they must have a positive net worth. Banks that become insolvent (with liabilities exceeding assets) must cease operations. Formerly, even in prosperous times, many hundreds of banks failed every year in the United States, with grievous losses to depositors. Stricter supervision has made failures much rarer, and deposit insurance has made losses to depositors still rarer. The *Fed-*

eral Deposit Insurance Corporation insures each deposit at member banks and almost all other banks, including savings banks, for up to $15,000. The cost to banks is small: one thirtieth of 1 percent of deposits annually. In the event of bank failure, the FDIC takes over the bank's assets and pays off the depositors.

Because all banks are solvent, the Fed is willing to lend banks Federal Reserve Notes on the basis of *any* asset they possess. The Fed stands ready to provide any amount of cash people desire. To use the example on page 198, if depositors requested $350 million of cash—items (7) and (8)—the Fed would, on the basis of $350 million of the bank's assets, lend it $350 million of newly printed Federal Reserve Notes to pay off all depositors. The entries would be:

FEDERAL RESERVE BANK OF BOSTON, MASSACHUSETTS

ASSETS	LIABILITIES AND NET WORTH

2. Discounts and advances
          + $350 million
	5. Federal Reserve Notes
	          + $350 million

SECOND NATIONAL BANK OF AMHERST, MASSACHUSETTS

ASSETS		LIABILITIES AND NET WORTH	

1. Cash	+ $350 million	9. Borrowings from the Federal
		    Reserve Bank of Boston
		          + $350 million	

1. Cash	— $350 million	7. Demand deposits
		    (a) of U.S. government
		    (b) of other U.S.
		        commercial banks
		    (c) all others
		8. Time deposits
			— $10 million
			
			— $50 million
			— $240 million
			— $50 million

Note that entries (2) and (9) are two sides of the same thing (the bank's IOU). The Fed's own IOU's outstanding (paper bills) increase, are first in the hands of the Amherst bank, then go to the public whose deposits disappear. The total money supply is increased: $240 million of it (7c) has disappeared (replaced with cash), but the public also holds cash in place of near-money (8). If no time deposits were held by the government or banks, the money supply is up by these $50 million (in the form of cash). The cash held in place of (7a) and (7b) is still not counted in the money supply, by definition.

Because of the Fed's readiness to *provide elastically any amount of cash the public wants,* a "run on the banks" is very unlikely. If it did occur, people would find that they all, at the same time, could get cash, although each bank holds *ordinarily* only a tiny amount compared to its deposit liabilities. The public would probably redeposit the cash the next day.

SUMMARY

1 Although we are apt to take it for granted, money is one of the most important of human inventions. Without it, specialized production and exchange would be impossible. We would be immeasurably less productive.

2 Historically, many things have been used successfully as money, ranging from animals to salt, from precious metals to pieces of paper. This alone should make us suspect that the link between money and precious metals is a historical accident rather than logical necessity.

3 All types of money in the United States today are nothing but different forms of IOU's. There are three types: token coins, paper bills, and demand deposits. They perform the functions of medium of exchange (hence, as a store of generalized purchasing power in between exchanges) and unit of account.

4 The U.S. money supply is defined as the total of coins, paper bills, and demand deposits owned by the public (that is, by anyone other than the U.S. Treasury, the Federal Reserve System, or the domestic commercial banks).

5 Demand deposits are transferred by check. The process of check clearing differs depending on whether it involves a single bank, two banks in the same Federal Reserve district, or two banks in different Federal Reserve districts.

6 The process of check clearing is best illustrated by studying balance sheets. The balance sheet shows someone's wealth at a particular moment of time. It shows assets always equaling liabilities plus net worth.

7 The Federal Reserve System is the central bank of the United States. As such, it is the bank of commercial banks, foreign central banks, and the U.S. government. Although nominally owned by its member banks, it is really an institution responsible first and foremost to Congress. As we shall see in the next chapter, it is the agency administering monetary policy, responsible for influencing the levels of GNP, employment, and prices by regulating the supply and cost of money.

8 Money can be created or destroyed by any one of three institutions: the U.S. Treasury, the Federal Reserve System, or commercial banks. Furthermore, different types of money can be easily transformed into one another.

TERMS[3]

advances	cash
asset	check
balance sheet	checking account
Board of Governors	check clearing

commercial bank   money supply
demand deposit   near-money
discounts   net worth
Federal Deposit Insurance Corporation   paper bills
Federal Reserve Note   representative full-
Federal Reserve System   bodied money
full-bodied money   savings account
gold certificates   Silver Certificate
greenback   solvency
legal tender   time deposit
liability   token coins
monetary policy   U.S. Note

QUESTIONS FOR REVIEW AND DISCUSSION

1 "If people link the value of money by necessity to the value of precious metals backing it, they are caught in a myth. Such link is a historical accident, not logical necessity." Explain.

2 "Money *by itself* is nowadays about as valuable as a ticket. A nation cannot become richer by creating more money, just as the owner of a theater cannot increase its seating capacity by printing more tickets." Evaluate. Is the analogy correct? Write down your answer and check it again after you have read Chapter 10.

3 Show how IOU's may serve as money. Show that all U.S. money consists of IOU's. Why are some IOU's money and others are not?

4 Take a look at some of the paper bills you are carrying and show which ones have rather archaic inscriptions. Why are they archaic?

5 "The term demand *deposit* is misleading." Explain.

6 What are the functions of money?

7 "The Federal Reserve System is more public than private." Explain.

8 Show how any artificial contrivance could perform the unit-of-account function of money. It need not be the dollar, pound, or franc, it could be the biblical shekel, the ancient guinea, even bushels of tomatoes or cucumbers.

9 Take the following list of a student's assets and liabilities: cash $100; money owed roommate $10; clothing $500; car $1,000; U.S. taxes due $200; tuition due $1,900; stock $50; books $120. Calculate his net worth and set up a balance sheet.

10 Write out a list of your assets. Of your liabilities. What is your net worth?

11 The text shows that the money supply in a recent year was less than $200 billion. Yet, the Federal Reserve allegedly cleared checks worth $2 trillion. How is this possible?

[3] Terms are defined in the Glossary at the end of the book.

12 If you were a commercial banker, would you like or dislike inflation? Explain. (Consider the effects of inflation discussed in Chapter 4, as well as the kinds of assets and liabilities a bank has.)

13 Show how money is created if a commercial bank makes a loan to you, how it is destroyed when you pay it back. (Would it make any difference whether this is done with cash or demand deposits?)

14 Use bank or Treasury balance sheets to show that it is possible for all Americans at the same time to convert (a) all coins into paper money, (b) all coins into demand deposits, (c) all paper money into coins, (d) all demand deposits into cash (coins or paper money). What happens to the money supply in each case?

15 "Gold certificates once were representative full-bodied money in the United States when they were freely circulating and redeemable in gold. They still exist but they are now no money at all." Explain.

16 "When the U.S. government in 1963 began to issue dimes and quarters made from copper and nickel rather than silver, it reduced the value of money." Discuss.

17 Which of the following are part of the U.S. money supply:
  a. A checking account owned by a college in an American bank
  b. A 1 cent coin in a child's piggy bank
  c. A dime that fell into a sewer and cannot be retrieved
  d. A five dollar bill held by a collector in Belgium
  e. A checking account in an American bank owned by an American commercial bank
  f. A five dollar bill in the vault of an American savings bank
  g. A $1,000 gold certificate held by the Federal Reserve Bank of Boston
  h. A one cent coin held by the Federal Reserve Bank of Boston
  i. A checking account of the U.S. government in an American bank
  j. A checking account of the New York City government in an American bank

18 Suppose you wrote a check on your bank and sent it to someone who deposited it in a commercial bank in Honolulu (part of the San Francisco Federal Reserve District). Trace the process of check clearing via balance sheets. What do you think would happen if he deposited it in Tokyo?

19 COMMERICIAL BANKER X: "I cannot create money. I only lend what people deposit with me."
    Evaluate.

20 Indicate the effects on a bank's balance sheet of the following:
  a. The bank buys $10,000 of government bonds.
  b. A depositor repays a $1,000 loan.
  c. A depositor deposits $12,000, of which $2,000 is cash, $1,000 checks of other depositors at this bank. The rest are checks on other banks.
  d. The bank borrows $50,000 at the Federal Reserve.

FEDERAL RESERVE SETS RISE TO 6% IN DISCOUNT RATE

Reserves Required of Banks Will Also Be Increased in a Tight-Money Step

INFLATION SPURS ACTION

By EDWIN L. DALE Jr.
Special to The New York Times

WASHINGTON, April 3 — The Federal Reserve Board, in what it called a "further move against inflation," raised today both its discount rate and the reserves required of the nation's banks.

The double-barreled step was designed to convince the banking and business communities that the Federal Reserve continued to mean business in its tight money policy. . . .

The discount rate—the interest rate charged to banks when they borrow from the Federal Reserve—was raised from 5½ to 6 per cent, the highest rate in 40 years. . . .

$650-Million Frozen

Reserve requirements were raised by one-half percentage point against demand deposits with the effect of "freezing" about $650-million of lendable funds in the hands of banks. The 6,000 member banks of the Federal Reserve System are required to hold a percentage of their funds as reserves with their local Federal Reserve banks.

The discount-rate increase, which will go into effect immediately at each of the 12 Federal Reserve banks except Boston, was approved unanimously by the seven-man board. . . .

The increase in reserve requirements means that larger banks' requirements will go from 16 ½ to 17 per cent on demand deposits under $5-million and from 17 to 17½ per cent on deposits over $5-million. For smaller or "country" banks, the requirements will go from 12 to 12½ per cent for deposits under $5-million and from 12½ to 13 per cent for deposits over $5-million.

Effective Today

The reserve requirement change is effective for deposits starting today, but the banks will not actually have to put up the extra money for two weeks.

Under the nation's complex fractional reserve system, the banks as a whole can lend or invest 3 to $4 for each dollar of reserves. Thus, theoretically the freezing of $650-million of reserves by today's move could cause a contraction of bank loans and investments by more than $2-billion.

MONEY COST RISES AS BIG BANKS SET 7½% PRIME RATE

4th Rise Since December Expected to Have Uneven Impact on Consumer

By H. ERICH HEINEMANN

The Government's drive against inflation pushed the cost of money to a new high yesterday.

For the fourth time since December, the nation's largest banks raised the minimum charge on loans to their biggest, most creditworthy borrowers —this time to 7½ per cent, up half a percentage point.

Economists said yesterday that the new rise in the banks' prime rate— to the extent that the soaring cost of money causes businessmen, municipalities and consumers to defer their spending plans — should dampen the demand for goods and services and thus help to cool the overheated American economy. . . .

Since corporate borrowers are normally required to keep a portion of their loan on deposit as a "compensating balance"—20 per cent is the most common figure—the true cost of funds that actually can be used may be more than 9 per cent.

Pressure on All Rates

Furthermore, most major banks are now rationing credit, so that loans for some purposes, such as corporate takeovers, are not available at any price.

For consumers, the impact of yesterday's increase in the cost of business loans is likely to be uneven and uncertain.

The prime rate is a basic interest cost, from which other money charges tend to be scaled upward, so its increase should put further upward pressure under interest rates everywhere.

However, in many areas (New York State for one) many interest rates are already at the maximum levels permitted by law. So, barring action by the Legislature, consumers here are not likely to see major changes in the cost of borrowing to buy a house, an automobile or a refrigerator.

Rather, money will simply be harder to get, as lenders divert some of their funds into areas where interest rate ceilings do no apply. . . .

The political reaction to yesterday's increase in the prime rate was mixed.

Representative Wright Patman, the Texas Democrat who heads the House Banking and Currency Committee, called on the Nixon Administration to take action to roll back the rate increase, which he compared to "legalized robbery." . . .

The course of money rates now becomes hard to predict.

On the one hand, the Federal Reserve has already sharply reduced the rate at which it is pumping new funds into the economy and shows every intention of continuing to do so.

The nation's money supply, for example, increased at a 2.2 per cent annual rate from December through February, against a 6.5 per cent growth rate through all 1968. The money supply is the total of most checking accounts at the banks, plus currency and coin in the hands of the public.

10

monetary

policy

W̲E HAVE SEEN in the previous chapter how money can be created and destroyed. This does not mean, however, that money should be created or destroyed at random without regard to consequences. The main reason for the existence of the Federal Reserve is indeed not the clearing of checks, the supervision of member banks, or the provision of paper bills. Its main function is to *regulate the supply and cost of money with a view to the consequences on the levels of real GNP, employment, and prices.* Like a helmsman in a boat, the Fed can help steer the economy along a path that avoids the twin perils of unemployment and inflation. In this chapter, we shall learn about the techniques used to achieve this aim.

THE TOOLS OF MONETARY POLICY
Setting Reserve Requirements

We saw in the previous chapter how commercial banks can create demand deposits, our principal form of money. They might accept a $100 IOU from you while adding $100 to your checking account. We noticed that this involved nothing more difficult than changing an entry in the bank's books. If you previously had $31.25 in your account, the bank would simply change that figure to read $131.25. The reverse would happen when you pay back the loan. If your account at the time reads $421.11, the bank would just change it (on your instruction) to $321.11 and give you back your IOU.

It is time now to ask whether banks can create such new money without limit. From what we have learned so far, the answer seems to be yes. After all, it only takes paper and ink to make out IOU's and to change figures on the banks' books! So far as we can see right now, the only trouble that could arise is that the recipients of the new demand deposits, or the people who receive checks written on them, might go to the bank and ask for *cash*, that is, paper bills or coins. Because our commercial banks cannot make cash, they might not be able to honor such demands, unless, of course, they have enough cash in their vaults. In ages past, therefore, bankers used to limit on their own the amounts of checking accounts created by them. They would note from experience, for example, that for every 1 dollar of demand deposits created by them someone would sooner or later want to cash in 25 cents. If they had $25,000 of cash in their vaults, therefore, they might feel free to create demand deposits of $100,000, but no more. If they created more demand deposit money, and people as in the past cashed in a quarter of this, bankers would not have enough cash. Then the "soundness" of their operations would be questioned. Everybody would want to have cash. There would not be enough, and the bank would have to close. Thus, bankers in their own interest (which was to stay in business making loans and earning interest thereon) would limit the total of loans made and thus of checking account money created.

You will also remember that the Federal Reserve System nowadays makes successful runs on the banks impossible. The Federal Reserve Banks stand ready to lend to their member banks any amount of cash needed to redeem demand deposits in paper bills and coin. All the banks have to do is to pledge some asset as collateral. And such assets the money creating bank will always have, namely, its customer's IOU. Thus, it seems that under the Federal Reserve System the old cautiousness of bankers (not to create too much money) is quite unnecessary. For every dollar of demand deposits they create they get a dollar's worth of IOU. For every dollar's worth of IOU, the Fed will lend the bank a dollar in cash. Hence, even if customers were to cash in their new deposits 100 percent, as they never do, there would be enough cash to honor the demand! In order to avoid this unlimited creation of money, however, the Federal Reserve System has laid down certain ground rules. These rules in effect assure that commercial banks, as in days long past, must limit the amount of demand deposits created by them to a certain multiple of their own cash and deposits at the Fed.

reserves of member banks   Federal Reserve Banks do not want their member banks to create demand deposits (our checking accounts, item (7), page 198) without limit. To avoid excessive money creation, they could, of course, simply set a dollar ceiling to the amount, such as $180 billion. Whenever desirable, this ceiling could then be raised or lowered. The Fed is achieving the same result differently. It has defined the maximum size of commercial banks' demand deposit liabilities as a multiple of another item, namely the banks' vault cash plus deposits at the Fed (items (1) and (2), page 198). Just suppose the multiple is 8. For every dollar of vault cash and deposits at the Fed owned by them, the member banks may then create up to $8 of the public's demand deposits. Put in another way, in this hypothetical example, vault cash and Federal Reserve deposits must be owned at least equal in value to 12.5 percent (100/8) of the checking accounts owned by the public. This percentage is called the commercial banks' *reserve requirement*. Vault cash and Federal Reserve deposits are the commercial banks' *reserves*.

Do not get the idea, however, that vault cash and Federal Reserve deposits are given this role *to give value to* our checking accounts. Nothing is further from the truth. It may look as though the former "back up" the latter, but their only role is to *limit the dollar amount of demand deposits created by commercial banks*. The value of demand deposits depends on what we can buy with them.

If the Fed wanted to double the aggregate size of demand deposits, it would simply alter, to continue our example, the reserve requirement to 6.25 percent. Then, every dollar of vault cash or Federal Reserve deposits owned would allow the commercial banks to create not $8 (that is, 100/12.5), but $16 (100/6.25) of checking accounts. Similarly, if the Fed wanted to halve the maximum total of demand deposits, it would, in our example, change the reserve requirement from 12.5 to 25 percent. Then, every dollar of vault cash or Federal Reserve deposits owned would allow the commercial banks to create not $8, but only $4 of checking accounts.

Returning to the above example, the Fed could achieve the same result more directly by changing the maximum limit from our hypothetical $180 billion to $360 (or to $90) billion. It could achieve the same result in other indirect ways by tying the maximum to *any* other figure, expressing it, say, as a multiple of the commercial banks' loans or net worth. In that case, loans or net worth would become "reserves," and the percentage their size holds in the desired size of demand deposits would become the "reserve requirement."

At the time of this writing, in May 1969, Congress allowed the Fed to set the reserve requirement anywhere between 7 and 14 per cent for country banks, and between 10 and 22 percent for city banks. The Fed actually set this percentage at 12.5 percent for country, and 17 percent for city banks. For every dollar of cash in vault or of deposit at the Fed, they could create up to $8 or $5.9, respectively, of demand deposits. Put differently, vault cash and Federal Reserve deposits are the commercial banks' reserves. For every dollar of demand deposits owed,[1] a country bank had to own 12.5 cents, a city bank 17 cents of such reserves (cash or deposits at the Fed).

Finally, the Fed also sets reserve requirements for time deposits (or savings accounts) on the basis of reserves identically defined. The reserve requirement for all banks is between 3 and 10 percent. In early 1969, it was 3 percent.

A HYPOTHETICAL BALANCE SHEET OF A COMMERCIAL BANK (IN MILLION DOLLARS), SECOND NATIONAL BANK OF AMHERST, MASSACHUSETTS, JANUARY 1, 1970

ASSETS		LIABILITIES AND NET WORTH	
1. Cash	$ 20	7. Demand deposits	
2. Deposit at Federal Reserve Bank		(a) of U.S. government	$ 10
of Boston	20	(b) of other U.S. commercial banks	50
3. Deposits at other U.S.		(c) all others	240
commercial banks	1	8. Time deposits	50
4. U.S. government securities	108	9. Borrowings from Federal Reserve	
5. Loans	250	Bank of Boston	10
6. Other assets	1	10. Net worth	40
	$400		$400

Let us now take a look at the statement of the hypothetical bank on page 198. Its balance sheet is reproduced here for easy reference: Now assume this bank is subject to the May 1969 requirements for a country bank: 12.5 percent requirement for demand deposits and 3 percent for time deposits. Then, every dollar of reserves could support exactly $8 of demand deposits (100/12.5) or $33.33 of time deposits (100/3). Owing net, item (7) minus (3), $299 million, our bank would need, we can figure, 12.5 percent, or $37.375 million of reserves for demand deposits. It would also need, owing $50 million of time deposits, 3 percent, or $1.5 million of reserves for them. This gives a total of $38.875 million of *required reserves*. The bank has in fact more, $40 million, of *actual reserves*. Hence, it has $1.125 million of *excess reserves*. It could use them to pay off its indebtedness to the Fed—decreasing items (1) or (2) and (9). Or it could on their basis create new deposits—increasing items (5) and (7). But, as you can now see, its ability to create new deposits would be quite limited.

The difference between excess reserves and indebtedness to the Fed is frequently used as an indicator of a bank's likelihood of creating more deposits. If the difference is positive, it is called *free reserves*. If it is negative, we speak of *net borrowed reserves*. In our example, the bank has net borrowed reserves of $8.875 million (item (9) less excess reserves).

---

[1] Strictly speaking it is *net* demand deposits, or item (7) minus (3) on this page. Also, the reserve requirements were slightly higher for banks with deposits over $5 million. (See also the news reports introducing this chapter).

What has been said about member bank reserves can essentially be repeated for non-members. They have reserves, often in the form of deposits at large member banks. Their reserve requirements are set by state laws or state authorities. Typically, they are also higher on demand than on time deposits and for larger than smaller banks.

reserves of the Fed   Until recently, the Federal Reserve Banks themselves were also subject to a reserve requirement. This applied to their own Federal Reserve Note and deposit liabilities (items (5) and (6), page 201). Congress had defined the maximum size of the Fed's paper money and deposit liabilities as a multiple of gold certificates held by the Federal Reserve Banks. For a long time, this multiple was four. For every dollar of gold certificates, the Fed could create up to $4 of paper bills and demand deposits. Thus, gold certificates were the Fed's *reserves*, and the *reserve requirement* was 25 percent (100/4).

As in the case of the commercial banks, however, this link to gold was not to give value to paper bills and Federal Reserve deposits, but to limit the total dollar amount of them created. Thus, if the Fed had $10 billion of gold certificates (or, at the official price, a claim on some 286 million ounces of gold at Fort Knox), it could legally create $40 billion of paper bills and deposits. If $20 billion of this were deposits, and these were owned by member banks, they could, in turn, create our checking accounts on this basis. At a reserve requirement of 12.5 percent, they might create up to $160 billion of them (that is, $20 billion times the multiple of 100/12.5). No wonder, member bank deposits at the Fed are called *high-powered "money"*. A relatively small amount of them might be turned into a much larger amount of the public's demand deposits. And notice something else. Because the Fed's own reserves were gold certificates, the amount of gold owned by the Fed ultimately limited the money supply. In our example, it might consist of $20 billion of circulating Federal Reserve Notes and $160 billion of checking accounts.

This limit depended entirely on a number of our own arbitrary decisions and our willingness to abide by them: Congress had arbitrarily fixed the price of gold at $35 per ounce. It could have changed that price and thus made 286 million ounces be worth any dollar amount it liked! Similarly, Congress could have changed the Fed's reserve requirement up or down to any desired percentage figure. Finally, it could have let the Fed change the member banks' reserve requirement beyond the existing legal limits. Thus, it was clear that the amount of gold we had limited our money supply only if we let it. In recognition of this fact, Congress in early 1965 removed the gold certificate reserve requirement from Federal Reserve deposits. In early 1968, it removed it also from Federal Reserve Notes. Thereby the last link between our money supply and gold was severed. The Fed itself has now no gold reserve requirement at all. Gold plays no further role in our domestic economic relations. The Fed uses essentially its own judgment as to what is desirable when it creates paper bills and deposits. But private commercial banks are still subject to the reserve requirement set by the Fed, as we noted above.

raising the reserve requirement   Now let us return to our earlier example and see what would happen if the Fed were to raise the reserve requirement on net demand deposits to 12.88 percent. Our bank's actual reserves are unchanged at $40 million (items (1) + (2)). Required reserves are now 12.88 percent of $299 million plus 3 percent of $50 million, or $40 million also. Excess reserves, the bank's power to create new deposits, have been eliminated! Customers will be discouraged from borrowing by higher interest rates, by more selective credit standards, or by refusal.

The figure of 12.88 was chosen, of course, not to make the arithmetic difficult for you, but to demonstrate how the Fed might eliminate excess reserves exactly (Just ask yourself: if the bank needs $1.5 million of reserves for time deposits, and has a total of $40 million of reserves, which percentage figure would make the remaining $38.5 million of reserves just required for our $299 million of net demand deposits? Of course, (38.5/299) × 100, or 12.88.

What if the Fed had instead raised reserve requirements on net demand deposits further to the maximum allowed by Congress, 14 percent? Actual reserves are still $40 million, but required reserves rise to 14 percent of $299 million plus 3 percent of $50 million, or $43.36 million. Our bank has *deficient* reserves of $3.36 million. Not only can it *not* create new deposits, it must reduce its deposits liabilities by deficient reserves times the multiple of 100/14, or about 7.1—or by $24 million to $275 million. It may call in loans payable on demand, reducing both items (5) and (7c) by this amount. It may, as loans become due, not renew them until (5) and (7c) have fallen by this amount. It may try to sell U.S. securities to its depositors, charging their accounts and again reducing (4) and (7c) by the amount needed. Unless the bank can somewhere get more reserves of $3.36 million, it must reduce its demand deposit liabilities by $24 million. At that point, required reserves will be 14 percent of $275 million plus 3 percent of $50 million, or $40 million, equal to actual reserves. The money supply is down. Banks and borrowers have a hard time: Banks earn their living by holding the IOU's of others (items (4) or (5)). They now have to reduce these holdings. Borrowers find it hard or impossible to borrow, and "money is tight." To the extent that any of the remaining loans fall due (reducing items (5) and (7c) below the new maximum), they can be renewed, but banks will do it only at higher interest rates, so eager is the demand for money.

reducing the reserve requirement   Now let us reverse the situation. The Fed *reduces* the reserve requirement from the maximum to the minimum, from 14 to 7 percent. Our original situation, let us assume, is as on page 216, except that in the period of tight money both items (5) and (7c) have been reduced by $24 million. (You might want to pencil in the new figures of $226 million and $216 million). With one stroke, required reserves now change from $40 million (equal to *actual* reserves) to 7 percent of $275 million plus 3 percent of $50 million, or to $20.75 million. Our bank has excess reserves of $19.25 million! Now it can do a great number of things. First, it may choose to do nothing at all. It is not illegal to have excess reserves. Second, which is more likely in the United States, it may get rid of its indebtedness to the Fed, reducing by $10 million both items (2) and (9). This would still leave excess reserves of $9.25 million. Third, it may try to create new money by offering to lend at low interest and by reducing credit standards. Suppose it decides to follow this course: "money is easy." Yet, nothing may happen at all—people may not want to borrow. As the Fed puts it, "you cannot push on a string, although you can pull on it (refuse to lend)." But suppose people do want to borrow. How much can our bank lend, having excess reserves of $19.25 million? It would probably start out cautiously, lending only an amount *equal to* its excess reserves. Note the words "equal to." The bank never touches the reserves themselves. It does *not* "lend out its reserves." It creates *new* money (7c), an entry in the books, in return for customers' IOU's. The balance sheet would change as in step A below: Then our bank waits.

SECOND NATIONAL BANK OF AMHERST, MASSACHUSETTS (IN MILLIONS)

ASSETS		LIABILITIES AND NET WORTH	
A. 5. Loans	$+\$19.25$	7(c). Demand deposits (public)	$+\$19.25$
B. 1. Cash	$-\$19.25$	7(c). Demand deposits (public)	$-\$19.25$
C. 5. Loans	$+\$17.90$	7(c). Demand deposits (public)	$+\$17.90$
D. 2. Deposit at Federal Reserve Bank of Boston	$-\$17.90$	7(c). Demand deposits (public)	$-\$17.90$

Possibly the customers want to cash the new accounts. Then, as in step B above, the bank may pay the amount from its vault cash, canceling the new accounts. The money supply is up by $19.25 million, first in demand deposits, then in paper bills. Here the story ends.

But Americans typically do not behave this way. More likely than not, they spend new deposits forever via check, as described in Chapter 9. If our bank finds that the new money created in step A simply circulates from account to account *in this bank* (as on page 199), it can safely create *more* money. It still has excess reserves, for its *actual* reserves are $40 million, but its *required* reserves are now 7 percent of $294.25 million ($275 million plus $19.25 million) plus 3 percent of $50 million, or $22.10 million instead of $20.75 million. This is no surprise, in that demand deposits are up by $19.25 million, requiring extra reserves of $1.35 million. *Excess* reserves are $17.90 million. Our bank can in step C repeat on a smaller scale what it did in step A (provided step B did not occur). Even if these new deposits are cashed (as in hypothetical step B), the money supply is up by $19.25 million + $17.90 million = $37.15 million.

As we said before, this is unlikely. Much more likely, however, is this: checks are written on the new accounts and they fall into the hands *of other banks* (as on pages 202–204). Then our bank will experience the entries shown as step D. This does not change our conclusion about the money supply, for somewhere another Bank X will experience the opposite of step D (gaining, as the Springfield or Sacramento banks above, reserves and deposits). This is shown in step E. If the demand deposits remain with Bank X (not being cashed but

BANK X (IN MILLIONS)

ASSETS		LIABILITIES AND NET WORTH	
E. 2. Deposit at Federal Reserve Bank	+$17.90	7(c). Demand deposits (public)	+$17.90
F. 5. Loans	+$16.65	7(c). Demand deposits (public)	+$16.65

G. 2. Deposit at Federal Reserve
    Bank
    1. Cash
	− $16.65
	+$16.65		

H. 1. Cash	− $16.65	7(c). Demand deposits (public)	− $16.65

continually changing hands as on page 199) Bank X has excess reserves. It gained actual reserves of $17.90 million, but its new deposits only *require* additional reserves of $1.25 million. Hence, it has excess reserves of $16.65 million. It can safely do what the Amherst bank did in steps A and C: create new money equal to excess reserves. If people want to borrow, we may get what is shown in step F. Now the aggregate money supply is up by $19.25 million + $17.90 million + $16.65 million = $53.8 million. This conclusion is not changed if people cash the latest new deposits, forcing Bank X to cash its Federal Reserve deposit (G) and give the cash to its customers (H). Bank X still has left reserves of (millions) $17.90 − 16.65 = 1.25, enough to "support" its remaining customers' deposits of $17.90 million. In short, as long as people want to borrow and the new demand deposits are not cashed, the money supply, although it may move from bank to bank (steps D and E), keeps rising. It clearly does not rise forever, because each addition to demand deposits converts some excess reserves into required reserves. When they are all required, the process comes to an end. In our case, where the reserve requirement is 7 percent and the original excess reserves $19.25 million, the latter figure is 7 percent of the maximum new deposits banks can create. This maximum is (in million dollars)

$$19.25 + 17.90 + 16.65 + 15.48 + 14.40 + 13.39 + \ldots = 275.$$

This will only happen, of course, if banks choose not to hold excess reserves, do want to lend, do find borrowers, and borrowers do not cash the new deposits. In the United States, this is usually true. If you want a precise formula for the assumptions stated above, multiply excess reserves by 100/RR, where RR is the reserve requirement in percent. Above,

$$19.25 \times 100/7 = 19.25 \times 14.285 = 275$$

summary   In summary, we can state that an increase in reserve requirements eliminates excess reserves, if any, and thereafter *forces* a reduction in the money supply, entailing higher interest rates and difficulties for borrowers. Lower reserve requirements create excess reserves and the *possibility* for easier borrowing, lower interest rates, and a larger money supply.

Setting the Discount Rate

The Federal Reserve Banks can also hope to influence the money supply by varying the rate at which member banks can borrow at the Fed, be it via discounts or advances. This rate of interest is called the *discount rate*. Take another look at the position of our hypothetical bank on page 216.

raising the discount rate   Suppose the Fed wanted to make money harder to get. Instead of raising the reserve requirement from 12 to 12.88 and then to 14 percent as we did above, it may raise the discount rate from 4 to 5 percent. This means that our bank will have to pay 5 percent on $10 million—item (9)—or $500,000 per year instead of $400,000. This may cause the Amherst bank to pay off the entire debt, reducing both item (2) and item (9) by $10 million. But now note the consequence of this. Although the reserve requirement is unchanged at, say, the originally assumed 12.5 percent, the amount of actual reserves has dropped by $10 million to $30 million. Yet required reserves are, as we saw on page 216, $38.875 million. Our bank has *deficient* reserves of $8.875 million. It may try to correct this illegal position by reducing demand deposit liabilities by $71 million to $228 million, hence reducing required reserves (for the remaining demand and time deposits) to actual reserves. It may achieve this by persuading depositors to buy government securities—reducing item (4) along with (7c)—or by refusing to renew loans as they fall due—reducing items (5) and (7c). Or it may try to borrow some other bank's excess reserves in what is called the *federal funds market*. As in the case of an increased required reserve percentage, given the amount of reserves, we now have tight money, given the required reserve percentage, but with a reduced amount of reserves. Interest rates are up, borrowing is difficult or impossible, the money supply is down.

lowering the discount rate   What if the Fed wanted to make money easier to get? Instead of lowering the reserve requirement, it may encourage banks to borrow from it by *lowering* the discount rate, as from 4 to 3 percent. This means that our bank will only have to pay $300,000 per year on the $10 million borrowed—item (9). It may decide to borrow more, say a total of $13.33 million, leaving the annual interest cost at $400,000, as before. In this case, both items (2) and (9) would rise by $3.33 million. The amount of actual reserves is now $43.33 million. The required reserves, still assuming the original required percentage of 12.5, are $38.875 million. Our bank has excess reserves of $4.455 million ($3.33 million newly borrowed and $1.125 million in excess originally). It may, as a result, try to lend more, increasing items (5) and (7c) by at least this amount of $4.455 million. As we have seen above, if people do want to borrow and do not cash the new deposits created, the money supply may ultimately rise until the excess reserves are all required, that is, until $4.455 million are 12.5 percent of the new deposits, which can thus equal $35.64 million. Money is easy, banks encourage borrowing by low interest rates and relaxed credit standards.

summary   In summary, we can state that an increase of the discount rate may discourage member bank borrowing at the Fed, possibly leading to a fall in the supply and a rise in the cost of money. A decrease of the discount rate may encourage member bank borrowing at the Fed, leading possibly to an increase in the supply and a fall in the cost of money. Note the careful wording, however. This *may* happen. Banks may also borrow *more* at the Fed despite higher discount rates, borrowing at 5 percent while lending new money to their customers at 8 percent! The Fed discourages this, however. Its inspectors will not permit a member bank to maintain part of its loans *continually* on the basis of Federal Reserve borrowing. The "discount window" at the Fed has the primary function of tiding a bank over a period of adjustment, because it often cannot reduce its deposit liabilities overnight. Beyond that, American banks traditionally do not like to be indebted to the Fed and such "moral suasion" on the part of Federal Reserve inspectors is often quite unnecessary. In the same way, banks need not react to a lower discount rate at all, and even if they do, as here contemplated, no one may want to borrow from them.

Because the immediate effects are so uncertain, we can best describe a discount rate change as a kind of flag, signaling the intentions of the Fed.

Open-Market Operations

The most important means of Federal Reserve action to influence the money supply is through their purchase or sale of domestic IOU's, especially U.S. government securities. This is referred to as *open-market operations* because the Fed buys and sells securities through dealers in New York City exactly as everyone else does.

For illustrative purposes we shall act as if all such operations are done with interest-bearing U.S. government securities, popularly called government bonds, but officially designated as bills, certificates, notes, and bonds. At the end of March 1969, there existed $359.5 billion of such securities. Of these, $79.0 billion were held by U.S. government agencies and trust funds, $52.4 billion were held by Federal Reserve Banks, $60.6 billion by commercial banks, and the rest by all others. Of the total, furthermore, $237.3 billion were marketable and could be freely bought and sold. They are the object of open-market operations.

federal reserve sales   Imagine that the Federal Reserve persuaded the nonbank public to buy $10 million of U.S. securities from it by offering them for relatively low prices. What would happen? Typically, the public would write checks on their accounts (for example, in Amherst), handing them (via a securities dealer) to the Fed. The Fed would do what it *always* does when receiving checks drawn on a member bank, namely, deduct that amount from the member bank's account at the Fed. The resultant entries, if we imagine this to involve the Amherst bank described above and the Boston Federal Reserve, are:

FEDERAL RESERVE BANK OF BOSTON (IN MILLION DOLLARS)

ASSETS		LIABILITIES AND NET WORTH	
3. U.S. Government securities	—$10	6(b). Demand deposit (Amherst bank)	—$10

SECOND NATIONAL BANK OF AMHERST (IN MILLION DOLLARS)

ASSETS		LIABILITIES AND NET WORTH	
2. Deposit at Federal Reserve Bank of Boston	—$10	7(c). Demand deposits (public)	—$10

For the Amherst bank the result is disastrous. (Unlike the two cases on pages 202–204, furthermore, there is no bank in the United States that has gained the reserves Amherst lost. This is a loss to the system as a whole.) It had (page 216) reserves of $40 million but has left only $30 million. It now has net demand deposits of $289 million, requiring (again assuming the original reserve requirement of 12.5 percent) $36.125 million of reserves. Another $1.5 million are needed for time deposits (at 3 percent). Hence, there are *deficient* reserves of $7.625 million. Unless our bank can get new reserves from somewhere, it must reduce demand deposits by another $61 million down to $228 million, for example, by calling in loans or selling government securities to its depositors. Money is tight; the money supply is down by a total of $71 million; interest rates are high; borrowing is next to impossible. (Had the bank not had excess reserves to begin with, the money supply would have had to drop by $80 million.)

federal reserve purchases   Imagine, instead, the Federal Reserve *buying* $10 million of U.S. securities from the nonbank public, persuading the public to sell by offering relatively high prices. The public would receive checks from the Fed drawn on the Fed itself, and it would promptly deposit them at commercial banks. The consequences would be exactly the reverse of the above, because the commercial banks would send the checks in turn to the Fed to be credited to *their* accounts. On the commercial banks' balance sheets, items (2) and (7c) would go *up* by $10 million, so would items (3) and (6b) on the balance sheet of the Fed, which now holds more government securities while owing more to its members. The commercial banks would find their deposit liabilities up by $10 million. But, by our assumption, required reserves are up by only $1.25 million, with actual reserves up by $10 million. Excess reserves are up by $8.75 million (previously they were down by the same amount, because we moved from $1.125 million of excess to $7.625 million of deficient reserves). As we have seen so often, money becomes "easy": banks are willing to lend at low rates and to lower credit standards. As people borrow—increasing items (5) and (7c)—the money supply rises, potentially by another $70 million over the $10 million depositors have already received from the Fed in return for their securities.

summary   In summary, we can state that Federal Reserve open-market sales to the nonbank public will reduce the commercial banks' reserves, eliminating excess reserves and, if large enough, creating deficient reserves, *forcing* a further fall in the availability of and rise in the cost of money. Federal Reserve open-market purchases will increase commercial banks' reserves, making it *possible* for the money supply to rise by a multiple.

THE CONSEQUENCES OF MONETARY POLICY

Monetary policy is undertaken solely for the purpose of achieving certain *consequences*. That, of course, is why we study it.

Expanding Aggregate Demand

Suppose GNP and resource use are below potential. Then the Fed might do one or all of the following: (1) lower reserve requirements, (2) lower the discount rate, (3) buy securities in the open market.

immediate consequences   We know the immediate results. Action (1) will create excess reserves, although the amount of total reserves is unchanged. Action (2) will probably create excess reserves, as at least some banks are encouraged to borrow more from the Fed, getting larger amounts of reserves. Action (3) will create excess reserves by giving banks larger amounts of reserves. If the securities are bought from the nonbank public, it will also increase the money supply immediately by an equal amount (as the Fed's checks are deposited).

later consequences   What happens hereafter and when it happens is only *conjecture*. These things do not have to happen. Quite probably, banks will stand ready to make more loans at lower rates and under easier conditions. (They do not earn anything on excess reserves, but they do earn interest on loans made by creating new money on the basis of excess reserves.) Hence, it is conceivable that at least some consumers borrow more than before. Others have already more cash in hand, having sold securities to the Fed. Conceivably, consumers as a group spend more out of any income. Our consumption demand line shifts upwards, as shown in Figure 6.2(b) MOVEMENT ALONG VS. SHIFT OF THE CONSUMPTION DEMAND LINE. Or consider the shift of line *x* to line *y* in Figure 6.5 CONSUMPTION VS. GNP STATISTICS.

Private businesses may also be encouraged to put more of their dreams into reality. Previously, when interest rates on business loans were 5 percent per year, a certain sum might have been borrowed only for a monthly payment of $100,000. Now it may be borrowed at 4 percent, at a smaller monthly payment. Or the same monthly payment may be able to get a larger loan. In any case, business spending on buildings, equipment, and inventories may be encouraged, raising the investment demand line, as in Figure 6.6 INVESTMENT DEMAND. This would also be true if businesses always finance investments from retained profits. When interest rates on government bonds are 5 percent, businesses with funds might *save* them in the form of bonds if they thought they could only make 4.7 percent by investing in the business. Yet, after government bond yields fall to 4 percent, they will find it more advantageous to *invest* by buying equipment. Household purchases of new residential houses are also strongly affected by the interest rate. The FHA-insured and VA-guaranteed mortgages, making possible very low down payments, may not legally carry more than a certain interest rate. Hence, in periods of high interest rates above the FHA and VA ceiling, no bank will lend for this purpose.

State and local governments may well be in a similar position. Their expenditures for highways, schools, sewers, and so on are frequently tied to the possibility of long-range borrowing. These levels of government cannot create money, and they may be reluctant to increase taxes to cover huge capital expenditures all in one year. Frequently, such governments are even limited by statute to borrowing below a certain percentage, say 4.5. Hence, a fall in the rates they have to pay on their bonds, for example, from 4.6 to 4.1 percent, may be just the thing needed to go ahead and raise the level of government demand (see Figure 6.7 GOVERNMENT DEMAND).

Finally, if easy monetary policy does increase these autonomous demands, it also may increase somewhat spending on imports, because the borrowing households, businesses, and governments may well increase spending on both domestic *and* foreign goods. In that case, net export demand, or exports minus imports, may decline—unless, of course, foreigners also buy more from us (Figure 6.8 NET EXPORT DEMAND). In any case, aggregate demand is likely to rise. As we have seen in Chapter 7, this will (in a period of general unemployment) raise real GNP and employment. In a period of full employment or demand-pull inflation, however, it would create or intensify demand-pull inflation. In that case, of course, the Fed would not wish to raise aggregate demand.

a graphic exposition   We can also return to our earlier graphical analysis. Consider Figure 10.1 HOW EASY MONETARY POLICY WORKS. Suppose we are at a position of general unemployment equilibrium, such as at the aggregate demand and aggregate supply inter-

Figure 10.1   HOW EASY MONETARY POLICY WORKS

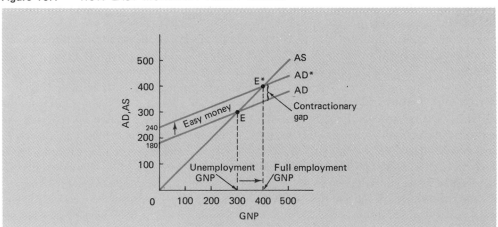

Easy monetary policy (lowering reserve requirements, lowering the discount rate, open-market purchases) raises aggregate demand from AD to AD*. This displaces an original equilibrium GNP at E to a higher full employment level at E*.

section E of $300 billion, but potential GNP is $400 billion. To get to full employment, we need an increase in aggregate demand by the size of the excess supply gap as we find it at full employment. This we can try to do by *easy monetary policy*. The Fed states: we have to "lean against the prevailing wind." If there is an excess supply gap at full employment GNP, forcing the economy into unemployment, we must try to expand aggregate demand to force it right back to full employment. In terms of Figure 10.1, we should encourage an increase in the money supply and a reduction in interest rates just enough to raise the AD line until it goes through point E*. Then *full employment* GNP of $400 billion becomes an *equilibrium* GNP, capable of being maintained.

Every increase in the money supply up to this point is for the good, for its only consequence is an increase in output, a reduction in involuntary general unemployment, and hence a reduction in scarcity. Whatever the money supply is at full employment is its "natural" limit, if we want to use that term. To limit it by anything else, such as gold, would be uttter folly, for if the money supply is lower, aggregate demand will be lower. We will have more scarcity than is necessary.

Reducing Aggregate Demand

If the money supply were higher than necessary to give us just full employment, aggregate demand would be too large. The AD line would shift up beyond its intersection at E* with the AS line in Figure 10.1. *Then*, we would have encouraged people to demand more goods than we could possibly produce at full employment. If the aggregate demand line in Figure 10.1 were to intersect the aggregate supply line above and to the right of E*, we would have an excess demand or expansionary gap at full employment. But expansion would be impossible in terms of *real* output beyond $400 billion. The only thing that could happen is that prices of all goods rise. We would have *demand-pull inflation*.

In such a situation, the Fed would (4) increase reserve requirements, (5) raise the discount rate, or (6) sell securities in the open market. (Note the first news story introducing this chapter.) We have seen the immediate results. Action (4), if carried on forcefully enough, *will* create deficient reserves, although the amount of total reserves is unchanged. Action (5) *may* encourage banks to repay their loans from the Fed, reducing the amounts of reserves. Action (6), if carried on forcefully enough, *will* create deficient reserves by reducing the amounts of reserves owned by banks. If the securities are sold to the nonbank public, it also will decrease the money supply right away by an equal amount (as checks are given to the Fed). As a result, the following *will* happen. Banks must reduce the money supply still further, make loans much harder to get or refuse to make any. Interest rates soar. (Note the second news story introducing this chapter.) From here on, it is conjecture. Probably aggregate demand will fall (for reasons analogous to the above rise in it). That is just what we want, because until aggregate demand falls to intersect the aggregate supply line at E*, we have demand inflation. This is shown in Figure 10.2 HOW TIGHT MONETARY POLICY WORKS. The way to stop demand-pull inflation is to reduce the supply and raise the cost of money. Again the Fed "leans against the prevailing wind." If there is an excess demand gap at full

Figure 10.2   HOW TIGHT MONETARY POLICY WORKS

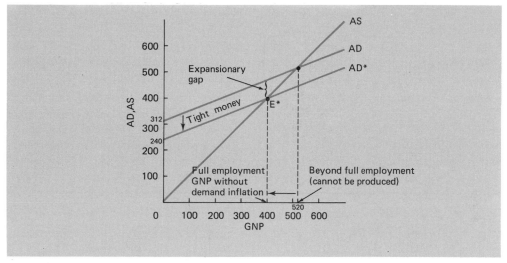

Tight monetary policy (raising reserve requirements, raising the discount rate, open-market sales) reduces aggregate demand from AD to AD*. This replaces an inflationary situation by full employment GNP at E*.

employment GNP, forcing the economy into inflation, we must try to *contract* aggregate demand to force it right back to full employment without inflation.

Summary So Far

In summary, let us just remember this. Most people believe that the money supply should be limited by the amount of gold we have. They believe that an increase in the money supply, independent of an increase in the supply of gold, must cause inflation. You should be able to show why this is not so. There is nothing automatic about money going up and prices going up. Tying the money supply to the quantity of gold is as foolish as tying it to the population of grasshoppers. Suppose the gold supply allowed only a money supply of sufficient size to raise aggregate demand to a $300 billion level, as in Figure 10.1 HOW EASY MONETARY POLICY WORKS. Then we would have eternal unemployment. Suppose new discoveries raise the gold stock tenfold. Then the money supply would rise, encouraging aggregate demand until we demanded the impossible real GNP of, say, $520 billion in Figure 10.2 HOW TIGHT MONETARY POLICY WORKS. Then we would have eternal inflation. Human judgment is the only reasonable way, *tying the size of the money supply to nothing but its consequences.* If increasing the money supply has desirable consequences (raising real GNP), we should *increase* it, even if the gold supply or the population of grasshoppers is going *down.* If increasing the money supply has undesirable consequences (causing demand-pull inflation), we should not increase it (if we are at full employment without demand-pull inflation) or decrease it (if we already have demand-pull inflation). This we should do even if the gold supply is going up. It is best to forget about gold as well as grasshoppers. They are equally irrelevant.

JUDGING THE EFFECTIVENESS OF MONETARY POLICY

Theoretically, monetary policy can assure full employment without demand-pull inflation. However, we should understand that this policy is a very difficult one. In reality, it may not work at all or not very satisfactorily or not fast enough. Let us see why. Look again at Figure 10.1 HOW EASY MONETARY POLICY WORKS. Let us assume that the relationships underlying it depict accurately those in the United States and that we are in a position of general unemployment equilibrium, as at E. The country is in a major depression if we assume that potential GNP equals $400 billion. It is easy enough to conclude that we should engage in expansionary or easy money policy. Beyond that we have troubles.

The Recognition Lag

First, for a perfect determination of the dose of medicine required we have to know exactly the severity of the disease. We may not be able to know exactly where we are because (1) all statistics are somewhat imperfect and (2) it takes time to collect and process them. Hence, we may now only know where we were a year or several months ago. It may be obvious that we still have unemployment on a large scale, but perfect policy-making requires knowledge of its extent, whether our real GNP is still, as some time ago, at $300 billion, or is now at $350 billion, or $280 billion. This unavoidable problem is called the *recognition lag*. So we have to guess that GNP is still at $300 billion, and in this case, we happen to be right.

The Administrative Lag

Second, we have to decide on the dose of medicine to be given and we must actually administer it. By how much shall we lower reserve requirements or the discount rate? How many billion dollars' worth of securities should the Fed buy? The time elapsed between recognizing where we are (even if it *is* a guess) and doing something about it is called the *administrative lag*. It could be extremely short. Reserve requirements and the discount rate can be changed at a moment's notice; billions of dollars of securities can be bought from security dealers with a few telephone calls! Although this can be done fast, the decision on the extent of this action also involves fallible human judgment. If the policy-makers have a workable model of the economy (such as implied by Figure 10.1) and are convinced that the economy is in the position shown at E, they know that aggregate demand should be raised by $100 billion. This is the amount by which actual GNP falls short of potential GNP.

Suppose now that the monetary authority decides to raise autonomous demands through easy money. It may seem only reasonable to raise demand by the whole $100 billion. There is a problem, however, if the Fed succeeds in this. If we had a model such as this one, we would also know what would happen in the future. Owing to the kind of multiplier and accelerator process discussed in Chapter 8, in later years consumption spending would rise *induced* by the higher real income. Investment spending would rise *induced* by the rise of income. If autonomous demands are still up by $100 billion then, aggregate demand (autonomous plus induced) would exceed $400 billion, that is, would exceed what the economy can produce. Prices would then rise; we would have exchanged general unemployment for demand-pull inflation! Hence, later years would call for a tight money policy, reducing autonomous demands by exactly the amount that was added to induced demands. Whenever the aggregate demand needed for full employment (here $400 billion) does not come about naturally, monetary policy must expand or contract actual demand by just the right amount.

The Operational Lag

If this looks simple, let us remind ourselves of the following. The estimate of the economy's original position may have been wrong. Policy-makers also do not have a perfect model of the economy, and they may estimate incorrectly the changes in induced demand that have to be compensated for by changes in autonomous demand. Other unforeseen changes (such as the types of unforeseeable autonomous demand shifts discussed in Chapter 8) may completely alter the picture. Hence, the result may not be so accurate as we wished. Even if all estimates of required changes in demand are made correctly and there are no unforeseen changes, there is no way short of trial and error to determine when how much monetary ease or tightness brings about an actual change in demand of the required magnitude. This also involves the *operational lag*, a serious lag between policy action taken and its effect on spending and the GNP.

the expansionary case   The Fed can increase the supply of money and lower interest rates, but it can never force people to borrow and spend. Hence, easy money policy may *never* raise aggregate demand. Banks may refuse to lend (as they did in the 1930's) despite huge excess reserves, because they consider potential borrowers poor credit risks. Businesses may not want to borrow, because their decision to invest depends on lots of things other than cheap money. If they think that they will make losses, they will not invest no matter how cheap credit may be. Sellers of securities to the Fed may hold money idle or buy stock instead of goods. Or they may buy only foreign goods, which in no way helps *our* GNP and employment (unless foreigners buy more from us as a result). Instead, easy money policy may raise aggregate demand, but only a year later (as voters debate whether to build that new school now that money is cheap). It may raise it right away, but by too little or too much, keeping us below full employment or pushing us into demand-pull inflation.

the contractionary case   Clearly, it is easier to force people to spend less by refusing to lend. As the Fed puts it, "you *can* pull on a string, even though you can't push it." Yet tight money policy, too, may not have effect until much later, or it may have an immediate effect of wrong magnitude, failing to avoid inflation or pushing demand down too far, thereby causing unemployment.

In addition, *financial intermediaries* (which cannot create money), such as savings banks, may seriously hamper monetary policy. When the Fed lowers the money supply and raises interest rates to discourage spending, these institutions are likely to encourage people, through higher interest rates, to part with idle money balances. Households and businesses economize on their money balances and exchange unused portions of their checking accounts at commercial banks for savings accounts at savings banks or the newly invented negotiable time certificates of deposit or for government securities held by savings banks. In fact, during the 1960–1965 period, the holdings of time certificates of deposit by nonfinancial corporations rose by $17 billion, while their holdings of money and U.S. securities fell by $7 billion. Savings banks, in turn, lend the greatest part of the proceeds to those eager to borrow and spend but unable to obtain loans of new money from commercial banks. As a result, most of the formerly idle checking accounts fall into the hands of eager spenders at a time when the Fed wants to *discourage* spending. The money supply may go down, but the rate at which the remaining supply is spent—the *velocity* of money—may rise so much as to increase spending. Then, of course, the Fed can decrease the money supply further, but for a time at least its efforts may be frustrated.

Less than Perfection

Historically, the Federal Reserve System, as central banks in other countries, has been very cautious in administering policy. It has been especially fearful of inadvertently causing inflation. In a situation such as that depicted in Figure 10.1 HOW EASY MONETARY POLICY WORKS, it may only encourage autonomous aggregate demand permanently by the amount *ultimately* needed, that is, $60 billion a year, not by the $100 billion we first considered. This $60 billion is the size of the excess supply gap at full employment if aggregate demand is shown by AD. Economists also call this the *contractionary gap*, because without government intervention, GNP will contract to a lower unemployment level, here $300 billion. Even if this could be done just right (and were not upset by other unforeseen disturbances), inflation may not be avoided. Because of the tendency of the economy to generate accelerator effects, aggregate demand may still exceed aggregate supply temporarily on the way to full employment without demand-pull inflation. Then, although the *whole* economy may have more goods, those whose spending rises by less than prices will have fewer goods.

More Power to the Fed?

Some people have in fact argued that the Fed should be given additional and more *direct* powers to influence aggregate demand. If for the many reasons now indicated, monetary policy fails to work or fails to work with enough force or at the right time, the Fed might use these additional weapons. It might, for instance, be given the power to determine minimum down payments on the purchase on credit of consumer goods or residential houses, as well as maximum periods for repayment of consumption and mortgage loans. Increasing the down payment and shortening the repayment period would powerfully reduce spending and vice versa. In 1968, for instance, the *net* increase in installment credit was $9 billion, whereas mortgage debt increased *net* by $27 billion. The kind of Federal Reserve power discussed (power it did have in World War II and during the Korean War) could greatly increase or reduce such borrowing and spending. (A tough policy in 1968 might have prevented *any* extension of installment credit, undoubtedly reducing consumption demand. Extensions of such credit, including renewals of earlier credit, were $89.9 billion.) At the present time, such *selective monetary controls* (hitting on particular people, such as home buyers) are not authorized by Congress, except for the Fed's power to set minimum down payments on stock purchases (*margin requirements*). This has only the most indirect effect on spending on *goods*. By making it harder or easier to buy stocks on credit (most of which are old issues being continually resold), stock prices *may* be kept from rising or falling; this *may* dampen or encourage businessmen's optimism and *may* reduce or increase investment demand. A highly tenuous link! On the other hand, the present *general* monetary policy, allegedly discriminating against no one, is in fact often discriminatory. Note our discussion of statutory interest ceilings on certain mortgages and types of government spending. The result: higher interest rates in *general* hit *selected* groups of spenders.

In short, monetary policy is an art. To engage in it with perfect success requires omniscience. We must know exactly where we are (hence the need for accurate, comprehensive, and timely statistics). We must know how and when people's demand will react to how much of what kind of monetary policy. We must know how and when producers will react to this in turn. And we must know whether and when what kinds of other disturbances working in the same direction with or opposite direction to monetary policy can be expected! No wonder policy-makers at times go wrong. Yet, if they were able to lift real GNP from an average of 12 percent below potential to an average of 7 percent below, it would be worth it to try.

A NOTE OF DISSENT: THE AUTOMATIC MONETARY PILOT

Not all economists agree with the tenor of this chapter. There are some who would reduce rather than increase the Fed's power to engage in consciously determined monetary policy.[2] They argue that human judgment is more fallible than can be tolerated and that the Fed, continually tightening and loosening the monetary tourniquets, will, with the best of intentions, make things worse. Being overly preoccupied with fluctuations in GNP, employment, and prices, the Fed is conditioned, so the argument goes, to overreact. Its stop-go policies will not avoid booms and busts, but make *bigger* booms and *bigger* busts. They point to the early 1930's when the Fed, operating as it does today, with imperfect data and imperfect theories, and hampered, as it is today, by policy lags that are uncertain and may vary

[2] This view is often associated with Milton Friedman of the University of Chicago. For an excellent brief statement in Professor Friedman's own words, you might wish to consult Milton Friedman and Walter W. Heller, *Monetary vs. Fiscal Policy* (New York: Norton, 1969).

from 3 to 18 months, allowed the money supply to *contract* by a third. This contributed to the greatest depression ever experienced by Americans.

Some economists would, therefore, prefer a radically different approach: The economic boat should not be steered by a human helmsman at all (who is free to make one wrong decision after another), but by an *automatic monetary pilot*. Human authority should be replaced by one simple rule: for example, to increase the money supply by 4 percent a year through thick and thin (or perhaps by at least 2 and at most 6 percent). This percentage is to reflect roughly the observed and expected growth rate of our potential GNP. Hence, this automatic increase in money is to encourage aggregate demand about as much as we can expect aggregate supply to grow, giving us on the average just full employment, but without demand-pull inflation. If autonomous aggregate demand ever were to fall, the continued increase in the money supply would put a quick stop to any massive collapse in demand, avoiding any *major* dip in real GNP. If autonomous aggregate demand ever were to rise too fast, the continued policy of not raising the money supply by more than, say, 4 percent a year would quickly put a massive restraint on the demand rise. Because there is an upper limit for the velocity of money, this restraint in the rise of demand prevents the economic machinery from "overheating" and avoids any *serious* inflation.

To be sure, we will have a business cycle, but we will not have a serious one, the argument goes. This is not a counsel of perfection; it is only a practical, reasonable way of avoiding the capricious actions of a bungling group of Federal Reserve Board officials.

As mentioned above, most economists do not subscribe to these views. They feel that binding ourselves forever to a fixed rule of action in an ever-changing world, tying our hands in face of all unforeseen contingencies, is a greater error than all repeated acts of foolishness imaginable. Most economists would subscribe to the words of Justice Oliver Wendell Holmes: "Every year, if not every day, we have to wager our salvation upon some prophesy based on imperfect knowledge." The simple rule of the automatic pilot is an illusory escape from the practical problem of decision-making in the face of uncertainty. It is like refusing to provide a patient with crutches because using them he may fall or because, 100 years from now, we may discover a way to heal his limbs.

SUMMARY

1   All private banks are required to hold reserves, dollar amounts of certain assets equal to at least a stated percentage of the dollar amount of certain liabilities. Commercial member banks of the Federal Reserve System must have cash in vaults or must own demand deposits at the Fed as reserves for their own demand and time deposit liabilities. The role of reserves is *not* to give value to the mentioned liabilities, but to limit their amount. The Federal Reserve Banks themselves once were required to hold gold certificates as reserves for Federal Reserve Notes issued and their demand deposits. This requirement is now eliminated, and gold plays no role at all in our domestic monetary affairs.

2   If the Fed raises reserve requirements, excess reserves of member banks (if any) are reduced, possibly eliminated, and potentially become negative. In the latter case, banks unable to get new reserves must reduce their deposit liabilities by a multiple. If the Fed lowers reserve requirements, deficient reserves of member banks (if any) are reduced and possibly eliminated; positive excess reserves appear. In the latter case, they may be held idle, be used to reduce indebtedness to the Fed, or become the basis for money creation by a multiple.

3 An increase in the Fed's discount rate may discourage member bank borrowing; a decrease may encourage borrowing. This, in turn, may lead to a fall in the supply and a rise in the cost of money, or vice versa, respectively.

4 Open-market operations by the Fed directly affect the amount of actual reserves in the banking system without changing the amount of required reserves. The effect is the same as if the reserve requirement had been changed without a change in the amount of actual reserves.

5 The purpose of monetary policy (changing reserve requirements, changing discount rates, open-market operations) is to affect aggregate demand so as to bring about the elimination of unemployment and the production of the potential GNP without demand-pull inflation. As long as such a goal is furthered, and no other undesirable side effects occur, *any* change in the availability and cost of money can be called desirable.

6 This can be shown graphically, as in Figure 10.1 HOW EASY MONETARY POLICY WORKS. Given aggregate demand, AD, there is a *contractionary gap* at full employment. Hence, output contracts below potential and reaches equilibrium at a $300 billion GNP. By easy monetary policy (lowering reserve requirements, lowering the discount rate, open-market purchases), the Fed can hope to shift up the autonomous components of aggregate demand by the amount of the contractionary gap. AD becomes AD*. Full employment GNP becomes equilibrium GNP.

Now look at Figure 10.2 HOW TIGHT MONETARY POLICY WORKS. Given aggregate demand, AD, there is an *expansionary gap* at full employment. Output, however, cannot possibly expand beyond potential, such as to a $520 billion GNP. Only $400 billion can be produced, yet demand is continually larger. Prices rise, and we have demand-pull inflation. By tight monetary policy the Fed can shift down the autonomous components of aggregate demand by the amount of the expansionary gap. AD becomes AD*. Full employment GNP becomes equilibrium GNP without demand-pull inflation.

7 Monetary policy, however, is an art. Its perfect execution is hampered by the recognition lag, the administrative lag, and the operational lag. Actual policy must be expected to yield less than perfect results. It is doubtful that more direct powers given to the Fed (such as selective monetary controls) could overcome these problems. Nor could an "automatic monetary pilot."

TERMS[3]

actual reserves	automatic monetary pilot
administrative lag	contractionary gap

deficient reserves   net borrowed reserves
discount rate   open-market operations
excess reserves   operational lag
expansionary gap   recognition lag
federal funds market   required reserves
financial intermediary   reserve requirement
free reserves   selective monetary controls
margin requirements   velocity of money

QUESTIONS FOR REVIEW AND DISCUSSION

1 "The role of reserves is not to give value to anything." Discuss.

2 Look at the hypothetical balance sheet on page 216. If we were interested in keeping items (7) minus (3) at or below $299 million, we could designate loans (or net worth) as "reserves" and set the reserve requirement at what percentage?

3 What happens when the Fed raises or lowers the reserve requirement? When it raises or lowers the discount rate?

4 "If each bank creates new money equal to excess reserves (and if no one cashes newly created demand deposits, but transfers them only via check), all banks together will end up creating money equal to a multiple of any increase in excess reserves." Trace this process through a series of hypothetical bank statements.

5 "If, under the assumptions of question 4, new excess reserves of $10 million appear, while the reserve requirement is 20 percent or 1/5, the total of new money created will equal 100/20 or 5/1 multiplied by $10 million." Do you agree? Explain your answer.

6 "In the absence of reserve requirements, banks could create money without limit." Evaluate. Under what circumstances might it be true? Or false?

7 "Changing reserve requirements is a relatively heavy, blunt tool of credit control, compared with the gradual, flexible way open-market operations can be used." Comment.

8 Member bank deposits at their Federal Reserve Banks, although not part of the money supply, are often referred to as *high-powered money*. Try to explain.

9 The text describes the effect of open-market operations involving the Fed's trading of U.S. securities with the *nonbank* public. Would the process and its effects differ if the Fed dealt with *commercial banks*?

10 Suppose you were a commercial banker at a time when your long-standing customers want more money, but the Fed is pursuing restrictive policies. What would you do?

11 "In many periods of prosperity, it is difficult to get loans, although the Federal Reserve does nothing at all." Evaluate. Could this be true? If so, why?

[3] Terms are defined in the Glossary at the end of the book.

12   MR. A: "Money is indeed the root of all evil. We would be doing all right, if banks wouldn't be allowed to manipulate all economic affairs to their own ends."

   MR. B: "You are going too far. Banks are merely passive creatures which respond to the changing needs people have for money."

   Evaluate. With whom do you agree? Why?

13   What is the nature of the three lags hampering economic policy-makers?

14   "The impact of restrictive monetary policy can be highly uneven. For one thing, it hits hardest those sectors particularly dependent on credit and even among these it hits some more than others." Discuss.

15   Financial intermediaries may provide a buffer to restrictive monetary policy. Explain.

16   Suppose all banks had to meet 100 percent reserve requirements. How different would monetary policy be?

17   "Whenever the quantity of money in existence goes up, the value of each dollar naturally goes down." Discuss.

18   Do you think we can judge what monetary authorities did in years past by just looking at interest rate statistics? Why or why not?

19   In 1968, as usual, the Federal Reserve System handed over its net profit to the Treasury, but this time it was an all-time high of $2.5 billion. The $600 million increase over 1967 reflected both higher interest rates on newer issues of Treasury securities acquired by the Fed in its open-market operations, an official said, as well as a higher level of such securities holdings. On the basis of this information what kind of policy do you think the Fed pursued in 1968? Can you guess why?

20   Consider the news stories introducing this chapter. Explain their meaning.

Nixon Panel Will Advise Revenue Sharing

Staff Reporter of The Wall Street Journal

WASHINGTON—A Nixon task force studying the problems produced by proliferating Federal programs will recommend a Democratic-devised solution: Revenue sharing. Its aim is to increase local initiative and diminish central direction from the nation's capital.

Under this approach, state and city governments would receive an earmarked proportion, say in the range of 3% to 5%, of Federal tax revenues to spend largely as they see fit to meet pressing public needs. The prime purpose is to strengthen local government by enabling it to tap, at least in a limited fashion, the massive fiscal resources of the Federal tax system.

In theory, decision-making, along with money, would be transferred from Washington back to state capitals and city halls. In addition, future expansion of highly specific Federal spending programs, which range from aid for measles immunization to support of consumer and homemaking courses in vocational schools would be slowed. Many experts argue that such "categorical" grant-in-aid programs, which have more than doubled during the Johnson Administration, unduly limit the discretion of state and local officials. Their cost has climbed to an estimated $17.3 billion a year from $8.4 billion in the fiscal year ended June 30, 1963. . . .

Heller Proposed System in 1964

Revenue sharing was initially advanced as an alternative to restrictive Federal grant-in-aid programs in 1964 by Walter Heller, then chairman of President Johnson's Council of Economic Advisers, and Joseph Pechman, a Brookings economist. Though ignored by the President, mainly because of its cost, the system was well received by key Republicans, such as Reps. Laird of Wisconsin[1] and Goodell of New York (now a Senator), who were searching for substitutes for Great Society programs. Governors and mayors who saw revenue sharing as a partial solution to their fiscal woes and politically unpalatable local tax increases also became enthusiasts. . . .

But the key obstacle is expense. The Nixon Administration will struggle with the same budget stringencies that ruled out many new initiatives by President Johnson. Even in modest form, most revenue-sharing proposals would cost $2 billion a year, and the outlays could steadily climb as tax revenues rose. The original rationale rested on the assumption of a steadily growing Federal tax surplus, which could be turned back to states and cities without unbalancing the Federal budget. But such optimistic expectations of large "fiscal dividends" have

eroded under the pressure of the Vietnam war and demands of some domestic programs.

Thus, some enthusiasts would settle for establishing the principle of revenue sharing even though the actual financial benefit to states and cities was small at first. The local share could be expanded in later years, when more money was available, it's reasoned. "Revenue sharing without any expenditure limitations expresses most fully what the new approach is to do," says one expert.

Several Systems Proposed

A variety of revenue-sharing methods have been proposed. Many allocated a fixed proportion, usually 3% to 5%, of the Federal personal income-tax receipts—running at about $75 billion a year. Another approach takes a smaller percentage of the steadily growing total taxable personal-income base—estimated at $345 billion—in an effort to avoid the effects of undue year-to-year fluctuations in tax receipts.

Either way, revenue-sharing advocates argue, the Federal income tax is the most equitable way to finance state and local outlays for such public services as schools, police, public health and fire protection. The major existing sources of such spending, local property and sales taxes, are particularly burdensome on the poor because they aren't adjusted for income. Revenue sharing "meets state and local needs and relies on the highly growth-elastic Federal income tax. Many people feel the total tax system ends up being stronger," maintains Brookings' Mr. Nathan.

The earmarked Federal revenues would be allocated by formula to each state, based on its population, local taxing effort and probably some kind of equalization factor. This final adjustment would favor states with lower incomes and larger social needs, such as Mississippi. An important consideration is whether distribution of the money is left entirely to the states or whether some portion, perhaps half, is specifically allotted to the cities to ensure that rural-dominated legislatures don't ignore the needs of the urban population centers.

There is also debate over the extent to which revenue sharing should be hedged in with Federal limitations to ensure that states and cities spend the money on socially useful purposes rather than on political patronage or lavish buildings. Most advocates are eager to risk giving the states and cities wide leeway; the central concept is to enhance their autonomy.

The Wall Street Journal, December 11, 1968

---

[1] President Nixon's first Secretary of Defense.

11

government spending and taxes

OUR DISCUSSION OF monetary policy in the previous chapter revealed one possible approach to the problems of unemployment and inflation. If aggregate demand is too large, resulting in inflation, the monetary authorities can try to cut the spending ability of households, businesses, and even some governmental units by lending less money to them. If aggregate demand is too small, resulting in unemployment, the monetary authorities can try to stimulate household, business, and certain types of state and local government spending by making it easier for spenders to borrow. Yet, as we saw, such monetary policy is not a "sure-fire" weapon in the assault on our problems. It is only natural to look for substitutes. One other weapon that naturally suggests itself is fiscal policy, variations in the federal government's spending or taxing deliberately undertaken for the purpose of influencing the levels of real GNP, employment, and prices.

This is a story we shall pursue in detail in the following chapter. In this one, somewhat as a preliminary, we take a more systematic look at the role of government in our economy. We have already noted in earlier chapters that this role is hardly negligible. Now we ask exactly how big a role is played by government.

GOVERNMENT SPENDING

Government spending is not undertaken by a single unified authority. There are, on the contrary, tens of thousands of governmental units in the United States, ranging from the federal government to the states and to the complex overlapping jurisdictions of counties, municipalities, townships, and even school districts.

Government spending comprises, in a most general sense, two categories: expenditures on commodities and services (denoted by G earlier) and transfers. Let us recall that the latter are payments made without any current receipt of commodities or services in return. Taking all levels of government as a whole, such government spending in fiscal 1970 amounted to over $300 billion, or over $1,500 for every single person living in the United States.

Federal Spending

In 1970, federal government spending accounted for about 60 percent of that total. Figure 11.1 THE MAKEUP OF FEDERAL GOVERNMENT SPENDING helps us to see the uses to which this vast total of expenditures was put.

The largest category of expenditure was national defense, which includes Department of Defense expenditures as well as atomic energy programs and foreign military assistance. Yet spending connected with war really goes beyond this item. Interest on the public debt is intimately war-connected, because most of the debt was incurred as a result of past wars. The same goes for veterans' benefits and services (such as compensation payments, pensions, and medical care). These expenditures would not exist but for past wars. Much of present expenditures on space research and technology is of tremendous military significance and can be regarded as preparation for future wars. Finally, much of what is spent on international affairs (the conduct of foreign affairs, foreign information and exchange activities, and a variety of economic programs) serves the overriding purpose of preventing future wars. Thus, it is not too much to say that approximately 60 cents of every federal dollar of expenditures is connected with war in one way or another. This is indicated by the shaded portion of Figure 11.1.

The largest expenditure item of the nonmilitary portion of federal expenditures is labeled health and welfare. This includes health services and research, economic opportunity programs, and above all social security programs. The latter is an area into which the federal government stepped in the 1930's. Until then Americans were completely unprotected from destitution in old age or loss of all income owing to involuntary unemployment. Under the influence of the Great Depression, it was decided that society must insist that people save for their own retirement and unforeseen contingencies. The main piece of legislation in this

Figure 11.1   THE MAKEUP OF FEDERAL GOVERNMENT SPENDING

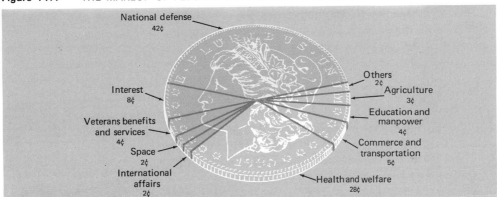

Federal government spending in fiscal year 1970 amounted to $195.3 billion in the United States. Here we see the purposes to which each dollar was put. About 60 cents of each federal spending dollar went for war, past, present, and future (shaded). Source: Bureau of the Budget estimates.

area is the Social Security Act of 1935 (and a variety of amendments since). At present, it provides compulsory old age, survivors, and disability insurance for nine out of ten jobholders, including many self-employed. Retired insured workers over 65 (or 62 if they choose) receive a monthly check. Its size depends on the age at which retirement occurs, on the average monthly wage earned in the past (excluding a period of lowest income), and on the number of dependents. In 1969, maximum monthly benefits were $177 for single retired workers, $375 for a widow with two or more dependent children. This maximum applied only where the insured worker had participated in the program for a long period. Actual average payments made were substantially lower. Free hospitalization is also provided to people over 65 for up to 60 days a year (Medicare). Payments are also made to widows or widowers of insured workers, if they are over 65, to disabled workers over 50, and to children under 18 of deceased workers. In addition, under a joint federal-state program, many involuntarily unemployed receive a weekly payment. However, this part of social security is less liberal. Checks cover roughly half of the average wage and stop entirely after 26 weeks, when workers may become eligible for welfare assistance. Unemployment insurance covers less than three quarters of the civilian labor force. Notably excluded are farmers, farm workers, domestics, and employees of small establishments and of state and local governments.

The remainder of federal spending covers only about 14 percent of the total. Commerce and transport include expenditures on aviation, water transport, highways, postal service, and programs to advance or regulate business, including area redevelopment. Education and manpower covers all levels of education and basic research as well. Agricultural expenditures cover farm income stabilization policies (to be discussed in Chapter 19), rural housing, electrification, and telephones, as well as agricultural research and a variety of services to farmers.

All other expenditures, in order of decreasing importance, include (a) legislative, judicial, and executive functions, (b) housing and community development (public housing programs, urban renewal, the national capital), and (c) natural resources (such as land, water, forest, mineral, fish, wildlife, and recreation). Interestingly, item (a), which is apt to come first to mind when considering government functions, is near the very bottom of the list.

types of federal budgets   It should be noted that the data of Figure 11.1 are based on the latest federal "unified" budget figures. This requires at least a brief comment. Anyone studying federal government finances will quickly discover that in the past there have been three different budget concepts in use.

First, there was the *administrative budget*. It was the budget traditionally submitted by the President to Congress each January and referred to the *fiscal year* beginning the following July 1. Although this budget has for many years past received the greatest attention, it was not at all the most useful of the three when it came to determining the impact of the federal government on the economy. This budget included only those expenditures that required congressional appropriations and mostly only those receipts which entered the general account of the Treasury, that is, were not earmarked by law for a specific purpose. A number of important receipt and expenditure items were completely omitted in this budget, and there was no distinction made between transfer payments and government spending on commodities and services. The most conspicuous omission in this budget concerned trust fund operations, which consist of funds held in trust by the federal government (such as highway and social security taxes or medicare premiums) for use in carrying out specific programs in accordance with the terms of a trust agreement or statute. In recent years, trust fund operations have grown very rapidly, and the financial transactions between the federal government and the rest of the economy were considerably larger than indicated by the administrative budget alone.

Second, there was the *consolidated cash budget*. It covered not only funds wholly owned by the federal government, but also the financial transactions of the federal trust funds, the largest being the social security and highway trust funds, and the transactions of five government sponsored enterprises: the Federal Deposit Insurance Corporation, the federal intermediate credit, land, and home loan banks, and banks for cooperatives. This budget was superior to the administrative budget when it came to judging the size of federal government activities. In 1969, there was roughly a difference of $50 billion between the two.

Third, there was the *national income budget*. It was a refinement of the consolidated cash budget and was deliberately set up to measure the federal government's impact on the economy. It included trust fund transactions, but it excluded such purely financial transactions as loans, mortgages, and the purchase or sale of existing assets, which represent neither the production of current output nor incomes earned in the productive process. Also, whereas the other two budget concepts counted taxes when collected and expenditures when paid, the national income budget recorded some taxes as they accrued and purchases when delivery was made. It was argued, for instance, that the impact of taxes on the behavior of the public is more likely to be felt when taxes accrue rather than at the time of actual payment.

Corresponding to the three budgets, there were three different surplus or deficit figures. The national income budget usually showed the smallest deficit or largest surplus. The administrative budget was at the other extreme. (In mid-1968, for instance, the President estimated the minimum federal deficit for fiscal 1968–1969 at $6.4 billion under the national income budget, at $11.5 billion under the consolidated cash budget, and at $14 billion under the administrative budget.) Naturally, the President was likely to choose the most convenient figure when making speeches, and he never failed getting accused of gimmickry. Worse yet, one budget could be in deficit, while the other was in surplus. This easily led to confusion, as you might expect, but there can be no doubt that the national income budget was the most appropriate for purposes of analyzing the effect on the economy of federal government spending and taxing. To avoid the confusion, the President in 1967 appointed a Commission on Budget Concepts that proposed the use of a single new concept. This concept, simply referred to as *the federal budget*, has just been introduced in fiscal 1969. It includes federally owned and trust funds, distinguishes between expenditures proper and loans, and separates receipts arising from the government's compulsory powers from others stemming from its business-type activities.

State and Local Spending

State and local government spending in recent years accounted for only 40 percent of total government spending. However, these governments employed 9 of the 12 million people working for government. Figure 11.2 THE MAKEUP OF STATE AND LOCAL GOVERNMENT SPENDING, based on 1967 data, gives a convenient picture of the types of spending involved.

The largest category of state and local government spending was education. One fifth of this total went for institutions of higher education, the rest to all other schools. Second in importance came public welfare spending and all expenditures on health, including hospitals. Third came highways which should surprise no one.

Spending on utilities includes water supply, electric power, transit, and gas supply sys-

Figure 11.2   THE MAKEUP OF STATE AND LOCAL GOVERNMENT SPENDING

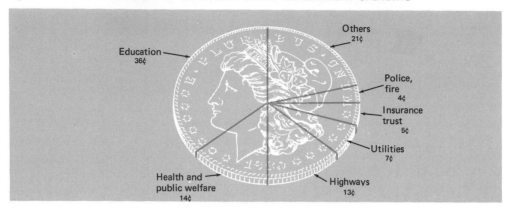

State and local government spending in 1967 amounted to $106.7 billion in the United States. Here we see the purposes to which each dollar was put. Source: U.S. Department of Commerce.

tems, as well as liquor stores. Insurance trust expenditures cover employee retirement checks and unemployment compensation. Police and fire protection is self-explanatory.

This leaves the "others" category. It includes a great variety of spending: general administration, natural resources, housing and urban renewal, parks and recreation and interest on the public debt.

The Historical Record

The relative importance of federal and state-local government spending has, however, not always been what it is today. Figure 11.3 THE HISTORY OF GOVERNMENT SPENDING IN THE UNITED STATES provides a clear picture of that.

At the turn of the century, federal spending was only about $500 million per year, a far cry from today's almost $200 billion. (If you want to know how much that is, consider that it would take you 63 years to earn that amount, provided you earned $100 every second, day and night!) State and local spending at the turn of the century was twice as important as federal spending, and continued to be larger than federal spending until 1917 inclusive. Then came World War I which took federal spending beyond the $20 billion mark in 1919, or to a level over five times as large as only 3 years earlier. However, the increase was in *military* spending. State and local spending have continued to be larger than federal *non*military spending until 1967 (with the exception of 1943 and 1944).

What explains the tremendous growth in total government spending? The first answer is "war." War involves, as we have seen, not only government spending while it is fought, but also in peacetime years because of the aftermath of old wars and preparation for new ones. The technology of war, furthermore, has changed incredibly since 1900. Today's planes, only a dream at that time, cost millions of dollars each, and the development of atomic bombs and rockets costs billions. All this is reflected in the expenditure figures of the 1950's and 1960's (Korean War, Cold War, Vietnam War).

Second, there has occurred, as we have also seen, a change in the public's attitude toward internal security. Ever since the Great Depression, the public has demanded (and legislatures have provided) protection from the economic burdens imposed by unemployment, sickness, disability, and old age. This trend, together with an increasing number of people over 65 and improved benefit levels, has greatly expanded expenditures at all levels of gov-

Figure 11.3   THE HISTORY OF GOVERNMENT SPENDING IN THE UNITED STATES

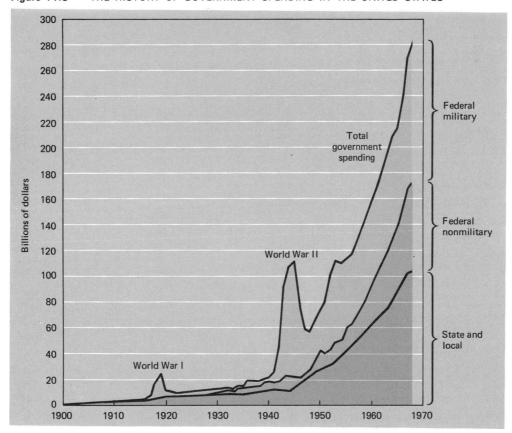

All types of government spending have risen during this century in the United States. Federal spending has become increasingly important, and expenditures connected with wars (top portion), such as national defense, interest, veterans benefits and services, space, and international affairs, are swallowing a large portion of federal spending. Source: U.S. Department of Commerce.

ernment. It is interesting to note in this connection that the "vast" expansion of the role of the federal government in the 1930's is largely a figment of the imagination of the more rabid anti-New Dealers. In dollar terms that expansion was a drop in the bucket.

Third, changing times have also brought changed attitudes and needs in other areas of life. Take the attitude toward education. A much greater percentage of teenagers, for instance, go to high school today than in 1900, and people would not want to have it any other way. Or note the need for highways created by the invention of the automobile. People would not want to go without them. There is also the need for more public utilities as people decide to live closer together in large numbers. America has seen a great degree of urbanization, and this process requires all kinds of governmental activity unnecessary in a rural society. (This is discussed further in Chapter 28.)

All the above explain why government spending *per head* has risen as it has. In addition, of course, total government spending has risen with the number of people. The U.S. population has grown from 76 to over 200 million since the turn of the century. Even without war, social security and an increased desire for education, private cars and city living, population growth would explain a lot of the increase in government spending. The particular data of Figure 11.3, furthermore, also reflect an increase in prices since 1900, because they are given at the prices current in each year. The purchasing power of each dollar was probably at least three times greater in 1900 than in 1970. Thus total government spending in real terms has risen less than indicated in Figure 11.3, but even so it has risen significantly. (To make them comparable with data in the 1960's, the figures early in the century should probably be raised threefold.)

TAXES

Although a household, as we all know too well, usually has to fit its expenditures to its income, governments do not. They may well decide on expenditures *first* (and that is why we discussed them first) and think about income later. Governments are in the position of a housewife who goes out shopping one afternoon and afterwards reaches into her husband's pocket to finance the adventure. In the same way governments can and do reach into everyone's pockets. They have the power to tax, to require compulsory payments from people without bestowing any special benefit on those making payment. As the saying goes, "Nothing is surer than death and taxes." It is too bad they do not come in that order.

Although we shall discuss taxes in this chapter at some length, and although most governments finance most of their spending by taxation, let us keep in mind that governments do not have to tax in order to spend. Government enterprises, discussed in Chapter 5, have regular sales revenues and can finance expenditures from these; but this is of no great importance in the United States. More significantly, general government can finance its spending by borrowing, and the *federal* government can even do so by creating new money. (You might want to take another look at Chapter 9.) In the next chapter, we shall have occasion to evaluate these last two possibilities. Then we shall see why governments frequently prefer direct taxation to borrowing or money creation as a revenue source.

Federal Taxation

Reflection will show that taxes pervade the entire economy. Taxes are levied on all kinds of income, on all sorts of purchases, and on many varieties of property. The federal government alone in fiscal 1970 collected a total of 198.7 billion in taxes. Figure 11.4 THE MAKEUP OF FEDERAL GOVERNMENT REVENUE shows the relative importance of the various kinds of federal taxes.

First and foremost stands the individual income tax, which was introduced in 1913 and now provides close to half of federal tax revenue. It is levied on the income of natural persons, regardless of whether this income is derived from work or property services. (Profits of un-incorporated enterprises, whether or not withdrawn from the business, are also treated as personal income of the owners.) Certain types of incomes, such as state and municipal bond interest and federal government pensions, are not taxable, however. Other incomes are taxable only after certain exemptions and deductions have been excluded. A nontaxable exemption of $600 per year is granted to the taxpayer, as well as to each of his dependents. (Further exemptions are granted to the blind and those over 65 years of age.) Deductions from income are allowed for certain contributions to charity, medical expenses, interest payments, state and local taxes, and a variety of other expenses.[2]

The tax rate, or the percentage which is applied to the taxable income so calculated,

Figure 11.4   THE MAKEUP OF FEDERAL GOVERNMENT REVENUE

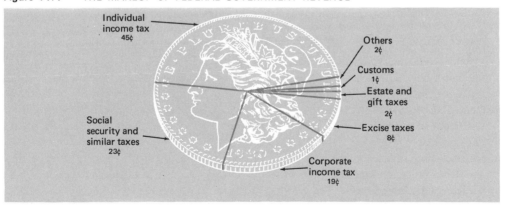

Federal revenue in fiscal year 1970 amounted to $198.7 billion in the United States. The typical revenue dollar shows clearly the relative importance of the various types of taxes. Source: Bureau of the Budget estimate.

[2] At the time of this writing, in early 1969, President Nixon had put tax reform high on his domestic agenda. Many powerful congressmen were predicting passage in late 1969 of a sweeping tax reform bill. This bill was to close tax "loopholes," such as abolishing the tax-free status of income from state and municipal bonds. It was also to alter significantly the types and amounts of deductions allowed. For an up-to-date and more detailed account of these matters, you might wish to read one of the popular books on the preparation of income tax returns, such as J. K. Lasser Tax Institute, *Your Income Tax,* 1970 edition (New York: Simon & Schuster, 1969).

varies with the type of income and with its size. The first $1,000 of ordinary taxable wage income may be taxed at 14 percent, the next $1,000 at a higher rate, and so on, until (at present) a maximum of 70 percent is taken out of the last $1,000 portions of very high incomes.[3] Yet income derived from the sale of property which appreciated in value while being held for more than 6 months (so-called realized long-term capital gains) is never taxed more than 25 percent. In fact, if the property is not sold by the owner before his death, it is never taxed at all.

Second in importance among federal taxes are social security taxes and certain unemployment and retirement taxes. These are compulsory insurance "contributions" stemming mostly from the above-mentioned Social Security Act of 1935, as amended. Half the payments are exacted from the insured employees, half from their employers. In 1969, both paid the current tax rate on the first $7,800 earned a year by the insured. The earnings base taxed has frequently been raised. The rate is to rise gradually to 5.6 percent by 1987. Payments go into a trust fund out of which the type of health and welfare expenditures discussed in connection with Figure 11.1 THE MAKEUP OF FEDERAL GOVERNMENT SPENDING are made. Third in place is the corporate income tax. (You might wish to take another glance at our discussion of the corporation in Chapter 5 at this point.) Corporate income tax rates are very simple. The first $25,000 of corporate profit (*before* any decision is made as to payment in dividends or retention) is liable to a 22 percent tax, all profits above that to 48 percent.

Next we come to excise taxes. These are taxes on the purchase of specific domestically produced goods; on liquor, tobacco, cars, tires, gasoline, television sets, jewelry, cosmetics, and telephone service, for instance. Such taxes are levied either on the manufacturer or at the wholesale or retail level. Back in 1900, such taxes provided half the federal government's revenue of $567 million.

Estate taxes are placed on the estate (that is, the net worth) of deceased individuals. Gift taxes are levied on gifts they have made (presumably in contemplation of death) within 3 years of death, presumably to avoid the estate tax. However, only the part of an estate above $60,000 is taxable if the deceased was unmarried, the part above $120,000 if he was married. To these taxable portions tax rates are applied varying from 3 to 77 percent.

Finally, we have 1 percent of federal tax revenue coming from customs duties, which are taxes levied on the importation of foreign goods. According to the U.S. Constitution, only the federal government may use this type of tax. Interestingly, 41 percent of federal revenues came from this source in 1900, and more before that.

The "other" tax category includes a great variety of minor taxes.

State and Local Taxation

State and local governments levy taxes similar to the federal government plus other types of their own. They also receive some revenues, allocated for specific purposes, in the form of

[3] At the time of this writing, in early 1969, Congress had legislated a temporary 10 percent surcharge on all of these rates. Although this surcharge was due to expire in mid-1969, President Nixon had asked Congress to extend this legislation for another year.

Figure 11.5   THE MAKEUP OF STATE AND LOCAL GOVERNMENT REVENUE

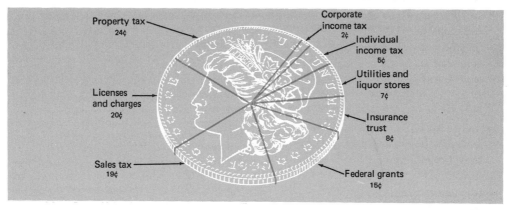

Property tax
24¢

Corporate
income tax
2¢

Individual
income tax
5¢

Utilities and
liquor stores
7¢

Licenses
and charges
20¢

Insurance
trust
8¢

Sales tax
19¢

Federal grants
15¢

State and local government revenue in 1967 amounted to $107.3 billion in the United States. The typical revenue dollar shows clearly the relative importance of the various types of taxes. Source: U.S. Department of Commerce.

federal grants and others still from the operation of government enterprises. Figure 11.5 THE MAKEUP OF STATE AND LOCAL GOVERNMENT REVENUE gives us the familiar overview.

The largest chunk of state and local revenue is provided by the property tax. It is usually levied locally on buildings, land, and improvements thereon. In some places, it is also based on tangible personal property, such as livestock, grain, furniture, autos, and jewelry. Less frequently it is levied on intangible property, such as stocks, bonds, and mortgages. Unlike income tax, which is levied once on the income, property tax is levied again and again on the same piece of property. Furthermore, it is levied regardless of whether the piece of property is fully owned or the owner has any income at all. Property taxes used to be even more important in the past. At the turn of the century, two thirds of state and local revenue came from this source.

Sales taxes are next in importance. They are usually levied as a percentage of the retail price of broad groups of commodities and services. Sometimes certain items, such as food or medicines, are excluded from the tax base.

The great variety of licenses and charges made by state and local governments bring in an amount equal to sales tax revenues. This category includes nonfederal inheritance taxes levied on individuals inheriting estates or portions thereof.

Federal grants are also quite significant. They are allocated to particular purposes, such as public welfare, highways, education, and social insurance. They often require matching funds from state and local sources to be spent for the same purpose. The first large federal grant programs go back to the 1930's and were concerned with emergency relief and public assistance. Federal grants declined during World War II and grew rapidly in the 1950's, especially highway construction grants. Recent years have brought an acceleration of federal aid, especially for elementary and secondary education and to combat poverty. As the news story introducing this chapter illustrates, there is widespread support for an extension of federal aid to other governments, especially in the form of general purpose grants. In mid-1969, President Nixon was planning on having a regular revenue-sharing program in effect by 1971, with grants rising to 1 percent of the federal income tax base by 1976.

The insurance trust revenues listed in Figure 11.5 refer to retirement and unemployment insurance taxes. The utilities (water, electric power, gas, transportation, sanitation, and sewerage) and liquor store revenues represent genuine government enterprise revenues.

Interestingly, revenues from individual or corporate income taxes, so important at the federal level, are of minor significance only. Only thirty-five states have a personal income tax; relatively few large cities have one.

The Historical Record

The relative importance of federal and state-local taxation in the United States in historical perspective can most easily be seen from Figure 11.6 THE HISTORY OF TAXATION IN THE UNITED STATES. The importance of property and sales taxes within the total tax revenue of state and local governments is also shown in the chart. Similarly, the significance of individual income and social security taxes within the total tax revenue of the federal government is indicated. At the turn of the century, the federal government collected $567 million in taxes (and spent less). In 1970 it collected close to $200 billion. World War I brought the first major change in federal taxation. In 1917, tax collections crossed the $1 billion mark, but only a few years later, in 1920, they reached almost $7 billion. Thereafter, federal tax collections dropped again, to under $2 billion by 1932. The real change came with World War II. From $5 billion in 1940, federal tax collections jumped to almost $45 billion in 1945. On the way, in 1942, federal tax collections permanently seem to have passed the level of state and local taxes. Since the postwar period, taxes have crept up inexorably. The reasons, of course, are the same as the ones we referred to when discussing the rise in government spending.

THE THEORY OF GOVERNMENT SPENDING

It is one thing to note, as we have, what governments are doing. It is another to argue about what they should be doing. As we have noted, for example in Chapter 2, there is a strong tradition of private enterprise in the United States. This tradition has often argued for a very limited role of government. "What can be done privately, should be done privately." The classical economists would have approved of only three types of government spending, on collective goods, on goods with external effects, and on unusually large and risky under-takings.

Collective Goods

Collective goods are goods that benefit everyone regardless of whether the individual pays for them. National defense and police protection are cases in point. It is impossible to with-hold the benefit from those who do not pay, to separate the buyers from the freeloaders. As

Figure 11.6   THE HISTORY OF TAXATION IN THE UNITED STATES

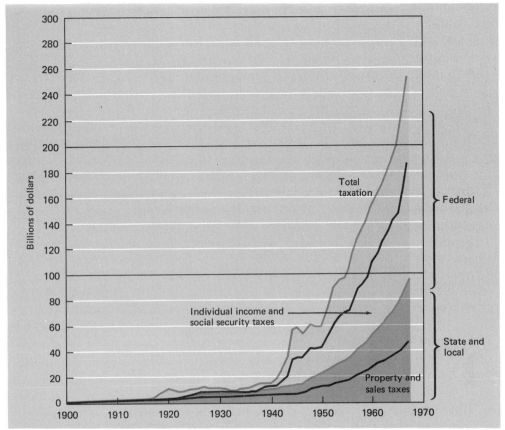

Taxation by all types of government has risen during the twentieth century in the United States. Federal taxation has become increasingly important. Note how property and sales taxes have throughout provided a significant portion of total state and local tax revenues. Since the late 1920's, individual income and eventually social security taxes have come to play an equally important role among federal taxes as major revenue getters. Source: U.S. Department of Commerce.

a result, it would be rational for any one individual *not* to pay. After all, he gets the good anyway. Hence, collective purchase, with everyone paying his share, and being assured that everyone else pays his, seems reasonable.

Goods with External Effects

Some goods are similar to collective goods in that many others besides the private producer may benefit from them without incurring any cost. If a farmer dams up a river, not only he gains from the resultant flood control, but so do his neighbors, and possibly city dwellers 100 miles away. Here is a good case again for governmental action, for government alone can assure that all who gain also pay. The case for public education rests on similar grounds. Not only do the educated gain personally (as did our enterprising farmer), but so does society as a whole. Employers have a more reliable and productive labor force, democratic political institutions would be unthinkable without an educated citizenry, and so on. Hence there is reason to make everyone pay for what benefits all.

Large and Risky Undertakings

Finally, even the classical economists would have agreed that some undertakings are simply too large and risky for any private party to undertake. Think of the enormous research cost and the long time involved in developing atomic power for peaceful uses. Or think of communications via space satellites. Even our industrial giants may be too small to undertake the risks and costs involved, at least initially. Thus, the government steps in.

No Market Test

Yet many people still would look askance at even these types of government activity. They fear that purchase of goods through government may lead to a massive waste of resources. There is no test of the market in the sense that unjustified costs lead someone to make losses and to be eliminated from the scene. A government agency may well dip into the pockets of taxpayers forever, and ever more deeply, they fear, paying outrageous sums for purposes that could be achieved much more economically. Certainly such fears are not completely unjustified. They have led in recent years to increasing application of *cost-benefit analysis* to government projects. Although it may be worthwhile, for instance, to let government build a dam, it would not be worthwhile to build just any dam. One might consider a number of alternative flood protection plans (with different annual operating costs) and compare the benefits derived by farmers, industry, and households from each plan with its costs. As long as a more ambitious plan raises benefits by more than costs, it pays to undertake it. When the opposite is true, it pays to be less ambitious. This kind of analysis can be applied to a wide variety of governmental activities, from the automation of the post office to building supersonic transport planes to subsidizing shipbuilders. Having been pioneered by Defense Secretary McNamara, President Johnson instructed the Budget Bureau in the mid-1960's to push the spread of this type of *programming-planning-budgeting*, or PPB, throughout the federal government.

No Consumer Sovereignty

Another reason why people look askance at governmental economic activity is that it necessarily involves a significant modification of consumer sovereignty. In one sense, this may be welcome. Though the private economy operates on the principle of "one dollar—one vote," giving greater power over the use of resources to the relatively rich, the public economy operates on the principle of "one man—one vote." If democracy functions as it should, the poor man has as much to say about defense spending or school construction as has the rich one. Yet there is one major drawback. People do not vote for public spending item by item, as they do "vote" when going out into the supermarket. The special vote on a new school bond issue is the exception, not the rule. Typically, people vote for legislators, and this means voting for an ill-defined complex of public goods. Suppose I am against new roads and for more public parks and airports. Candidate A is for roads and parks, but against airports. Candidate B is against roads and parks but for airports. I have no choice but to take B's failings with the good. He will deliver two of the things I want, A would deliver only one. But will it work out that way? I can never be sure. During the legislative process, influenced by pressure groups within and without the legislative halls, B may in the end vote for roads and against parks and airports! Worse yet, if he wins, I will be *forced* to pay for all this, although I am against it all. Nobody ever forces me to buy oranges or steaks. Thus, voting for public goods in a package, as we must, is most unsatisfactory. *Citizens' sovereignty* is a poor substitute for consumer sovereignty. Which is not to say that we have a better alternative.

State and Local vs. Federal Spending

Some people argue that there is one simple way to solve the dilemma just described. Because private production and purchases of some goods is out of the question or undesirable and because government production and purchase may be of questionable value owing to the absence of a market test and of consumer sovereignty, we should keep such government activities as close to the people as possible. Of all things that cannot be done privately, let local government do as much as possible. Let state government do only what local governments cannot do. Let the federal government do only what state governments cannot do. President Eisenhower, for instance, was most sympathetic to this idea and appointed a commission to look into the possibilities. Essentially, it is hoped that following this path will give people a greater chance to pick directly the public goods they want and to keep a closer eye on whether the benefits justify the costs. A typical example of this kind of thinking is provided by some proposals concerning our urban problems.

The Problems of Metropolitan America

Almost two thirds of all Americans live in metropolitan areas. Most cities have been deteriorating physically and economically for some time. Manufacturing industry, once attracted by the railroads and a steady labor supply, has been moving out. It prefers to locate near highways and airports in an age of trucking and air freight and a mobile labor supply. This is accentuated by the fact that nowadays one-story plants are cheaper to build and operate than multi-story ones, but land values in the cities are too high to afford their construction there.

Together with manufacturing industry, middle and upper income families have been fleeing the cities for the suburbs in search for their own homes and more space, and in flight from city slums, crime, and congestion. In city after city, neighborhoods began to deteriorate and landlords found it uneconomical to maintain their buildings. And they could get away with it. Lucky for them, there was first the general housing shortage of World War II and then the artificial one (in the central cities) created by discrimination (in the suburbs). As a result, landlords have found it easy to rent dilapidated slum dwellings to a captive market. Apart from a few very rich who live in luxury apartments, the unskilled poor now inhabit the cores of our cities, amidst miserable housing, rutted streets, crumbling curbs, abandoned parks, polluted rivers, smoggy air, crowded busses, delinquency and crime. More on this in Chapter 28.

For urban governments these trends have spelled financial disaster. Their tax base (middle and high income families and industry) has failed to grow, but their needs have multiplied: massive costs for welfare, transportation, education, fire, and police protection. City after city has found it impossible to deal with urban blight. City after city lives in an atmosphere of crisis. Watts and Harlem and Chicago's South Side are well-known symbols. They do not stand alone. Everywhere are the crying unmet needs for good schools and teachers, for sewers and sidewalks, for street lights and playgrounds, for more garbage collection and fewer rats.

Here then is a classic case for government action. Private parties will not and cannot do much. How are we going to deal with this? The "Washington reflex," of throwing money at a problem hoping that it will somehow go away, may help little. Federal officials may not have the skill, knowledge, wisdom, and ingenuity that is available in the afflicted localities. But the federal government does have the most powerful system of collecting revenues in the world. This is, some people argue, where the solution must be sought. Massive and regular transfers of federal revenues should be made, without strings attached, *to state and local authorities*. Such general purpose grants would bring to bear the federal bounty on the local burdens. Nor would it be a matter of charity, for the healing of our urban wounds serves national purposes as well. As Walter Heller, former Chairman of the President's Council of Economic Advisers, put it:[4] "The good life will not come, ready-made, from some federal assembly line. It has to be custom built, engaging the effort and imagination and resourcefulness of the community." Thus one way to solve the problems of urban America may indeed be to let local government, with massive financial support of the federal government, do what private parties cannot do and to involve the afflicted population directly to ensure that the right things are done and in the most economical way. Again, see the news story introducing this chapter.

---

[4] Walter W. Heller, *New Dimensions of Political Economy* (New York: Norton, 1967), p. 171.

THE THEORY OF TAXATION

As you can well guess, the great variety of taxes now in existence in the United States has not come about according to a master plan. Instead, many taxes are first imposed on the basis of expediency, and this may create many inconsistencies and injustices. As a result of the haphazard imposition of taxes by legislatures, some people may end up sharing a disproportionate burden, even if no one planned it that way originally. Just take one example. Suppose you are unmarried and receive an annual income of $100,000. Under present law, if it is all from wages, you will roughly pay a federal tax of $55,000. If it is all from long-term capital gains (for example, you bought common stock for $50,000 in January and sold it for $150,000 in October), your federal tax will not exceed $25,000. If it is all interest on municipal or state bonds, your federal tax is zero. Although one can find such examples, the amazing thing about the American tax system is not its faults, but how well it works. Imagine collecting close to $300 billion in taxes, almost a third of our GNP, and doing so with a voluntary program, without violence and bloodshed and only a little bit of griping! This can only be true because most people believe that the system is essentially fair and everybody pays his share.

Principles of Taxation

Naturally, economists have considered the question of what an ideal tax system (one which would avoid inconsistencies and injustices) might look like. This turns out to be a thorny problem, indeed. First, one might wish to set up general principles relating to the fairness of taxation.

the benefit principle   Some argue that fairness requires that people be taxed in proportion to the benefit they receive from general governmental activity. This may be possible in some cases. Local government may assess the homeowner for the cost of a sidewalk in front of his house. State governments may assess the automobile driver for the cost of highways on which he drives (for example, by earmarking gasoline tax revenues for highway maintenance and construction). The federal government may exact "contributions" for social security trust funds from those who get rights to social security benefits.

In most cases, however, it would be impossible to apply this principle. Some people derive benefits but are unable to pay taxes because they are too young, too old, too poor, or too sick. It would be manifestly absurd to tax the unemployed in order to pay them unemployment benefits. In any case, it is hard to measure the benefit. What exactly is the benefit *you* receive from the FBI, space research, and the administration of justice?

the ability-to-pay principle   Other economists have argued that, given the nature of general government, everyone should contribute to it according to his financial ability. This may sound fine and just, but can still lead us into many arguments.

Does this mean that taxes should be *proportional*, everyone paying the same *percentage* of his income? Suppose the income tax rate is 11 percent. If you earn $100 a week, you pay $11; if you earn $1,000, you pay $110.

If we interpret ability to pay in this way, some people will immediately point out "injustices." The man with $1,000 weekly income may be a bachelor who owns a $20,000 house free and clear and has $500,000 in the bank. The man with the $100 weekly income may have ten children and live in a $100,000 house, but have a mortgage of $90,000 and no liquid assets. Can he really be expected to pay a tax of $11? Couldn't the bachelor easily pay more than $110?

This leads to the argument for a *progressive* tax, one which takes a larger percentage of higher than of lower incomes. This argument is made even if people are alike in every respect except income. If both the above had ten children and $100,000 houses (with $90,000 mortgages) and no liquid assets, it may still be argued that the $1,000-a-week man should pay a larger percentage of his income than the $100-a-week man. This argument rests on the belief that each additional dollar becomes subjectively worth less as more dollars are being earned, and that therefore 11 percent taken away from *both* people represents an unequal burden. "Eleven dollars means a lot more to the one than $110 to the other." If this were true, one might want to take only $5 out of the $100, yet $200 out of the $1,000. Sacrificing 5 percent of highly valued dollars is perhaps equally burdensome as sacrificing 20 percent of lower valued ones.

Even if we agree with this argument, a baffling question remains: how much more percentagewise shall the man with higher income pay? There can be no objective, scientific answer to that question. It is a matter of opinion, and everyone will have to make up his own mind. More than that. What if the thing being taxed, what if our tax base, is not income at all? Suppose it is property instead. Shall we then have an equal tax rate for all?

As with income, an equal rate may appear fair at first sight. Going back to the original case, suppose a 1 percent tax is levied on real estate. Our bachelor would then pay 1 percent of $20,000 or $200 a year. The father of ten would pay 1 percent of $100,000, or $1,000 a year. If we knew nothing else, this may seem fair indeed. Yet, looking at income, we see that the bachelor paid $200 on a yearly income of $52 \times \$1,000 = \$52,000$ or about 0.4 percent of his income. The father of ten paid $1,000 on a yearly income of $52 \times \$100 = \$5,200$, or 19.2 percent. The lower the income, the greater the percentage of tax taken: a *regressive* tax. Many would consider this highly unfair.

What is to be done? If we charge the same percentage of everyone's income, we may fail to measure accurately ability to pay. If we charge the same percentage of everyone's property, the same may happen. (Incidentally, if we charge the same percentage of everyone's purchases, the same can happen.) Yet, it is not at all clear which (possibly differential) percentage of tax applied to what base would distribute the tax burden fairly.

principles applied in the United States   We have already noted above that the benefit principle is to some degree applied in the United States (social security taxes and licenses, for instance). Most actual taxes, however, would come under the ability-to-pay principle. In any case we can find examples of progressive and regressive taxes. Income, estate, gift, and inheritance taxes are progressive. Property taxes, customs, sales, and excise taxes tend to be regressive. If we relate the amounts of property, customs, sales, and excise taxes paid to the *incomes* of the taxpayers (rather than to property value, sales value, and the like), most of these taxes, as in our example above, turn out to be regressive. We have seen an example above of why this may be true for property taxes.

In the case of sales taxes it is true because the poor tend to spend a much larger proportion of their income on taxed items than the rich, so they end up paying a greater portion of their low incomes for such taxes.[5] Social security taxes, levied as a certain fixed percentage of income below a certain ceiling, are also regressive, because not everyone's income is completely below that ceiling. Suppose that the tax rate is 3 percent on income up to $7,000 a year. Then a man with a $5,000 income will pay $150, or 3 percent, but a man with a $10,000 income will only pay 3 percent on $7,000, or $210, that is, 2.1 percent on his income.

practical considerations   The foregoing discussion should have made one thing clear. It is practically impossible to make a tax system "fair." What is fair according to one criterion is undoubtedly unfair according to another equally valid one. Since no two people are alike, one simply *cannot* treat people in the same way on the grounds that they are alike.

Leaving aside fairness, tax collectors try to satisfy a number of other criteria in practice. They try to make a tax simple to compute, convenient to pay, and economical to collect. They do not always succeed. A 3 percent general sales tax is certainly simple to compute, the federal income tax is harder, and the federal estate tax is close to impossible. Sales taxes are conveniently paid with the purchase price of taxed items; many income taxes are withheld at the source. This has been true, for instance, for the federal income tax since 1943. Employers must withhold their employees' estimated tax liability and pay the amount directly to the Treasury. Because this shifts much of the burden of tax collecting on to others, it is no wonder that the federal income tax is also one of the most economical ones (from the standpoint of government, which collects it at an administrative cost of .5 percent of total revenue).

Another matter tax collectors must consider about taxes is whether the tax will provide a stable, dependable, and growing revenue. The revenue received from an excise tax on a particular good will fluctuate with the sales of that good and cannot be relied upon to the same degree as the revenue from *general* sales taxes or income taxes. The revenue received from sales taxes in one community is far from dependable if people can avoid the tax by shopping in a neighboring town. The revenue from income taxes in a community is much more apt to grow than that from property taxes, even without any change in tax rates.

Finally, tax collectors must worry about possible harmful side effects of taxation. Will a tax discourage initiative and incentive, thereby stultifying economic progress? This certainly

---

[5] Actually, it is quite difficult to establish these effects, because one must know who exactly bears the burden of a tax, or what the tax "incidence" is. The person who *pays* the tax may be able to *shift* it on to other people. The above results have been derived from a very careful study by eminent experts. They are by no means always self-evident. We shall return to the problem of tax incidence in Chapter 27.

would be true if taxes were imposed indiscriminately and tax rates were set at extremely high levels. What man with ability would put forth his maximum effort to improve a product, for instance, if all resulting extra income were to be taxed at 95 percent?

These are just some of the philosophical and practical considerations any government must face when it imposes taxes. In the next chapter, we return to the main track of this section when we ask how the inevitable impact government has on the economy may be deliberately planned so as to shape the course of economic events.

SUMMARY

1 Government spending can be grouped into two categories: spending for which commodities and services are received and spending for which nothing is currently received. The latter expenditure is called transfer payments.

2 Presently, about 60 percent of over $300 billion of annual governmental spending is done by the federal government. About three fifths of federal spending goes for wars, past, present, and future. Somewhat over a quarter goes for health and welfare programs. It should be noted that federal government transactions have in the past been reported in three different ways, via the administrative budget, the consolidated cash budget, and the national income budget. In the future, all these concepts are to be replaced by *the federal budget*.

3 One third of state and local government spending is directed toward education. Health and welfare expenditures and highways are next in importance.

4 Historically, government spending has risen during this century from as little as $1.5 billion in 1900 to over $300 billion today. Much of this rise can be attributed to military spending, to a growing public demand for economic security, and to an increased desire for education, private cars, and city living. Population growth and inflation have, of course, also contributed to higher spending by government. State and local spending have almost always been larger than federal nonmilitary expenditures.

5 Although there are other ways of gaining revenue, most of the time governments finance most of their spending by taxation. The federal government gains most of its revenue from income taxes, social security taxes, and excise taxes. State and local governments' favorite revenue sources are property and sales taxes, followed by licenses and federal grants.

6 The theory of government spending concerns itself with the question of the proper role of government. Traditionally, this role has been limited to providing collective goods, goods with external effects, and large and risky undertakings.

7 As many people see it, the trouble with governmental provision of goods is that this activity is not subjected to a market test and that consumer sovereignty is replaced by citizens' sovereignty. To overcome these handicaps, one might make greater use of cost-benefit analysis in the public sphere and emphasize local and state, as opposed to federal, government activities.

8 The theory of taxation deals with an "ideal" tax system. The establishment of an "ideal" tax system is next to impossible. The question of what tax is fair is ultimately a matter of opinion. Neither the benefit nor the ability-to-pay principle of taxation provides a clear guide to fairness. The actual taxes levied in the United States follow

partly one, partly the other principle. Their effects vary from progressive to regressive. As with fairness, the other attributes of an ideal tax system are only partially fulfilled.

TERMS[6]

ability-to-pay principle	fiscal policy
administrative budget	gift tax
benefit principle	inheritance tax
capital gains	national income budget
citizens' sovereignty	progressive tax
collective goods	proportional tax
consolidated cash budget	regressive tax
cost-benefit analysis	sales tax
customs duties	tax (amount)
estate tax	tax base
excise tax	tax incidence
external effects	tax rate
federal budget	trust fund

QUESTIONS FOR REVIEW AND DISCUSSION

1   Write a brief essay on the present composition of government spending in the United States.

2   Why has government spending in the United States increased so much during this century? Does that make the United States more socialistic in 1970 than in 1900?

3   What are the major taxes imposed by the federal government? By state and local governments?

4   How would you go about making a tax system fair?

5   Mr. A pays a tax of $500 on a $30,000 income, while B pays $600 out of $33,000 of income. Is the tax progressive, proportional, or regressive?

6   What would your answer be if the $30,000 and $33,000 figures in question 5 referred to taxable *property*?

7   "Poll taxes (identical taxes per head) are regressive." Discuss.

8   "Even if all families had equal incomes, a property tax on family dwellings could be regressive." Discuss.

[6] Terms are defined in the Glossary at the end of the book.

9   The social security program is compulsory. Maybe some people do not want to be insured against old age, sickness, disability, and unemployment. Why not make it a voluntary program?

10 In 1966, U.S. personal income was $580.4 billion, yet federal individual income tax collections were only $55.4 billion. How is that possible with tax rates ranging from 14 to 70 percent?

11 It has been argued that urbanization, and the breakup of the multi-generation family household that went with it, is directly responsible for the "socialized" financial support of our aged. Evaluate. Could it be true? Why?

12 Figure out by how much each family's federal taxes could be reduced if we had no defense spending. If we had no defense spending and did not lower taxes, what might we do instead with the money?

13 "If all taxes were placed on corporations and no one else, we would all be a lot better off." Discuss.

14 Which tax would you abolish to make the over-all affect of U.S. taxes more progressive? Explain.

15 Is individual freedom consistent with a law that places a tax on you, even if you do not personally benefit from the government spending so financed?

16 What would happen if one applied the benefit principle of taxation to public welfare programs? To education?

17 "Citizens' sovereignty is preferable to consumer sovereignty, because museums, police protection, and parks are preferable to mink coats, night club entertainment, and auto model changes." Comment.

18 The text says that "state and local governments in recent years accounted for only 40 percent of total government spending. However, these governments employed 9 of the 12 million people working for government." How do you account for this? Is the federal government more efficient?

19 Do you think we should differentiate for income tax purposes among wages, rent, interest, and profit? Justify your answer.

20 Should a Massachusetts resident be taxed to help residents of Connecticut? Of California? Of Vietnam?

A NIXON ADVISER ASKS ADJUSTMENT OF SURTAX YEARLY

Suggests New Device for Stabilizing Economy With Minimum of Inflation

By EDWIN L. DALE Jr.

Special to The New York Times

WASHINGTON, Nov. 28—A high-level economic policy adviser to . . . Richard M. Nixon suggested today a new device for regularly adjusting taxes to stabilize the economy at high employment with a minimum of inflation.

The adviser, Herbert Stein, director of economic studies of the Brookings Institution,[1] proposed routine annual Presidential recommendations and Congressional consideration of a "moderate" income tax surcharge that would vary in amount and might in some years "be zero or even negative." . . .

Problem of Inflation

Mr. Stein was chosen to tackle the problem of "unemployment, inflation and economic stability," the title of his essay, before it was known that he would have an advisory role to Mr. Nixon. . . .

Mr. Stein's essay drew few sharp and clear conclusions. But he did express a clear preference for "more flexibility in taxation" while recognizing as impractical previous proposals that Congress give the President advance discretionary authority to make modest changes in tax rates to fight excessive boom or recession in the economy by varying the deficit or surplus in the budget.

Would Debate Proposal

On his proposal for regular annual consideration of a one-year surcharge, Mr. Stein wrote:

"The President would recommend the rate of the surcharge, which might be zero or even negative, on the basis of whatever combination of considerations he thinks important. Congress would debate the proposal, and pass it, with or without amendments, or reject it. It might use the legislation in an attempt to force the President to change the expenditure side of the budget, as it did in 1968.

"In any case, both Congress and the President would have a vehicle for making an overall fiscal decision in a fairly routine way . . . with assurance that the decision would not bind the future . . . Moreover, there is reason to believe, after the experience of 1968, that an across-the-board equal percentage surcharge of moderate size would be accepted as a distributionally neutral tax change and would not stir protracted debate over the question of its equity."

On the basic question of inflation and unemployment, Mr. Stein displayed a clear preference for reducing the current 4 per cent rate of inflation at least to 2 per cent. . . .

'Prolonged Injustice'

Acceptance on a continued basis of a 4 per cent inflation, he said, "would impose serious and prolonged injustice on many whose incomes have been determined by an earlier and lower rate of inflation." He made clear his view that, once a 2 per cent inflation rate had been achieved, the economy could resume normal growth with low unemployment.

On the question of monetary policy —the other main tool besides the budget by which the Government influences the economy—Mr. Stein suggested abolishing the present ceilings on the interest that banks and savings institutions can pay. He suggested that a monetary policy of the Federal Reserve Board aimed at stable growth of the economy without inflation would involve a steadier rise in the nation's money supply but inevitable swings up and down in interest rates.

Removal of the ceilings would enable banks and thrift institutions to continue to attract savings deposits at times of high interest rates, he said, and this would mean that mortgage money could continue to be available to the housing industry, which now often suffers.

Detailed Estimates

Mr. Stein showed a cautious preference for some kind of "stabilization rule" for monetary policy, such as a prescribed range for the growth of the money supply, which consists of currency and checking account deposits. He indicated approval of the recent recommendation of the Joint Economic Committee of Congress that the Federal Reserve System, regardless of all other considerations, govern its actions in such a way that the money supply grow every year no more than 6 per cent and no less than 2 per cent.

[1] Mr. Stein was later appointed a member of President Nixon's first Council of Economic Advisers.

12

*fiscal
policy*

I

N THIS CHAPTER, we consider how the federal government can influence the course of the business cycle through *fiscal policy*, the deliberate exercise of its power to tax and spend in order to move real GNP, employment, and prices to desired levels. As in the case of monetary policy, this type of policy, also, runs head-on into the prejudices of the public, which is apt to reason from analogies that are not valid. The public, comparing the federal government with a household (which it is not) is likely to berate it for "irresponsible and unsound" taxing and spending when undertaken for the "mere" purpose of influencing the level of economic activity.

Let us face the problem directly and investigate the *consequences* of fiscal policy. What would happen, if the federal government, without any change in tax rates, varied only its spending on domestically produced commodities and services?

VARIATIONS ONLY IN FEDERAL GOVERNMENT SPENDING ON DOMESTIC GOODS

The consequences of variations in federal government spending on domestic goods are so easily perceived that they hardly need mentioning. An increase in government spending *without* a change in taxes immediately and by the same amount increases aggregate demand. A decrease in government spending without a change in taxes immediately and by the same amount decreases aggregate demand. Hence, we can influence output and employment. In a period of unemployment, raising government demand *by just the right amount* will bring us full employment without demand-pull inflation. In a period of demand-pull inflation, lowering government demand *by just the right amount* will eliminate the inflation while maintaining full employment. Modern economists would call this sound fiscal policy.

The question that arises immediately is, of course, what is "just the right amount." Actually, our earlier discussion in Chapter 7 of equilibrium GNP can help us find the answer. (For simplicity, we will ignore throughout this chapter the further complications introduced by the accelerator discussed in Chapter 8.)

The Unemployment Case

Suppose full employment GNP is $400 billion per year, but actual and equilibrium GNP is only $300 billion. Should government go ahead and spend another $100 billion per year? It might, of course, do so, buying army trucks and new computers, and schools and hospitals and roads. Before we knew it, we would reach full employment. But as we have also learned, and as common sense tells us, we must expect further consequences. The people, previously unemployed, who now make trucks and computers, schools, hospitals, and roads, as well as the owners of nonlabor resources that helped make these goods, will want to spend a great portion of their extra income. The new income recipients will want to buy toys and clothes for their children, refrigerators and furniture for their wives, and new cars for themselves. As we put it, there will be "induced" consumption demand, because income is up. At this point, clearly then, aggregate demand will come to exceed $400 billion per year. In the aggregate, people would be trying to buy more goods than the economy is capable of producing. Unless government then quickly reduces its demand for every extra dollar of induced consumer spending, we will have generated demand-pull inflation. Because there are not enough resources to produce more trucks and schools for the government *as well as* more clothes and furniture for the newly employed, the prices of everything will begin to rise. People will succeed in spending each year more than $400 billion of money all right. They will not succeed in getting more than $400 billion of real goods.

Using our formula on page 158, we could have predicted this. Autonomous demands divided by (1 − mpc) gives us equilibrium GNP. Put differently, autonomous demands times the multiplier (which is 1/1 − mpc) equals equilibrium GNP. Or, as we put it on page 160, a change in autonomous demands times the multiplier equals the change in equilibrium GNP. If the government, by spending $100 billion per year more, regardless of its income, raises autonomous aggregate demand by this amount, we should expect equilibrium GNP to rise by more. After all, the whole idea of the multiplier formula is to show us how any initial autonomous spending change gets multiplied into a larger figure by rounds of responding. Say, as in Chapter 7, that the mpc is 0.4; hence the multiplier is 1/1 − 0.4, or 1.67. Then we can predict an equilibrium GNP increase of $100 billion (what the government spends extra) × 1.67, or $167 billion. Equilibrium GNP rises from $300 billion to $467 billion per year. Because we can only produce each year (at current prices) $400 billion of goods, we naturally run into the problem just discussed.

But our formula also holds the key to the right answer. Because change in autonomous spending times multiplier gives us change in equilibrium GNP, why not start with the latter? We want GNP to rise from $300 billion to $400 billion per year. Thus our desired change in equilibrium GNP is $100 billion. Because the multiplier is 1.67, we can easily perceive that the required change in autonomous demands must be $100 billion ÷ 1.67, or $60 billion. If the government spent each year this extra amount on new trucks, schools, and so on, the new income recipients can be relied on to spend another $40 billion, raising aggregate demand by just the $100 billion desired. Real GNP would rise to its full employment level, and there would be no inflation.

If you like graphs, you can see that this correct increase in government spending can be measured by the size of the contractionary gap existing at full employment GNP. See, for instance, Figure 10.2 HOW EASY MONETARY POLICY WORKS.

The Case of Inflation

What we have said about eliminating unemployment can be repeated, with appropriate changes, for eliminating inflation. This would call for a *reduction* in government spending of just the right amount. You can find the right amount by dividing the desired cut in equilibrium GNP by the multiplier. Say, aggregate demand is $520 billion per year, but maximum possible output each year (at current prices) is only $400 billion. If we want to eliminate this inflationary pressure from the economy by fiscal policy, this situation calls for a cut in government demand of $72 billion per year. Why? Because this is $120 billion (the desired cut in equilibrium GNP) divided by 1.67 (our assumed multiplier). If government spends each year this much less on army trucks, schools, and so on, people who earn this much less can be relied upon to buy, in turn, fewer toys, refrigerators, and the like. This induced cut in consumer demand will add to $48 billion, bringing the total cut in aggregate demand to the desired goal of $120 billion per year.

Again, if you like graphs, you can see that in this case the correct cut in government spending can be measured by the size of the inflationary gap existing at full employment GNP. See, for instance, Figure 10.3 HOW TIGHT MONETARY POLICY WORKS.

Conclusion

Thus proper fiscal policy can change the course of the economy so as to avoid unemployment and inflation. This is not to deny that raising government demand by too little can fail to eliminate general unemployment. And raising government demand by too much can bring us demand-pull inflation. Lowering government demand by too little can fail to eliminate demand inflation. And lowering it by too much can bring us general unemployment. Modern economists would call such incorrect variations in spending unsound fiscal policy. But note that the public would consider *all* these actions highly "unsound." This is so because people, rather than looking at consequences, are apt to look at the means used to achieve them. And whenever the government spends more without taxing more, it tends to create a *deficit*, and this for most people is a sure sign of irresponsibility. An analogy is made to the household. "After all," people say, "if I keep spending more than I earn, I am headed for bankruptcy; if I take in more than goes out, I am on the way toward great wealth. Who could approve of the former? Who could disapprove of the latter? One just doesn't spend one's way to prosperity." This homely appeal is unfortunately quite wrong, for the *federal* government at least does not have to live within its means. It is not a household. What is true for a household is not true for the federal government. We shall return to this point shortly.

A Graphical Exposition

As already noted, we can also utilize our earlier graphical analysis. Consider Figure 12.1 HOW EASY FISCAL POLICY WORKS—SPENDING MORE. Suppose we are at a position of general unemployment equilibrium, such as at the aggregate demand and aggregate supply intersection E of $300 billion, but potential GNP is $400 billion. To get to full employment, we need an increase in aggregate demand by the size of the excess supply, or contractionary, gap as we find it at full employment. This we can do by *easy fiscal policy*. If there is an excess supply gap at full employment GNP, forcing the economy into unemployment, the federal government, like the Fed, must "lean against the prevailing wind." Unlike the Fed, which can only hope to influence demand indirectly, the federal government can *directly* expand aggregate demand through higher governmental purchases of domestic goods. This forces the economy right back to full employment. In terms of Figure 12.1, we could raise government spending on domestic goods just enough until the AD line goes through point E*. Then *full employment* GNP of $400 billion becomes an equilibrium GNP, capable of being maintained.

One may well argue that every increase in government spending on domestic goods up to this point is for the good, for its only consequence is an increase in output, a reduction in involuntary general unemployment, and hence a reduction in scarcity.

Figure 12.1   HOW EASY FISCAL POLICY WORKS—SPENDING MORE

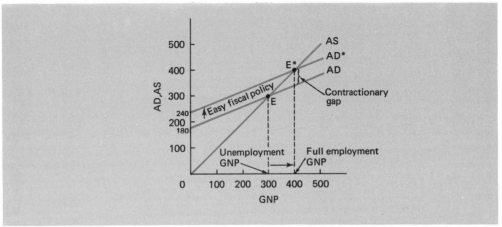

Easy fiscal policy (increasing government spending on domestic goods) directly raises aggregate demand from AD to AD. This displaces an original equilibrium GNP at E to a higher full employment level at E*. Note how the autonomous demand increase (which shifted the AD line up) can be measured on the vertical axis.*

If the increase in government spending were higher than necessary to give us just full employment, aggregate demand would be too large. The AD line would shift up beyond its intersection at E* with the AS line in Figure 12.1. Then we would have engaged in unsound fiscal policy, having encouraged people to demand more goods than we could possibly produce at full employment. If the aggregate demand line in Figure 12.1 were to intersect the aggregate supply line above and to the right of E*, we would have an excess demand, or expansionary, gap at full employment. But expansion would be impossible in terms of *real* output beyond $400 billion. The only thing that could happen is that prices of all goods rise. We would have *demand-pull inflation*.

In such a situation, the government could reduce its spending on domestic goods. Aggregate demand would fall. That is just what we want, because until aggregate demand falls to intersect the aggregate supply line at E*, we have demand-pull inflation. This is shown in Figure 12.2 HOW TIGHT FISCAL POLICY WORKS—SPENDING LESS.

Figure 12.2   HOW TIGHT FISCAL POLICY WORKS—SPENDING LESS

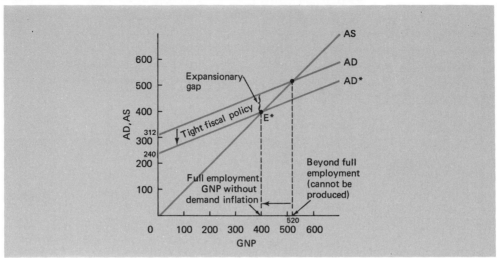

Tight fiscal policy (reducing government spending on domestic goods) directly reduces aggregate demand from AD to AD*. This replaces an inflationary situation by full employment GNP at E*. Note how the autonomous demand decrease (which shifted the AD line down) can be measured on the vertical axis.

Again the federal government must "lean against the prevailing wind." If there is an excess demand, or expansionary, gap at full employment GNP, forcing the economy into inflation, we must *contract* aggregate demand to force it right back to full employment without inflation.

A Professional Value Judgment

Now we have shown how it is possible for variations in government spending on domestic goods to bring us full employment without demand-pull inflation. Most economists would add: government demand *should* be so varied until we have real GNP at full employment without demand-pull inflation. They are saying, in fact, that the federal government should buy goods not on the basis of whether it can "afford" to (having enough tax revenue), but on the basis of what is needed to reach and maintain full employment GNP. Or, to turn it around, at full employment, even if the government could (because of high revenues) "afford" to spend more, it should refrain from so doing.

To most people this is simply shocking, but it is really only stating a simple truth. As long as you have a disease (real GNP below potential or demand above potential GNP), you must take medicine (increase or lower aggregate demand, for example by increasing or lowering the government demand component). Once you are healthy (full employment without demand-pull inflation), you should stop taking medicine (varying government demand), even if you have medicine left (could vary government demand). People practice this every day when taking their own medicine!

Practical Problems?

Those who understand the argument of how variations in government demand can make aggregate demand just right for full employment, at this point usually retreat to another position. "It is all fine and good," they say, "but we simply *cannot* follow the type of expansionary policy described in this section, no matter how desirable. Suppose the government budget is originally balanced, how could we possibly *finance* additional government demand *without* taxes?"

There are two answers, and both are typically received with a shocked raising of eyebrows. First, the federal government could finance government demand by borrowing, and it could borrow *without limit.* Second, it could make new coins and paper money, and it could do so *without limit.* In fact, it does not need taxes at all! It is not hard to understand that eyebrows are raised, for people immediately think of a household, and they are quite right that a household cannot do with no income at all, nor can it borrow without limit, nor can it create new money at all. However, the government is *not* a household.

borrowing from the public   Let us take borrowing first. The Treasury can at any time print up any amount of interest-bearing IOU's, popularly called government bonds, and offer them for sale to the public. These are highly desirable securities and are usually eagerly bought up by the public (households and private businesses alike, including private banks), for they are the safest way in which to hold savings. The U.S. government having the power to create money could *never* go bankrupt. It could always pay off its debts by making new money, if need be. We will have more to say about this later on. At this point, it is only necessary to see that quite likely the government can get any amount of money it wants by borrowing the public's savings. But let us just consider the unlikely case that *everyone,* all households and all businesses, including commercial banks, refused to buy government bonds even at extremely high rates of interest. Then what? Nothing is simpler than that.

borrowing from the fed   The Treasury can always sell bonds to the Fed. Items (3) and (6a) on the Fed's balance sheet (page 201) would rise equally. The Treasury can buy anything it wanted with these deposits; hence, it could raise government demand to any level desired. As the deposits are spent, the Treasury checks are deposited by the recipients in commercial banks, adding to their deposit liabilities and deposits owned at the Fed (items (2) and (7c), page 216). As the checks are cleared, only the ownership of deposits changes on the Fed's balance sheet (from (6a) to (6b)). In the end, government demand is up (as in Figure 12.1 HOW EASY FISCAL POLICY WORKS—SPENDING MORE). The Fed holds more bonds and owes more deposits to member banks. Member banks hold more reserves and owe more deposits. In fact they could now, as we saw in Chapter 10, increase the money supply further, and this may well stimulate other demands: consumption demand, investment demand, and state and local government demand. To that extent, federal government demand can be reduced in subsequent years.

What if Congress, as it has in the past, *forbids* the Fed to buy bonds from the Treasury? The Treasury, wishing to raise government demand because of general unemployment, would have no trouble selling bonds to security dealers. The reason is as follows. The Fed, in a period of unemployment, is supposed to pursue an easy money policy. This involves, as we saw, buying bonds from security dealers. Hence, the Treasury's bonds end up in the Fed anyway, and the checks given for them fall into the hands of the Treasury anyway, which spends its deposit as before!

creating new money   Now let us take the alternative. We have seen in Chapter 9 how the Treasury can at any time make coins and paper money, *non*interest-bearing IOU's. It can hand these to the Fed (as on page 204) in return for deposits to be spent, or it can spend the new cash directly. In any case, government demand can rise without limit. It is of little consequence *how* it is done.

_____

More Objections

At this point, the questioner is likely to shift his position again. "O.K.," he will say, "so the federal government is not a household. It can borrow without limit; it can make money without limit; hence it can vary government demand to any level to create full employment. But haven't you forgotten something? The public debt surely cannot grow forever lest we wish to court disaster, and pumping in more money will surely cause inflation. Just look what happened to prices last month!" Well, again, our questioner is wrong. What happened to prices last month is quite irrelevant, unless he can show that they rose because of *too big* an increase in government demand (which is not what we intend to do). The public debt *can* grow forever without disaster, as we shall see in the next chapter. And, as we saw in Chapter 10, more money is *not* synonymous with inflation. Demand-pull inflation is caused by too much spending, by people trying to buy more than can possibly be produced. Yet the purpose of fiscal policy is exactly to regulate government demand to *avoid* demand-pull inflation. Hence, new money used to finance a rise in government demand is not inflationary because the government would spend only as much new money as is necessary to raise government demand to such a level as is needed to have aggregate demand equal to potential GNP. If the new money in the economy subsequently lowers interest rates and encourages private spending beyond what it was, government demand will then have to be *lowered* to keep aggregate demand at the right level. The new money will never be inflationary. It will only be allowed to be *expansionary,* to raise real GNP to its potential.

As we said above, sound finance, just as sound monetary policy, reasonably defined, depends on *consequences,* not on the means used to achieve them. Increasing government demand without new taxes *can* be sound. Whereon the questioner usually says: "It sounds all right, but I just *know* it's wrong somewhere." What about you?

VARIATIONS IN TAXATION ONLY

The above road to full employment is not the only one at the disposal of fiscal policy-makers. It should be noted, however, that many economists favor it over other methods, at least when it comes to eliminating unemployment (Figure 12.1). Foremost among these is Harvard's John Kenneth Galbraith, who has argued that we overemphasize the gratification of private wants at the neglect of public wants with the only exception of spending for war. Being constantly lured by the multibillion dollar voice of private advertising, people have come to prefer mouthwashes to clean cities, new model cars to education for the young, Galbraith says. As a result, we have the kind of urban problems discussed in Chapter 11 above (pages 251–252) and in Chapter 28. To redress this imbalance, argues Galbraith, we should enlarge the provision of public goods in our economy. Therefore, even though there may be other ways to do it, if unemployment needs to be eliminated, an increase in government demand is the proper course to be followed. As we also noted in the earlier section just referred to, this may well take the form of federal funds being transferred to and actually spent by state and local governments, as proposed by Walter Heller.

Let us now consider another possible approach. What if we left government spending unchanged, only changing tax rates? This again is considered an irresponsible fiscal action by many people, because taxing less without spending less tends to create a *deficit*, whereas taxing more without spending more tends to create a *surplus*, which some people at least would regard as unnecessary. As before, a false analogy is made to the household. The argument made in the previous section applies fully. The federal government can at will vary tax collections at any GNP by manipulating rates, because it does not need any taxes (as a household needs income) *at all*. It could at any time borrow, or easier still, manufacture its own money. "Then why," you will say triumphantly, "do governments *ever* tax?" The answer to that question is the point of this section.

National governments tax more not because they need more money but because they want to make someone else (who cannot manufacture money) spend less. They tax less not because they need less money, but because they want to make someone else spend more. As the government, through variations in tax rates, collects a greater or smaller amount of taxes at each level of GNP, the net incomes of households and private businesses fall or rise at each level of GNP. Consumers as a group will therefore, by a somewhat smaller amount that depends on the marginal propensity to consume, decrease or raise their spending. More likely than not, at least some of the businesses, left with lower or higher net profits, will decide to lower or raise investment demand. Hence, given governmental demand for goods, a decrease in taxes will increase aggregate demand. A rise in taxes will decrease aggregate demand. Thus, we have yet another tool for reaching full employment without demand-pull inflation. If real GNP is below potential, lowering taxes *by just the right amount* (to a *negative* figure if need be) will bring us full employment without demand-pull inflation. In a period of demand-pull inflation, raising taxes *by just the right amount* will eliminate the inflation, while maintaining full employment. This is what "unsound" fiscal policy *may* do.

Again the obvious question arises: what is "just the right amount"? We can use the same technique employed earlier.

The Unemployment Case

Suppose, again, that actual GNP is at $300 billion a year, but the potential is $400 billion. We want to raise equilibrium GNP by the $100 billion difference. Again we look at the formula:

> autonomous demands times multiplier equals equilibrium GNP.

At present, equilibrium GNP is $300 billion. The marginal propensity to consume gross national income being 0.4 (we still assume), the multiplier is $1/1 - 0.4$, or 1.67. This implies that, presently, autonomous demands are $300 billion *divided by* the multiplier of 1.67. They equal $180 billion per year. In short, if we put numbers in the above formula, it would read:

$$\$180 \text{ billion} \times 1.67 = \$300 \text{ billion.}$$

Yet we want equilibrium GNP to be $400 billion. There are two obvious routes to achieve this. We can raise autonomous demands by $60 billion and write

$$\$240 \text{ billion} \times 1.67 = \$400 \text{ billion.}$$

This we did in fact above, when we raised government spending by $60 billion. (See Figure 12.1 HOW EASY FISCAL POLICY WORKS—SPENDING MORE.)

But we can also raise the size of the multiplier, writing

$$\$180 \text{ billion} \times new \text{ multiplier} = \$400 \text{ billion.}$$

The new multiplier would have to be 2.22. Can we really do that? Of course, we can! Remember that the multiplier equaled $1/1 - mpc$. Hence, the marginal propensity to consume gross national income that is implied by our new multiplier is 0.55. This is so because $1/1 - 0.55$ equals 2.22.

In plain English, what does this tell us? It says that one other way to raise aggregate demand and real GNP to the full employment level of $400 billion a year requires making induced consumption spending equal to 55 cents, rather than 40 cents as before, of each dollar of GNP.

This we have the power to do. Recall from earlier chapters how we derived the mpc of 0.4. We assumed that consumers spend (on top of a certain minimum expenditure) 80 cents of every dollar of disposable personal income (recall, for instance, Table 6.2 AN AGGREGATE CONSUMPTION DEMAND SCHEDULE). We also noted that disposable personal income equals the gross national income minus certain deductions, such as depreciation, retained corporate profits and taxes, plus transfer payments (Figure 6.3 INCOME CONCEPTS). For simplicity, we assumed all this to amount to a net deduction of half of GNP (Table 6.2). Hence, every extra dollar of GNP brought with it an extra half-dollar of disposable personal income and an extra 40 cents of induced consumer spending. Thus, the mpc, the change in induced consumer spending divided by the change in gross national income causing it, equaled 0.4.

Now, for the sake of the argument, let us assume these deductions and additions from gross national income were as follows: depreciation took 10 percent, retained corporate profits took 10 percent, taxes took 35 percent and transfer payments *added* 5 percent. As we said, the net effect would be a 50 percent deduction. Every dollar of gross national income would finally yield only 50 cents of disposable personal income (of which people then consumed 40 cents).

Can you now see how we can get people to consume, in addition to a certain minimum, 55 cents of each dollar of GNP, even though they continue to insist on spending 80 cents of every dollar of disposable personal income? We must make sure that they get more disposable personal income per dollar of GNP! The government may not be able to influence the deduction for depreciation or retained corporate profits. But it surely has the power to lower the deduction for taxes or to increase its transfer payments (make negative taxes).

Suppose the tax rate were cut from 35 percent of gross national income to 16.25 percent. Immediately, each dollar of GNP would be subjected to a net deduction of 31.25 cents only: 10 cents each for depreciation and retained corporate profits, 16.25 cents for taxes, offset by 5 cents of transfer payments. Each dollar of GNP would yield 68.75 cents (rather than 50 cents) of disposable personal income. People would spend eight tenths of that, or 55 cents, rather than 40 cents, on consumer goods.

This, as we calculated above, would raise aggregate demand just enough to reach full employment production. As each income recipient found his net income up, he would start spending more. The increased purchases by households of private cars and furniture and vacation trips would put other people to work. The formerly unemployed would suddenly find jobs and start spending in turn! Thus, a tax cut can achieve the same that a rise in government spending could have achieved.

Finding the New Tax Rate

Perhaps you are curious how the correct tax rate of 16.25 percent was found? It is very simple. Start with the required new multiplier, as calculated above, and figure out the new mpc implied by it (as we did above). Let us call the marginal propensity to consume *personal disposable income* (our 0.8) by the symbol MPC. Let us call the fraction that personal disposable income is of gross national income by the symbol f (our 0.5). Then mpc always equals f × MPC. (Using our original numbers, 0.4 = 0.5 × 0.8.) Given the new required mpc of 0.55, we can calculate the new required f: 0.55 = f × 0.8, or f = 0.6875. In short, disposable personal income must become 68.75 percent of gross national income. At present, each dollar of gross national income is already reduced by 10 cents of depreciation and 10 cents of retained corporate earnings, then partially offset by 5 cents of transfer payments, yielding, before taxes are figured, 85 cents of income. Thus, taxes can at most take 85 cents minus 68.75 cents, or 16.25 cents per gross national income dollar. The earlier tax rate of 35 cents per dollar was too high and responsible for our unemployment!

Conclusion

All this, of course, can be applied also to the case of demand-pull inflation. Then, a tax hike, like a cut in government spending, could discourage aggregate demand sufficiently to stop inflation.

This is not to deny that lowering taxes by too little can fail to eliminate general unemployment. Or that lowering taxes by too much can cause demand-pull inflation. Similarly, raising taxes by too little can fail to eliminate demand-pull inflation. Raising them by too much can bring us general unemployment.

A Graphical Exposition

What we have said can again be shown graphically. Consider Figure 12.3 HOW EASY FISCAL POLICY WORKS—TAXING LESS. Suppose we are at a position of general unemployment equilib-

Figure 12.3   HOW EASY FISCAL POLICY WORKS—TAXING LESS

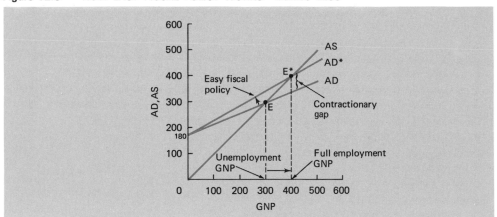

Easy fiscal policy (a uniform decrease in the tax rate) raises aggregate demand from AD to AD*. This displaces an original equilibrium GNP at E to a higher full employment level at E*. Note how the multiplier increase (which tilted the AD line up) shows up as a greater slope of that line.

rium, such as at the aggregate demand and aggregate supply intersection E of $300 billion, but potential GNP is $400 billion, as in our earlier examples. By lowering tax rates, the government could stimulate aggregate demand just sufficiently to tilt the aggregate demand line up to become AD*. Note that what is needed is an increase in aggregate demand *at the full employment level* by the size of the contractionary gap. Hence, tax *collections* at the full employment level have to fall by *more* than the size of this gap. Although every dollar tax cut raises disposable personal income by a dollar, part of any increase in disposable personal income goes into increased saving, rather than increased demand. Thus, it may take a tax cut of $75 billion at full employment GNP to raise private demands by $60 billion (the size of the gap), if $15 billion of the lowered taxes are saved.

Note also that the possibility of a tax cut is in no way limited by the amount of taxes actually collected prior to the cut. Taxes can always be reduced to below zero, if necessary. This means that people, rather than having to send a smaller amount to the tax collector, can be asked to send nothing and be *given* a check instead, possibly in the form of a refund of past years' taxes.

The making of such *transfer payments* is then, of course, very similar to the earlier case of increasing government spending. The only differences are that private individuals, rather than the government, will get the goods and that the cost to the government of raising demand by a dollar are larger here. If the government spends a dollar directly for its own purchases, demand is up by that much. If it hands the same dollar to a household as a gift, demand may well rise by less.

If a tax cut is excessive, however, aggregate demand can become too large. The AD line would tilt up beyond its intersection at E* with the AS line in Figure 12.3. We would have created demand-pull inflation. In such a situation, the government can raise taxes, reducing aggregate demand. This type of case is illustrated in Figure 12.4 HOW TIGHT FISCAL POLICY WORKS—TAXING MORE. By contracting aggregate demand just sufficiently to close the expansionary gap at full employment GNP, the economy can be forced back to full employment without demand-pull inflation.

Having seen how it is *possible* for changes in taxes to get us to full employment without

Figure 12.4   HOW TIGHT FISCAL POLICY WORKS—TAXING MORE

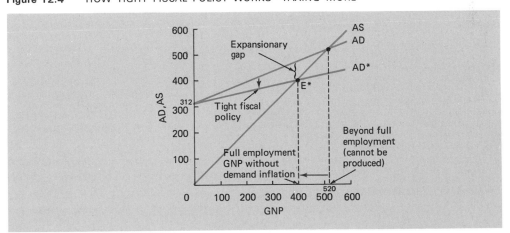

Tight fiscal policy (a uniform increase in the tax rate) reduces aggregate demand from AD to AD*. This replaces an inflationary situation by full employment GNP at E*. Note how the multiplier decrease (which tilted the AD line down) shows up as a smaller slope of that line.

demand-pull inflation, economists would again argue that this *should* be done, as long as the consequences are desirable ones. Government, in short, should not tax more to get money, but to destroy money in the hands of the public so as to lower aggregate demand. Government should not tax less if it wants to spend less, but if it wants to leave more income in the hands of the public so as to increase aggregate demand. In the previous section, we have seen how this *can* be done, because federal government spending on goods, government demand, does in no way depend on tax collections.

Considering what we have said above about some economists' preference for greater public provision of goods, you can guess that they would prefer a tax hike to fight inflation (Figure 12.4 HOW TIGHT FISCAL POLICY WORKS—TAXING MORE), but increased government spending to fight unemployment (Figure 12.1 HOW EASY FISCAL POLICY WORKS—SPENDING MORE). The former would cut excessive aggregate demand at the expense of private demands. The latter would raise deficient aggregate demand by raising public demand. On the other hand, other people have argued that it is just as important to raise certain types of private demands, such as the demand of the poor. They would prefer to fight unemployment by tax cuts, but selective cuts favoring the poor. But such preferences aside, you should see that in principle either unemployment or demand-pull inflation can be combatted by government spending changes alone (Figures 12.1 and 12.2) or by tax rate changes alone (Figures 12.3 and 12.4).

COMBINING THE TWO APPROACHES

What can be achieved by varying spending or taxes separately can also be achieved by varying them together. What would happen if the federal government varied both its spending on commodities and services and, by a change in tax rates, its tax collections by an equal amount?

"Sound" Fiscal Policy

Most people would consider only such an equal variation in spending and tax collections as "sound" fiscal policy, for they compare tax collections to the "earned income" of a household. They argue that "a household (hence the government) must live within its means, lest dire consequences befall it." Most people would also argue that equal increases or decreases in taxing and spending by government would have *no* effect on aggregate economic activity. "After all, $10 taken away from the public in taxes means $10 less spent by the public. If the $10 are then spent by government, *total* spending is unchanged. Output and employment will be unchanged. The only thing changed will be the distribution of output. The government will have more, the public less."

Yet these arguments, so frequently encountered and so "obvious" on the surface, are wrong! Let us begin with the latter.

If you have studied the preceding sections carefully, you should already know the answers. What happens if $10 more (or less) are taken away from the public in taxes? The immediate effect is only to lower (or raise) the disposable personal income of the public by $10. What then happens will vary greatly if we look at any *one* individual at a time. You may, indeed, spend $10 less (or more), someone else may spend $30 less (or more), I may spend 1 cent less (or more). But, as we have argued, and as empirical evidence bears out so clearly, the public *as a group* reacts in a very predictable fashion. It spends less (or more) for each dollar variation in income, but not less (or more) by a full dollar, for it also reduces (or raises) its saving. On the average, people behave like our man in Table 6.1 AN INDIVIDUAL'S CONSUMPTION DEMAND SCHEDULE. As disposable personal income falls from $100 to $90 weekly, because, let us say, taxes were raised by $10, consumption demand falls from $90 to $82 and personal saving from $10 to $8. Private spending goes down by *less* than the increase in taxes. It goes down by $8, while taxes went up (and disposable personal income down) by $10. On the other hand, were disposable personal income to rise from $100 to $110 weekly, because taxes were lowered by $10, consumption demand would rise from $90 to $98 and personal saving from $10 to $12. Private spending goes up by *less* than the fall in taxes. Now we can state the consequences correctly.

1. An increase in personal income tax collections by any amount will lower consumer demand by less. Hence, aggregate demand will rise if government demand rises by the amount of higher taxes. If we are below full employment to begin with, output will rise. If we are at full employment originally, more will be demanded than can possibly be produced and we will have demand-pull inflation. If we have demand-pull inflation originally, it will be intensified.

2. A fall in personal income tax collections by any amount will increase consumer demand by less. Hence, aggregate demand will fall if government demand falls by the amount of lowered taxes. If we are below full employment to begin with, output and employment will fall. If we are at full employment originally, we will end up below it. If we have demand-pull inflation to begin with (trying to buy more goods than can be made), it will decrease in intensity. Depending on the magnitude of aggregate demand decline, we will end up, in this last case, with lesser demand-pull inflation, full employment without demand-pull inflation, or even general unemployment.

3. What most people consider "sound" fiscal policy may bring about full employment without demand-pull inflation if taxes and spending on goods are raised together *by just the right amount* in a period of general unemployment, or lowered together *by just the right amount* in a period of demand-pull inflation. In all other instances, sound fiscal policy may not turn out to be so sound at all, failing to eliminate or even *creating* demand-pull inflation or general unemployment!

A Numerical Exposition

We can show the implications of this with the help of our familiar example. Suppose we are again at the $300 billion GNP position of general unemployment.

As we saw in Figure 12.1 HOW EASY FISCAL POLICY WORKS—SPENDING MORE, we could just raise government spending by the size of the contractionary gap at full employment. All would be well *as long as we did not raise taxes*. Yet, if we raised taxes to cover the increased spending in a situation such as the final one depicted at E* in Figure 12.1, the AD* line would tilt down. True enough, it would tilt down by less, given people's propensity to cut their saving as well as spending in the face of a tax hike. But tilt down it would. Hence, at least *part* of the contractionary gap would open up again. We would not get full employment. Not yet, anyway.

The increased spending by government on army trucks, schools, and so on puts some people to work. But the decreased spending by all those hit by higher taxes puts others out of work!

If increased government spending is to be financed by increased taxes (which reduce private demand to *partially* offset the increased public demand), we must raise government spending by *a great deal more* than would be necessary without the accompanying tax hike. If, for example, every $10 increase in government demand reduces private demand by $8 (owing to our insistence on raising taxes by $10 also), we can raise *aggregate* demand by $10 per year only if we raise annual government demand by $50. The accompanying tax hike of $50 will then cut private demand by $40. This leaves a net rise of $10 per year in aggregate demand. In our case, we could achieve the necessary increase of autonomous demand by $60 billion per year only if government spent and taxed $300 billion more each year. The $300 billion per year rise in government demand would be offset in large part by a $240 billion fall in private demand.

The case is similar for an inflationary situation. Instead of just reducing government demand by the size of the expansionary gap (see Figure 12.2 HOW TIGHT FISCAL POLICY WORKS—SPENDING LESS), we must reduce government demand by more. Then we must cut taxes simultaneously (and by an equal amount). Because every cut in government demand is partially offset by a rise in private demand resulting from the tax cut, the total cut in government demand (and taxes) must be larger than the size of the expansionary gap.

In our case, we could achieve the necessary decrease in autonomous demand of $72 billion per year only if government spent and taxed each year $360 billion less. The $360 billion per year cut in government demand would be offset in large part by a $288 billion rise in private demand. Clearly all this is very awkward. But, in principle, full employment without demand inflation can be reached by equal variations in both spending on goods and taxing. Only in cases of extreme general unemployment may this policy not be practical, as it then becomes impossible to raise taxes sufficiently to cover the required increase in governmental demand.

JUDGING THE EFFECTIVENESS OF FISCAL POLICY

Theoretically, fiscal policy can assure full employment without demand-pull inflation. Since the 1930's, this has become in liberal circles an increasingly favored way of dealing with the business cycle. However, like monetary policy, fiscal measures, too, are difficult to undertake in practice.

The Recognition Lag

There is, as before, the *recognition lag,* the fact that policy-makers are in a position of a man driving a car with only a view toward the past via a rear-view mirror. They have to guess about where the economy is precisely at present and even more about where it is going. Economic policy-makers, like doctors, do not always agree even on the diagnosis. Faced with a 30 percent chance for demand inflation and a 70 percent chance for worsened general unemployment in the next six months, the policy-maker is in a dilemma (and an elected official would hate to be blamed for either of these events). Act he must, and he could create a disaster. For example, in the early 1930's, the federal government was faced at given tax rates with *falling* tax revenues as GNP declined in respone to lower private demand. So the government followed what the public considers to this day sound fiscal policy, *reducing* its spending on goods. This clearly made the depression worse. (Can you show why?) Faster collection and processing of data and improvements in forecasting may over time reduce the lag involved. But the need for someone to act wisely on the basis of this information will remain.

The Administrative Lag

Even when the decision to act in a certain way has been made, the fiscal policy-maker, unlike the maker of monetary policy, can under present circumstances, not act very fast. A few phone calls to sell or buy securities or an official announcement on reserve requirements will not do. The *administrative lag,* until something is done, is likely to be very long. Changes in government spending or taxes require *congressional* action. Unfortunately, the human race is not particularly prompt in dealing collectively with urgent problems. In addition, congressmen may be under pressure from constituents to pursue sound fiscal policy (as in 1933!). Then they may refuse to act at all. Even barring misinformation and ignorance, congressmen may be in recess or busy with other matters. Even if they do act and act wisely, a tax or spending bill is assured of a lengthy trip through a ponderous Congress. (For example, the tax cut law of February 1964 was proposed by President Kennedy in early 1963, the tax hike of June 1968 was urgently demanded by President Johnson ever since 1966.) This is made worse by the fact that such measures, under present circumstances, are hard to reverse. If continued general unemployment is foreseen in early 1963, taxes should be cut *then* (or government spending be raised, or spending and taxes raised equally). Yet, they may finally be cut only in 1964 or even later, and it just might be that unforeseen changes have by then made the need for a tax cut obsolete; in fact, by that time the opposite may be required. Imagine doctors prescribing drugs to be taken a year after diagnosis!

However, this problem is not unsolvable in principle. Even now the President has certain powers with respect to the exact timing of spending authorized by Congress for a given fiscal period. He could, for instance, accelerate or retard expenditures in certain months of a fiscal year. President Kennedy tried to combat a recession in this way by speeding up post office construction and tax refunds. Yet such powers are very limited. In other countries, such as Sweden, there are much broader powers.

In 1962, President Kennedy proposed procedures for making quick, temporary, pre-fabricated cuts in personal taxes when needed. The proposal caused scarcely a ripple in Congress. Other proposals have been made since. (Note the news story introducing this chapter.) Similarly, the President could be given standby authority to initiate or terminate *previously approved* government spending programs for specified purposes and up to specified magnitudes under certain conditions. Such conditions could be spelled out in detail by Congress—for example, a continued rise in unemployment or prices, respectively, for so many months, or unemployment or the price index, respectively, going above a certain percentage. This could even be made subject to congressional veto to preserve congressional prerogatives. But even such contingency legislation would only cut, not eliminate the lag. Blueprints on the shelf are not enough. The government must advertise for bids and let contracts and builders must get organized before work is actually begun. Once under way, increased spending is hard to stop. A bridge halfway across the river is of no use and has to be completed, even though the time has come for a cut in government demand. Yet, spending can possibly be slowed down, as it has in the interstate highway program.

Similarly, Congress could enact *in advance* a great variety of alternative tax laws, giving the President the power under agreed conditions to change effective rates at a moment's notice, as by announcing the replacement of tax rate Table A by Table B. A *fast and flexible* policy could not do without this.

The Operational Lag

However long at present the administrative lag may be, the *operational lag* for fiscal, as opposed to monetary, policy is likely to be much shorter. Demand may never respond to easy money, but it usually responds fast to lower taxes, and a government spending change is itself a change in demand. Once fiscal measures are in operation, their effectiveness can, of course, again be strengthened or impaired by unforeseen changes in the economy.

Political Problems

We must also face political considerations that may override economic ones. Just as demand inflation threatens and when economists see the need for lower aggregate demand (which could be accomplished through raising taxes or lowering government demand or lowering government demand and taxes equally), we might have a war requiring *higher* government demand. Or we might have elections making politicians desirous of *lowering* taxes. These matters do not make truly sound fiscal policy impossible, but they make it more difficult. But, to eliminate our historical underutilization of resources and with it unnecessary scarcity, it surely is worth a try.

It would be a pity, if public ignorance, masquerading as morality, kept us from using perfectly good weapons in the fight against scarcity. The problem of the economists is not so much what to say, but how to get people to listen. They must reconcile sensible economic policy with popular values that, however mistaken, cannot be transformed overnight. Every one of you should work hard to understand the simple logic of sound monetary and fiscal policy. Imagine yourself in the process of learning to swim. It seems so difficult at first because it involves movements in conflict with those you normally make. Yet, with practice it becomes a habit, and then you can never understand what was so hard about it. It is the same way here. Money creation, money destruction, eternal federal deficits, and so on, are not synonymous with inflation, robbery, disaster, and profligacy. To a household, like swimming motions on land, this may seem odd and out of place and downright dangerous. For the economy as a whole, like swimming motions in the sea, this is just what comes natural and is downright necessary.

AUTOMATICITY VS. DISCRETIONARY STABILIZATION

Just as some people have argued for an automatic monetary pilot (see Chapter 10), others would like to rely on automatic forces in fiscal matters also. They point out how there exist already a variety of "built-in stabilizers" in our economy that tend to dampen any swings in real GNP and employment. Take the progressive federal personal income tax, for example. If real GNP and employment rise, aggregate money income in the economy rises. Without any change in the tax rate table whatsoever, tax collections will also rise. This will happen for two reasons: there is more income to be taxed, and more and more people move up into higher tax brackets, possibly from a no-tax bracket. Thus, a $20 billion rise in GNP, being accompanied by, say, a $5 billion rise in personal income tax collections, will at best leave room for a $15 billion rise in disposable personal income. Given people's propensity to save part of any additional income, this will, in turn, lead to an even smaller rise in consumption demand. The same principle works in reverse. A fall in employment and GNP is accompanied by a reduction in tax collections (without any change in the tax law, mind you). Hence, it leads to a smaller fall in disposable personal income and a smaller one still in consumption demand.

In short, the existence of the federal personal income tax (and in addition its progressivity) has the effect of cushioning the impact of swings in GNP on demand. This ultimately limits the swings of GNP itself.

There are other automatic stabilizers: potentially all the elements intervening between GNP and disposable personal income (compare Figure 6.2 INCOME CONCEPTS). To the extent that depreciation, indirect taxes, corporate income taxes, social security taxes, and undistributed corporate profits decline or rise with declines or rises in GNP, disposable personal income declines or rises by less. The same is true if transfer payments rise as GNP declines and fall when it rises. This is, in fact, most likely. A higher GNP, for example, most likely involves a higher rate of capital utilization and higher depreciation charges. Taxes other than personal income taxes also flow in increased quantities into governmental coffers as sales, corporate profits, and employment rise with the rise in GNP. Undistributed profits are likely to be larger in boom times. Unemployment compensation benefits, welfare payments, farm subsidies, and so on are likely to be smaller as fewer people are in economic difficulties. When GNP falls, the opposites would happen. All of this would moderate the swings of disposable personal income compared to those of GNP. (The Council of Economic Advisers estimated in 1969 that each $1 change in GNP led to only a 65 cent change in disposable personal income plus retained corporate profits).

But one thing should be noted. Automatic stabilizers tend to mitigate, but by no means offset, swings in aggregate demand, GNP, and employment.

To this some people would retort that the economy's automatic shockproofing should be improved. Transfer payments, for instance, should be liberalized. At the moment, over a quarter of the unemployed are unemployed for over 6 months. Yet, unemployment benefits run out after 6 months, nor do they start until a person has been unemployed for 2 weeks. Even for this limited period, such transfers now offset at most a third of any income loss.

Another possibility is to "automate" tax changes. One may legislate, for instance, that tax rates are cut automatically by 5 percent for each percentage point by which unemployment rises above 3 percent. Then, if the unemployment rate is 5.3 percent, it would trigger automatically a tax cut by 2.3 × 5, or 11.5 percent. A powerful stimulus, indeed! Congress is unlikely to enact any such law, however. And for the same reason that it has denied standby authority to Presidents Kennedy and Johnson in fiscal policy matters. Congress is very jealous of any infringement of its powers of the purse. It certainly would not want to tie them to statistics that are far from foolproof. In fact, in 1966, the Senate-House Fiscal Policy Committee, which considered these matters, spoke out against such legislation. Most economists nowadays look to *discretionary* fiscal policy (of the types discussed in the body of this chapter) to reverse the course of a recession or of inflation. Only a quick deliberate change in tax rates and in government demand can reverse the trend of GNP with certainty and quickly. Moreover, argue most modern economists, the aim should go beyond an attempt to smooth out the business cycle. It should be to lift aggregate demand at all times to the level of potential GNP. Any deviation of private aggregate demand from this potential should be compensated for by deliberate countermeasures in the public sector. This is why fiscal policy is often referred to as *compensatory* policy. Note how adherence to the principle of the balanced budget would paralyze such policy and reinforce rather than offset swings in GNP. A fall in GNP during a depression, bringing with it an automatically reduced flow of taxes, would dictate deliberate cuts in government spending or deliberate hikes in tax rates. Nothing better could be devised to strengthen the fall in GNP! Similarly, in a period of inflation, rising tax revenues, occurring automatically, would require higher government spending or lowered tax rates to keep the budget balanced. What better prescription is there for enhanced inflation? Following the principle of the annually balanced budget would mean allowing the blind forces of the economy to be our master.

The Full Employment Budget

Because the public is so intent on looking at the federal budget, economists have in recent years tried a new approach to escape the paralyzing grip of economic myth. They, too, have talked of budget balance, but of balance *at full employment*. This approach soothes the public's fears, while allowing for all the necessary flexibility of compensatory fiscal policy. Congress should determine, argue these economists, the size of government demand without regard to revenues, solely on the basis of their merit. Then it should legislate tax rates such that they would yield a balanced budget *under conditions of full employment without demand-pull inflation.* If then the actual budget is not in balance, it can be attributed to the automatic and passive budget response to GNP deviations away from full employment.

Using this approach, it becomes very educational to compare the actual budget (net tax collections minus government spending on goods) with what it would be like at full employment. Figure 12.5 REGULAR VS. FULL EMPLOYMENT BUDGET provides such data. It turns out that at current tax rates, had there been full employment, given actual government spending on goods, the federal budget would have been in surplus from mid 1954 through 1965. In fact, it was often in deficit. The meaning of this is clear and simple: tax rates were too high, imposing a major *fiscal drag* on the economy. As GNP rose, tax collections rose so fast as to stop the rise in GNP long before full employment was reached. Paradoxically, lower tax *rates* would have allowed aggregate demand and GNP to expand further, leading to full employment and higher tax *collections.* (Collecting a 30 percent tax on a $100 income brings in less revenue than collecting a 25 percent tax on a $150 income!)

Figure 12.5   REGULAR VS. FULL EMPLOYMENT BUDGET

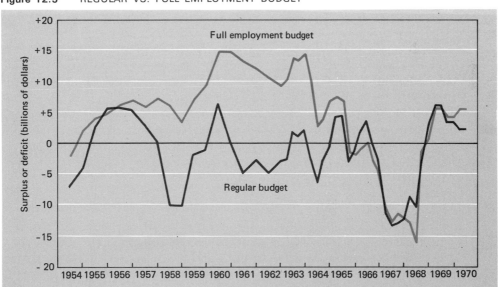

The full employment and actual federal budget have differed significantly during the 1950's and 1960's. Economists use the former as a gauge of the impact of federal government operations on the economy. Source: Federal Reserve Bank of St. Louis, based on national income accounts budget figures. The 1969 and 1970 data are estimates of the bank.

If you look at Figure 12.5, you will note the particularly sharp increases in the full employment budget surplus in 1960 and 1963. The 1960 Eisenhower budget message had called for a policy that "not merely balances expenditures with revenues, but achieves a significant surplus for debt retirement." This led to strict expenditure control by the administration and to increased social security and excise taxes. If there had been full employment, a substantial surplus would have been achieved. But the high rates needed to achieve the much smaller actual surplus prevented the attainment of full employment. The administration's policy to be fiscally responsible resulted in high unemployment. In 1961 and 1962, increased government spending on defense and space, liberalized public assistance payments and social security benefits, and certain tax cuts led to a decline in the full employment budget surplus. But it was still a surplus, dragging the economy into unemployment and presenting it with an actual budget deficit in addition. Congressional failure to pass the Kennedy tax cut in 1963 led to a rise in the full employment surplus. Only in 1964, when the tax cut was enacted, did the surplus decline significantly. As a result of increased Vietnam spending, it turned into a deficit in the mid-1960's. This deficit reached its peak in early 1968 and pushed the economy into inflation. The full employment deficit was eliminated (and the actual deficit also) by late 1968. In that year, Congress had enacted the tax hike (retroactively to April 1). It had also forced President Johnson to pare down his January spending proposals by $6 billion. (President Nixon, in 1969, asked Congress to extend the tax surcharge, as well as certain excise taxes. He cut the budget further. Hence, the 1969–1970 surpluses.)

Thus, the hypothetical full employment budget can be used as a fiscal gauge. If it is in surplus, the federal government is dragging the economy below its potential. Then, even though the actual budget is in deficit, a still greater deficit should be incurred to get rid of it (and of unemployment).

If the full employment budget is in deficit, the federal government is pushing the economy above its potential. Then, even though the actual budget may be in surplus, a still greater surplus is required to get rid of it (and of inflation).

In any case, it seems wisest to forget about budget balance, except perhaps at full employment, and make any deliberate fiscal changes necessary to assure the continual production of potential GNP.

SUMMARY

1   Fiscal policy is the deliberate exercise by the federal government of its power to tax and spend in order to bring about the elimination of unemployment and the production of the potential GNP without demand inflation. As long as such a goal is furthered, without undesirable side effects, *any* change in government spending or taxation can be called desirable.

2   We have shown that the goal of full employment without demand-pull inflation can be attained by (a) variations in federal government spending on domestic goods alone, (b) variations in taxation only, or (c) simultaneous and equal variations in federal government spending on domestic goods and in tax collections. Of course, appropri-

ately thought out policies of simultaneous and unequal variations in spending and taxing (where neither variation is zero) can also accomplish the goal. Within limits, such policies could also be carried out by state and local governments.

3 Any amount of federal government spending can be financed without taxes by borrowing (if need be from the Fed), or by creating new money. Whether this is desirable depends on the *consequences*.

4 As monetary policy, fiscal policy is somewhat of an art. Its perfect execution is hampered by the recognition lag, the administrative lag, and the operational lag. Actual policy must be expected to yield less than perfect results. It is quite possible that more authority given to the executive branch of government (such as standby powers to change spending and taxing at a moment's notice) could appreciably improve the chances of successful policy.

5 Probably the greatest obstacle to successful fiscal policy is public misunderstanding. Though some people would advocate reliance on automatic stabilizers, others would allow discretionary policy measures, provided they are guided by the rule of the balanced budget. Following such rule would have disastrous consequences. Economists propose instead the use of the full employment budget as a gauge for needed policy actions.

TERMS[2]

automatic stabilizers vs. discretionary stabilization fiscal drag	fiscal policy full employment budget

SYMBOLS

MPC

QUESTIONS FOR REVIEW AND DISCUSSION

1 Give a verbal description of what happens in a period of general unemployment when government spending is raised.

2 How would you answer question 1 for a period of demand inflation?

3 Suppose GNP is in equilibrium at $700 billion. The mpc equals ⅓. At full employment, we could produce $1,000 billion of goods. By how much should government spending be raised to get the economy to full employment?

4 Can you graph the answer to question 3?

[2] Terms and symbols are defined in the Glossary at the end of the book.

5 Which method of eliminating unemployment would Galbraith prefer? Why? How about you?

6 Suppose GNP is in equilibrium at $700 billion. The mpc equals 0.4. At full employment we could produce $1,000 billion of goods. By how much should the tax rate be lowered to get the economy to full employment? (Assume that presently the MPC equals 0.8, that depreciation and retained corporate profits take 10 percent of gross national income combined and that transfer payments equal 10 percent of gross national income also.)

7 MR. A. "Equal and simultaneous increases or decreases in government spending and taxing obviously have no effect on aggregate demand."

MR. B. "There is no way to leave aggregate demand unaffected by varying government spending and taxing simultaneously."

Discuss. With whom do you agree? Why? (Hint: the word *equally* does not appear in this second statement.)

8 MR. A. "Equal increases in government spending and taxing may bring about an increase in output or cause or intensify inflation. Hence, we better never use this type of policy."

MR. B. "Equal decreases in government spending and taxing may bring about a fall in output or stop or dampen inflation. Hence, we better never use this type of policy."

Discuss. With whom do you agree? Why?

9 "What is true for a private household is not true for the federal government." Explain. Give as many examples as you can.

10 "Unsound" fiscal policy may be very sound. Explain. Why did the statement say "may be?"

11 Which of the statements made about the federal government in this chapter could *not* be made about state and local governments? Which could? (Suggestion: go carefully through the whole chapter and reread every paragraph with this question in mind.)

12 Just as there are three types of fiscal policy capable of eliminating unemployment, there are three types capable of eliminating demand inflation. Which of the three would tend to create the largest *surplus*, given a certain target *reduction* in aggregate demand? Explain.

13 MR. A: "Let us assume for simplicity that only taxes account for the fact that disposable personal income differs from gross national income."

What is Mr. A assuming away?

14 Suppose there is an expansionary gap at full employment of $20 billion and the marginal propensity to consume disposable personal income equals ⅔. To eliminate this inflationary pressure
   a. by how much and in what direction would we have to change government spending on domestic goods?
   b. by how much and in what direction would we have to change full employment tax collections?
   c. by how much and in what direction would we have to change government spending and taxing together, if we insisted on equal changes in both?

(Disregard any accelerator effects and assume that all spending changes as a result of tax changes affect domestic goods only.)

15   In 1967, Harold M. Somers proposed the establishment of a "national inflation trust fund." Because a tax hike to fight inflation may cut demand too much and bring about unemployment, he proposed an easy way out if the need should arise: make the tax hike refundable once the inflation danger has passed. Evaluate the proposal. (Think of the consequences.)

16   Maurice H. Stans, Director of the Bureau of the Budget under President Eisenhower and President Nixon's first Secretary of Commerce, said that "the federal government should have a balanced budget; its expenditures . . . should not exceed its income. As a matter of fact, I find it difficult to understand why there are still some people who do not seem to agree." Do you find it difficult?

17   "An attempt to eliminate federal deficits may well increase them." Explain why this is true.

18   "What may be true in theory, often fails to work out in practice. Why, for instance, should any reasonable man believe in modern fiscal policy? Consider the fact that we tried to spend our way out of the depression in the 1930's, but still had 15 percent of our labor force unemployed in 1940." Comment.

19   The balanced budget provided an excellent yardstick for a public evaluation of government spending. Now modern fiscal principles take the curse off deficits. How can the public tell whether spending is reckless?

20   "If the private sector of the economy willingly only spends less than its income, the public sector must spend more than its income, or GNP will fall." Evaluate. (Hint: remember the connection between GNP, aggregate income and aggregate demand.)

Debt-Limit Boost Passed by House In 313-to-93 Vote

Dramatic Passage Was Due To Republicans Acceding To GOP President's Plea

Rise of $12 Billion Is Voted

By a WALL STREET JOURNAL *Staff Reporter*

WASHINGTON—The House, in a dramatic realignment of voting patterns, approved and sent to the Senate a bill raising the national debt ceiling by $12 billion to $377 billion.

The vote of 313-to-93 was the most lopsided of 16 roll-call votes on the issue in the past 11 years. In 1967, a debt-limit increase was defeated once; later that year, a scaled-down version passed by only 21 votes.

Yesterday's wide margin, in contrast, resulted from the fact that Republican Congressmen voted overwhelmingly in favor of the request of a Republican President. They have consistently opposed debt-ceiling increases requested by Democratic Administrations. In the two 1967 votes, for instance, Republicans voted 176-to-0 against the increases.

The debt-limit increase isn't expected to encounter much trouble in the Senate.

Raising the Congressionally imposed limit on the amount of debt the Government may incur is an annual, and occasionally semiannual, ritual that's regarded on Capitol Hill as more of a political exercise than an economic issue.

It's taken more seriously by the Treasury, however. Shortly before the House vote yesterday, the Treasury reported that the public debt, as of Friday, was only about $283 million below the legal ceiling of $365 billion.

The period just before March 15 traditionally is one of the tightest times of the year for the Government's debt managers. The Treasury squeaked past that point Friday by the slimmest margin in at least two years.

Treasury officials are apprehensive about their ability to avoid trouble again unless Congress grants a ceiling increase before early April, another traditionally tight time.

Chairman Mills (D., Ark.) of the House Ways and Means Committee, who sponsored the bill, told the House that imposition of a debt-ceiling isn't an effective way to control Government spending. Congress, instead, should place item-by-item limitations on authorized spending during its annual consideration of Administration budgets, Mr. Mills said.

He said the Nixon Administration may find it impossible to achieve significant spending reductions, and that "at the rate we're going" Congress will be asked to extend the 10% income-tax surcharge in mid-1969 and again in mid-1970 "just to meet the increased costs of Government from fiscal 1969 to fiscal 1970."

The influential Mr. Mills declared that "I would have a great problem bringing myself around to sponsorship of such an extension" unless Government expenditures are reduced.

The final tally showed Republicans favoring the bill by a margin of 140-to-41. The Democratic breakdown was 173 for and 52 against.

The Wall Street Journal, March 20, 1969

13

the national debt

W E HAVE SEEN how it may be useful for the federal government to increase its spending on goods without increasing taxes. Or, it may be desirable to decrease taxes without decreasing spending on goods. This may bring the economy to full employment, but it may also mean incurring federal deficits. Such deficits could be financed by the creation of new money, and this would not be inflationary if spending and taxing are adjusted continually to keep aggregate demand at the right level. Hence, deficits, should they occur, are neither synonymous with a growing public debt nor with inflation. However, deficits could be financed by borrowing, and then the public debt would grow. Historically, deficits have usually been financed by borrowing (although they have by no means usually been deliberately incurred to eliminate unemployment). Many Americans profess to be terribly worried about this. Therefore, we discuss it at some length in this chapter.

THE SIZE OF THE DEBT

It is easy to see why people are worried and like to "put a lid on the debt." Consider Figure 13.1 THE HISTORY OF THE NATIONAL DEBT IN THE UNITED STATES. It shows the incredible rise in federal indebtedness since the turn of this century. (You might wish to compare this figure with Figure 11.3 THE HISTORY OF GOVERNMENT SPENDING IN THE UNITED STATES and Figure 11.6 THE HISTORY OF TAXATION IN THE UNITED STATES.) The U.S. national debt has grown from a mere $80 million in 1791 to $1.3 billion in 1900 to $365 billion in 1969. On a per capita basis, this growth has been from $21 in 1791 to $17 in 1900 to $1,800 in 1969. Interest payments alone are now in the billions each year. Newspaper editorialists love the subject. Like sex and crime, it always finds eager readers. And it is so easy to picture the American citizen, weighed down by an unbearable burden, tottering on the road to national bankruptcy.

A FALSE ANALOGY

Nor are newspaper editorialists alone with their complaints. As Benjamin Franklin put it: "Who goeth aborrowing, goeth asorrowing," and most people in America are convinced that something horrible is going to happen as a result of all this heedless prodigality. They know that no household could long run its affairs as the federal government is trying to do. Right here, of course, they miss the whole point. *The federal government is not a household.* What is true for the latter, is not always true for the former. The entire analogy of private debt with national debt is a false one. When a household borrows from someone else, it is enabled in that period to receive more goods than it could have otherwise gotten, to live *beyond its income.* When it repays, it must give up in *that* period some goods it could otherwise have enjoyed, to live *below its income.* The added *benefit* in one period is followed by a *burden* in a later period. That is not all, however. There is the *additional* burden of interest, which has to be borne as long as the household's debt is in existence. Each year, some goods that could have been enjoyed have to be sacrificed because income has to be given up to someone else as interest. And finally, a household's debt eventually has to be *paid off.* Failing to do so, one

Figure 13.1   THE HISTORY OF THE NATIONAL DEBT IN THE UNITED STATES

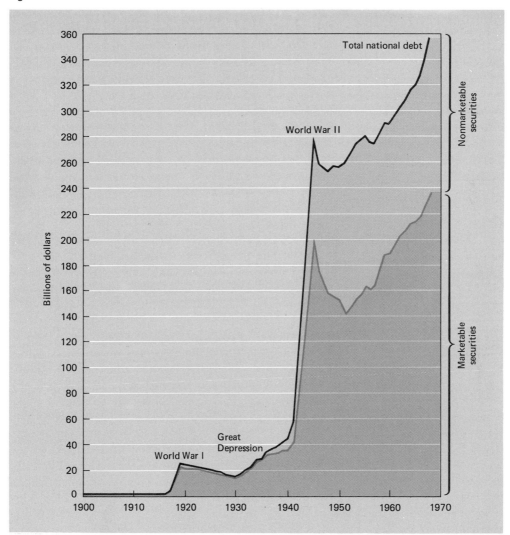

The U.S. national debt has risen significantly during this century. Note in particular the impact on its size of the two world wars and the Great Depression. A large portion of the total consists of marketable securities, that is, federal IOU's that can be sold from one holder to another until they are eventually repaid by the federal government. Source: U.S. Department of Commerce.

may be taken to court and end up in jail. A household's debt cannot grow forever, unless it wants to risk such "bankruptcy." From this common knowledge, people generalize, and this is where they go wrong.

Internal Debt: The "Burden" of Repayment

To see why, we have to know one more fact about the U.S. national debt. Let us consider the net national debt, that is, the value of federal government IOU's issued that are not held by the federal government itself, for instance, those in the social security trust fund. In early 1969, 95.8 percent of the net national debt was owed to Americans (39.9 percent to private businesses including banks, 27.2 percent to households, 18.7 percent to Federal Reserve Banks, and 10.0 percent to local and state governments). Only 4.2 percent was owed to foreigners. This has always been typical of the U.S. debt. Now let us look first at the large domestically owned portion of the debt.

What happens when the American people *borrow*, through their federal government, *from Americans*, as they typically do? Do Americans (as our household above) in that period receive more goods than they could otherwise have gotten because they receive some goods from someone else? The answer must clearly be no! Part of this very period's real GNP, which Americans could have bought individually, is not so bought. The money is given to the federal government, which can buy the goods instead. Americans *as a group* are not able, unlike our household, to live beyond their income (GNP) because the debt has been incurred by Americans from Americans.

What happens when the American people, through their federal government, *repay* this debt *to Americans*? Do Americans (as our household above) in that period receive fewer goods than they could otherwise have gotten because they have to give them to someone else? The answer again is no! The money for repayment of principal, as for all kinds of federal government expenditure, can come from three sources: taxes, borrowing, or money creation. Wherever it comes from, it is given to American bondholders. Americans refrain from buying part of this very period's real GNP collectively; bondholders (who are also Americans) can buy it individually. Americans *as a group* are not required, unlike our household, to live below their income (GNP) because the debt has been repaid by Americans to Americans. In short, *internal* borrowing or repaying by the federal government only reshuffles part of the real GNP of the period from Americans to Americans of that same period! It involves no benefit or burden corresponding to that of a household. When the federal government borrowed in 1943, Americans refrained from buying cars and refrigerators individually, releasing resources for use elsewhere. This enabled those Americans to buy airplanes and bombs collectively. Part of the 1943 real GNP was hurled at the enemy! Americans in 1943 as a group received no benefit from anyone *else*. If the federal government in 1970 were to repay that 1943 debt, 1970 Americans would have to refrain from buying rockets and schools collectively (releasing resources for use elsewhere) in order to let 1970 Americans buy cars and homes individually. Just as resources in 1943 were diverted from making private to making public goods, 1970 resources would now be diverted from making public to making private goods. But the people living in 1943 had in 1943 *no* benefit whatsoever from those living in 1970. They did not fight the war with 1970 GNP! Nor do the people living in 1970 suffer any burden whatsoever in 1970 from actions of those living in 1943. They do not have to give up one bit of 1970 GNP to fight a war in 1943! Hence the common argument about "our grand-children paying for our profligacy" is an absurdity. We are now borrowing from *ourselves;* we cannot possibly now borrow what our grandchildren will produce in 1989. If the debt is repaid, grandchildren will repay it *to themselves*. They cannot possibly in 1989 send 1989 GNP down the dusty road of time to 1970.

Internal Debt: The "Burden" of Interest

This brings us to the second burden of a household's debt, the burden of interest. True enough, as long as the national debt owed to Americans is in existence, interest will have to be paid. This involves no burden corresponding to that of a household either. For one thing, as we saw, about 19 percent of the net debt is owed to Federal Reserve Banks. These are public corporations, owned in name only by member banks. The gross earnings of these banks (including receipt of interest on U.S. securities held) are used to cover operating costs and to pay a 6 percent dividend to the member banks on the amount originally contributed to establish the Fed. The rest is customarily paid into the U.S. Treasury. In recent years, the Treasury has received back most of the amounts paid in interest to the Fed. (See question 19, Chapter 10.)

What about the rest of interest payments? They will have to be made, but involve, as in the case of a hypothetical debt repayment, only a reshuffling of currently available real GNP. Whatever the real GNP is, as money goes from the Treasury to American bondholders as interest, Americans are losing the opportunity to enjoy goods collectively, while gaining the opportunity to demand them individually. Unlike a debtor household, which does lose part of its income to someone *else*, Americans as a group lose nothing of their GNP to anyone!

Internal Debt: An Upper Limit?

Which brings us to the third point, that eventually interest payments will be so large as to be impossible and the debt will have to be paid off or bankruptcy will occur. If meant liter-ally, this is clearly nonsense. No judge can send the United States to jail. In fact, no one could do anything about it if she defaulted on her debts! But she never would have to de-fault. She could *always*, unlike a household, pay *any* amount of interest by borrowing or creating money for the purpose, even if she did not want to tax, or were unable to collect fees (as from a toll road) and get revenue that way. If that raised aggregate demand too much, she could take back in taxes what she pays out in interest. Hence, the debt could grow to any size, from its present $365 billion to $365 trillion or even a thousand times that! Further, the debt *as a whole,* no matter what its size, would never *have* to be paid off, because the federal government can always borrow anew (if need be from the Fed) the amounts needed to pay off individual maturing IOU's. (This is called refunding the debt and is usually done.) Yet, the debt as a whole *could* be paid off in the same way as interest may be paid, by appropriate taxation or money creation! Whether any of these things should be done is another question taken up below.

THE RIGHT ANALOGY

Let us now turn to the (insignificant) foreign-owned portion of the U.S. debt. In this case, many common prejudices happen to be correct, for what an interpersonal debt is to a person, an international debt is indeed to a nation.

External Debt: Repayment Is a Burden

When the American people borrow, through their federal government, *from foreigners*, as they hardly ever do, they do (as our household) in that period receive more goods than they could otherwise have gotten. Americans *as a group* can live beyond their income when they receive part of foreigners' real GNP. (The same holds if Americans, having lent to the federal government by buying its bonds, turn around and resell the bonds to foreigners.) In the same way, when Americans, through their federal government, *repay* this debt *to foreigners*, they will have available *as a group* fewer goods than otherwise. They must ship part of their real GNP abroad. Hence, *external* borrowing or repaying, exactly as in the case of a household, involves for the nation as a whole a benefit or burden, respectively. Had the federal government in 1943 borrowed *abroad* (like households borrow from *other* households), 1943 Americans would have received part of another nation's 1943 GNP (a benefit from someone else). In this case, 1970 Americans could have inherited a burden, because they might have to give up in 1970 part of 1970 GNP to someone else (the foreigners), belatedly paying for a war long gone. This is the grain of truth in the public's fear of the national debt. Under the present U.S. circumstances, it is largely an unjustified fear, but in other countries it is not. Repayment of a foreign-held debt, whether incurred through borrowing (as in Great Britain) or imposed by force (as the reparations were in East Germany[1]) has in many cases been a real burden on future generations by reducing their living standards as a group. However, the ability to repay a foreign debt can be increased if the foreign debt was used to import capital goods from abroad, raising our potential GNP. Hence, the future may inherit a benefit as well as a burden.

External Debt: Interest Is a Burden

Similarly, when the American people, through their federal government, pay interest on the foreign-owned portion of the national debt, they suffer an additional burden. Just like a household paying part of its income as interest to someone else, Americans as a group, as

---

[1] A study of this dramatic instance can be found in my *Economic Integration in the Soviet Bloc: With an East German Case Study* (New York: Praeger, 1965), Chapter 1.

long as a foreign-held debt exists, have to give up part of each year's real GNP to foreigners, and live to that extent below their income. Americans are losing the opportunity to enjoy goods collectively when the Treasury pays interest. Foreigners are gaining the power to demand those goods as they receive that interest.

External Debt: True Limitations

Can a foreign-held debt, too, grow forever? Its growth can clearly be limited by foreigners' willingness to lend. It can be limited, if the debt is in dollars, by foreigners' inability to lend. *They* cannot manufacture dollars. It can be limited, if the debt is in foreign money, by our inability to service the debt, that is, to pay interest in foreign money on it. No one can legally make someone else's money. The U.S. Treasury cannot make foreign money. Within these limits only, the debt could grow.

Would it ever have to be paid off? As long as foreigners are willing and able to lend and relend and we are able to service the debt (which is forever, if it is in *dollars*), the answer is no. If foreigners demand repayment, the answer is yes—except there is nothing they can do if we refuse! No one can take the United States to jail, although one could hate her and wage war against her. If we want to avoid this, the debt would have to be paid off, unlike the domestic debt, which could always be reborrowed from someone else, the Fed if need be.

EFFECTS OF THE EXISTENCE OF THE NATIONAL DEBT

Are we to conclude that the size of the U.S. national debt is a matter of indifference, as long as most of it is domestically held and, therefore, involves no effects corresponding to those felt by a household? Essentially this is true, although the fact that there are none of the benefits or burdens corresponding to those felt by a household borrower does not mean there are no effects at all. We must make sure that the effects that do exist are desirable or, if not, somehow taken care of.

Creation of Financial Markets

First, the existence of the national debt enables households and businesses to transform at any time, for any period desired, idle cash into first-class, safe, interest-bearing securities. There are many types of securities to choose from. As you can see from Figure 13.1 THE HISTORY OF THE NATIONAL DEBT IN THE UNITED STATES, most federal IOU's are marketable. That is, any buyer does not have to hold on to the security until it matures (is due for repayment by the Treasury). He can at any time sell the security to someone else. Whoever happens to hold it on the due date will get repaid by the government. Such marketable securities include short-term Treasury bills, certificates of indebtedness, and notes, as well as longer-term bonds. Nonmarketable securities must be held to maturity by the original purchaser. They include mainly U.S. savings bonds and notes and investment bonds. Thus, there is some kind of security for many different financial investors.

Also, the existence of such a volume of marketable U.S. securities allows the Fed to engage in monetary policy via open-market operations. Without the national debt, this powerful weapon for full employment without inflation would not exist or the Fed would have to rely on less safe, private securities.

Some people, however, argue that the existence of a national debt, especially a large one, may also *hinder* Federal Reserve policy by straining relations with the Treasury. When inflation threatens, the Fed would make money tight by selling government securities. Typically, this practice lowers security prices and raises their yield and interest rates generally. But the Treasury is continually refunding the debt by selling billions of dollars worth of new securities each month, when individual, older IOU's mature and must be paid off. To persuade the holders of old IOU's, or other people, to buy the new issues, the Treasury must offer interest rates in line with the general level of rates prevailing at the time. Thus, the Fed's tight money policy has the effect of forcing the Treasury to pay higher rates along with everyone else. (During the tight money period of mid-1969, the Treasury had to pay 7.82 percent interest on 18 months notes, the highest rate since 1859.) Thus, the Treasury, in an attempt to avoid higher tax collections to finance higher interest costs, may try to persuade the Fed *not* to pursue a policy of tight money. Before 1950, it was indeed successful in this. Thereby the Fed's power to fight inflation was nullified.

Yet you should be able to show that such a dilemma results from the misunderstanding of economic principles. If indeed inflation threatens, the Treasury should be happy to raise taxes, for that is exactly what is needed to cut aggregate demand. A Treasury-Federal Reserve policy clash can only mean that the two do not agree on the analysis of the situation (is there too much demand or not?) or that one of the agencies is making a policy mistake or unwilling to use proper economic tools for fear of side effects.

Redistribution of Income

Second, although interest payments are made by Americans to Americans, the Americans involved may be different Americans. There *may* occur a redistribution of real GNP toward the recipients of interest. Take the case where interest payments are made from taxes (which is only *one* possibility). It is quite possible that "poor" Americans and "rich" Amercians each pay $5 billion of such taxes, but only the "rich" receive $10 billion of interest. If this is undesirable, a change in tax rates can eliminate it.

Incentives

Third, if interest payments are made from taxes (which is only *one* possibility), those who receive less interest than the taxes they pay, and perhaps others too, may be discouraged, whether that be rational or not, by the high taxes to work hard or to engage in risky ventures promoting technical progress. This would tend to lower the *potential* GNP or keep it from rising as rapidly as otherwise. In this case, interest payments should not be made from taxes.

Stimulating Aggregate Demand

Fourth, those holding federal IOU's may be made to feel rich, making them spend more out of any income than they otherwise would. This would tend to shift up the consumption demand line with each increase in the national debt. (Had, in the past, private investment replaced all government demand, the effect might be the same. People would hold stocks and corporate bonds instead of government securities.) Once consumption demand is so high as to lift aggregate demand to the full employment level, the debt *should* not grow further lest we have further stimulation of demand and inflation. Of course, at full employment, the debt *would* not grow further, because there would be no need to raise aggregate demand by raising government demand without taxes or lowering taxes with no change in government demand.

Another Burden?

The first effect of the debt's existence (creation of financial markets) is quite desirable; the others can most probably be coped with. Yet there persists, even among those who understand the meaning of truly sound fiscal policy, a rumor. It is the claim that even a *domestic* national debt imposes a burden on the future, only it is *different* from what the public thinks! The argument goes like this: "If we pursue a truly sound fiscal policy (one with desirable consequences), we are incurring a debt only when it is desired to finance in this way a deficit to raise aggregate demand. If we cut tax collections (as in Figure 12.3 HOW EASY FISCAL POLICY WORKS—TAXING LESS), this is fine, for government demand remains the same but consumption and investment demand rise as we go to full employment. If instead we increase government spending (as in Figure 12.1 HOW EASY FISCAL POLICY WORKS—SPENDING MORE), and this we have usually done, the result is terrible. Although private demand rises again on the way to full employment, ultimately government demand is also higher. The amount by which government demand is higher could have been used privately, for instance to raise investment. Borrowing made possible this shifting of billions of full-employment GNP from private to public uses. Hence, our grandchildren will inherit a smaller capital stock (which we could have created by privately investing more). Although they do not have to give up any part of their actual GNP to anyone else, the resources they inherit, hence their actual GNP, will be smaller than it would have been had we not incurred the national debt."

Now this is a most peculiar argument, for it should be quite clear from Figure 12.1 that, without the assumed government policy, we would never have produced full employment GNP *at all*. We would have stayed right at the position shown at E with less government demand (and less consumption demand also) and no more investment demand at all. If the government stopped spending the extra billions each year shown by the size of the contractionary gap, we would go right back to the position at E. Private businesses do not want to invest what they could invest if government demand were reduced. Reducing government demand would only release resources *into unemployment*, not for private uses. You cannot blame a growing debt that happened to finance deficit spending for the fact that grand-children inherit a lower than possible capital stock. The same would also be true without deficit spending (which would have kept us in the position at E) or with it, but financed by new money!

In fact, one can almost turn the argument around. It is quite possible that our grand-children *gain* from the fact that we have replaced unemployment with increased production for government and consumers at E*. Who says government demand must be a waste? Government demand may have been used to wage successfully a defensive war. Do not future generations gain from the fact that we kept an enemy from destroying the capital stock we had and that they do inherit? (Consider your own expenditure made on an appendectomy instead of a television set. Was it not a "productive" expenditure, enabling you to inherit a longer life and enjoy other goods possessed, even if not a television set?) Furthermore, is it not conceivable, and in fact true, that government expenditure can add to the *collectively* owned capital stock, can add to *assets* as well as to liabilities? Just think of the structures, equipment, inventories, and land owned by the U.S. government: hospitals, power plants, housing projects, airports, dams, roads, space research and exploration facilities, ships, planes, vehicles, stocks of foods and metals, national parks, and so on. They are worth hundreds of billions of dollars and are inherited by future generations. They also inherit intangible assets, such as the stock of knowledge, partly acquired and transmitted with the help of federal expenditures on research and education. As of June 30, 1966, the U.S. federal government listed tangible personal and real property, in part valued at *acquisition costs,* of $347 billion. If you inherited a business with assets of more than $347 billion and net debts of $260 billion, you would consider yourself rich. Strangely, people only look at one side of the ledger when complaining about the national debt.

Even if government demand were a waste (hiring people to dig holes for other people to fill), the private sector of the economy, if brought to full employment, is still better off. In Figure 12.1 HOW EASY FISCAL POLICY WORKS—SPENDING MORE, the private sector ends up with goods at E* worth $40 billion more per year than at E. (Increased government spending of $60 billion—the size of the contractionary gap—leads via the multiplier to a $100 billion rise in real GNP.) Certainly the *present* generation gains, even if a gross gain of $100 billion should be frittered away to the tune of $60 billion per year, leaving us only with a net gain of $40 billion per year. But mostly government demand is not a waste in this sense. If it involved sweeping streets instead of building them, the present generation would gain something worth the entire $100 billion increase in GNP, although such services could not be inherited by the future. And it would be silly to blame government spending for a lower than conceivable capital stock inherited by the future. We might just as well blame present *consumer* spending, for every resource used to satisfy individual needs is also a resource taken away from potential capital formation. If we performed heroic feats of austerity now (neither making shoes to walk nor sweeping streets to walk on), we could enormously increase the provision for the future (by adding to capital instead). Are we imposing a burden on the future every time we eschew this path?

CONCLUSIONS

The national debt is mostly domestically held. It has none of the consequences usually ascribed to it. There is no reason why it cannot be raised permanently to any level desired to finance government spending to raise aggregate demand to full employment. Paying off the entire debt is unnecessary. Individual IOU's, of course, must be paid off. But faster than this, new ones can be issued. Thus the debt as a whole can grow. This is exactly what happens with the national totals of household and business debt also. Nevertheless, though unnecessary, paying off the entire national debt could be accomplished at any time through taxing or creating money. Taxing would certainly drastically lower private demands as net incomes are reduced. Receipt of cash for bonds would only constitute an asset transformation toward more liquidity. It would not constitute income. It would *possibly* reduce interest rates and stimulate consumption and investment demands, partially offsetting the tax effect on aggregate demand. As a whole, paying off the debt via taxation would almost certainly lower aggregate demand. Hence, it would be absurd to do it, except when one *wants* to lower aggregate demand as in a period of demand inflation.

Paying off the debt via money creation would probably raise aggregate demand just as easy monetary policy does. Hence, it would be absurd to do it, except when one *wants* to raise aggregate demand, as in a period of unemployment. But why fight inflation and unemployment by this curious mixture of fiscal and monetary policies brought about by the fixation on the national debt? How inefficient it would be to fight inflation by the above-mentioned combination of very tight fiscal and easy money policy! How inefficient it would be to fight unemployment by nothing else but the just-mentioned policy of easy money accompanying debt repayment! It seems wisest to pursue monetary and fiscal policies as we studied them in Chapters 10 and 12, without any undue concern about the size of the national debt. National administrations, Democratic as well as Republican, have in fact done just that. As the news report introducing this chapter indicates, Congress has again and again raised the legal ceiling on the national debt whenever Treasury expenditures made it necessary. Given the public's reaction to the national debt issue, all Presidents, however, are defensive about their request for a higher debt ceiling. President Nixon's 1969 approach is a case in point. Instead of asking Congress to raise the national debt ceiling above the $365 billion limit he inherited, he asked for a reduction in the ceiling to $300 billion. He got all the headlines you might expect. But the President also asked Congress for permission not to count in the national debt at all some $82 billion of government securities held by the social security and other trust funds. In short, he wanted the ceiling applied only to what we have called the net national debt. Deduct $82 billion from $365 billion, and you get $283 billion. If Congress had agreed, the debt would have been counted as $283 billion, the new ceiling would have been $300 billion. Hence, the President would have had the authority to borrow $17 billion *more*, while all the time getting headlines about having *reduced* the national debt! The House Ways and Means Committee called this "gimmickry." The news story introducing this chapter tells you what did happen.

SUMMARY

1. If deficit spending is financed by borrowing, the national debt grows. There are many misconceptions about the national debt. Most arise from a false analogy between a private household and the federal government.

2. It is important to distinguish between an internally owed and a foreign-owed national debt. Only the latter benefits the nation as a whole when it is incurred, and burdens it when interest and principal are repaid. Even in this case, however, a benefit may be inherited together with the burden.

3. There is no reason why the federal government's internal debt cannot grow without limit. Nor is there any reason why it ever must be paid off. Yet, it could be paid off quite easily, but this may not be desirable. These statements are not necessarily true for an external debt.

4. The above does not mean that an internally held debt has no effects at all. The effects that do exist are either desirable or can most probably be counteracted.

TERMS[2]

internal vs. external national debt
national debt
national debt refunding

QUESTIONS FOR REVIEW AND DISCUSSION

1. The text says that easy fiscal policy "may also mean incurring federal deficits." Why "may"?

2. "Proper fiscal policy does not *require* a growing national debt." Comment.

3. "It is impossible to put a burden on future generations by incurring a national debt." Discuss.

4. MR. A: "The national debt is a problem because we are passing a burden to our grand-children."

   MR. B: "The debt is no problem because we owe it to ourselves."

   Comment.

5. How might future generations *benefit* from our incurring of a national debt?

6. If we were intent on hurting future generations, what would we have to do?

[2] Terms are defined in the Glossary at the end of the book.

7 Some people make a great issue of the fact that the U.S. national debt, as well as interest payments thereon, have both declined *as a percentage of GNP*. This is supposed to show that the burden of the debt has declined. Evaluate this approach.

8 What are the effects of the existence of a national debt?

9 The text states that some effects of the existing national debt can "most probably" be coped with. Why "most probably?" (Hint: Think of a situation in which we have full employment, taxes do hurt incentives, and no one, not even the Fed, will buy new government securities. How can and should interest payments then be financed?)

10 The text suggests something incredible: that the U.S. debt could grow to $365 *trillion* and that interest on it could be paid with newly created money that could then be taken right back in taxes. If this should make people refuse to buy any new government securities, could the government still pursue *both* expansionary and contractionary fiscal policy?

11 Do you think there should be a lid on the national debt of the United States?

12 Can you think of any economic situation in which it would be desirable to pay off all or part of the national debt? (Hint: Consider several means of doing this. In each case consider the *consequences* and ask yourself whether you like them.)

13 "An economy without private and public debt is unthinkable." Evaluate. (You might also want to find out what has happened to private and all types of public debt in the United States recently. How about your family's?)

14 Is the debt of the State of California an internal or an external debt? What difference does it make?

15 THOMAS JEFFERSON: "I wished it were possible to amend the Constitution taking from the federal government the power of borrowing."

ALEXANDER HAMILTON: "A national debt, if it is not excessive, will be to us a national blessing."

Comment.

16 Read the news report introducing this chapter. Do you understand it? All of it?

17 Someone once proposed that Congress should not put a lid on the national debt. Rather it should limit new borrowing to a given percentage of each year's GNP. Do you think such a policy would decrease or increase GNP fluctuations?

18 ADAM SMITH: "What is prudence in the conduct of every private family can scarce be folly in that of a great kingdom."

Is he right? Is he wrong?

Jobs and Prices

Analysts Doubt Inflation Will Slow Without Rise In Unemployment Rate

Nixon Policy Aims at Averting Big Layoffs, but Aides See Joblessness Approaching 4%

The Threat of Urban Unrest

By Richard F. Janssen

Staff Reporter of THE WALL STREET JOURNAL

WASHINGTON—A statistical time bomb—the threat of higher unemployment—is ticking away in the White house.

Despite three straight months of joblessness at the exceptionally low level of 3.3% of the work force, Nixon Administration men recognize that the politically sensitive indicator has not been defused. The question isn't whether the rate will rise, one says, but only "when and how much."

The reason for this sober outlook is the fight against inflation. Officials figure they'll have to slow the economy through tight credit and a black-ink budget so that new jobs probably won't be created fast enough to accommodate quite all of the rapidly expanding work force. While Chairman Paul McCracken of the President's Council of Economic Advisers calls any unemployment "a personal tragedy," it's clear that officials are willing to risk a little more of it in the near future. . . .

Administration aides carefully avoid precise public forecasts, but they are privately poring over projections that range from some slight upticks in the jobless rate to more than a full-percentage-point increase by late 1969. If the worst fears are realized, one strategist says with a shudder, it would mean "almost a million more people out of work"—and a socially explosive situation that could force the Administration to let up in the inflation fight.

An Ominous Curve

The President's planners are acutely aware that a chart economists call the "Phillips Curve" (after its developer, British economist A. W. Phillips) shows that there usually is a close relationship between inflation and employment. While this relationship can vary from time to time, the chart shows that so far in the 1960s U.S. price rises have been small only when unemployment was rather high.

Thus, the Administration is pinning its hopes on "gradualism," a strategy intended to skim off excess demand for goods and services so carefully as to prevent large layoffs. . . .

But the rub, insiders admit, is that these ways aren't readily at hand. Mr. McCracken concedes that "no one can be certain" whether the inflation from three years of overheating "can be cooled with no adverse unemployment effects."

Consequently, other key officials say, no one can be sure how far and how effectively the White House and the Federal Reserve Board will press their battle against inflation.

The "critical issue," says board member Andrew F. Brimmer, is how long the public will tolerate a jobless rate drifting back toward the 5% plus levels of the early 1960s, when prices were rising only about 1% annually. "There is little likelihood" of ending or even appreciably reducing the inflation rate "without some increase in unemployment," he warns. . . .

With a wary eye on possible fresh unrest in urban slums, Government economists fret that the first sizable increases in the rate are likely to come in early summer, when the high schools will likely pour out more job-seeking youngsters than business can absorb. Of those arrested in riots of recent years, the Joint Economic Committee reports, some 20% to 30% usually were jobless, and most of the rest voiced frustration about low-paying and erratic employment.

Moreover, Mr. Brimmer warns, in an economic slowdown the jobless rate among nonwhites (usually about double the average for the whole labor force) climbs more than twice as fast as that of whites. Even now, some of the "hard-core" unemployed laboriously recruited by auto makers are being affected by layoffs in the industry because their seniority is the lowest.

The specter of widespread layoffs of Negroes only recently trained—at substantial Federal and corporate cost—clearly haunts White House aides. . . .

"I don't think there's any way out of the box we're in unless we do let the rate drift up," a well-placed aide says. . . .

For the longer run, though, Government economists appear increasingly optimistic that they can "shift the Phillips Curve." That's their way of saying that the efficiency of the U.S. economy can be increased enough to keep prices reasonably steady even at a jobless rate consistently below 4%.

The main reason the Phillips Curve is plaguing the U.S. now, the economists say, is a Vietnam-related bulge in Federal spending and borrowing. The extra demand has forced employers to increase pay sharply to retain skilled employees and to scramble for many marginal workers, whose ability to produce doesn't match the pay they can command.

Peace in Vietnam and then an avoidance of sudden Government-caused surges in demand would be a big help in combating the Phillips Curve, officials figure.

The Wall Street Journal, March 26, 1969

14

simultaneous
unemployment
and inflation

I N THE PREVIOUS chapters, we have seen how general unemployment and demand-pull inflation can, in principle, be cured by sound monetary and fiscal policies undertaken by the federal government. We have also seen that truly sound policies (those having desirable consequences) often involve means that the public calls unsound. Therefore, it may be difficult to undertake them in the face of an irrational resistance thereto. Even if they are undertaken, we can expect such policies at best to bring us *closer* to potential real GNP without demand-pull inflation, for only an omniscient and clairvoyant policy-maker could achieve the goal with perfect precision in an economy of continuous change.

For these reasons alone, we should not be surprised to find remnants of unemployment or inflation in the real world. However, so far our discussion may leave the impression that we will never find both *at the same time*. Either aggregate demand is too small, relative to potential GNP, and we have general unemployment, or it is too large, and we have demand-pull inflation. Because aggregate demand cannot be too small and too large simultaneously, it seems that we cannot have unemployment and inflation at the same time. But we do. In this chapter, we look at the reasons and at possible cures.

THE DILEMMA

There are a number of reasons why we may experience the dilemma of involuntary unemployment and inflation simultaneously. Perhaps the simplest explanation is that not all unemployment is general unemployment and not all inflation is generalized demand-pull inflation. Our discussion so far has been aggregative, all inclusive. We have always looked at the whole economy, ignoring its parts. We have talked of *aggregate* demand, and we have neglected the fact that it is the sum of the demand for steel and for cars, for bread and for shoes, and so on. We have argued as if deficient aggregate demand meant deficient demand for *all* goods and general unemployment, that is, unemployment in all sectors of the economy. We have argued as if excessive aggregate demand meant excessive demand for all goods and generalized demand-pull inflation, that is, rising prices everywhere. This may not be so in fact. There may be deficient demand for steel (and 100,000 steel workers unemployed), excessive demand for shoes (and 100,000 more workers needed), and neither deficient nor excess demand for cars and other goods (and full employment in the auto industry and elsewhere in the economy). This is a situation in which there is certainly neither excess demand nor deficient demand in the economy as a whole. Thus, there is no general unemployment, nor is there generalized demand-pull inflation. But there is short-run frictional or chronic unemployment, depending on the ease or difficulty with which steel workers can be turned into shoemakers.[1] Also, as long as the economy is not perfectly competitive (in the way described, for instance, in Chapter 2), we cannot expect prices to move freely in all directions in response to localized excess demand or excess supply, either. Thus, in our example, steel prices, rather than falling, owing to excess supply, may stay constant. Shoe prices will probably rise, owing to excess demand, and other prices stay constant, too. Although there is no *gener-*

---

[1] Compare pages 55–57 above for a discussion of short-run frictional and chronic unemployment.

alized demand-pull inflation, excess demand (in shoes) is pulling prices up, but deficient demand (in steel) is not pulling them down. So our over-all price index will move *up*. Even worse, this rise in some prices owing to localized excess demand (sometimes called "bottleneck inflation") may be intensified by cost-push inflation.[2] Fully employed auto workers and bakery workers and shoe industry workers will find themselves in a fairly good bargaining position. As the cost of living rises (in our case, the price of shoes), their unions may insist on higher wages. Auto makers, for instance, may grant such wage hikes, but raise the price of cars in spite of the absence of excess demand. Firms operating near capacity are often unwilling to risk a strike. They are likely to have high profits. They are not afraid to lose business to competitors who are equally busy. Thus a price hike is "safe." This may, in turn, lead other strong unions and strong businesses to force their prices up. Before we know it, we have unemployment and inflation at the same time!

THE ROLE OF MONETARY AND FISCAL POLICIES

Can we confidently expect monetary and fiscal policies to deal with frictional and chronic unemployment in the same way they deal with general unemployment? Can they take care of bottleneck and cost-push inflation as they do of generalized demand-pull inflation? The answer in either case is *yes, but not without undesirable side effects.*

Combating Short-run Frictional and Chronic Unemployment

Some people advocate that easy monetary-fiscal policy should be used to check short-run frictional and chronic unemployment after we have raised aggregate demand enough to have eliminated general unemployment. "Just increase aggregate demand *beyond* the level needed to eliminate *general* unemployment," they say, "and watch what happens. Everywhere, all kinds of employers will be faced with a demand so strong that they cannot satisfy it. On the other hand, it is then impossible to find *everywhere* unemployed people of *all* skills, *all* ages, *all* races, *all* creeds, *both* sexes. What will employers do? To be sure, many will start raising the prices of their products. We will have demand-pull inflation. But many will also take another hard look at the resource markets, for they could increase their profits by producing more with additional resources. And such additional resources—*frictionally* and *chronically* unemployed—do exist! In this situation, employers will be delighted to take a man with the wrong skill and retrain him on the job, to take a person of the "wrong" age, the "wrong" race, the "wrong" creed, the "wrong" sex. Employers will be delighted to take over buildings, machines, and land not perfectly suited for the job, because these, too, can often be adjusted to different needs. Employers will be delighted to spread widely information on available jobs and even to pay moving expenses, if that is the only thing keeping a man away. In

---

[2] Compare pages 81–83 above for a discussion of cost-push inflation.

short, they will hunt in every nook and cranny for labor, land, and capital, and, when they find them, they will not mind making any adjustments needed to get them and make them suitable for the job to be done. Frictional and chronic unemployment will tend to disappear."

There is undoubtedly something to this argument, as the United States' experience during the height of World War II has shown. At that time, employers did engage in exactly the kind of practices just described. They were willing to train and retrain anyone, even people considered unemployable before, just to squeeze the most output from our scarce resources. The unemployment rate reached its lowest point in U.S. history (see again Figure 3.2 THE SERIOUSNESS OF INVOLUNTARY UNEMPLOYMENT).

As the above argument also shows, however, one should not be surprised, after the elimination of *general* unemployment, to find all kinds of prices going up. Some goods simply cannot be produced in greater quantities; more of others can be produced only after a delay used to hunt down, retrain, adjust, and put to work frictionally and chronically unemployed resources. In World War II, the government prevented much of this type of price rise by establishing and enforcing maximum prices on many goods. However, in the absence of wartime price controls, we would have inflation. This has also been demonstrated vividly in the countries of Western Europe since World War II. They have consistently had less unemployment than the United States, but also more inflation.

Combating Bottleneck and Cost-Push Inflation

Other people argue that tight monetary-fiscal policies should be continued to check bottleneck and cost-push inflation after they have cut aggregate demand enough to have eliminated demand-pull inflation. "Just lower aggregate demand *below* the level needed to eliminate demand-pull inflation," they say, "and watch what happens. Everywhere all kinds of producers will be faced with a demand so weak that they could easily more than satisfy it. It is easily possible to find *all* kinds of unemployed resources and to produce more. What will producers do? In past ages, they might have lowered prices of products, as the classical economists assumed. Owners of labor, land, and capital might have accepted lower prices for their services, too. This is too much to hope for nowadays, in a world of powerful monopolies and labor unions. Even in a period of *deficient* aggregate demand and *general* unemployment, they are unlikely to *lower* prices. But they will also think twice before *raising* them! A producer who raises prices in the face of deficient demand for his product may find people buying so much less that revenues *drop*. His competitors will be more than glad to satisfy his customers at the old prices. A union that insists on higher wages in the face of general unemployment may find the demand for labor dropping so much that those remaining employed earn less as a group than those previously employed. And the union leader may be blamed for the increased unemployment. Therefore, it is quite likely that bottleneck and cost-push inflation will disappear."

There is a lot to this argument, also. If we were willing to create general unemployment deliberately, the further we proceeded along this road the more likely it would become that all kinds of inflation can be stopped. (President Johnson, in his last economic report, called this policy a "prescription for social disaster as well as for unconscionable waste.")

The Phillips Curve

The above proposals have one obvious disadvantage. We cannot follow both simultaneously. We cannot eliminate all types of unemployment by raising aggregate demand to whatever level required (thereby causing all types of inflation) and at the same time eliminate all types of inflation by cutting aggregate demand to whatever level required (for this again causes unemployment). For this reason, reliance on monetary-fiscal weapons alone would never free us from the simultaneous unemployment-inflation dilemma.

A British economist, A. W. Phillips of The London School of Economics, has investigated the relation between the rate of unemployment and inflation. A neat graphical device, the *Phillips curve*, has been named after him. It can be used to put our discussion in perspective. Consider Figure 14.1 THE PHILLIPS CURVE. The horizontal axis measures involuntary unemployment as a percentage of the civilian labor force. The vertical axis measures changes in the price level. Annual data for the United States for 1948 through 1968 have been used to plot the scattered dots in the figure. (Ignore the encircled dots for the time being. They refer to World War II years.) The dot labeled 1957, for instance, shows that in that year the unemployment rate was on the average 4.3 percent, while the price level rose by 3.7 percent.[3] The highest dot (not encircled) to the left of the line shows, in turn, that the unemployment rate stood at 3.3 percent in 1951, but prices rose by 6.7 percent. The only dot below the horizontal axis shows how in 1949 a 5.9 percent unemployment rate was accompanied by a 0.6 percent decline in the price level.

Is there in the modern capitalist economy some kind of *stable* relationship between unemployment and inflation such that a fall in the former brings a predictable intensification in the latter long before full employment is reached? Mr. Phillips thought so. Such a possible relationship is illustrated by the line drawn through the 1957 data. It is a purely hypothetical construct, very much like the consumption demand lines in Figure 6.5 CONSUMPTION VS. GNP STATISTICS. This Phillips curve indicates the alternative combinations of unemployment and inflation that might have been open to the policy-maker in 1957. Given the nature of the economy in that year, he could have, this curve tells us, eliminated all types of inflation completely by vigorously cutting aggregate demand. Graphically, this would have meant moving down and to the right along the curve. Such policy would have raised unemployment to 6.3 percent. Similarly, he might have moved from the actual 1957 dot upward and to the left by raising aggregate demand. This would have reduced unemployment to, say, 3.2 percent, but only at the cost of raising inflation to 7 percent. Raising ag-

[3] The price level data used in Figure 14.1 are more comprehensive than the consumer price index discussed in Chapter 4. They are based on the "GNP deflator," which is constructed by dividing each year's GNP at current prices by that year's GNP at (in this case) 1958 prices. The resultant is a (in this case 1958-based) price level index covering all the goods entering the GNP.

Figure 14.1   THE PHILLIPS CURVE

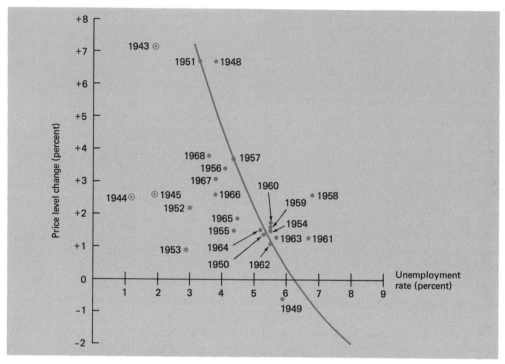

The dots in this figure show the historically observed combinations of the U.S. rates of unemployment and price level change from 1948–1968. The starred data represent the years of Korean War price controls, the encircled ones the years of World War II price controls for comparison. A Phillips curve is drawn through the dot for 1957. The curve is a hypothetical construct indicating the rate at which in 1957 higher unemployment might have been traded for lesser inflation, or vice versa. Tight monetary-fiscal policies, if pursued vigorously enough, allow us to move down along the curve. Monetary-fiscal ease allows us to move up along it. Over time, as economic institutions change, the curve itself may shift right or left. Source: Economic Report of the President, *January 1969, pp. 230 and 255, and Figure 3.2* THE SERIOUSNESS OF INVOLUNTARY UNEMPLOYMENT.

gregate demand further might have eliminated all unemployment, but possibly at a cost of an 18 percent inflation (not shown in graph).

Neither moving down nor moving up the curve would have been an unmixed blessing. Would it have been worth it in 1957 to eliminate inflation by throwing 1.3 million more people into unemployment? Would it have been worth it to find work for another 469,000 of the unemployed if prices had risen by 7 rather than 3.7 percent? If you were a politician, you would certainly hate to be in such a dilemma. You would call in your economic advisers and ask them how you might *avoid* this undesirable trade-off between jobs and prices. How could you get to that most desirable of all spots in Figure 14.1, the origin 0, where the general level of prices is stable and involuntary unemployment is eliminated? The answer to this question will concern us in the remainder of this chapter.

ALTERNATIVE POLICIES

There have been essentially two sets of proposals made to avoid this undesirable ride up or down the Phillips curve. The first would destroy presently existing institutional arrangements. The second would create new institutional arrangements. Though the former are unlikely to be followed, the latter are increasingly being put into practice. Graphically, all these proposals involve moving the Phillips curve itself, rather than moving along it.

Destroying Present Economic Institutions

labor unions and minimum wages   Let us take the case of short-run frictional and chronic unemployment first. Some private students of the labor market argue that much frictional and hard-core chronic unemployment can be explained by government and union interference in the process of buying and selling labor. "Normally," they say, "an excess supply of any kind of labor (that is, more people wanting to work than are wanted by prospective employers) would lead to a fall in the wage of this kind of labor (see Figure 3.4 THE MARKET FOR HIGH SCHOOL SOCIAL SCIENCE TEACHERS). As a result, some of these people would leave the labor force and become *voluntarily* unemployed. Others would be hired by employers who find it profitable to do so at the lower wages. Wages would continue to fall until all the involuntary unemployment *of whatever kind* is eliminated in this way. However," continues the argument, "the government interferes with this process, partly by supporting unions who resist wage cuts, partly by legislating minimum wages and raising them every few years.[4] What is the result? As the supply of relatively unskilled labor increases (women and teenagers enter the labor force, farmers migrate to cities, coal miners lose their jobs as oil replaces coal), the demand for such labor does not increase. Who wants to hire people at the minimum wage and maybe even train them for a new job if these people's output sells for less than they have to be paid? The best thing one can do for the frictionally and chronically unemployed," concludes the argument, "is to smash all institutional resistances to a decline in wages."

In terms of Figure 14.1 THE PHILLIPS CURVE, such policy, which abolished labor unions and rescinded protective government labor legislation, is supposed to move us from a point as the 1957 dot to the left toward the horizontal axis. It is also supposed to move us down to the extent that it eliminates, say, union-caused cost-push inflation. But we need not dwell on the merits or deficiences of this proposal. It is totally unrealistic to expect that it could be implemented in the United States in the foreseeable future.

---

[4] A 1966 amendment to the Fair Labor Standards Act increased minimum wage coverage to about 80 percent of all nonsupervisory employees and set the minimum hourly wage at $1.60 as of February 1, 1968.

direct price controls   The same can be said for proposals that hope to bring about full employment by whatever means and then to eliminate all inflation by direct governmental control of all prices (including wages). Graphically, this would amount to moving down along the Phillips curve toward the horizontal axis by demand-raising policies and then to the left via comprehensive price (and wage) controls. Now note the starred and encircled data in Figure 14.1, which indicate what such policies achieved while they were in effect in the Korean War period and during World War II, respectively. Such controls have been used in the United States only during World War II and the Korean War (not during the Vietnam War), and they are most unlikely to ever be used in peace time.

There are a number of reasons for this. For one thing, labor unions and businesses resent interference with their prerogative of setting prices of things they sell. Only in cases of extreme national emergency can any U.S. government take such drastic action and hope to stay in office. Second, there are millions of prices to be controlled. The bureaucracy required to administer direct controls is truly huge. Its task is extremely complicated even in the best of circumstances. No administration that can possibly avoid it would want to have the headaches this involves. Finally, and probably most importantly, any interference with the price system has, and inevitably has, a great number of undesirable side effects, requiring further and further interference. One cannot just legislate a maximum price and leave it at that.

Consider Figure 14.2 PRICE CONTROLS ILLUSTRATED. Suppose free forces of demand and supply, shown by lines D and S, respectively, have established an equilibrium price of $20 per pair of shoes, with 20 million pairs traded each year. Now suppose demand-raising policies raise the demand for shoes, together with the demand for other goods. Curve D becomes D*. A free market would establish a new equilibrium at b. Price would rise to $43.50, quantity to 43.5 million. Could the government just legislate that the new quantity be sold at $20 per pair, as before?

Obviously not. If it did, and did nothing else, a shortage of 31 million pairs of shoes would occur (distance ac) at the legal maximum price. Although demand has risen from D to D*, as long as the price is $20, sellers will offer only 20 million pairs. Quickly, frustrated buyers would bid up the price toward the $43.50 equilibrium at b. In the process, quantity demanded would fall (along cb), quantity supplied rise (along ab). Together, these two forces would exactly eliminate the shortage (ac). Thus, legislating a price alone is not enough. If this new price is to be held, the government must also take steps to enforce its law.

It could, for instance, take over the firms involved and, irrespective of profit or loss, *force* them to produce more at the old price. Such direct government management or production control would be most cumbersome, quite apart from the ideological problems involved.

Second, the government could impose stiff penalties for any buyer or seller who sells at a higher price than $20 per pair. As in Hitler's Germany, Stalin's Russia, or modern Vietnam, this may even involve execution of anyone caught violating the law. This will prevent the open-market price from rising above $20 to the new equilibrium at b, but it will surely not eliminate the shortage. Actual trade will take place at point a, not at point c. Although at the $20 price 51 million pairs are wanted, only 20 million will be supplied. Who decides who is to get shoes and who goes without?

If the government doesn't, an informal rationing system will evolve. It may be as simple as "first come, first served." Once the supply is sold, the remaining would-be shoppers go home empty-handed. This immediately leads people to stand in line and is not exactly designed to make people happy. Besides being a nuisance of major proportion and being extremely frustrating (you cannot stand in line simultaneously at the meat counter and the bakery shop and the shoe store), it creates a great deal of social tension. Working people cannot go shopping until evening and may be continually out of luck by then. They are unlikely to take this lying down. Thus, the "first come, first served" system is doomed from the start. It would create too many injustices.

Retailers, like everyone else, hate to be hated. So they may set up an informal rationing system of their own. "Half a pound per customer" or "Regular customers only." This may work well in some cases, but it will be hard on those who usually shop around (and have no regular store) or on those who have just moved to a new town. People being what they are, it will also tempt many to cheat on the rules.

Eventually, pressures will grow, and the government simply has to step in with a system of *formal* rationing. People are issued ration coupons and will need them, as well as money, to buy anything. The red tape involved, for households, businesses, and government alike, will be enormous. So will be the chances for mistakes and mix-ups. In terms of Figure 14.2, it will be a lucky government, indeed, that just issues coupons for 20 million pairs. More

Figure 14.2   PRICE CONTROLS ILLUSTRATED

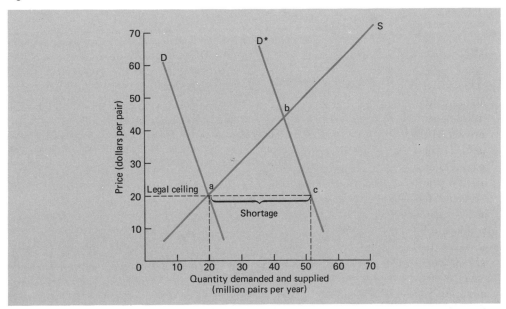

Demand and supply curves can illustrate the effects of a legal price ceiling below the equilibrium price. Given curves D* and S, a $20 per pair ceiling price would create a shortage of 31 million pairs of shoes (distance ac).

likely, it will issue too few or too many with all the resultant waste and frustration this implies. Nor does a formal rationing system put an end to social tension. The reliance on necessarily clumsy and arbitrary rules, the inevitably imperfect decisions of government officials, will have people fighting over coupons in no time, possibly forging them, possibly using them more than once. Working people will demand more than other people get. "Important" jobholders will wish to find special favors, too. No one will be content.

Above all, the price system, tied hand and foot by an ever-growing web of government control of prices, output, and distribution, will sneak in through the back door. *Black markets* will develop, in spite of all the penalties, for people suffer countless temptations to evade or violate the rules set by the vast administrative apparatus. Everyone will hope that he will not be caught. Often he will be right. People who are well to do will offer high prices. Sellers who are pinched between high costs and a price ceiling will find it hard to refuse. Only one thing could really put an end to black markets: if the government gave up its controls and let prices find their equilibrium levels! How true this is can be seen from the fact that war time price controls have always led to open inflation at the end of the war, when controls were removed. While controls are in effect, we have *suppressed* inflation (except for the black market). The government does not cure the disease; at best, it only suppresses its symptoms. Demand that does not find an outlet in the black market is pent-up and reappears after the war. With all these problems, it is little wonder that governments hate to touch direct controls. (President Nixon made it clear in mid–1969 that he would absolutely not fight inflation by direct controls.)

Creating New Economic Institutions

increasing labor mobility   One approach to the simultaneous unemployment-and-inflation dilemma that has a reasonably good chance of success involves programs to increase the mobility of labor. Particularly important are attempts at quick conversion of chronic unemployment, whenever it appears, into general unemployment and then employment. This can be done by retraining and relocating people and by abolishing discriminatory hiring practices prior to raising aggregate demand. Without the programs increasing labor mobility, the chronically unemployed are doomed to the position of standby equipment that is only sporadically employed in periods of general excess demand.

Furthermore, as we noted in Chapter 3, chronic unemployment is highly conducive to social tension. Half our chronically unemployed, for instance, are concentrated in the slums of our fifty largest cities. Most are handicapped, either physically or by discrimination. They are blacks, Mexican Americans, Puerto Ricans (and in the countryside American Indians). Many are either teenagers or older people. All are in need of literacy training, job skills, and even work experience to develop motivation. They cannot be helped by the old system of employment offices, which was about the only type of manpower program in existence until a few years ago.

Here are some instances of the recent frontal assault on short-run frictional and chronic unemployment by the federal government:

The Area Redevelopment Act of 1961 offered aid to areas of chronic unemployment via loans and grants. These funds were to finance community projects and private undertakings employing the chronically unemployed. They were also to help the displaced to train for new jobs in the industries of the area.

The Manpower Development and Training Act of 1962 was also designed to cope with short-run frictional and chronic unemployment. The U.S. Employment Service was to spread information on jobs, while funds were made available for retraining people for producing goods in excess demand and for maintaining their families while they were being retrained. However, at first, the typical trainee was a white, male, high school graduate. Only one third the trainees were from the disadvantaged groups that form the bulk of the chronically unemployed. In the late 1960's, efforts were being made to raise to two thirds the proportion of the disadvantaged in the program: older workers displaced by technological change, persons in correctional institutions, handicapped workers, the paroled, the illiterate, and the young. Special emphasis was put on intensive on-the-job training. In fiscal 1969, 275,000 trainees were involved in the program. The act also required the Secretary of Labor to submit to the President and Congress an annual *Manpower Report*. This has been done since 1963.

The Vocational Training Act of 1963 was another step of many geared to fight chronic unemployment. In 1966, about 5.8 million persons were enrolled in vocational education programs. Yet these programs also had a serious fault. As in 1918, when federal concern with vocational education started, they stressed traditional areas of home economics and agriculture to the extent of two thirds of the trainees, quite the opposite of what the changing patterns of the economy require! Apprenticeship programs operated in cooperation with the federal government by labor unions, civil rights group, and others were much more directly focused on providing the skills needed by industry. In 1966, about 25,000 workers, mostly in the construction trades, completed such programs.

The Economic Opportunity Act of 1964 had the purpose of combating frictional unemployment by providing work experience, basic education, and training. It was from the start aimed wholly at the disadvantaged. In 1967, 46,000 persons on unemployment relief became part of a *work experience program* teaching basic skills. Training was also given to 31,000 youths in residential *job corps* camps (100,000 in fiscal 1969) and to 350,000 others (from 16 to 21 years of age) in *neighborhood youth corps* centers. When first enrolled, 50 percent of job corps participants failed to read at the fifth-grade level, and 30 percent could not read a simple sentence. The neighborhood youth corps program reaches annually several hundred thousand needy students who receive aid (in 1966 an average of $500) from in-school and summer programs helping them to continue in school. It also trains youths no longer in school. In fiscal 1969, some 560,000 poor persons were involved in programs designed to serve the participants and their neighborhoods simultaneously.

The Appalachia Program of 1965 was begun to develop employment opportunities in 350 counties and 12 states from New York to Alabama. This is a huge economically depressed area. The program is to pave the way for private industrial development through the public construction of roads and health facilities, as well as land erosion control and the restoration of water and timber resources.

In addition to the programs emphasizing immediate relief of chronic unemployment, there are longer-range programs to avoid such unemployment in the future. This is the objective of the federal support of education, ranging from the basic *Elementary and Secondary Education Act of 1965* and the *Higher Education Act of 1965* to the more specific *Allied Health Professions Personnel Training Act of 1966.*

The armed forces have also entered the act. They have long had specialized training programs. Some 2,000 courses, from auto repair to aerospace technology, are available. The Armed Forces Institute allows members to receive the equivalent of a high school diploma. In 1966, *Project 100,000* was added, an attempt to make military service a path to a productive career by accepting and training a third of the 300,000 persons annually labeled unfit for service by previous standards.

In 1966, the *National Commission on Technology, Automation, and Economic Progress* presented proposals to the President. Among them were that the federal government become an "employer of last resort," providing presently at least 500,000 full-time public service jobs for those unable to find work. Also recommended was the extension of free education to 14 years to meet the increasing needs for *educated* labor, and a "nationalization" of the present state-federal unemployment service via a computerized national job availability service matching workers and jobs. (The West European success in depressing the level of unemployment has, among other things, been attributed to an excellent employment service and broad industry training and internship programs.) A 1968 law, in fact, authorized the development of a comprehensive system of labor market information using electronic data processing and telecommunications equipment for up-to-the-minute contacts among recruitment, job training, and placement agencies. An experimental computerized job bank at the Maryland State Employment Service was called a great success. A similar one was to be installed in thirty other cities by mid-1970. Also with federal help, a statewide matching system was working in Utah when President Nixon took office, and the President expressed a desire to make this a nationwide system.

In 1968 a program entitled *Job Opportunities in the Business Sector* (JOBS) was initiated. It was designed to bring the "flexibility and imagination of the private sector into full partnership with the government." With the federal government contributing $350 million in the first year, private industry was to train and hire 500,000 of the hard-core unemployed by mid-1971. (The goal was later raised to 614,000.) The government was to identify and locate the unemployed; private companies were to train them and offer them jobs. Under the arrangement, the private employer would pay normal training costs, and the government would pay any additional expenses. These would, for instance, involve costs for individualized teaching of reading and writing, for the correction of special health problems, for transportation, and for counseling on all kinds of matters ranging from personal care to work proficiency and follow-up assistance to assure the newly trained keep their new jobs. (These costs turned out to be an average of $3,000 per enrollee per year.) To do the business part of the program, a *National Alliance of Businessmen* was formed in late 1967. The government part of the program was carried out as part of a new *Concentrated Employment Program* of the Labor Department aimed at employing the disadvantaged in poverty areas through federal, state, local government, and private cooperation. In addition, this program was being coordinated through the *Cooperative Area Manpower Planning System* (CAMPS) with others pursued by other government agencies. Such other programs were mushrooming in the late 1960's: The Model Cities Program, New Careers, Operation Mainstream, The Work Incentive Program (WIN). All these, in one way or another, were aimed at helping the chronically unemployed in the nation's slums.

Along the same lines, the Economic Development Administration of the Commerce Department was giving subsidies in the late 1960's for training the unskilled and chronically unemployed in slum-based plants. The Office of Economic Opportunity offered "success insurance" (initially insuring businesses in four cities against losses incurred in private job training of 4,000 persons) and insured loans to private persons to upgrade their skills. Although the idea was hardly sweeping American businesses like wildfire, partly on their own and partly after government prodding, companies have begun to go where the jobless are and agreed to forget about high school diplomas, prison records, age, sex, race, and similar barriers to employment. Examples are the Control Data Corporation's new plant in the north side slum of Minneapolis, the Avco Corporation's new commercial printing plant in the Roxbury section of Boston, and the Aerojet plant in Watts, Los Angeles.

President Nixon, who had talked much of "black capitalism" during his campaign, established a new Office of Minority Business Enterprise in 1969. Its aim was to help blacks, but also Mexican Americans, Puerto Ricans, and American Indians, to get jobs and business ownership in new "industrial complexes" to be created in the urban ghettos with federal aid.
Conclusion so far.   It remains to be seen how effective these programs (as well as certain sections of the *Civil Rights Acts of 1964* barring discrimination) will be in eliminating short-run and chronic unemployment. There can be no doubt that monetary and fiscal policies *alone* cannot eliminate all types of unemployment, *unless we are willing to pay the price of deliberately created inflation.*

The large and rapid expansion of federal training activities clearly helps meet a major need: to make the disadvantaged employable and to retrain those who suffer no special disadvantage, but who lack the specific skills in demand. After frictional and chronic unemployment has been reduced into general unemployment in this way, monetary and fiscal policies can then be relied on to turn general unemployment into employment. However, the proliferation of federal, state, and local government as well as private training programs, often designed to serve the same people, is bound to lead to confusion and inefficient management.

Most of the programs are still very new. Little has as yet been done in a systematic way to motivate all the chronically unemployed to undertake training and to isolate the most effective approach to the problem. Should training bonuses be provided? How about relocation assistance? How about earning allowances for persons receiving public assistance? How about day care centers for mothers of dependent children, and training allowances for chronically unemployed who have exhausted their unemployment insurance benefits? What is the best way of preparing illiterate youths from the slums for employment as opposed to improving the skills of a literate adult with previous work experience? How can we truly enforce antidiscrimination laws?

These questions must be answered if we want to avoid the painful choice between large short-run frictional and chronic unemployment without inflation, on the one hand, or full employment with inflation, on the other. To get full employment *without* demand-pull inflation by monetary and fiscal policies, we must first prepare the ground, so to speak, by making resources responsive to a rise in aggregate demand. This requires providing the skills needed by an economy undergoing continual technological change, helping those who are presently unemployable to attain skills (as well as teach them to become more disciplined and motivated), reducing discrimination, and improving job counseling and placement. The benefits from such activity, furthermore, go clearly far beyond economics.

moral suasion   Controlling all prices directly to deal with bottleneck and cost-push inflation is, as we saw, a difficult and thankless job. Other ways may well be preferable, although hardly easier. The U.S. government has in recent years increasingly relied on *moral suasion,* on attempts to hold back "inflationary" price increases by unions and management through special White House appeals. In this way, erstwhile private behavior has become subject to a kind of federal government screening for "social responsibility." To determine whether a price increase is "inflationary" (is likely to raise prices in *general*), the President's Council of Economic Advisers in 1962 suggested certain *wage-price guideposts* for unions and management. Although government officials had talked of "restraint" before, it had become abundantly clear that, in the absence of clear-cut criteria, everyone identified his actual behavior with desired behavior. The purpose of the guideposts was to make clear to all that increased *real* income can only come from increased productivity. If everyone followed the guideposts when setting his *money* income, cost-push inflation could be eliminated, leaving room for monetary and fiscal policies to do the rest. The guideposts involve the following.

Wage-price guideposts explained.   Money incomes (including fringe benefits in *every* industry should be raised only to the extent that average productivity rises *in the long run* in the nation *as a whole.* Average productivity is defined as real GNP *per person employed.* (It has recently risen by 3 percent per year, and the President's Council of Economic Advisers in 1966 recommended a guidepost of 3.2 percent.) Suppose we take an example, illustrated by Table 14.1 GUIDEPOSTS EXPLAINED: I. Let real GNP (in 1958 dollars) per person employed

Table 14.1   GUIDEPOSTS EXPLAINED: I

YEAR	REAL GNP PER PERSON EMPLOYED (AVERAGE PRODUCTIVITY) IN 1958 DOLLARS		
	TOTAL	PORTION GOING TO LABOR (60 PERCENT OF TOTAL)	PORTION GOING TO OTHERS (40 PERCENT OF TOTAL)
1965	7,800	4,680	3,120
1966	8,034	4,820.40	3,213.60

Hypothetical data show that everyone's income can rise by 3 percent, if total income rises by 3 percent.

equal $7,800 in 1965, labor receiving 60 percent of this, or $4,680, nonlabor income recipients the rest, or $3,120. If average productivity rises by 3 percent, it would be $8,034 in 1966. If labor's and everyone else's money income everywhere rose by the same percentage, the labor and nonlabor portions wouid also rise by 3 percent to $4,820.40, and $3,213.60, respectively. In short, if we produce 3 percent more on the average, *everyone* can in fact get 3 percent more exactly. All money incomes (wages, rents, interest, profits) can rise by 3 percent. There will be no *general* price rise because 3 percent more output is also there to be bought.

However, the guideposts suggested that *individual* prices possibly should change. If a *particular industry's* productivity rose as the national average, everything would be as above: no price change, 3 percent more output, 3 percent more money income for everyone. If a particular industry's productivity rose more than the national average, its prices should fall. (If it rose by less, they should rise.) Table 14.2 GUIDEPOSTS EXPLAINED: II provides an illustration.

Table 14.2   GUIDEPOSTS EXPLAINED: II

YEAR	REAL GNP PER PERSON EMPLOYED (AVERAGE PRODUCTIVITY), IN 1958 DOLLARS, AND MONEY INCOMES SET BY GUIDEPOSTS					
	CASE A (PRODUCTIVITY INCREASES 20 PERCENT, INCOMES ARE RAISED ONLY 3 PERCENT)			CASE B (PRODUCTIVITY INCREASES 1 PERCENT, INCOMES ARE RAISED 3 PERCENT)		
	OUTPUT VALUED AT 1958 PRICES	MONEY INCOMES GOING TO		OUTPUT VALUED AT 1958 PRICES	MONEY INCOMES GOING TO	
		LABOR	OTHERS		LABOR	OTHERS
1965	10,000	6,000	4,000	10,000	6,000	4,000
1966	12,000	6,180	4,120	10,100	6,180	4,120
	10,300			10,300		
	Reduce output prices until output per person employed sells for $10,300 instead of $12,000.			Raise output prices until output per person employed sells for $10,300 instead of $10,100.		

Hypothetical data show how an industry's prices have to be adjusted under the wage-price guideposts. If the industry's productivity rises faster than national average productivity (case A), but its incomes are raised according to the latter, that industry's output value at current prices exceeds the value of incomes earned. Prices must be reduced sufficiently to equalize the two. If the industry's productivity rises more slowly than national average productivity (case B), but its incomes are raised according to the latter, that industry's output value at current prices falls short of the value of incomes earned. Prices must be raised to equalize the two.

Suppose the value added per person employed in the auto industry in 1965 were (in 1958 prices) $10,000, but in 1966 it equaled $12,000, a 20 percent rise, clearly above the national average of 3 percent. If in the auto industry, too, labor gets 60 percent and nonlabor resources get 40 percent of value added, we had in 1965 respective income shares per person employed of $6,000 and $4,000 (case A). Following the guidelines, these would be raised by the extent of average productivity rise of the nation *as a whole*, or by 3 percent to the 1966 figures of $6,180 and $4,120, respectively. That is, money incomes of $10,300 per person employed would be paid out in the auto industry.

But, because, in 1966, the auto industry's output per person employed at unchanged prices would sell for $12,000, something would be wrong! The value of output produced per person employed would be more by $1,700 than the value of incomes paid out per person employed. Therefore, in this case, prices of output must be adjusted downward such that what would sell at $12,000 at old prices sells in fact at $10,300 at new prices.

Case B is analogous. In 1966, value added, we now assume, rises by only 1 percent, to $10,100 per employee. Yet, if we raise money incomes according to the guidelines (by 3 percent), we are paying out $10,300 per employee. Thus, there is a $200 discrepancy between output value (at old prices) and incomes paid out. We resolve it by raising output prices such that what would sell for $10,100 at old prices sells in fact for $10,300 at new prices.

If every industry followed this simple policy (raise *all* incomes by the increase in *national* average productivity, adjust output prices, if needed, to make value of output equal to value of incomes paid), the *general* price level could never rise owing to cost-push inflation. Everyone working would share equally in the fruits of progress.

Guidepost exceptions. The guideposts further suggested that certain exceptions be made to this rule to correct major inequities and to encourage the solution of structural problems. The pay for particular types of chronically unemployed resources may be raised by less than the average to encourage greater use and smaller supply of such resources. The pay for particular types of resources that are relatively overpaid because of past successful use of exceedingly strong bargaining power should also rise by less to correct injustices. This would involve raising wages by less and raising prices by less or lowering them by more than otherwise called for. The opposite might be done with resources in chronically short supply to encourage smaller use and greater supply and with resources relatively underpaid because of exceptionally weak bargaining power.

The degree of success. These guideposts, although strongly supported by President Kennedy and Johnson, ran into increasing opposition by mid-1966. Strong unions, such as those in the construction industry, had ignored them all along. They would hear nothing of governmental interference with free collective bargaining. Other unions, such as in the airlines, New York subways, electrical equipment, and telephone industries, negotiated wage hikes far above the guideposts in 1966. Others still, as in the steel industry, observed the guideposts reasonably well. The situation was similar for business firms. A number of price reductions, which the guideposts would have recommended, failed to materialize. In 1966, this was particularly noted in automobile, aluminum, newsprint, gasoline, and agricultural machinery production.

We should not be surprised about this. Without powers of *enforcement*, moral suasion (that is, asking people to forgo potential private gain for the national good) is a weak weapon. People do not want to share *equally* in the fruits of progress, to maintain in fact their relative shares of real GNP as of 1962. The existence of cost-push inflation stems exactly from the fact that people are using economic *power*. No union that *could* get a 5 percent wage boost is likely to settle for 3 percent (although it is clear that, real GNP having risen only by 3 percent, not everyone can succeed in this game in real terms). No business that *could* get a 20 percent profit boost it likely to settle for 3 percent by lowering its prices. In fact, this is the *fun* of the whole game. *On the average*, everyone's real income can only rise by 3 percent if real GNP rises by 3 percent. Yet everyone can (legitimately) hope to get more by raising money income by more, letting the subsequent inflation decide *whose* excessive claim to a nonexistent part of real GNP must be canceled, Man's instinct to gamble is strong, and more likely than not, some *will* win (raise their share of real GNP) even if at the expense of others.

The federal government was fully aware of this problem. Under Presidents Kennedy and Johnson, an all-out effort was made to get the guideposts understood and accepted by the relevant parties and the general public. Members of the Council of Economic Advisers, Cabinet and sub-Cabinet officials, the President himself, made numerous addresses, including radio and television appearances on the subject. They appeared before congressional committees, especially the Joint Economic Committee. Behind the scenes, efforts were equally intense.

Continually, there were private, and usually secret, meetings between government leaders, on the one hand (the council members, the Secretaries of Labor, of Commerce, of Agriculture, of the Treasury, of the Interior, of Defense), and labor or business leaders, on the other. The aim was to underscore as forcefully as possible the public interest factor in wage-price decisions and to solicit the voluntary cooperation by labor and business. In 1966, the Council of Economic Advisers resorted to urgent letters, telegrams, and phone calls in over fifty cases in which price hikes had just been announced or were imminent. Those responsible were invited to high level "discussions" and were urged to rescind, reduce in amount or coverage, or delay price increases.

In addition to this private pressure, the council began to issue formal statements to the public on particular wage-price decisions. In 1966, this was done about actions of the New York Transit Authority, the airlines, and the steel, aluminum, copper, and molybdenum industries.

There can be no doubt that this policy of moral suasion was partly successful. Many have ridiculed the policy as an "open-mouth policy." Nevertheless, if you were a business or labor leader, you would find it difficult to act contrary to a direct and personal Presidential appeal. Consider the following example of Presidential pressure that succeeded in holding back price increases: President Kennedy's Press Conference Statement on the Steel Price Rise, Washington, D.C., April 11, 1962.

Simultaneous and identical actions of United States Steel and other leading steel corporations increasing steel prices by some $6.00 a ton constitute a wholly unjustifiable and irresponsible defiance of the public interests. In this serious hour in our Nation's history, when we are confronted with grave crises in Berlin and Southeast Asia, when we are devoting our energies to economic recovery and stability, when we are asking reservists to leave their homes and families for months on end and service men to risk their lives—and four were killed in the last two days in Vietnam—and asking union members to hold down their wage requests at a time when restraint and sacrifice are being asked of every citizen, the American people will find it hard, as I do, to accept a situation in which a tiny handful of steel executives whose pursuit of private power and profit exceeds their sense of public responsibility can show such utter contempt for the interest of 185 million Americans.

If this rise in the cost of steel is imitated by the rest of the industry, instead of rescinded, it would increase the costs of homes, autos, appliances, and most other items for every American family. It would increase the cost of machinery and tools to every American businessman and farmer. It would seriously handicap our efforts to prevent an inflationary spiral from eating up the pensions of our older citizens and our new gains in purchasing power.

It would add, Secretary [of Defense, Robert S.] McNamara informed me this morning, an estimated $1 billion to the cost of our defenses, at a time when every dollar is needed for national security and other purposes. It would make it more difficult for American goods to compete in foreign markets, more difficult to withstand competition from foreign imports, and thus more difficult to improve our balance-of-payments position, and stem the flow of gold. And it is necessary to stem it for our national security, if we're going to pay for our security commitments abroad. And it would surely handicap our efforts to induce other industries and unions to adopt responsible price and wage policies.

The facts of the matter are that there is no justification for an increase in steel prices. The recent settlement between the industry and the union which does not even take place until July 1st, was widely acknowledged to be noninflationary, and the whole effect of this administration's role, which both parties understood, was to achieve an agreement which would make unnecessary any increase in prices. Steel output per man is rising so fast that labor costs per ton of steel can actually be expected to decline in the next twelve months. And in fact, the acting Commissioner of the Bureau of Labor Statistics informed me this morning that, and I quote, "employment costs per unit of steel output in 1961 were essentially the same as they were in 1958."

The cost of the major raw materials, steel scrap and coal, has also been declining, and for an industry which has been generally operating at less than two-thirds of capacity, its profit rate has been normal and can be expected to rise sharply this year in view of the reduction in idle capacity. Their lot has been easier than that of 100,000 steel workers thrown out of work in the last three years. The industry's cash dividends have exceeded $600 million in each of the last five years, and earnings in the first quarter of this year were estimated in the February 28th *Wall Street Journal* to be among the highest in history.

In short, at a time when they could be exploring how more efficiency and better prices could be obtained, reducing prices in this industry in recognition of lower costs, their unusually good labor contract, their foreign competition and their increase in production and profits which are coming this year, a few gigantic corporations have decided to increase prices in ruthless disregard of their public responsibilities.

The Steelworkers Union can be proud that it abided by its responsibilities in this agreement, and this Government has responsibilities which we intend to meet. The Department of Justice and the Federal Trade Commission are examining the significance of this action in a free, competitive economy. The Department of Defense and other agencies are reviewing its impact on their policies of procurement. And I am informed that steps are under way by those members of the Congress who plan appropriate inquiries into how these price decisions are so quickly made and reached and what legislative safeguards may be needed to protect the public interests.

Price and wage decisions in this country, except for a very limited restriction in the case of monopolies and national emergency strikes, are and ought to be freely and privately made. But the American people have a right to expect, in return for that freedom, a higher sense of business responsibility for the welfare of their country than has been shown in the last two days.

Some time ago I asked each American to consider what he would do for his country, and I asked the steel companies. In the last twenty-four hours we had their answer.

In 1967, the Council of Economic Advisers stood by its guideposts, yet the attitude of unions in particular shifted away from cooperation with the government. The median money wage hike negotiated by large unions was 2.9 percent in 1962. It rose steadily to 3.8 percent in 1965, 4.8 percent in 1966, 5.6 percent in 1967, and 7.5 percent in 1968. The unions' refusal to abide by the guideposts was largely owing to the fact that consumer prices rose more than usual in the late 1960's and corporate profits also rose and rose relative to labor income. Although the violation of guidepost criteria in the past cannot be blamed for this (most of the consumer price increases occurred in areas not covered by the guideposts, such as agriculture and professional services; corporate profits increased relative to labor income because average productivity rose by more than the long-term trend), the "recalcitrant" attitude of labor was understandable. But the government was not giving up. President Johnson established a Cabinet Committee on Price Stability. It consisted of the Secretaries of the Treasury of Commerce, and of Labor, the Director of the Budget, and the chairman of the Council of Economic Advisers. This committee was to

1. Prepare and publish studies in depth of economic conditions in industries that are persistent sources of inflationary pressure, be it because of inefficiency or abuse of market power;

2. Study and propose government policies affecting prices, including federal procurement and construction, manpower and labor programs, imports and exports, research and development, and natural resource supply;

3. Work with representatives of business and labor and the public to enlist their cooperation toward responsible wage-price behavior and to work out a consensus on standards to be applied;

4. Recommend legislation.

Thus, the battle, in which public opinion and Presidential persuasion were pitted against the market power of strong businesses and strong unions, continued. The government hoped to bring a sense of the public interest to private decision-making and to convince everyone that it is not in his self-interest to contribute to the inflationary spiral, at least not in his long-run self-interest. Just before he left office, President Johnson's Cabinet Committee on Price Stability issued a report. In view of the "disturbing, but understandable" wage hikes of 1968, it urged a 1969 wage guidepost of just under 5 percent, about halfway back to the long-run productivity ideal. For the first time, the committee also recommended a guidepost for business profit: businesses were asked to absorb without a price increase up to 1 percent increases in unit costs of production. They were also asked to aim for profit margins in 1969 not greater than the 1967–1968 average and not to pass the tax surcharge on to consumers. The committee and President Johnson reemphasized belief in the value of moral suasion. We must call attention, they said, to flagrant departures from the standards of responsible decision-making.

President Nixon, however, has scuttled numerical guidelines as public policy. This focuses "on the symptoms, rather than on causes of inflation," he said. His advisers have returned to the Eisenhower policy of issuing *general* requests for restraint. Yet, one can be almost certain that any future Democratic administration will go back to specific guideposts. Certainly the Joint Economic Committee of Congress has deplored President Nixon's decision. It has even advocated the establishment of a high level office that would be both a competent factfinder and mobilizer of public opinion against unrestrained increases in prices.

CONCLUSION

To sum up, monetary and fiscal policies *alone* cannot eliminate all types of inflation, unless we are willing to pay the price of deliberately created general unemployment. At present, there is no really effective weapon against cost-push inflation. Figure 14.3 OUTPUT VS. PRICES

Figure 14.3   OUTPUT VS. PRICES

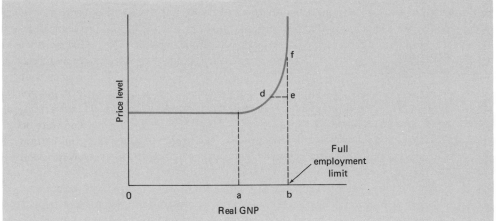

The level of real GNP will be determined by aggregate demand. The closer aggregate demand pushes real GNP to its potential at b, the more likely inflation becomes.

puts the whole problem in a nutshell. It illustrates a hypothetical relationship between the levels of real GNP and prices in general. When aggregate demand is very low, demanding a real GNP of a or less, the general price level is constant. Anywhere between O and a, monetary and fiscal policies affecting demand can change real GNP without affecting prices in general. (Note again Figures 10.2 HOW EASY MONETARY POLICY WORKS, 12.1 HOW EASY FISCAL POLICY WORKS—SPENDING MORE, and 12.3 HOW EASY FISCAL POLICY WORKS—TAXING LESS.) When aggregate demand is excessively high, demanding a real GNP beyond its full employment limit at b, the general price level will be rising. In this situation, monetary and fiscal policies affecting demand can change the price level without affecting real GNP. (Note again Figures 10.3 HOW TIGHT MONETARY POLICY WORKS, 12.2 HOW TIGHT FISCAL POLICY WORKS—

SPENDING LESS, and 12.4 HOW TIGHT FISCAL POLICY WORKS—TAXING MORE.) The real world is likely to be in the middle. That is where the Phillips curve becomes relevant. Operating below potential, but not excessively so, as between a and b, expansionary monetary and fiscal policy can raise, contractionary policy can reduce, real GNP. We can "move up or down the Phillips curve" (Figure 14.1). Even if neither action causes or eliminates generalized demand-pull inflation, it may cause or reduce bottleneck inflation and may encourage holders of economic power to foster or restrain, respectively, cost-push inflation.

Imagine we are at a point such as d. Real GNP is close to full employment GNP. The price level has been rising somewhat. We could go to f or above by *indiscriminate* use of monetary and fiscal weapons. That is, we could get to potential GNP, all the way to it, but the price level would rise greatly. This is "riding up the Phillips curve." Yet, we are trying to get to e. We are trying to go to potential GNP *without* raising prices further. We can do it by *carefully* raising aggregate demand with monetary and fiscal policies, converting general unemployment into employment, while (1) busily converting short-run frictional and chronic unemployment into general unemployment, and (2) persuading the holders of economic power to follow the wage-price guideposts. To the extent that we fail with (1) we will end up to the left of ef (with less than full employment) and above de (with some demand-pull inflation). To the extent that we fail with (2), the move above de is intensified (by cost-push inflation). At the present time, there seems to be no way of completely avoiding this undesirable trade-off between unemployment and inflation. All we can hope for is that the programs discussed above "shift the Phillips curve" left and down, making it possible to "trade" at better terms than heretofore. (You might want to draw in such a curve in Figure 14.1 THE PHILLIPS CURVE. Suppose the new curve went through the 1944 dot and were otherwise parallel to the one printed in the book. What would it mean? It would tell us that we can now, for example, reduce unemployment to 2 percent with only a 1 percent inflation per year. Previously it would have required a much greater inflation.)

SUMMARY

1   This chapter dealt with a major policy dilemma: although monetary and fiscal policies in principle can eliminate general unemployment and demand-pull inflation, they cannot by themselves eliminate, without undesirable side effects, all types of unemployment and all types of inflation simultaneously.

2   Short-run frictional and chronic unemployment are much less responsive to demand-raising policies than is general unemployment. Unless a situation of intense excess demand is created, private businesses have little incentive to train or relocate people with the wrong skills or no skills, or of the "wrong" sex, age, or race. Only a state of substantial excess demand can substantially reduce such chronic unemployment. This will simultaneously create demand-pull inflation and create favorable conditions for intensified cost-push inflation.

3   Bottleneck and cost-push inflation are similarly much less responsive to demand-cutting policies than is generalized demand-pull inflation. Unless a situation of extremely deficient demand is created, these types of inflation are likely to exist. Only a state of greatly deficient demand can substantially reduce them. This will simul-

taneously create general unemployment on top of short-run frictional and chronic unemployment.

4 As a result, we observe in reality unemployment and inflation simultaneously. The Phillips curve is a graphical device showing how less unemployment may be "traded" for more inflation, or vice versa. The effects of changes in aggregate demand can be shown graphically by movements along the curve.

5 Policy-makers clamor for alternatives to the dilemma. They do not like to compromise with the devil by accepting inflation as the price of full employment. Nor do they wish to live with unemployment as the cost of stable prices.

6 Some propose to destroy presently existing institutional arrangements "to get off the Phillips curve." Others would prefer to create new institutional arrangements to "move the Phillips curve" into a more acceptable position (wherein we can reduce unemployment a lot without any significant increase in inflation and vice versa).

7 The former proposals are unlikely to be followed, because they are unrealistic or highly undesirable. They include abolition of labor unions, annulment of protective labor legislation, and direct governmental control of all prices, as well as probably of output and distribution.

8 The latter proposals include attempts to improve on the imperfectly working price system, rather than to replace it, for example by increasing labor mobility and administering massive doses of moral suasion. Public policies may be directed toward systematic and massive *public* retraining and training of workers, as well as improved job counseling and placement services. This would essentially convert short-run frictional and chronic unemployment into general unemployment, which would be less impervious to demand-raising policies. Similarly, for the avoidance of inflation *without* the creation of unemployment, more is needed than tight monetary-fiscal policy. The federal government has experimented with direct persuasion of labor and business leaders to consider the public interest (in avoiding inflation) by making wage and price decisions on the basis of the President's wage-price guideposts. Such policy has been less than perfectly successful (and is being de-emphasized by the Nixon administration). Yet, such policy could theoretically overcome the problem posed by the use of excessive economic power. If everyone followed the guideposts, the results would be very much like those achieved by supply and demand in perfect competition with freely flexible prices and freely mobile resources.

TERMS[5]

average productivity	moral suasion
black market	Phillips curve
bottleneck inflation	price controls
GNP deflator	suppressed inflation
minimum wage	wage-price guideposts

[5] Terms are defined in the Glossary at the end of the book.

QUESTIONS FOR REVIEW AND DISCUSSION

1 "Eliminating chronic unemployment by easy monetary and fiscal policy alone is like compromising with the devil." Explain. (Think of the Phillips curve.)

2 Describe some of the major federal programs designed to combat short-run frictional and chronic unemployment.

3 "Because society at large benefits immeasurably from technological progress, the government should aid all who are displaced by it however long it takes them to find a new steady job." Discuss.

4 Republican politicians frequently chide Democrats for proliferating public programs of the type discussed above to deal with chronic unemployment. Can you think of *private* programs that could effectively deal with chronic unemployment? With general unemployment? With inflation?

5 In 1980, private retirement plans will cover 40 million workers, that is, three fifths of private nonfarm employees. Many of them (80 percent) lose the right to their pension if they terminate their employment. As you might expect, this seriously interferes with labor mobility. Should one do something about this? Would you? What?

6 "Just like all types of unemployment are responsive to the sun of strong aggregate demand, so all types of inflation can be choked off by the noose of tight monetary-fiscal policies." Evaluate.

7 "It may be easy enough to distinguish demand-pull inflation from cost-push inflation in theory. In practice it is next to impossible." Discuss.

8 In early 1969, President Nixon took the Job Corps away from the Office of Economic Opportunity. He placed administration of the camps under the Department of Labor. He also closed half the existing centers (old military camps in the countryside). But he promised to open up others in or close to *cities*, where, he said, the trainees will have to live and work. (The affected job corpsmen answered with howls of protest and a letter writing campaign.) Do you think the President's was a wise move? Why or why not? What other information might you want to have before you make up your mind?

9 In recent years, there has been much talk about "inflationary" and "noninflationary" price increases. How can any price increase possibly be *non*inflationary? (Hint: reread the section on the President's wage-price guideposts, then answer the question by explaining those guideposts.)

10 Wage-price guideposts have been criticized because they would (a) preserve the past distribution of income between labor and others, and (b) make it impossible for fixed-income recipients to share in the fruits of progress (because the general price level would become stable). Evaluate these criticisms.

11 "Wage-price guideposts will never work, for it is impossible to thwart the instinct of self-enrichment." Comment. (How would you react as a businessman or labor leader?)

12 "The trouble with wage-price guideposts is this: those naïve enough to comply get punished; those who have the cleverness or gall to evade and resist them get rewarded." Comment.

13 MR. A: "Direct price controls are infinitely better than the creeping admonitionism of guideposts."

MR. B: "There are no acceptable alternatives to guideposts."
Comment.

14   If a government, knowing full well that a black market existed, wanted to keep the black market price as low as possible and black market transactions as small as possible, whom should it threaten with the most severe punishment: buyers or sellers? Or should it threaten both equally? Justify your answer.

15   "Price controls distort the allocation of resources." Explain. (Hint: consider the lessons of Chapter 2 before answering this question.)

16   "The simultaneous unemployment-and-inflation thesis is an illusion. Price indexes lie, for they fail to take account of quality changes in products, they ignore productivity increases in the government sector (a higher salary *always* means a higher cost for the *same* output), and so on." Comment.

17   What does it mean if the Phillips curve shifts to the right or left? Steepens or flattens?

18   If you had to choose between decreasing unemployment or inflation, how would you decide?

19   "Prices are rising at 3 percent a year. Unemployment has been declining, but still stands at 5 percent. It looks like the recovery is slackening, but no one is sure." What would you do as a Federal Reserve Governor? As Secretary of the Treasury?

20   Do you think President Kennedy should have acted the way he did in the steel price controversy? Why or why not?

Peril for the Dollar

A Sizable 1969 Deficit
In Balance of Payments

Fed May Face a Hard Choice

By Richard F. Janssen
Staff Reporter of THE WALL STREET JOURNAL

WASHINGTON—Relaxation is the watch-word of the Nixon Administration's balance-of-payments policies—but not of its policy-makers.

Instead, the White House decision to ease controls over foreign investment is perceptibly increasing tensions among many officials who were already apprehensive about fresh trouble ahead for the dollar and gold.

While relieved that Mr. Nixon was dissuaded from his election-campaign pledge to abolish the controls altogether, a key strategist worries that even the more modest steps "won't come cheap." In proclaiming the Good Friday grant of more freedom to business, banks and individuals to lend and invest abroad, Treasury Under Secretary for Monetary Affairs Paul A. Volcker cautioned that the dollar outflow problem remains "urgent." . . .

Soaring imports make the foreign-trade flank of the payments balance so vulnerable, officials admit, that even today's tight credit policies may not be enough to fully protect the dollar from foreign political and speculative sniping. Moreover, they advise, three or four months from now the Federal Reserve Board may well face a crucial choice: Keep credit policies stringent longer for balance-of-payments purposes or ease the money supply to prevent a deflationary "overkill" of the domestic economy.

In a sharp swing from the payments surplus of $990 million that the Johnson Administration enjoyed in last year's final quarter, insiders say, the Nixon Administration will have to report a "considerable" deficit for the quarter ended March 31. Such a deficit occurs when foreigners acquire more dollars than they return; those dollars ending up in foreign central banks may generally be used to buy Treasury gold.

Even if the fingers-crossed forecasts of Nixon aides are accurate and the loosened investment controls don't let out a cascade of dollars, the Administration is bracing anyway for what Commerce Secretary Maurice Stans calls a "very substantial" payments deficit for the full year. Very tentatively, specialists estimate a deficit of at least $2 billion for all 1969. And they stress that this forecast assumes near-perfection in the way domestic policies dampen inflation and thus make U.S. goods more competitive again at home and abroad. . . .

The Administration decided to accept "some risk to the balance of payments" in order to "push as far as it could" toward more economic freedom, says Herbert Stein of the President's Council of Economic Advisers. But the push poses some thorny new problems.

Certainly a pivotal one, economists figure, is the pressure present policy puts on the Federal Reserve to prolong its current tight credit policy, lest lower interest rates prompt U.S. investors to seek higher yields abroad and diminish the inflow from foreign investors.

Also, some analysts say, a return to substantial dollar outflows could weaken the Nixon Administration's argument that other nations should agree to a swift and sizable outpouring of "Special Drawing Rights"—or "paper gold." The rationale for this reform, slowly approaching ratification by the 111-country International Monetary Fund, is that supplies of real gold and foreign-held dollars won't grow enough to support expanding world trade.

Postponed Crises

In the meantime, others caution, the apparent melting away of last year's surplus will leave the U.S. dollar less of a bastion of confidence in any new international currency crisis. "All the crises have been postponed," says a financial aide, referring to lingering doubts about whether the French and British can avoid devaluations and the continuing suspense over whether the Germans will raise the value of the mark.

If another major currency upheaval erupts at a time when an aura of weakness may be enveloping the dollar again, strategists see much more likelihood of some foreign central banks panicking and cashing in large holdings of dollars for the Treasury's gold at the fixed price of $35 an ounce. From this could evolve the Administration's ultimate monetary crunch: A decision either to halt sales from the $10.8 billion gold stock or—much less likely—to stretch the supply by increasing the official price. . . .

Whether businesses and banks take maximum advantage of the $800 million more leeway they have just received for investing and lending abroad this year is ranked as a . . . major uncertainty. . . .

But, analysts reason, if foreign ventures do prove appealing, it would likely become evident just about the time the Federal Reserve's tight money policy has prevailed to the domestically dangerous point . . . Most likely, officials conjecture, the Fed would be easing credit at that point to avoid the more pressing economic and political repercussions of a recessionary upsurge in unemployment. Thus the burden of battling the payments deficit would be put back on the White House.

How the Nixon Administration would react can scarcely be guessed at present, insiders say, but one expert says the Government would be "highly reluctant" to clamp on tighter payments controls again. About the only option that would seem feasible, he suggests, would be a return to the original Johnson tactic of badgering the big businesses that account for the bulk of foreign investment to "voluntarily" hold down outflows of dollars. And, others note, Mr. Nixon is taking the precaution of asking Congress to extend the interest equalization tax for another 18 months beyond its slated July 31 demise.

The Wall Street Journal, April 11, 1969

15

unemployment, inflation, and the balance of payments

W E HAVE SEEN in the previous chapters how monetary and fiscal policies, properly used, can eliminate general unemployment and demand-pull inflation. We have also seen, however, that the great problems of unemployment and inflation cannot be solved completely unless we take special supplementary measures to deal with chronic unemployment and cost-push inflation. In this chapter, we have to become acquainted with another hurdle yet standing in the way of full employment and price stability. This hurdle results from the country's involvement in economic relations beyond its boundaries. As we shall see in Chapter 21, the quantity of goods available to a country may be greatly increased if it participates in international specialization and exchange. But this requires the use of foreign monies. Frequently, the amounts of foreign money, or *foreign exchange*, that a country earns and that it needs to pay its bills abroad are not equal. Then special consideration has to be given to its international *balance of payments*. Consideration for this balance may at times seriously circumscribe the economic policy-maker's freedom to use his monetary and fiscal weapons at all. Then, as we shall see, he faces a serious dilemma of having to choose between full employment and price stability, on the one hand, and unrestricted international trade and lending on the other. At times, he cannot have them both.

THE BALANCE OF PAYMENTS

To get an idea of the problem, we must first consider the meaning of a *balance of payments*. It is nothing more difficult than a systematic record of all economic transactions having occurred during a specified period between two parties. Usually, the parties concerned are nations and the period is a year. In principle, however, one could set up a balance of payments for any period desired and between one person and all others, between one town and all others, and so on. An economic transaction is the exchange of anything at all that has value. A balance of payments is set up in T-account form with everything that is *given up* on the left and everything that is *received* on the right side of the account.

BALANCE OF PAYMENTS

Things given up or Exports or Credits or (+)	Things received or Imports or Debits or (−)

Frequently, the items on the left are called *exports,* those on the right *imports*. Sometimes the items on the left are called *credits* or denoted by a plus sign, those on the right are called *debits* or denoted by a minus sign. All these terms are interchangeable. We must remember that "exports," "credits," and (+) mean nothing else but *things* of *value given up*. Often, people think automatically of exports *of commodities* when hearing the word "exports," and they think that something *good* has happened when hearing the word "credit" or seeing a big fat plus sign. Such interpretations are quite out of place. Similarly, "imports," "debits," and (−) mean nothing else but *things of value received*. It does not mean something *bad* has happened. Nor does it necessarily mean commodities have been received.

Types of Transactions

It is convenient to talk of five, and only five, categories of "things" one can give up or receive in an economic transaction. These include (1) all commodities, excluding monetary gold, (2) all services, (3) thank-you-notes, (4) titles, and (5) gold. Category (1) is self-explanatory and includes all physical objects except gold used in the monetary system, rather than for industrial purposes. Gold plays a special role in international trade, being regarded by all countries as a readily acceptable means of payment. This is, of course, just a matter of custom and it being so, we list monetary gold movements in a separate category (5). Category (2) is also easily understood. Whenever services of labor, land, or capital are rendered or received, their value is entered in the balance of payments. Category (3) is a tricky little item. If something of value is given up in return for *nothing*, we imagine that a thank-you-note *of equal value* is received. If something of value is received for nothing, we imagine that a thank-you-note of equal value has been given up in return. This is then entered in the balance of payments to indicate the occurrence of such one-sided transactions. However, the fancy term "unilateral transfers" is substituted for the words "thank-you-notes." Do not let that confuse you. Wherever you see the words "unilateral transfers," just substitute "thank-you-notes" in your mind. That is *all* it means. Category (4), finally, involves the giving up or receipt, of certificates of ownership or indebtedness. Typical certificates of ownership would be deeds to real estate or common stocks. Typical certificates of indebtedness would be government or corporate bonds, personal IOU's, and, as we saw in Chapter 9, all types of money. When given up, these constitute title exports; when received, title imports. The giving up of coins, paper bills or demand deposits is called a *short-term* title export; the receipt of them, short-term title import. With minor exceptions (which we shall ignore in this book), all other titles are referred to as *long term*. Unfortunately, movements of titles are referred to as *capital movements* and are so recorded. This has *nothing* to do with the term capital as used throughout this book, in the sense of buildings, equipment, and inventories. Even worse, short-term or long-term *title exports* are recorded as short-term or long-term *capital imports* (and quite properly on the export side). Short-term or long-term *title imports* are recorded as short-term or long-term *capital exports* (and quite properly on the import side). Whenever you see the term "capital exports," just substitute "title imports" in your mind. Whenever you see "capital imports," substitute "title exports." That is *all* these terms mean.

An Illustration

Let us develop further the concept of the balance of payments by recording a number of hypothetical transactions for the United States. Note that each transaction *must* involve two entries, something given up and something received, even if only a thank-you-note. Furthermore, the only things of value one can possibly give up or receive must be commodities (excluding monetary gold), services, thank-you-notes, titles, or monetary gold. *Always think in these terms first.* When they are given up, record it on the export side; when they are received, on the import side. *Then* you can substitute fancy language. Here are a few transactions that are recorded in Table 15.1 A HYPOTHETICAL BALANCE OF PAYMENTS:

1. American businesses export $5 billion of automobiles to France. They are paid by check drawn on a Paris bank. We are giving up commodities (cars). We are receiving a title (a demand deposit, which was something owed by the Paris bank to Frenchmen, is now owed by it to us; hence we imported a form of IOU, a "certificate" of indebtedness). The entries are recorded in Table 15.1 under (a) in accounts A and D, the title import being (unfortunately) called capital export.

2. A Greek shipping company ships for the U.S. government supplies to American troops abroad. The U.S. government pays in full by handing over $2 billion of Italian paper money. We are giving up titles (noninterest-bearing certificates of indebtedness issued by the Italian government were owned by Americans, are now owned by Greeks). We are receiving services of Greek labor (sailors) and capital (ships). The entries are recorded under (b) in accounts B and D, the title export being (unfortunately) called capital import.

3. The U.S. government gives India a gift of $3 billion of wheat. We are giving up commodities (wheat). We are receiving a thank-you-note (at least potentially) in return. Entries are as under (c) in accounts A and C.

4. American households buy $15 billion of corporate stock, bonds, and land from foreigners. They pay by check on New York banks. We are giving up titles (demand deposits previously owed to American households are now owed to foreigners). We are receiving other titles (corporate certificates of ownership, certificates of indebtedness, and deeds previously owned by foreigners, are now owned by us). Entries are as under (d) in accounts D and E.

5. Foreign central banks (which under present international agreements have the right to do so) convert $9 billion of their demand deposits at the Fed in the United States into gold. We have to give up gold. We receive titles (demand deposits owed by the Fed to foreigners are now owed to itself, that is, to no one). Entries are as under (e) in accounts D and F.

The Balance of Payments as a Whole

Assuming this is to be a complete record of all international transactions of U.S. residents with all others in 1970, the U.S. balance of payments would look like Table 15.1. Immediately we perceive the consequence of the system of double-entry bookkeeping (which we already met when discussing a firm's balance sheet, which must not be confused with a balance of payments). *The balance of payments necessarily always balances.* In this particular case, American residents gave up (exported) $34 billion of valuable things (cars, wheat, foreign paper money, American demand deposits, and gold). They also received (imported) $34 billion of valuable things (shipping services, thank-you-notes, foreign demand deposits, American demand deposits, stocks, bonds, and deeds).

Table 15.1   A HYPOTHETICAL BALANCE OF PAYMENTS (United States, 1970, IN BILLION DOLLARS)

ACCOUNTS	EXPORTS (1)	IMPORTS (2)	BALANCE (3) = (1) − (2)
A	(a) Commodity exports (cars) 5 (c) Commodity exports (wheat) 3		+8
B		(b) Service imports (shipping) 2	−2
C		(c) Unilateral transfers 3	−3
D	(b) Short-term capital imports (decrease in American-owned foreign paper money) 2 (d) Short-term capital imports (increase in foreign-owned American demand deposits) 15	(a) Short-term capital exports (increase in American-owned demand deposits abroad) 5 (e) Short-term capital exports (decrease in foreign-owned demand deposits here) 9	+3
E		(d) Long-term capital exports (increase in American-owned stocks, bonds, and deeds) 15	−15
F	(e) (Monetary) gold exports 9		+9
A through F	Total 34	Total 34	0

The balance of payments is usually subdivided into a number of "accounts," reflecting the types of things exported or imported. The account labeled A contains only commodities, excluding monetary gold. The difference between their exports and imports, here + $8 billion, is called the *balance of trade*. The account labeled B contains only services. The difference between exports and imports, here—$2 billion, is called the *balance of services*. The account labeled C contains only thank-you-notes. The difference between their exports and imports, here − $3 billion, is called *balance of unilateral transfers*. The account labeled D contains only short-term titles (movements of coins, paper bills, and deposits, essentially). The difference between their exports and imports, here + $3 billion, is called the *balance of short-term capital*. The account labeled E contains only long-term titles. The difference between their exports and imports, here − $15 billion, is called the *balance of long-term capital*. Finally, the account labeled F contains only (monetary) gold. The difference between exports and imports, here $+\$9$ billion, is the *balance of gold*. The sum of all these balances necessarily always equals zero, because the balance of payments *as a whole* always balances. Because of the difficulties of data collection, however, any actual balance of payments contains another item: errors and omissions, which is put on whichever side necessary to balance the account. This in no way contradicts the fact that a balance of payments always balances in principle.

The Balance of Payments and the GNP Accounts

Let us further note that the combined accounts A, B, and C are called the *current account*, and the *balance of current account*, here $+\$3$ billion, is exactly what we have called net export demand throughout earlier chapters. We can easily see why. When we wanted to measure aggregate demand with a view to what happens to our real GNP and employment of resources, we wished to measure aggregate demand for *American-made* commodities and services. (See also our discussion on pages 138–140 above.) Therefore, we deducted from *total* expenditures on commodities and services by American households, private businesses, and governments $(C + I + G)$ and by foreigners in the United States (X) their expenditures on commodities and services previously imported into the United States. In the balance of payments, such imports would be goods *received* from abroad (entries in column (2), accounts A and B) minus those received as gifts (measured by entry in column (1), account C) and hence not part of *expenditure*. On the other hand, foreign expenditure on American goods (X) equals goods given up by us (entries in column (1), accounts A and B) minus those given up as gifts (measured by entry in column (2), account C) and already counted as expenditure of Americans who bought them. In our case, the exports of goods relevant for the GNP accounts equal (in billion dollars) $(5 + 3) + 0 - 3$. The relevant imports equal (in billion dollars) $0 + 2 - 0$. Hence, net exports, NX, of the GNP accounts equal $\$3$ billion. Entries in accounts D to F are in no way part of our GNP. (Remember how GNP is defined.)

Balance vs. Equilibrium

Now we can move a step closer to the main point of this chapter. Although the balance of payments as a whole always balances, individual accounts only balance by accident. Sometimes such imbalance *in individual accounts* can clearly not be sustained for long. Hence, we must expect imminent change. This we call a situation of balance-of-payment *disequilibrium*. Take another look at Table 15.1. We may argue that this balance of payments is in disequilibrium (although it is in balance and will always remain so) for at least two reasons. First, the United States is losing $9 billion of monetary gold per year. Unless the United States is a large gold producer, this cannot go on for long. Things are bound to change. Second, the United States has a net short-term capital import of $3 billion per year. And this means that foreigners are getting more of our money than we of theirs. (In this case, we lost foreign paper money, but gained more foreign deposits, a net gain of $3 billion. However, foreigners, though losing deposits here, gained more, a net gain of $6 billion.) This *could* go on forever, especially if foreigners use American dollars to trade among one another (very much like Mr. Jones and Smith and Brown in Chapter 9 used John Doe's IOU). Something like this has in fact happened for many years after World War II. However, *eventually,* foreigners may be unwilling to accumulate *further* dollars. Then something will have to change.

Many economists would in fact measure the *extent* of disequilibrium by the magnitude of the combined balances of all accounts *other than* D and F. In our case, this would be −$12 billion. It would be called the balance-of-payments *deficit* (if negative) or *surplus* (if positive). Such a deficit must be covered by net gold exports and short-term capital imports (that is, money exports that are *potential* gold exports). It cannot possibly be maintained forever, because *we* will run out of gold (unless we are a large enough gold producer).

A surplus, on the other hand, must be covered by net gold imports or short-term capital exports (that is, money imports which are *potential* gold imports). It cannot possibly be maintained forever, because *foreigners* will run out of gold (unless they are a large enough gold producer).

In the last decade, the U.S. government worried about the fact that our balance of payments has looked very much like Table 15.1, with large deficits year after year. Notice, however, that a deficit is not bad per se. A deficit enables a country to get more commodities, services, thank-you-notes, and long-term titles *from* foreigners than it gives *to* them. This would correspond to your getting lots of commodities and services and good will (for making gifts), while becoming other people's creditor and owning more and more land and corporate stock. This is wonderful. The only trouble is that a deficit cannot go on forever. Just as you would run out of money, the United States could run out of gold. Just as other people one day will refuse to give you more of these lovely things for your IOU's, foreigners one day will refuse to take more U.S. IOU's (money!). *This* is why one worries about a deficit. It is a good thing that cannot last.

INTERNATIONAL MONETARY ARRANGEMENTS

Exactly how a balance-of-payments disequilibrium is cured depends on the framework within which international economic relations are being carried on. A survey of such possible frameworks will help us decide what the United States might do about its problem.

The Old-Fashioned Gold Standard

During the last century and partly in this one (before World War I and again in the 1920's) all the important countries of the world were on the gold standard. We call this old-fashioned, because no country is on it today. This arrangement operated very simply.

the rules   First, each government enacted a law, defining its currency unit in terms of a fixed quantity of pure gold. The United States, for instance, declared the dollar to be equilvalent to 23.22 grains of gold, whereas the United Kingdom evaluated the pound sterling (£) at 113 grains.

Second, each government announced its willingness to buy from anyone and sell to anyone unlimited amounts of gold at this price. There were no restrictions to trading in gold.

Third, each government promised to pursue all necessary policies to maintain the gold standard.

the consequences   It is fairly easy to figure out the consequences of such an arrangement. First, the price of gold in each country was fixed at the official level designated by law. This was so not because people are naturally law abiding (remember our discussion of black markets in the previous chapter), but because the governments stood ready to trade gold with anyone, citizen and foreigner alike, without limit *at this price.* No one who wanted to get rid of 23.22 grains of gold had to sell them for less than a dollar, for he could always get a dollar at the U.S. Treasury. At a lower price, there simply were no sellers. Similarly, no one who wanted to get 23.22 grains of gold had to pay more than a dollar. He could always go to the Treasury and buy there. Thus, the price could not be higher, either. There simply were no buyers at a higher price.

A further consequence concerned international trade. The price of foreign moneys was fixed, too, within a very narrow range. Take an American who wanted to buy British goods and needed pounds to do so. He could count on getting sterling for somewhere between $4.85 and $4.89. The reason was simple. He could always spend $4.87 and get 113 grains of gold at the U.S. Treasury. He could spend, perhaps, another 2 cents for shipping, insurance, and commissions and have the gold in London, where a ready government would exchange 113 grains of gold for one British pound. Thus he could get a pound for $4.89 at most. Actually, American banks could be counted on to perform this operation. No one needed to carry it out personally. For this reason no one ever needed to pay more than $4.89 for £1.

At the same time, no one could ever hope to get a pound for less than $4.85. A British importer needing dollars could always get 113 grains of gold at home for £1. By spending perhaps 2 cents more, he could move them to Washington, D.C., where a ready government would exchange them for $4.87. His net proceeds would be $4.85. Therefore, nobody would ever sell pounds for less than this.

In short, whenever two governments defined their monetary unit in gold and announced their readiness to trade at this price, they also (indirectly) set the rate of exchange between their currencies. Because 23.22 grains of gold (defined as one dollar) go 4.87 times into 113 grains (defined as one pound), the *gold parity* rate of exchange was about $4.87 per £1. The actual rate prevailing was sure to be within pennies of this parity. This assured equivalence in terms of gold. Anyone who traded across national frontiers was assured of getting paid in his own currency and of getting paid at a rate he could predict for years in advance.

But consider what this type of arrangement involved in the way of governmental economic policy. Governments promised, as we saw, "to pursue all necessary policies to maintain this arrangement." Suppose the United States had a deficit in its balance of payments, like in Table 15.1. Suppose foreigners were accumulating dollars and converting some of them into gold. This meant a severe threat to the system. Sooner or later, the United States would run out of the yellow metal and could not continue to sell gold. Thus, a policy aimed at avoiding this contingency was called for. He who promises the impossible (to sell, if need be, unlimited quantities of gold) can keep his promise only by making sure of never being put to the test! Indeed, under these circumstances, the U.S. government would have vigorously pursued a *tight monetary policy*. The idea was this:

Higher interest rates might have persuaded foreigners to use their dollars to buy our bonds rather than our gold (raising the entry in account E, column (1), Table 15.1, from zero to some positive figure). They would have persuaded Americans to buy securities at home rather than abroad (lowering the entry in account E, column (2)). Tight money would have also cut aggregate demand (as we saw in Chapter 10), including that for foreign goods (lowering entries in accounts A and B, column (2), Table 15.1). In addition, the slackness of aggregate demand, together with the accompanying declines of real GNP and employment, would have put a quick end to any signs of inflation. Prices might have actually fallen. In either case, exports of commodities and services would have been encouraged (raising entries in accounts A and B, column (1), Table 15.1). And the relatively lower prices here would have further discouraged imports from abroad. The deficit would have tended to disappear!

Foreign governments, equally committed to making the gold standard work, would have reinforced all these effects. Countries with a balance-of-payments surplus that were importing our gold and accumulating our dollars would have pursued a vigorous policy of *easy money*. Their increased aggregate demand would have spilled over into increased demand for foreign, including American goods. This would have been strengthened by inflationary pressures there and deflationary ones in the United States. The low interest rates there would have led to greater purchases of securities abroad, including the United States, where rates were higher. The balance-of-payments surplus, mirror image of the American deficit, would have declined and disappeared.

As people used to put it, the gold standard would "automatically" take care of balance-of-payments deficits and surpluses. The taking care part was true enough, but there was little truth to the claim about automaticity. For the system to work, governments had to be willing to abide by the "rules of the game." They had to be willing not to change the gold content of their currency (a purely arbitrary law). They had to be willing to trade gold freely at the legal price. They had to be willing to pursue policies contracting or expanding aggregate demand with a view *solely to the balance of payments*. The eradication of unemployment or inflation at home had to be *subordinated* to the needs of the international economy. A balance-of-payments deficit meant tight money cutting aggregate demand, even if it should lead to unemployment. A balance-of-payments surplus meant easy money raising aggregate demand, even if it should lead to inflation. Unless a deficit country just happened to be bothered by inflation, or unless a surplus country just happened to be engulfed by unemployment, equilibrating the balance of payment meant deliberately creating turmoil in the domestic economy. No responsible government nowadays is willing to allow this to happen. That is why the old-fashioned gold standard died during the Great Depression.

Direct Controls

Under the old-fashioned gold standard, complete freedom of trade and lending across national frontiers was viewed as an ideal. As we saw, achievement of this ideal required a willingness to pay a high price if needed: complete tolerance of domestic unemployment and inflation. The United Kingdom, for instance, suffered from a prolonged depression even in the 1920's, when most countries enjoyed a hitherto unequaled prosperity. This happened precisely because the British government was determined to preserve the gold standard at the pre-World War I gold and foreign exchange value of the pound sterling. Winston Churchill, then Chancellor of the Exchequer, considered it a matter of national honor and prestige. Millions of people unemployed for a decade were the price paid for achieving this dubious goal. In the end, Britain, like everyone else and earlier than most (1931), went "off gold." Governments everywhere proceeded to institute direct controls to deal with their balances of payments. You may use Table 15.1 as a kind of checklist of the kinds of policies that were involved. To cut imports of commodities and services (accounts A and B, column (2)), governments levied higher and higher taxes on such imports (tariffs). They also limited them by fixing directly maximum amounts of certain goods that could be imported (quotas) and maximum amounts that travelers could spend abroad. Capital movements were strictly controlled by requiring special permits for them. Sometimes, *exchange controls* were introduced. All export proceeds had to be sold to the government, which doled out the foreign money so received as long as it lasted to whomever it considered engaged in "desirable" import activities.

Note that no country has complete control over its balance of payments, even when it uses such radical policies. Other countries are likely to react to anything done by the first. If you limit your imports, they will limit theirs in turn. Thus, a fall in your imports is followed by a fall in your exports, too. What looked like an improvement in your balance-of-payments deficit may end up as no change at all with a reduced volume of international trade and lending all around. This happened in the 1930's. The volume of trade and lending fell precipitously as countries tried desperately to isolate, through direct controls, their domestic economies from international complications.

The Modified Gold Standard

Contemplating the postwar period and hoping to avoid a recurrence of domestic and international economic chaos of the 1930's, representatives of forty-four nations met at Bretton Woods, New Hampshire, in 1944. Their aim was to reach an international agreement that would allow postwar governments to pursue full employment and price stability at home without having to restrict the flow of trade and lending across their frontiers. They did reach such an agreement. It led, in 1946, to the establishment of the International Monetary Fund. This organization has presently over 100 members—almost every country in the world, excluding those of the Soviet bloc.

The International Monetary Fund, or IMF, as it is called for short, is the present-day equivalent of the old-fashioned gold standard. As in the olden days, member countries have defined their respective currency units in terms of gold. Unlike the period before the Great Depression, however, this has been done by mutual agreement, rather than unilaterally. The gold content of the dollar, for instance, has been set at 13.71 grains of pure gold, that of the British pound sterling at 32.91 grains.

Unlike previously, however, governments are not willing to trade gold freely with all comers. Private citizens in many countries, including the United States, are even forbidden to hold any gold except for specified "legitimate" purposes, such as for dentistry or the industrial arts. Central banks of member countries buy gold freely at the established legal price, but they sell gold only to other member central banks (and the aforementioned "legitimate" users). As a result, the old mechanism by which exchange rates were held stable (private export or import of gold) does not function.

the foreign exchange market   Foreign monies are nowadays exchanged in what may on the surface appear as completely free markets. Actually, they are not that free. As we shall see shortly, governments strongly influence the forces of supply and demand in those markets.

Foreign exchange is traded through foreign exchange dealers, mostly banks in financial centers, such as New York, Chicago, or San Francisco. They buy and sell dollars and foreign moneys through branch offices or other banks in foreign financial centers, such as London, Paris, or Tokyo. They establish prices to equilibrate supply and demand. Figure 15.1 THE FOREIGN EXCHANGE MARKET illustrates the process. On the vertical axis, we measure the dollar price per unit of foreign money, or the exchange rate. On the horizontal axis, we measure the quantity of foreign money traded. As an illustration, let us just consider foreign trade with Great Britain (or with countries using its currency unit, the pound sterling, or £). For simplicity, we shall assume that any purchase abroad requires in the same period a corresponding purchase of foreign money. If you want to buy a watch in Britain, for example, you must first buy British money. In any given period, there will then be a certain demand for pounds (because we want to import the kind of things listed in accounts A to E of Table 15.1). There will be a certain supply of pounds because we export similar items. If an Englishman wants to buy an American tennis racket, say, he must first offer pounds to get American money. The exact quantity of pounds demanded or supplied will vary with their price. We are assuming here that more pounds will be demanded at a lower exchange rate. Thus the demand curve slopes down to the right. For instance, if each pound costs $7, we have to pay $14 for a watch costing £2 in Britain and we may buy 100 million watches. This requires us to buy £2 × 100 = £200 million (point c on the graph). If each pound costs only $2.40, we have to pay only $4.80 for the British £2 watch. Thus, we may buy more, say 170 million watches. This requires us to buy £2 × 170 = £340 million (point d on the graph).

We are also assuming that fewer pounds will be supplied at a lower exchange rate, thus the supply curve slopes down to the left. For instance, if each pound trades for $7, British citizens have to pay £1 for a tennis racket costing $7 in the United States. They may buy 200 million rackets. This requires them to buy $7 × 200 = $1,400 million, or to offer 1400/7 = £200 million (point c on the graph). If each pound trades for only $2.40, however, the British have to pay £2.9 for the American $7 racket. Thus they may buy less, say 38 million rackets. This requires them to buy $7 × 38 = $266 million, or to offer 266/2.40 ≐ £110.8 million (point e on the graph).[1]

Figure 15.1   THE FOREIGN EXCHANGE MARKET

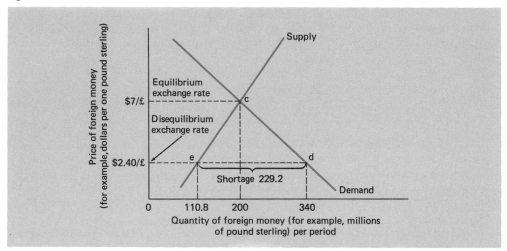

A supply and demand diagram can help us understand the functioning of the market for foreign money. The demand curve shows alternative quantities of foreign money people would buy at alternative exchange rates. The supply curve shows alternative quantities of foreign money that would be offered. Given the curves in the graph, only an exchange rate of $7 per pound would assure equilibrium in the foreign exchange market and (we assume) in the balance of payments. If the rate were, say, below equilibrium, as at $2.40 per pound, the balance of payments would be in disequilibrium. As long as it can supply a quantity such as 229.2 million pounds per period, a government can keep the market rate below the equilibrium, however.

Now suppose that the example just discussed, and illustrated in Figure 15.1, represented all U.S. foreign trade in a year. Given a completely *unrestricted* market in foreign money, foreign exchange dealers would trade at an exchange rate of $7/pound, with quantity supplied and demanded equal at £200 million per year. Trade would not take place at $2.40 per

---

[1] Note that this is just one possibility. As advanced texts would show, the British might also offer *more* pounds, although buying *fewer* American goods. What if their purchases had dropped in response to the tennis racket price increase (as *they* see it from £1 to £2.9), from 200 to 190 million rackets? Then they would have had to buy $7 × 190 = $1,330 million, which means offering 1,330/2.40, or £554 million. *More* than before!

£, for that would create a shortage in the market. The exchange rate would rise to equilibrium in a free market.

Under the old-fashioned gold standard, what would have happened? If the Americans had defined 13.71 grains of gold as a dollar, and the British 2.4 times that much, or 32.91 grains, as a pound sterling, nobody would have been willing to buy or sell pound sterling at any price far removed from the gold parity rate of $2.40 per pound. At that exchange rate, to be sure, Americans would have been earning only £110.8 million (exporting 38 million tennis rackets). They would have been trying to spend £340 million (importing 170 million watches). And they could have, for that deficit of £340 million − £110.8 million, or £229.2 million, would have been financed by exports of gold. Before paying $7/£, American importers or their banks would have exchanged dollars for gold, shipped the gold to Britain and exchanged it for £229.2 million. They would have ended up paying at most $2.42 for a pound. There would have been no shortage. Tennis rackets *and gold* would have paid for the watches bought at the parity rate of exchange.

In the meantime, as we saw above, the governments involved would have taken measures to eliminate the gold flow. Graphically, these measures would have shifted the supply curve to the right and the demand curve to the left until they intersected somewhere between e and d *at the parity rate of exchange* of $2.40/£. This would have converted the disequilibrium to an equilibrium rate. See Figure 15.2 GOLD STANDARD: DEFICIT FINANCING AND REMOVAL.

The moment we remove the possibility of private gold purchase and export in the face of a balance-of-payments deficit, we seem to remove the stability of the exchange rate. What is there to prevent it from rising to $7/£, if private demand is so eager and private demanders have no alternative sources of pounds?

the exchange stabilization fund   The founders of the International Monetary Fund, well aware of this problem, designed an alternative procedure to keep exchange rates stable at the parity rates implied by their currencies' official gold content. They agreed to establish "exchange stabilization funds." These are governmental agencies that buy or sell foreign monies in whatever amounts necessary to keep the market exchange rate within a narrow range of the desired parity rate. Take a situation such as that depicted in part (a) of Figure 15.2 GOLD STANDARD: DEFICIT FINANCING AND REMOVAL, for instance. The U.S. stabilization fund would "support" the desired exchange rate of $2.40/£ by selling £229.2 million per year. (These pounds may have been accumulated in the past, or they may be acquired presently with gold from the Bank of England.)

The situation would be similar if it were desired to support a gold parity rate at say $9/£, *above* the market equilibrium at c. Then our exporters would be earning more pounds than our importers would care to buy and use. To prevent the exchange rate from falling to the market equilibrium level, the exchange stabilization fund would then intervene and buy the surplus foreign money. In this way, the exchange stabilization fund is designed to do what private citizens and banks did under the old-fashioned gold standard: keep the exchange rate stable at the gold par.

Figure 15.2   GOLD STANDARD: DEFICIT FINANCING AND REMOVAL

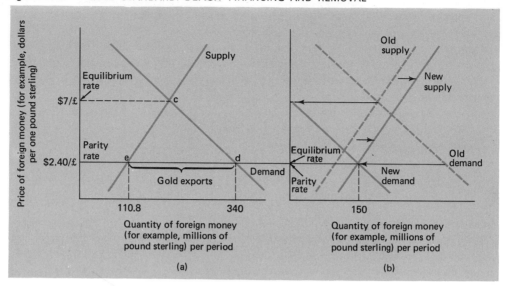

This graph illustrates how a balance-of-payments deficit was financed, and then removed, under the old gold standard. Part (a) is a duplicate of Figure 15.1. If the gold parity rate was below the free market equilibrium rate of exchange, nongold exports would bring in less foreign money (here 110.8 million pounds) than was needed for nongold imports (here 340 million pounds). Gold exports would bring in the difference, thereby preventing the exchange rate from rising to its equilibrium. Because it could not export gold forever, the deficit country government would pursue a tight monetary policy. This would stop any inflation. It might even create unemployment. The result is seen in part (b). The demand for foreign goods, stocks, bonds, and so on would drop. Hence, the demand for foreign money to buy these things would drop. Note the leftward shift of the demand curve. With less inflation and possibly even lower prices in the deficit country, foreigners would buy more goods. Interest rates being higher, they might buy more bonds, too. Thus the supply of foreign money to the deficit country would rise. Note how the supply curve shifted right. If the surplus country deliberately created inflationary full employment by easy money, all these effects would be reinforced. Thus gold exports would cease to be necessary. The deficit would disappear. The parity rate of exchange would become an equilibrium rate. Nongold exports (of 150 million pounds) would pay for nongold imports of equal value.

the need for liquidity   Note, however, what this involves. If a country has a balance-of-payments surplus, it requires purchases of foreign money by the fund. If it were willing to accumulate foreign money forever, this could easily be continued without limit. If a country has a balance-of-payments deficit (as pictured here), it requires perpetual sales of foreign money by the fund. Although it is easy enough for a U.S. government agency to *buy* unlimited quantities of foreign money (it can always manufacture the dollars needed to do so), it cannot *sell* unlimited quantities of foreign money. It will run out of its reserves of pounds, for instance, and it cannot manufacture them. For a time, it can replenish its supply of pounds by buying them from the Bank of England with gold, but it can also run out of gold. Then, if it still has to sell pounds to the public, there are only three choices left: borrow gold to buy more pounds, borrow pounds, or quit supporting the rate of exchange at the disequilibrium level. Because the International Monetary Fund members prefer to keep exchange rates stable, maintaining "liquidity," that is, owning or being able to borrow gold and foreign currencies is of major importance to them. As the name suggests, the organization revolves around a *fund* of gold and member country currencies, a total now exceeding $10 billion. Each member has contributed to the fund in accordance with a "quota" related to the member's GNP. The U.S. contribution is about a third of the total. This fund is available for lending to members who can borrow gold and foreign currencies for the purposes described above, up to a quarter of their quota in any 1 year. However, such loans are designed to be temporary. They must be repaid promptly, at interest. They are to allow a country, faced with a temporary deficit, to maintain a stable exchange rate without having to engage (as under the old-fashioned gold standard) in economic policies possibly destructive to its domestic economy.

devaluation by agreement   But suppose a country's balance of payments deficit (as illustrated by the $2.40/£ rate in Figure 15.1) is not temporary. It persists. The country supports the rate as long as it can. It runs out of owned gold and foreign money to sell, it exhausts its possibilities to borrow at the IMF. Then, according to IMF rules, the country may "devalue" its currency without having to fear retaliation by the other countries. Devaluation simply means reducing the official gold content of the currency unit. Suppose the United States reduced it from the aforementioned 13.71 grains to 4.70 grains per dollar. Collaboration within the IMF would assure that other countries do not act likewise. Given the British gold content of 32.91 grains per pound, the gold parity rate of exchange would change to become 32.91 divided by 4.70, or $7.00/£. (Had the British retaliated and devalued also to, say, 11.28 grains per pound, the new exchange rate would have remained at the old level of $2.40/£.) In terms of Figure 15.1, the deficit would have disappeared. This would have been owing to two facts. The rise in the exchange rate following devaluation would make U.S. imports more expensive and discourage them. It would make U.S. exports cheaper to foreigners and encourage them. Although there is no guarantee for it, a forceful devaluation thusly might eliminate a payments deficit entirely. According to the IMF agreement, any member nation, faced with a persistent payments disequilibrium, may change its exchange rate by up to 10 percent by just notifying the fund. Any larger change (as contemplated in our example) requires prior approval by the fund's directors. The overriding goal of the IMF is to preserve as much freedom of international trade and lending as possible at basically stable exchange rates without eroding the member nations' power to fight the business cycle at home.

THE U.S. BALANCE-OF-PAYMENTS PROBLEM

As we mentioned earlier, the United States has had a balance-of-payments deficit for many years, but it has only been regarded as serious in the last decade. The reasons for this go back to the end of World War II. At that time, Europe and Japan lay devastated. The

United States was more prosperous than ever before and unbombed. From 1940 to 1945, U.S. real GNP had risen by 56 percent, real consumption by 18 percent, in spite of the war. Our allies were deeply indebted to the United States and without foreign assets. Though they first bought war material and civilian goods from the United States, they eventually received huge loans. At the war's end, far from being able to repay, they were now eager for more. The vast productive power of the United States and seemingly limitless reconstruction needs abroad seemed made for each other. But Europe had nothing to offer in exchange. This was the time of the *dollar shortage*.

The Marshall Plan provided billions of dollars of aid as an answer. Europeans used the dollars so received, with no strings attached, to buy goods in the United States, from each other, and elsewhere. They were eager also to add dollars to their depleted reserves of foreign exchange, to buy U.S. securities, or to buy U.S. gold. While the U.S. balance of trade was in surplus, its balance of payments was in deficit (like Table 15.1 above). The United States, however, did not need to worry. We were the world's banker, providing through our deficits the means of financing a swelling volume of world trade. These deficits were welcome; foreigners seemed to have an unending appetite for more dollars. They were the world's key currency—as good as gold.

Then came the mid-1950's. Western Europe, Japan, and the U.S.S.R. had recovered. Their prosperity was restored. Their rate of GNP growth soared to more than twice that of the United States. And their appetite for dollars ebbed. Yet the United States continued to pour more dollars into the rest of the world than it took back in. U.S. aid, private investment abroad, and defense expenditures around the world more than offset a continued large surplus in the U.S. balance of trade. Like the man who came to dinner, the U.S. deficits, though invited, stayed too long. The dollar shortage became a *dollar glut*. America's trading partners began to cash in more and more dollars in gold. Their needs for dollars to finance imports from the United States and to finance trade among one another were more than satisfied. At this point, in the late 1950's, it became obvious that the U.S. deficit was not sustainable any longer. Counteraction was required. It is the need for this action that has been throwing an ever longer and darker shadow over U.S. domestic policies for the past several years.

Dealing with the Deficit

measures short of devaluation   At first no one seriously suggested changing the gold content of the U.S. dollar. Under these circumstances, what could the United States do to eliminate its deficit? There are many possibilities. Just consider what you could do if you had a deficit in your balance of payments. You could export more commodities or services (sell or rent commodities you own, work more). You could try to get more gifts (exporting thank-you-notes). You could try to get long-term loans or reduce your claims on others (borrow long-term or sell stocks, bonds, deeds, and the like). And, of course, you could import less of these same things (buy fewer commodities, fewer services of other people's property and labor, give fewer gifts, make fewer long-term loans, buy fewer stocks, bonds, deeds, and so on). The U.S. government must make Americans *as a group* do these very same things if it is to eliminate a deficit in the U.S. balance of payments. Here are some things it *could* do:

1. The United States could encourage commodity and service exports by vigorously fighting inflation here or by government subsidies to exporters. If this is successful, while foreign prices remain the same or rise, U.S. prices compared to foreign prices fall (*relatively*, if not absolutely), and foreigners may buy more here. If moral suasion does not eliminate inflation, tight monetary and fiscal policies creating large general unemployment will work (as we saw in the last chapter). In addition, exports can be pushed by "tying" foreign aid, that is, foreign recipients can be forced to spend aid money in the United States, even if better bargains can be struck elsewhere.

2. The United States could encourage foreigners to make gifts to us (as for the maintenance of American troops abroad) or to others in our place (as for foreign economic development).

3. The United States could ask foreigners to make more long-term loans to the United States at high interest rates brought about by tight money policy. (Such external debt, whether public or private, *would* put a burden on the shoulders of future generations. However, we might also give them a possibly larger *benefit*, if we use the proceeds to import capital goods enabling the future to produce a lot more. Since 1966, something like that seems to be happening in that borrowing by United States businesses abroad has been rising after Commerce Department encouragement.)

4. The United States could encourage foreigners to buy here all types of ownership interests. The tight monetary and fiscal policies pursued under (1) will probably help to create a general feeling of pessimism, depressing prices of stocks, land, and so on.

5. The United States could discourage commodity and service imports by reducing aggregate demand in general through the same tight monetary and fiscal policies. This may be strengthened by raising tariffs and instituting direct quantitative import restrictions (quotas on commodities, forbidding dependents of servicemen to live abroad, forbidding Americans to travel abroad on foreign ships, and the like). As evidence of this kind of policy, in 1959, Defense Secretary McNamara ordered U.S. military supplies and services bought in the United States as long as their cost here exceeded their foreign cost by no more than 50 percent. In 1968, the President ordered cuts in troop spending and in civilian government employment and travel abroad. He also asked all Americans to defer for two years nonessential travel outside the Western Hemisphere. And note the fears expressed by experts in 1969, as shown in the news report introducing this chapter: The Fed might have to choose between eliminating our payments deficit or unemployment. Because one calls for tight money, the other for easy money, it cannot do both.

6 . The United States could encourage Americans to make fewer gifts abroad (cut immigrants' remittances, cut foreign aid).

7. The United States could ask or force Americans to make fewer long-term loans abroad and to buy fewer ownership interests abroad. This has become particularly relevant since the establishment of the European Common Market. From 1960–1965, as U.S. com-

panies crossed the Atlantic to set up their beachheads, U.S. direct investment in West Germany rose 165 percent, in Italy 150 percent, in France 130 percent, in Holland 115 percent, in Belgium and Luxembourg 100 percent. A *voluntary program of restraint* was introduced in 1965 under the aegis of the Federal Reserve System and the Department of Commerce. In 1968, it was made mandatory for private businesses, with a lower permitted level of capital exports, including reinvestment of earnings abroad. This was especially directed toward continental Europe. This was reinforced by Federal Reserve guidelines to U.S. financial institutions as to restricted lending to foreigners. (As noted in the news report introducing this chapter, these restrictions were somewhat relaxed in 1969, possibly prematurely.)

High interest rates at home may also help to keep funds here; a tax on earnings made abroad may strengthen this effect further. (Such an *interest equalization* tax was introduced in 1963 on foreign securities issued in developed countries other than Canada. It hit Americans who had increasingly been buying "high-flying" issues of growing firms in Western Europe and Japan. Again, however, note the introductory news report.)

It hardly needs mentioning that many such policies are, or would be, highly unwelcome here and abroad. If the U.S. government interferes with free international trade through tariffs and quotas, foreigners are likely to retaliate in kind. The net effect would be less trade both ways and (for us) possibly the same deficit. A cut in foreign aid interferes with foreign policy. A cut in private aid, loans, and acquisition of equity abroad interferes with the freedom of American households and businesses and is highly resented. Equally resented would be increased foreign control of American business. And most resented of all, and indeed intolerable, would be a depression deliberately brought about. In short, a balance-of-payments crisis can be cured, but (under present international arrangements and at the present rates of exchange) probably not without seriously interfering with a variety of goals, including that of bringing about full employment without inflation! On the other hand, pursuit of the latter goal at a time when general unemployment and a balance-of-payments deficit coexist would probably worsen the deficit.

devaluing the dollar

An increasing number of economists have therefore suggested that the United States make use of the mechanism provided by the IMF and devalue the dollar drastically. The U.S. government, however, has rejected and continues to reject that possibility out of hand.

One reason given is that our trading partners simply could not afford to abide by the IMF agreement and *not* retaliate in kind. The entire international monetary system would collapse, returning us to the dark and chaotic days of the 1930's. The reason why our partners would have to retaliate, these people argue, is that a successful U.S. devaluation would raise U.S. exports and lower U.S. imports of goods (as hoped for) by many billions of dollars. This would constitute an increase in the United States of net export demand and, given some unemployment, a welcome, even though relatively small, rise in GNP and employment. Abroad, however, there would occur a corresponding fall in net export demand. Given the smaller size of the economies of some of our trading partners, this would lead to a *drastic* fall in their GNP and employment. Restoration of full employment by monetary and fiscal measures abroad would lead to balance-of-payments trouble abroad, not to mention the serious structural adjustments required as former export industries wither away and must be replaced by new kinds of activities.

Furthermore, these people argue, we have repeatedly given our word that we would not devalue. By breaking that promise, we would punish those friendly nations that refrained in years past from cashing in their dollars for gold. We would be unnecessarily rewarding those nations (such as France) that precipitated the run on the dollar by continually demanding gold and others (such as South Africa and the Soviet Union) that are big gold producers.

Moreover, argue the opponents of devaluation, we should avoid it from a purely selfish reason: devaluation worsens a country's *terms of trade*. Because our import prices go up relative to our export prices, from a barter point of view we will end up giving more goods away for fewer goods received.

replacing the IMF   Yet these arguments notwithstanding, some people would go even further than this. They argue that the only reasonable cure of the dilemma in the long run would be a complete *change* of present international monetary arrangements. It is only because of these arbitrary arrangements that the balance of payments (if in deficit) may put a certain restraint on easy monetary and fiscal policies needed for full employment. It seems only reasonable to change the arrangement, such as by forgetting about gold and stable exchange rates entirely.

Exchange rates, like prices of stocks or bonds, could become *freely flexible,* adjusting with supply and demand.

In terms of Figure 15.1, the exchange rate should be allowed to become $7/£ or any other figure necessary to balance supply and demand from day to day. Then monetary and fiscal policies would be freed from the shackles of the balance of payments to do whatever is necessary for eliminating demand inflation and general unemployment. Exchange rates would continually adjust to equilibrate the balance of payments as at point c in Figure 15.1. The frantic search for expedients to solve the balance-of-payments problem would come to an end. Flexible rates would put the small U.S. foreign trade sector in its proper place instead of blowing it up to dominate our economic policies. While flexible rates continually take care of the balance of payments, issues could finally be decided on proper grounds. Military expenditures could be decided on the basis of military effectiveness, not on the basis of saving foreign exchange. Aid to underdeveloped nations could be spent with a view to getting the most out of it, not with concern how to spend all of it in the United States. Congress could debate issues of aid on the basis of what is best for the United States, not worrying what best preserves our gold stock. Congress could set taxes on the basis of what is equitable, not on the basis of what helps along exports of goods, while discouraging imports and capital exports. American businessmen could build plants wherever it is profitable, not just in places where our balance of payments is not put in jeopardy. Moreover, the need for international liquidity, in fact for the entire IMF, would disappear.

This argument, too, has serious opponents. Continual movements of exchange rates introduce a large degree of uncertainty into foreign trade. After all, international economic transactions do not occur in a timeless world. Between buying and selling, investing and reaping profit, certainly days, more likely weeks, months, and years will pass. Flexible exchange rates, argue some, will kill the goose that lays the golden egg, that is, eliminate all international trade and lending. Who, hoping to sell an imported watch for $5 in the United States, would dare order it for German marks not knowing how many dollars they will cost when the bill is due? And how would he decide whether to invest in a firm abroad if he had no inkling whatsoever what the rate will be at which future earnings can be converted back into dollars?

It is probably true that through flexible exchange rates long-term capital movements (in the balance-of-payments sense) will be discouraged. Yet, in the short run, uncertainty could probably be borne by professional speculators and need not be borne by those who engage in trading goods.[2]

strengthening the IMF   Rather than replacing the IMF, one could strengthen its effectiveness. This seems to be the road its member countries are most likely to take. There have already been increasingly closer cooperative efforts among the central banks of the member nations. Ten central banks, for instance, have reached an agreement to aid one another in calming fears and uncertainties about exchange rate stability. They have provided for supplements to the IMF lending facilities. In 1964, they arranged a $3 billion loan on 2 days' notice to support the British pound. Similar action was taken in 1968 to "save the French franc."

In 1967, at a conference in Rio de Janeiro, the members went further in this direction by agreeing to increase the power of the IMF itself through the deliberate creation of *special drawing rights* (SDR's), whenever an 85 percent member majority decides to do so. (This percentage gives an effective veto to the United States as well as the Common Market countries should they vote as a bloc.) SDR's are distributed in proportion to member quotas. They give holders the unconditional right to obtain convertible currencies from fund members. The SDR's have a gold value guarantee and have been called *paper gold*. They can be used as reserves in addition to and exactly like gold and member currencies have been used so far.

This arrangement was reached as a solution to the increased needs for international liquidity as world trade annually grows by 50 to 200 billion dollars. (At the time of this writing, in mid–1969, the 111 IMF member countries had just ratified the Rio agreement.)

Others, such as Yale's Robert Triffin, would have liked to go even further beyond the Rio agreement and create an international central bank. This bank would create and hold reserves of national central banks. Thus, it would regulate the supply of all international means of payments in exactly the same way as the Fed regulates that of our domestic means of payments. It would dispense with the need internationally for gold and its equivalent

---

[2] Speculators buy goods or money now for future delivery at a price agreed on now. Those interested in this point may wish to consult the brilliant little essay by Abba P. Lerner, "What Would We Do without the Speculator?" in *Everybody's Business* (New York: Harper, 1961).

(convertible currencies and SDR's) the same way as gold and gold certificates have been dispensed with domestically. International reserves would be created as needed. There would be no tying of the volume of international reserves to the rate at which gold is being dug from the ground, the price at which it is being bought by the U.S. Treasury, the size of U.S. payments deficits, and similar arbitrary arrangements. Runs on national central banks would be eliminated just like runs on individual commercial banks have been.

However, this scheme is likely to founder on the rock of politics for some time. It goes too far too fast. Countries are unlikely to give up the degree of national sovereignty that would be required for this.

CONCLUSION

Given present international monetary arrangements, consisting of the IMF strengthened by the Rio agreements, it is more likely that the United States will insist on preserving the present gold value of the dollar and fixed exchange rates. As a result, we can expect continued efforts to solve the balance-of-payments problems by policies that clash with other goals, including those to achieve and preserve full employment without inflation.

SUMMARY

1 A country's balance of payments is a systematic record of all its economic transactions during a period with the rest of the world. The balance of payments is set up by double-entry bookkeeping and always necessarily balances. Yet it may be in disequilibrium owing to imbalances in particular accounts. The balance-of-payments deficit or surplus measures the extent of disequilibrium.

2 The disequilibrium in the balance of payments can be cured in a variety of ways. Under the old-fashioned gold standard, governments defined their currencies in gold and freely traded gold at this rate. This led to stable exchange rates and gold exports in the face of deficits, gold imports in the face of surpluses. Central banks put an end to such gold movements by creating monetary tightness in the face of deficits and gold losses, monetary ease in the face of surpluses and gold imports. Resulting changes in GNP, employment, and prices led to a restoration of balance-of-payments equilibrium.

3 During the 1930's, sacrificing the domestic goals of full employment and price stability for equilibrium in the country's external accounts became politically unacceptable. As a result, the gold standard broke down. Direct controls of foreign trade and lending led to a disastrous decline in the volume of international transactions.

4 The International Monetary Fund was founded in 1946. It aims at avoiding both the bad experiences of the 1930's and of the gold standard. It hopes to achieve free international trade and lending at essentially stable exchange rates without sacrifice of domestic policy goals. For this purpose, the IMF provides liquidity (gold and convertible currencies and now SDR's) to member countries that wish to be helped over temporary balance-of-payments difficulties without a change in the exchange rate. This liquidity allows the operation of governmental exchange stabilization funds. For persistent balance-of-payments trouble, the IMF provides a machinery for orderly exchange rate adjustment by international agreement.

5 The United States has had a persistent balance-of-payments deficit for most of the post-World War II period. This was at first welcome because dollars provided needed world liquidity. More recently, however, the previous dollar shortage has turned into a dollar glut, accumulation by foreigners of *undesired* dollar balances. This calls for measures to eliminate the U.S. deficit.

6 The United States has engaged in a great variety of stopgap measures to cut its deficit. Most of them are highly unpalatable curbs on free trade and lending. They even include Federal Reserve measures that tend to increase unemployment and keep real GNP below potential.

7 There seems to be little taste for a U.S. devaluation under IMF auspices at present. Nor is a replacement of the IMF by freely flexible exchange rates likely. Most likely, there will be continued reliance on the type of U.S. policies presently being pursued. There will be additional pressures, however, to guide the IMF toward a supernational central bank that can create its own means of international payments. This would eliminate the role of gold and U.S. dollars as the key currencies of the international economy.

TERMS[3]

balance of capital	dollar glut
balance of current account	dollar shortage
balance of gold	exchange controls
balance of payments	exchange rate
balance-of-payments deficit or surplus	exchange stabilization fund
	foreign exchange
balance-of-payments disequilibrium	gold parity rate
balance of services	gold standard
balance of trade	international liquidity
balance of unilateral transfers	International Monetary Fund
capital export	quota
capital import	short- vs. long-term capital movements
credit	
current account	special drawing right
debit	tariff
deflation	title
devaluation	unilateral transfer

[3] Terms and symbols are defined in the Glossary at the end of the book.

SYMBOLS

IMF
SDR

QUESTIONS FOR REVIEW AND DISCUSSION

1   Consider the following transactions of a student during a 3-day period and set up his balance of payments in conventional terminology (as in Table 15.1).
   a. He works for $10, but does not yet get paid.
   b. He sells a $5 book to a friend for cash.
   c. He sends a $5 check to his brother as a gift.
   d. He spends $2 on a haircut.
   e. He spends $1,500 of his demand deposit on all kinds of commodities he likes.
   f. He borrows $100 at a bank and pays his tuition.

2   Do you think our above friend's balance of payments is in equilibrium? Why or why not? (Hint: This depends on whether the situation can be maintained. Thus you may answer either way by making appropriate assumptions.)

3   Show how the balance of payments differs from a balance sheet (a) verbally; (b) by showing how each transaction in question 1 would *change* the student's balance sheet (if it affects his balance sheet at all).

4   Show why the balance on current account equals net export demand.

5   Describe the U.S. balance-of-payments problem.

6   Make a list of the actions one might conceivably undertake to solve a balance-of-payments deficit. How about a surplus? Would that be equally urgent?

7   "Policies to cure a balance of payments disequilibrium and domestic policies for full employment without inflation need not always clash." Explain. (Hint: what if the deficit exists at a time of demand inflation; what if a surplus exists at a time of general unemployment?)

8   "Short-term capital movements that seek protection abroad from monetary and political uncertainty at home (so-called "hot money") should be outlawed." Evaluate. What could this statement mean?

9   "A tight monetary policy may worsen rather than help a balance-of-payments deficit: it may generate a recession and falling profits, causing Americans to invest directly abroad by buying plant and equipment there in search for higher profits." Evaluate. Could this happen? Why or why not?

10 MR. A: "A tax cut to reduce unemployment is likely to worsen a country's balance of payments, because a more prosperous economy will import more."
   MR. B: "Profitable operation of domestic businesses at full capacity will keep wayward investment funds at home, and this will strengthen the balance of payments."
   Evaluate. Who is right? Why?

11 What is there to prevent the U.S. government from subsidizing all its export industries so that we can undersell all foreigners in everything? Why not solve our balance-of-payments problem this way?

12 At one point in the 1960's the Fed engaged in "operation twist," raising short-term interest rates while keeping long-term interest rates stable. Can you think of a reason?

13 In mid-1959, the Federal Reserve System abandoned its role as stabilizer of the domestic economy. It gave priority, as central banks have always done historically, to the balance of international payments. Should it have?

14 In the 1930's, countries imposed import duties to solve their balance-of-payments problems. They also hoped to solve their domestic unemployment problems in this way. Such policies, if successful, would "export" a country's unemployment to other countries. On the basis of your knowledge of the theory of output determination (Chapter 7), how would such "beggar-thy-neighbor" policy work?

15 The text says that "although there is no guarantee for it, a forceful devaluation might thusly eliminate a payments deficit entirely." Even assuming other countries do not neutralize the move by also devaluating, why isn't there a guarantee?

16 What would you think are the effects of a devaluation on real GNP, employment, and domestic prices?

17 What do you think would happen to its balance of payments if a country experienced rapid inflation?

18 Two of the most widely used definitions of the U.S. balance-of-payments deficit are the "liquidity" concept and the "official settlements" concept. Both include the net loss of U.S. reserves (gold and foreign monies convertible into gold). The former adds to this figure all net increases in liquid dollar claims by foreigners. The latter adds only net increases in liquid dollar claims by foreign monetary authorities, not by private parties. How reasonable, do you think, are these definitions? How do they differ (if at all) from the definition used for illustrative purposes in the text?

19 "European central bankers, by complaining continually about the 'soundness' of the dollar and by withdrawing gold from the United States or by threatening to do so, have pressured the Fed into giving the balance of payments priority over domestic policies. This is preposterous. It is time to change the present international monetary system." Discuss.

20 Stanford's Emile Despres has proposed to create a frankly dollar-based international monetary arrangement. To counter those speculators who buy and hold gold (in the hope that the United States will devalue the dollar and thus raise the dollar price of gold), he advised the U.S. Treasury to *reduce* the price of gold by the device of refusing to buy gold, while continuing to sell it at $35 per ounce while the supply lasts. When it is gone, gold would be demonetized, and reduced to the status of any other metal. Evaluate the proposal. What would be the effects? Are they desirable?

АКАДЕМИЯ НАУК СССР
ИНСТИТУТ ЭКОНОМИКИ

ПОЛИТИЧЕСКАЯ ЭКОНОМИЯ

-УЧЕБНИК-

★

ТРЕТЬЕ, ПЕРЕРАБОТАННОЕ И ДОПОЛНЕННОЕ ИЗДАНИЕ

МОСКВА
Государственное Издательство
ПОЛИТИЧЕСКОЙ ЛИТЕРАТУРЫ
1959

ACADEMY OF SCIENCES, USSR
INSTITUTE OF ECONOMICS

POLITICAL
ECONOMY

TEXT

3RD, REVISED
AND ENLARGED EDITION

MOSCOW
GOVERNMENT PUBLISHER
OF POLITICAL LITERATURE
1959

Every society requires . . . certain proportions in the distribution of labor and nonlabor resources over the various sectors of the economy. Under capitalism these necessary proportions are brought about during the process of production spontaneously, by continuous fluctuations which correct disproportions, by periodic crises of overproduction. This shows the basic flaw of capitalism. As Lenin put it: "Capitalism *requires crises* in order to bring about economic proportionality that is continually upset."

The socialist economy is free from this basic flaw of capitalism. The collective character of production [in any society] is in socialism based on the collective ownership of the nonlabor means of production. This collective ownership of the nonlabor means of production implies the necessity and possibility of a planned development of the socialist economy. As Engels said, the nationalization of the nonlabor means of production "makes finally possible a collective production in accordance with a predetermined plan."

Due to the collectivization of the nonlabor means of production, the necessary proportionality in the distribution of the nonlabor means of production and of labor over the sectors of the socialist economy is determined by plan. Spontaneity and free enterprise are incompatible with the existence of the collective ownership of the nonlabor means of production. Private property in the nonlabor means of production *divides* producers from each other and results in competition and anarchy in the process of production. In contrast, collective ownership *unites* numerous firms into a unified whole, subordinates them to one goal. . . .

Lenin showed the necessity for a planned development of the socialist economy. He pointed out that one cannot guide the economy without a long range plan and that the massive task of the socialist revolution is this: "Transforming the entire economic mechanism into a single giant machine, into an economic organism that works in such a way that hundreds of millions of people allow themselves to be guided by a single plan."

Just as capitalism is unthinkable without competition and anarchy in production (which imply a waste of resources), one cannot imagine socialism without a planned development of the economy (which guarantees a rational and frugal utilization of resources and their products).

The planned, proportional development of the economy is an economic law of socialism.

Translated from the Soviet textbook *Politicheskaya Ekonomiya* (Moscow, 1959)

16

the nature
of the centrally
planned economy

I N THE PREVIOUS chapters, we pursued a single theme: how the developed capitalist economy might deal with the great problems of unemployment and inflation. Inflation is a serious social evil that capriciously redistributes people's power to buy what has already been produced; unemployment is a problem that lies closer to the heart of economics. Our success or failure in eliminating unemployment determines how much is produced in the first place. It determines to what extent we succeed in reducing overall scarcity.

But what we have learned so far is only part of the story. As we shall see in Parts 2 and 3 of this book, scarcity can be reduced further, even after resources have been fully put to work. Before we proceed along these lines and discuss the importance of economic efficiency and economic growth, however, it is worthwhile to remind ourselves in this chapter and the next that our story is incomplete in still another sense. So far, we have completely neglected to account for the completely different framework within which economic activity is being carried on in many other countries. How, if at all, do they deal with unemployment and inflation?

In this chapter and the next, we look at the centrally planned socialist economies and their traditional methods of resource allocation. Although we shall refer mainly to data and institutions in the Soviet Union, the theoretical analysis presented here can be regarded as applicable to most fully socialist countries in the world. By making only appropriate changes in the descriptive material, we could just as well be telling the story of mainland China or the other East European countries, such as Albania, Bulgaria, Czechoslovakia, East Germany, Hungary, Poland, or Rumania.

A DIFFERENT FRAMEWORK

Before we can intelligently discuss how the Soviet economy performs when it comes to using resources fully and how it might do better, we must have a general idea of what it is like. It differs in every important respect from the type of economy in which most readers of this book are likely to have been brought up. As we saw in Chapter 2, the U.S.-type economy is preponderantly a *market* economy. In it *private* owners of labor, land, and capital, if they wish, sell the services of their resources for money in markets to *private* firms, which try to produce the kind of goods and the quantities of goods recipients of money income demand. This basic relationship was sketched in Figure 2.1 THE CIRCULAR FLOW.

We saw subsequently how government may be introduced into this basic framework. The government of a capitalist country can prevent its citizens (through taxes or borrowing) from getting all of potential output. It can then demand some of it itself (with money taxed, borrowed, or newly created) for collective use. It can do more than that. If all of potential output is not being produced to begin with, it can raise actual output toward the potential and eliminate involuntary unemployment by stepping into the circular flow with its own demand *without* cutting anybody else's demand. It can also raise private demand (by cutting taxes or by easy money) without cutting its own demand, achieving the same desirable consequence. And there are, of course, possible combinations of these policies. And there is room for the opposite policies if aggregate demand is too large. This framework will never do for the Soviet-type economy.

In the first place, all nonhuman resources (land and capital) are collectively owned and cannot be put to use by private owners. Firms are run not privately for profit, but by government-appointed salaried managers according to a *central economic plan*. This plan guides economic life. Theoretically, it could do so in any desired detail, prescribing what is to be produced in what quantities, how it is to be produced, and who is to get the output. In fact it will be most useful before discussing the actual Soviet economy to consider a model of a centrally planned economy. This will provide a most convenient framework for discussing socialist reality.

THE NATURE OF CENTRAL PLANNING

Imagine a socialist government appointing a Central Planning Board to plan all economic activity for the next year and to supervise the execution of this plan. Scarcity in socialism would also be *the* basic economic problem, for resources do not become more abundant by being publicly rather than privately owned. Hence, *full* utilization of available resources would be the first goal established by the board. Beyond that, it could simply proceed to assign to socialist firms physical output targets for hundreds of thousands of different goods (tons of this, numbers of that, square meters of the other thing), making sure that their production in the aggregate does not require more or fewer resources than are available. In one case, the plan would be unworkable. In the second case, they would produce below potential and be left with idle resources. Proceeding in this way, the board would very quickly stumble on a basic fact of economic life: *the production of any one good is intricately bound up with the production of all other goods.* Each output, by requiring inputs, affects other outputs, and so on, in a never-ending chain! The possibility of drawing up a plan that is internally inconsistent is, therefore, great and must be avoided. You will recall from Chapter 2, when you were asked to pretend being an economic dictator, how very difficult is the task any central planning board faces. Such a board would have to do a great deal more than, say, the U.S. government. As we saw, the U.S. government has a hard enough time trying to assure the proper level of *aggregate* demand. At least, it does not have to worry about the production of every single good, about the detailed *composition* of this aggregate. The price system takes care of that. (Note the news story introducing Chapter 2.) The socialist central planner, however, has to do both. He must worry about producing enough in the aggregate to avoid unemployment of resources. He must worry about the exact composition of this aggregate to avoid inconsistencies. That is, he cannot hope to get tractors unless he carefully plans for the steel needed to make them, for the iron ore to make steel, for freight cars to transport ore to steel mills, and so on. In theory, this planning could be performed with the help of *input-output analysis*. It could assure the full use of resources (the proper level of aggregate demand) as well as the proper allocation of resources (their correct use for the making of different goods).

The Input-Output Table

Input-output analysis is a mathematical technique revolving around the notion of economic interdependence just referred to. A basic part of it is the input-output table. Such a table shows systematically how (for instance, during 1969) each type of output and resource was distributed among all its users. A hypothetical input-output table is presented as Table 16.1 THE INPUT-OUTPUT TABLE AS A HISTORICAL DOCUMENT. For illustrative purposes, it has been enormously simplified by reducing the number of outputs and types of resources from millions to a few. Let us assume that this shorthand description of a country's economic activity during 1969 is a *complete* description of everything that has occurred. For illustration's sake, let it also be assumed that the products and resource services listed in the five rows are completely *homogeneous*. There exists only one kind of car, one kind of aluminum, one kind of corn, one kind of labor, and one kind of machine. To the extent that these assumptions do not hold in reality, a realistic input-output table would have to be greatly expanded, listing all products and resources as well as all types of qualities of each as a separate row.

The table is easily interpreted. Rows (1) to (3) (reading from left to right) show the *output* (of physical commodities) delivered by each type of producer listed on the left side of the table to each user listed on the top. The disposition of resource services (labor and capital) is also shown—rows (4) and (5). Hence each *column* (reading from top to bottom) shows the *inputs* received by each user listed on top from the producers or resource owners at the left. Therefore, the name *input-output table*.

The upper left corner of Table 16.1 has been set off by heavy lines. It is the *processing sector*, containing all the output of this year which was *in this year both produced and completely used up* within the processing sector. This is output, therefore, that cannot become available for what is called *final demand*, which means to households—column (4)—to the government—column (6)—to foreigners—column (7)—or for addition to the capital stock—column (5). Note that the entries in the processing sector columns measure the production of intermediate goods, a term we have learned in Chapter 5. The entries in the final demand sector columns measure the production of final goods.

The processing sector always contains an equal number of rows and columns. In a completely realistic table, it would include all types of manufacturing output (not just automobiles and aluminum), all types of agricultural output (besides corn), as well as other economic activities such as construction (number of houses built), transportation (million tons transported so many miles), communications (number of phone calls relayed), and trade (number of transactions negotiated).

The remaining rows, read all the way across the table, show the disposition of the services of *resources*, here of labor and capital. In our abbreviated version, this is represented by rows (4) and (5) only. In reality, there would be many rows, one of each *type* of labor, land, and capital (as defined in Chapter 1).

Table 16.1 THE INPUT-OUTPUT TABLE AS A HISTORICAL DOCUMENT

SOURCES →	USERS →							
	PROCESSING SECTOR			FINAL DEMAND SECTOR				
	(1) AUTOMOBILE PRODUCERS	(2) ALUMINUM PRODUCERS	(3) CORN PRODUCERS	(4) HOUSEHOLDS C	(5) CAPITAL FORMATION I	(6) GOVERNMENT G	(7) NET EXPORT NX	(8) TOTAL GROSS OUTPUT
Processing sector (1) Automobile producers (million cars)	1	1	1	5	2	3	−1	12
(2) Aluminum producers (million tons)	20	0	0	0	12	0	3	35
(3) Corn producers (million tons)	0	0	5	6	1	2	220	234
Resources (4) Labor force (million man-hours)	100	50	320	10	0	57	2	539
(5) Capital stock (million machine-hours)	30	0	0	0	0	0	5	35

An input-output table of a past year (1969, for example) shows how the output of producers and the services of resource owners listed on the left were delivered to a variety of users listed on the top (hypothetical figures).

A Detailed Interpretation

the rows   Row (1) tells us that 12 million cars were produced in 1969. Yet 1 million cars each were delivered to and during 1969 *completely used up* by the makers of automobiles (for example, for testing), of aluminum, and of corn (for transportation), respectively. Five million cars were delivered to households, 2 million cars were added to the capital stock (becoming some firm's equipment or inventories), and 3 million cars were delivered to the government. How could 13 million cars be delivered, if only 12 million were produced? Obviously because imports exceeded exports of cars by 1 million—row (1), column (7).

Row (2) tells us that of 35 million tons of aluminum produced in 1969, 20 million tons were delivered to and *completely used up* by automobile producers during the same year. No newly produced aluminum was used to make aluminum or to make corn. None was delivered to households or government, but 12 million tons were added to capital (inventories), and (net) 3 million tons were exported.

Row (3) informs us that of 234 million tons of corn produced in 1969, none were used in the production of automobiles or aluminum, but 5 millions tons were used up to make corn (for instance, as seed). Of the rest, households received 6 million tons, the capital stock (inventories) 1 million tons, government (as for the army) 2 million tons, and foreigners (net) 220 million tons.

Row (4) tells us that 539 million man-hours of labor were performed in 1969. (This might mean that 269,500 persons worked 50 weeks each for 40 hours.) Of these millions of man-hours, 100 were performed in the making of automobiles, 50 in aluminum production, 320 in corn production, while 10 were received by households directly (services of doctors, barbers, and the like), 57 by government directly (services of typists, judges, soldiers, and so on), and 2 by foreigners (advisers working abroad, barbers here serving foreign tourists, and so on). The entry in column (5) *must* be zero. It is logically impossible to add 1969 labor hours to the capital stock *as* buildings, equipment, or inventories to be used in 1970. Labor not performed cannot be stored.

Finally, row (5) tells us that existing machines (produced prior to 1969) were used for 35 million hours. (This might mean that 17,500 machines were used for 50 weeks, each for 40 hours.) In our case, 30 million hours of machine time were used by automobile producers and 5 million hours (net) by foreigners (we might have rented machinery to them). Nowhere else were machines used at all. Note that the entry in row (5), column (5) *must* be zero. One cannot logically add machine-hours to the capital stock. Capital services not performed (like the services of all resources) cannot be stored. That is exactly the tragedy of unemployment. The output not produced is gone forever. Not using machines may keep our capital stock from shrinking via wear and tear, but it will never enlarge it.

monetary equivalents   Note that we *could* translate all entries into monetary units. Reading across the rows, we would then get the total money *receipts* of each producer or resource owner on the left from each user on the top of the table. If the price were $1,000 per ton of aluminum, row (2) would tell us that aluminum producers had sales receipts of $35 billion—of which $20 billion came from automobile producers (who bought and used up new aluminum to that extent), $3 billion from foreigners, and $12 billion from all others (possibly including automobile producers) who added aluminum to inventories. Furthermore, the entries in the resource rows would correspond to the money incomes earned by resource owners. The money receipts for labor hours performed would be wages; those for allowing the use and using up of capital and land would be interest, rent, depreciation, and profit. In fact, the sums in column (8) of the resource rows (the *value* of 539 million man-hours, plus the value of 35 million machine-hours, and so on) would add exactly to the gross national income, equaling the GNP. However, we shall continue to use the input-output table in *physical,* rather than monetary, terms.

the columns   The meaning of the columns should be clear by implication. Let it be stressed, however, that the column labeled capital formation would list this year's new accumulation of new buildings, equipment, and inventories by all firms, *regardless of who exactly received them.* The 12 million tons of aluminum accumulated in inventories—row (2), column (5)—may be held by aluminum producers, corn producers, or automobile producers. If received by the latter, it would mean that automobile producers, while receiving 32 million tons, used up completely 20 million tons, storing the rest. Were we to turn the entries in the table into monetary units and read *down the columns*, we would again recognize an old friend. The processing sector columns would list the *cost* (including profit) involved in production. The automobile producers, for instance, would have bought and used up so many dollars worth of automobiles and aluminum (raw material costs), while incurring so many dollars worth of labor and other costs (wages, row (4); interest for the use, depreciation for the using up of capital, row (5); rents and profit in a more detailed table). The final demand sector columns would list the total *spending* by the familiar groups of demanders. Households would have bought so many dollars worth of automobiles, so many dollars worth of corn, and so many dollars worth of labor services, adding to personal consumption expenditures. Businesses would have bought so many dollars worth of new capital goods, adding to investment expenditures (*actual* investment), and so on for the other final demand columns. Hence, the sum of the totals under columns (4) to (7), if expressed in value terms, would add to the gross national expenditure, equaling the GNP. An input-output table in value terms could therefore give us the familiar two measures of the GNP (see page 95), once as the total value under the final demand columns, and again as the total value of the resource rows.

Planning Next Year's Economic Activity

Now let us return to our Central Planning Board. Imagine it to have gathered physical statistical data on what *actually* happened in a past year, as in our Table 16.1. The board can now proceed to plan *next* year's economic activity on this basis. First, it will determine the quantity of each resource available for use. There clearly is much room for arbitrary judgment at this point. Shall we consider a person working, as above, 40 hours a week for 50 weeks per year as fully employed? He *could* work more or less, and the same is true for the use of land and capital. Shall we allow voluntary unemployment? This, too, will have to be decided and has in the case of labor, of course, an immediate impact on the degree of human freedom maintained. This decision having been made, however, there will be certain maximum entries in column (8) of the resource rows above which the new economic plan cannot go. This limitation of resources is the ultimate source of scarcity in the economy, the restraint under which the socialist planner must also work. Suppose the entries in rows (4) and (5) and column (8) could at most be 580 million man-hours and 45 million machine-hours, respectively. Then there was unemployment in 1969 (at least by the planner's definition of the term). The planner could now plan for a fully employed economy in 1970 by raising one or all output targets. The targets of interest to him are obviously the entries in *the final demand columns*. As long as there is no waste, he does not care about intermediate goods or production used up in the processing sector. The important thing is how many final goods can be produced, how many commodities and services can be made available to final demand. Thus the planner might decide to raise next year's target for final automobile production, delivered to government, from 3 million cars to 6 million cars—row (1), column (6). What does this involve? Can he just raise total gross output—row (1), column (8)—by 3 million cars, too, leaving it at that? Obviously not! As we see from column (1), automobile production last year required not only the use of labor and machine services (which he can draw out of unemployment), but also the using up of automobiles and aluminum. Unless he wants to deliver less of those to someone else (and more to automakers), or unless he can use a different production technique, he must produce more of these to have the inputs needed for the additional cars to go to government. The planner is here confronted with the kind of difficulties we became aware of in Chapter 2 when we imagined what it would be like if you had to plan a country's economic activity for a year. How easy it would be to make a mess of things!

Let us suppose our planners are unwilling or unable to use a different production technique; nor are they willing to reduce deliveries of anything to anyone else. Then they may well proceed like this:

intermediate goods coefficients and resource coefficients

Planners could establish from the processing sector columns of Table 16.1 THE INPUT-OUTPUT TABLE AS A HISTORICAL DOCUMENT a table of *direct intermediate goods and resource coefficients*. Because it has just been assumed that the *same* production technique must be used next year as this year, this table conveniently shows the inputs directly required *per unit* of output. See Table 16.2 TECHNICAL COEFFICIENTS.

Just as a gross output of 12 million cars used up in production 1 million cars (Table 16.1), so the gross output of 1 million cars is expected to use up in its production 1/12 million cars—Table 16.2 row (1), column (1). Just as a gross output of 12 million cars used up in production 20 million tons of aluminum, so the gross output of 1 million cars is expected to use up in its production 20/12 million tons of aluminum—Table 16.2, row (2), column (1). And so it goes. Column (2), Table 16.2, for instance, tells us that each 1 million tons of aluminum is expected to be produced by 1/35 million cars (being used up) and with 50/35

Table 16.2   TECHNICAL COEFFICIENTS

GROSS OUTPUT OF / INPUT OF		1 MILLION AUTOMOBILES REQUIRES (1)	1 MILLION TONS OF ALUMINUM REQUIRES (2)	1 MILLION TONS OF CORN RE-QUIRES (3)
Intermediate goods coefficients	(1) million auto-mobiles	$\dfrac{1}{12}$	$\dfrac{1}{35}$	$\dfrac{1}{234}$
	(2) million tons of aluminum	$\dfrac{20}{12}$	$\dfrac{0}{35}$	$\dfrac{0}{234}$
	(3) million tons of corn	$\dfrac{0}{12}$	$\dfrac{0}{35}$	$\dfrac{5}{234}$
Resource coefficients	(4) million man-hours of labor	$\dfrac{100}{12}$	$\dfrac{50}{35}$	$\dfrac{320}{234}$
	(5) million machine-hours	$\dfrac{30}{12}$	$\dfrac{0}{35}$	$\dfrac{0}{234}$

Each entry in a table of direct intermediate goods and resource coefficients shows how much of the inter-mediate good or resource service listed on the left is needed to produce the amount of gross output listed on the top. Hypothetical figures. (Source: Table 16.1)

million man-hours of labor. In short, we are assuming that the technical requirements for production are unchanged regardless of the *scale* of production. If we want to produce 1/35 of what we produced last year, we must reduce all inputs equally to 1/35 of what they were last year. If instead we were to produce 25 percent more than last year, we must increase all inputs by 25 percent. (These are *assumptions,* let it be repeated, usually made in input-output analysis, but reality must not necessarily be like this. It might well be possible to produce 25 percent more by increasing some input by 30 percent and another one by 21 percent, thus *substituting* one for the other.)

using the coefficients   Back to our problem. Planners want to increase the entry in row (1), column (6), Table 16.1 from 3 to 6 million. They want to eliminate unemployment of men and machines by producing 3 million more cars for government use. Hence gross automobile output—row (1), column (8)—must be raised by 3 million *at least*. Table 16.2, column (1) now shows us the *immediate* consequences. We need as input for this additional gross output three times all the entries in column (1), that is, additional 3/12 million cars plus 60/12 million tons of aluminum plus 300/12 million man-hours plus 90/12 million machine-hours. The addition of 3 million cars to gross output (to satisfy a projected final demand increase) requires another 3(1/12) million cars (to make those 3 million cars)! Yet this cannot be the end. The latter 3/12 million cars, in turn, require for *their* production 3/12(1/12) million cars, and so on. Following this dwindling chain, we get a total required increase in gross automobile production of *at least* (in million cars) $3 + 3(1/12) + 3(1/12)$ $(1/12) + \cdots = 36/11 =$ about 3.2727.[1]

This still is not the end. Our original increase of 3 million car gross output required $3(20/12) = 60/12 = 5$ million tons of aluminum as input. Hence, our final $36/11 = 3.2727$ million cars need $(36/11)(20/12) = 720/132$ million tons of aluminum. Worse than that! As Table 16.2, column (2), teaches us, each million tons of aluminum requires 1/35 million automobiles for *its* production. Thus we need *at least* $(720/132)(1/35) = 720/4620 = 12/77$ million automobiles more. These again need automobiles for *their* production, giving us another total addition (in million cars) of $12/77 + (12/77)(1/12) + (12/77)(1/12)(1/12)$ $+ \cdots = 144/847 =$ about 0.17. This equals about a 5.2 percent increase over the original increase of 3.27. It will require, in turn, another 5.2 percent increase, for *these* additional cars (0.17 million) require aluminum also, which requires more cars for *its* production! Fortunately for us, neither the production of automobiles nor aluminum requires corn (and indirectly *more* automobiles) as an input. Nor do, of course, already available resources—rows (4) and (5)—require anything for *their* production. So we have reached one conclusion: to raise car deliveries to government by 3 million cars, we must, to take account of the economy's interdependence, raise car gross output by 3.2727 plus $0.17 + 0.0088 + \cdots = 3.4519$ million, or from 12 million to 15.4519 million. (If you are confused, reread this section slowly. This is important material, and it will be worth your while to learn it.)

The New Plan

Now we can begin to fill in a table indicating our plan for economic activity in the future, such as Table 16.3 THE INPUT-OUTPUT TABLE AS A PLAN DOCUMENT. The entries in the final demand sector columns (4 through 7) are autonomous, that is, set by the wishes of the Central Planning Board. (You may want to place a check mark beside each figure to indicate you understand how it got there.) From here originate all changes in economic activity. The entries are, as we assumed, identical with those in Table 16.1 THE INPUT-OUTPUT TABLE AS A HISTORICAL DOCUMENT, except for the encircled entry in row (1), column (6). We have just calculated the required entry in row (1), column (8). (Check it.) From it and our coeffi-

---

[1] There is a simple formula for finding the sum of such an infinite series. Adding $1 + 1/12 + (1/12)^2 + (1/12)^3$, and so on, yields

$$\frac{1}{1 - 1/12} = \frac{1}{11/12} = \frac{12}{11}$$

In the text example, every element was still multiplied by 3; therefore, the result was 3(12/11), or the 36/11 given there.

Table 16.3 THE INPUT-OUTPUT TABLE AS A PLAN DOCUMENT

SOURCES / USERS →		PROCESSING SECTOR			FINAL DEMAND SECTOR				(8) TOTAL GROSS OUTPUT
		(1) AUTOMOBILE PRODUCERS	(2) ALUMINUM PRODUCERS	(3) CORN PRODUCERS	(4) HOUSEHOLDS C	(5) CAPITAL FORMATION I	(6) GOVERNMENT G	(7) NET EXPORT NX	
Processing sector	(1) Automobile producers (million cars)	1.2877	1.1644	1	5	2	6	−1	15.4519
	(2) Aluminum producers (million tons)	25.7532	0	0	0	12	0	3	40.7532
	(3) Corn producers (million tons)	0	0	5	6	1	2	220	234
Resources	(4) Labor force (million man-hours)	128.7658	58.2189	320	10	0	57	2	575.9847
	(5) Capital stock (million machine-hours)	38.6298	0	0	0	0	0	5	43.6298

An input-output table for a future year (say, 1970) can be calculated from the technical and resource coefficients implied by past economic activity, given the desired composition of final demand. If there are at least as many resources as needed (in column (8) of the resource rows). this can become a blueprint of future economic activity. Hypothetical figures (rounded).

cients column (1), Table 16.2, we can calculate all entries in column (1), Table 16.3, by multiplying 15.4519 by the entries in column (1), Table 16.2. (Check them off.) Next, because no aluminum ever gets used in aluminum and corn production, we can fill in the entire row (2) in Table 16.3. (Check it.) From its sum in column (8) and from column (2), Table 16.2, we can now likewise derive column (2) by multiplying 40.7532 by the entries in column (2), Table 16.2. (Check it off.) Furthermore, because no extra corn was needed to make extra cars or aluminum and final demand for corn is unchanged, the entire row (3) and column (3) of Table 16.3 are unchanged. (Check them off.) With these entries all that remains is checking the sums of rows (1) to (3) and finding the sums of rows (4) and (5). Our calculations were correct. Table 16.3 represents an *internally consistent* plan for 1970. Were we to calculate intermediate goods and resource coefficients from *it*, we would again derive Table 16.2, showing that we have indeed kept technology unchanged. (Try and see!)

Consistency vs. Feasibility

This plan is internally consistent. As the many changes compared to Table 16.1 indicate, we are taking account of all the *indirect* as well as direct effects of the single change in final demand. This plan is also *feasible*, as we assumed the availability of 580 million man-hours and 45 million machine-hours. We still do not have full employment, but we are closer to it. By increasing some final demand target further, our Central Planning Board might work it out on paper until it has set up a plan that uses resources as fully as fixed technology allows. (If all production required labor as well as machines, it would be impossible to eliminate the unemployment of one if that of the other is eliminated first.) In every case, it would be necessary to figure out all indirect effects of any change in columns (4) to (7) in addition to the direct effect given by Table 16.2. In our case, we found that directly (so far as we could tell from column (1), Table 16.2) only $3/12 = 0.25$ million cars were needed in addition to the 3 million extra cars to go to government. Yet in the end gross output had to rise by 3.45, not 3.25 million! In our case, directly only $60/12 = 5$ million tons of extra aluminum were needed, yet it took 5.75 million more tons. In our case, directly only $300/12 = 25$ million more man-hours were needed, yet in the end we needed 36.98 million more. Finally, directly only $90/12 = 7.5$ million more machine-hours were needed, but to accomplish the goal without a hitch we needed to provide for 8.63 million more.

You can well imagine how unbearably complicated central planning of this type must be in reality where we have *millions* of rows and columns (all interrelated), *multiple* production techniques for each product, and thousands of changes desired by the planner in the final demand sectors! Even the gathering of data for a *past* period such as our Table 16.1 would present enormous difficulties. With the best of will on the part of planners, it would be subject to large errors. Beyond that, nothing short of a gigantic battery of electronic computers could calculate a consistent and feasible plan, as our Table 16.3.[2]

---

[2] A detailed elementary description of how this might be done can be found in my *Welfare and Planning* (New York: Wiley, 1966), Chapters 7 and 8.

CARRYING OUT THE PLAN

Having established such a plan, it is theoretically very easy for an all-powerful Central Planning Board to turn it into reality *without any use whatsoever of money and prices.*

Output Quotas

Using our example, socialist managers in the automobile industry would simply be *ordered* to produce in 1970 a total of 15.45 million cars. They would be *ordered* to deliver 1.29 million to themselves (where they will be used up in 1970), to deliver 1.16 million to aluminum producers (where they will be used up in 1970), to deliver 1 million to corn producers (where they will be used up in 1970), to deliver 5 million to households, to deliver 2 million to a variety of places to be added to inventories, to deliver 6 million to government agencies, and to import (net) 1 million cars from abroad.

In the same way, aluminum producers would be *ordered* to produce in 1970 a total of 40.75 million tons of aluminum. They would be *ordered* to deliver 25.75 million tons to automobile producers (where they will be used up in 1970), 12 million tons to all kinds of places to be added to inventories, and to export (net) 3 million tons to foreign countries.

Finally, the corn producers would be *ordered* to produce in 1970 a total of 234 million tons of corn, delivering 5 million tons to themselves (to be used up in 1970), 6 million tons to households, 1 million tons to places here not specified to be put into inventories, 2 million tons to government, and 220 million tons abroad.

Input Quotas

In addition, the Central Planning Board, having complete control of all nonhuman resources, would make sure that, as in row (5), 38.63 million machine-hours are made available to automobile producers and 5 million more to foreigners.

All that remains to be done is to make sure that the labor force is distributed as in row (4) of the plan. Labor, even in socialist countries, is not owned by the people collectively as slaves. Hence it is not under the Central Planning Board's control in the same sense as land and capital. If the government were totalitarian, however, it might simply announce that 575.98 million man-hours will have to be worked, whether people like it or not.

Then people would be *ordered* to work 128.77 million man-hours in the automobile industry, 58.22 million man-hours in the aluminum industry, 320 million man-hours in corn production, 10 million man-hours providing services to households, 57 million man-hours providing services to government, and 2 million man-hours providing services to foreigners. This *could* be done without thought, assigning almost everybody to a job he *dislikes* (remember that we have been assuming here that labor is homogeneous, that everybody is equally *able* to do all jobs).

It could also be done by asking for volunteers first and assigning people, as far as possible, to jobs of their choosing. If, for example, 100 million man-hours were voluntarily offered for the auto industry, only 28.77 million would have to be gotten through force. If 17 million man-hours were voluntarily offered for household services, at least 10 million of these could be accommodated. In short, it would not be necessary to force *everybody* into something he dislikes. But almost surely the totalitarian government would have to rely to some extent on force.

In this totalitarian solution, money and prices would be completely unnecessary. Because the plan was internally consistent to begin with, all firms—columns (1) to (3)—will find that they receive just the right inputs needed to fulfill the plan. Others have been ordered to give them just enough of intermediate goods—rows (1) to (3)—and resources—rows (4) and (5)—to enable them to fulfill the output quotas they have received.

Households who supply labor, as in row (5), can be given income in kind, as provided for in column (4), rather than in money. Real income, furthermore, can be distributed unequally or equally. If distributed equally, households would simply share equally the 5 million cars provided for them, and the 6 million tons of corn, and the 10 million man-hours of labor performed for them. Every individual person has to work wherever he is placed, and although he receives no money income, he knows that he will receive "free" so many cars, so much corn, so much medical care, and so on. In the same way, the government's program of enlarging the capital stock—column (5)—of collective consumption—column (6)—and foreign trade—column (7)—would be carried out as commanded by government planners.

Monetary Incentives

Socialism and totalitarianism, however, are not synonymous. It is also conceivable that our socialist state was established democratically and that our Central Planning Board is a group of democratically elected officials. In that case, they would hesitate forcing people to work against their will. Hence, their original definition of full employment would be akin to ours, the absence of *involuntary* unemployment. Suppose our plan of Table 16.3 has been set up on this basis and at least 575.98 million man-hours are *voluntarily* offered. In that case, the Central Planning Board could still have trouble executing the plan unless people wanted to work in just the "right" amounts in the various places. What if now, too, only 100 million man-hours are offered for the auto industry, but 17 million for household services? Unwilling to rely on the stick—that is, force—our Central Planning Board would have to do one of two things: abandon its plan or rely on the carrot, that is, monetary incentives. Presumably it would *try* to do the latter. It would try to offer people *money* income for work and keep raising the wages where more people are needed (as in the automobile industry) and lowering the wages where fewer are wanted (as for household services) until the correct total is correctly distributed. That is, wages might be adjusted until just the right number of people required by the plan *want* to work in the various occupations. Potential barbers and lawyers decide to become auto workers and executives instead. If for some reason people are so immobile as not to respond to wage differentials or are willing to respond only to undesirably huge differentials, the board, unwilling to use force, would have to abandon the plan.

For the democratic solution, the introduction of money and prices *could* be limited to the household sector. Having received money income for labor—performed as shown by row (4)—households naturally should not be given their real income—column (4)—"free" as above. Then they would still want to spend their money income on something, but there would be nothing left to buy! Thus they would lose all incentive to work. As a solution, the real income provided for households in the plan—column (4)—could be *sold* to them for money (as in capitalism). The Central Planning Board would have to make sure to set the *prices* of things delivered to households (cars, corn, services) such that after all is bought, households' money income is exactly exhausted.

CONCLUSION

We have said enough to see how a centrally planned socialist economy *might* be organized. In theory, it would be no problem at all to plan in physical terms all the economic activity of a country for a future year via input-output analysis. One could set up a plan which uses resources fully (however defined). Subject only to the provision of a minimum of subsistence for the population, as in column (4)—such plan could give any desired priority to capital formation (accumulating buildings, equipment, inventories), collective consumption (schools, hospitals, roads, space ships), or foreign trade. Such plan could in theory be executed with a minimum of monetary variables and a maximum of direct orders couched in physical terms. In fact, no monetary variables at all would be needed in a totalitarian setting.

SUMMARY

1   In many socialist countries, all or much of economic activity is centrally planned by a Central Planning Board. The production of any one good, by requiring other goods as inputs, is intricately bound up with the production of all other goods. Therefore, drawing up an internally consistent plan is a difficult task. In addition, the plan must be feasible. That is, it must require no more scarce resources than are available.

2   Consistent planning is made possible with input-output analysis. Its basic tool is the input-output table, which illustrates the interdependence of economic sectors by showing how the output of producers and the services of resource owners are distributed among their users.

3   From an input-output table of a past year, a table of direct intermediate goods and resource coefficients can be computed. These coefficients indicate the amounts of intermediate goods or resource services needed as inputs per unit of gross output of a good. They can be used in turn to set up a consistent plan for a future year by starting from the desired composition of final goods to be produced and determining the inputs their production would require directly and indirectly.

4 Having established an internally consistent plan, a Central Planning Board can turn it into reality if the plan is also feasible (enough resources are available). This can be done by command, without the use of money and prices. Yet, such direct commands of output and input quotas are apt to involve a certain degree of compulsion when it comes to assigning people to jobs. A central plan can possibly also be realized without compulsion by the use of monetary incentives.

TERMS[3]

central economic planning	final demand sector
Central Planning Board	input-output table
direct intermediate goods coefficient	input quota
direct resource coefficient	output quota
processing sector	

QUESTIONS FOR REVIEW AND DISCUSSION

1 The Soviets often claim that their central economic planning must be superior to capitalism because the capitalist government forgets to plan certain things altogether. Hence, there must be chaos in capitalism.
  a. What do you think they mean by this?
  b. Could they be right? Could they be wrong?

2 What is the most basic difference between capitalism and socialism?

3 Explain the notion of economic interdependence illustrated by the input-output table.

4 Distinguish intermediate from final goods.

5 Interpret the meaning of the following in Table 16.3 THE INPUT-OUTPUT TABLE AS A PLAN DOCUMENT: row (2), row (4), column (1), column (7), column (8).

6 Below is given a hypothetical and extremely oversimplified input-output table for the Soviet Union. (To simplify matters, all data are in rubles.)
  a. Interpret each row and column.
  b. Set up a new *internally consistent* plan for 1971 in which final demanders get 500 billion rubles of industrial output, and (as before) 200 billion rubles of agricultural output and no labor. Assume technology is unchanged.
  c. If the labor resources available are worth 650 billion rubles, is your 1971 plan *feasible*?

[3] Terms are defined in the Glossary at the end of the book.

HYPOTHETICAL INPUT-OUTPUT TABLE, SOVIET UNION, 1970 (IN BILLION RUBLES)

USERS SOURCES	AGRICULTURE	INDUSTRY	FINAL DEMAND	GROSS OUTPUT
Agriculture	0	800	200	1000
Industry	800	0	400	1200
Labor	200	400	0	600

(Hint: You can check your result for accuracy by calculating an intermediate goods and resource coefficient table, such as Table 16.2, from the table given here and another from your 1971 plan table. The two must be identical, because technology was assumed unchanged.)

7   "What is wrong with taking account only of *direct* input requirements when planning an output target? After all, if each car requires five tires (including one spare) and I want one more car, I need only plan for five more tires. If I produced six or seven more tires, I would have a surplus." Discuss.

8   Explain the difference between a central economic plan which is internally consistent and one which is also feasible.

9   Point 4 of the summary says that "a central plan can possibly also be realized without compulsion by the use of monetary incentives." Why *possibly*?

10   "Even a totalitarian central planning board would not have to force *everybody* into a job he dislikes." Explain.

11   What is the monetary equivalent to input-output table rows?

12   What is the monetary equivalent to input-output table columns?

13   What are output quotas? Input quotas?

14   Explain the role of monetary incentives in a centrally planned economy.

Soviet Input-Output Analysis

In the last 10 to 15 years input-output analysis has come to be generally accepted as a highly useful and versatile tool of analysis of national and regional economic data. Most Western countries have prepared, or are in the process of preparing, one or more input-output tables for their economies.

After some initial reluctance to use an analytical tool developed and perfected by "decadent bourgeois science," economists, statisticians, and planners in the U.S.S.R. and other countries of the Soviet bloc are also finding more and more use for input-output analysis. However, complete integration of input-output techniques with more traditional tools of central economic planning has not yet occurred. Most countries of the bloc have by now prepared one or several input-output tables of varying degrees of detail and statistical sophistication, and interest in the exploration of input-output techniques continues unabated. In the U.S.S.R. alone, to date a total of 10 national input-output tables have been completed or are in preparation, ranging from an 83-industry table in value terms for 1959 to a mammoth 600-product table in physical units being prepared for 1970, the terminal year of the current 5-year plan. Some 20 regional or interregional tables have also been prepared.

Needless to say, an input-output table is not only useful to government agencies of the country in question but is also of singularly great interest to an outside analyst. This is especially true when dealing with a country like the U.S.S.R. where, all the recent improvements in the flow of published statistics notwithstanding, our knowledge of economic data is severely limited. It must be emphasized that an input-output table need not necessarily be used as a whole entity for the study of overall national capacity, industrial interrelations, or national projections. A table with even a modest degree of detail offers a wealth of specific information on production techniques, distribution patterns, allocations to final uses, generation of national income, or foreign trade flows for a given industry or product.

From a study for the Joint Economic Committee, 1966

17

central
planning
in the
soviet union

W E HAVE SEEN that central economic planning would be enormously complicated. Yet, as shown in the previous chapter, detailed and accurate central economic planning is at least a *conceivable* alternative to the market economy. But does it also work in practice? In this chapter, we study how the Soviet economy has been directed from the late 1920's to the mid-1960's. After all, this is the largest as well as oldest centrally planned economy functioning today. How well has it done in banishing scarcity? Has it succeeded, better than capitalism, in fighting the evils of unemployment and inflation?

A study of the traditional Soviet methods of planning and guiding the economy will go a long way in answering these questions. Note, however, that some features of the Soviet economy are in a state of flux. The likely effect of current economic reforms is discussed further in Chapters 23 and 25.

SETTING UP THE PLAN

Although central planning in the Soviet Union is *not* correctly described by the model discussed in the previous chapter, at least since the mid-1950's that model has been regarded by many as an ideal after which planners should strive. In reality, ever since the late 1920's, central planning has been performed by a board, called Gosplan. And planning is a 12-month job.

Data Collection and Analysis

A Central Statistical Administration, during the first half of a planning year, collects data on the past performance of the economy. These are data on inputs and outputs of the previous year and estimates for the first half of the current year. With these data, naturally imprecise, Gosplan makes projections for the second half of the year in order to have a basis for next year's plan. (Although the data are not set up in this form, they correspond to our Table 16.1 THE INPUT-OUTPUT TABLE AS A HISTORICAL DOCUMENT.) This information is studied by a Council of Ministers and the Presidium of the Communist Party's Central Committee. They determine the major objectives to be sought during the following year. These are sent to Gosplan and are usually cast in very general terms, such as "increase the share of resources devoted to capital formation by 5 percent" or "reduce the importance of road building in favor of school construction." This, of course, amounts to giving general directives as to the desired makeup of the GNP. In fact, these are called *party directives*.

Original Plan Formulation

The party directives are used by Gosplan in the second half of the planning year to specify in physical terms, for maybe 1,000 "important" commodities in great detail and for about 16,000 other "important" ones in lesser detail, the exact output targets, the distribution of output, and the major inputs required to make the output. (This detailing of party directives amounts to filling in the final demand columns—(4) to (7), Table 16.3. The setting of output targets is equivalent to calculating gross outputs—our column (8), Table 16.3. The simultaneous calculation of output distribution and input requirements corresponds to our calculation, on the basis of technical information (as Table 16.2), of all other entries in the plan table—columns (1) to (3).)

Note, however, that not all of reality's millions of goods and resources are included in this physical plan. Oskar Lange, a famous economist and a high official in the Polish government, put it this way:

> There was the famous joke in Poland—really, it was not a joke, but it was true—that the production of pickled cucumbers was in the national economic plan. Another case, which again was not a joke but a fact, was that the State Planning Commission made a plan of the number of hares which were to be shot during the year by hunters. At the same time, you could not get, for instance, buttons or hairpins for ladies, simply because they had been forgotten in the plan.[1]

As you might guess, such examples were not confined to Poland. East European central planners were attempting to be as detailed and accurate as possible, but they inevitably failed. What does this mean in terms of last chapter's input-output model? Simply this: just as we did for the sake of illustration, planners simply neglected many rows and columns in the table entirely. This, although good enough in an illustration, is not good enough when planning reality. It introduces serious gaps and inconsistencies into the plan, as a great number of outputs and inputs are completely neglected or incorrectly planned.

Second, it must be noted that Soviet planners have historically only taken account of *direct* input requirements (as suggested by our Table 16.2) for each output target. As we saw even in our simple example, this introduces further error, for it neglects interdependencies. Producing an extra 3 million vehicles may *not* be enough to deliver that many more to government, if, for instance, further vehicles are needed to transport the steel required to make vehicles.

Finally, we must note that the Soviet economic plan for "important" goods is not actually set up in the form of an input-output table. Rather it is set up in the form of *material balances*. A typical material balance would look like Table 17.1.

A material balance lists in any desired detail and in physical units (such as tons, or numbers produced) all the sources and uses of a given commodity (material), making certain that they are equal (balance). (This is only a special way of writing down a *row* of an input-output table. Table 17.1 here corresponds exactly to the information contained in row (1), Table 16.3. The specific sizes of imports and exports were hidden there, since only the net amount, NX, was given. Similarly, the fact that car inventories both decreased and increased was hidden there in the figure showing a net increase only.) Setting up a number of material balances, as is done by Gosplan for "important" goods, corresponds, thus, to setting up an input-output table *in disaggregated form*.

[1] Oskar Lange, *The Political Economy of Socialism* (The Hague: Institute of Social Studies, 1958).

Table 17.1   A MATERIAL BALANCE

MILLIONS OF AUTOMOBILES (HYPOTHETICAL FIGURES)

SOURCES		USES		
Production	15.45	Manufacturing		
Imports	2.00	(a) automobiles	1.29	Intermediate
Inventory decrease	1.00	(b) aluminum	1.16	uses
		Agriculture		
		(a) corn	1.00	
		Households	5.00	
		Inventory increase	3.00	Final uses
		Government	6.00	
		Export	1.00	
Total sources	18.45	Total uses	18.45	

A material balance (here of the 1970 plan) shows all the sources from which a given good will be received and all the uses to which it will be put.

It is set up, as we noted above, with innumerable gaps and inconsistencies, as "unimportant" goods, and all but the direct input requirements of the "important" ones are neglected. This does not show up, of course, in any one material balance that is made to balance, but it is implicit *in the system* by the fact that some material balances that should have been set up have not been set up at all, while those that have been set up may not fit together. This part of the plan is, furthermore, set up by different groups of people, in different offices, at different times during the planning process that stretches through much of the year preceding the one for which economic activity is being planned.

After an original elaboration of material balances by Gosplan, *monetary balances* are also set up for "unimportant" goods. As in Table 17.1, they would specify (at governmentally set prices) the *value* of, say, garden tools to be produced or imported or taken from inventories and how the total is to be distributed. As our hypothetical Planning Board in Chapter 16, Gosplan attempts to set output targets (physically for "important," in terms of value for "unimportant" goods) in such a way as to use available resources fully (however defined).

Elaboration of the Plan

The first material and monetary balances of the Central Planning Board are called *control figures.* They are then passed down the administrative hierarchy to various ministries and regional planning centers. The Ministry of Vehicle Production, for instance, might be told to plan on producing 15.45 million cars in 1970, the Foreign Trade Ministry to import 2 million (and export 1 million), the Agriculture Ministry to expect delivery of 1 million cars for corn production, and so on.

As a next step, each ministry or regional agency will split up the aggregate into sub-totals. The Ministry of Vehicle Production might allocate the production of 15.45 million cars among the Soviet Republic planning agencies, which, in turn, will pass the plan down to smaller geographic administrations and individual plants. Finally, auto plant X in Irkutsk will have before it the control figures for 1970, telling it to produce 77,000 cars, to be delivered in a specified way, and to be produced with so many units (in physical or value terms, depending on the "importance" of the item) of aluminum, labor, machine-time, and the like.

Changing Control Figures

At this point, the planning process is reversed. Plant officials suggest changes in the control figures. Even if the control figures (in the aggregative form set up by Gosplan) had been perfectly comprehensive and consistent and feasible so far as resource availability is concerned (and we saw that this is *not* the case, except in our idealized model in chapter 16, there may be inconsistencies at the detailed level of individual plants. Auto plant X may have been assigned too much labor and too little aluminum and (by mistake) cabbage planting machines. Auto plant Y may have been assigned too little labor and too much aluminum. And state farm Z may not have received much needed cabbage planting machines! Such mistakes made in the process of detailing a *perfect* aggregate plan could now be ironed out, if loyal managers reported to their superior planning agencies the projected receipt of inputs not needed (here labor and cabbage planting machines for X, aluminum for Y), while also reporting projected deficiencies in inputs required to fulfill the plan (here aluminum for X, labor for Y, and cabbage planting machines for Z). Planners could simply reassign inputs until everybody has exactly what is needed to fulfill his output target. Then the control figures would become the *draft plan*, be approved by parliament to make it a *plan law,* and be put into operation the next year. Having been perfectly comprehensive and consistent and feasible, the country would produce exactly its potential real GNP without unemployment and consisting of just the kinds of goods desired by Gosplan.

A Problem of Disloyalty

We saw, however, that the control figures, as set up by Gosplan in the Soviet Union, are *not* consistent and, except by accident, *not* feasible. (Frequently output targets are set so high as to require more resources than exist.) As a result, *most* plants will find, when the control figures reach them, that they have been assigned not enough of *all* inputs needed to fulfill the target, as well as having been assigned some useless inputs by mistake. This sort of problem *cannot* be ironed out at the local level, because *all* plant officials *at the same time* will try to get higher input assignments. Gosplan must *cut* output targets until they are feasible. In practice this does not work. The reason: plant managers are a lot less loyal than the state would hope. This is owing to the way in which their *personal* incentives have been set up.

Like the managers of a modern capitalist corporation, they are motivated to work hard by the lure of salary and promotion. Beyond that, however, the environment in which they function is obviously different. They do not respond to market demand for their product, but are asked to fulfill a centrally determined plan of output with centrally determined inputs. Fulfilling such a plan well means receipt (on top of the salary) of a monetary bonus (which can be translated into a home, a car, and vacations at the Black Sea). Failing to fulfill the plan (as in the United States, failure to manage well) can bring loss of job or demotion, but (unlike in the United States) also prosecution for criminal negligence with people's property, and under Stalin possibly a bullet in the head. Extreme as the punishment are the rewards. A manager quite possibly can receive as a bonus up to 50 percent of his basic salary for plan fulfillment alone and up to 4 percent more for each percentage point of overfulfillment. Thus, the difference between 99 and 100 percent plan fulfillment can mean up to 50 percent difference in the incomes of the managing group. A manager overfulfilling his plan by 10 percent may receive up to 90 percent above his basic salary. No wonder that output plan fulfillment receives the managers' undivided attention! And this is where trouble enters the planning process itself.

The lower the plan target, the easier it can be fulfilled. Thus, there is the strong urge to *hide from Gosplan the true productive capability* of the plant. Yet, to plan centrally, nothing is more vital to Gosplan than to have an exact idea of the economy's capacity to produce. There is also a strong urge to *overorder and hoard inputs*. This stacks the deck beforehand in favor of the managers. By pretending that more inputs are needed than is in fact the case, more might be received, making it easier to fulfill or overfulfill plans. In addition, inputs received and unusable (such as our cabbage planting machines) may be traded secretly in a black market for other inputs.

As a result of all this, what happens when control figures reach individual plants? As you might expect, whether true or not, managers will unanimously complain of too high output targets and too low input assignments (and they will *not* report the projected receipt of inputs not needed at all). Gosplan knows this, yet it is unable to check the veracity of reports from hundreds of thousands of firms. Thus it is in a dilemma. For perfect planning it must know the truth, and the truth is intentionally hidden. So it arbitrarily rejects many proposals for higher input and lower output assignments. This may be just what is needed to "flush out" hidden capacities and hoarded inputs, leading managers to fulfill plans nevertheless. But it may also set up an utterly unfeasible plan, eliminating bonuses and incentives and bringing criminal prosecution on the innocent. In any case, it is most likely that the draft plan emerging from this "bargaining session" between managers and planners and being rubber-stamped by parliament into the law of the land for the coming year's economic activity is in a million different ways incomplete, inconsistent, and unfeasible.

This is not to say that Soviet output plans are never fulfilled or that all output is of low quality. In fact, the "important" goods contained in the material balances (capital formation, military goods, foreign aid) are frequently produced in just the right way because central planners lavishly provide required resources for them. It is the "unimportant" goods that bear the brunt of the defects of planning. Their producers are eventually left with insufficient resources, and thus agricultural, industrial consumer goods production, or residential construction targets have typically been underfulfilled.

CARRYING OUT THE PLAN

The Soviet economic plans are carried out with the help of money flows, and therefore the economy may appear *on the surface* to be very much like that of the United States. This, as we have just seen, is not true.

State Bank Control

Soviet industrial firms, having received their individual plans, "sell" outputs (as directed by the plan) to others. They "buy" inputs (as directed by the plan) from others. Such monetary transactions among firms are all made via the State Bank and the "acceptance method." Instead of the buyer writing a check, the seller initiates the process by billing the State Bank. The State Bank delivers the order to pay to the buyer who by signing it "accepts," thereby gaining legal title to the goods. Then the buyer's account at the State Bank is reduced, the seller's account increased, just as if a check had been written. The only difference is that the State Bank could (and is supposed to) check the purpose, timing, and size of every transaction, preventing it unless it fits into the plan. The State Bank becomes in theory the overseer of the economy! In fact, however, the administrative burden of overseeing billions of transactions per year makes this impossible, and it is bound to fail in this role.

Thus, disloyal managers, following their personal self-interest rather than that of the state, may get away with sabotaging the execution of the plan just as much as its formulation. Managers with bad luck (having ended up with *truly* unfeasible plan targets) will, for instance, try to "fulfill" the plan anyway by cutting corners. They may do so by producing ten tons of low quality aluminum rather than eight tons of high quality. This will have further repercussions. For example, it could make it impossible for car producers to produce as many cars as they normally could with ten tons of aluminum of the right quality, and hence cause them, in turn, to produce the right number of cars but of lower quality than desirable or without a single spare part.

Money Income to Labor

Labor is also allocated via money flows. It is guided into various occupations in the short run by wage differentials established by the state and in the long run by the state determination of openings for various types of education. In addition, graduates are *assigned* to their first job, but after 4 years they can go wherever they please (although the housing shortage seriously limits geographical mobility). In industry and state-owned farms, once on the job, things are very much like in any advanced capitalist country. Wages, which are paid in cash, differ within an occupation with skill required, unpleasantness of work, effort exerted. Personal effort leads to promotion, lack of it to demotion or loss of job.

Collective farmers, on the other hand, until mid–1966 received *residual* money income plus earnings from private production. *Collective* farms are not collectively owned by the people as a whole, as *state* farms or most other businesses. They are owned by the group of peasants living on them. They are also subject to the central plan and must sell their output to and buy inputs from state enterprises at prices set by the government. Any money left over between sales and costs has traditionally been shared by the collective farmers as residual income. In addition, they may grow food on small private plots and sell it freely at any price to anybody. As of July 1, 1966, the collective farmers in the Soviet Union are receiving for work on the collective land twice-monthly guaranteed wages in cash, as well as, at harvest time, payments in kind. The State Bank is obliged to give credits to collective farms for this purpose if needed. This new method is to help correct tremendous wage differentials among classes of workers. In 1965, for example, even after the government raised prices paid to and lowered prices and taxes paid by collective farms, the monthly (residual) cash income of the average collective farmer was only 47 percent that of the average worker on state farms and 35 percent that of the average industrial worker.

Free Consumer Choice

The money income earned by managers, workers, and peasants can be freely spent. However, unlike in the U.S.-type economy, such consumer demand does not determine the size or composition of consumer goods production. The plan has already done that. Thus, the "consumer is king" in a very limited sense: he can choose only among what the government provides, not decide what is provided.

The government sets the prices of planned consumer goods production—column (4), Table 16.3—in such a way that it just could be bought exhausting households' money incomes. This, too, leads to lots of trouble even if the production plans in this area were fulfilled (as they usually are not). Look at column (4), Table 16.3 THE INPUT-OUTPUT TABLE AS A PLAN DOCUMENT. If the money income of households, which is to be "mopped up," were 21 million rubles, one could set the prices as follows: 1 ruble per car, 1 ruble per ton of corn, 1 ruble per hour of service bought (of barbers, doctors, and so on). If households bought exactly what has been provided them (and the output plan *is* really fulfilled), they would spend 5 million rubles on cars, 6 million rubles on corn, 10 million rubles on services. Now watch what can go wrong: if output is lower than planned because of faulty planning, some households will be left with money burning in their hands after all goods are gone. This is bad for incentives, for these households would see no further reason for work. If the output is produced as planned, households may want to buy no services, 1 million tons of corn, and 20 million cars! Then some households will be left with money they wanted to spend on cars they could not get. Unsold corn will accumulate in the stores, and potential services will not get performed. This is equally bad. Hence, output must be changed, prices must be changed, or "something else" must happen. In the United States, output *would* be changed, as the strong demand for cars induced private car producers to make more (as long as resources allow it) and at the same time induced private producers of corn and services to offer less. In the Soviet Union, output would *not* be changed, as firms do what the plan tells them to do.[2] In the United States, prices *would* be changed, at least raising that of cars (if resources are not available to make more), possibly lowering those of corn and services. The Soviet government has traditionally preferred *not* to change prices either. In fact, "something else" typically has happened in the Soviet Union. To the extent that they were unable to spend money in retail stores, workers have spent it in the free collective farm markets bidding up the prices of privately grown onions and plums to any level required to get rid of their money! This by itself does not solve the problem, however, for now the *peasants* hold useless money. This money can, in turn, be eliminated in a number of ways, all of which have been used at times: (1) expropriating it directly in a "currency reform" (for example, everybody might have to hand in 10 rubles to get 1 ruble of slightly different design), (2) forcing people to buy government bonds or pay higher taxes, (3) reducing the collective farmers' residual income from their collective farm activities by lowering prices paid for their produce (which *has* to be delivered) or raising prices they have to pay for their inputs (such as fertilizer), or (4) actually producing more consumer goods.

This is not to say that consumers have become worse off. Quite the contrary. Goods available for the average consumer have become continually more plentiful since World War II, *but* this rise in living standards has been usually much slower than planned and also much slower than in many other countries.

IMPROVING THE SYSTEM

The traditional method of central economic planning in the Soviet Union is, as we have seen, a highly time-consuming and imprecise process. During Stalin's lifetime, no one dared worry about this openly, for Stalin himself did not care. In 1963, Premier Khrushchev gave this amazing picture of the extent of Stalin's indifference:

I will mention a fact to show how plans were approved at that time. This happened shortly before Stalin's death. The Council of Ministers met to approve the annual plan and Stalin came to the meeting. Ordinarily he did not preside over the Council of Ministers. This time, however, he presided. He picked up the folder containing the draft plan and said: "Here is the plan. Who is against it?" The ministers looked at each other and said nothing. "Then it is accepted," Stalin said, and the meeting ended. As we left the meeting he said: "Let's go to a movie." He arrived at the movie theatre and said: "We took them for a good ride!" Who had been taken for a ride? It was the ministers.

---

[2] A New System of Economic Planning and Management is, however, now being experimented with. It might change this. It is discussed in Chapter 23.

The plan went awry. Great miscalculations were made in it because the ministers had had no real hand in its preparation and did not agree with it. Other officials who had read it also disagreed with it. But Stalin himself did not pay much attention to questions of planning, and he was not anxious for others to pay much attention to these questions.[3]

Essentially, Gosplan is using the same crude techniques of planning now that it used then (and it is very doubtful that the "hand of ministers in plan preparation" can improve the degree of plan consistency and feasibility). This is why some Soviet economists are dreaming of creating a complicated mathematical model of the economy (of the type discussed in the previous chapter) and of using a large network of computers to control every aspect of economic life. Such a network would receive data from all levels of the economy and grind out a number of alternative plans (like our Table 16.3), all of which would be internally consistent and feasible. The top leadership would merely select one plan, and the computer would take over. It would break down the plan into any desired detail, disseminate it to individual enterprises, watch the progress of plan realization, make continual corrections when needed. (Note the report introducing this chapter.)

Yet the problems, theoretical and practical, of establishing such a system of planning are enormous. Many are unsolvable. Soviet leaders are quite aware of the difficulties of training the necessary personnel, producing the computers, and solving conceptual and organizational problems. They are talking of replacing routine tasks of planning by computers, but they envision a *gradual* automation of the planning process, which is to take at the very least 10 years. However, as we shall see in Chapter 23, there is a substantial number of influential people who favor *de*centralization of economic control, rather than improvement of the present system of central planning by the infusion of computers and mathematical planning techniques.

FULL EMPLOYMENT AND INFLATION

Let us now consider how well the traditional planning system has done with respect to full employment and price level stability. Soviet textbooks on economics invariably repeat a familiar tune, namely that "unemployment in the Soviet economy has been liquidated fully and forever." This is supposed to have happened in the late 1920's, and unemployment statistics in fact have neither been compiled nor published since then. In this section, we shall examine to what extent such claims are correct, hence to what extent actual real GNP equals the potential, and whether it is reached without inflation.

Labor Resources

According to the Soviet Constitution (article 12), "Work in the U.S.S.R. is a duty and a matter of honor for every able-bodied citizen, in accordance with the principle: 'He who

---

[3] *Pravda,* June 29, 1963.

does not work, neither shall he eat.' " The able-bodied population is considered to consist of all healthy males between 16 and 59 and females between 16 and 54. We could call this the Soviet conception of potential labor force. Deducting from this the members of the armed forces, we can arrive at the potential number of people available for *civilian* employment. Ideally, from the planners' standpoint, all these people should be employed in the "socialist sector." That is, the potential civilian labor force should equal socialist civilian employment. This means people should be working in state enterprises or in collective farms, unless they are full-time students at educational institutions. In short, socialist ideology (1) equates the actual civilian labor force with the potential civilian labor force and (2) expects that actual employment occurs in the socialist sector of the economy. However, neither of these expectations and possibilities is enforced. Actual employment in the socialist sector of the Soviet economy has always been below the potential civilian labor force. Ideology notwithstanding, some people are working outside the socialist sector as domestics or artisans or on small private plots of land, and others, such as housewives, full-time students, and the involuntarily unemployed, if any, are not employed anywhere. This has been possible because labor resources always have been allocated by a combination of central direction *and market forces.* Here we may add some detail.

labor laws and labor unions   The Labor Code of 1918 introduced direct industrial conscription. In 1922, this was reduced to exceptional cases (such as fighting the elements or high priority state work), and people could terminate their employment with seven days' notice. Thereafter, labor was largely allocated through wage differentials among industries and regions and reflecting training, effort, and working conditions. This was supplemented by major voluntary recruitment drives (to get millions of women to enter the labor force, to shift millions from farms to the cities, from western to eastern regions, and so on), and the careful channeling of the "right" number of young people into various types of education required by the industrialization plans. In 1938, however, permanent "labor books" were introduced, giving each person's identification, a record of his education and training, a list of the jobs he held and rewards received, and reasons for previous separations. Without these books, no one could be hired, and people were now required to give a month's notice before leaving a job. This was designed to decrease an excessive labor turnover, as the newly recruited peasants moved restlessly from job to job in search of a better arrangement. (In 1934–1935, for instance, 97 percent of manual industrial workers and 86 percent of construction workers changed jobs during the year.) In 1940, the government stepped in. New decrees prohibited anyone from quitting or being absent from his job without the permission of the enterprise director and provided for the compulsory transfer of specialists. Violators became criminally liable, and, as the war began, these laws were drastically enforced. People were drafted for industrial and agricultural jobs and frozen to them. Since the early 1950's, however, there has been an unmistakable change from compulsion toward choice. The 1940 decrees were repealed in 1956, restoring legally what had become true in fact for some years, people's right to quit working entirely or to look for another job (with two weeks' notice). In 1960, further restrictions were removed. for example, the previous denial of sick leave and temporary disability pay for 6 months to those who quit their job. In 1961, another feature hindering labor mobility, length-of-service bonuses, was abolished, except in underground mining.

On the other hand, managers have also in the last decade been free to fire or hire employees (whether that was legal or not) and to pay them what they had to (even if it meant manipulating officially fixed job classifications and wage norms). New laws recently enacted will even increase the power of managers to bid for workers or to fire them.

Labor unions, we might note, play a very different role in the Soviet Union than in the United States. For very good reasons, labor-management disputes in the Soviet Union do not exist. Labor unions are instruments of the state (that is, the principal employer). Their function is to enforce labor discipline, not to bargain. Strikes are in fact illegal. This is rationalized in two ways. First, factories are owned by all the people; hence any strike by workers would be a strike against themselves. Second, because no private owners are receiving any profit, all gains in output automatically accrue to all the people, thus workers can hope to improve their living standard only by harsh discipline. Interestingly, Premier Khrushchev pointed out in 1956 what all Soviet workers knew too well:

> The quality of union work clearly lags behind life's needs. . . . Our trade unions primarily lack militancy in their work. They need creative ardor, initiative. . . . Everyone knows that labor-management agreements are reached in the enterprises. But everywhere these contracts are not carried out, and the trade unions remain silent as though everything were in order. Generally, the trade unions have stopped having disputes . . ., peace and harmony reign supreme. . . . However, . . . sometimes it is even desirable to have a hard fight.[4]

Khrushchev, seeing that Soviet workers did not regard trade unions as their own organizations but as a device of the state to make them work harder and accept bad working conditions, wanted to increase the unions' prestige. Then, as he well realized, they could be much more helpful to the state in getting the most out of workers. In fact, there have been a number of decrees recently increasing the role of unions in maintaining the interests of their members. Yet, their ultimate task remains to help increase production by whatever means are best.

In 1970, the Soviet labor market can be described as basically free, with employers and employees responding to economic incentives very much as in the United States, but with unions playing a negligible role. There are, to be sure, vestiges of force. A nationwide network for redistributing the labor force from farms to cities (Orgnabor) still must give collective farmers the permission to leave the land. So-called antiparasite laws can be used to make "recalcitrants" take a job from 2 to 5 years in specially designated places.[5] Graduates of colleges and specialized (agricultural and industrial) secondary schools are assigned to

---

[4] *Pravda,* February 15, 1956.

[5] The 1961 Law "Concerning the Intensification of the Fight against Persons Who Avoid Socially Useful Work and Lead an Antisocial Parasitic Way of Life" limited this to special court decrees against persons who "derive unearned income from the exploitation of land plots, automobiles, or housing, or commit other antisocial acts that enable them to lead a parasitic way of life."

their first job for periods ranging from 2 to 4 years to "repay the state for a free education" (very much like an American boy goes to the Navy for 4 years after the ROTC arrangement paid for his college education), and often Soviet graduates do not get their diploma until they have worked for a year. Graduates may, however, also select their first job, but cannot quit it for the period specified (just like an American boy under the ROTC arrangement may select the branch of the armed forces in which he serves). Finally, as in the United States, people do get drafted into the armed forces.

voluntary unemployment   With these exceptions, most people could choose whether and where they wanted to work, subject only to monetary incentives and the fact that no income other than from labor is to be had. To the extent that able-bodied citizens do not want to work for pay, they are allowed to do so. Thus, reality differs from ideology. These people are by both U.S. and Soviet definitions *voluntarily* unemployed.

To the extent that able-bodied citizens want to work but are not employed in the socialist sector, reality again differs from ideology. These people in the Soviet Union, too, are considered *voluntarily* unemployed. By the U.S. definition, however, they might be *employed* or *involuntarily unemployed*. For instance, a U.S. statistician would count all Soviet citizens employed outside the socialist sector, such as a private artisan or a collective farmer's wife and children working on the private plot, as employed. He would do so (as we saw in Chapter 3) even if it involved only 1 hour a week for pay or profit or involved no work because of illness, strike, vacation, bad weather, and personal reasons, or involved work without pay done by a family member working at least 15 hours a week. On the other hand, people employed nowhere, but currently available for work and looking for a job, or not looking because of temporary layoff or because they are about to start new work soon, would by the U.S. definition be counted as involuntarily unemployed.

involuntary unemployment   Is there, by the U.S. definition, such involuntary unemployment in the Soviet Union? Experts on the Soviet economy agree that *general* labor unemployment there has indeed been eliminated since the beginning of the central planning era in the late 1920's. Production targets set by Gosplan have typically been extremely high relative to the resources available. Incentives of industrial managers were set up in such a way as to make them desirous of *overfulfilling* these targets. Hence, their demand for inputs, including labor, was so strong as to employ anyone who could possibly be persuaded to enter the industrial labor force, training them, if need be, in special factory schools for the job. This does not mean, however, that other types of involuntary unemployment have also been absent. Quite the contrary. Let us look at *short-run* frictional unemployment first.

short-run frictional unemployment   As we saw, the central economic plan is likely to contain gaps and inconsistencies. Hence it is bound to happen that every year something goes wrong. Plans may not mesh. Raw materials do not arrive or arrive late. Machines break down and spare parts are not available or only after much delay. Thus workers will be laid off or have nothing to do. In addition, workers with the right skills in the right numbers may be available in European Russia, but jobs for them exist only in Siberia or the Far East. Or again, for a million different reasons, workers are fired or quit voluntarily or have just entered the labor force (out of school, back from the army, married women having reared their children). It takes time to find a job even if it is available in the same town.

The Soviets are quite frank about these problems. In 1961 the Central Statistical Administration reported losses of labor time for industry which resulted from work stoppages, inadequate organization of work places, and the like, amounting to 231 million man-days. This would amount to permanent involuntary unemployment of 0.8 percent of the potential civilian labor force. One can find numerous reports of geographic maldistribution of labor also. The Asiatic part of the U.S.S.R. contains 75 percent of the territory, and in 1959 had 88 percent of its fuel and power, a capital stock four times larger than in the European part, and a severe labor shortage with only 20 percent of the population. Yet, people tend to shun the new eastern industrial complexes, preferring the older and larger cities in the west which have better housing, lower prices and better medical and cultural facilities, but also labor surpluses.

Nor has there ever been scarcity of complaints about excessive labor mobility *within* geographic regions. In 1954, Premier Bulganin reported that 23 percent of manual industrial workers and 48 percent of construction workers changed jobs. In 1964, it was reported that a third of industrial workers changed jobs (60 percent on their own) and were out of work for almost a month in between. The percentage was considerably higher in the Far East, lower in the old areas of European Russia. Such turnover would be equivalent to permanent involuntary unemployment of 1.6 percent of the potential civilian labor force.

There also seems to be, since the mid-1950's, increased frictional unemployment among teenagers, although discrimination of any kind (as by age or sex) is illegal. However, Soviet laws force managers to give teenagers special privileges (such as 8-hour pay for 4 to 6 hours of work, time off for study, generous vacations, and the like), and although there are hiring quotas for teenagers and local Juvenile Placement Commissions to help enforce them, managers have increasingly been able to avoid hiring youngsters at all. To some extent, this has been countered by the recent extension of elementary and secondary education.

chronic unemployment—open and disguised   There is likely to be chronic unemployment, too. Automation and technical change make existing skills obsolete. People will be unemployed although many jobs exist for people with different skills. The growth of entirely new industries and the decline or disappearance of others is likely to have the same effect and, as in the United States, this kind of unemployment is especially prevalent in small towns. Also as in the United States, the gradual shortening of the work day has not eliminated, but only mitigated the problem. Often such structural unemployment is hidden, furthermore, by the fact that "despite mechanization, the introduction of automatic lines, etc., the total number of personnel, especially workers . . . is rising from year to year. . . . The result is that not infrequently there are many people employed at enterprises who are not needed at all."[6] In short, there is little doubt that the Soviet Union is experiencing short-run

---

[6] E. Manevich, *Voprosy ekonomiki,* **6,** 1965.

frictional and chronic involuntary unemployment in addition to genuine voluntary unemployment.

a matter of semantics   However, the Soviets are always surprised to see any but general unemployment referred to as involuntary unemployment. They would never think of calling such a person involuntarily unemployed because "he is bound to find a job soon if he tries." Let us remember that "unemployment," as defined in the United States, is an arbitrary definition and the Soviets have a perfect right to define it differently. Given their definition and the circumstances of excess demand on firms made by the planners, they are indeed correct in claiming to have abolished unemployment! Anybody unemployed (by the U.S. definition) can probably find a job relatively soon, even if he has to wait for raw materials, has to move to the Far East, or go to school first. Those refusing to do so, might then be called voluntarily unemployed (even by the U.S. definition). If we want to compare the degree of resource use in the United States and the Soviet Union, however, we should use the identical definition. Using that of the United States, we do find in the Soviet Union frictional and chronic unemployment. This means there as here that output could be higher if this kind of unemployment could be avoided.

dealing with unemployment and underemployment   What is being done about the unemployment that does exist? Much depends on the unemployed themselves. Employment agencies do not exist. A person out of work has to rely on advertisements at the factory gates or in newspapers and street bulletin boards, on announcements over the radio, or on what his friends happen to have heard. Only major recruitment needs for distant areas are filled with anything resembling an official machinery to match men and jobs (Orgnabor). But even here great reliance is placed on mass appeals in union meetings and newspaper editorials. "Go east, young man" is the phrase used to appeal to the sense of adventure and patriotism of the youth, as was the case after the 1954 decision to develop agriculture in Kazakhstan and to concentrate further industrial development in Siberia and the Far East.

Beyond that the government does nothing at the moment. To be sure, it organizes public opinion against "rolling stones" and "flitters" (that is, those responsible for the high labor turnover). Others are urging it to do more. "It is evident," thundered E. Manevich,

that we should now set up special organizations to deal with the problems of finding jobs for workers and employees. This (along with other measures) will enable enterprises to rid themselves of surplus workers and employees. And finally, this will create conditions under which jobs can be found for personnel in the best possible way, with due account of their specialties, professions, age, inclinations, family status, etc. At present, even the large industrial cities of the U.S.S.R. have no special organization that tabulates manpower requirements, has the necessary data on personnel in need of jobs and deals with the distribution and redistribution of manpower. Under the conditions of our planned economy . . . such a situation is abnormal. In the interests of both the working people and socialist production, it would be desirable to provide workers and employees who have been released from their jobs because of technical progress with material security during the period in which they are seeking new employment. If one considers how much money the state is compelled to spend on the maintenance of superfluous workers and employees at enterprises . . . it becomes clear that this material security is completely justified economically.[7]

Mr. Manevich urged further to improve the system of retraining workers, to elaborate a well thought-out system of measures for the development of small towns, and to find effective economic stimuli for the voluntary migration of workers to regions in need of manpower. (Among the latter, he proposed higher wages plus payments for long service plus construction of dwellings with all amenities plus improvement of communal and cultural facilities.) Interestingly, the 1966–1970 economic plan called for the construction of new enterprises mainly in medium size and small cities.

We should also note that in addition to frictional and chronic unemployment (or underemployment) in industry, there must be a great deal of *under*employment in agriculture. Thirty-seven percent of Soviet employment is in agriculture. As is inherent in agriculture in the temperate zones, it is typically short of labor in the summer, but there is great labor redundancy in the winter. In 1960, the adult able-bodied collective farmer worked on the average only 196 days. Even in the United States, such not working because of the weather would be called "employment." Yet there is clearly room for expanding production in such a situation. The draft directives of the latest Five Year Plan, issued in 1966, showed awareness of these problems by stating the party's desire to "ensure the rational use of manpower in all regions of the country" and to "make better use of manpower in the countryside all the year round," as well as to "achieve more intensive utilization of the means of production." This brings us to the next point.

Nonlabor Resources

How well are Soviet *nonlabor* resources utilized? In this area, too (just as in the United States) systematic statistics are neither gathered nor published. On the one hand, one might guess that managers of enterprises, being under constant pressure to fulfill or overfulfill very demanding plan targets and having strong personal incentive to do so, would try to use capital and land resources as fully as possible. Indeed, it is very unlikely that there has been since the late 1920's at any time any significant degree of general unemployment of these resources. On the other hand, other types of unemployment are bound to exist. When parts of the central plan do not mesh, inventories, equipment, buildings, and natural resources will go unused for lack of other materials or equipment or labor at the right place and time. As technical progress occurs, specific types of capital and land, just as labor, might be displaced. The mechanism for making use of such chronically or frictionally unemployed resources, furthermore, is very weak. Although this may soon change, enterprises until recently have been endowed free with capital and land. Although they had to pay into the state budget cash payments to cover depreciation of capital (that is, its being *used up*), no payments of interest and rent for the privilege of *using* these scarce resources were required. (This is discussed at greater length in Chapter 23). As a result, enterprise managers have

---

[7] *Ibid.*

always regarded capital and land as "free gifts." Although they certainly had the incentive to use them if possible, they also knew that it cost them nothing not to use them. Thus, especially capital and land resources unsuited for the particular enterprise which held them were likely to be "just kept around," possibly for future (illegal) trading with other enterprises. And though such unused resources do really cost nothing to the enterprise holding them idle, they do cost society plenty, namely, the goods forgone that might have been produced with them somewhere.

The Soviet literature is filled with hints about such unemployment of "the means of production." Because of imprecise planning, for instance, capital goods are reported to be installed very slowly or be used insufficiently for many years after installation, while managers wait for complementary inputs. The Siberian branch of the U.S.S.R. Academy of Sciences estimated that it takes an average of 5 to 6 years for new capital goods to be fully used. They reported the following instances. In 1962 capacity for the production of phosphorous fertilizer was completed in Estonia; 1 year later, only 5 percent was being used. In 1961, capacity for the production of polyethylene was completed in Grozny; 2 years later, only 45 percent was being used. In 1960, a giant blast furnace was readied at the Karaganda iron and steel works; yet even 3 years later, it was used to only 77 percent of capacity.[8] Similarly, a Moscow University publication complained that most enterprises "have extensive untapped possibilities as regards the employment of means of labor. . . . The presence of a large quantity of uninstalled and superfluous equipment means that a considerable part of the value of the means of labor is lost to society because they do not take part in the production process."[9]

Nor is imprecise planning solely to blame for this state of affairs. The pressure on managers to fulfill output targets frequently leads to quantitative fulfillment only at expense of quality. As a result, 90 to 100 percent of all technological equipment in the Soviet economy is repaired *every year,* 20 to 25 percent being subjected to medium-type overhaul, 11 to 12 percent to a complete overhaul.[10] This, plus the notorious lack of spare parts, causes managers to keep certain generous reserves of essential capital idle to be put to use in the frequent emergencies. At any one time, as is quite clear from numerous Soviet sources, a sizable portion of the capital stock does not work because it is thus being kept for emergencies, is being repaired, or is in the hands of managers who cannot possibly use it. There are even reports in the Soviet press describing a kind of discrimination, the fact that *imported* types of equipment are at times simply not used at all under any circumstances.

Soviet GNP Movements

The presence of short-run frictional and chronic unemployment in the Soviet Union implies that there, too, real GNP is lower than it might be. By how much it is lower, however, is anybody's guess, because exact data on the unemployment of resources are absent com-

---

[8] *Voprosy ekonomiki,* **6,** 1964.

[9] *Vestnik Moskovskogo Universiteta, seriia ekonomiki,* **1,** 1965.

[10] In 1958, equipment maintenance and repair workers constituted the largest skill category of workers in the Soviet economy. Their number was 3.2 million, while there were only 2.1 million production workers making *new* machines.

pletely. All we can really say is that Soviet real GNP seems to have grown rather rapidly, although unevenly so, and that it undoubtedly, like that of the United States, is typically below potential. Although we do not know by how much, there is no evidence that the Soviet Union has ever experienced a major economic downturn that would correspond to the Great Depression in the rest of the world. Many of its short-run declines in real GNP or in its growth rate seem to be related to the weather and bad harvests (agriculture accounting easily for a quarter of Soviet GNP but less than 5 percent of U.S. GNP). The gradual decline in growth rates during the past decade, furthermore, cannot possibly be explained by a lack of aggregate demand, as one might explain such a phenomenon in a U.S.-type economy. Central planners have continued to demand the production of a GNP that would fully use available resources. However, the old ways of doing things are becoming increasingly inadequate as the economy grows. Hence, fast and accurate *central* planning for more and more firms and products becomes ever more difficult. The observed slowdown in Soviet growth in the 1960's can almost certainly be explained by ever-growing internal inconsistencies in central plans, leading to ever-worsening degrees of short-run frictional and chronic unemployment of labor, land, and capital. Indeed, Soviet planners are in the midst of widespread debate on how the management of their economy can be improved. Some suggest that this be done by bringing reality more into line with the kind of central planning model discussed above. Such comprehensive planning with high-speed electronic computers is, however, as was already noted, music of a distant future. Others suggest that a variety of measures be taken to *decentralize* planning, as we shall see in Part 2 of this book. In any case, it is quite clear that the types of expansionary monetary and fiscal policies discussed in earlier chapters are quite irrelevant to the present Soviet economy. The problem of insufficient resource utilization does not stem from an incorrect level of aggregate demand, but from the failure of resources to move quickly to where they *are* demanded.

Inflation

Yet we cannot say that monetary or fiscal policies play no role at all in the Soviet Union. In fact, their main role is exactly to prevent inflation, rather than to stimulate aggregate demand. In a sense, of course, *undesired* demand-pull inflation as well as cost-push inflation can be said to be impossible in the Soviet Union. If the government, as it does, sets all prices (excepting those in the free collective farm market), prices can never rise unless the government agrees to raise them. If people have more money than is needed to buy goods available for sale at current prices, they will simply take the goods at given prices, accumulating unneeded cash in the process. In short, any government rigidly setting prices *can* prevent cost-push inflation entirely (with nothing but anger in people's hearts to show for it). It *can* suppress demand-pull inflation also (although at the cost of rising idle money balances in the hands of firms and households and possibly bad effects on their incentives).

the historical record   Yet the Soviet economy suffered severe inflation from 1928 to 1940.[11] Wages rose sixfold, consumer goods prices in state stores twelvefold, in the collective

[11] I am indebted for the following remarks to Franklyn D. Holzman, "Soviet Inflationary Pressures, 1928–1957: Causes and Cures," *The Quarterly Journal of Economics*, May 1960.

farm markets twentyfold, and basic industrial goods prices rose two-and-a-half-fold. The basic causes seem to have been the central planners' shift in the composition of real GNP from the production of consumer goods toward the production of goods for investment and the government. The reduced availability of consumer goods at unchanged prices and money incomes would create open demand-pull inflation if prices were allowed to move, or suppressed inflation if they were held steady by government decree.

In the 1930's, however, this tendency toward open or suppressed inflation was reinforced by the existence of a free labor market. In a situation in which managers were being ordered to produce more than was typically possible, they tried to bid labor away *from each other,* causing the aforementioned rise in wage rates and excessive labor turnover. The State Bank, furthermore, pursued a policy of freely making loans to businesses for this purpose. (Short-term loans outstanding rose from 4.4 billion rubles in 1930 to 55 billion rubles in 1941.) As a result, *larger* money incomes and reduced availability of consumer goods went hand in hand.

Instead of preventing inflation by directly taxing away excessive money incomes, the Soviet government decided to condone inflation. It raised consumer prices deliberately through increasing the sales tax component in them (called *turnover tax*) from an average of 21.5 percent in 1928 to 60.5 percent in 1940. Thus, people had to spend more money to get fewer goods. If they had money left over, they spent it in the collective farm market, bidding up prices there. Industrial firms, on the other hand, began to make losses at increased wage costs and fixed selling prices. For a while, the government paid them subsidies. Then, it raised their selling prices also.

It should be noted, however, that none of these things had to happen. Direct controls on people's mobility could have prevented wage hikes in the first place. So could a stringent monetary policy on the part of the State Bank, had it refused to provide funds to managers to pay higher wages to try to get workers who (in the aggregate) did not exist.

During World War II, consumer goods production was restricted even further. Wages rose more, but given the restrictions to labor mobility introduced in 1940, as well as a tight money policy started in 1939, they rose only by 70 percent. Applying stricter direct controls, consumer goods prices in state stores were raised only fourfold, other prices kept constant. People could do nothing with excess money but spend it in the collective farm market where prices by 1943 had risen fifteenfold over 1940.

At the end of the war, the government introduced a currency reform, exchanging the idle money (mostly in peasants' hands) at a rate of 10:1. In a way, this was a belated type of fiscal policy: expropriation by a direct tax.

Since World War II, there has been deflation, a reduction, rather than increase in the price level. Real GNP has grown rapidly, the availability of consumer goods has grown also, even though at a slower pace. Through strict bank controls, firms have received funds only sufficient to raise money wages slowly, in spite of increased freedom of the labor market. Considerable declines in all prices have been administered, making possible the distribution of consumer goods, which have multiplied faster than money incomes.

government policies   To sum up, various combinations of fiscal and monetary policies, together with direct controls, are being used in the Soviet economy to manipulate the level of prices. Central planners prefer to determine directly by command what gets produced, and they try to set their targets such as to fully use available resources. They do, however, pay money income to labor, selling the consumer goods, produced on the basis of the central plan, for money at state-administered prices. A fall (or rise) in the quantity of consumer goods available requires obviously that people's ability to buy goods is reduced (or increased). This can be done by fiscal policy, as by increasing (or decreasing) direct taxes (hence affecting money incomes) or indirect taxes (affecting prices). It can be done by monetary policy, as by reducing (or increasing) loans and grants to business enterprises destined for wage payments. Obviously, if money incomes change differently from prices or if different types of prices change unevenly, not only can consumers' real income in general be affected, but also its distribution among consumers. The redistributive effects of inflation or deflation can occur in the Soviet economy as everywhere else. As everywhere else, they can be countered by proper monetary and fiscal measures preventing general price changes or offsetting their undesirable effects.

SUMMARY

1 Central planning in the Soviet Union is not correctly described by the input-output model discussed in the previous chapter. Yet, that model can be used to illustrate how planning is done, and that model is also regarded by many as an ideal after which actual planning should strive.

2 On the basis of data collected by the Central Statistical Administration, the Soviet Council of Ministers and the Presidium of the Communist Party Central Committee issue party directives to Gosplan on the desired composition and growth of real GNP.

3 Party directives are turned by Gosplan, on the basis of technical coefficients, into a preliminary physical plan of economic activity. This plan covers the production of several thousand "important" goods and their direct input requirements. It is set up in the form of material balances.

4 The material balances are supplemented by monetary balances for "unimportant" goods. Material and monetary balances together are called control figures. They are adjusted, after a series of "discussions" with enterprise managers and subordinate planning agencies, leading to the draft plan.

5 Given the way incentives of enterprise managers are set up, there is no guarantee that mistakes made when setting up the control figures will be ironed out when elaborating the draft plan. Quite the opposite may be true.

6 Thus, Soviet planning may be described as setting up, in disaggregated form, of an input-output table in which many rows and columns are left out. For this reason, as well as the disloyalty of managers, this plan is bound to be internally inconsistent and quite possibly unfeasible.

7 Money and prices, which in principle would not be needed in a centrally directed economy, are used in the Soviet Union to provide a means (theoretically) of super-

vising via the State Bank all transactions among enterprises. They are used in part to allocate labor among occupations and jobs and provide work incentives, and, finally, to distribute goods to households.

8   Plans to improve the present system of planning and management of the economy include a computerization of the process of planning and plan execution. Their realization, if ever, is bound to take a long time.

9   The Soviets claim that "unemployment in the Soviet economy has been liquidated fully and forever." They define the potential labor force as all healthy males between 16 and 59 and females between 16 and 54. A portion of this group is in the armed forces, the rest comprises the potential civilian labor force. The greatest part of this group is employed in the socialist sector of the economy, that is, in state enterprises or on collective farms. Others are voluntarily unemployed (*Soviet* definition).

10   This "voluntary" unemployment includes (by the U.S. definition) employment outside the socialist sector, voluntary unemployment (including students), and involuntary unemployment.

11   Soviet labor resources have been allocated over the years by a mixture of central commands and market forces. Labor laws have been very stringent at times, lax at others. Labor unions play a role quite different from U.S. practice, serving primarily the interests of the state.

12   Given excessively high aggregate demand in the form of output quotas from Gosplan for all enterprises, and given managers' incentive to meet that demand, it is no surprise that general involuntary unemployment in the Soviet Union has, indeed, been eliminated. Short-run frictional and chronic unemployment, however, exist.

13   Short-run frictional unemployment of labor and nonlabor resources arises from faulty planning, because of voluntary labor turnover, new entry into the labor force, and so on. Chronic unemployment arises from technological change and other structural changes in the economy, and it may persist, as when people are unwilling or unable to be retrained or relocated. It may also be disguised by underemployment. Such underemployment exists both in industry and agriculture, for labor and nonlabor resources. Exact measurements of involuntary unemployment do not exist.

14   There are no employment agencies in the Soviet Union. Those who are involuntarily unemployed have to fend for themselves. There are no governmental programs designed to deal with chronic unemployment.

15   As a result, real GNP can be expected to be below potential. The observed fluctuations of Soviet GNP cannot be attributed to capricious fluctuations in aggregate demand (as might be done in the United States), but rather to the weather and to varying degrees of frictional and chronic unemployment arising from inconsistencies in the central plan.

16   The Soviet government controls all prices directly (except for the free collective farm market). Hence, it could prevent any open inflation, just as other countries do in wartime. Yet, at times it has deliberately manufactured inflation when the value of goods produced fell short (at current prices) of the money demand for them. Instead of taking people's money away by income taxes, the same was accomplished by raising the prices of goods via a turnover tax.

17   At other times, the Soviet government has suppressed inflation and dealt with the underlying causes for excess monetary demand. This has involved tight monetary policy, such as preventing State Bank loans to enterprises attempting to pay higher wages. It has also involved tight fiscal policy, such as a tax on everyone via a currency reform or via forced bond sales to the public and subsequent repudiation of the bonds. It has involved other measures: forbidding people to move to higher paying jobs or producing more of some goods in excess demand. In recent years, there has actually been deflation, as money incomes were allowed to rise more slowly than the availability of goods, and prices were than reduced.

TERMS[12]

acceptance method	labor books
collective farm	material balance
collective farm market	monetary balance
control figures	Orgnabor
currency reform	party directives
draft plan	plan law
Gosplan	state farm
	turnover tax

QUESTIONS FOR REVIEW AND DISCUSSION

1 Describe the process of Soviet economic planning with reference to Table 16.3 THE INPUT-OUTPUT TABLE AS A PLAN DOCUMENT.

2 Who or what is Gosplan? What does it do?

3 Consider row (3) of Table 16.3. Set it up as a material balance. (Make any assumptions you like regarding detail.)

4 What is the trouble with Soviet material balance planning?

5 Explain in detail why Gosplan discussion of the control figures with enterprise managers may make the plan less rather than more precise. Do you think Gosplan can afford not to have such discussions? Explain your answer.

6 Can you think of any way in which the disloyalty of Soviet managers can be avoided? (Hint: If you have an answer, ask yourself why the Soviet government has not introduced your solution long ago. They have probably thought of it, too.)

7 Are Soviet economic plans really made in Moscow?

8 Who in the Soviet Union decides on the types and quantities of consumer goods produced? How are these goods distributed to consumers? What kinds of problems may arise in this process?

9 The material balance given as Table 17.1 shows that it is planned to deliver 1.16 million cars in 1970 to aluminum manufacturers. Where would you find those cars

[12] Terms are defined in the Glossary at the end of the book.

on January 1, 1971, if things work out exactly as planned? (Hint: watch the differentiation between intermediate and final uses.)

10   What does the State Bank do in the Soviet Union?

11   Distinguish free consumer choice from consumer sovereignty.

12   What is the difference between the United States and Soviet definitions of "potential labor force"? (Suggestion: reread the discussions in Chapters 3 and 17, respectively.)

13   Summarize the history of Soviet labor legislation and describe the role of labor unions in the Soviet Union.

14   Make a list of all the types of short-run frictional and chronic unemployment existing in the Soviet Union. Think of labor and nonlabor resources. Compare the lists to the corresponding discussion in Chapter 3.

15   "Soviet teenagers, like their American counterparts, often have trouble finding jobs." Explain.

16   Why has the growth of Soviet real GNP slowed in the 1960's?

17   "The Soviet Union could not possibly have open inflation unless the government planned it that way, but it could easily have suppressed inflation contrary to plan." Discuss. How could the Soviet government deal with suppressed inflation? How could the U.S. government deal with it?

18   "Prices in the collective farm market can become a measure of the degree of suppressed inflation in the rest of the Soviet economy." Explain. (Hint: what could make prices in the collective farm market go up?)

19   Why would anyone *want* to plan an economy centrally?

20   Find out as much as you can about computers and evaluate the ease or difficulty of planning an entire economy with their help by, for instance, the input-output method.

epilogue

This brings us to the close of Part 1 of our endeavor which dealt with the full utilization of resources. As we have seen, full employment is achieved neither in the U.S.-type economy (because of insufficient aggregate demand or frictions impeding resource mobility), nor in the Soviet-type economy (because of frictions arising from the difficulties inherent in central planning). One could undoubtedly show the same for the underdeveloped nations of the world. Of course, no one has really accurate data on the resource availability, resource use, and real output of these nations. But most of them are agricultural economies and it is not hard to guess that a great portion of the labor force, however busy in *some* months, will be considerably underemployed during the rest of the year. Even in tropical countries, where agriculture has less of a seasonal character, labor may be underemployed much of the time. It is up to the reader whether he wants to regard this as "employment" (following the U.S. definition) or as unemployment. The same problem would arise with respect to natural resources that are known to exist but are not being utilized (because of, say, lack of skilled labor or of capital goods or technical knowledge). Is that voluntary unemployment or is it involuntary? Clearly, whatever definition one finally chooses, one would find instances of involuntary unemployment in any country in the world, and thus mankind is poorer than it has to be.

In the United States at least, fiscal and monetary policies could eliminate general unemployment. Possibly (at the price of demand-pull inflation) these policies could eliminate much of short-run frictional and chronic unemployment also. Other measures, however, may be more appropriate in dealing with frictional and chronic unemployment. In the Soviet Union nothing short of a complete change of the planning system might do (as we shall discuss further in Part 2). In the underdeveloped world, things may be more difficult still. The full use of resources may require a complete upheaval of society (as we shall see in Part 3). One obviously cannot pursue monetary and fiscal policies in a "vacuum" (say, in a preponderantly subsistence-type barter economy), and one cannot improve on central planning when there is none to begin with. Thus, much of the experience gained by economists in the U.S. economy, or in the Soviet economy for that matter, may be completely inapplicable to the *identical* problem of scarcity when met in the profoundly *different* environment of the underdeveloped world.

We now turn, in Part 2, to completely different matters. Even if we had full employment, the challenge of scarcity would not yet be met. There are other things one may do to reduce scarcity further. This requires taking a close look at exactly *how* resources that are fully employed are being used.

394

In this part of the book we shall discuss whether
the modern economy is likely to use it scarce resources
in an economically efficient way. Although we shall refer mostly
to data and institutions in the United States, the theoretical
analysis presented here can be regarded as applicable to most
developed capitalist countries in the world.
A final chapter, however, looks at the same issue in the very
different context of the socialist economy.

efficient
employment
of resources

Trust-Case Sentences: A Pattern for Future?

By EILEEN SHANAHAN

Special to The New York Times

WASHINGTON — For the first time since the famous electrical equipment industry cases of eight years ago, some executives of large, established corporations are going to jail for violations of the antitrust laws.

The sentencing last week of five top officials of plumbing-fixture companies for price fixing has raised some fresh questions about future trends in antitrust law enforcement.

The questions come at a time when most corporate executives and antitrust lawyers were concentrating their thoughts on the antitrust policies they could expect from the Nixon Administration in such relatively new areas as the treatment of conglomerate mergers. They were certainly not expecting any changes of status in such settled areas of antitrust law as price fixing.

The plumbing-fixture cases do, however, represent something almost brand new in antitrust law, and something that must be considered when the expected policies of the Nixon Administration are being weighed.

Unusual Sentencing

This is the simple fact that the jail sentences were meted out not after any conviction nor after a guilty plea, but after pleas of nolo contendere.

The sentences, which ranged from 24 hours to 30 days in terms of the amount of time that will actually be served in jail, presumably should not have come as any surprise to the defendants, despite the fact that such sentences are almost unprecedented.

Judge Louis Rosenberg of the United States District Court for the Western District of Pennsylvania, before whom the case was tried, asked each of the defendants whether he understood that the plea constituted an acknowledgement that there was a factual basis for the charge against him. A nolo plea, which literally means that the defendant is not contesting the charge, has not generally been defined as such an acknowledgement in antitrust cases in the past.

Thus, traditionally, corporate executives involved in price-fixing charges have often been willing to plead nolo contendere. That way, they escaped the cost and publicity of a long trial, but needed fear nothing worse than fines, corporate or individual.

Avoiding Costs

The Justice Department, for its part, was generally, though not always, willing to accept the plea to avoid the cost of litigation—and the possibility that it might fail to obtain a conviction.

In the plumbing fixtures case, the department fought a long history of convictions for price fixing and that the offense in this case had been particularly grievous, consisting not only of a criminal conspiracy to fix prices but also of a conspiracy to discontinue entirely the manufacture of a lower-priced line of plumbing fixtures. Literally every significant manufacturer of plumbing fixtures was indicted in the case, although only five of the eight defendant corporations pleaded nolo and the rest remain to be tried.

In the electrical equipment cases, the department had also fought the court's acceptance of nolo pleas, on the specific ground that it wanted to punish the conspirators with jail sentences.

In this case, the Justice Department seemed to lose the battle but actually won the war. The judge accepted the nolo pleas but imposed jail sentences anyway.

The wisdom of nolo pleas in criminal antitrust cases seems certain to be reassessed by many in the light of this case.

Resolutions Made

Judge Rosenberg actually required resolutions from the boards of directors of the companies that pleaded nolo stating that they recognized that their pleas were an admission of guilt for the purposes of this case. The companies that entered the nolo pleas were the Wallace-Murray Corpora-

tion, the Universal Rundle Corporation, the Rheem Manufacturing Company, the Crane Company and the Briggs Manufacturing Company, in addition to the Plumbing Fixture Manufacturers Association.

Those who refused to plead nolo include the largest manufacturer of plumbing fixtures, American Standard, Inc., the Kohler Company and the Borg-Warner Corporation. Their trial is scheduled to begin in mid-January.

Justice Department lawyers who are jubliant about the outcome of the case so far believe it will have a meaningful deterrent effect on would-be price-fixers, who will now know that the Justice Department may be able to put conspirators in jail without the burden and cost of tying up manpower in a full trial.

They also believe that an interesting precedent in antitrust enforcement has been set that will be difficult for the Nixon Administration to turn away from.

Regardless of what antitrust policies the new administration follows, it is generally believed here that it cannot turn away from prosecution of hard-core antitrust violations, such as price-fixing.

Of course, it remains entirely possible—some informed persons even say probable that the Nixon Administration will follow a strong antitrust policy in all areas.

A large proportion of the cases that broke new legal ground in recent decades were filed during the Eisenhower Administration, especially the second, under acting Antitrust Director Robert A. Bicks.

Matter of Confidence

Mr. Bicks used to argue that any Republican Administration was bound to pursue vigorous antitrust enforcement to prove to the public that it was not a captive of its business constituency.

Mr. Bicks and others have also reasoned that a Republican Administration that does not believe in direct government regulation of business must, perforce, see to it that the market functions freely as a regulator. Such are certainly the views of some of Mr. Nixon's currently prominent economic advisers. . . .

18

big business

and

antitrust laws

IN PART 1 we dealt with the great problems of full employment and price level stability. Analyzed in the light of Keynesian ideas, one thing became inescapable: a great deal can be done by government to counter the obvious evils of unemployment and inflation. In this second part of the book, we proceed on a much more difficult road. We leave behind us macroeconomics. We cease to look at the economy as a whole (note that the word *macroeconomics* derives from the Greek *macros*, meaning large). We turn instead to its parts, to individual firms, individual resources, or individual industries. We now deal with *microeconomics* (a word deriving from the Greek *micros*, meaning small). We do this to pursue a much more subtle and less dramatic theme. Assuming resources are fully employed, how can we be sure that we employ them in the right way, that we really get the most out of them? How can we be sure to employ them in an *economically efficient* way? It is extremely difficult to give a full exposition, at an elementary level, of the meaning of economic efficiency. By concentrating on a few selected problems, we can, however, gain a feeling for the importance of the issue. This chapter will proceed along this road by discussing the issue of "big" business vs. antitrust laws. In the following chapters, we shall deal, in turn, with selected problems posed by agriculture, labor unions, and foreign trade, with a final chapter making a summary judgment on the economic efficiency of the American economy.[1]

THE BIG BUSINESS NEWS OF 1961

Early in 1961, the newspapers headlined one of the biggest pieces of business news in many years. A federal judge in Philadelphia, claiming that the survival of the free-enterprise system was at stake, had imposed fines totaling $2 million on twenty-nine electrical equipment industry firms and dozens of their employees after they were convicted of conspiracy to fix prices and rig bids. Seven prominent executives of the electrical equipment industry, coming from such renowned firms as General Electric, Westinghouse, and Allen-Bradley, were convicted of the same conspiracy and were sentenced to jail. All defendants had pleaded guilty or no defense. Here is what had happened.

In addition to such common items as refrigerators, washers, and electric motors, which were sold to millions, these firms were producing gigantic pieces of apparatus, such as power transformers, switchgear assemblies, and turbine-generator units, built to specification for relatively few customers. Such items, understandably, had no common price and were sold, mostly to private electric utility companies and to various levels of government, in sealed bids with the lowest bidder getting the business. The prices involved were gigantic, too. A 500,000 kw turbine generator, producing electricity from steam, cost $16 million, for instance. As a result, the economic position of many a firm in this field was one of feast or famine: either there were large orders for the giant and expensive pieces of equipment or there were none at all.

Naturally, the executives of the industry were less than enthusiastic about this situa-

---

[1] Those who wish to pursue the subject of economic efficiency in greater depth and more systematically than is provided here may turn to my *Scarcity Challenged* (New York: Holt, Rinehart and Winston, 1968), Chapters 15–19.

tion. Their anxiety was reinforced by the marked overcapacity with which the industry had come out of World War II. The industry was equipped to meet peak government demands of the war, but that demand had vanished and was not yet replaced by growing private needs. No wonder they all wanted to appropriate for themselves whatever private demand there was for these products. This urgent desire led in 1955, and again in 1957, to price wars among the firms involved. In a famous "white sale," prices of some equipment were cut in successive rounds by as much as 50 percent, that is, by millions of dollars! As you might expect, that was no solution. Profits throughout the industry plummeted. There was red ink in some cases.

While all this was going on, the executives of the firms involved saw one another frequently. They had common interests. They met at industry association meetings and technical conferences. Some were personal friends and met socially. Naturally, they talked about their mutual desire to ensure their firms' survival.

What each needed was secure minimum prices and a minimum share of the market. They needed not to be told that their past behavior had been mutually destructive. Was it difficult to formulate the idea of a common response to a clearly recognized common danger? Of course not.

Before long, beginning in 1956 and continuing into 1959, the executives exchanged information on costs, prices, and intentions. They decided to fix prices and divide markets so that everyone could "get along." Nominally sealed bids were rigged in advance so that each company would be assured a certain percentage of the available business. In order to preserve the secrecy of the operation, the executives referred to their companies by code numbers in their correspondence. They made telephone calls from public booths or their homes, rather than from their offices. They also falsified expense accounts for their meetings to cover up the fact that they had all been in a certain place at the same time.

Yet, as so often happens, there is no honor among thieves. An employee of a small conspirator company told all to federal officials in 1959. As a result, 2 years later, the American business community had the exhilarating spectacle of watching some of the nation's most highly paid (and impeccably dressed) executives being marched off to jail! Some watched in horror, others with glee. Meanwhile, customers were suing the convicted companies for hundreds of millions of dollars' worth of damages for having paid "artificially high" prices.

THE ANTITRUST LAWS

The story of the electrical equipment industry conspiracy is by no means unique. Every year brings new instances of governmental power being brought to bear against the "noncompetitive" behavior of private businesses. In 1967, for instance, the Supreme Court voided the 1957 merger between Procter and Gamble (the largest U.S. manufacturer of soap) and the Clorox Corporation (dominant in the liquid bleach market). At the same time, the Department of Justice indicted Pfizer and Co., Cyanamid, and Bristol-Myers Co. for having monopolized the sale and rigged the price of certain "wonder drugs." The government claimed these actions to have been agreed on orally. But it also cited visible evidence of cooperation: how, for instance, in 1953 and 1954, Cyanamid had secretly sold a million grams of a drug (at a 64 percent profit) to its main "competitor" Pfizer (which promptly resold the same quantity to the public at a price three times higher). The companies were convicted and promptly sued by their customers. In 1969, the convicted companies and two others involved offered to pay $120 million in damages. The American Hospital Association rejected its $20 million share. Instead it sued for treble damages on an alleged overcharge of $250 million.

In 1968, the Supreme Court ruled against a Florida-based Concentrated Phosphate Export Association. It had handled U.S. foreign aid deliveries of phosphate to Korea in the early 1960's. Five producers had allocated the available business among themselves and set minimum prices. They were convicted of illegal activities directed against the American taxpayer. The Supreme Court also ordered the Continental Oil Company to divest itself of the Malco Refineries, Inc., acquired in 1959. Malco sold gasoline to more than 200 distributors and retailers, mostly in New Mexico. This was said to lessen competition too severely. Also in 1968, the Justice Department sued Hart Schaffner and Marx, a major maker of men's clothing, to divest itself of thirty-three companies operating forty-eight men's clothing stores. Continued control of these companies, acquired since 1965, was said to substantially lessen competition. Note also the news report on the 1968 plumbing case that introduces this chapter.

Indeed, this activity has continued under the Nixon administration. In 1969, the Florists Transworld Delivery Association was convicted of price fixing. IBM (according to sales the seventh largest U.S. industrial corporation) was sued for monopolizing the computer industry. The acquisition by Atlantic Richfield of Sinclair Oil was attacked in court. So was the merger of the nation's sixth largest steel company (Jones and Laughlin) with the nation's thirty-eighth largest industrial corporation (Ling-Temco-Vought). And so was the acquisition of one of the largest food vendors (the Canteen Corporation) by ITT, the twenty-first largest industrial corporation.

All such governmental actions are based on a set of laws, commonly referred to as the *antitrust laws*. Their avowed purpose is to maintain competition to assure that resources are used in an economically efficient manner. Let us consider what the laws are all about, what they should accomplish ideally, and what they do achieve in fact.

A Brief Look at History

During the last century, the American economy underwent a thoroughgoing transformation. As we all know, the family farm and the small business serving a local market, once dominant, began to recede into the background. The United States was joining the *industrial revolution*. A significant factor in this development was the creation of a nationwide reliable system of transportation and communication. The building of a network of railroads was in no small degree the work of government. Although private enterprise did the building and owning and operating, government made it possible. It authorized the corporate form of business without which, as we saw in Chapter 5, the accumulation of the required huge sums of money would have been impossible. Government also gave the railroad companies the right to take land by eminent domain, a right usually preserved for government itself through which it can force the sale of private land. Finally, government land grants in the West, which (some people think) were considerably more generous than necessary for laying the tracks (they included a 6-mile-wide stretch along one side of the tracks), provided an enormous subsidy to the railroad companies.

emerging giants   By having thus assured the building of a nationwide rail network and by also granting other forms of business the right of incorporation, the government set the stage for their growth. Technological advances made possible a size and complexity of manufacturing plants hitherto undreamed of. The above factors made them economically possible also. The railroads vastly expanded the size of the market from which supplies could be drawn and to which products could be shipped. Advanced communication also drew the United States closer together. The corporate form of business allowed the amassing in a few hands of huge sums required for large-scale operations of buying, manufacturing, and selling. What was physically possible became profitable.

Business entered the age of mass production, because under the new technology increases in output led to cuts in cost per unit until very large output volumes were reached. But there was one further consequence. Businesses also became more vulnerable to competition. The huge quantities of capital and land employed by a single business saddled it with huge *fixed* charges: interest and depreciation on capital, rent on land, as well as wages for administrative personnel. These charges, now large relative to the wages of production workers and raw material costs, remained fixed, regardless of the volume of sales. Capital, land, and administrative personnel could not be laid off, as production workers could. Their costs, unlike the bill for production workers and raw materials, could not quickly be reduced in the face of declining sales. Hence, declining sales, by requiring a cutback in output, now led to a rise in cost per unit. Naturally, this happened without a corresponding rise, and possibly with a fall, in sales price per unit. Hence, a loss of market meant a severe profit squeeze and quite possibly bankruptcy. For the emerging big business, furthermore, it meant bankruptcy on a multimillion dollar scale. No wonder that more and more American businesses sought one goal above all others: maintaining or increasing their share of the market. Being able to sell a lot meant being able to produce a lot. And being able to produce a lot was the only economic justification for the giant technically advanced production facilities being installed everywhere. Large output was needed to spread fixed costs over many units and hold down costs per unit.

competition among the giants   Competition became increasingly drastic during the last third of the nineteenth century. The giants locked horns. Oil producer against oil producer. Steel mill against steel mill. Railroad against railroad. Mining company against mining company. The 1870's and 1880's saw a series of price wars, and "wars" with other, and less civilized methods, too. (Standard Oil, for instance, bought up pipelines and refused service to competing oil companies. It drove competing pipelines to the wall by buying up refineries which then refused to take oil from the competing pipelines. It even forced railroads into giving it rebates of up to 50 percent, not only on Standard's own shipments, but even on those of its competitors!)

But then, just like the electrical equipment companies discussed above, they decided that there must be a better way. They formed *trade associations*, and *gentlemen's agreements,* and *pools*—all of which were informal agreements to divide up markets and avoid suicidal price wars among them. In the 1880's, there emerged a coal pool, a cordage pool, a salt pool, a whiskey pool, and numerous railroad pools. But there was one problem. When times were good for all members of the pool, things worked out as planned. Each member became effectively the only seller in a given area and soaked his captive customers to his heart's content. When times were bad, however, his co-conspirators tried to cheat on the agreement. Thus, the pools broke down. This could not very well be avoided by reaching more formal and written agreements. The English common law (unwritten law) invalidated contracts binding competitors to fixed prices, output, or market shares.

the end of competition   Nevertheless, the emerging new world of big business was determined to survive. And it did. Three ideas provided the necessary boost. First among these was the *trust*. Stockholders of competing companies would surrender their stock certificates (and the right to run enterprise affairs) to a group of "trustees" in return for trust certificates. The trustees would then run all the companies as if they were a single enterprise, eliminating all competition among them. Holders of trust certificates would, as before, be entitled to all the profits made by the trust. Because most stockholders are more interested in earning something on their financial investment than in running a business and because the elimination of competition through the device of the trust was expected to stabilize, if not raise, profits, the number of trusts grew rapidly. Most famous was the oil trust under John D. Rockefeller. Other large ones existed in whiskey, cordage, lead, and sugar.

A second device used to replace competition with complete market control by a single seller (monopoly) was the *merger*. Most important for this purpose was the "horizontal" merger in which competing firms selling a like product in the same area would merge into one. As giants gobbled up their smaller competitors, and eventually their larger rivals, the trend of monopoly or near-monopoly to win over competition was further strengthened. In manufacturing and mining alone, the number of mergers rose from 43 in 1895 to 1,208 in 1899. It involved assets of $41 million in 1895, but assets of $2.3 billion 4 years later.

A third method of escaping competition was the formation of *holding companies*. This was made possible by an 1888 New Jersey law permitting one corporation to buy stock in another, supplemented by a later law permitting a New Jersey corporation to do business anywhere. As a result, a New Jersey corporation could be formed for the sole purpose of buying a controlling share of stock in a variety of other corporations. This holding company (holding the stock certificates of others) could then be used as a device to run all the firms in an industry as a unit and to eliminate competition among them. The holding company itself needed in no way to own directly any productive assets, as land or machinery.

With a minimum of financial investment and some luck, the owners of the holding company could control a vast industrial empire.

Consider a hypothetical example. Take an oil company with real estate and equipment of $1 billion. Suppose it has acquired these assets by selling $500 million of bonds and $500 million of stock certificates. Suppose further that half the stock is nonvoting preferred stock.[2] Then you will be able to control the corporation with certainty by owning just a little bit over half of the common stock that alone carries the right to vote. That is, you can control all of the $1 billion of assets by owning just a little more than $125 million of common stock. Because in fact most stockholders do not bother to vote, especially if the common stock ownership is widely dispersed, you can probably control the company by owning a much smaller block of common stock. Suppose instead of owning a fraction above 50 percent, you can get away with owning as little as 10 percent and still control the firm. Then you can control the $1 billion of assets with only $25 million of common stock. And you can control ten companies like this (with $10 billion of assets) with only $250 million of common stock.

Better than that! Let a holding company A own those $250 million of common stock. If you are smart and lucky, you can endow company A with 250 million *dollars* by again selling bonds (of say, $125 million), nonvoting preferred stock (of, say, $62.5 million), and voting common stock (of the remaining $62.5 million). Making the same assumptions as above, you can control company A (and indirectly all ten oil companies) with as little as 10 percent of its common stock, or $6.25 million.

Nor need you stop here. Let holding company B hold those $6.25 million of common stock. By the same procedure used above, you can control company B (and hence A and hence all ten oil producers) with as little as $156,250. Or you can let holding company C own those $156,250 of common stock of B, while you control C, *and ultimately $10 billion of oil companies,* with no more than $3,906.25.

This may seem fantastic, but it is not. Many actual holding companies exceeded vastly in complexity the above example. They included such well-known companies as American Can, American Tobacco, U.S. Rubber, and U.S. Steel, established around the turn of this century. Prior to World War I, Standard Oil of New Jersey controlled seventy operating companies directly and thirty others indirectly by this device. The Morgan banking interests held 341 directorships in 112 corporations. Their aggregative wealth exceeded three times all the real and personal property of New England. The billion dollar Associated Gas and Electric Company was controlled by a man holding $100,000 of voting stock.

the Sherman Act   By the above devices, business empires grew in America. With them grew the public fear of big business. The need to restrain competition became an issue in the national election campaign of 1888. Both major parties promised "to do something about monopoly." They did, in 1890, by enacting the *Sherman Act*. Thus, the "wickedness"

[2] See pages 109–110 above for a discussion of the various forms of corporate securities.

of monopoly, long asserted by common law, was affirmed by statute. The Sherman Act probably is one of the shortest pieces of legislation on record:

Section 1. Every contract, combination in the form of trust or otherwise, or conspiracy, in restraint of trade or commerce among the several States, or with foreign nations, is hereby declared to be illegal. Every person who shall make any such contract or engage in any such combination or conspiracy, shall be deemed guilty of a misdemeanor, and, on conviction thereof, shall be punished by fine not exceeding five thousand dollars, or by imprisonment not exceeding one year, or by both said punishments, in the discretion of the court.

Section 2. Every person who shall monopolize, or attempt to monopolize, or combine or conspire with any other person or persons, to monopolize any part of the trade or commerce among the several States, or with foreign nations, shall be deemed guilty of a misdemeanor, and, on conviction thereof, shall be punished by fine not exceeding five thousand dollars, or by imprisonment not exceeding one year, or by both said punishments, in the discretion of the court.

Without defining its terms, the act thus forbade individual or joint efforts to restrain trade and to "monopolize." It was not clear whether it outlawed already *existing* monopolies or only the attempt or even only the successful attempt to get a monopoly. Nor was it clear whether it outlawed every or only every unreasonable combination in restraint of trade. The act was to be enforced by the U.S. Attorney General, and its vague language gave wide latitude of interpretation to him and to the courts.

For instance, the Supreme Court in 1911 enunciated its famous "rule of reason" for interpreting the Sherman Act. Both the Standard Oil Company (then controlling 91 percent of the refining industry) and American Tobacco (controlling 90 percent of the market for tobacco products except cigars) were found guilty under both Sections 1 and 2 of the Sherman Act. They were dissolved into several independent firms. However, they were guilty for having restrained trade *unreasonably*, having used vicious tactics to dispose of smaller competitors. This interpretation by the court narrowed the scope of the Sherman Act considerably. Subsequently, International Harvester, United Shoe Machinery Corporation, Eastman Kodak, and U.S. Steel were found *not* guilty, precisely because they held near-monopolies which they had "thrust upon them," that is, without having made predatory attacks on competitors. Mere size, or the existence of unexerted power, the court held in 1920, was no offense. Yet, in 1945, in a case involving Alcoa (then controlling 90 percent of aluminum production), the court reversed tradition. Alcoa was found guilty because of bigness alone, even though its conduct had not been offensive.

the Clayton Act   In the years following its enactment, the Sherman Act was hardly ever enforced. In many industries (such as steel, farm machinery, and tin cans) powerful new business combinations came into being. Again and again, practices used to achieve them were held not to violate the act. When the American Sugar Refining Company bought controlling stock interests in its four largest competitors, the Supreme Court found no Sherman Act violation, because sugar refining was manufacturing, not commerce. Hence, there was no restraint of *trade*. All this became another national issue by 1912. President Wilson eventually recommended that the meaning of the Sherman Act be spelled out in detail (listing monopolistic practices item by item) and that a special agency be created to enforce the law. It was found impossible to follow the first proposal, except in part. The *Clayton Act* of 1914 specifically outlawed a number of practices, *but only if* their effect was "to substantially lessen competition or tend to create a monopoly."

The Clayton Act specifically forbade sellers "to discriminate in price between different purchasers of commodities." But it allowed such differences if due to "differences in the grade, quality, or quantity of the commodity sold," if making "only due allowance for differences in the cost of selling or transportation," and if made "in good faith to meet competition." This price discrimination section of the law was primarily designed to protect small firms from larger rivals who frequently slashed prices on particular goods in particular markets only in order to eliminate small competitors.

The act also outlawed exclusive contracts, forbidding sellers to "lease or make a sale or contract for sale of . . . commodities . . . on the condition that the lessee or purchaser thereof shall not use or deal in the . . . commodity . . . of a competitor." It similarly outlawed tying contracts wherein the seller sells good A only if the buyer also takes good B from him.

Firms were forbidden to acquire shares of competing corporations or to have interlocking directorates between each other if one of them had a net worth of more than $1 million.

the Federal Trade Commission Act.   At the same time, the *Federal Trade Commission Act* was passed. The law forbade all "unfair methods of competition." The commission newly created was empowered to issue "cease and desist" orders and to bring suits against "unfair methods of competition," such suits being financed by the Treasury. Previously, such suits had to be brought on private initiative and at private expense. As in earlier legislation, it was not spelled out what was and was not "unfair."

the Robinson-Patman Act   The next legislation of importance in this area was the *Robinson-Patman Act* of 1936. Its concern was price discrimination; in particular, the protection of small independent wholesalers and retailers from mass distributors (such as chain stores or mail order houses). The latters' bargaining strength (argued the smaller independent distributors) enabled them to pay "unjustified" lower prices for their purchases and then to undercut competitors. (In fact, as subsequent developments showed, much of their superior competitive strength came from streamlining internal operations.) The act forbade differential quantity discounts among buyers buying the same quantity. It forbade *any* quantity discounts *if* they helped to create monopoly; and, given the same effect, it forbade the charging in one locality of lower prices than elsewhere. Fines up to $5,000 and imprisonment up to 1 year, or both were provided for violators.

amendments   These are the basic antitrust laws on the books today (fines are now $50,000 on each count, however). Later legislation has only slightly amended these laws:

The *Wheeler-Lea Act* of 1938, for instance, outlawed in addition to "unfair methods of competition" also "unfair or deceptive acts or practices" in and of themselves, even if they did not hurt competitors. If all competitors lie equally to consumers, for instance, they are now violating the law. Ever since that time, the Federal Trade Commission has been able to control deceptive advertising practices.

The *Celler-Kefauver Antimerger Act* of 1950 was designed to close a loophole in the Clayton Act. It forbids not only the acquisition, for purposes of monopolization, of competitors' shares of stock, but also the use of such stock by proxy or the direct acquisition of the assets of a competitive firm. The act has been used to block any "horizontal" merger (between firms in the same industry) that would give the new firm control of at least 15 percent of the market. For instance, it was used in 1956 to block the merger of Bethlehem Steel Corporation with the Youngstown Sheet and Tube Company, the second and sixth largest steel producers, respectively. From 1951–1966, one of four such mergers was attacked by the government. The act has also been used to prevent "vertical" mergers, as when manufacturers combine with their suppliers or with their customers, such as the retail stores handling their products. From 1951 to 1966, one of six such proposed mergers was attacked by the government. Finally, the act has been used to prevent even "conglomerate" mergers, as in the Procter and Gamble-Clorox case mentioned earlier. Such mergers in which one company moves into other fields by acquiring diversified companies have been least discouraged however. Only one of twenty-eight proposed has been challenged.

The permissive government attitude toward conglomerate mergers, however, may well change during the Nixon administration. Both the administration and Congress have been increasingly disturbed by a current wave of such mergers between groups of companies operating in separate markets. The above-mentioned International Telephone and Telegraph Company (ITT) is a case in point of an empire held together solely by financial and administrative authority. It started out as a communications company and still operates as such in 123 countries. As a natural move, it branched into the manufacture of telephone equipment. But now it also rents cars (Avis). It builds homes (Levitt and Sons). It bakes bread (Continental). It operates hotels and motor inns (Sheraton). It makes consumer loans. It produces glass and sand. It processes data. It manages mutual funds. So Congressmen have been wondering whether such a giant might not curtail competition just as much as a large firm producing only a single good. Might such a giant not use profits from one market to subsidize losses in another (while prices are held low there to drive out competitors)? Might not potential new firms in any of the fields mentioned above be simply scared away by the prospect of being unable to match the advertising budget or established distribution channels of ITT? Might a conglomerate, such as ITT, not force its suppliers into purchases from it they would rather not make? ITT, for instance, is the nation's twenty-first-ranking industrial corporation (by sales). Its many suppliers employ among themselves a third of the nation's industrial labor force. Now just suppose, Congress has asked, ITT acquires the Canteen Corporation, one of the largest food vending companies. And just suppose it forces its suppliers (by threatening not to buy from them) to buy their in-plant food services from its Canteen Corporation division. The difficulties then encountered by other food vendors are obvious. Thus, conglomerate mergers, however harmless they may look at first sight, may also lead to monopoly.

THE EVIL OF BIG BUSINESS

The time has come to look at the economic significance of any governmental campaign against bigness in business. What, if anything, is wrong with the acquisition and use of significant private economic power? And if something is wrong with big business, how big is "too big?"

Most people would probably answer that any private business large enough to exploit its workers by paying too low wages or its customers by charging excessive prices is too big. It is then reaping *monopoly profits*, they will say, and that is what is evil about big business. Like a bully, big businesses drive the little man to the wall and tyrannize him. The government, like a policeman, should protect the little man. Antitrust laws, the Department of Justice, and the courts serve the function of the policeman.

Ask any economist, and this is exactly the answer he will *not* give you. Monopoly profits are not the problem at all. Economists know that there is a very simple and reliable way to deal with any person, business, or group in the population that is deemed to have too high an income. They can be forced to pay a percentage of that income as a tax to the government. Thus, big businesses, if we disliked their monopoly profits, could simply be forced to pay 30 or 50 or even 99 percent of them in taxes. If we wanted to, we could give that money to the people exploited by the monopoly. This would solve the problem, and we could save ourselves the trouble of legislating antitrust laws and taking businesses to court under them. Moreover, a tax taking a *percentage* of business income would in no way change the behavior of the businesses involved. If, as is likely, they produce an output volume designed to maximize their profits, they cannot escape the tax by producing more or less. That would reduce their gross profits and hence their net profits, which are a percentage of them. Even if the tax rate is 99 percent and pretax "monopoly profits" are $50 million, it is better to get 1 percent of $50 million than 1 percent of any smaller figure.

The real problem, as economists see it, is much more subtle. The existence of big business is most likely to lead to a use of resources such that output derived from them is less than it could be. Big business, furthermore, in the economist's sense, is not just the giant firm discussed above. It is, in fact, *any business large enough to influence its selling price through its own actions*. The economist calls such business an *imperfect competitor*. This is to distinguish it from the *perfect competitor*, briefly discussed in Chapter 2, who has absolutely no control over price. We can best bring out the issues involved by briefly considering the typical behavior of the two types of firms.

The Perfect Competitor

As we said, a perfect competitor has no control over price. Take a farmer growing Irish potatoes, for instance. Even if he is a large farmer, he will be supplying at best a negligible portion of the nation's crop. (In 1966, U.S. farms produced over 15 million tons.) In a fashion described earlier by Figure 2.5 DEMAND AND SUPPLY CURVES SUPERIMPOSED, demand and supply will establish an equilibrium price for Irish potatoes such that the total quantity brought to market at that price is gladly bought, leaving neither shortages nor surpluses. Suppose the equilibrium price, as in part (a) of Figure 18.1 THE PERFECTLY COMPETITIVE OUTPUT MARKET, is $45 per ton. For simplicity, we are assuming here that the total annual crop is thrown onto the market no matter what the price. Hence, the supply curve is a vertical line. If the crop can be stored, we could, of course, have a more normal supply curve (of the type we met in Chapter 2) with quantity supplied lower at low prices and higher at high prices, as potatoes are put into or taken out of inventories, respectively. Now consider a single farmer. He may be growing 1,000 or 2,000 or even 15,000 tons of potatoes a year. Whichever he does, he has no chance of influencing the equilibrium price set by the market. He can double his sales offer or reduce it to zero. He will still be faced with a price of $45 per ton. His actions would change market supply from 15 million tons to, perhaps, 15,002,000 tons. Try to envisage this in the graph. It would shift the market supply curve in part (a) so negligibly that the market would not react. The equilibrium price would change by a tiny fraction of a penny. That is, it would stay put. To the single seller that price is a datum.

This is illustrated by the horizontal line in part (b). That is how the demand curve looks to the single farmer. People are demanding, *at $45 per ton,* any quantity he can sell. No matter what he sells, 1, 1,000, or 5,000 tons, he can get $45 for each. He could not get a cent

Figure 18.1   THE PERFECTLY COMPETITIVE OUTPUT MARKET

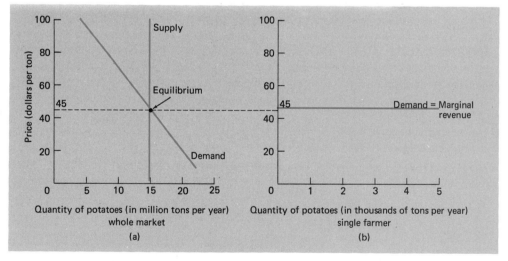

In a perfectly competitive market, here for Irish potatoes, demand and supply in the aggregate set the equilibrium price. In this case (part a), the total crop of 15 million tons is thrown onto the market for whatever it will bring (hence the vertical supply line). It is bought for $45 per ton. The single farmer is helpless in the face of this price. To him it is a given at which, it appears to him, he can sell any quantity he likes (part b). Each extra ton sold brings him extra, or "marginal" revenue equal to the market price.

more, for there are hundreds of thousands of competing farmers selling potatoes just as good as his. He need not sell for a cent less. Everybody in the country would then want to buy from him. He could not possibly handle the business. He would only be giving money away needlessly.

profit maximization   As economists put it, the equilibrium market price is our farmer's *marginal revenue*. It is the figure that shows how his total revenue would change if he changed output and sales by a ton. It shows the extra (or marginal) revenue he can obtain if he sells another ton. It is also the revenue he loses if he sells a ton less. In fact, economists *define* a perfect competitor as a business whose marginal revenue is constant no matter what the volume of its sales.

How much will our farmer produce and sell? This depends on more than what he can get. It depends also on what it costs him to produce. In fact, argue economists, if he is interested, as businessmen usually are, in maximizing his profits, our farmer need only compare his marginal revenue (how his total revenue changes with a unit change in output) with his *marginal cost* (how his total cost changes with a unit change in output). If he produces another ton and his total cost rises from $700 to $720, his marginal cost was $20. If he sells that extra ton, and his total revenue changes from $800 to $845, his marginal revenue was $45. Clearly, as long as marginal cost is below marginal revenue, it pays to produce more. Another ton produced and sold would then add more to total revenue than to total cost. Hence, it would increase total profit, which is the difference between the two. When marginal cost is above marginal revenue, it pays to produce less.[3] Producing and selling a ton less would then reduce total cost more than total revenue. It again would increase total profit. Our farmer, indeed any business, would *maximize* his *total profit where marginal cost and marginal revenue are equal*. This is the point where producing a unit more or less would change total costs by exactly as much as total revenue. There would then be no change in total profit.

the law of diminishing returns   The above leaves us with one question. Can we be sure that there is a level of output at which marginal cost and marginal revenue will be equal? What if marginal cost is always above or always below marginal revenue?

The answer is simple. If marginal cost exceeds marginal revenue at all levels of output, our firm will go bankrupt and disappear from the scene. If marginal cost is below marginal revenue, our firm will expand its operations, but it will not grow to infinite size. Sooner or later, marginal costs will rise to the level of marginal revenue and limit the volume of output produced by our firm. This is owing to a technological fact, the famous *law of diminishing returns*.

This law states that, given technical know-how, *successive additions to output brought about by equal additions of quantities of resources used will get smaller and smaller, provided at least one resource remains fixed.*

---

[3] Advanced texts would show that this is strictly true only if marginal costs are not falling.

This is not difficult to understand. Consider our farmer. In any given year, he has a given know-how relating to farming. He has, let us suppose, certain fixed quantities of land and equipment. To these he applies labor, fertilizer, pesticides, and seed potatoes. How many tons of potatoes will he produce?

This clearly depends on the amounts and proportions of labor, chemicals, and seed potatoes applied to the fixed quantities of other inputs. Take the simplest possible case in which he arbitrarily chooses amounts of chemicals and seed potatoes and then varies only the hours of labor put in. If he experiments, he might get the kind of results shown in Table

Table 18.1   THE LAW OF DIMINISHING RETURNS

QUANTITY OF LABOR (HOURS PER YEAR) (1)		TOTAL OUTPUT (TONS OF POTATOES) (2)	
3,000		1,000	
6,000	→ +3,000	1,500	→ +500
9,000	→ +3,000	1,800	→ +300
12,000	→ +3,000	1,900	→ +100
15,000	→ +3,000	1,920	→ + 20

Given all other inputs as fixed, the law of diminishing returns becomes evident when equal additions of one input (1) bring forth smaller and smaller additions to output (2).

18.1. These results are not surprising. They simply show that sooner or later the ability of one input (here labor) to increase output, while other inputs are held fixed, becomes exhausted. More tender loving care may raise output by keeping the weeds down and providing water through irrigation ditches, but it cannot make up for lack of seed potatoes, fertilizers, or land. Eventually, a greater dose of labor *by itself* cannot add more to output. The same would have been true had we added more and more labor *and* chemicals *and* seed potatoes to fixed amounts of land. There would have come a time when the available land was saturated with the other inputs and further output was impossible. Because all businesses in the short run are subject to the fixity of some inputs, they are all subject to this law of diminishing returns.

Notice what this implies. It implies that marginal costs of all businesses will be rising after some level of output is reached. Here is why. In the above case, going from 3,000 to 6,000 hours of labor per year raises output by 500 tons. That is, when total output is 1,000 tons, the labor cost of extra output, or marginal cost measured in labor hours, is 3,000 hours per 500 tons, or 6 hours per ton.

Now go from 6,000 to 9,000 hours. This raises output by another 300 tons (note the *diminishing return* compared to the earlier addition of 500 tons). That is, when total output is 1,500 tons, the marginal cost measured in labor hours is 3,000 hours per 300 tons, or 10

Table 18.2   DIMINISHING RETURNS AND RISING MARGINAL COSTS

	TOTAL OUTPUT (TONS OF POTATOES) (1)	MARGINAL COST (IN LABOR HOURS PER TON) (2)	(IN DOLLARS PER TON, IF WAGE IS $2 PER HOUR) (3)
A	1,000	6	12
B	1,500	10	20
C	1,800	30	60
D	1,900	150	300

Diminishing returns imply rising marginal costs.

hours per ton. And so on, as we move further down the table. Columns (1) and (2) of Table 18.2 DIMINISHING RETURNS AND RISING MARGINAL COSTS summarize this information.

Column (3) shows how we can also express marginal costs in dollars, once we are given the hourly wage. This information is graphed in Figure 18.2 below. Superimposed also is the marginal revenue curve from Figure 18.1(b). We perceive immediately how our farm's best profit output would be about 1,750 tons of potatoes per year—given the fixed amounts of land, equipment, chemicals and fertilizer we have assumed. At any smaller output, mar-

Figure 18.2   PERFECT COMPETITION: BEST PROFIT OUTPUT

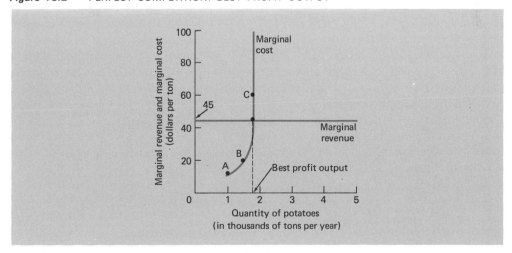

A firm's best profit output is found where marginal revenue equals rising marginal cost.

ginal cost would be below marginal revenue. Profits could be raised by producing more. At any larger output, marginal cost would exceed marginal revenue. Profits could be raised by producing less.

the economic efficiency of perfect competition   We can now see why perfect competition is economically so efficient. Self-interest will cause *all* our potato farmers to select such a volume of output that marginal cost equals marginal revenue. Because all are faced with the *same* marginal revenue (it equals the market price common to all), they are, in effect, without being aware of it, equalizing one another's marginal costs. This means that *wherever* Irish potatoes are being produced, they are being produced at the identical marginal cost. This is not to say that all farms produce identical quantities or make identical total profits. Our above friend may produce 1,750 tons and make a profit (total revenue minus total cost) of $2,000 a year. Some other farmer, with more land and equipment, with better technical know-how, may produce ten times that much and earn a great deal more. But everywhere it would take exactly another $45 of resources to produce *another ton*. Everywhere we could release $45 of resources if we produced a ton less.

And this is most efficient, indeed. Suppose it were otherwise. Suppose the marginal cost of farmer Brown were $28 per ton and that of farmer Green $56 per ton. This would mean a serious misallocation of resources. By forcing Green to produce a ton less, we could release $56 of resources. By giving them to Brown, they could increase his output by two tons. Even though Green and Brown were doing their best from a *technical* standpoint (they got the most out of the resources at their disposal), there was inefficiency from the *economic* standpoint. Green had too many resources. He had advanced too far along the road of diminishing returns. Correspondingly, Brown had too few resources. He had not gone far enough along that road. As we switch resources from Green to Brown, Green's output and marginal cost would fall, Brown's would rise. Eventually, their marginal costs would become equalized. But as long as Green's exceed Brown's, Brown's output would rise by more than Green's falls. Although resources may have been fully employed, they were employed in the wrong places. Scarcity was greater than necessary because of economic inefficiency. In perfect competition, this would never happen. At a price of $45 per ton, Green would never dream of producing when his marginal cost is $56. He would lose $11 on the last ton produced. He would voluntarily produce less. Brown would not be content to produce when his marginal cost is $28. At a price of $45, he could gain $17 by producing another ton. He would be eager to produce more.

The Imperfect Competitor

It is a relatively short step from here to understanding the economist's concern with big business, if by *big* business we mean any enterprise large enough in relation to its market to be able to influence market price. Like all firms, this firm would maximize its profits by producing a volume of output such that marginal cost equals marginal revenue. But unlike in perfect competition, the imperfectly competitive firm—by definition—*can* influence price. Its demand curve, like that for the market in the aggregate, is downward sloping. The only way it can sell more (such as 17.5 million tons of aluminum per year rather than 8.5 million tons) is to *lower* price (as from $4.50 to $3 per ton). What happens in this case to total revenue? In one period, 8.5 million tons are sold for $4.50, yielding $38.25 million of total revenue. In the next period (or in the same period instead), 17.5 million tons are sold for $3, yielding $52.5 million, a gain of $14.25 million. Because 9 million extra tons were sold, extra revenue per unit, or marginal revenue, was

$$\frac{\$14.25 \text{ million}}{9 \text{ million tons}} = \$1.58 \text{ per ton.}$$

Yet, each extra ton was sold for $3! This apparent inconsistency is easily resolved. Although 9 million more tons were sold for $3 (bringing in extra $27 million), the only reason they could be sold was that the price on *all* units was lowered. Whereas, previously, 8.5 million tons sold for $38.25 million (at $4.50 each), they now also sell for $3, yielding $25.5 million, that is, $12.75 million *less*. Thus, the change in total revenue consists of two parts: + $27 million and − $12.75 million, yielding net + $14.25 million. This very significant conclusion can be summarized thus.

Unlike the perfectly competitive firm that could sell more at the same price, the imperfectly competitive firm can sell more only at a lower price. Therefore, it cannot consider price equal to marginal revenue. At any output above one unit, for the imperfect competitor, *price always exceeds marginal revenue* (as $3 exceeds $1.58). Some of the gain it makes from selling more just goes to offset the loss from selling its original (or an alternative) quantity for less!

This implies something else. Because profits are maximized for all firms when marginal cost equals marginal revenue, but the imperfect competitor's price exceeds his marginal revenue, the imperfect competitor's price also exceeds his marginal costs. Hence, what follows? Unless every imperfect competitor's price just exceeds marginal cost by the same percentage (a most unlikely case), marginal costs of imperfect competitors of the same good may differ even if they sell at identical prices.

the possible economic inefficiency of imperfect competition   Thus, in imperfect competition, self-interest does not necessarily operate for the public good: There may be two producers of aluminum. They may both sell at $3 per ton. But the marginal cost per ton of company A may be $2, that of company B $1. If only we could force A to produce less and B to produce more! Every ton less produced by A would release $2 of resources. B could produce two extra tons with those resources. However, unlike the case of farmers Brown and Green above, there would now be no incentive whatsoever for A to release resources in favor of B. Both would already be maximizing their profits as long as their different marginal costs equal similarly different marginal revenues. We may have full employment, but resources are employed in the wrong places. Although the companies concerned have not the slightest inkling of it, resources are employed in economically inefficient ways. Scarcity is larger than it has to be! This is the major evil of big business.

AN EVALUATION OF ANTITRUST LAWS

What do antitrust laws do to overcome such inefficiency? Not much. For one thing, they have been directed mainly against big business in the popular sense, against the General Motors and IBMs and ITTs, our economy's giants. Even so, they have not been enforced very vigorously. Even if they were, it would not be enough. For, as we have just seen, the real problem is "bigness" in a more sophisticated sense. Firms quite small by popular standards may qualify for this group by the economist's criterion.

The Degree of Enforcement

The antitrust laws have not been enforced vigorously enough to achieve market structures even *resembling* perfect competition. The reasons lie partly in powerful forces tending to move the economy in the opposite direction.

technical reasons for large-scale production   The main force tending to destroy perfect competition or tending to keep it from ever coming about is the development of *modern techniques of production*. Modern production techniques often require plants (that is, physical production facilities) of considerable size. As we noted earlier, they must produce a large output volume (relative to existing demand) to achieve *technical* efficiency.

Suppose, for instance, that the best-known technical way of producing cars is to utilize three types of modern machines in the production process, first A, then B, then C. Let us suppose further that machine A can handle 1,000 cars, B can handle 5,000 cars, and C can handle 6,000 cars per day. If engineers want to use all machines fully, the scale of the producing plant must be such as to produce at least 30,000 cars per day (using 30A, 6B, and 5C). If market demand is 90,000 cars per day, even a single technically efficient plant would supply one third of the market!

Beyond that, it may well pay to have a *firm* (that is, the administrative and legal entity undertaking to produce a good) operate more than one *plant* of optimum size. To keep unit costs as low as possible for any volume of output, it may be best for any managerial, research, promotional, or distributive setup to serve more than one plant. Say, in the above example, that administrative talent needed for the firm's existence could just as well handle two as one plant. Then the *firm's* optimum size is two plants, and it supplies at this size two thirds of the market.

To turn from mere speculation to facts, consider the data of Table 18.3 THE CONCENTRATION OF FIRMS. Column (2) shows the optimum plant size for twenty important industries (they together accounted for 20 percent of all 1947 shipments in manufacturing). Optimum plant refers to the technically best size of the production unit, giving lowest possible costs per unit. The optimum is expressed as a percentage of the national industrial capacity, which we can take to be a rough measure of the size of the national market. Even experts differ on estimates of this sort. The range of values given in the table shows the extent of disagreement among engineering authorities on the subject. As Table 18.3 shows, in eleven of the twenty industries studied, the optimum plant would produce only a small fraction of the industry total (below 3 percent). In five cases, however, it might produce 10 or more percent of the total. In the latter cases, there would be room for only ten technically efficient firms in the entire United States, assuming each firm contained only a single plant. If, furthermore, these ten firms did not compete on the national market, but each restricted its activities by choice or necessity to a smaller region, these firms could easily be monopolies. Breaking them up into many small units would create technical inefficiency.

Column (3) shows the optimum size of *firm* for the same twenty industries. Firm, as always, refers to the business unit (single proprietorship, partnership, or corporation). Each can, of course, operate a number of *plants*. Expert opinion shows that in a number of cases (shoes, cement, steel, and so on) technical efficiency can be further increased by operating several plants under one management. In such cases, the firm would require a larger market share for technical efficiency than the plant. This is not always true, however. Where optimum firm and plant are of the same size, this is indicated in column (3). In other cases data could not be ascertained (shown by n.a.).

The total amount of money required (in about 1951) for constructing an optimum plant is given in column (4). In many cases these are truly staggering amounts. This partly explains the fact that new firms do not easily enter such industries as petroleum refining, steel, cigarettes, automobiles, and tractors.

The last two columns lead us to one inevitable conclusion. The actual market share held by a few firms must often be large for technical efficiency. Actual shares are often larger than this. For instance, the four largest firms together typically exceed the share justifiable for reasons of technical-managerial efficiency. The values of column (5) are the same as in column (3)—or column (2) if missing in (3)—multiplied by four. This indicates the market share one could expect for technical reasons for the four largest firms. This share is, as column (6) indicates, exceeded in almost all cases. This is apt to be even worse if we could look at the largest firm only. Though the optimum steel firm for technical reasons needs 2 to 20 percent of the market, U.S. Steel alone holds 30 percent. Though the optimum auto firm needs at least 5 to 10 percent, General Motors holds 50 percent of the auto market. This kind of market power of existing firms, in addition to large initial money requirements, will also keep potential newcomers at bay.

breaking up the giants?   It is no wonder under such circumstances that the enforcement of antitrust laws has typically *not* taken the route of *breaking up existing firms*. Courts may understandably be afraid to promote economic efficiency by creating technical inefficiency through atomizing the industry into too many units compared to what is technically desirable. Furthermore, data such as those in column (3) of Table 18.3 are usually

Table 18.3   THE CONCENTRATION OF FIRMS

INDUSTRY	PERCENTAGE OF NATIONAL INDUSTRY CAPACITY CONTAINED IN ONE		TOTAL MONEY REQUIRED FOR ONE OPTIMUM PLANT (MILLION DOLLARS)	PERCENTAGE OF NATIONAL MARKET HELD BY FOUR LARGEST FIRMS	
	OPTIMUM PLANT	OPTIMUM FIRM		IF THEY HAD OPTIMUM SIZE	ACTUAL
(1)	(2)	(3)	(4)	(5)	(6)
Flour milling	0.1 to 0.5	n.a.	0.7 to 3.5	at least 0.4 to 2	40
Shoes (excluding rubber)	0.14 to 0.5	0.5 to 2.5	0.5 to 2	2 to 10	30
Canned fruits and vegetables	0.25 to 0.5	as col. (2)	2.5 to 3	1 to 2	28
Cement	0.8 to 1	2 to 10	20 to 25	8 to 40	31
Distilled liquors	1.25 to 1.75	n.a.	30 to 42	at least 5 to 7	64
Petroleum refining	1.75	as col. (2)	193 excluding, 250 including transport facilities	7	33
Steel	1 to 2.5	2 to 20	265 to 665	8 to 80	55
Metal containers	0.5 to 3	n.a.	5 to 20	at least 2 to 12	14
Meat packing					
fresh	0.02 to 0.2	as col. (2)	very small	0.08 to 0.8	39
including processing	2 to 2.5	as col. (2)		8 to 10	16
Gypsum products	2.5 to 3	27 to 33	5 to 6	100	90
Rubber tires and tubes	3	n.a.	25 to 30	at least 12	79
Rayon (yarn and fibre)	4 to 6	n.a.	50 to 135	at least 16 to 24	80
Soap and detergents	4 to 6	8 to 15	13 to 20	32 to 60	85
Farm machinery (excluding tractors)	4 to 6	n.a.	n.a.	at least 16 to 24	38
Cigarettes	5 to 6	15 to 20	125 to 150	60 to 80	82
Automobiles	5 to 10	n.a.	250 to 500	at least 20 to 40	75
Fountain pens	5 to 10	as col. (2)	6	20 to 40	57
Copper	10	as col. (2)	n.a.	40	87[a]
Tractors	10 to 15	n.a.	125	at least 40 to 60	74
Typewriters	10 to 30	as col. (2)	n.a.	40 to 100	83

[a]1958.   n.a.—not ascertained.

Data for the United States show that the percentage of the national market actually held by the four largest firms is in many manufacturing industries larger than necessary for technical efficiency—compare column (6) with (5). The technically optimum market share—column (5)—takes account of both technically efficient plant size—column (2)—and firm size—column (3). The data also reveal one reason for the failure of more firms to enter the market: prohibitively large capital requirements—column (4). Sources: Columns (1) to (4) from Joe S. Bain, "Economies of Scale, Concentration, and the Condition of Entry in Twenty Manufacturing Industries," The American Economic Review, March 1954. Data refer to 1950–1952. Column (5) calculated from column (3) or estimated from column (2). Column (6), Bureau of the Census; see U.S. Senate, Subcommittee on Antitrust and Monopoly of the Committee on the Judiciary. Concentration Ratios in Manufacturing Industry 1958, Parts I and II (Washington, D.C., 1963). Data for 1954.

hard to come by and can never be anything more than good guesses. This may not be good enough for a court. No wonder then that courts have preferred to look not at business size but at the *motives* of businessmen brought before them. They have argued for a long time, as we saw, that "bigness as such" is not bad, but *actions deliberately undertaken to destroy rivals* are. However understandable this attitude of the courts, from the standpoint of the economist it matters little whether firms are big or small (in the popular sense). It matters little what the motive is. All that matters is the *result* of any business practice. If the result, whether accompanied by "good" or "evil" intentions, is to create imperfect competition, we have (probably) economic inefficiency. Economists are bound to deplore this, for it means having more scarcity than there has to be.

the actions of the courts   Furthermore, it is extremely difficult to *prove* motive. Hence, this approach to antitrust law enforcement is bound to reap few results. And few results it has reaped.

This is not entirely owing to the attitude of the courts. Few cases of "monopolization" are ever brought to court in the first place, if for no other reason than lack of funds appropriated to the Antitrust Division of the Department of Justice. Funds until the 1930's were only sufficient to go after a dozen cases per year. Since then fewer than fifty cases per year have been given intensive investigation and litigation. This is still an insignificant number. Furthermore, many of the big cases against monopoly take an incredibly long time (5.5 years on the average!) and create an impossible volume of evidence (hundreds of thousands of pages!).

For this reason, the U.S. Attorney General has preferred action in "open and shut" cases of collusion by *several* firms. The courts have consistently held collusive agreements as illegal per se, that is, regardless of motive. Penalties have mostly taken the form of fines, but they have been incredibly insignificant. A 1950 *Study of Monopoly Power* by the House Committee on the Judiciary, for instance, revealed the following for a group of twenty-five major companies: During the preceding 12 years, they had been given fines on seventy-seven occasions for violating the antitrust laws. The total of fines paid by a single firm ranged from $3,500 (Socony-Vacuum Oil Company) to $75,000 (A & P). Relating the total of fines paid over 12 years to the firms' assets as of 1948, the percentages ranged from 0.0002 (Socony-Vacuum Oil Company) to 0.05 (Bausch and Lomb Optical Company). Relating the total of fines paid over 12 years to the firms' *net* profits of a *single* year (1948), the percentages ranged from 0.002 (General Motors) to 2.402 (Bausch and Lomb Optical Company). Since that time, things have not changed, either. From 1955 to 1965, the average fine handed corporations was $12,778, that for individuals $3,226. It is hard to believe that such fines for conviction (which is very improbable anyhow) would deter collusive behavior. However, such behavior may be discouraged by *other factors*. Those include, as noted above, possible treble damage action by injured parties, consumer brand switching owing to injury to the firm's "image," refusal of the government to do business with such firms, sanctions by administrative agencies (such as refusal to renew licenses for broadcasting), and so on.

imperfect competition remains   Even if the U.S. Attorney General were to sue in every single instance of antitrust violation, even if courts convicted all those guilty of collusion and broke up all firms guilty of monopoly, eliminating both, so far as the *economist* is concerned the problem would just have begun to be tackled. We would then still have a world of imperfect competition. So far as economic inefficiency is concerned, it matters little whether excessive market power is exercised by a single firm or a few. Yet, this is not even considered by the existing laws as anything to be discouraged. Thus, just a different kind of imperfectly competitive market form is likely to be created by the dissolution or prevention of monopoly. This is likely to be called *desirable* by the courts and the general public, for it is in the dramatic advertising wars of few competitors that they see "how competition works." It is for this reason that many economists would join Harvard's John Kenneth Galbraith in calling our antitrust laws a "charade."[4] Monopoly itself is illegal, but all other forms of imperfect competition, *with the same economic consequences*, are not. It is as though you were guilty of assault, said Mr. Galbraith, when hitting your neighbor heavily over the head with a sledge hammer, while remaining innocent if you use a lighter instrument or show a poorer aim. Thus the laws are sadly at odds with the real problem.

Conclusion

In summary, we can state that the enforcement of the antitrust laws has been lax. The public makes no particular demand for action, and any vigorous enforcement is quickly labeled as witch hunting by the National Association of Manufacturers. Government spokesmen argue at times that "the ghost of Senator Sherman is an ex-officio member of every board of directors." This is supposed to mean that businessmen think twice before any action on pricing, expansion, and the like, so as not to come in conflict with the law, however vague the statutes, however lax their enforcement, however ridiculous the penalties. The law to such spokesmen has primarily *preventive* effects. This, by nature of the statement, is unprovable. Yet, there is overwhelming evidence that the laws are continually violated on a large scale. It may well be, however, that they would be violated even more without the threat of fines, without the frequent use of court injunctions halting "undesirable" behavior, and without the fear of the other indirect effects of indictment or conviction alluded to above. Be that as it may, when it comes to antitrust laws, as with speed laws, everyone is in their favor, everyone breaks them, and hardly anyone gets caught. At best, these laws are a constant irritant to the business community. So far as the *economic* issues are concerned, however, it matters little. Even the complete abolition of monopoly, even the complete absence of collusion, even the complete absence of any attempts by anyone to destroy his competitors, would not yet assure economic efficiency as long as competition remains imperfect. This is the important point to see in this chapter.

[4] See his best-selling book, *The New Industrial State* (Boston: Houghton Mifflin, 1967).

SUMMARY

1   This chapter introduces the meaning of economic efficiency via a discussion of governmental efforts to enforce the antitrust laws.

2   These laws were the outcome of a basic transformation of the American economy that began in the latter half of the nineteenth century. Industrialization led to a decline in the importance of the agricultural sector. Technological advances in manufacturing, transportation, and communication led to the rapid growth of large businesses. Price wars among them and ruthless competition against smaller competitors worried the public. So did the growth of trusts, mergers, and holding companies, all of which tended to concentrate economic power in fewer hands.

3   As a reaction against this trend, Congress enacted the Sherman Act of 1890. It was designed to foster competition and restrain monopoly. So were later laws, such as the Clayton Act and Federal Trade Commission Act of 1914, the Robinson-Patman Act of 1936, the Wheeler-Lea Act of 1938, and the Celler-Kefauver Act of 1950.

4   What is the economic significance of such laws? From the standpoint of the economist, they serve a useful function only if they eliminate the "evil" of big business. That evil lies not in excessive monopoly profits, for they could easily be taxed away. It lies rather in an economically inefficient use of resources that leads to smaller output than otherwise possible.

5   Under perfect competition, when businesses have no control over selling price, self-interest leads to economic efficiency. Self-interest dictates that each producer choose that output volume at which rising marginal costs equal marginal revenue. The latter is identical with market price. Because all producers maximize their profits by equating marginal costs with the identical market price, they equate, unknowingly, one another's marginal costs. This makes it impossible to reallocate resources among firms and raise output. Thus, an "invisible hand" creates economic efficiency.

6   Such efficient resource use is only accidental, however, when businesses have influence over their selling prices. Economic inefficiency is probably inherent in the system of imperfect competition, although it in no way derives from mismanagement. Imperfect competitors may be most efficient from a technical standpoint. They may get the most output possible from the resources they have. They may also be doing well economically, maximizing their profits where marginal cost equals marginal revenue.

7   Yet, their price will surely exceed marginal revenue, hence marginal cost. Thus, there is no guarantee that the marginal costs of one producer of a good will be equal to those of another producer of the same good. More likely than not, a reallocation of resources among imperfectly competitive producers could lead to higher output. Yet, there is no incentive for this to happen.

8   Seen in this light, antitrust laws do nothing to eliminate economic inefficiency. This is so because they have not been enforced very vigorously. Nor do they go far enough. The reasons are easy enough to perceive. Modern technology requires plants and firms that are large relative to demand. One is rightfully hesitant to limit the size of firms in the search of economic efficiency if it means creating technical inefficiency. Further, as the laws stand, they do not hold imperfectly competitive behavior illegal at all if it does not tend to create a monopoly.

TERMS[5]

antitrust laws	monopoly
conglomerate merger	optimum firm
exclusive contract	optimum plant
fixed costs	perfect competitor
horizontal merger	plant vs. firm
imperfect competitor	pools
law of diminishing returns	Rule of Reason
macroeconomics	trust
marginal cost	trust certificate
marginal revenue	tying contracts
microeconomics	vertical merger

QUESTIONS FOR REVIEW AND DISCUSSION

1 Explain the principle of increasing marginal costs. Show how the *law of diminishing returns* is related to the principle of increasing marginal costs.

2 Explain why marginal revenue equals price only if price does not vary with quantity sold.

3 "Perfect competition is impersonal. Although each firm competes with every other, none feels hurt by the success of others. Imperfect competition is highly personal in contrast. Competitors readily are identified and singled out. The success of each affects the others distinctly."
Evaluate. Is it true? Can you give examples?

4 Show how the invisible hand, under perfect competition, transforms selfishness into public benefit.

5 How is one to measure "bigness" in business? Shall we look at assets, sales, employment, market share, or what?

6 "Unless an imperfectly competitive firm makes unreasonable profits, it is clearly not injuring the consumers." Discuss.

7 "Perfect competition's invisible hand fails to work in the real world. Self-interest and the requirements of economic efficiency may diverge. There may be inefficiency, yet no one may have an incentive to change." Explain by showing how economic efficiency in imperfect competition
a. May be violated even though prices to all are alike
b. May be fulfilled by accident.

[5] Terms are defined in the Glossary at the end of the book.

8 "In imperfect competition, we probably have economic inefficiency." Why *probably*?

9 "What's good for General Motors is good for the U.S.A." Discuss.

10 Describe the antitrust laws. Do they promote economic efficiency?

11 "Any government that pursues a vigorous antitrust policy must hate business." Discuss.

12 "The antitrust laws still have one large loophole: they cannot prevent the growth of giant firms through spontaneous *internal* sources, such as the reinvestment of earnings." Discuss.

13 The government recently noted in its indictment of Pfizer and Co., Cyanamid, and Bristol-Myers Co. that they and others, such as Upjohn and Co. and Olin Mathiesen Chemical Corporation, were charging "strangely identical" prices. It is strange? Does it make any difference?

14 "There is nothing wrong with a conglomerate merger. Why shouldn't a chemicals factory buy itself an electronics firm, a shoe factory, and a string of motels?" Evaluate. Consider the likely consequences.

15 "In 1966, a merger between two Los Angeles grocery chains, together holding less than 8 percent of the market, was forbidden (Von's Groceries case). This is an abuse of the antitrust laws. It protects inefficient firms, not competition." Discuss.

16 "Modern technology does not require large firms. After all, U.S. Steel is simply a dozen or so Inland Steels strewn around the country. There is no need for that." Evaluate in light of the lessons of this chapter.

17 "Technological progress is the real enemy of economic efficiency. By determining the technically most efficient size of the firm, technology determines also the firm's size in relation to its market." Evaluate. If you had to choose between economic and technical efficiency, how would you do it?

18 In 1967, the Justice Department admitted that it had prepared a draft of a legal complaint aimed at breaking up General Motors. Newspapers called it an "antitrust bomb," and the "biggest antitrust news since President Theodore Roosevelt's crusade early in the century." Would you favor such a move? Justify your answer.

19 "We should attack achieved market power as much as aspired-to-power. We should stop pouncing on small companies that wish to merge and instead concentrate on breaking up General Motors, Ford, General Electric, U.S. Steel, IBM, DuPont, Boeing, and the like." Evaluate. What would be the pros and cons of such a policy?

20 "The only good thing one can say about antitrust laws is this: they effectively prevent the extreme kind of naked economic aggression practiced in the last century (for example, by the old Standard Oil Company)."
Evaluate. Is it the only good thing one can say?

Soybean Price Support Cut 25c
In First Nixon Farm Policy Step

Agriculture Secretary Links Move to Mounting Supplies, Loss of Markets and Cost of Government Storage

By WILLIAM M. BLAIR

Special to The New York Times

WASHINGTON, March 6—The Nixon Administration, in its first major farm policy decision, cut the Federal price support of soybeans today by 25 cents a bushel.

Mounting supplies, a loss of dollar markets at home and abroad and the possibility that record stocks will wind up in Government storage at a cost of more than $500-million forced the reductions, Secretary of Agriculture Clifford M. Hardin said.

The support level for 1969 crop soybeans will be $2.25 a bushel for No. 1 grade against $2.50 in the last year. The price support on another oil crop, cottonseed, was reduced to $37 a ton from $48.

Some Republican members of Congress from the Middle West, have blamed former Secretary of Agriculture Orville L. Freeman for the overabundance of soybeans and have accused him of causing disaster for producers. Mr. Freeman raised the support to $2.50 and permitted soybeans to be planted on acreage diverted from corn and other livestock feed grains and from cotton.

Major Income Crop

There were no estimates of what effect Mr. Hardin's action would have on farm income. But the Secretary said at a news conference that a cutback in production and stocks could strengthen the market and enable producers to "ride up with the market."

"The lower supports will permit soybean producers to compete effectively in the market and thus provide a basis for growth of the industry," he said.

Soybeans have soared from a minor crop to a major income producer in less than 15 years. The farm value of the 1968 crop was estimated at $2.6-billion, compared with less than $1-billion in the late nineteen-fifties. Soybeans were ranked third in total value of production among all crops last year.

Soybeans have been priced out of dollar export markets by competitive oils, such as fish meal. Synthetic proteins and amino acids have also made inroads on soybean sales as feed for ruminant animals.

Secretary Hardin coupled his price support reduction with a prohibition on Government sales of soybeans during the current marketing year, which ends Aug. 31.

Sets Sales Price Floor

He also said that, beginning with the new marketing year, sales will not be made at less than the higher of the market price or 110 per cent of the 1969 crop support plus carrying charges.

And he said that soybeans planted on feed grain acreage would not be eligible for feed grain price support payments.

Clarence D. Palmby, Assistant Secretary of Agriculture for International Affairs, said that the effective reduction in the price support could range as high as 30 cents a bushel. This would come about because the price support, previously based on No. 2 grade soybeans, has now been based on No. 1 grade.

Secretary Hardin said that if the present support level of $2.50 a bushel had been permitted to run another year "the resulting [Government] investment could prove to be disastrous."

Economists, he said, estimate that the high price level would cause a build-up in carryover stocks of soybeans to 600 million bushels or more by the end of the 1970–71 marketing years.

19

the trouble
with
agriculture

T HE PREVIOUS CHAPTER has introduced the notion of economic efficiency. In this one, we continue to pursue this theme, but turn from the industrial to the agricultural sector of the economy. This will reinforce the major lesson drawn from our earlier study. A business enterprise, or indeed an entire sector of the economy, may be extremely successful from a technical or from its own economic standpoint. Technically, it may have succeeded in wringing more physical output from fewer resources than ever before. Economically, it may make more profit than ever before. Yet, there may exist economic inefficiency if, for instance, a reallocation of resources among enterprises could result in higher output still. Thus, let us remember, the charge that an economy is economically inefficient is not necessarily a reproach of its technical experts or its business administrators. Rather, it is a statement about the framework that coordinates these people's activity. That framework may stand in the way of the largest possible satisfaction of human wants. It may allow firm A to get resources though firm B can produce more with them. Or it may lead to the production of one set of goods, though households would want others more, that might have been made instead. It is this kind of inefficiency, unseen by the individual firm or industry, that the economist rightly deplores.

A CLASSIC SUCCESS STORY

In one sense certainly, the story of American agriculture is one of uproarious success. Consider the ancient problem of mankind to provide food and fiber even just sufficient for survival. For centuries all over the world, this task absorbed the efforts of the great majority of the labor force. In many parts of the world, it still does today. But not in the United States. When the United States was founded, almost everybody lived and worked on farms. A hundred years ago, three quarters of all people did. In 1929, we only had 22 percent of the civilian labor force working on farms. By 1967, the figure was lower than 5 percent. By 1980, farm labor needs are expected to drop again by a third. Even the acreage from which crops are harvested has declined recently, from 365 million acres in 1929 to 308 million acres in 1967. All the while, mind you, farm production has been going up. The total of crops raised in 1967 exceeded those of 1929 by 59 percent. The output of livestock and livestock products went up by 86 percent in the same short period.

Indexes of productivity, showing what happened to output per man-hour or per acre, are setting new records year after year. No other sector in the American economy can boast of similarly spectacular results. For instance, the man-hours needed to produce 100 bushels of wheat dropped from 373 in 1800 to 108 in 1900 to 11 in 1965. The corresponding figures for corn are 344, 147, and 10. They are 601, 280, and 43 per bale of cotton. Equally spectacular gains were made for all other crops and for livestock.

What accounts for this success? Part of it is explained by revolutionary improvements in agricultural machinery and its widespread use. For instance, from 1790–1800, when the cotton gin was introduced, cotton output increased twentyfold. It doubled again in the next decade. In the 20 years following 1834 and the invention of the reaper, wheat output doubled. Such stories could be multiplied manifold. Year after year, output grew with new and more machines. In 1910, there were practically no tractors and trucks in agriculture.

There were 2.6 million in 1940 and 7.9 million by 1968. The use of grain combines since 1940 has increased fivefold, of corn pickers sixfold. Over all, capital used on farms easily quadrupled since 1940 alone. Correspondingly, the number of mules and horses declined by 80 percent since 1940. The acreage once used for growing feed was released for other purposes. There were 40 million acres needed for this purpose in 1940 that were not needed in 1965.

A second reason for the vast increases in agricultural productivity lies in federal government support of research and education in agriculture. This goes back to at least 1862 and the enactment of the Morrill Act to which many state universities owe their origin. In addition to private efforts, this massive agricultural research sponsored by government led to better seeds, fertilizers, pesticides, and general knowledge about wise agricultural practices. The federal government consequently instituted a system of county agents to induce farmers to use hybrid seeds, to breed and feed livestock scientifically, to use the right kind of fertilizer and pesticides, correct techniques of plowing, crop rotation, and so on. As a result, from 1850–1900, the use of fertilizers in the United States increased by a multiple of twenty-five. It tripled again in the next 40 years. Since 1940, the use of fertilizers has quadrupled once more.

Finally, there were other factors most conducive to the agricultural miracle in this part of the New World. By luck, there was lots of flat land with rich soil and a suitable climate. Had the terrain been rougher, the temperature a little colder, and rain less frequent, we might have found ourselves in quite a different spot. Similarly, there were man-made factors that were helpful. The pattern of land ownership, the ready social acceptance of new methods, the widespread availability of credit to privately owned farms, all these helped to make effective the powerful potential stimulus inherent in technological and scientific advance.

WHERE THE TROUBLE LIES

The trouble with American agriculture, therefore, certainly does not lie in failure to produce enough. On the contrary, farmers are getting into trouble exactly because they are able to produce so much so easily. Coupled with a certain peculiarity in demand for agricultural products, producing much can spell economic disaster for the farmer in both the short run and the long run.

The Short Run

The demand for most farm products does not respond very much to changes in their price. Cut the price of many farm products in half and quantity demanded may go up by 5 percent. Double the price, and it may fall by 10 percent. This should not surprise us. For instance, the quantity of vegetables or bread or meat we eat in a year is not only determined by their price and our income, but largely by the capacity of our stomachs and by the number of stomachs to be filled! When the price falls, we hardly buy more. We rather save the difference or spend it on nonfarm goods. When the price rises, we won't cut purchases by much, either. We have to spend less elsewhere or save less. Even a large *percentage* change in price will result only in a small *percentage* change in quantity demanded.

On the other hand, quantity supplied is also likely to be unresponsive to price. This is especially true in the short run. Once a crop is harvested, a farmer may as well supply it, even if he dislikes the price. Storage may be costly or impossible. So may be use as feed. Some income is better than none. Suppose we consider wheat used for bread production. Suppose quantity supplied is 240,000 bushels regardless of price. The demand schedule by millers, which is, of course, derived from households' demand for bread, may be as in Table 19.1 HYPOTHETICAL DEMAND FOR AND SUPPLY OF WHEAT. Notice how unresponsive quantity demanded is to price. Were price to double as from $1 to $2 per bushel, quantity demanded would only fall by 20 percent, from 300,000 bushels to 240,000 bushels per period.

Table 19.1   HYPOTHETICAL DEMAND FOR AND SUPPLY OF WHEAT

PRICE PER BUSHEL	QUANTITY DEMANDED	QUANTITY SUPPLIED
$1	300,000 bu.	240,000 bu.
2	240,000 bu.	240,000 bu.
3	210,000 bu.	240,000 bu.

Were price to rise 50 percent, as from $2 to $3 per bushel, quantity demanded would only fall by 12.5 percent, from 240,000 bushels to 210,000 bushels. In a free market, a price of $2 per bushel would be established. The entire crop would be taken off the market at this price. Farmers' total revenue would be $480,000.

Now consider the effect of a change in demand or supply.

a change in demand   For some reason, consumers decide to eat less bread. Millers buy 60,000 bushels less at any price. Our schedule changes to read as shown in Table 19.2.

Table 19.2   HYPOTHETICAL DEMAND FOR AND SUPPLY OF WHEAT AFTER FALL IN DEMAND

PRICE PER BUSHEL	QUANTITY DEMANDED	QUANTITY SUPPLIED
$1	240,000 bu.	240,000 bu.
2	180,000 bu.	240,000 bu.
3	150,000 bu.	240,000 bu.

Notice how the change in demand has, as it must, affected every single price-quantity-de-manded combination. As a result, a new market equilibrium results at $1. Farmers' total revenue tumbles to $240,000. A 25 percent fall in quantity demanded (at the old price) leads to a 50 percent fall in total revenue. Because there is no reason to believe that total costs have changed, this may completely wipe out the *net* income of farmers.

a change in supply   Now suppose we have a year of perfect weather. A bumper crop appears on the market, say 300,000 bushels. Given the demand schedule of Table 19.1, equilibrium price again tumbles to $1. Although sales go up from 240,000 bushels to 300,000 bushels, total revenue drops from $480,000 to $300,000. Total costs probably go up, as the larger crop certainly requires additional expenses for harvest, transport, and storage. Again, net income is certain to go down.

This, then, is agriculture's problem in the short run. The unresponsiveness of quantity demanded and supplied to price in the short run produces in a free market drastic changes in prices and revenues if supply or demand changes. Such change in revenue quickly translates itself into *equally drastic changes in net income.* Such changes can be counted on to occur frequently if for no other reason than the unpredictability of the weather.

Go back to a time when there was no government intervention in farm markets. In 1913, for instance, the price of butter was 27 cents a pound. It rose to 54 cents by 1920, fell to 37 cents in 1921. Wool was 17 cents a pound in 1913, but 46 cents in 1920 and again 17 cents in 1921. Wheat was 79 cents a bushel in 1913, $1.83 in 1920, but $1.03 in 1921. Apples rose from 89 cents a bushel in 1913 to $1.24 in 1920, to $1.64 in 1921. Take a look at the Department of Commerce's *Historical Statistics of the United States* and you will find the same to be true for shorter periods, other times, and for all farm commodities. Prices fluctuated widely from one year to the next, regardless of whether you look at butter or milk, wool or tobacco, wheat or rice, apples or eggs.

The Long Run

The above instability of prices, revenues, and net incomes in the short run is bad enough for the farmer. Yet this has not been his only problem, nor the worst. At least it is conceivable that a low income in one year is offset by an extremely high one in the next. This has not happened, however. Farming, even in the long run, has not been a rewarding occupation for most farmers.

Average farm incomes, in relation to incomes earned in the rest of the economy, have been perpetually low. The data of Table 19.3 FARM VS. NONFARM INCOME show this.

Table 19.3   FARM VS. NONFARM INCOME

YEAR	FARM FAMILIES	NONFARM FAMILIES	FARM AS PERCENT OF NONFARM
1935–36	$951	$2,020	47.1
1946	3,385	4,573	74.0
1956	4,015	6,986	57.5
1966	6,231	9,842	63.3

Average family personal income in current dollars. Source: U.S. Department of Commerce.

Do not think that farmers need less money because they can produce their own food. These data include an estimate of the farm families' own production of food. They also include farm families' income earned off the farm. This has recently exceeded four tenths of their total income. Were we to exclude the nonfarm portion of farm family income, we could even detect a worsening trend in the relation of farm to nonfarm income.

The reasons for this are not hard to figure. Over the years, demand for farm output tends to grow only slowly, the primary determinant being population growth. Aggregate income grows considerably faster than population, but it has much less effect on the demand for farm products than on the demand for other types of output. Individual diet-conscious Americans today eat little more than their grandfathers despite the fact that they are richer. Foreign demand contributes little to the growth of demand for U.S. agricultural products because (among other things) underdeveloped countries have difficulties acquiring dollars to import food. Other advanced capitalist countries have agricultural programs of their own restricting such imports. Industrial demand for agricultural products often grows slowly, too. The demand for farm-produced fibers, for instance, is slowed by the increased use of synthetics.

By itself, the increase in demand over time, however slow, would, of course, lead to rising agricultural prices and incomes. But, as we saw, farm output has not been constant, nor has it risen slowly, as has demand for farm products. Farm output has grown spectacularly. The resultant of these two forces has been the poor showing in the development of farm income illustrated in Table 19.3 FARM VS. NONFARM INCOME.

a graphic illustration   If you wish, you can also illustrate this with the help of the familiar supply and demand diagram. Lines D_1 and S_1 in Figure 19. . LONG-RUN SUPPLY AND DEMAND CHANGES may represent, respectively, the demand for and supply of wheat in 1910. For illustrative purposes, we use again the completely hypothetical data of Table 19.1 HYPOTHETICAL DEMAND FOR AND SUPPLY OF WHEAT.

Given our assumed data, the 1910 price is $2 per bushel and the quantity traded 240,000 bushels, as we observed earlier. Now let demand rise to D_2 by 1935. If supply rises to S_2, price will be lower, or $1.50 per bushel with 450,000 bushels traded. Next, let demand rise further to D_3 by 1970. If supply continues to rise faster, such as to S_3, price drops again. This time, it reaches 92 cents per bushel with 750,000 bushels traded. Total revenue, to be sure, has risen: from $480,000 to $675,000 to $690,000. Quite likely, though, total cost has risen also. Hence, we cannot tell from this graph what happened to wheat farmers' *net* income. But we do know from other data (such as those in Table 19.3 FARM VS. NONFARM INCOME) what happened. Farm net incomes rose, too, but by less than nonfarm incomes.

FIGHTING BACK

Left to themselves, farmers of any one crop come closest of any group of producers to the economist's ideal world of perfect competition. This is owing to their large numbers, the standardized product they produce, and the relative ease with which people can become,

Figure 19.1   LONG-RUN SUPPLY AND DEMAND CHANGES

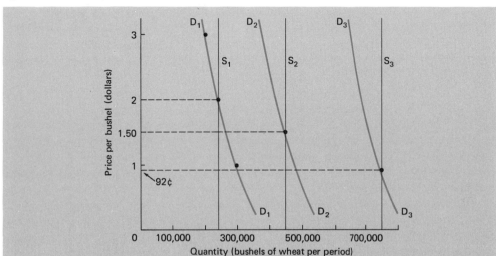

Over time, demand for many farm products has risen at a slower rate (from D_1 to D_2 to D_3) than supply (from S_1 to S_2 to S_3). As a result, prices have been under pressure to fall.

or can cease to be, the producer of any one crop. Ironically, as we have seen, the unequaled success of farmers in producing a lot has also meant economic hardship for many of them. No wonder they have come to look at the price system with suspicion. They have naturally thought of ways to escape the unwelcome dictates of the market.

Nor was there difficulty in finding precedents. "Look at the big manufacturing firms," farmers have said. "Do they, as we do, produce all their factories can produce and then throw the output on the market to sell for whatever it will bring? Not at all. If you are an auto maker, you first set your own price. Then you produce what you think you can sell at that price. No more, no less. Even if you produce way below capacity. It would never occur to you to act otherwise, for you are in the business to make *profit,* not cars! True enough, there is a difference. There are few auto makers. Each has a large market share. Each knows he can sell more only at a lower price. He can sell less and get a higher price. That is why he can set the price he likes. This would not be true for any one of half a million wheat farmers. *But it would be true, if they acted as one.* If farmers want to control price, they must get together."

Thus goes the argument. And it is quite correct at that. Just consider once again Table 19.1 HYPOTHETICAL DEMAND FOR AND SUPPLY OF WHEAT. As it stands, farmers sell 240,000 bushels per period, at $2 per bushel, with $480,000 of total revenue. Now let them get together. Let them hold back or destroy or fail to produce 30,000 bushels. This cuts supply by 12.5 percent to 210,000 bushels. The market will buy this quantity at $3 per bushel, or for a total of $630,000. An increase of almost a third in total revenue! And there would be no increase in total cost, possibly a decline if less is produced. Net income would soar.

Private Schemes

Thus endeth the lesson from the world of big business. As attempts by the National Farmers Organization to organize farm output destruction show, it is by no means a lesson that has been ignored. Yet, it is doubtful whether any private collusion of this type can work for long. Consider yourself to be one of some half million farmers who have just agreed to hold back or destroy output and thus raise prices and their economic fortunes. Suppose you used to produce 5,000 bushels, getting $10,000 of gross revenue at the old price. Now you know that you will have to destroy 12.5 percent (like everyone else). Then you will sell 4,375 bushels at $3. This will gross $13,125, a clear gain of $3,125. But you know something else. You know that you play an insignificant part in this whole scheme. Nobody would ever notice if you, just you, did *not* cut your output. Total supply would then be cut, you might figure, from 240,000 bushels to only 210,625 bushels instead of the ideal 210,000 bushels. That would surely make no difference. Price would still rise to $3, or almost that. And then your gross income would rise to almost $15,000, not just to $13,125. It pays you to cheat!

As you might expect, there are others who will have the same bright idea. There may be even some who are brighter than that. They may *raise* their output in the hope of making a killing when everyone else cuts his and causes price to go up. As a result, private schemes of output control have all had a rather sad ending. Output never falls by very much. Thus, the schemes founder on the rock of human greed.

Governmental Schemes

There are ways, however, to get around this problem. They involve *governmental* support and enforcement of the scheme. It may seem odd to expect governmental help in a conspiracy to escape the results of the price system. This is particularly true in light of the support the government has given to the price system through the enactment of the antitrust laws. As we saw in the previous chapter, the government sets itself up as a guardian angel of competition whenever it attacks the monopolistic tendencies of big business. Yet the ways of the world are strange indeed. This same government has been most willing to make an alliance with the farmers to help them restrict output and raise prices and incomes. It is party to the same kind of rapacious treatment of the public for which it sends electrical equipment industry executives to jail! In both cases, the idea is the same: to make the public pay more money for less output. There are essentially three ways in which this can be accomplished. In one way or another, all have been tried in the United States.

purchase and storage   In order to prevent the short-run fluctuation and the long-run decline in the prices of certain farm commodities (and thus to prevent the wide fluctuations of the incomes of farm families as well as the continuous and drastic decline in their number), the government began programs in 1933 wherein it would promise to "support" farm prices at an "appropriate" level. The appropriate level was to be found by comparing the prices of nonfarm goods with that of the commodity to be supported. The latter price was originally to be set in such a way that a quantity unit of the farm good sold at the support price could buy the same quantity of nonfarm goods as in the "good old days" of 1909–1914 before World War I. What would be the effect of setting such a "parity" support price, as it is called?

If, as is to be expected, this price is set above the equilibrium market price, quantity supplied will rise. Quantity demanded will fall. Hence, farmers will be left with a surplus that cannot be sold to households. Unless the government now purchases and stores that surplus, price will be bid right back down to its free market equilibrium level. In fact, government has done just that. Its purchase has involved many commodities, including barley, beans, butter, cheese, corn, cotton, cottenseed, dried milk, honey, peanuts, flaxseed, mohair, sorghum, oats, potatoes, rice, rye, sugar beets, sugar cane, soy beans, tung nuts, tobacco, wheat, and wool. The actual device used is often the *nonrecourse loan*. A farmer who has surpluses can get loans equal to the support price value of these surpluses from the government, but must pledge the surpluses involved as collateral. If the farmer does not repay the loan, the government simply takes title to the goods involved. If the free market price should rise above the support price, however, the farmer can sell the goods and repay the loan. Thus, the farmer is in a beautiful "heads I win, tails Uncle Sam loses" situation. By mid-1960, the Commodity Credit Corporation, which is the federal agency accumulating surpluses, held stocks valued at $6 billion. By 1967, however, they had fallen to $1.9 billion. Storage costs alone were $1.3 million a day in 1960, still $414,000 a day in 1967.

All this can be easily illustrated with the simple supply and demand diagram of Figure 19.2 GOVERNMENT PRICE SUPPORT: BUYING SURPLUSES. Suppose supply and demand establish a price of $1 per bushel with 360,000 bushels traded per period. Thus, the free market would give farmers a gross revenue of $360,000. Now let the government enter the picture.

The government sees that frequent small shifts of supply and demand cause continuous drastic fluctuations in price, total revenue, and income. It wants to protect farmers from that. It also sees how, in the long run, prices tend to decline as demand grows more slowly than supply. The average farmer lives in poverty; others flock to the city slums. To "preserve the rural way of life," which is apt to be pictured in idyllic terms in the history books, Congress announces a "parity" support price of $2.50 per bushel. Farmers are told that they can "count on that price." So they naturally supply 410,000 bushels (as the aggregate supply curve indicates). In the long run, this price guarantee may even shift the supply curve to the right, as farmers put in more land, fertilizer, and effort than ever before to produce wheat. But let us stick with the short run. A quantity of 410,000 bushels appears on the market, every law-abiding farmer charges $2.50 per bushel, and what happens? At that price, only 290,000 bushels are bought, as the aggregate demand curve indicates! Farmers are left, it seems, with a *surplus* of 120,000 bushels. Thus, *announcing* a support price is not enough. The government must do more. Otherwise, frustrated sellers will bid down the price to get rid of the surplus. Price will end up right where it was at $1 per bushel.

In our illustration, government would offer to buy those 120,000 surplus bushels at

Figure 19.2   GOVERNMENT PRICE SUPPORT: BUYING SURPLUSES

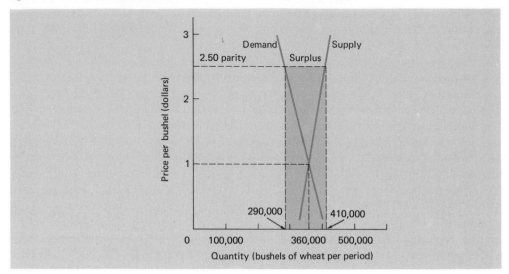

*By announcing its willingness to support wheat prices at $2.50 per bushel, government can raise farmers'
gross revenue, here from $360,000 to $1,025,000. Private buyers have to pay more for a lower quantity.
Government has to buy the surpluses. The amount it spends is shown by the shaded area.*

$2.50 each. Government would spend per period $300,000 and end up owning 120,000 bushels
of wheat. Farmers would receive a total revenue of $1,025,000 of which $725,000 come from
private purchases. The government has, of course, *additional* costs for storing or eventually
disposing of the surplus crops. So far as farmers are concerned, this method of price support
has the same effect as if private demand had risen to intersect supply at the $2.50 price.
Society pays the price for all this. Higher price ($2.50 rather than $1 per bushel) for fewer
agricultural goods (290,000 rather than 360,000 bushels) plus eternal governmental purchase
and storage of surpluses.

restrict supply   Government could support price in still another way. It could announce a support price of, say, $2.50 per bushel and then induce farmers as a group to *act like
a monopoly firm.* Given aggregate private demand, farmers can get the market price to be
$2.50 per bushel if they restrict, with governmental prodding, their supply sufficiently. As
we noted earlier, ironically, one arm of government is asking farmers to do what another
arm (the antitrust division) forbids industrial firms to engage in, namely, to get together
and raise price by restricting output. In fact, government has been the prime "conspirator"
against the public, proposing one trick after another to make aggregate supply fall. If this
could be done, government would neither have to buy and store, nor pay a single cent for
this program. Market price would rise and private demanders would buy all of restricted
output, providing all of farmers' revenue.

The question is *how* to restrict supply. Direct quotas to all farmers would be the only sensible method. Tell *everyone* how many *bushels* of wheat he could sell and make sure that the total at the support price adds exactly to what is demanded at this price. Farmers, however, do not like that. That is Big Bad Government *dictating* to them what they must do. "We might as well live in Russia."

So the government has tried other methods. Farmers have been cajoled into taking some land out of the production of surplus crops altogether and putting it into woods or grassland. This *Soil Bank program*, introduced in 1957, has not been very successful. In the first place, it is costly to "bribe" farmers to put land to such uses when they could instead produce high-priced wheat or some other "supported" commodity. At the peak of the program in 1960, it cost $350 million a year to keep 29 million acres out of production. Second, farmers will naturally put the poorest land into the Soil Bank (the acres suited best for growing cacti anyway), and they will then just *pour* fertilizer and care into the remaining acres. This, combined with the march of technical progress (knowledge of which is forever spread by government agents!), may well result in *larger* output from fewer acres, increasing, rather than decreasing, supply. Then government has to buy up more surplus than ever. Acreage allotments to each farmer, unconnected with the Soil Bank program, have run into the identical snags.

All this can also be illustrated graphically. Consider Figure 19.3 GOVERNMENT PRICE

Figure 19.3   GOVERNMENT PRICE SUPPORT: RESTRICTING SUPPLY

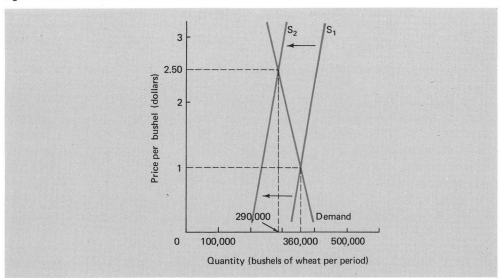

By helping farmers to get together and restrict supply (through marketing quotas, acreage allotments, and so on), government can support a parity price above the free market equilibrium. At $2.50 per bushel, private buyers have to pay more for a lower quantity. Farmers' gross revenue rises from $360,000 to $725,000.

SUPPORT: RESTRICTING SUPPLY. Supply and demand establish a price of $1 per bushel with 360,000 bushels traded per period. Farmers' gross revenue in this free market situation is $360,000. Now let supply be restricted. Farmers as a group supply less at every price. Line S_1 becomes S_2. Market price then rises to $2.50. Only 290,000 bushels will now be supplied and demanded. But farmers' gross revenue is up to $725,000. Furthermore, all this comes from private buyers. They get all the output. Government spends nothing.

cash subsidies   There is a third method of supporting farmers. This avoids the necessity of purchasing and storing surpluses. Government could tell farmers to produce whatever they wish at the guaranteed price and sell that quantity to *private* demanders for whatever it will bring. The government can then pay a monetary subsidy to bring total revenue up to the amount farmers would have received had they sold at the support price. In this case, farmers will produce more than at the free market price, but they can sell it to private demanders only at a lower price. Thus, the government, without buying anything, will have to pay quite a sum. Private consumers are clearly better off insofar as they get more for a lower price. Government may or may not spend more than under the purchase-storage program. This depends on whether the subsidy is larger or smaller than purchase costs plus storage costs minus possible revenue from sale abroad.

This method of price support has, interestingly, never found favor with farmers or Congress. Farmers prefer hidden subsidies to "charity," and Congress is shocked when the real cost of the program is made so obviously visible to all. Yet, what else than charity is the purchase and storage program, where the government buys what it does not want? Or what is the Soil Bank program where the government often "rents" land to be used for nothing? If one wants to support the incomes of a particular group, one might as well do it directly.

Figure 19.4 GOVERNMENT PRICE SUPPORT: CASH SUBSIDIES illustrates the cash subsidy program. The moment government guarantees a $2.50 per bushel price, farmers produce (as the supply curve indicates) 410,000 bushels. As they throw them on the market, they bring only 13 cents each (as the demand curve indicates). Private consumers get all the output for a total of $53,300. Note how they are better off. In a free market, they would have spent $360,000 for 360,000 bushels. Under the purchase and storage program, and under the supply restriction program as well, they would have spent $725,000 for 290,000 bushels. Yet, government has to pick up the remainder of the tab. Shown by the shaded area, it would have to pay a total of $971,700 or a $2.37 subsidy for each of the 410,000 bushels privately sold.

Note also that the supply restriction program (unless the government pays farmers not to produce) is always cheapest for the government. In our case, the purchase and storage program is probably next in costliness, unless storage costs, not shown in Figure 19.2, are extremely large and sale abroad by government is impossible. In our case, cash subsidies are most expensive to the taxpayer. Yet, this must not necessarily be so. It depends entirely on the nature of supply and demand. By experimenting, you can easily come up with supply and demand curves that yield a different result and make the cash subsidy program come out

Figure 19.4   GOVERNMENT PRICE SUPPORT: CASH SUBSIDIES

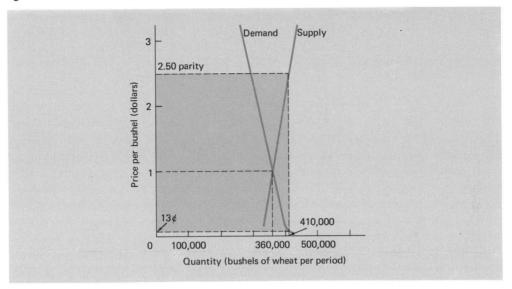

Government can guarantee a support price by promising cash subsidies to bring actual receipts per unit up to this level. In this case, farmers supply 410,000 bushels at the support price. They sell all for what private demanders are willing to pay: 13 cents per bushel. Then, government must pay a subsidy of $2.37 per bushel, a total of $971,700, shown in tint. Farmers' gross revenue rises from the free market's $360,000 to $1,025,000.

ahead of the purchase and storage program. In reality, too, the costliness of the latter two programs differs from crop to crop and year to year.

recent programs   In recent years, the U.S. Department of Agriculture has experimented with a mixture of the above programs. For instance, the voluntary Soil Bank program has been in effect. So have been acreage allotments. The latter have been mandatory, although only after a vote by those directly affected. Usually, a two-thirds majority is necessary, but often 80 or 90 percent of farmers have voted for the acreage allotments and the accompanying nonrecourse loan program. In some cases, this has been supplemented by direct cash subsidies. Farmers get a letter before the crop year starts telling them the maximum acreage they can plant for each crop to qualify. Those who care to participate then get immediately a 35 percent subsidy of expected receipts. The nonrecourse loan is available in addition when the crop is ready for sale. Thus, farmers have to gamble: which brings more revenue, producing as much as they like and selling at the free market price or restricting output and relying on price supports and subsidies? All this, however, may change soon. In 1969, a member of President Nixon's Council of Economic Advisers expressed the government's desire to end all farm price supports in 3 years. "A price level that I would like," said

Mr. Houthakker, "is one that would approximate equilibrium between supply and demand." Quite possibly, the step reported in the news report introducing this chapter is a move in this direction. In addition, the Soil Bank program is about to die. Although the Nixon administration encourages voluntary cropland retirement, no new Soil Bank contracts have been signed since 1961. Only 8,000 acres will remain in the Soil Bank in 1970.

EVALUATING AGRICULTURAL PROGRAMS

It is somewhat difficult to evaluate the agricultural programs pursued so far by the U.S. government. This is so because they are clearly designed to achieve a variety of goals. If we look at the programs in terms of their capacity to raise agricultural output, they have clearly been successful, spectacularly so. If we then consider the dire predictions of population specialists about the future of mankind if it continues to grow at the present rate, we might even conclude that in the long run this increased capacity of ours to produce food is all that really matters.

If we look at the programs with the eyes of those who wanted to preserve the family farms and the rural way of life, we will become less optimistic. Our government programs may have slowed down the exodus from the land, but there is no denying that the rural way of life has been on the way out for a long time. Our farm population has declined by the millions and is likely to continue to do so.

If we look at the programs in terms of their capacity to help the poor farmer and to achieve economic efficiency in the use of our resources, we can easily become downright depressed. Let us consider these two points in detail.

The Question of Poverty

Have the aforementioned programs really helped support the income of the American farmer? Before we answer this question, we must come to realize that there is no such thing as *the* American farmer. Not all farmers have been hurt by short-run price instability and long-run downward pressure on prices. Some were able to produce a lot and keep their income up by adjusting to the new technology using little labor, much machinery and chemicals, and the right amount of land. But for those unable to produce more, for those farming in very much the same way as their grandfathers did, the long-run decline in prices spelled a long-run decline in incomes at the very time when incomes outside agriculture were growing rapidly. Farmers have a choice to maintain income: be progressive and adopt the new, or leave agriculture for greener pastures elsewhere. Neither road is easy to follow. The former requires huge amounts of capital an individual family cannot get. The latter has to be accomplished on a massive scale. Under normal conditions, when the demand for a product rises more slowly than the capacity to supply it, the tendency for incomes in this line of production to fall can be forestalled if enough resources move to other occupations. If we look at labor in any industry, there are always some people better informed about alternative opportunities than others, some who are financially, geographically, by training, family status, or temperament better suited to move than others. They will move as conditions in their industry deteriorate, and any small reduction in resources needed is readily achieved in this way. But in agriculture, given such rapid improvements in technology plus, on top of it, a high rural birth rate, the number of people that must be moved out to maintain income levels is exceedingly large. It requires moving people who are in every way badly suited for any other kind of work. Thus, although only 5.2 percent of the American population lived on farms in 1968 as opposed to 30.1 percent as late as 1920, the exodus from agriculture has not been fast enough. Too many have stayed in agriculture *without* adjusting to the twentieth century, trying to tend to farm units too small and ill-equipped for modern technology. Their reward: a perpetual low living standard compared to the rest of the economy and compared to the best of farmers. Table 19.4 CLASSES OF FARMERS, helps us see the extent of the problem.

At the pinnacle of American agriculture we find what we may call class 1 farmers.[1] There are some 30,000 of them. Each annually markets produce valued at over $100,000. Together, they produce as much as the bottom three quarters of American farms! And there can be no doubt about the reason for this amazing productivity. It is not a matter of differences in quantity or quality of labor only. It is the most modern technical know-how, embodied in the most massive doses of capital equipment, put to work on large pieces of land that yields such results. Here is *big* agriculture and that is big business. Here we are dealing with corporations holding thousands of acres across the continent, with empires held together by airplane and teletype.

Equally far removed from the Jeffersonian image of the family farm are the farms labeled as class 2 below. Although not the biggest, they are big enough. Together with the operators of class 1, these first two classes of American farms each sell more than $40,000 of output annually. On the average each holds about 2,000 acres and $290,000 of real estate alone. Together they account for only 4.5 percent of farm units. Yet they operate a third of all agricultural land and produce 42.6 percent of total agricultural output, that is, about as much as the bottom 87 percent of all farmers! In short, if we had not 142,000, but 333,000 of such farms, we could get rid of *all* others. This is, in a nutshell, why most others are in trouble.

Looking at the first three classes of farms, selling each over $20,000 per year, we still find only 12.7 percent of farmers. They average over 1,100 acres, real estate of $175,000. They hold 47.8 percent of the land, employ 78.5 percent of hired farm workers, own 31.8 percent of tractors, use 56 percent of all fertilizer. They produce, as Table 19.4 indicates, 62.8 percent of agricultural output.

Now look instead at Appalachia, New England, the Ozarks, the Piedmont Plateau, the cutover regions of the Great Lake states. In such places you will find 1.3 million of class 7 farmers. They sell each year less than $2,500 of agricultural produce. And this is gross rev-

---

[1] The remainder of this section is indebted to the excellent analysis by Edward Higbee, *Farms and Farmers in an Urban Age* (New York: The Twentieth Century Fund, 1963).

Table 19.4   CLASSES OF FARMERS

CLASS	ANNUAL SALES VALUE	FARMS		VALUE OF OUTPUT	
		NUMBERS	PERCENT	BILLIONS	PERCENT
1	over $100,000	31,401	1.0	$8.5	24.2
2	$40,000–99,999	110,513	3.5	6.5	18.4
3	$20,000–39,999	259,898	8.2	7.1	20.2
4	$10,000–19,999	467,096	14.8	6.6	18.7
5	$ 5,000– 9,999	504,614	16.0	3.7	10.4
6	$ 2,500– 4,999	443,918	14.1	1.6	4.6
7	$ 50– 2,499	1,340,417	42.4	1.3	3.5
Total		3,157,857	100.0	$35.3	100.0

The U.S. Census of Agriculture for 1964 reveals the amazing fact that less than 13 percent of American farmers produce more than 60 percent of agricultural output. Source: U.S. Census of Agriculture, *1964.*

enue before costs! It takes almost 300 of them to match the output of a *single* progressive farmer of class 1. Unbelievable as it may seem, here we have 42.4 percent of all farmers producing only 3.5 percent of total farm output. The average size of their farms is below 100 acres. This compares with almost 4,000 acres for class 1 farmers. The average value of their real estate is just over $10,000. Even if we threw in the value of all his livestock and (antique) machinery, such a farmer could not even match with all his productive assets the value of one of the giant diesel tractors and plows used by his class 1 colleagues. (The cost goes into the tens of thousands of dollars.) The real estate owned by the average class 1 farmer alone exceeds $600,000.

It is important to take a close look at people in this class 7 category. One statistic is particularly revealing. In 1964 the average *net* annual income from farming of farmers in this group was well below $500. But their average income from other sources was almost $4,000. This can mean one of two things. Perhaps these people are farmers who are doing so miserably that they have to take part-time nonfarm jobs. Perhaps these people are only part-time or retired cultivators who should not be counted as serious farmers at all. An inquiry reveals that the Census Bureau counts anyone with ten acres who markets annually at least $50 of produce as a farmer. Of farmers in class 7, fully 47.7 percent were in fact part-time cultivators under age 65 who worked at least 100 days a year off the farm. Another 26.2 percent were in part retirement being over 65 years of age. Only about a quarter of class 7 farmers were genuine commercial farmers. They, too, were doing badly. They accounted for 11 percent of all farmers, but produced only 1 percent of total output. Holding 122 acres on the average, they held 4 percent of the land. They had 6 percent of the tractors, only 2 percent of all fertilizer. Their net income from farming was $472.

Certainly one thing is sure. However large the number of farmers in class 7, their individual and combined output is absolutely negligible. If all American farms were like this, the U.S. population would be fed worse than that of any other country! The exact opposite is true because a small percentage of farms have reorganized as big corporations to amass the capital needed for modern agriculture. Thus, less than one seventh of them produce almost two thirds of a record volume of output. Many other farmers are in trouble. And they are not being helped at all by governmental farm policies. This is so because government policies are directed toward helping a (nonexistent) "average farmer." By looking at average data only, the real problem in agriculture is hidden. If we include class 7 farmers in agricultural statistics, all of agriculture begins to look sick, just as the retail business would if we included the Girl Scout cookie enterprises in its statistics. On the basis of such average trade data, even the A & P might qualify for government support! Thus, the public has been bombarded with propaganda about "the poor farmer" in an effort to get it to help out. Because election districts did not reflect accurately the pattern of population settlement and gave enormous power to agricultural interests,[2] program after program of the types described above have been enacted. Yet, they inevitably end up helping those (giant) farmers who lobbied for them, but not those (classes 6 and 7) farmers on whose behalf they were enacted. Who can possibly be helped by high and stable farm prices? Only those upperclass farmers who are better off than most taxpayers and who bring the greatest quantities to market! They receive the greatest help. Thus government aid has preponderantly gone to those who do not need it, has been a welcome but quite unnecessary bonus to the efficient technical units. The problem of rural poverty has not begun to be solved. In a recent year, the 56 percent poorest farmers got less than 7 percent of federal support money.

There can be little doubt that a sensible farm program *directed to alleviate poverty* must take a completely different approach. Although the present winners (the big operators) will not like it, if the agricultural program to help the average farmer is really meant to help the *poor* farmer, a direct subsidy program *to the poor*, while allowing a completely free market in farm products, would be much more sensible. In fact, just imagine what would be the effect if all inefficient class 7 farmers were asked to get out of agriculture *entirely*. To the extent that they are unable to find jobs elsewhere, they could each be paid $3,500 per year as long as they live on the condition that their children learn skills usable outside agriculture. The cost of such a program, which would involve no government purchase and storage, would be $4.7 billion in the first year and then continually decline, eventually to zero. This is almost exactly the cost of present federal subsidy programs for agriculture that will *never* solve the problem of poverty and perpetuate quite unnecessary surplus and storage problems, barring a drastic change in demand relative to supply.

Whether we *want* to support the incomes of a particular group is a question we shall take up again in Part 4 of this book. But it is evidently absurd to spend over $4 billion a year to help the poor *average* farmer, if the real-life technically inefficient poor farmer is not even being helped. In fact, he should not be treated as a farmer at all. No one can help him *as a*

---

[2] Often rural districts with a minority of the population elected a majority of legislators. To give one example, in 1962, one state senator each was chosen from Burlington, Vermont (population 33,000) and from Victory, Vermont (population 48). Such examples could be multiplied with no end, and for all levels of government. However, the Supreme Court in 1962 ruled that election districts with greatly differing populations violate the rights of citizens in the more populous districts by diluting the value of their ballot.

farmer. Price supports do not help him who does not sell. And no *family* farm can ever hope to amass enough capital to be efficient enough to sell much. Help must come by making mobility to city jobs less slow and painful. Protecting resources in uses where they are not needed is hardly a good solution.

The Question of Economic Efficiency

Finally, we come back to the main question of this book. What do agricultural programs do to economic efficiency and the reduction of scarcity? Unfortunately, they do not do much that can make us happy.

On the surface, it may appear that American agriculture has done more than any other line of activity to reduce scarcity. After all, don't we rightly talk of agricultural *abundance*? Remember, though, that this is a technical achievement. Economists always ask perturbing and unpopular questions. They are not blind to the wonders of our agricultural productivity. But they do ask this: is it a wise use of our resources to produce some crops that (at present) nobody wants, while people would love to get more of others or of nonfarm goods? We *know* we are very good at combining labor, land, and capital to produce a record volume of wheat. But should we use labor, land, and capital to make wheat when people would prefer meat? Should we build fertilizer plants and railroads and trucks helping to produce wheat, if people would prefer refrigerators instead? This is again the issue of economic efficiency, of doing the right thing with our scarce resources.

Economists are not so sure that we are doing the right things. By interfering with the price system, we have distorted agricultural prices away from marginal costs of production. Note that this is the same problem we met in discussing big business in the previous chapter. There, as here, the consequence is the same. It may be possible to shift resources from one farm to another, or from agriculture to the nonfarm economy *and to produce more than before or to produce goods more urgently wanted*. But there is no incentive to do it.

Given their acreage allotments, farm A may produce wheat with a marginal cost of $1 per bushel, farm B with one of 50 cents. That is, with another dollar's worth of resources, A could produce another bushel, B could produce two more. By moving $1 of resources from A to B we would lose one bushel to gain two. Yet, this will not happen, as it would under perfect competition. Both A and B are "locked into" their present position. Neither may produce more; both get, say, $2.50 per bushel, our hypothetical support price. Thus, there is economic inefficiency. In a free market, as we saw in Chapter 18, each would be driven to adjust his output volume to the point where marginal cost equals free market price. Because that price would be the same for both, their marginal costs would be alike. Economic efficiency would prevail.

Similarly, the resources used to grow a bushel of wheat on either farm, and all the resources indirectly used (for transportation, storage, fertilizer production, and so on) may be capable of producing a completely different good somewhere else in the economy. That good may be beef, an electric toaster, or toys. It may be anything, and it may be wanted a great deal more than wheat. Yet, the governmental price supports may prevent resources from leaving agriculture and its supporting industries for these other ones. Or it may slow down their exodus from agriculture. Again, we have economic inefficiency. In a freely competitive market, self-interest would bring about the move. People who produce what people want less (such as wheat) would be punished by losses. Those who produce what people want more (such as beef or toys) would be rewarded by profits. Thus, resources would be moved. If anything, we should help resources to move from wrong occupations to right ones. This would mean more refrigerators, beef, toasters, and toys for people who want them and less wheat that nobody wants.

This is not to say that we cannot or should not help the poor wheat farmers who are forced out of agriculture and whose sons must learn to grow cattle or make refrigerators or toasters or toys. We can always help the poor—be they farmers or not—by subsidizing them directly. The rich can share their good fortune with the poor. But it is foolish, is it not, trying to help the poor to produce something nobody wants or at least not as much as other things. Doing that means impoverishing all of us—rich and poor alike.

SUMMARY

1 The story of American agriculture is in one sense a story of unbounded success. Nowhere in the world has man been so successful in wringing from nature such an abundance of product. The man-hours needed to produce 100 bushels of wheat dropped from 373 in 1800 to 11 in 1965. This is typical of all farm commodities.

2 This success is mainly explained by revolutionary improvements in agricultural machinery and its widespread use, as well as by federal support of agricultural research and education, leading to the widespread use of improved practices, seeds, and chemicals.

3 Yet, American agriculture has been plagued by extremely unstable prices, revenues, and net earnings, as well as by relatively low and relatively declining incomes. The former can be explained by frequent short-run shifts of supply and demand coupled with small responsiveness of quantities supplied and demanded to price changes. The latter is owing to a faster long-run increase in supply than demand.

4 Given the unwelcome effects of free agricultural markets, farmers have sought ways to escape the dictates of the price system. With an eye to imperfectly competitive firms in the industrial sector, they have tried to restrict output and raise price by collective action, hoping to raise gross revenue and net income as well. Unfortunately for the farmers, such private schemes usually fail.

5 Farmers have, however, succeeded in enlisting the federal government in their cause. This is strangely at odds with the governmental insistence that industrial firms do not restrict output and raise prices. Governmental *price support* programs involve purchase and storage, direct supply restriction, and cash subsidies.

6 Our agricultural programs are successful so far as technical ability to produce is concerned. They have not, however, been able to stem the exodus of people from the farms and to preserve the rural way of life. They have been spectacularly unsuccessful in dealing with the problems of agricultural poverty and economic efficiency.

7 To understand the poverty issue, one must see that the problem of poverty in agriculture does not equally apply to all farmers. One has to be aware of tremendous differences among farms, as shown by the fact that the 13 percent most progressive farms produce over 60 percent of agricultural output. Governmental policies toward agriculture (including purchase and storage programs, output restriction, and direct cash subsidies) have resulted in stabilizing farm prices. They have, however, not eliminated farm poverty. High prices only help him who can sell a lot. Poor farmers have little to sell. This is vividly shown by the fact that, in a recent year, the 56 percent poorest farmers got less than 7 percent of federal support money.

8 Government programs designed to help a (nonexistent) poor average farmer help distort agricultural prices away from marginal costs. Thus, they help create economic inefficiency throughout the economy. This is the very thing that antitrust laws, for instance, are designed to eliminate.

TERMS[3]

nonrecourse loan
parity price
Soil Bank

QUESTIONS FOR REVIEW AND DISCUSSION

1 What are the main reasons for the spectacular rise in U.S. agricultural productivity?

2 In the Soviet Union, unlike in the United States, agriculture has been anything but successful. Considering the reasons for the American success, what do you think are the reasons for the Soviet lack of it?

3 What is the "trouble with agriculture"?

4 Use supply and demand curves to illustrate the instability of farm prices in the short run.

5 "A parity policy in agriculture makes as much sense as one for the buggywhip industry." Comment.

6 "The whole concept of the parity price is very foolish. What if it costs less now to produce a unit of agricultural produce than in an earlier period? What if nonfarm goods used now did not exist earlier?" Comment.

7 "The agricultural purchase and storage program is akin to a pawnshop arrangement." Explain. What do you think would happen if the government "supported" the producers of all commodities in this way?

---

[3] Terms are defined in the Glossary at the end of the book.

8   "Farmers are only trying to imitate industrial producers when restricting supply." Evaluate. (Recall the discussion of imperfectly competitive firms in Chapter 18.)

9   Why are private attempts to restrict agricultural output likely to fail?

10   If you had to choose one of the three government programs to support farm prices, which would you choose? Why?

11   "The federal government must ensure the profitability of farming, for without farms we would have no food and starve." Evaluate.

12   "Farm programs are forced on unwilling farmers by a foolish government." Comment.

13   "If the government stayed out of the picture entirely, supply and demand would solve the farm problem." Evaluate by considering the consequences.

14   "The farm problem is really a problem of resource *immobility*, of labor, land, as well as capital." Discuss.

15   "Government aid to farmers may reduce their mobility by reducing their desire to leave farming, yet the same aid may well increase their ability to move." Evaluate this apparent paradox.

16   About 40 percent of the broiler chickens produced in the United States come from highly automated, factory-like farms run by a dozen big corporations, such as Ralston Purina Co., Pillsbury Co., Swift and Co., and Textron, Inc. Similarly, big canners, such as Minute Maid, a subsidiary of Coca Cola Co., and Libby, now own an estimated 20 percent of Florida's citrus groves. Gates Rubber Co., a Denver-based tire maker, started a chicken farm to produce eggs and now produces 300,000 eggs a day. More recently, it bought ranches that raise 18,000 head of cattle. And it is "looking at other agricultural opportunities." Some farmers believe that such corporate farms should be outlawed. The North Dakota branch of the National Farmers Union even got the issue before voters in the 1968 general election. What do you think?

17   "The U.S. government is in effect trying to solve the problem of agricultural poverty by creating economic inefficiency." Discuss.

18   In 1968, the Federal Reserve Bank of Kansas City wrote:

The changing mix of resources used in farming can be attributed largely to changing relative prices and the impact of changing technology on the use of specific resources. The influence of changing prices on the mix of resources used is verified by the fact that, from 1950–1967, real estate prices increased 157 percent, [but prices of] farm labor 95 percent, of farm machinery 66 percent, and of fertilizer 6 percent. It can be illustrated that technology also had an impact by pointing out that efficient use of modern day techniques for soil preparation, application of chemicals, and harvesting methods frequently require sophisticated machinery and equipment.—*Monthly Review*, November 1968, p. 11

Explain. (Use supply and demand curves if you like.)

19   "In view of the world population explosion agricultural surpluses are the last thing we should worry about." Evaluate.

20   Compare this chapter's discussion of government intervention in agricultural markets with our earlier discussions in Chapter 14 of price controls to combat inflation and in Chapter 15 of measures to maintain stable exchange rates. Take note of the differences as well as similarities.

In Addition to Guaranteed Wage

Reuther Demands Profit Sharing Pact

By Robert W. Irvin

Special to The Washington Post

DETROIT, July 10—United Auto Workers President Walter P. Reuther opened new contract talks with General Motors today by demanding a profit sharing agreement as well as a guaranteed annual wage in this year's negotiations.

"What we call equity sharing will be a firm demand of this union," Reuther told a press conference before meeting with GM Vice-President Louis G. Seaton and other company officials.

Reuther said what he wants would be "within the framework of the American Motors agreement." AMC signed the industry's first and only profit sharing contract in 1961, when it was prosperous and selling record numbers of cars. There have been no earnings to split lately.

The UAW has tried before but always failed to win an agreement containing profit sharing at the big three. If Reuther is serious about winning this in 1967, it could be another sign pointing to strikes in the industry when the contracts expire Sept. 6. . . . Reuther acknowledged there "has been a lot of talk about strikes," but added "we hope to work out a satisfactory agreement. We are not looking for a strike, but we will settle for nothing less than equity." . . .

Asked about profit sharing, Reuther said earnings of executives and dividends of stockholders are geared to the annual financial results of a company and the same should be true for blue collar workers.

"With all its managerial know-how, GM is only able to guess at the equity of a worker in 1968 or 1969. We want to get out of the guessing stage by giving the worker a basic annual wage and then a second year-end increment like an executive gets."

Reuther maintained that none of this would be inflationary and insisted that [with] the current supplemental unemployment benefits (SUB) program the workers are already two-thirds of the way to a guaranteed annual income. "We intend to take the final step this year and will spell out the details to GM on Wednesday," Reuther said.

Until then, GM reserved comment, although Seaton said "I believe we have a fairly substantial guaranteed income now" with the SUB plan which guarantees a laid-off worker 66 per cent of his pay for a year.

Asked about the chances of a strike, Seaton said, "We always approach these negotiations with the idea that we are going to work out an equitable agreement on a peaceful basis — and we have a good record of doing that."

He called for "wisdom and restraint" and admitted he had talked with Federal mediation chief William E. Simkin in recent weeks. The Government is keeping a close watch on the talks.

The Washington Post. July 11, 1967

PICKERS ADAMANT IN GRAPE DISPUTE

Coast Boycott Continues in Bid to Force Bargaining

DELANO, Calif., Oct. 4 (AP) — "La Huelga!"

The last four years, those Spanish words—"the strike!"—have been the rallying cry of an epic California labor dispute in the hot vineyards of one of the world's richest agricultural belts. The end is not in sight.

Technically, no strike exists. Members of the United Farm Workers Organizing Committee, affiliated with the American Federation of Labor and Congress of Industrial Organizations, are merely refusing to accept jobs. Non-union members are available and are working.

For four years, however, matters have grown steadily more bitter, reaching a peak early this year when a national boycott was called against the sale of California table grapes.

The key word in the dispute is table. Wine and raisin grapes are not involved—the union has signed contracts with a number of vintners and raisin producers. No table grape grower has signed.

Every major political candidate—and some minor ones—has been pressured to take a position. Many church councils have endorsed it. Some grocery chains have discontinued the sale of table grapes.

Stickers Urge Boycott

Bumper stickers have appeared all over California, proclaiming: "Boycott Grapes," "Don't Buy New York Products"—a retaliation to New York City supporting the boycott—and "Buy Grapes."

The boycott is designed to force growers, who share in California's $3.8-billion agricultural industry, to the bargaining table.

On one side of the issue are the growers, whose lands lie among fields producing 37 per cent of the fruits and vegetables sold in the United States. On the other are Mexican-Americans who bring in the harvest, traveling from one spread to another in season. When the harvest is done, so is their job—until the next time. The average farm worker toils 134 days a year. About 84 per cent earn less than the Federal poverty level of $3,100, with an average annual income of $1,378, the union contends. Growers contend grape pickers average more than $2 an hour.

Cezar Chavez is head of the United Farm Workers Organizing Committee and architect of the boycott. Devoted to the nonviolence teachings of Gandhi, he is a religious man who says frequently, "No union movement is worth the life of one farm worker or his child, or one grower or his child."

Early this year, Mr. Chavez, 41 years old, demonstrated his dedication to the strike with a 25-day fast.

Since the fast, broken in a celebration that brought Senator Robert F. Kennedy to his side, Mr. Chavez has been under treatment for a spinal disc disease, aggravated by the fast.

Housing Is Poor

He insists that grape pickers must come under the National Labor Relations Act. He contends that growers exploit the farm workers, paying low wages, providing poor housing.

The table grape growers have refused to meet with committee representatives. They refused to appear at a House subcommittee meeting on farm labor relations.

Mr. Chavez countered with the boycott.

Growers call this move an admission of failure. They say that grape picker earnings are well over $2 an hour, higher than the $1.60 an hour minimum set by Congress for industrial workers.

The growers also insist that their refusal to meet with Mr. Chavez does not mean they are antiunion. They say, that because grapes are perishable they must stipulate a no-strike clause in any collective bargaining agreement with farm unions.

20

the role of
labor unions

I N THE PREVIOUS two chapters, we have studied the industrial and agricultural sectors of the American economy. We did so in order to assess the degree of economic efficiency likely to prevail in the economy. In this chapter, we continue this quest. However, we look at the problem from a different point of view. Rather than concentrate on the conditions surrounding the pricing, purchase, and sale of goods, we study the framework that governs the pricing, purchase, and sale of resources. To simplify matters, we shall concentrate on one productive input only, human labor. What we say about labor could be said about other inputs, too. Here, as before, it is not our aim to provide encyclopedic detail. We only want to gain a feeling for the concept of economic efficiency and its importance in the fight against scarcity.

When considering the process of selling, buying, and pricing labor in the American economy, we are immediately confronted with the existence of labor unions. As the newspaper reports introducing this chapter vividly remind us, labor unions are an integral part of the American scene. As the reports also show, some unions, such as the auto workers, are firmly entrenched. They have become so powerful that they can seriously demand a share in business profits in addition to high wages and guaranteed employment. Other unions, on the other hand, such as farm workers, are still struggling, even for their very existence. Clearly, these two will have a very different impact on the setting of wages, levels of employment, and, ultimately, the degree of economic efficiency prevailing in the economy. As a way of introduction to the economics involved, let us take a more detailed look at unions in America.

THE HISTORY OF LABOR UNIONS IN THE UNITED STATES

Early Beginnings

In one form or another, labor unions have existed in the United States almost since the days of independence. In Boston, New York, and Philadelphia, carpenters, shoemakers, and printers banded themselves together as early as 1791. These organizations of workers, however, were weak and short-lived. Their growth was hampered by legal impediments and the militant opposition of employers. Legally, the first labor unions faced the severe handicap of the *conspiracy doctrine*. Just like courts in France, Germany, and Great Britain, U.S. courts looked at workers who "conspired" to raise wages as common criminals. A Massachusetts Supreme Court decision as late as 1842 finally established the legality of unions. Still, they were of no general importance for many decades thereafter. The public attitude was one of disapproval. Even by the end of the Civil War, an attempt to organize all workers into one big National Labor Union (with the goal of achieving certain ends, such as the 8-hour day, through political means) met with no success. Limited success was reached by the Knights of Labor founded in 1869 as a secret society to avoid reprisals of employers. Strikes against the railroads and coal mines in the 1870's made the public take notice of the new movement. In the 1880's, the organization dropped secrecy and vigorously fought against child and convict labor, for higher wages and a shorter working day. It called for the establishment of a cooperative noncapitalist society and quickly gained 700,000 members. These comprised 7 percent of nonfarm workers. Just as quickly, however, the organization vanished.

The Labor Movement Comes to Stay

After the 1880's, labor unions in the American economy never again were negligible. Although the Knights of Labor vanished quickly from the scene after reaching their peak of influence in 1886, other unions gradually took their place. More and more, the public's attitude shifted toward sympathy with the nascent labor movement. As powerful corporations appeared in increasing numbers on the economic stage, the public came to look on unions of laborers as a kind of welcome countervailing power.

Most important among unions for half a century was the American Federation of Labor (AFL). Founded in 1886, it remained under the leadership of Samuel Gompers until 1924. As the earliest unions that had sprung up a century earlier, the unions belonging to his federation were *craft unions*, or unions of *skilled workers only*. Workers of a given skill, such as plumbers or carpenters, would combine in the same union, regardless of their place of employment. Under the leadership of Gompers, they developed a very practical-minded philosophy that has been summarized in the words "more—now." Quite unlike unions in other countries, the AFL was not interested in political action that gradually (by legislation) or suddenly (by revolution) would change the character of society. It was concerned with bread and butter for its members, as long as it was *more* and *now*. The union was content to live within the existing political framework. Unlike its predecessors, the National Labor Union and the Knights of Labor, and unlike its foreign counterparts, the AFL had no aspirations to reform or revolutionize society.

After the sudden demise of the Knights of Labor, membership in all unions grew to 447,000 by 1897 and 868,000 by 1900. The latter figure exceeded in absolute terms the peak membership of the Knights of Labor. Yet, it was still a smaller percentage (under 5 percent) of the nonagricultural labor force than had belonged to the earlier union. By 1910, however, union membership had grown to over 2 million, comprising over 8 percent of workers outside agriculture. By 1920, membership climbed to a peak of 5 million, or 16 percent of nonfarm workers. Thereafter, union membership declined to below 3 million by 1933, or 10 percent of nonfarm workers.

The Heyday of Unionism

In the 1930's, the growth of unions took on new life. Public opinion blamed big business for the Great Depression and began to favor more than ever before the self-protection of workers via unions. In this situation, it was easy for the advocates of *big labor* to secure public support. All they had to do was to conjure up a picture of how General Motors' chief of personnel might overwhelm each of hundreds of thousands of workers separately until he accepted the lowest wage possible! Whether this popular image was true or not does not matter. It certainly was reflected in legislation helpful to union organization.

the laws   The *Norris-La Guardia Act* of 1932 took a first and giant step protecting labor unions. It outlawed one of the most powerful weapons employers had used against union activities: the injunction. Although, as we have seen, unions as such had been legalized in 1842, many of their *actions* could still be blocked. Employers found it very easy to obtain court decrees enforceable by arrest and jail, forbidding strikes, peaceful picketing, and even membership drives. Such injunctions, once obtained, automatically made the union a wrongdoer in the eyes of the law if it persisted in actions that were vital to its functioning.

President Roosevelt's New Deal very quickly broadened the new freedoms granted to labor. The *National Industrial Recovery Act* of 1933 gave unions the right to organize and bargain collectively, free from employer interference and coercion. Such right had frequently been called into question before. Until 1914, when the Clayton Act exempted unions from the antitrust laws, unions were frequently charged with violating the Sherman Act and barred from their activities by court orders based on this Act. As we just saw, right up to the 1930's the courts had been willing to issue injunctions enforceable by arrest and jail against strikes, picketing, and even organizing itself.

When the Supreme Court, 2 years later, declared the act unconstitutional, Congress quickly reenacted its labor provisions in the *National Labor Relations Act*, or *Wagner Act*, of 1935. It reaffirmed unions' right to organization and collective bargaining free from interference. It made collective bargaining contracts legally enforceable. It went further than that. First, it *guaranteed* a union recognition by an employer. It *ordered* employers to bargain with the duly elected representative of their workers if a majority of them wanted to bargain collectively. Second, the law outlawed a number of anti-union practices that were specifically named. A National Labor Relations Board was set up to enforce the provisions of the act. The board supervises elections in cases of dispute about whether a majority of a group of workers wants to be represented by a particular union. The board may order *employers* to cease and desist from *unfair labor practices*, which order can be enforced through the courts. Such unfair practices include firing men for joining a union or refusing to hire them if sympathetic to unions, threatening to close the firm if workers join a union, interfering with or dominating the administration of a union, and refusing to bargain with a union.

The *Fair Labor Standards Act* of 1938 continued the wave of pro-union legislation. It set a federal minimum wage and maximum basic hours for workers employed in industries engaged in interstate commerce. It prohibited child labor. The minimum wage at the time was 25 cents an hour. By 1968, it had climbed to $1.60 per hour. The law allows work above the maximum weekly limit, but only on the basis of overtime pay.

a change in strategy   Government threw its support to labor in the 1930's, and the labor movement itself underwent significant change. Some labor leaders abandoned the principle that union membership be limited to specific skills (to electricians, carpenters, and the like), which had been the basis of the AFL. Instead, workers were to be organized on an industry-wide basis without regard to particular skills. As a result, millions in the mass production industries (steel, autos, electrical products) qualified for membership in the new Congress of Industrial Organizations (CIO). Under the fiery leadership of John L. Lewis, the CIO engaged in the 1930's in massive organization drives. Often there was violence. In famous sitdown strikes, the new unions seized the auto plants. These were the days when Walter Reuther was beaten up by the hired strongmen of the Ford Motor Company. What a contrast to the news report introducing this chapter!

One by one, the industrial giants—Ford, General Motors, U.S. Steel—succumbed. They recognized, for the first time in history, a CIO union as their workers' bargaining agent.

Union membership soared. From below 3 million in 1933 it went to 9 million by 1940 and almost 15 million by 1945. As a percentage of nonagricultural employment, union membership grew to 27 percent in 1940 and 36 percent in 1945. The latter figure has never been exceeded since.

The Swing of the Pendulum

Something happened since World War II that put an end to vigorous union growth in the United States. To be sure, membership had grown further to 18 million by 1955, a figure unchanged by 1967. In relative terms, the importance of unions has declined: to a third of the nonagricultural work force in 1955, and only 26 percent of it in 1967. There are at least two reasons for this.

the laws   The Wagner Act of 1935 had said nothing about "unfair" practices on the part of labor. To these Congress turned in 1947 when it passed the *Taft-Hartley Act*. It was passed, over President Truman's veto, against the background of a postwar wave of strikes, as the now giant unions for the first time learned to use their strength. Paralyzing strikes in steel, coal, and shipping alarmed the public. So did *jurisdictional* strikes, resulting not from disputes with employers, but from two unions fighting each other for jurisdiction over a group of workers. Labor, it was argued, had been given an overdose of power. To counter it, the new act outlawed the closed shop (but not the union shop) and a number of other *unfair union practices.*

The closed shop existed where a firm operated under a collective bargaining agreement not to employ nonunion workers. Before nonunion members were employed, they had to become union members. As a condition of employment, they had to remain members of the union with which the employer had a contract. The closed shop has been regarded by unions as necessary for their security. If it has all the workers on its side, the union is assured recognition by the employer and has unquestionable power to make requests concerning wages and working conditions. Because all employees enjoy the benefits of union contracts, unions felt that they should all support the union. On the other hand, employers argued that a fundamental principle of freedom is violated if people are forced to join an organization, that they, as employers, find it difficult to hire the best workers for a job (because they must take those whom the union admits to its membership), and that union leaders, having an assured membership, are likely to become irresponsible and deal dishonestly with their members. Apparently, Congress favored these arguments.

Under the union shop arrangement, anyone may be hired. But he must, to retain his job, join the union within 30 days or at least pay union dues. Some twenty states, however, have passed so-called right-to-work laws, outlawing the union shop also.

Other unfair union practices outlawed by Congress in 1947 include refusal of the union to bargain with the employer, forcing the employer to pay for work not done (featherbedding), striking without 60 days' notice, striking to force the recognition of one union where another has already been certified, and so on.

Under the Taft-Hartley Act, employers may also sue unions for breach of contract and may engage (without coercion) in anti-union activities. Unions must make financial reports to their members and disclose their officers' salaries; they cannot use dues for political contributions, nor charge excessive initiation fees. The act also allowed the President to ask for court suspension for 80 days of strikes or lockouts that "imperil the national health and safety." The idea is to give the parties more time to come to a peaceful settlement. At the end of this *cooling off period*, there must be a secret union ballot on the latest company offer.

Although existing unions vigorously denounced the Taft-Hartley Act, it seems to have had little effect on them. There is some evidence, however, that the law made it much more difficult to establish new unions and thus to *raise* union membership.

In 1959, the *Landrum-Griffin Act* amended the Taft-Hartley Act. It was passed against a background of hearings of the McClellan committee into labor racketeering. It had exposed "gangsterism, bribery, and hoodlumism" in the affairs of some unions. Some union leaders had used union funds for personal use, had taken payoffs from employers for union protection, and even were involved in blackmail, arson, and murder. In answer to such labor racketeers who fattened themselves by extortion from both workers and employers, the act put still more curbs on union power. It was particularly concerned with the misuse of union funds. Members of unions were guaranteed the right to vote in secret. The list of unfair practices was lengthened.

other causes   Undoubtedly, there are other reasons for the recent stagnation in union growth. Consider Table 20.1. Table 20.1 shows the present membership of the largest unions. It also shows something else. Union strength is concentrated among *blue collar workers outside agriculture*. The percentage of blue collar workers in the labor force has, however, been steadily declining. That of white collar workers, typically unsympathetic to unions, has risen from 18 percent in 1900 to 48 percent in 1968. In manufacturing, where unions have been strongest, only 5 percent of white collar workers are unionized, over all perhaps 12 percent are. In general, the outlook for organizing white collar workers, excepting possibly government employees, is bleak. No wonder union growth has stagnated since the 1950's.

Even apart from these difficulties arising from the changing structure of the labor

Table 20.1   UNION MEMBERSHIP*

Teamsters (Ind.)	1,651	Plumbers	285	Oil, chemical	165
Automobile workers	1,403	State, county	281	Ironworkers	162
Steelworkers	1,068	Railway and steamship		Bricklayers	149
Electrical (IBEW)	875	clerks	270	Papermakers	144
Machinists	836	Musicians	252	Postal clerks	143
Carpenters	800	Mine workers, District		Maintenance of way	141
Retail clerks	500	50 (Ind.)	232	Boilermakers	140
Laborers'	475	Painters	201	Packinghouse	135
Garment, ladies'	455	Government (AFGE)	200	Transport workers	135
Hotel and restaurant	450	Letter carriers	190	Railway carmen	126
Clothing workers	382	Railroad trainmen	185	Teachers	125
Meatcutters	353	Textile workers	182		
Building service	349	Pulp, sulphite	171	Firefighters	115
Engineers, operating	330	Retail, wholesale	171	Printing pressmen	114
Communications		Rubber	170	Typographical union	107
workers	321	Electrical (UE)		Transit union	103
Electrical (IUE)	320	(Ind.)	167	Sheet metal workers	100

* All unions not identified as independent (Ind.) are affiliated with the AFL-CIO.
Labor unions with headquarters in the United States having more than 100,000 members in 1966, in 1,000's.
Source: Statistical Abstract of the United States, 1968, p. 240.

force, the "fighting spirit" has left many unions. Most union members are now middle income workers, well above the poverty level. Their general well-being makes the union less necessary to them. This feeling of apathy is reflected in the unions' lessened drive to expand. In recent years, this has become a hot issue within existing unions. In 1955, the AFL under George Meany and the CIO under Walter Reuther had joined into the AFL-CIO. In 1968, they split over the CIO's dissatisfaction with the status quo. George Meany, head of the joined federation, was accused of "undemocratic, heavy-handed leadership" that prevented any "positive program to get labor moving again." The CIO demanded nothing less than an all-out crusade to organize the unorganized. As our second newspaper report introducing this chapter shows, this is likely to be tough going.

WHAT WORKERS GET FROM UNIONS

As we have noted already, American unions have a distinct *bread-and-butter personality.* Unlike their foreign fraternity brothers, they are not out to change the world through political action. They do not care about establishing socialism. They pursue no radical designs. First and foremost, American workers want their unions to improve the terms and conditions of their employment.

Direct Benefits

The direct benefits workers seek are, before all else, better terms of employment. They want higher wages and pensions. They want health insurance and jury pay. They want vacations and holidays. They want a *steady* job.

And workers want to have some say when it comes to setting and interpreting the rules of work. They want seniority for layoffs and promotions. (Workers with more years of service get laid off last and promoted first.) They want prior notice before layoff. They want to be protected from arbitrary reassignments, from discrimination as to race, sex, or age. They want, at least as much as they want more pay, a *jointly administered grievance procedure*. They want to see union representatives and the employer together enforcing and interpreting the contract agreement. They want to have a way of protesting unfair disciplinary action. They hate to be helpless before their foreman. If he makes arbitrary and unwarranted decisions, they want to be able to protest and protest with impunity. Ask any union man, and he will stress the overwhelming importance of this. Even if the wage hike won is modest (and might in any case have come about without the union), workers pay their union dues. To them it is like buying insurance: insurance against arbitrary decisions by the boss, assurance of equitable treatment of each individual.

Other Benefits

The benefits of a union to the worker go beyond the terms and conditions of his work. To many a laborer, the union is far more than a mechanism to raise wages, cut hours, and keep the boss off his back. The union also gives him status. It makes him important, accepted, part of a group. It gives him self-respect. And somebody he can trust. He may not understand about balance sheets, profit and loss statements, recessions, and inflation. The union can and does help him understand.

In fact, there can be little doubt that unions, through their educational efforts on their own members, have created a significant base for public support of measures designed to alleviate unemployment and poverty. Union members have strongly supported liberal measures compatible with the present political system: social security, progressive income taxes, higher minimum wages, higher welfare and unemployment benefits, public housing, federal school subsidies, and, in general, all the policies directed at maintaining full employment, which we discussed in Part 1.

In addition, unions may help their members to improve their skills, learn of job opportunities, even buy insurance and get consumer loans. In many ways, therefore, unions have been a very good thing. Still, the economist is at times not too happy with them. We already noted one reason in Chapter 14. Unions may cause cost-push inflation. And inflation, as we noted in Chapter 4, is a serious evil. In the remainder of this chapter, we will look at another kind of trouble. Unions, too, can cause economic inefficiency.

THE TROUBLE WITH LABOR UNIONS

The very existence of labor unions may lead to a national output that is smaller than it might be. As we did earlier when discussing big business (Chapter 18), we can best bring out the issues involved by imagining a world of perfect competition in the labor market. What would be the typical behavior of a firm buying labor (and selling its output) under perfect competition?

The Perfect Competitor

As we have noted so often, a perfect competitor has no control over price. Take again the above farmer growing Irish potatoes. But this time let us look at him not as a grower and seller of potatoes, but as a buyer and user of farm labor. Even if he is a large farmer, he will be hiring at best a negligible portion of the agricultural labor force. (In 1969, 3.7 million people worked on the nation's farms.) In a fashion described earlier by Figure 3.4 THE MAR-KET FOR HIGH SCHOOL SOCIAL SCIENCE TEACHERS, demand and supply will establish an equilibrium wage for farm labor such that the total quantity offered for sale is gladly bought, leaving neither shortages nor surpluses. Suppose the equilibrium wage, as in part (a) of Figure 20.1, is $2 per hour.

Now consider a single farmer. He may be hiring 10, 100, or even 1,000 workers per year. Whichever he does, he has no chance of influencing the equilibrium wage set by the market. He can double his hiring or reduce it to zero. He will still be faced with a wage of $2 per hour. His actions would change market demand from 3.7 million workers to, perhaps, 3,700,050 workers. Try to envisage this in the graph. It would shift the market demand curve in part (a) so negligibly that the market would not react. The equilibrium wage would change by a tiny fraction of a penny. That is, it would stay put. To the single employer that wage is a datum.

This is illustrated by the horizontal line in part (b). That is how the supply curve looks to him. People are offering, *at $2 per hour*, any quantity of labor he can hire. No matter how many workers he hires, 10, 100, or 1,000, he has to pay each $2 per hour. He could not get them for a cent less, for there are hundreds of thousands of competing farmers offering $2. He need not pay a cent more. Everyone in the country would then want to work for him. He could not possibly use them all. He would only be giving money away needlessly.

profit maximization   As economists put it, the equilibrium wage in the market is our farmer's *marginal outlay*. It is the figure that shows how his hourly cost would change if he changed employment by a man. It shows the extra (or marginal) outlay involved if he hires another man. It is also the hourly outlay he saves if he hires one man less. In fact, economists *define* a perfect competitor as a business whose marginal outlay is constant no matter what the volume of resources it buys. How many men will our farmer hire and put to work? This depends on more than what he has to pay them. It depends also on what the fruits of their labor bring him. In fact, argue economists, if he is interested, as businessmen

Figure 20.1   THE PERFECTLY COMPETITIVE LABOR MARKET

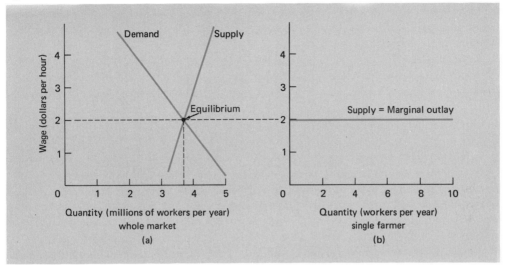

In a perfectly competitive market, here for farm labor, demand and supply in the aggregate set the equilibrium wage. In this case (part a) it equals $2 per hour. At this wage, the services of 3.7 million farm workers are offered and bought. The single farmer is helpless in the face of this wage. To him it is a constant at which, it appears to him, he can hire any quantity of labor he likes (part b). Each extra worker hired involves an extra or "marginal" outlay of $2 per hour.

usually are, in maximizing his profits, our farmer need only compare his marginal outlay (how his total cost changes when he changes employment by a man) with his *marginal revenue product* (how his total revenue changes in consequence of the change in production caused by the employment change). If he hires another man for an hour and his total cost changes from $700 to $702, his marginal outlay was $2. If the man produced two bushels and each is sold for $2, his total revenue may change from $800 to $804. His marginal revenue product was $4. Clearly, as long as marginal revenue product exceeds marginal outlay, it pays to hire more men. Another man hired and put to work would then add more to total revenue than to total cost. Hence, he would increase the farmer's total profit, which is the difference between the two. When marginal revenue product is below marginal outlay, it pays to produce less.[1] Hiring and using one man less would then reduce total cost more than total revenue. Hence, it would again increase total profit. Our farmer, indeed any business, would maximize total profit where marginal outlay and marginal revenue product are equal. At this point, hiring a man more or less would change total costs by exactly as much as it would change total revenue owing to the change in production and sales. There would then be no change in total profit.

[1] Advanced texts would show that this is strictly true only if marginal revenue product is not rising.

declining marginal revenue product   The above leaves us with one question. Can we be sure that there is a level of resource use at which marginal outlay and marginal revenue product will just be equal? What if marginal revenue product is always above or always below marginal outlay?

The answer is simple. If marginal outlay exceeds marginal revenue product at all levels of output, our firm will go bankrupt and disappear from the scene. If marginal revenue product exceeds marginal outlay, our firm will expand its operations, but it will not grow to infinite size. Sooner or later, marginal revenue product will fall to the level of marginal outlay and limit the quantity of resources hired by the firm. This results from a technological fact, already met in Chapter 18, the *law of diminishing returns*.

Consider once more Table 18.1 THE LAW OF DIMINISHING RETURNS. It showed us how, given at least one input as fixed, equal additions of one input, such as labor, brought forth smaller and smaller additions to output. If the farmer hired 3,000 hours of labor per year, he produced 1,000 tons of potatoes. By adding another 3,000 hours of work, he could add 500 tons to output. Hence, the marginal *physical* product, the extra output per hour of work measured in physical units, was 500 tons divided by 3,000 hours, or ⅙ ton per hour.

Starting at 6,000 hours hired and a total of 1,500 tons produced, our farmer could add another 3,000 hours and raise output by another 300 tons. Hence, the marginal physical product would fall to 300 tons divided by 3,000 hours, or ⅒ ton per hour. As we noted in Chapter 18, these diminishing returns to extra work give rise to increasing marginal costs of production. That is, because equal increases in effort led to smaller and smaller increases in output (declining marginal physical product), only larger and larger increases in effort (rising marginal costs) could bring about equal increases in output.

Now we can put the same story differently. If equal increases in effort lead to smaller and smaller increases in output (declining marginal *physical* product), they also lead to smaller and smaller increases in revenue (declining marginal *revenue* product). After all, marginal revenue product is only the monetary value of the marginal physical product. Table 20.2 DIMINISHING RETURNS, MARGINAL PHYSICAL PRODUCT, AND MARGINAL REVENUE PRODUCT, using the data of Table 18.1 THE LAW OF DIMINISHING RETURNS, shows why this is true.

Columns (1) and (3) of Table 20.2 repeat the data of Table 18.1 in slightly rearranged form. Columns (2) and (4) have been calculated from these data. (They can also be seen in Table 18.1.) Dividing column (2) by column (4), we derive the marginal physical product in column (5), or the extra tons of potatoes produced per extra labor hour. Reflecting the law of diminishing returns, these data in column (5) are declining. Now suppose the market price for potatoes is $45 per ton, as we assumed in Chapter 18. Then we can derive the data of column (6) by simply multiplying each entry in column (5) by $45. This is the marginal revenue product.

The first row of Table 20.2 tells us the following. If the farmer's total output is 1,000 tons of potatoes, he can add 3,000 labor hours and increase output by 500 tons. In the 1,000–1,500 ton total output range, he adds ⅙ ton per extra labor hour to his physical output. Given

Table 20.2 DIMINISHING RETURNS, MARGINAL PHYSICAL PRODUCT, AND MARGINAL REVENUE PRODUCT

RANGE OF TOTAL OUTPUT (TONS OF POTATOES)	CHANGE IN TOTAL OUTPUT (TONS OF POTATOES)	RANGE OF TOTAL QUANTITY OF LABOR (HOURS PER YEAR)	CHANGE IN QUANTITY OF LABOR (HOURS PER YEAR)	MARGINAL PHYSICAL PRODUCT (TONS OF POTATOES PER HOUR)	MARGINAL REVENUE PRODUCT (DOLLARS PER HOUR)
(1)	(2)	(3)	(4)	$(5) = \dfrac{(2)}{(4)}$	$(6) = (5) \times \$45$
1,000–1,500	500	3,000–6,000	3,000	$\dfrac{500}{3,000} = \dfrac{1}{6}$	\$7.50
1,500–1,800	300	6,000–9,000	3,000	$\dfrac{300}{3,000} = \dfrac{1}{10}$	4.50
1,800–1,900	100	9,000–12,000	3,000	$\dfrac{100}{3,000} = \dfrac{1}{30}$	1.50
1,900–1,920	20	12,000–15,000	3,000	$\dfrac{20}{3,000} = \dfrac{1}{150}$	.30

The law of diminishing returns is reflected in declining marginal physical product and declining marginal revenue product as well.
Source: Table 18.1 THE LAW OF DIMINISHING RETURNS.

the market price of \$45 per ton, he also adds ⅙ ton times \$45, or \$7.50 per extra labor hour, to his revenue.

Should he do it? As we saw, the answer is yes, if the hourly wage (his marginal outlay) is \$7.50 or less. In fact the data of columns (3) and (6) are his demand schedule for labor! If total employment is in the range of 3,000 to 6,000 hours per year, he will at most pay \$7.50 per labor hour. Given the technical facts of production and the market price of output, he cannot afford to pay more. If, instead, total employment is in the range of 6,000–9,000 hours per year, he will at most pay \$4.50 per labor hour. Although the "earlier" worker added more to his revenue, the last ones only add this much. The law of diminishing returns has cut their productivity. Clearly, he cannot in practice differentiate between "earlier" and "later" workers. If he fires *any one* of them, he loses \$4.50 for each hour he works less. So they all get \$4.50 at most.

The data of columns (3) and (6) are graphed below in Figure 20.2 PERFECT COMPETITION: BEST PROFIT INPUT as the demand curve for labor. By assuming that each farm laborer works 1,000 hours a year, the hourly data have been transformed into "workers per year."

Superimposed also is the marginal outlay curve from Figure 20.1(b). We perceive immediately how our farm's best profit input would be about 8.5 workers, that is, 8,500 hours, per year—given the fixed amounts of other inputs we had earlier assumed in Chapter 18. As Table 18.1 THE LAW OF DIMINISHING RETURNS tells us, this would produce somewhat less than 1,800 tons of potatoes per year. It is no accident that this is the same result we obtained earlier in Figure 18.2 PERFECT COMPETITION: BEST PROFIT OUTPUT.

Figure 20.2 PERFECT COMPETITION: BEST PROFIT INPUT

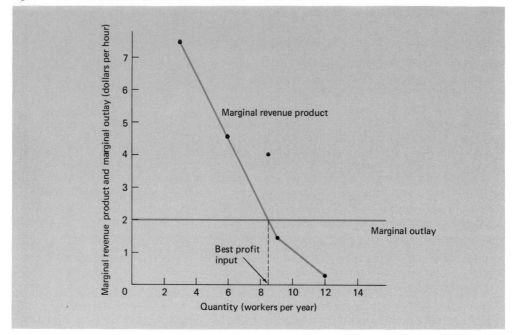

A firm's best profit input quantity is found where falling marginal revenue product equals marginal outlay.

At any smaller input use, marginal revenue product would be above marginal outlay. Profits could be raised by hiring more men. At any larger input use, marginal outlay would exceed marginal revenue product. Profits could be raised by hiring fewer men.

the economic efficiency of perfect competition   We can now see the reason why perfect competition is economically so efficient. Self-interest will cause *all* our potato farmers to hire such a quantity of labor that marginal outlay equals marginal revenue product. Because all are faced with the *same* marginal outlay (it equals the market-determined wage common to all), they are in effect, without being aware of it, equalizing their workers' marginal revenue product. This means that, *wherever* farm labor is bought, it is producing the same marginal revenue product.

This is not to say that all farms hire the identical number of workers, produce identical output quantities, or make identical total profits. These can vary widely among them. But everywhere *another hour of labor* would add exactly $2 to output. Everywhere would an hour worked less cut output by $2.

This is most efficient, indeed. Suppose it were otherwise. Suppose the marginal revenue product of farmer Brown were $5 per hour and that of farmer Green $1. Given the market price of wheat of, say, $2 per bushel, this would imply that labor's marginal *physical* product is two and one-half bushels per hour on Brown's farm and one-half bushel on Green's. This would indicate a serious misallocation of resources. By forcing a man to work for Brown rather than Green, we could raise output. For every hour he does not work for Green, Green loses half a bushel. For every hour he works for Brown, Brown gains two and a half bushels. We could gain two bushels without increasing the total quantity of resources used.

Even if Green and Brown were doing their best from a *technical* standpoint (they got the most out of the men at their disposal), there was inefficiency from the *economic* standpoint. Green had too much labor. He had advanced too far along the road of diminishing returns. Correspondingly, Brown had not enough labor. He had not gone far enough along that road. As we switch labor from Green to Brown, Green's output would fall, his remaining workers' marginal physical product would rise. Brown's output would rise, his workers' marginal physical product would fall. Eventually, their marginal physical products would become equalized. But as long as Green's falls short of Brown's, Brown's output would rise by more than Green's falls. Although resources have been fully employed, they were employed in the wrong places. Scarcity was greater than necessary because of economic inefficiency.

In perfect competition, this would never happen. At a wage of $2 per hour, Green would never dream of hiring a man whose efforts only added output worth $1 per hour. He would lose $1 on the last hour's work. He would voluntarily hire less labor. Brown, on the other hand, would not be content in a situation in which another man costs $2 per hour, but brings in $5. He could gain $3 from another hour's work. He would be eager to hire more as long as such discrepancy persisted.

The Imperfect Competitor

It is a relatively short step from here to understanding the economist's concern with big labor. Labor unions, unlike individual workers in a perfectly competitive market, can influence wages. As we saw, this is one of their main functions. It is why workers unite in unions to bargain as a single unit with their employers. There are many ways in which unions can raise wages. Some restrict the supply of labor in an industry. They may insist on long apprenticeship periods, costly training programs, or high entrance fees. This is the method used by the medieval craft guilds and also by modern professional organizations, such as of lawyers and doctors. Supply restriction, analogous to that by farmers depicted in Figure 19.3, can thus raise hourly labor income even without collective bargaining. It also leads to a fall in the number of those employed.

But let us consider another case. Suppose a union does bargain collectively about both the wage and the level of employment. By threatening to strike, or to withdraw all labor completely, such a union may force an employer into a situation he would never voluntarily choose: where marginal revenue product falls short of marginal outlay. Thus, a firm may end up on a point *off* its demand curve for labor, as indicated by the lone dot in Figure 20.2 PERFECT COMPETITION: BEST PROFIT INPUT. A firm that would have hired about nine workers at $2 per hour in perfect competition may be forced to hire them at double that wage. Naturally, this would cut into the firm's profits. The last man hired, using the data of Figure 20.2, would cost $4 each hour and add only $2 to revenue. Yet, as long as *total* profit is not wiped out completely, the firm may live with this situation.

Now watch what this implies. The wage paid by this firm now exceeds marginal revenue product. The same may be true for other firms. But only by the sheerest of coincidences would wages everywhere exceed marginal revenue product by the same percentage. In non-unionized sectors of the economy, wages may, in fact, equal marginal revenue product. Hence, there will be innumerable instances in which marginal revenue products differ among firms. As we saw, this means labor's marginal physical products differ, and a switch of resources is indicated.

The invisible hand of self-interest ceases to bring this switch about. There may be two producers of steel, both selling steel at $3 per ton. A laborer's marginal revenue product may be $6 per hour in company A (his marginal physical product being two tons per hour). A laborer's marginal revenue product may be $9 per hour in company B (his marginal physical product being three tons per hour). If only we could switch a man from A to B! For every hour worked, we could then gain a ton of steel! Yet, unlike in the case of farmers Brown and Green above, there might now be no incentive whatsoever for A to lay off men to be hired by B. Both might be locked into their positions by union demands. We might have full employment, but resources would be employed in the wrong places, in economically inefficient ways. Scarcity would be larger than it has to be. This could be the "trouble with labor unions."

A Word of Warning

As all our discussions in Part 2, the above is only to convey a general feeling for the issue of economic efficiency. Labor unions must not necessarily have the bad effect indicated above. Just briefly consider the case in which the shoe is on the other foot. Suppose employers get together and, through a "you-take-it-or-leave-it" offer, force nonunionized workers "off their supply curve." That is, workers may be forced to accept a wage-hours combination they would never voluntarily choose. They may be exploited, paid a wage *below* their marginal revenue product.

As a result, wages will again differ from marginal revenue product. Only this time they are below, rather than above, it. Most likely, we would again have economic inefficiency. In this case, unions may be just the thing needed to restore efficiency. They may force the wage right back up to marginal revenue product, restoring the efficiency of perfect competition.

CONCLUSION

It is difficult to evaluate the effect unions have on economic efficiency in such a general discussion as this one has to be. If unions were facing perfectly competitive firms, one could be practically certain that firms would be forced to buy a quantity of labor different from that where wage equals the marginal revenue product of labor. In short, firms might be forced away from the profit-maximizing position by an all-or-nothing offer backed up by the threat of strike. As a result, we could say without hesitation that labor unions, however desirable for other reasons, are contributing to economic inefficiency. What is good for unions is not necessarily good for the country!

If, however, unions are facing imperfectly competitive firms (as they are likely to do), they might again force firms away from the profit-maximizing position. In this case, however, they may, as we just noted, restore the condition of efficiency originally upset by the firm.

Yet this need not happen. We have no guarantee that unions will just undo the harm imperfectly competitive firms have made. In fact, this would be a most unlikely coincidence. Some studies estimate that American unions have raised wages of their members from 5 to 15 percent above the levels that would probably have prevailed otherwise. Thus, there is a presumption at least that unions do succeed in causing economic inefficiency and thereby increased scarcity. Because labor unions serve a great variety of important functions other than raising wages, however, we might hesitate to propose their dissolution even if their economic effects were clearly negative.

One other point should be noted. In an imperfectly competitive world, what is a firm likely to do if forced by a union to pay a wage above the workers' marginal revenue product? It may well raise the price of its output, thereby pushing up its marginal revenue product. In terms of Figure 20.2 PERFECT COMPETITION: THE BEST PROFIT INPUT, if unions push up the marginal outlay curve to $4, firms may react by pushing up the marginal revenue product curve until it intersects the new marginal outlay curve at the lone dot indicated on the graph. This then would be a classic case of cost-push inflation, discussed in Chapters 4 and 14. Even though workers' productivity has not risen, if workers insist on getting paid more than they are producing, a firm can simply increase the value of its product by charging more for it.

If you have read Chapter 14, you will note that the tools developed in this chapter can be easily used to illustrate the meaning of the wage-price guideposts. Wages are supposed to be raised everywhere in accordance with the nationally observed long-run rise in productivity. Suppose they are raised at 3.2 percent a year. Graphically, our marginal outlay curve shifts up at 3.2 percent each year. If this particular firm's marginal physical product of labor has also risen at 3.2 percent, the marginal revenue product would rise likewise, with no change in product price. Our marginal revenue product curve would shift up to intersect the higher marginal outlay curve at the same volume of employment.

If, however, the particular firm's marginal physical product of labor has risen faster than the national average, its new marginal revenue product would lie above the new marginal outlay. Firms are then supposed to bring it down to marginal outlay by reducing their output prices. (This is case A illustrated on page 315.)

If the particular firm's marginal physical product of labor has risen more slowly than the national average, its new marginal revenue product would lie below the new marginal outlay. In that case, firms are supposed to raise their output prices to bring marginal revenue product up to marginal outlay. (This is case B illustrated on page 315.) Thus, the tools developed in this chapter do more than illuminate the important issue of economic efficiency.

They can also help us see the mechanism that creates cost-push inflation. They have been instrumental in shaping a new social invention: the wage-price guidepost as a means of dealing with cost-push inflation.

SUMMARY

1 This chapter continues the discussion of economic efficiency via an analysis of the role of labor unions.

2 Labor unions have existed in the United States since the days of independence. Until the Civil War, however, they were of no importance. The Knights of Labor was the first major union. After its influence faded, the American Federation of Labor (AFL) gradually became the dominant labor organization.

3 Union membership once reached 700,000 in the 1880's, but dropped to less than half a million by 1897. Then it slowly grew to reach a peak of 5 million by 1920, only to fall below 3 million in the depth of the Great Depression. Unionism had its heyday in the decade after 1935. Membership jumped to 15 million by 1945—36 percent of nonagricultural employment.

4 The tremendous growth of unions was owing to two factors: favorable legislation and a change in union strategy. Laws protecting labor included the Norris-La Guardia Act of 1932, the National Industrial Recovery Act of 1933, the National Labor Relations (Wagner) Act of 1935, and the Fair Labor Standards Act of 1938. These laws outlawed use of the injunction as an antilabor weapon and established securely labor's right to organize and bargain collectively. They also outlawed unfair antiunion practices. The change in union strategy involved the establishment of industrial unions in addition to craft unions. Most notable among these was the Congress of Industrial Organizations (CIO).

5 Since World War II, union growth has stagnated. There were, in 1967, 18 million members, but they comprised only 26 percent of the nonagricultural work force.

6 The stagnation in union growth was influenced by two factors: legislation unfavorable to unions and changes in the structure of the labor force.
    The Taft-Hartley Act of 1947 outlawed the closed shop and a number of unfair *union* practices. The Landrum-Griffin Act of 1959 put further curbs on unions. Union growth was also slowed by a decline in the importance of blue collar workers and general apathy caused by economic well-being.

7 American unions have a distinct *bread-and-butter personality*. Harboring no radical designs for society at large, they are content to live within the existing political framework. They aim for better terms and conditions of employment. Nonpecuniary functions, such as provision for a grievance procedure, are at least as important as pecuniary goals.

8 Unions, like big business, can contribute to economic inefficiency in the economy that means smaller output than otherwise possible.

9 Under perfect competition in the labor market, when no single buyer or seller has control over price, self-interest leads to economic efficiency. Self-interest dictates that each employer hire that quantity of labor at which falling marginal revenue product equals marginal outlay. The latter is identical with market-determined wage. Because all employers maximize their profits by equating marginal revenue product

with the identical wage, they equate, unknowingly, their respective workers' marginal revenue products. This makes it impossible to reallocate resources among firms and raise output. Thus an "invisible hand" creates economic efficiency.

10   Such efficient resource use is only accidental, however, when labor unions appear on the scene and influence labor's selling price. Superimposed on an otherwise perfectly competitive market, wage may come to exceed marginal revenue product. Thus, there is no guarantee that labor's marginal revenue product in one firm equals that in another. More likely than not, a reallocation of labor among producers could lead to higher output. Yet, there is no mechanism to bring this about.

11   On the other hand, not all is this clear-cut. Businesses can also create economic inefficiency by exploiting workers and paying wages below their workers' marginal revenue products. If they do, unions just may re-establish economic efficiency if they force wages back up to the level of the marginal revenue product. However, there is no guarantee, and it is in fact unlikely, that unions just do that.

12   Still, one is rightfully hesitant to limit or abolish labor unions. Their economic effects are somewhat uncertain. Their noneconomic ones are often desirable.

TERMS[2]

closed shop	injunction
conspiracy doctrine	jurisdictional strike
craft unions	marginal outlay
exploitation	marginal physical product
featherbedding	marginal revenue product
grievance procedure	right-to-work law
industrial unions	seniority
	union shop

SYMBOLS

AFL
CIO

QUESTIONS FOR REVIEW AND DISCUSSION

1   As noted in Chapter 12, the government suggests that parties to collective bargaining take into account the public interest when setting wages and prices. Labor unions were less than happy with this intrusion into their affairs by government. Strangely,

[2] Terms and symbols are defined in the Glossary at the end of the book.

even management, usually opposed to unions, defended *free collective bargaining.* How do you account for this?

2   Should the government through antitrust laws forbid industrial firms to get together and raise the prices of what they sell, while encouraging farmers and labor groups to do these very things?

3   What effects, do you think, has the imposition of a minimum wage law?

4   Federal laws insist that unions and management "bargain in good faith." What if one party makes its best offer right away and then refuses to make concessions? Would you call this bargaining in good faith?

5   "Increasing productivity, such as output per man, is attributable to the workers themselves, to investors making capital available, and to improvements in managerial skills." Evaluate. (Consider the lessons of Chapter 1.)

6   American unions since the 1930's have become adherents of government intervention in the economy. Yet, their main concern is still private collective bargaining, not political action. The prospects of a separate *labor party* in the United States are almost nil. To foreign labor leaders this is somewhat of a mystery. How do you account for it?

7   "Some economic groups obtain their income objectives partly through political processes rather than those of the market." Explain.

8   Do you think unions should have the right to strike? Justify your answer.

9   "People always get paid what they are really worth." Evaluate. (Consider the discussion of marginal revenue product.)

10   "In the final analysis, a worker's marginal physical productivity determines what he can earn." Evaluate.

11   "Rising marginal costs and declining marginal revenue product are brothers under the skin." Explain.

12   The market supply curve of Figure 20.1(a) is sloping upward to the right. Explain the meaning of this.

13   "Unions are firmly entrenched in many sectors of the American economy. The power of unions, however, is not necessarily indicated by their membership. Some unions are too weak to have any effect. Others have effects far beyond their membership." Discuss.

14   Why have labor unions never been important in agriculture?

15   Thirty-five years ago, cartoons would depict businessmen sitting on sacks full of money, smoking fat cigars, and torturing little men trying to earn bread for their children. Nowadays, you are more likely to see a different picture, such as poor Ford Motor Company cringing before a grinning monster labeled "Labor." What, if anything, is true about these cartoons?

16   "Union members enjoy little or no differential wage advantage over unorganized workers. The unions' main contribution to their members lies in nonpecuniary matters." Explain.

17   "Labor unions (however desirable for other reasons) *by themselves* contribute to economic inefficiency in a perfectly competitive world. When superimposed on an imperfectly competitive situation to begin with, as happens in the real world, the outcome is uncertain." Discuss.

18 "Working persons should be given a much wider set of options than now as between work and leisure. Why should not someone who could satisfy his needs for goods in 15 hours a week be allowed to do so? Why shouldn't everyone be allowed several months' paid vacation a year, in return for lower pay during the remaining months? Casting everyone into the same mold (the standard work week) not only restricts freedom, it is also inefficient." Evaluate.

19 "Unions should only be allowed to exist where workers are being exploited." Comment.

20 "The invisible hand of the perfectly competitive market may allocate labor such as to assure economic efficiency, yet it does so at a great sacrifice of other values. It provides no compensation for men injured at work, for men out of work against their will, for retired workers. Nor does it protect anyone from unjustified discharges. For the sake of compassion, we should forget about efficiency." Evaluate.

GATT Releases a 'Gripe Book'

Trade Complaints Listed

Special to The New York Times

GENEVA, Oct. 17—The world's leading trading nations began examining today a 300-page "gripe book" that catalogues all the evils that each sees in the others' way of doing business.

The catalogue of the so-called nontariff barriers to trade was compiled by the staff of the seven-nation General Agreement on Tariffs and Trade.

The gripe book's examination by a 32-member GATT Committee on Trade in Industrial Products is viewed by many qualified sources as a necessary preliminary to what could develop into a major Kennedy-round type of negotiation to liberalize world trade further.

However, these sources emphasize that several years of hard study of nontariff barriers will be required to identify the issues and goals and permit an international assault on them.

Today's first meeting of the Industrial Products Committee was said to have brought out a general desire to get on with this preliminary work. Nevertheless, delegates were said to have been "cautious" in their initial statement because in many countries the recriminated practices are deeply rooted in domestic legislation, sanitary regulations and other politically sensitive areas.

The Industrial Products Committee was established last November by a decision of the GATT Assembly of Member States with the mission of exploring the "opportunities for making progress toward further liberalization of trade."

The committee was specifically asked to go into nontariff barriers to trade because of the successful conclusion in the summer of 1967 of the Kennedy round of tariff-cutting negotiations.

Once these cuts become complete in 1972, it was felt, tariffs will no longer be a significant obstacle to trade in industrial products. On the other hand, it was believed, with the reductions in tariffs, other trade barriers will take on more importance and offer a fruitful area for future negotiations.

Dairy Import Controls Tightened by President To Reduce 1969 Inflow

Quotas on Low-Priced Cheeses, Canned Milk Made Permanent; Limits on Other Items Added

By a WALL STREET JOURNAL *Staff Reporter*

WASHINGTON—President Johnson further tightened dairy import controls to try to reduce 1969 imports to around 1.3 billion pounds of milk equivalent from an estimated 1.9 billion pounds in 1968 and 2.7 billion pounds in 1967.

The President's order, based on Tariff Commission findings, made permanent previous temporary quotas on canned milk and most low-priced foreign cheeses, including Edam, Gouda and Gruyere-process.

In addition, a 17-million-pound annual quota was established for chocolate milk "crumb." Also, butterfat-sugar mixtures in consumer packages were included in limitations that previously applied only to commercial quantities.

The latest actions reflect the continuing problem for the Federally supported U.S. dairy industry caused by mounting European dairy surpluses. With their milk products surpluses soaring, West European governments are subsidizing efforts to dump excess supplies in this country, government and industry officials contend.

The consumer packages of butter-fat-sugar mixtures offer a recent example. Although only half-pound and one-pound packages have been permitted to enter the U.S. quota-free, they are priced so low that ice cream manufacturers have found it worthwhile to purchase these inconvenient units for use in their products, a department official notes. As a result, more than six million pounds of these small packages have entered this country since the imports began in September.

The Wall Street Journal, January 7, 1969

21

the
free trade
question

I N THE PREVIOUS three chapters, we explored the concept of economic efficiency. We concentrated on the domestic economy. We considered the production and sale of goods, both industrial and agricultural. We also studied the sale and use of resources, in particular of labor. We saw how imperfections in competition, brought about by excessive private economic power (big business and big labor) or by government interference may result in more scarcity than necessary. In this chapter, we turn our attention beyond the confines of national boundaries. We focus our attention on the *international* movement of resources and of goods. We consider the age-old question of *free trade vs. protectionism*. Can we reduce scarcity by allowing resources and goods to move freely across our borders? Or should we protect our economy from international competition?

THE DRAMATIC EVENTS OF 1967

Somewhat unnoticed by the general public, the year 1967 saw a great deal of action on these very questions. It was the final year of 3 years of bargaining at Geneva, Switzerland, among more than fifty of the world's nations. This bargaining was known as the *Kennedy round* of trade negotiations, because it was started under the impact of a new law pushed through Congress by President Kennedy. Representatives of nations generating 80 percent of world trade had met in exhausting sessions ever since May 1964. Their aim: promoting freer international trade by agreeing on less restrictive commercial policies.

Such policies include primarily the setting of tariffs or customs duties and of import quotas. Tariffs are taxes levied on imports only. They are designed to discourage imports by raising the price to domestic buyers and lowering quantity demanded. If buyers substitute domestic nontaxed goods, their domestic producers are then "protected" from foreign competition. Quotas are to achieve the same goal, but they do so with more certainty. They establish a fixed maximum amount of specific foreign goods (such as 100,000 bales of Egyptian cotton) that are allowed to enter a country from abroad in a specified period. Tariffs provide no such certainty, because unlimited amounts of goods can enter as long as the customs duty is paid. In addition, commercial policies set a variety of rules, such as those concerning governmental procurement abroad, foreign shipping and airlines operating in the domestic economy, movement of resources across a country's borders, and certificates of health, origin, and so on. Often such rules tend to delay, make costlier, and discourage foreign trade.

So important did the U.S. government consider the Geneva negotiations that President Johnson, in the final days of the Geneva conference, kept hour-by-hour track of developments there. For fear of wiretapping, U.S. officials used a "scrambled" telephone line. And then, one day, the President flashed the go-ahead to U.S. Ambassador William Roth: "The man is wearing a white hat." It was the prearranged code, signaling Roth to accept the latest conditions proposed by our trading partners.

The results, announced in June 1967, included the following. First, over a 5-year period, the United States, Great Britain, the Common Market countries, and Japan would cut tariffs on 60,000 industrial and agricultural goods. The weighted average cut would be 35 percent of the existing tariffs. The United States would put the cut into effect in five equal annual installments, beginning on January 1, 1968. Some of her trading partners would do the same. Others would wait until mid-1968, but then make 40 percent of the agreed-on cut. Second, the United States agreed to reduce tariffs on chemicals by 40–45 percent, whereas the Common Market countries in Europe would only reciprocate with a 25 percent cut. This differential was to make up for a 1922 U.S. law providing for a special valuation method for benzenoid chemical imports. To protect the then-infant U.S. chemicals industry from competition by established European firms, Congress had ordered U.S. tariffs based on (high) U.S. chemicals prices, rather than on the actual (lower) European prices at which imports were being bought.

Third, an antidumping agreement was reached. It was to protect businesses from foreign competition if foreigners sold abroad below cost.

Fourth, as an extension of domestic agricultural policies (of the type discussed in Chapter 19), an international grain agreement provided for a minimum worldwide wheat export price of $1.73 per bushel.

Finally, the developed nations set an important precedent by agreeing on a program of multilateral food aid to the underdeveloped nations. These nations would be provided, over a 3-year period, with 4.5 million metric tons of wheat and other food grains annually. Of this aid, the United States would provide 42 percent, the Common Market countries another 23 percent.

The U.S. government considered the Geneva accords as the most significant achievement in the area of international trade in many decades. A brief look at the background can show us why.

U.S. COMMERCIAL POLICY IN PERSPECTIVE

Let us just briefly consider the history of U.S. tariff legislation. The U.S. Congress has a long heritage of protectionism. In 1821, only 5 percent of imports could enter the United States free; the remainder was charged with a 45 percent tariff, on the average. By 1830, 8 percent of imports were allowed in free, but the remainder paid an average tax of 62 percent. A hundred years later, in 1930, two thirds of imports came in free of customs duties, the remainder paid on the average 45 cents tax on the dollar. In the 100 years intervening, the ratio of duties to dutiable imports had been as low as 16 percent (in 1920). Yet, in 55 of those years it was above 40 percent. In only 8 years was it below 25 percent.

In 1930, Congress passed the *Smoot-Hawley Act* for higher tariffs. In a matter of 2 years, it helped raise the average tariff rate from 45 to 59 percent.

Since that time, however, successive administrations have persuaded an always reluctant Congress to liberalize trade restrictions. In 1934, under pressure from Secretary of State Cordell Hull, Congress passed the *Reciprocal Trade Agreements Act*. It was regularly renewed thereafter. It gave the President authority to swap tariff cuts with individual countries in bilateral negotiations. Through use of this power, the average tariff level in the United States was whittled down to 19 percent of dutiable imports by 1947, but the percentage of imports coming in free did not change.

After World War II, which had established a strong spirit of international cooperation among the victorious powers, a number of attempts were made to extend that collaboration into the postwar period. One of these was the *General Agreement on Tariffs and Trade* (GATT), an executive agreement that required no congressional action. It provided a framework for *multilateral* discussion among some forty members concerning a reduction in trade barriers. Before the Kennedy round mentioned above, such discussions occurred in 1947, 1949, 1951, 1956, and 1961. So far as the United States was concerned, the effect was not great. Although the average tariff was reduced further by 1961 to 12 percent of dutiable imports, the percentage of imports that came in free fell from 61 percent in 1947 to 40 percent in 1961.

Postwar renewals of the Reciprocal Trade Agreements Act tied the hands of the U.S. government increasingly. Negotiations had to be conducted, after hearings, product by product. An *escape clause* made it possible to revoke concessions if a domestic industry was seriously hurt as a result. *Peril points* were set. These were limits below which tariffs could not be lowered by the administration. The allowable reduction in tariffs was reduced again and again. In the meantime, giant steps were taken elsewhere in the world to liberalize trade. In 1957, six European countries (Belgium, France, Italy, Luxemburg, the Netherlands, and West Germany) formed the *European Economic Community* (EEC), more generally known as the European Common Market. These countries decided to eliminate all trade barriers among one another over a period of 12 to 17 years and to "harmonize" their national economic policies. Though there would be unhindered movement of goods as well as resources among them, these countries would erect common trade barriers to the outside world by the end of this period. (Actually, progress toward this goal was made much faster than planned. By 1967, 80 percent of the tariff walls had disappeared within the EEC.)

Seven other countries set up a parallel organization in 1960, known as the *European Free Trade Association* (EFTA). These "outer seven" comprise Austria, Denmark, Norway, Portugal, Sweden, Switzerland, and the United Kingdom. The United Kingdom had been hesitant to join the Common Market, because it would have required giving up the special trading preferences accorded the Commonwealth countries. Since then, Great Britain has tried three times to link up with the EEC, however. Each time, in 1963, 1967, and 1968, her membership application was in effect vetoed by France.

Considering the growth of free trade blocs abroad and unhappy with the postwar record of trade liberalization in the United States, President Kennedy sponsored the *U.S. Trade Expansion Act of 1962*. This act authorized the President to negotiate across-the-board tariff cuts of up to 50 percent in exchange for comparable concessions from abroad. The act eliminated tariffs on tropical products. The act also provided for adjustment assistance to American workers and businesses injured as a result. It was this act that gave rise, in 1964, to the sixth postwar assault on tariff walls under the auspices of GATT. As we saw above, it was the most successful venture so far. Even before the end of the Kennedy round at Geneva, the height of U.S. tariff walls had been reduced by 1966 to 6 percent of dutiable imports. But the percentage of imports coming in free fell further to 37 percent.

This reflects the grudging congressional attitude toward trade liberalization. Although the administration has continued to advocate free trade strongly, Congress has at least tried to slow down this effort. In 1967 alone, a wide variety of bills were introduced in Congress to compensate for tariff cuts by the imposition of new and the lowering of old import quotas on almost anything, ranging from textiles, apparel, and mink furs to steel, lead, and zinc to meat, groundfish fillets, baseball gloves, scissors, and flat glass. So far, most of such efforts have failed.

Nevertheless, there have been exceptions even to the administration's liberal trade attitude. Note President Johnson's dairy import quotas described in the news report introducing this chapter. Just before leaving office, he also got the European Coal and Steel Community and nine Japanese steel companies to agree on "voluntary" export quotas to the United States. These exporters accounted for over 80 percent of American steel imports. President Nixon has pursued a similar policy. Although generally affirming a free trade stand, he imposed higher duties on Italian steel imports. He tried to get Europeans and Asians to agree on "voluntary" textile export curbs to the United States. At the time of this writing, he was studying the imposition of lower oil import quotas.

Once the present Geneva agreement goes into effect fully in 1972, however, and barring unforeseen events, U.S. tariff barriers are going to be reduced to the nuisance level. On the U.S. side, such barriers to world trade in goods will then be negligible.

This alone, of course, will increase the *relative* importance of nontariff barriers. As shown by the other news report introducing this chapter, the members of GATT are planning to deal with these in turn. Commerce Secretary Maurice Stans has shown great eagerness to dismantle such barriers also. These include the quotas already mentioned. They include a great number of *consumer protection laws*. Here are some cases in point. West Germany, which imports a great deal of feed for poultry and swine from the United States, established a maximum fat content of 5 percent for such feed for "health reasons." U.S. exports contain 10 percent of fat. France put "highway safety regulations" on imported U.S. farm tractors, requiring them to have headlights. This increased their cost by 2 percent, offsetting a 2 percent Kennedy Round tariff cut. West Germany required farm tractors to have two sets of brakes and two seats. Great Britain required her importers to deposit an amount of money equal to half the import value with the British Treasury for 6 months without interest. The loss of interest again raises the cost of foreign goods. Mexico forbade the import of electric drills .5 inch or less in diameter. This cut out U.S. exports. The United States set a minimum size for imported tomatoes. This cut out Mexican tomato exports. Brazil required U.S. vehicles to be imported without tires. The additional labor involved raised their cost. Israel required special licenses for the import of power tools. The fees involved raised their cost. Believe it or not, Italy put a "sanitary tax" on foreign snake poison. Thus, there is much left to talk about in the "gripe book" sessions at Geneva.

ARGUMENTS ABOUT BARRIERS TO TRADE

We have become acquainted with the major facts surrounding U.S. policies with respect to trade barriers. We now turn to a discussion of the arguments for and against the imposition of such barriers. Then we shall evaluate their impact on the efficiency of resource use in the present U.S. economy.

Arguments in Favor of Trade Barriers

There are a great many arguments used by those who lobby for legislation imposing restrictions on trade. We shall look at some of the most commonly used ones.

keeping money in the country   Centuries ago, the "mercantilists" used to argue for an excess of commodity and service exports over corresponding imports in the hope of importing gold for the difference, thereby making the nation "rich." This argument still crops up nowadays, for instance, when people argue that domestic purchases leave our country in possession of the goods *and* the money, whereas purchase abroad gives us the goods but the foreigner the money.

To advocate tariffs or quotas on that account is absurd. After all, a country's wealth consists of the *goods* it has and not of its money. If we continually give up more goods than we import from abroad, we are *reducing* our standard of living. Scarcity is reduced by getting goods, not by giving them away.

Furthermore, such a mercantilist policy is self-defeating in the long run. Our money in the hands of foreigners tends to return to us via their purchases here. If we don't buy from them, they cannot long buy from us. Our exports will decline together with our imports. So far as our money is concerned, it is something we can manufacture anytime and in any quantity, as we learned in Chapter 9 above. If tariffs do keep money in the country, it certainly does not make us richer.

raising government revenue and employment   Another frequently used argument for tariffs is that they bring in revenues for government; at the same time, they help domestic employment. As a moment's reflection will show, only if tariffs do not sufficiently discourage imports will revenues be collected. If, however, tariffs are so high as to discourage imports completely, there will be no revenue at all. If there are no sales, a sales tax brings in nothing! In any case, there are better ways for government to get revenue.

Furthermore, the effect on employment is uncertain. Possibly it works out as argued. But it will also happen that tariffs, which cut our imports, lead to cuts in our exports. This can happen either because foreigners impose retaliatory tariffs or because their employment and income have fallen. Thus, our employment may not be affected at all in the aggregate. We may raise our level of employment by importing less and producing substitutes at home. But we will put our export industry workers out of work. Thus, we may only shift employment among industries in the end, with lots of suffering in between. In fact, our level of employment may even fall, if the foreign demand for our exports falls by more than our demand for import substitutes rises. In any case, as we saw in Chapters 10 and 12, there are certainly better ways of dealing with unemployment than its "export" via tariffs.

protecting our high wages   Perhaps most often heard is the argument that American workers must be protected against "cheap foreign labor." On that basis, people sometimes propose the introduction of a "scientific tariff" designed to equalize foreign costs (now including the tariff) with domestic costs. This, too, rests on many misunderstandings.

For one thing, a truly "scientific" tariff of this nature would end all foreign trade completely. Second, although many foreigners receive lower wages *per hour* than Americans, they are often also much less productive, being endowed with less capital, land, and education. Thus, they may still have a higher cost *per unit produced*. This is recognized by foreigners who complain, in equally confused fashion, that "Americans with their cheap capital are bound to undersell us in everything." This is as false as the pauper labor argument above.

Consider an American getting $3.00 per hour and a Japanese getting 50 cents per hour. Being skilled and endowed with lots of machinery and cheap raw materials, the American worker may produce 300 flashbulbs an hour. Thus, the labor cost is 1 cent per flashbulb. The Japanese, being less skilled and endowed with inferior tools, may produce only twenty-five flashbulbs per hour. Thus, the labor cost is 2 cents per flashbulb. Thus, lower wages per hour do not have to mean lower cost per unit produced.

This is, in fact, often the case. As statistics bear out clearly, American output per man-hour is frequently higher than anywhere else in the world. As a result, the United States is often able to compete successfully with the lowest wage in the low-wage countries. Our high wages simply reflect our high productivity. We do not need tariffs to protect these high wages.

protecting "young" industries and economies   There are some reasonable arguments for interfering with international trade. There is the *infant industry,* or *young economy*, argument, for instance. It holds that a country or industry within it may be kept by foreign competition from ever developing and that protection is needed temporarily until the new industry can develop to the point where it can compete.

It is frequently a technical fact that unit costs of production fall until very large output volumes are achieved. If you produce 1,000 cars a year, they may cost you $19,000 each on the average. If you produce 500,000 cars instead, the cost per unit may be down to $1,900. This may reflect increased possibilities for specialization as the scale of production is enlarged, as well as the spread of fixed costs (for buildings and equipment) over many units. This effect is often called the *economies of scale*, or *mass production*, effect. The U.S. iron industry in the last century grew up behind a protective tariff wall keeping out competition of established British firms. We saw a similar example above with respect to the U.S. chemicals industry.

The *young economy* argument is similar. It holds that a country must diversify its economic activities. Otherwise, like some of the countries producing primary products, it is too vulnerable to changes in foreign demand. If Brazil, for example, produces mostly coffee and cotton, most of which is exported, it can be in the position of the individual farmer described in Chapter 19. A bumper crop, or a slight fall in foreign demand, can lead to a drastic fall in price and revenue. Hence, the quantity of goods Brazilians can buy abroad can fluctuate violently from year to year. The solution: reduce the importance of agriculture in the economy by developing industries. It is argued that one needs for this reason initial trade barriers keeping foreign competitors out. Australia and Canada are examples of successful pursuit of this policy.

national defense   There is also the *national defense* argument. If a country's oil industry or merchant marine cannot survive in international competition, but their existence is deemed necessary for national security, we may wish to protect them from competition. Or, in general, whenever international tensions make national self-sufficiency seem preferable to specialization and trade, one may favor limitation of trade, even in nonstrategic goods.

However, arguments such as these are all too often abused, because those with selfish interests wrap their personal preferences around the flag to make them more acceptable to legislators. Nothing sells better than appeals to nationalism. Thus it has been argued, for instance, that the U.S. watch industry must be protected from Swiss competition, lest the United States be without fine-mechanical precision workers in case of war, an argument one can doubt.

conclusion   Many arguments in favor of erecting barriers to free trade rest on crude fallacies. This is certainly true of the first three discussed in this section. It is somewhat different with the latter two. Economic development and national defense are goals reasonable men can be expected to pursue. Yet, one can doubt that tariffs and similar barriers are the best way to grant the desired protection. In fact, they may well contribute to international tension conducive to war. If it is truly desired, for reasons of economic development or national defense, to protect certain industries, this may be done better by outright subsidies. These can bring the protected industries' prices down to those of foreign competitors instead of bringing the prices of foreign competitors up to those of domestic producers. In this case, too, the cost of the game is clearly obvious, something that is never the case with tariffs.

Most economists are free traders. This is a reaction against the nonsense arguments. It is also an indication of their belief that the goals of economic development and national defense can be better served in other ways than restricting free trade. Yet, economists may well have jumped to the wrong conclusion. The failure of an argument does not automatically prove the opposite! I may be unable to prove the existence of God. That does hardly prove that He does not exist. In the same way, failure of some arguments for tariffs and quotas and similar barriers does in no way prove that free trade is the best of all possible worlds. Nor does it preclude the existence of other arguments for tariffs and quotas not considered so far.

Arguments against Trade Barriers

There are a number of powerful arguments, however, that seem to tip the scale in favor of free international movement of goods and resources. Let us consider two of them.

the case for free movement of resources   Recall the case of steel companies A and B in the last chapter. Owing to imperfections in the labor market, the marginal physical product of a worker in A was two tons of steel per period, that of a worker in B was three tons. Although we could see the obvious advantage of moving men from A to B until this difference was eliminated, there was no incentive for this to happen. Hence, resources were inefficiently employed from the standpoint of the economy as a whole. Scarcity was larger than necessary.

Now extend your horizon. Suppose steel company A stands for the Japanese steel industry and company B for that of the United States. Again, seen from the world standpoint, it would now be worthwhile to transfer resources outright between producers, as from the high- to the low-cost producer. If, as in our earlier example, the same resources could produce higher outputs in the United States than in Japan (the marginal physical product of an American worker exceeds that of a Japanese), it would be worthwhile to transfer resources from Japan to the United States. As a result, U.S. output, like company B's, would rise by more than that of Japan, which, like company A's, would fall. World output would be up, and everyone *could* be made equally well or better off. Thus, any obstacles to resource mobility, be they physical inability to move them, language barriers, insufficient transport routes, immigration laws, or psychological factors, are obstacles to the achievement of economic efficiency. If, for instance, there is much capital (buildings, equipment, inventories!) in the United States relative to labor, while the opposite holds for Japan, the addition to output (marginal physical product) a unit of labor could make in the United States would probably be larger than the output forgone (marginal physical product) by its loss in Japan. Hence, it would be wise *for the sake of economic efficiency* to move people from Japan to the United States. Here you feel immediately that noneconomic considerations (whether they be rational or not) are likely to override economic ones. For all the reasons just given, it is exceedingly difficult to move resources across national borders.

As a result of natural or man-made barriers to resource mobility, some international cost differences remain permanent. To the extent that one country has a permanent absolute cost advantage in the production of a good (and so far as we can tell at this point), it pays other countries to buy the good involved in this country. It pays the United States to import coffee, tea, and bananas. It would be foolish for her to grow such products in the artificial climate of New England greenhouses. She does much better producing machine tools and exporting them in return. Tropical countries, on the other hand, would be foolish to produce machine tools without the easy access to raw materials and the lavish endowment with capital and skilled labor enjoyed by the United States. Without such sensible division of labor, world output would be much lower than it is.

Note, however, that the above proves relatively little. It only proves that some trade is better than none! It does not prove that free trade is better than trade partially restricted. Yet, 150 years ago, economists developed an argument that would seem to prove just that.

the case for free movement of goods   The argument for completely free movement of goods was developed, among others, early in the nineteenth century by the British economist David Ricardo. It is the theory of *comparative* advantage. Take the worst of all possible cases, Ricardo would argue. Consider two countries, the United States and Japan. Suppose it is impossible to move resources internationally between them. And suppose that the United States is capable of producing *every* good at a lower resource cost. No matter what good you pick—steel, bicycles, even rice—the United States needs less labor, land, and capital than Japan to produce another unit of it. It seems that Japan would do well to buy *everything* in the United States, whereas the United States could not possibly gain by buying anything in Japan. Anything she could buy there, she could make more cheaply at home!

Still, argued Ricardo, mutually advantageous trade would be possible in *both* directions *as long as resources can be moved within a country.* Suppose the facts are those given in Table 21.1. The data show clearly what we have assumed. The marginal physical product

Table 21.1   INTERNATIONAL PRODUCTIVITY DIFFERENCES

| COUNTRY | ANOTHER UNIT OF LABOR, LAND, AND CAPITAL CAN PRODUCE | |
	STEEL	RICE
Japan	1 ton	1 ton
U.S.A.	3 tons	2 tons

The productivity of resources often differs between producers.

of a unit of resources in the United States exceeds that in Japan for all goods. Add or take away such a unit of labor, land, and capital in the U.S. steel industry, and output would change by three tons. In Japan, it would change by only one ton. Add or take away such a unit in U.S. rice farming, and output would change by two tons. In Japan it would change by only one ton. American resources are more productive no matter where they are employed.

Turned around, the American resource cost is lower for all types of output. At the margin, a ton of steel costs one unit of resources in Japan, but only one-third unit in the United States. At the margin, a ton of rice costs one unit of resources in Japan, but only one-half unit in the United States. Thus, Table 21.2 gives the same information as Table 21.1.

Still, argued Ricardo, this direct industry-by-industry comparison of marginal costs between countries is quite irrelevant. It does not matter that American marginal costs are lower for all goods than corresponding Japanese figures. What does matter is this: they are not lower for all goods *by the same percentage.* Comparatively, America is better at steel making than at rice growing. In steel, she has a 3:1 edge. Marginal cost is one third the Japanese figure. In rice, the United States has only a 2:1 edge. Marginal cost is one half the Japanese figure.

The United States, argued Ricardo, should specialize in that activity in which she has the comparative advantage: she should specialize in and export steel. Japan should similarly specialize in that activity in which she has the comparative advantage. (And that term may mean having the least disadvantage.) Although she is absolutely worse at mak-

Table 21.2 *INTERNATIONAL DIFFERENCES IN MARGINAL COSTS*

| COUNTRY | MARGINAL COST PER TON OF PRODUCT (IN UNITS OF LABOR, LAND, AND CAPITAL) | |
	STEEL	RICE
Japan	1	1
U.S.A.	$\frac{1}{3}$	$\frac{1}{2}$

Marginal costs differ between producers, reflecting differences in resource productivities.

ing everything, Japan has the least disadvantage in rice production. She should specialize in and export rice.

Now watch what would happen. Suppose the United States takes a unit of labor, land, and capital out of rice production. Rice output will fall by two tons. Suppose these resources are transferred to steel making. Steel output will rise by three tons. Let Japan do the opposite. Let her take two units of labor, land, and capital out of steel production and let them produce rice instead. Steel output falls by two tons; rice output is up by two tons.

What is the over-all result? Seen from the standpoint of the world as a whole, rice output has not changed, but steel output is up by one ton. The same resources, differently employed, yielded higher output. Thus, there was economic inefficiency before. Although resources could not be moved from Japan to the United States, they could be moved within Japan and within the United States, respectively.

Clearly, this gain from specialization could, argued Ricardo, be shared between the two countries. Japan could, for instance, export two tons of rice for two and one-half tons of steel. Thus, she would end up with half a ton of steel more than before. So would the United States. Her imports of two tons of rice would compensate for her lowered production. Only two and one-half of the three extra tons of steel would have to be given up in exchange.

Following the insights provided by the theory of comparative advantage, concluded Ricardo, could make us all richer.

Table 21.3 THE GAINS FROM TRADE summarizes the above discussion. Naturally, as long as the productivity differences depicted in Table 21.1 persist, it pays to carry specialization further. The above is just the first step. Quite possibly, in the end, Japan will produce nothing but rice and the United States nothing but steel. Through trading, they may have available a great deal more of both goods than before specialization and the opening of trade.

the mechanism   One thing remains to be seen. What is the mechanism that actually brings about what is theoretically possible? For that, too, nineteenth-century economists had a ready answer: the invisible hand of perfect competition would take care of all.

As we saw in Chapter 18, prices would come to equal marginal costs under perfect competition. Thus, the real data of Table 21.2 INTERNATIONAL DIFFERENCES IN MARGINAL

Table 21.3   THE GAINS FROM TRADE

	JAPAN		U.S.A.	
	STEEL	RICE	STEEL	RICE
(1) Initial production (assumed)	300 tons	500 tons	300 tons	200 tons
(2) Change through specialization (based on respective marginal costs)	− 2 tons	+2 tons	+3 tons	− 2 tons
(3) Final production	298 tons	502 tons	303 tons	198 tons
(4) Change through international trade (based on assumed world prices of 1 ton of rice for 1.25 tons of steel)	+2.5 tons	− 2 tons	− 2.5 tons	+2 tons
(5) Final amounts available	300.5 tons	500 tons	300.5 tons	200 tons

By specializing according to comparative advantage and trading, all countries could become better off. Compare rows (1) and (5).

COST would be reflected in monetary marginal cost and price data. Suppose a unit of labor, land, and capital costs $10 in the United States and 100 yen in Japan. Then, Table 21.2 can be converted into its monetary equivalent of Table 21.4.

Where in a free trade world would Americans and Japanese buy steel and rice? Naturally, where they are cheapest. But we cannot tell that until we know the exchange rate between yen and dollars. It clearly could not be 1:1. Then everything would be so much more expensive in Japan. No American would import from there.

All Japanese would want to buy American goods. There would be a great demand for dollars by Japanese wanting American goods. There would be no supply of dollars by Americans who wanted Japanese goods. "Cheap American capital," the Japanese would wail, "is underselling us in everything." Dealers in foreign money would have to raise the price of those scarce dollars in terms of yen above our hypothetical 1 yen for $1.

Suppose they raised the rate to 50 yen per dollar. That would make steel and rice both cost $2 per ton in Japan. Now we would be in the opposite spot. Everything would be more

Table 21.4   PERFECT COMPETITION: PRICES EQUAL MARGINAL COSTS

COUNTRY	MARGINAL COST AND PRICE PER TON OF PRODUCT	
	STEEL	RICE
Japan	100 yen	100 yen
U.S.A.	$3.33	$5

Under perfect competition market price everywhere equals monetary marginal cost.

expensive in the United States! No Japanese would import from here. All Americans would want to buy Japanese goods. There would develop a great supply of dollars by Americans wanting Japanese goods. There would be no demand for dollars by Japanese who wanted American goods. "Cheap Japanese labor," Americans would cry, "is underselling us in everything." Dealers in foreign money would have to lower the price of those abundant dollars in terms of yen below our hypothetical 50 yen for $1.

And somewhere in the middle, they would discover a wonderful thing. Steel would become cheaper in the United States, and rice cheaper in Japan. Trade would begin to flow both ways at a rate higher than 20 yen per dollar and lower than 33 yen per dollar. The former is the ratio of the Japanese to the American price of rice, the latter that of the Japanese to the American price of steel (Table 21.4). Somewhere in between, at say 25 yen per dollar, there would be an *equilibrium* rate of exchange exactly equating the demand for and the supply of dollars. In a world of perfect competition, the country with the comparative advantage (having the greatest absolute advantage or the least disadvantage) would become the country with the lowest money price. Thus, at the 25 yen per dollar rate, Japanese steel would cost $4 per ton, Japanese rice the same. Free trade would lead to an expansion of the American steel industry and exports to Japan of steel costing only $3.33 per ton. It would also lead to a contraction of American rice farming and imports from Japan of rice costing only $4 per ton. Perfect competition in the markets for goods as well as for money would see to it that the gains from trade, that we saw to be theoretically possible, would become reality!

conclusion   You can well imagine that the remarkable insight of David Ricardo, based on the most unfavorable of assumptions, impressed economists deeply. Any interference with the free international movement of goods is bound to lead, argued generations of economists, to a reduction in world output. Hence, the imposition of tariffs and import quotas and similar barriers can only impoverish all of us, for they create inefficiencies in the use of the world's resources. Given the Ricardian theory as a basis for rejecting tariffs, and the nonsensical arguments usually advanced in favor of tariffs, free trade became an article of faith in the academic community. As we saw above, successive administrations in the United States have also subscribed to that faith. Yet, the general public and the Congress have not. Who is right? To that question we now turn.

COULD THE FREE TRADERS BE WRONG?

Seemingly, the argument for free international trade is a strong one. Free trade can lead, we have seen, to a more efficient use of the world's resources and less scarcity. Arguments against free trade are either nonsensical or are supporting goals that could be reached by methods other than interference with trade. Could anything be more clear-cut?

Unfortunately, there is one fatal flaw in the armor of the free traders. True enough, free trade *could* lead to higher world output. True enough, free trade *would* lead to higher world output *in a world of perfect competition*. But our world, as we observed in the previous chapters, is not such a world. It is a world of *big* business, of *big* labor, of *big* government. It is a world in which prices typically are *not* equal to marginal costs. They are above marginal costs. What are the implications of that? They are serious indeed.

Consider Table 21.5 IMPERFECT COMPETITION: PRICES DO NOT EQUAL MARGINAL COSTS. Columns (1) and (3) repeat the marginal cost data of Table 21.4 on the assumption of an equilibrium exchange rate of 25 yen per dollar. Columns (2) and (4) show hypothetical price data. They have been chosen arbitrarily, except for the condition that prices exceed marginal

Table 21.5   IMPERFECT COMPETITION: PRICES DO NOT EQUAL MARGINAL COSTS

| | STEEL | | RICE | |
| | (1) | (2) | (3) | (4) |
COUNTRY	MARGINAL COST	PRICE	MARGINAL COST	PRICE
Japan	$4	$6	$4	$7
U.S.A.	$3.33	$8	$5	$6

Under imperfect competition, market price can diverge from marginal cost.

costs, as is likely in the real world. By accident, to be sure, all prices might exceed marginal costs by the same percentage. Then people, buying where prices are lowest, would still buy where marginal costs are lowest. All the above conclusions about the advantage of free trade would continue to hold. But this would be a most unlikely case. Much more likely is the case depicted in Table 21.5. Prices exceed marginal costs everywhere, *but by different degrees.* In the United States, it costs $3.33 of resources to produce another ton of steel, but price is $8, or 140 percent higher. On the other hand, the American price of rice exceeds marginal cost by only 20 percent. The Japanese prices of steel and rice exceed marginal costs by 50 and 75 percent, respectively.

As a result, it turns out that steel is cheaper in Japan and rice cheaper in the United States *so far as money outlay is concerned.* Under these conditions, if we had free trade, steel users would naturally buy steel in Japan and rice in the United States. After all, people buy goods where they are cheapest.

The only trouble is that prices that are not equal to marginal costs lie. In terms of real resources, as we saw in Table 21.2 INTERNATIONAL DIFFERENCES IN MARGINAL COSTS, the United States, having an absolute advantage in the production of both goods, has a *comparative* advantage in steel, not in rice. To raise world output, she should produce more steel. Japan should produce more rice. Yet, people buy rice in the United States and steel in Japan! Hence free trade, under conditions of imperfect competition, can lead a country into specialization according to comparative *dis*advantage. As nobody buys American steel and everybody wants her rice, the American steel industry withers away and rice farming expands. The opposites happen in Japan. Yet as Table 21.1 INTERNATIONAL PRODUCTIVITY DIFFERENCES shows so clearly, for every extra two tons of rice, the United States must sacrifice three tons of steel. Both require the same quantities of real resources. For two tons less rice produced, Japan is enabled to produce two extra tons of steel. Thus, world output is *down* by one ton of steel. Free trade has led to greater inefficiency, to more scarcity than before. The great promise of Table 21.3 THE GAINS FROM TRADE fails to get realized if we are guided by prices that distort the real forces they are supposed to reflect. Whatever prices may be saying, marginal costs still determine how production can be changed. Their ratio (such as the Japanese $4 to $4 or the American $3.33 to $5 in Table 21.5) shows what is technically possible: not to produce a ton of steel in Japan and to produce a ton of rice instead, or not to produce a ton of steel in the United States and produce two-thirds ton of rice instead.

Thus, free traders could be wrong, after all. Suppose a U.S. tariff of $3 per ton on Japanese steel prevented free Japanese steel imports into the United States. In the United States, Japanese steel would then cost $9 per ton, whereas U.S. steel could be had for $8. Suppose a Japanese tariff of $3 per ton of U.S. rice prevented free American rice imports to Japan. In Japan, American rice would then cost $9 per ton, whereas Japanese rice could be had for $7. Even if the reasons used for imposing the tariffs were nonsensical, the economic effect of such tariffs would be desirable. Given our example, which is by no means unrealistic, trade barriers would interfere with trade according to comparative *dis*advantage. They would, therefore, help to increase world output back to its pretrade level. Thus, we see that there may be quite valid reasons for imposing tariffs, namely, to adjust for the fact that money prices do not reflect marginal costs correctly. Better no trade than wrong trade!

Note that the same argument can be used, however, to subsidize the U.S. steel industry to undercut the internal Japanese price of $6 per ton. It can be used in Japan to subsidize Japanese rice farming to undercut the internal American price of $6 per ton. If this could be accomplished, we could move another step toward efficiency. Going from wrong trade to no trade helped restore output to the pretrade level. Now we can move from no trade to correct trade. This would raise world output in the fashion described above by Table 21.3 THE GAINS FROM TRADE.

Thus, international specialization and trade remains a desirable goal in that it helps raise world output. But that trade should be *free* trade only if prices accurately reflect marginal costs. If they do not, a complicated system of tariffs and subsidies may just be the thing needed to make them reflect marginal costs.

AN EVALUATION

What then can we conclude from the above for the real world? Should we rejoice whenever special interest groups pressure Congress to impose quotas and tariffs? Or should we stand behind the recent actions by the executive branch of government that have led and are going to lead to free international trade?

It is by no means easy to find an answer. The usual arguments advanced against free trade are wrong or support goals that could be achieved in other ways. The classic argument for free trade, the *theory of comparative advantage*, can be supported wholeheartedly only in a world of perfect competition in which prices reflect marginal costs. In such a world, tariffs, by distorting prices away from marginal cost, would distort behavior away from the optimum, thus leading to an economically inefficient use of resources. Tariff-distorted prices may cause people to have no foreign trade at all (thus forgoing the gains from trade) or may induce people to specialize according to comparative *dis*advantage, thereby causing a *reduction* in world output. In perfect competition, there is a clear case against tariffs and for free trade.

Yet, we do not live in this kind of world. Our relative prices are likely to deviate from relative marginal costs even in the absence of tariffs. Thus, it is conceivable that even without tariffs, free international trade leads to economic inefficiency, just as self-interest within the economy cannot be relied on to assure economic efficiency. In such a case, the imposition of a tariff or the raising of an existing one may even eliminate this inefficiency by discouraging the undesirable behavior. We cannot be sure, however. The higher tariff can also make things worse, as when it is imposed on a situation of (accidental) economic efficiency.

And there we stand. The clear-cut argument for free trade, which goes with perfect competition, becomes a matter of great uncertainty in the real world. Depending on the original situation of efficiency or inefficiency (which *cannot* be identified with certainty) and, in the latter case, depending on the exact change undertaken, higher tariffs may or may not stand in the way of fighting scarcity. Economists do not really know for sure whether human wants in the real world would be satisfied more with all tariffs removed. Those who argue that way, nevertheless, only show that they have forgotten that the real world is not a world of perfect competition. Or they show, as they very well may, of course, that their argument is based on other grounds.

Let us consider some of these other arguments.

Economies of Scale

Some people argue that we should not worry about specialization according to comparative advantage or disadvantage. Whichever we do initially, output will eventually go up. Specialization per se is what counts. By increasing the size of the market, it will allow industries to expand and reduce unit costs and marginal costs appreciably. Even if we do the wrong thing initially, such as letting, in our example, the Americans produce rice and the Japanese steel, economies of scale will overcome all this. In terms of Table 21.5 IMPERFECT COMPETITION: PRICES DO NOT EQUAL MARGINAL COSTS, expansion of Japanese steel making will eventually reduce Japanese marginal costs from $4 below the American level of $3.33. Expansion of U.S. rice farming will eventually reduce U.S. marginal costs from $5 below the Japanese level of $4. There may, of course, be something to this argument. Yet, one could also argue that the over-all gain in world output would be larger still if gains from mass production were added to gains from initially correct specialization and trade, rather than used to make up for and surpass losses from initially incorrect specialization and trade. Presumably, had the United States correctly specialized in steel and Japan in rice originally, the U.S. steel industry and

Japanese rice farming could also have enjoyed the gains from mass production. All these gains would then have been a net gain, instead of partly making up for the ill effects of specialization according to comparative disadvantage.

We might point out, however, that many scholars believe that the gains from comparative advantage that can be had under present circumstances are extremely small. They consider gains from mass production of much greater quantitative importance. The gains through comparative advantage achieved by the Common Market countries have, for example, been consistently estimated as low as .05 to 1 percent of GNP.[1]

Noneconomic Benefits

Other arguments for free trade are made on frankly noneconomic grounds. They are not concerned with higher or lower output. If world output should fall owing to free trade, they would still be in favor of it. Lower output, should it occur, is a price they gladly pay for achieving other goals. One such goal is peace and stability in the world.

Suppose we encourage free trade between East and West. This would strengthen, argue some people, the Communist countries' commitment to a peaceful status quo. Cooperation in practical matters of trade would help to erode the ideological passions that divide us. The more we see of each other, the more we work together, the less are we likely to fall victim to the propaganda machine that pictures us as man-eating monsters. Some people point to the Antarctic Treaty as an example. It has made the Russians America's cooperative associates in keeping the Cold War from the cold continent. Thus, it has helped to reduce tensions and to improve the general atmosphere in which we live together. Cooperation, like conflict, tends to feed on itself. Initial cooperation in trade can lead to broader cooperation in other areas. The Russians, like everyone else, value acceptance. If we discriminate against them in trade, we inflict a psychological scar that is all out of proportion to the economic wounds inflicted, if any. Freer trade, concludes the argument, leads to more freedom in the political arena, too. These political and psychological benefits far outweigh economic considerations.

In short, as in the case of labor unions discussed in the previous chapter, governmental policies concerning trade barriers have a variety of effects. The economic effect is in any case uncertain. Noneconomic ones are possibly of greater concern.

SUMMARY

1   This chapter focuses on the international movements of resources and goods with a view to their implications for economic efficiency.

[1] See T. Scitovsky, *Economic Theory and Western European Integration* (London: Allen and Unwin, 1958); Harry G. Johnson, "The Gains from Freer Trade: An Estimate," *Manchester School,* March 1958; or W. Welmesfelder, "The Short-Run Effects of the Lowering of Import Duties in Germany," *Economic Journal,* March 1960.

2 In recent decades, U.S. administrations have pursued policies tending to liberalize international trade. A large step in that direction was taken in 1967 at the end of the *Kennedy round* of trade negotiations in Geneva.

3 The U.S. Congress, however, has a long heritage of protectionism. In 1821, only 5 percent of imports could enter the United States free. The remainder was charged with a 45 percent tariff, on the average. By 1932, little had changed. After passage of the Smoot-Hawley Act, the average U.S. tariff rate was even 59 percent.

4 Trade liberalization began with the 1934 (Cordell Hull) *Reciprocal Trade Agreements Act*. It authorized the President to swap tariff cuts with individual countries in bilateral negotiations. The postwar *General Agreement on Tariffs and Trade* led to multilateral discussions on the same issue. By 1961, the average U.S. tariff had been reduced to 12 percent of dutiable imports. Yet, only 40 percent of imports came in free.

5 In the meantime, giant steps were taken elsewhere in the world to liberalize trade. These included the establishment of the *European Economic Community* and the *European Free Trade Association*. Their growth led to enactment of the (Kennedy) *U.S. Trade Expansion Act* of 1962. It led, in turn, to a reduction by 1966 of the average U.S. tariff rate to 6 percent and the 1967 Geneva accord to cut tariffs by another 35 percent.

6 Many arguments commonly used for imposing trade barriers are nonsensical. These include those wanting to keep money in the country, hoping to raise revenues and employment, or trying to protect high wage levels. Other arguments make a certain amount of sense. But the goals they support can be achieved in other and better ways besides restricting trade. Such arguments include those concerned about infant industries, young economies, and national defense.

7 There are powerful arguments in favor of a free international movement of resources or goods. The movement of resources to countries where they are more productive would increase world output. If that is impossible, world output can be increased by letting countries specialize and freely trade in goods they can produce with *relatively* fewer resources than other countries. Even if one country should have an absolute advantage in the production of all goods, it would be worthwhile for it to specialize and trade in those goods it can produce with comparative advantage, that is, where its absolute advantage is greatest. By letting other countries also specialize and trade in goods they can produce with comparative advantage, that is, where their absolute disadvantage is smallest, world output can again be raised.

8 The above arguments, however, are too general. Would free trade *assure* such benign forms of specialization and trade? It can be shown that this would happen in a world of perfect competition where prices reflect marginal costs. In the real world of imperfect competition, the result is uncertain. People buy goods where they are cheapest, and prices may not accurately reflect marginal costs. Hence, free trade in the real world may or may not bring about specialization according to comparative advantage. Correspondingly, tariffs and similar barriers may or may not be desirable instruments for raising world output.

9 One may, nevertheless, support free trade in the real world for other reasons. Two reasons mentioned are economies of scale achieved through large markets and noneconomic considerations of peace and stability.

TERMS[2]

absolute advantage	infant industry
commercial policy	mercantilism
Common Market	nontariff barriers
comparative advantage	peril point
economies of scale	scientific tariff
escape clause	tariff (customs duty)
import quota	young economy

SYMBOLS

EEC
EFTA
GATT

QUESTIONS FOR REVIEW AND DISCUSSION

1   "If I buy a foreign good, I have the good and the foreigner the money. If I buy the same good at home, I have the good and my country has the money. Therefore, we are better off." Evaluate this argument for tariff protection.

2   "A newly developing country may find that its young industries cannot compete against established foreign competitors. A tariff should protect these infant industries while they grow up. Once they are large enough and able to produce as cheaply as foreigners, they can stand on their own feet without tariff protection." Evaluate.

3   "The argument cited in question 2 is nonsense. What industry ever admits to growing up? They all cling to tariff protection long after they have ceased being infants." Evaluate.

4   Show why a tariff "to protect our high wages" may well *reduce* our real wages.

5   Can you think of any producer in the United States that should be protected by tariffs? Justify your position.

6   "Tariffs cannot be cut without hurting somebody, but it is worthwhile paying that price." Comment. When tariffs are reduced, should those who are injured by this be compensated?

7   "Lower tariffs mean higher unemployment." Discuss.

8   "The imposition of import quotas is inflationary." Comment.

[2] Terms and symbols are defined in the Glossary at the end of the book.

9 "As long as we pursue agricultural price support and crop restriction policies, we must set agricultural import quotas. Failure to do so would mean that we have to support the prices of all the world's farmers." Evaluate.

10 The U.S. Constitution forbids states of the union to impose tariffs on imports or exports. Evaluate the significance of this clause for the American economy.

11 Suppose all foreign trade came to an end for the United States. What would be the effects? (Hint: Consider the types of goods traded and their relative importance in the U.S. economy. Consider imports and exports.)

12 "The good thing about freer trade is not that we can export more, but that we can import more, thereby getting goods at a lesser sacrifice of something else than would otherwise have been possible." Evaluate.

13 "Free international trade brings about the most efficient use of resources. Any interference with free trade reduces efficiency." Evaluate. Could it be true? Could it be wrong?

14 "Free trade may raise output through specialization. Yet, it also makes a country more vulnerable to interruption in trade. Therefore, self-sufficiency is the better policy." Evaluate.

15 "The underdeveloped countries need growing markets in the industrialized western countries. They cannot get them through bargaining down tariff walls." Evaluate the statement. Suggest an answer to it.

16 Why, do you think, is it so important for members of a common market to "harmonize," that is, attune to one another, their national economic policies?

17 Take the following data on marginal costs per unit of product:
England: cloth 10 pounds sterling; wine 20 pounds sterling
Portugal: cloth 5 escudos, wine 5 escudos
a. Who has a comparative advantage in what?
b. Show how proper specialization could raise world output.
c. Show how both countries could gain through trade.
d. If exchange rates are flexible, between what limits would the pound-escudo rate find equilibrium?

18 The text describes the mechanism bringing about specialization and trade under perfect competition. It assumes exchange rates are flexible. What would have happened, if the rate had been *fixed*, at, say 1 yen per dollar or 50 yen per dollar?

19 The text showed how both countries could gain from specialization and trade. What assures that both *will* gain? Can't one country take all the gain or even more, leaving the other with no more or even fewer goods than before?

20 Consider the Communist countries in Eastern Europe, outside the Soviet Union. Can you show how free trade with them could greatly benefit them as well as the United States for *noneconomic* reasons?

1968 Joint Economic Report

The Joint Economic Committee, over the two decades since the passage of the Employment Act of 1946, has stressed the great importance of our competitive free enterprise system in achieving our broad policy goals. Effective monetary and fiscal policy alone cannot carry the enormous burdens of our society, without the aid of a well-functioning market system. In short, we rely upon the market system as the primary means of achieving our goals. The market system, in turn, history has demonstrated, has not performed satisfactorily without a vigorous antitrust program.

Extensive problems are developing at the present time and demand attention. The merger movement apparently has reached an alltime high. According to the Federal Trade Commission, preliminary data indicate that larger mergers, involving the acquisition of manufacturing and mining firms with $10 million or more of assets, rose approximately 50 percent in 1967 in terms of the number of firms acquired and over 100 percent in terms of the aggregate assets acquired. This suggests that fundamental changes are taking place in our economy which should be studied critically . . .

We also believe that the Council of Economic Advisers should explore the implications of the changing structure of the economy on its own program for achieving broad economic goals. The Council's strange silence on these serious problems in its report—in the face of the greatest merger movement in history—suggests that the Council should reassess its program. In the long run, the success of the wage-price guideposts depends for proper maintenance on a vigorous antitrust program.

1968 Joint Economic Report

22

efficiency in the united states economy: a summary appraisal

IN CHAPTER 2, we discussed the nature of the market economy. We admired the ease with which it allocates resources among the producers of hundreds of thousands of goods and does so without any central human direction at all. In the preceding chapters, we have learned something else, only hinted at in Chapter 2. The market economy, if perfectly competitive, assures more than a smooth allocation of resources according to consumer preferences. It also assures use of these resources in an economically efficient manner such that output and welfare could not possibly be raised by their reallocation. The actual U.S. economy, in contrast, is not *perfectly* competitive and, therefore, probably less economically efficient than it might be. In this chapter, we summarize this discussion.

THE ECONOMIC EFFICIENCY OF PERFECT COMPETITION

Perfect competition, as we have noted, is a market form that meets a number of important requirements. No individual buyer or seller is a big enough part of the market to have a personal influence on price. Traded goods and resources are standardized. That is, in the eyes of buyers, any one unit is as good as any other. People are well informed about the market. That is, everyone is aware of all available opportunities, of prices, qualities, and so on. People are free to enter and leave the market at will, to become or cease to be a buyer or seller in it at any time.

In this situation, market supply of and market demand for a good will establish its equilibrium price (compare Figure 2.5 DEMAND AND SUPPLY CURVES SUPERIMPOSED). That price will become a constant to the individual buyer or seller around which he can plan his own activities in the market (compare again Figure 18.1 THE PERFECTLY COMPETITIVE OUTPUT MARKET).

Similarly, market supply of and market demand for a resource will establish its equilibrium price (compare Figure 3.4 THE MARKET FOR HIGH SCHOOL SOCIAL SCIENCE TEACHERS). That price, too, will be regarded as a constant by the individual buyer or seller. On this price he will base his own decisions in the market (compare again Figure 20.1 THE PERFECTLY COMPETITIVE LABOR MARKET).

Households and firms in perfect competition are *pricetakers* and *quantity adjusters*. They must take the price as it comes. They can decide what quantity they want to buy or sell, and in so doing they have no reason to worry about the effects of their actions on price. Economic power is so diffused that anyone, acting alone, can be sure that he can sell or buy more or less at the *same* prevailing market price if he wishes.

In the Goods Market

Now consider a firm trying to decide on its volume of output so as to maximize profit. Any firm will do so, as we saw, only if its marginal cost equals its marginal revenue. If the change in total cost (marginal cost) when changing output and sales by a unit exceeds the accompanying change in total revenue (marginal revenue), the firm gains profit by producing less. If marginal cost falls short of marginal revenue, the firm gains by producing more.

Price is a constant to the firm. Price is unaffected by the firm's actions, although price could vary if *aggregate* demand or *aggregate* supply changed in the market for this good. Hence, the change in total revenue (marginal revenue) when changing output and sales by a unit equals the market price of the good. Hence, profits are maximized when marginal cost equals price (compare Figure 18.2 PERFECT COMPETITION: BEST PROFIT OUTPUT). If all firms follow their self-interest, they will all change their output volumes until marginal cost equals the price set by the market. Because all are looking at the same price, they will all, unknowingly, equate one another's marginal costs of producing any given good. Therefore, it will be impossible to get more output by shifting resources among firms. What is good for the firm (maximum profit) is good for the country (maximum output). "Private vice is public virtue."

If shoes are priced at $8 a pair, every shoe producer's marginal cost will tend to be $8. (If it is not, he will quickly change output until it is.) Ask one producer to produce a pair less, and he will release resources worth $8. Ask any other to take these resources to make shoes, and he will produce exactly one more pair. Resources are used in an economically efficient way. Reallocation does not yield higher output.

In the Resource Market

Consider a firm likewise trying to decide on its volume of resources used so as to maximize profit. It will do so, as we saw, only if its marginal outlay equals its marginal revenue product. If the change in total outlay when changing resource purchase and use by a unit exceeds the accompanying change in total revenue from selling the product so made, the firm gains profit by hiring less of the resource. Put more simply, if marginal outlay exceeds marginal revenue product, it pays to hire less of the resource. If marginal outlay falls short of marginal revenue product, the firm gains by hiring more.

Price is a constant to the firm. It is unaffected by the firm's actions, although it could vary if aggregate demand or aggregate supply changed in the market for this resource. Hence, the change in total outlay (marginal outlay) when changing resource purchase and use by a unit equals the market price of the resource, such as the wage of a unit of labor or the rent for a unit of land. Hence, profits are maximized when resource market price equals marginal revenue product (compare Figure 20.2 PERFECT COMPETITION: BEST PROFIT INPUT). If all firms follow their self-interest, they will all change their resource volumes in use until marginal revenue product equals the resource price set by the market. Because all are looking at the same price, they will all, unknowingly, equate one another's marginal revenue products of using any given resource in the production of any given good. But marginal revenue product is just the revenue derived from selling the marginal physical product of a unit of labor, land, or capital. It is the change in physical output owing to a unit change in resource use (marginal physical product) multiplied by the output price. Because the output price, as the resource price, is also the same for all firms, equal marginal revenue products imply equal marginal physical products. Therefore, it will be impossible to get more output by shifting resources among firms. What is good for the firm (maximum profit) is good for the country (maximum output). Again, private vice becomes public virtue.

If labor is priced at $16 per day, every shoe producer's marginal revenue product will tend to be $16. (If it is not, the quantity of the resource used will be changed until it is.) If shoes cost $8 a pair, this implies that every shoe producer employs labor with a marginal physical product of two pairs a day. Ask one producer to release a man for a day, and he will lose output worth $16 (two pairs of shoes). Ask any other to hire that man, and he will gain output of exactly $16 (two pairs of shoes). Resources are used in an economically efficient way. Their reallocation does not yield higher output.

A Sad Fact of Life

As we have seen in the previous chapters, and as we had hinted at in Chapter 2, ours is not a perfectly competitive economy in which no participant can determine the terms at which others must trade goods or resources. This by itself would not really matter. What matters is this: our economy does not meet, except by accident, the standard of economic efficiency toward which perfect competition would tend. The world of perfect and impersonal competition is not a portrait of the real mixed economy of the United States. It is an imaginary world that can be used as a sort of standard against which we can compare the performance of actual economies. Only if they meet that standard can we trust that social interest and self-interest are one and the same. The real world being removed from this standard, we cannot be sure of its economic efficiency. In fact, we can be almost certain that there are many instances where a shift of resources could increase output more in one place than reduce it elsewhere. Or that it could bring about production elsewhere that is wanted more than the output lost. It is time now to take a closer and more systematic look at the structure of the U.S. economy. (See also Chapter 5.)

THE STRUCTURE OF THE U.S. ECONOMY

In the real world, many buyers and sellers of goods or resources, even when acting alone, can and do influence the market price. Far from being pricetakers, they are pricemakers. They take or offer significant percentages of the total traded. If someone buys or sells 50 percent of the total, it is unrealistic to expect that he could double his quantity or reduce it to zero, while leaving the price unaffected. In such cases, the actions of *individual* buyers or sellers will be as powerful an influence on price as those of large *groups* of buyers or sellers in perfect competition.

Second, it is certainly *not* true that all units of a good or resource are homogeneous in the eyes of buyers. Many goods and resources are highly differentiated from one seller to the next. Even if they were physically identical, much advertising effort in the real world, appealing to emotion rather than logic, is directed toward making buyers believe that they are different. In fact, a great deal of effort is being spent to deliberately *misinform* and confuse the parties involved on such matters! For this reason alone, market participants in the real world are not so well informed as we assume them to be in perfect competition about opportunities in the market, about prices and characteristics of traded goods and resources.

Finally, entry into markets is in many ways restricted. Government may determine what farmers can grow. Labor unions or professional groups may refuse to admit people to membership, thus blocking their chance to engage in some occupations. Entrenched positions of existing firms, supported by massive advertising, massive capital requirements, and trade secrets, may keep new firms out of an industry.

As a result, there is little left in reality of our earlier conclusion with regard to a uniform price for any good or resource throughout the market. Nor are prices freely flexible over time. Because of different degrees of market power possessed by different groups in the market, actual or imagined differentiation of goods and resources traded, and imperfect knowledge and barriers to entry, prices even of identical goods or resources may differ among sellers. More than that, they may differ for a given seller depending on the buyer (as in the case of electricity used for lighting, cooking, heating, or manufacturing, to name just one instance). And prices are frequently less flexible than under perfect competition when market demand or supply changes.

Now let us turn to a more detailed study of the real world by considering various types of market power and how they differ from perfect competition.

Monopoly

The most extreme change we can envision is to think of a *monopoly*, a firm that is the *only seller of a good for which no close substitutes exist*. Other producers are somehow prevented from producing the good, so firm and industry are identical in this case. Those who want the good in question must buy from this one producer or go without. They cannot even find any similar goods. Such monopolies having complete market control are rare in reality.

regulated monopolies   There are two basic types of monopoly firms. *Regulated* monopolies (as public utilities) are deliberately created by government charter and supervised by government. They are found in areas where competition, although possible, is deemed undesirable for technical reasons or reasons of public safety. Thus, the government (unless it provides these goods itself) may allow only one private company to provide electric power or water or gas for a particular area. The duplication of power lines and water and gas pipes, if several companies could compete, would clearly represent a great *public nuisance*. It would also represent *technical inefficiency*, because most of the equipment of most of the competitors would not be used most of the time, and output could not be produced in the technically best way. To give just one example, many electric power producers can obtain lower average costs the larger the scale of operation up to enormous capacities. In the 1960's, these technically most efficient plant sizes were in excess of 300,000 kilowatts for conventional steam plants (generating about four-fifths of electric power in the United States).

Atomic power plants now being built promise further cost savings of 30 percent per kilowatt hour with 1 million kilowatt plants. Some of the hydroelectric stations have optimum plant sizes of millions of kilowatts. Because 1 million kilowatts is enough to meet the total power needs of many a large American city, it is clear that perfect competition among power producers without technical inefficiency is out of the question.

For similar reasons, governments franchise at times only one producer in such fields as transportation (railroads, buses, taxis, airlines) and communications (telephone companies, television, and radio stations). Yet, all these are not necessarily monopoly firms in the strict sense. Airline travel certainly is a substitute for railway travel. Telegrams and letters compete with the telephone, and although there may not be any good substitute for electric light, there are many substitutes for electric heat.

free monopolies

Besides regulated monopolies, there are *free* monopolies—free, that is, from government regulation. They often come into existence with government help, however, such as the granting of a license to the local barber or mortician or of a patent for the exclusive production of a unique product.

Patent laws, by assuring monopoly for a limited period (presumably to encourage innovation), usually have the effect of giving a firm an impregnable market position by the time the patent expires. A classic example is the United Shoe Machinery Corporation, the only producer in the United States of a full line of machines for making leather shoes. It gained and long maintained its dominant position through patents. Being the only supplier of certain vital machines, it eliminated rivals by forcing customers to buy all types of machines from it or go without the important ones. After a 20-year antitrust suit, United Shoe was forced in 1969 to set up two rival companies.

Until 1940, another example of a patent-created monopoly in the United States was Alcoa, then the only producer of aluminum. Although one may think that aluminum, being just one metal among many, should have a great number of close substitutes, it really does not. There is nothing to match the fact that it is lightweight, nontoxic, nonmagnetic, nonsparking, and at the same time is an excellent conductor of heat and electricity. Beyond that, it can be alloyed (giving it great tensile strength and resistance to corrosion) and processed by a variety of means (casting, rolling, drawing, and so on). Alcoa gained its monopoly through strategic patents covering the process by which alumina (aluminum oxide) is turned into aluminum ingots. By 1903, it was the only American producer of ingot, setting its price and determining its output volume.

In this case, as in others, monopoly was further strengthened by the *control of strategic inputs or markets*. Alcoa, for instance, controlled at least half of domestic bauxite deposits (bauxite is any ore containing at least 32 percent of alumina). It also became the only producer of alumina destined for aluminum production, and it controlled many strategic water power sites capable of generating the massive electric power needed for aluminum ingot production. It strengthened its position by also gaining dominance in the fabrication of other products from ingots. In 1940, it produced 100 percent of aluminum cable and aluminum pistons, 75 percent of cooking utensils. Another example of a monopoly created by possession of strategic inputs is American Metal Climax, which controls more than 90 percent of molybdenum in the world (all of it in one Colorado mountain).

These factors and a general *lack of knowledge* (outside the monopoly firm) about the techniques of working with the product, the unavailability (outside the monopoly firm) of trained personnel, and the absence of any published financial data often keep other competitors from entering the market. This was clearly the case with Alcoa. Thus, there was a complete lack of knowledge of the incredible profitability of Alcoa's operations: From 1909 to 1917, *annual* earnings as a percent of investment never were below 14 percent; they went as high as 31 percent. Throughout the 1920's, net profits were about 10 percent of invested capital.

Even if this knowledge had been available, however, potential competition would have found it very difficult to enter the market, because the *latest technology required a production volume that was large relative to the market.* Nothing less than an *initial* investment of hundreds of millions of dollars was needed. Thus, it is by no means true that a monopoly firm must keep competitors out of the market through price wars or campaigns of personal vilification among the rival's customers, suppliers, or bankers. There are many other "cleaner" methods that provide effective barriers to the entry of competitors into the market. The same factors limit the number of firms in other markets, even if there is more than one producer.

Oligopoly

Although pure monopoly may be rare, the existence in a market of just a few firms is quite common. Entry of additional firms may be blocked for the same reasons given above when discussing monopoly firms. Such a situation, in which *very few sellers exist,* is termed *oligopoly.* All units of the product sold in this market may be homogenous (for example, cement or steel of a certain grade or railroad transportation). Or they may be differentiated (for example, cars, heavy machinery, electrical appliances, soap, cigarettes, or aspirin tablets).

Unlike in the case of monopoly, where no rivals exist at all, or in the case of perfect competition, where no firm had to worry about rivals because all were equally insignificant, firms in an oligopoly situation are intensely aware of one another's existence. They know that the actions of one will appreciably affect the others of whom there are so few. Given any aggregate demand for the product in general, each producer knows that he cannot regard all of it as demand for *his* product, because somebody is bound to buy from his competitors. Hence, *the demand facing him is uncertain.* The perfectly competitive firm knew it could sell all it cared to at the market price (compare Figure 18.1(b) THE PERFECTLY COMPETITIVE OUTPUT MARKET). The monopoly firm knew it could sell more only at a lower price, yet whatever demand was, it was all "its own" and allowed the calculation of its marginal revenue (compare page 413 above). The oligopoly firm is in a bind.

nonprice competition and price wars   It must *guess* how much of market demand at each potential price would be directed toward its product. Suppose it guesses that it could capture half of market demand at each potential price and makes output and price decisions on that basis. More likely than not, competitors may have guessed that they could capture two thirds of the market at each potential price (which is inconsistent with our firm's guess). Or rivals may operate under different cost conditions. As a result, let us suppose, they offer the identical product (say, cement) at a lower price. The same could hold, of course, for a differentiated, but close substitute product (as when our firm sells Ramblers, and its competitor, Fords). Immediately, our firm will find sales less than expected, because customers go over to the competitors. Our firm could, of course, quietly acquiesce and adjust it own output volume and price to lower levels where its profits are maximized, assuming no reactions from its rivals. Or it may initiate a big advertising campaign, trying to convince buyers that it is worthwhile to buy from it, even at a higher price. (We'd rather fight than switch!) As a result, we find competitive advertising rampant in oligopolistic markets, but not in perfect competition, nor in monopoly. The perfect competitor, as we know, can sell all he wants at the market price. So it makes no sense for farmer Brown to advertise "Eat more of *farmer Brown's* potatoes!" The monopoly firm sets the price such as to sell what it wants. It might, nevertheless, engage in public-relations-type advertising to keep the firm's name before the public eye: "We are nice fellows, we don't exploit our workers or customers, we are owned by poor widows, we do a lot of important research, we are the backbone of the American economy," etc.

Instead of advertising, our oligopolistic firm may try to achieve the same end by offering better quality or better conditions of sale (such as different credit terms, prompter delivery, more "green stamps"). It may offer more reliable service, or try to fool people by distinct product designs and packaging suggesting on the surface basic differences that do not exist. Clearly, there is no telling where this will end. If our firm is successful, its competitors are bound to react. Then we may witness the beginning of a long price and advertising war in which firms forget all about profit in the short run in order to conquer their "rightful" share in the market. By slashing prices, possibly below the profit-maximizing level, and by raising costs sky high through exorbitant advertising campaigns each firm hopes to drive the others out of business.

Such price cutting happened, for instance, 100 years ago among railroads hauling freight between New York and Chicago; in the 1880's among oil companies; in the 1930's among cigarette producers; and in the 1950's, as we noted in Chapter 18, in the electrical equipment field. In 1968, there was a price war among steel companies. Extreme chaos results and, as in all wars, all participants lose. For a time, of course, consumers gain, getting a larger quantity for a lower price.

collusion and price leadership   Yet businessmen are not stupid. Just as everyone loses when everyone looks only after himself, everyone could gain if everyone got together. This, too, we saw in Chapter 18. Much of the uncertainty about one's demand can be eliminated through *collusion* among the oligopoly firms! If five out of five firms get together and in some way agree to share the market (for example, on a geographic or a percentage basis), the reactions of one's rivals are then known. Each firm can happily maximize its profits forever after. This collusion, furthermore, can in principle take many forms: the signing of a document (a *cartel agreement*), a handshake over lunch (a *gentlemen's agreement*), or an unspoken but deliberate parallelism of action derived by trial and error as when firm *A always* changes it price and output the same way and at the same time as *B*, the industry's *price leader*. Open collusion, as we saw, is outlawed by our antitrust laws. Tacit collusion, however, can be observed in the United States among firms in many industries. Take steel and cigarette producers, for instance. Steel prices have for many years been set by U.S. Steel and quickly copied by other steel producers. Since 1958, other steel companies have often "led the way." Reynolds (producer of Camels, Salems, and Winstons) used to initiate price changes in cigarettes. Or take an actual example from the aluminum industry. Alcoa announced in 1964 an increase in the price of aluminum ingot. On the same day it was followed by Reynolds (no relation to the cigarette producer) and Kaiser. Others followed the next day. By acting in this way, the oligopoly firms are in fact maximizing their *combined* profits (acting as if they were one monopoly firm) and then sharing them.

Things don't always work out smoothly, however. In 1953, Socony increased the price of gasoline in New York and New England. Others, such as Atlantic and Gulf followed, but Esso refused. A few days later, the price increases were rescinded. A more dramatic example happened in 1962. Several steel companies refused to follow U.S. Steel's 3.5 percent price hike, and U.S. Steel had to back down. This followed President Kennedy's intervention in steel labor negotiations in which the union settled without a wage increase for the first time in 13 years. The President thought he had a moral commitment from the steel producers to hold their prices constant in the face of a moderate settlement accepted by the unions. He successfully exerted tremendous pressure on Inland and Kaiser Steel not to "follow the leader." (See also pages 317–319 above.)

Monopolistic Competition

There are also markets combining some of the features of perfect competition and some of monopoly. A situation in which *many sellers sell differentiated products that are close substitutes* is termed *monopolistic competition.* Unlike in oligopoly, rivals are numerous. Entry into the market is typically easy, and no one worries about the reactions of others to his own actions. Unlike in perfect competition, the product is differentiated (in the eyes of the buyers) from one seller to the next (as in retail trade, clothing and shoe manufacturing, and such services as provided by doctors, barbers, or apartment rental).

Thus, one can find both price and nonprice competition. The monopolistic seller has a very mild sort of monopoly, for there are many substitutes for his product. By charging a price very much lower than that charged by others for similar products, an individual firm may attract a lot of business, possibly more than it can handle. So its willingness to lower price may be quite limited for this reason, even though it has no fear of retaliation as the adverse effect on others is spread thinly over so many. On the other hand, by charging a price very much higher than that charged by others for similar products, an individual firm may not lose all customers (as it would in perfect competition), but it may lose a sub-

stantial number of them. This may be even more true today than in the past. Think of re-
tailing, for instance. Consumer loyalties to a particular seller may be a lot weaker today
than at the turn of the century when the typical family did not have its own means of transportation nor any basis for judging manufacturers. So people relied on *reputable* merchants
nearby. In the meantime, people have acquired cars—and a lot more knowledge. Consider
Consumer's Union, an organization that engages in independent expert testing of products
and distributes its monthly *Consumer Reports* to about 1 million subscribers. People's
loyalty may be placed with the product of a national manufacturer rather than a particular
merchant. Thus, retailers are much closer to being perfect competitors than they used to be.

They are trying, of course, desperately, to make even an identical product sold in all
other stores seem different. There may be a new store closer to your home, more and friend-
lier clerks (you do not have to wait so long), music while you shop, carpeted floors, more
trading stamps, more advertising, charge accounts, faster repair and maintenance, and free
convenient parking, just to name a few examples.

An Overview

What is the relative importance of these various types of market structures in the U.S.
economy? One possible approach is to find out how many firms there are in the various markets of the U.S. economy and what their contribution to output is.

manufacturing   A study made by the U.S. Bureau of the Census revealed the data
of Table 22.1 CONCENTRATION IN U.S. MANUFACTURING. Although the data given here are
selective, they are typical of what the study revealed also for other industries. Regardless of
the number of firms in existence, an industry-by-industry comparison shows how significant
percentages of total industry shipments originate in a few large firms. In short, oligopolistic
or monopolistic competition seems to be typical, at least for much of U.S. *manufacturing*.
In fact, only in 90 among 417 industries studied did the 4 largest companies account for less
than 20 percent of the industry's shipments. Twenty-two of these were apparel industries.
But, of course, even if it takes twenty companies out of hundreds or thousands to supply 20
percent of shipments, we are a far way removed from perfect competition. Nothing can
better impress this fact than the knowledge that, in 1963, the 200 largest manufacturing
firms in the United States originated 41 percent of the $192 billion *value added* by all the
hundreds of thousands of manufacturing companies. The largest 100 firms alone originated
33 percent! In 1967, the five largest American corporations (General Motors, Standard Oil
of New Jersey, Ford, General Electric, and Chrysler) accounted for 11 percent of total manufacturing sales, net income, and employment.

Some words of caution.   Yet the kind of data contained in Table 22.1, as all data, should be
interpreted with care. To some extent these data may even *understate* the market power
of firms, for they refer to the nation as a whole. Many markets, however, are effectively
limited to a much smaller area because of such factors as prohibitive transportation costs,
perishable products, and so on. Suppose there are in a hypothetical industry 1,000 pro-

ducers, all of equal size. Then the four "largest" companies would ship 4/1,000 of output, or 0.4 percent. If producers compete on a national scale, buyers everywhere have 1,000 sellers to choose from, and we might approach closely, at least so far as *numbers* are concerned, what the low index of concentration seems to say, perfect competition. Yet, if each firm is the sole supplier in a three-county area and transportation beyond that area is impossible or difficult, each firm has something close to a monopoly. Yet, the index of concentration, calculated on a national basis, would be as low as before!

Table 22.1   CONCENTRATION IN U.S. MANUFACTURING (1963)

INDUSTRY	NUMBER OF FIRMS	INDEX OF CONCENTRATION = PERCENTAGE OF VALUE OF SHIPMENTS ACCOUNTED FOR BY LARGEST			
		4 FIRMS	8 FIRMS	20 FIRMS	50 FIRMS
Flat glass	11	94	99+	100	—
Steam engines	17	93	98	100	—
Telephone, telegraph apparatus	65	92	96	99	100
Cereal preparations	35	86	96	99+	100
Cigarettes	7	80	100	—	—
Motor vehicles and parts	1,655	79	83	90	94
Copper	13	78	98	100	—
Household laundry equipment	31	78	95	99+	100
Soap, detergents	641	72	80	88	93
Aluminum rolling, drawing	168	68	79	87	95
Cutlery	156	66	76	87	96
Photographic equipment	499	63	76	86	93
Aircraft	82	59	83	99	99+
Vitreous plumbing fixtures	34	57	78	98	100
Organic chemicals	343	51	63	79	93
Shipbuilding, repairing	305	48	63	81	92
Natural and process cheese	982	44	51	59	69
Farm machinery	1,481	43	55	67	77
Musical instruments	288	38	54	73	88
Sea food, canned and cured	345	38	51	66	80
Toilet preparations	673	38	52	75	90
Periodicals	2,562	28	42	59	73
Canned fruits and vegetables	1,135	24	34	50	66
Bread and related products	4,339	23	35	45	56
Meat processing	1,273	16	23	35	51
Men's suits and coats	1,031	14	23	38	56
Soft drinks	3,569	12	17	24	34
Dresses	4,577	6	9	14	23
Typesetting	1,271	6	10	18	30
Ready mixed concrete	3,999	4	7	13	22

Source: U.S. Senate, Subcommittee on Antitrust and Monopoly of the Committee on the Judiciary, Concentration Ratios in Manufacturing Industry 1963, *Part I (Washington, D.C., 1966).*

On the other hand, a high index of concentration does not necessarily denote imperfect competition. Imports from abroad may substantially alter the picture, especially for individual industries. Thus, the four largest firms may account for 100 percent of domestic shipments, yet they may only supply 1 percent of the total sold, if imports are of overwhelming importance. Thus, one may argue for a free trade policy as something like a substitute for effective antitrust action.

Finally, the meaning of the industry classification must be carefully assessed. "Organic chemicals," for instance, is a broad category. Although the four lagrest firms supply 51 percent of shipments, we might want to know what these shipments are. It may turn out that each of the four firms supplies 100 percent of *particular* organic chemicals, so the ratio understates what it is supposed to test. Vice versa, "canned fruits and vegetables" may be too narrow a category. Fresh fruits and vegetables are undoubtedly an excellent substitute. Even though four companies make 24 percent of shipments, their market power may be much less than this seems to indicate. You may try to find other instances of likely understating or overstating in Table 22.1.

Nevertheless, although Table 22.1 by itself does not prove it, imperfect competition *is* prevalent throughout American manufacturing. This should be clear from your personal observation also, especially if you remember that imperfect competition is defined by more than just the number of sellers in any market.

the rest of the economy   What about the rest of the U.S. economy? It is tempting to think of manufacturing as most important. It draws the greatest attention. After all, is not the United States the "mightiest industrial nation on earth"? Yet manufacturing accounts for less than 30 percent of GNP! Table 22.2 U.S. GNP AND NUMBER OF FIRMS BY SECTOR shows the origin of GNP by major sectors and the number of firms in each. The data refer to 1963, the same year for which the latest concentration ratios have been gathered. More recent data for 1968 show practically the same percentage breakdown.

We have already seen how public utilities, including much of transport and communications (just like government itself), by their very nature are localized monopolies. Because they are government regulated, however, they may or may not behave like free monopoly firms. Agriculture, trade, and services, each with millions of establishments, seem to be excellent candidates for perfect competition. If we restrict ourselves to numbers, this is true. It may even be true if we consider the other aspects of perfect competition. The categories given here, however, are much too broad to make such a judgment. We would have to look at particular groups of substitutable products, *within* agriculture, and so on. We would have to consider the effective market size served by firms producing them. We would find that even in these sectors a few large firms can and do have significant market power. To the extent that perfect competition tends to come about in agriculture, government intervention has destroyed it for about half of agricultural output.

With respect to trade and services, let us remember that local cleaners, beauty shops, retailers, or movie houses certainly do not compete with thousands of others, even if there are that many in the nation. If we consider, beyond numbers of firms, the existing differentia-

Table 22.2   U.S. GNP AND NUMBER OF FIRMS BY SECTOR (1963)

SECTOR	GNP BILLION DOLLARS	PERCENTAGE OF TOTAL	NUMBER OF FIRMS (1,000's)
Agriculture, forestry, fisheries	23.3	4.0	3,620
Mining	11.9	2.0	64
Construction	27.0	4.6	836
Manufacturing	160.4	27.5	407
Wholesale and retail trade	102.9	17.6	2,545
Finance, insurance, real estate	72.1	12.3	1,061
Transportation	24.5	4.2	⎫
Communications	12.3	2.1	⎬ 354
Public utilities	15.2	2.6	⎭
Services	66.0	11.3	2,450
Government	65.2	11.2	—
Other	3.2	0.5	—
	583.9	100	

Source: U.S. Department of Commerce.

tion of products, imperfections of knowledge, and barriers to entry, it is clear that here too, perfect competition does not exist. Monopolistic competition probably best describes the type of market found in trade and services. In mining, construction, and finance, we typically find a few dominant firms, in short, oligopoly, in any given market area.

Conclusion

Although one can find exceptions, imperfect competition prevails in most sectors of the American economy outside agriculture. Even in agriculture, the importance of big commercial farms is growing. Recall from Chapter 19 that less than 13 percent of farmers are producing over 60 percent of our agricultural output. Specifically we can conclude the following. In the goods markets, about one quarter of output derives from such imperfectly competitive producers as general government, government enterprises, or producers directly regulated by government. The latter include transportation and communications, public utilities, petroleum, and half of agriculture. Another quarter of output at the least derives from fields of few sellers, or what we have described as (unregulated) monopoly and oligopoly producers. This covers about half of manufacturing and mining and most of construction, banking, and insurance. This leaves at most half of goods output being traded in markets of many sellers (the rest of agriculture and manufacturing, and services, trade, and real estate), but many of these are also imperfectly competitive for reasons other than control over price.

In the resource market, a similar picture emerges. Looking at labor only, we found in Chapter 20 that a quarter of workers are union members, many of whom have considerable power over market price. The same goes for many employers who may be the only local purchasers of labor. The wages of another fifth of workers are directly regulated by government (if they are government employees) or indirectly so (if government restricts entry into the occupation by licensing). Thus, half of workers at most, including self-employed, can be regarded as selling their services in anything remotely resembling perfectly competitive markets.

CRITICISM OF THE U.S. ECONOMY

As the previous chapters have shown, there are serious consequences that flow from the imperfect competitiveness of the American economy. Unlike in perfect competition, where self-interest leads to socially desirable consequences, self-interest in the real world framework may not. What is good for the individual firm (maximum profit) may not be good for the country (may not bring maximum output). Marginal cost may diverge from price. Marginal outlay may diverge from marginal revenue product. As a result, except by sheer accident, the marginal costs of different producers making the same good may diverge. Any given resource may yield different marginal physical products in different places. Precious opportunities to raise output or to produce more urgently wanted goods by reallocating fully employed resources may be missed. In imperfect competition, the invisible hand that Adam Smith praised so well cannot work to perfection. We all are poorer for it. It is concern about this unnecessary degree of economic inefficiency that worries the Joint Economic Committee of Congress in its March 1968 statement opening this chapter. And remember one thing. Many people in the United States are apt to take it either as an insult or a joke when they are told that the American economy is inefficient. "What do you mean?" they will huff and puff. "Have you ever seen how miserably inefficient the Russians are in making cars? Have you ever seen how primitively rice is grown in Vietnam? Don't you realize that we are the richest nation on earth? Inefficient, don't make me laugh!" This reaction, although understandable, misses the whole point. Michigan's superiority in making cars and California's superiority in making rice is *technical*. Thus people confuse technical and economic efficiency. No one denies the great technical achievements of the United States. As was pointed out earlier, we may be producing a good in the best technical way known to mankind, yet we are inefficient economically if another good is demanded or if we produce too much of the good relative to other goods. It might even be true that we are the richest nation on earth. To say that we are economically inefficient is only to say that we could be richer still.

Other Wastes of Imperfect Competition

There are other criticisms people make of our mixed economy. They look beyond the subtle and unmeasurable waste of our resources in their inefficient allocation. They point to more obvious wastes.

advertising   As we noted above, there would be no advertising by individual firms in perfect competition. Therefore, people argue that we are wasting resources in advertising, when, as in 1967, we spend over $15 billion for that purpose in the United States. The resources used for that purpose could have better been used to make other goods, these people say. Instead of using up our forests to make billboards and paper, why not build houses for the poor? These critics point to the type of advertising occurring. Much of it, to be sure, is informative and, therefore, useful in spreading information needed for effective competition. Some of it, however, is meaningless, purely persuasive, and gives no hard information at all. It only serves to build prestige for the firm concerned by linking its product in people's minds with favorable circumstances.

"Blondes have more fun," we are told. "Ours is the most expensive perfume in the world." "This cigarette has the honest taste." Do these statements mean that the products, be they hair color, perfume, or cigarettes, are of higher quality than competing ones? Certainly, that is the impression the advertiser hopes to leave behind. But that is not what the advertisements are saying. (Read them again!)

In this way, every product produced by imperfect competitors is studied for all its selling points, however irrelevant they may be. From morning to night, we are informed by a million voices how the future of mankind depends on banishing dragons from our mouths, dripping faucets from our stomachs, and miniature sledgehammers from our heads. These voices are whispering at times, raucous and dissonant at other times. But they are always there. They promise everything from health to beauty, from calm nerves to popularity, from happy marriages to just sex. Minor and even imaginary qualities of a good are shown as conferring the greatest benefit and to be of the greatest importance. The whiteness that is "whiter than white" is deemed no less important than a special announcement by the President of the United States.

Having forsworn price competition, America's firms are pouring their aggressiveness into advertising, hoping to take customers away from one another. Is it all a waste? There are a few things we do get: some information on products, television shows, 10 cent newspapers. Many people think these gains small and that we might do better things with the resources used in advertising. They think that, as with national armament, much of advertising simply cancels that of the other fellow. And the resources would do better elsewhere. Others disagree. They believe that all advertisers gain because people spend less on goods produced by industries not engaged in advertising campaigns. They also believe that people save less and spend more in the aggregate owing to advertising. Thus, the advertisers are said not to take people away from one another. They are shown to all gain simultaneously by changing people's spending patterns among broad classes of goods and by changing their propensity to save. Is this desirable?

product differentiation   Advertising tries to build the image that "our product is different" (hence better). Imperfect competitors reinforce their words by action. They manipulate not just the consumer, but products, too. They remodel. They repackage. Occasionally, they even improve their product in the process. Many means of product differentiation, too, may waste resources. When blindfolded, coffee drinkers and smokers usually cannot tell the difference among various blends. There are probably better things we could do with our resources than spend billions of dollars annually on superficial changes. Take auto model changes. Each year, the product is changed just enough to make many households dissatisfied with last year's model. In the late 1950's, factory retooling, plus increased gas consumption owing to increased size and horsepower of cars, cost $5 billion a year. Critics call this "planned obsolescense." It has been estimated by critics of the auto industry that without this each of our cars would cost $700 less. Auto makers put the figure closer to $200.

On the other hand, our television pictures are clearer, our dishwashers more reliable, our clothes more varied, and our cars may be safer. So there are advantages also. Given their own peculiar needs and preferences, some buyers are served better with a great variety of choice provided by an imperfect market.

barriers to entry   Some barriers to entry in our economy are equally pernicious as resources wasted in useless advertising and imaginary product differentiation. Such barriers, too, can lead to less output than otherwise possible or to the production of one good where another is more urgently wanted. The American Medical Association, through its control over medical school accreditation, limits the number of medical students and doctors in the country. Many young people able and willing to become doctors are not allowed to do so. As a result, the incomes of those who do become doctors are very high, which is, of course, the purpose of this monopolistic practice. Another result is that the quantity of medical services available is lower than it otherwise could be. Infant mortality in the United States is a lot higher than elsewhere in the world where such artificial restrictions do not exist. By inducing some youngsters to become advertising managers rather than doctors, we are in effect trading cheaper television and more billboards and a lot of nonsense advertising for the lives of young children who might have been saved with more *and cheaper* medical care.

Or consider some of the craft unions. By charging high initiation fees and by other means, the carpenters or electricians may regulate the number of youngsters trained in their skill. They, too, have tried to keep the numbers down to assure themselves a greater income than might otherwise be available. In recent years, they have often been accused of racial discrimination, as they refused to admit blacks to their ranks. Frequently, this was only an indication of their determination not to admit anyone, be he white or black. Again, the consequences may be disturbing. The youngster refused a chance to be an electrician may end up selling brushes from house to house. Quite possibly, society would have preferred his services as an electrician had more of them been available at a lower price.

SOME COUNTERARGUMENTS

The section of the 1968 Joint Economic Report reproduced at the beginning of this chapter refers to the President's Council of Economic Advisers. It chides them for their "strange silence" on the serious implications of the imperfectly competitive structure of the American economy. Such silence is easily explained. Economists, although keenly aware of the subtle and obvious wastes of imperfect competition, do not always know what to do about them. In addition, there are some arguments against idealizing perfect competition.

Impracticability of Creating Perfect Competition

You cannot, for instance, use antitrust action against business and labor to forceably change the structure of the American economy toward a regime of perfect competition. You can try, take a step here and there, but you can never go all the way. That would involve measures intolerable from a political point of view. Most existing firms would have to be broken into fragments. None must remain large enough to control a significant percentage of the market. Brand names would have to be outlawed and give way to the faceless output of perfect competitors. Barriers to entry, such as patents and labor unions, would have to be eliminated completely. The same goes for all government interference with the price system. There could be no minimum wage, no agricultural price support, no tariff, quota, or subsidy in foreign trade.

Uncertainty about Benefits and Costs

We are not even certain whether the resultant increase in output or the resultant increase in welfare owing to a changed composition of output would be large or small. No one has measured all of it. In fact, no one can measure it with precision. One can hardly pursue such radical policies on the basis of the extreme degree of uncertainty regarding their desirability that is now prevailing. In addition, the institutions that may make for economic inefficiency are not all bad. As we noted, labor unions, for instance, serve important functions of a non-economic nature that we regard as valuable. Similarly, large firms may be important for technical reasons. Finally, even a regime of perfect competition would not be all perfect.

External Repercussions of Production and Consumption

Some people argue that we have wrongly elevated private output and consumption beyond all other goals. We have only eyes for new cars, new appliances, new detergents, new foods, new dentrifices, and new laxatives. We fail to see that society might and should achieve more than that. We are pround that ours is the highest GNP on earth. Seeing that we are productive, we conclude that we are good. That ours is a great society. That we would be greater by producing even more. But our quest for higher private output and higher private consumption has by-products that we ignore at our peril.

undesirable effects of production   Oftentimes private production involves costs to society at large for which the particular producer does not pay and of which he may not even be aware. Think of the tons of soot pumped into the air by the belching smokestacks of a steel plant. This will raise the cleaning bills and endanger the health of the neighborhood.

The noise and smells involved may play havoc with the nerves of workers and people living nearby (and raise their psychiatrist bills). The refuse dumped into the lake may decrease the catch (and thus raise the cost) of fish hundreds of miles away, and dozens of towns around the lake will be forced to build new treatment plants for drinking water. And we have not even mentioned how the steel plant itself, with blast furnaces and coal yards and a maze of railroad lines, with open pit mines, cranes and transmission wires, may spoil the beauty of the countryside for miles around and encourage, through the concentration of more and more people in the area, traffic congestion, the growth of city slums, and all types of social disorder. Furthermore, land erosion, the destruction of wildlife or the unnecessary destruction of other natural resources may constitute irreversible damage. In short, private costs of production may well understate the true costs to society, as the effects beyond the confines of the firm are neglected. (These matters are discussed at greater length in Chapter 28.)

There are *spill-over,* or *neighborhood,* effects. There are external repercussions of production. How does this affect efficiency?

Suppose the production of boats involves no external repercussion, but that of cars involves one of $1,000. This means that the production of one more car would, *in addition* to the producer's higher cost, involve costs *to others* of $1,000 more. We may call the producer's cost the marginal *private* cost of producing another car. We may call the resulting extra cost to others the marginal *external* cost. The two combined is then the marginal *social* cost. For example, as an automobile plant raises production of cars by one car per period, its total production costs rise by $2,000, by the marginal private cost. However, owing to the additional smoke, noise, refuse, and the like, cleaning and doctor bills of townspeople rise by $10 all together. Miles away, it now costs $30 more to get the same amount of fish as before (owing to the auto plant's pollution of a river). And cities in the neighborhood have increased expenditures of $960 in order to provide a growing population with drinking water, streets, parking space, traffic control, police protection, trash collection, and so on. We have a marginal external cost of $1,000. From society's point of view, an extra car costs $3,000 of resources, not $2,000 of them. Three thousand dollars is the marginal social cost involved here. Therefore, an economic system, such as perfect competition, that equated producers' marginal (private) cost with price would still be economically inefficient so long as there are external repercussions of production. Assume a boat, too, costs $2,000 and is priced at this marginal cost. Both prices being equal, people value a car and a boat equally. Yet, it is possible, by not producing a car, to free $3,000 of resources in the economy: $2,000 in the factory, $1,000 elsewhere. Because the extra cost of a boat is $2,000, output of boats can be raised by one and one-half units. Thus, consumers could be given one and one-half more boats for one less car. They would be better off, because they could get output worth $3,000 by sacrificing output worth $2,000.

Thus, it is argued, government must intervene to make relative prices truly reflect marginal *social* costs. Then consumers would buy any good in full awareness of what it *really* costs society at large and only to the extent that they felt gains in welfare justified such costs. In our case, government might force the producer of cars to pay for *all* the costs he inflicts on society. This can be done by taxing him (here $1,000 at the margin) and using the tax revenue to reimburse outsiders for the harm experienced through the production of cars. It can also be done by forcing the producer (by public health ordinances, zoning laws, conservation laws, and the like) not to harm others in the first place (making him spend whatever is necessary to avoid noise, pollution of air and water, land erosion, and so on). In either case, the external costs will become internal, for the producer to see.

desirable effects of production   Not all external repercussions must be undesirable. Some producers, while engaging in their private activities, are conferring *benefits* on others without being aware of it or without being able to collect a revenue for this. An agricultural enterprise that afforests a certain region may over the long run favorably affect the climate, thus raising the yield and lowering the costs of corn production nearby. Or imagine a pioneer firm coming into a backward region. By building roads, laying telephone lines, providing police protection, or training the local residents to work with complicated machinery, such a firm will make it considerably easier and cheaper for other firms to follow suit. Or think of a farmer who dams up a river (or a fisherman who builds a lighthouse). Not only he, but all his neighbors for hundreds of miles around, may gain from this. Or think of the favorable effects of private research throughout the world. It has greatly improved most of our lives.

It is not hard to guess that some of these activities, by the very fact that others gain as much or even more than the one who undertakes them, will not be undertaken at all or be undertaken in a limited fashion only. Everyone stands to gain by letting others do these things first, and, therefore, they do not get done! Government is again called on either to force people to buy such goods collectively (hence, the collective purchase of national defense, internal order, public education and research, roads, parks, flood control and lighthouses), or to reimburse private producers for the benefit conferred on others. As in this case private cost would be *above* social cost (if A spends $1,000 on a lighthouse privately, B half a mile down the coast can spend less on lighthouses and more on other goods, as A's lighthouse serves him as well), private producers (if they exist at all in this field) should be encouraged. This may be done, for example, through subsidies. This would induce greater production and consumption of such goods.

undesirable effects of consumption   External effects pervade the realm of consumption also. The generous use of alcohol or heroin by some forces others to pay for extra police protection, not to mention the misery suffered by the families of alcoholics or dope addicts. The widespread habit of smoking forces society to engage in extra medical research and the building and maintenance of hospitals. The enjoyment of television by the husband drives the wife to insanity. The car won in a contest by one family causes another to be consumed with envy. That new car on the road increases the inconvenience of everyone else, motorists, pedestrians, policemen, and town planners alike! Such inefficiency would exist in spite of perfect competition. By cutting consumption of those goods the use of which harms others, and substituting consumption of goods without such external effect, society's welfare could be increased.

Thus, it is argued once more that government should interfere to make relative prices truly reflect *social* preferences. Then goods would be consumed with full knowledge of the effect on everyone. In our case, government might force the buyer of alcohol to pay for *all* the costs involved in its consumption. This can be done by taxing his purchases and using the tax revenue to reimburse outsiders for the harm experienced through the consumption of it. Then we can assume the external net effect to be zero. It can also be done by forcing the consumer (by speed limits, ordinances forbidding the sale of alcoholic beverages to minors, prohibitions against noise in apartment houses, and the like) not to harm others in the first place. Then we would assume that the consumer incorporates the social viewpoint into himself. In either case, the external costs are brought to the attention of the consumer, hopefully making him consume more sparingly those goods with undesirable external repercussions.

desirable effects of consumption   External repercussions of consumption can also be beneficial. Consumption by one can confer benefits on bystanders. Neighbors enjoy beautiful gardens as well as does the gardener. The installation of a new telephone increases the satisfaction not only of the party concerned but also of others who can now call him. City dwellers who live in decent houses, who enjoy beautiful parks in the daytime and symphonies and drama at night, who have adequate medical care and good schools for their children, are less apt to riot than others for whom this is not the case. Their consumption benefits others as well. Hence, it may become desirable to encourage and expand the consumption of those goods with a social utility beyond the private one. Subsidies for medical care (polio shots, chest X rays), for education, the arts, housing and urban renewal are cases in point. (Again, see Chapter 28.)

In short, blind pursuit of the dream world of perfect competition may improve the quantity of output. It does not always improve automatically the quality of our lives also. To have the good life, we still would need government participation in the affairs of the economy. Such participation must discourage socially obnoxious activities, if people do not have the self-discipline to abstain from them. Government could do worse than encourage activities that have a favorable effect on the rest of society.

Economic Efficiency vs. Progress

We have seen how we cannot hope to achieve economic efficiency by creating a world of perfect competition. It would be utterly impracticable. Nor are we sure that the economic gains would be of sufficient magnitude to compensate for noneconomic losses.

We have also seen how even a perfectly competitive economy would have to face, as our economy must, the external effects of private production and consumption. There is nothing in the structure of a perfectly competitive economy to prevent certain undesirable effects from occurring. Nor would there be anything that would encourage activities with socially desirable side effects.

Thus, it is not surprising if economists show a "strange silence" on the issue of governmental policy designed to make the economy more competitive. In their hearts, they know that such policies (if carried to the necessary extreme) will never work. Nor are they sure that they really want them to work. The costs may be too high and the result not good enough. This feeling is considerably strengthened by another consideration.

Many people argue that we should forget about market structure, or the number and size of firms, the degree of product differentiation, and the ease of entry. We should forget about "static" efficiency, about getting the most output from *given* resources. We should instead concentrate on "dynamic" efficiency, on getting more output through growth of resources and above all through rapid technological change.

Their argument goes something like this: "Why burden ourselves with dismal thoughts about economic inefficiency, why worship at the throne of Perfect Competition which never was and never will be? Why not follow the example of many other advanced capitalist countries? Instead of forever crusading against trusts, they tolerate considerable restraints on competition not only in agriculture and in the labor market, but in all sectors of the economy. They even encourage business organizations, such as cartels, designed to foster monopoly. They have good reasons. It is true that at *any given time* economic inefficiency keeps us from overcoming scarcity to the extent that we might. But this is no tragedy, for it is the prerequisite for something much more important: technical change and rapid economic growth. Had we always had the many insignificant firms of perfect competition, none could have afforded the massive research and development carried on by our industrial giants. Which small-scale enterprise could support the types of laboratories run by DuPont, General Electric, General Motors, RCA, or the Bell System, employing thousands of scientists? None would have had the incentive, either. Any innovator would have been immediately copied by a swarm of imitators free to enter the market. He could never have recouped the massive outlays any significant technological breakthrough entails. *Economic inefficiency is the price of progress.*

"Oligopolistic firms are continually threatened by extinction through their powerful rivals. To keep from being supplanted, they are forever turning out improved and new products, developing new inputs, new markets, new types of production and organization. Even monopolies are continually threatened by the potential competition of new products. This is real and not just make-believe. Just watch how one new product after another comes along, attacking, upsetting and conquering long-held positions of seemingly impregnable monopoly (plastics vs. metals, television vs. movies, and so on).

"Imperfect competitors alone have the incentive and the means to finance such ventures. They can spread the costs over large output volumes and keep prices up until their outlay is recouped. The competition among the few and the large ones is a 'workable' competition. It 'works' because it is ultimately responsible for the enormous *growth* of U.S. per capita real income over the last century. To be sure, our economic system never does use its potentialities fully. Yet by so doing, it gives power to those who run the engine of progress. In the long run, under a regime of perfect competition, our output would never have become what it is. We would have been beautifully efficient and terribly backward and poor."

Shall we believe this argument? The evidence is mixed. We already noted in Chapter 18 how the actual size of plants and firms frequently exceeds the optimum required by modern technology. Thus, we may agree that modern technology requires large firms and imperfect competition without agreeing that all firms have to be as large as they in fact are. Corporate giantism is not the inevitable response to technological imperatives.

Nor is it clear that the large size of many existing firms is essential for rapid technological change and the rapid utilization of new techniques. For instance, the research and development expenditures per sales dollar are not any larger for our industrial giants than for their much smaller competitors. Nor are the former more productive of inventions than the latter. Nor are they faster in commercially introducing new developments. Often the contrary is the case. Big firms that do not fear competition can hold back introduction of the new.

True, some technological breakthroughs are the result of the efforts of large groups of scientists especially when expensive research instruments are involved (as in the case of missiles). Yet, many still come from individuals or very small groups. Cases in point are air conditioning, cellophane, the helicopter, insulin, the jet engine, the transistor, the laser, the Xerox machine. In fact, a study of the sixty most important inventions in recent years showed more than half made by independent inventors, less than half by corporate researchers.

Of thirteen major inventions introduced in the U.S. steel industry between 1940 and 1955, none was made by U.S. companies. Four were made by much smaller European companies, seven by independent inventors. The oxygen steel-making process, in particular, has been described as that industry's only major technological breakthrough since 1900. It was perfected by a tiny Austrian *firm*, less than one third the size of a single *plant* of U.S. Steel. Small American firms introduced it 4 years later. U.S. Steel and Bethlehem Steel lagged behind 14 years.

Similar stories can be told about other industries. The electric toaster was not introduced by giant General Electric. It was developed and marketed by a small firm (McGraw Co.). The same was true with electric ranges, deep freezers, refrigerators, clothes washers, dryers, dishwashers, vacuum cleaners, steam irons and shavers. Thus, imperfect competition may be the price of progress. Corporate giantism hardly is.

Conclusion

Government interference in the economy of the United States is not limited to the macro-economic attempts (which we discussed in Part 1) to maintain full employment of resources. The government is also concerned with matters of microeconomics, with the economically efficient use of resources once they have found employment. Yet as we go from one concern to the other, as we move from Part 1 to Part 2, it is as if we were passing from day if not into night, at least into fog. The theory of employment (Chapter 7) is well understood. So are the monetary and fiscal policy implications that follow from it (Chapters 10 and 12). These policies are *practical*; they *can* be carried out. Thus, we can have great hope that intelligent policy *will* be followed as needed to approximate full employment and thus reduce scarcity.

The importance of economic efficiency is also well understood (Chapters 18 to 21). Yet, its policy implications, the creation of a perfectly competitive economy, are *impractical*. We cannot even hope to carry them out. But this is no ground for despair. It only means that 100 percent economic efficiency is beyond our grasp. But remember this: what we have learned might be used to pinpoint the most serious deviations of our economy from the ideal. It might be used to take some action that may be better than none. Furthermore, although the evidence is by no means clear-cut, most economists would in any case argue that the sacrifice of some economic efficiency is the unavoidable price of having a progressive economy. Technical progress, after all, reduces scarcity, too. Finally as will be shown in Chapter 28, the very mode of thinking in terms of marginal costs and marginal benefits may be enormously useful for solving some of the most pressing problems of our time.

SUMMARY

1   Perfect competition by no means describes the heartland of the American economy. It is a market form in which no individual buyer or seller acting alone can influence price, traded goods or resources are considered to be homogeneous, people are well informed about the market and can enter or leave it at will.

2   Economists study perfect competition because of its amazing property. If all households and firms just follow their self-interest, the economy will tend toward a state of resource allocation that is economically efficient. It will then be impossible to reallocate fully employed resources and increase output or produce output more urgently wanted. "Private vice is public virtue."

3   The conditions defining perfect competition typically do not hold in real world markets. Even where some of them obtain, others are likely to be violated. In the goods market, for instance, we find that a large percentage of sellers have considerable power over price. Goods and resources are highly differentiated. Knowledge about the market is imperfect. Entry barriers are common.

4   This is true for monopolies (single sellers of a good without close substitutes), for oligopolies (few sellers of identical or differentiated, but substitute goods), and, to a lesser extent, for monopolistic competitors (many sellers of differentiated, but substitute goods).

5   One may try to gauge the extent of imperfect competition in the real world by studying such things as the index of concentration of firms. Yet, such data must be interpreted with the greatest of care. Nevertheless, it is clear that imperfect competition is rampant in U.S. manufacturing. Often the same is true in other sectors. General government, government enterprises, and producers directly regulated by government produce a quarter of output. The latter include transportation and communications, public utilities, petroleum, and half of agriculture. Another quarter of output, at least, derives from fields of few sellers (unregulated monopoly and oligopoly). This covers half of manufacturing and mining, most of construction, banking, and insurance. At most half of output is traded in markets of many sellers: services, trade, real estate, and the rest of agriculture and manufacturing. Even there other conditions of perfect competition (besides numbers) are often lacking. In the resource markets, a similar picture emerges.

6 In this real world of imperfect competition, sellers of goods, like perfectly competitive ones, maximize profits when marginal revenue equals marginal cost. Yet, having power to set price, marginal revenue is always below price. Therefore, it is in their self-interest to produce where price exceeds marginal cost. Similarly, marginal outlay may diverge from marginal revenue product. As a result, self-interest does not lead automatically to economic efficiency. Just as equilibrium and potential GNP could diverge in Part 1, so equilibrium of firms and households and economic efficiency are seen to diverge here. Just as in Part 1, the economy would reach equilibrium at full employment only by accident, so we see here that efficiency and equilibrium coincide only by accident in an imperfectly competitive world.

7 Thus, imperfect competition, in a subtle fashion that is not at all obvious to the individual firm or household, may lead to lower output than necessary or to the production of goods that are less urgently wanted than others that could have been made instead. Moreover, there are more obvious wastes: the waste of resources in noninformative advertising, in unnecessary or imaginary product differentiation, and owing to barriers to entry.

8 It is extremely difficult to deal with the bad effects of imperfect competition. It is impossible to create a regime of perfect competition by force. Even if one could, there is the question of whether the economic gains are large enough to compensate for noneconomic losses.

9 In addition, perfect competition would not eliminate the economic inefficiency caused by external repercussions of private production and consumption. When private producers or consumers confer benefits or impose costs upon others by their act of production or consumption, inefficiency is reintroduced into the economy. Self-interest does nothing to alleviate this. Government intervention may be needed.

10 Finally, people argue that perfect competition is not only impracticable (point 8) and an insufficient condition for maximum welfare (point 9), it is also undesirable. They consider the economic inefficiency of imperfect competition a necessary price that must be paid for progress. This may be true. Yet it may not justify the degree of imperfect competition (and inefficiency) actually observed in the U.S. economy.

TERMS[1]

cartel	marginal social cost
dynamic efficiency	monopolistic competition
external repercussion of consumption	oligopoly
external repercussion of production	perfect competition
free monopoly	price leadership
imperfect competition	regulated monopoly
index of concentration	static efficiency
marginal external cost	workable competition
marginal private cost	

[1] Terms are defined in the Glossary at the end of the book.

QUESTIONS FOR REVIEW AND DISCUSSION

1 "In ordinary discourse competition refers to personal rivalry. Yet, economists define (perfect) competition as exactly the opposite situation in which personal rivalry is completely absent." Explain. Can you think of any candidates for perfect competition in the U.S. economy?

2 "Both the perfect competitor and the monopolist are guided by the same motives. They even follow the same rules as to profit maximization (equate marginal cost and marginal revenue). Yet, the social consequences of their actions differ greatly." Explain.

3 The text claims that producers can change their marginal costs by changing their output volume. And that they can change their marginal revenue product (and by implication their marginal physical product) by changing their input volume. What is the mechanism that would bring about such changes in marginal cost or marginal physical product? (Hint: you might want to check in Chapters 18 and 20.)

4 Suppose you are an engineer designing steam engines. Your goal is to transfer as much of the potential energy contained in fuel into power produced by the engine. By careful design and construction you may get a highly efficient steam engine that loses only a tiny percentage of the potential energy stored in the fuel. Now suppose an economist comes along telling you that it would be much more efficient to mass produce much less perfect engines. Could the economist be right? Could he be wrong? Justify your answer.

5 "It is no trick at all to make someone better off by making someone else worse off. The important thing is making someone better off *without* making anyone else worse off. This is what economic efficiency achieves." Evaluate. (Consider the examples used in the text.)

6 Sometimes people complain that prices are too high. How would you decide whether prices are too high? Could prices ever be too low?

7 Marginal costs show the *change* in total costs if a unit more or a unit less is produced. Average costs show the *ratio* of total costs to number of units produced. Sometimes people argue that goods should be priced at average not marginal costs. What do you think and why?

8 "Improved transport and communications could prevent or foster monopoly." Explain.

9 "Oligopoly is an imperfect monopoly. It has some of the powers of monopoly, some of the restraints of competition." Evaluate by defining the two terms.

10 "Big business can be blamed for all the economic inefficiency in our economy. Without big business, we wouldn't have big government or big labor." Discuss.

11 "Concentration ratios lie." Evaluate.

12 Look through any magazine and consider the advertisements found therein. Are they informative or just persuasive? Which type occurs more frequently?

13 "Under perfect competition, advertising by an individual firm makes no sense." Evaluate. Why not strike the words "by an individual firm" in the above sentence?

14 The text says about advertisers: "They are shown to all gain simultaneously by changing people's spending pattern among broad classes of goods and by changing their propensity to save. Is this desirable?" Well, is it? Discuss.

15 Suppose the latest new car, compared to earlier models, has a more comfortable ride, is longer (and hence needs more space to park and does not fit into your garage), eats more gas, and needs fewer repairs. Is it a better car?

16 One reason for the existence of big businesses are barriers to entry of new firms. Among these barriers are extremely large initial investment requirements and lack of technical know-how. How could one lower such barriers?

17 Suppose you are operating a factory creating a great deal of smoke in its operations. State law requires you to install smoke control devices that are very costly. If your competitors in other states are not required to do likewise, how would you react to such a law? Does this mean we should never enact state or local laws concerning air or water pollution? How should this problem be tackled?

18 "Private industry should carry the cost of cleaning up our air and water, of rebuilding our cities, of fighting crime and delinquency. All these problems have been caused by private industry. It has destroyed the purity of our air and water, generated ugliness around us, displaced workers, created congested cities and social disorder." Discuss.

19 Harvard's Professor Galbraith, who does not regret the existing market structure in the United States, noted that the same firms we show proudly to foreign visitors as our economy's showpieces are the ones visited by the government's antitrust lawyers in pursuit of antitrust violations. Do you find this strange?

20 "It is just not true that bigness beyond the scale of maximum efficiency—column (3), Table 18.3—is needed to hasten economic progress. The first electronic computers were developed by tiny Ecker-Mauchly Computer Corporation, not giant IBM; the dial phone was inaugurated by small independents, not the giant Bell System. It is the small firm, the ambitious beaver in the competitive pond, that can be trusted to introduce new products and new production techniques. Monopolists and oligopolists, on the other hand, can choose to relax. They will drag their feet before they innovate and make their existing capital stock useless in the process." Discuss.

A RUSSIAN ASSAILS FOES OF REFORM

Economist Blames Rigid Party Bureaucrats

By BERNARD GWERTZMAN

Special to The New York Times

MOSCOW, March 5—A prominent Soviet economist has charged that progress in economic reform was being slowed by rigid theoreticians and well-entrenched bureaucrats who feared changes in the Soviet system.

Aleksandr M. Birman, an official of the Plekhanov School of Economics here, says in the current issue of the liberal journal Novy Mir that a prevailing conservative psychology must be overcome before the reform, now in its fourth year, can operate effectively.

The reform, putting more emphasis on profits and enterprise initiative, was proposed in the later years of the regime of Nikita S. Khrushchev by a number of economists, including Mr. Birman, and was put into practice in 1965.

Since then, about 26,000 Soviet enterprises have changed to the reform. They are said to represent 72 per cent of the goods produced and 80 per cent of the profits.

Many Opposed Reform

Mr. Birman, an expert in finance and credit, said the reform had been adopted only over the apprehension of many. He quoted one "leading economist" as having said, "My party conscience does not allow me to vote for profits."

"He undoubtedly was thinking that he was preserving the purity of socialist society from the dangers of bourgeois sin," Mr. Birman said.

The main problem is psychological, Mr. Birman said, adding, "Habits formed in the very complex decades of the past cannot be changed immediately."

He said the critics of the reform could be divided into two categories: the "theoreticians" and the "practitioners."

"Theoreticians are primarily those teachers of political economy who, unfortunately, are divorced from practical economic work, who for decades have not been in enterprises, and do not know life as it is, but have a good understanding of texts and citations," he said.

Doing It the Old Way

The "practitioners," he said, are accustomed to the system that prevailed before 1965, when every detail of an enterprise's work was directed by a central agency.

Many of these practitioners, he said, "continue to work in the old way, despite the hard will of the party and Government, as if there never had been a plenary meeting of the Central Committee or the 23d party congress [in 1965]," at which decisions about the reform were taken.

"It is completely obvious that people who were educated in this spirit for several decades believe that any appearance of initiative will cause chaos in the national economy, and they are trying with all their strength not to permit it, by putting brakes on initiative and creating bureaucratic blocks in its path," Mr. Birman said.

In the last two years, the debate over economic reform has seemed to be dominated by conservatives who want to limit the extent of the reforms, apparently fearful that too much change may erode the Communist system.

The Czechoslovak crisis last summer made the Soviet liberals' job more difficult because one of the leading targets of Soviet propagandists was Ota Sik, the economist who had pushed the Czechoslovak reforms beyond the limits set in the Soviet Union, where central agencies still control investment and price and wage structures.

23

economic efficiency in the socialist economy

THE PREVIOUS CHAPTERS led to a rather sad conclusion. Although we can imagine a type of capitalist economy that would automatically achieve economic efficiency, while also avoiding the need for central planning, ours is not that type of economy. We cannot rely on perfect competition's "invisible hand" in the real world to achieve 100 percent efficiency. Although our price system is a marvelous mechanism to allocate resources without central human direction, *perfect* competition does not now, never has, and never will exist. Hence, inefficiencies are likely to persist. Even under perfect competition, however, achieving efficiency would require government intervention to correct for external repercussions of private production and consumption. To achieve economic efficiency in the real world would require more than that. Real-life market imperfections would have to be removed by further government action. Otherwise, we are leaving it up to chance whether economic efficiency prevails. However, such government intervention, *in the framework of existing capitalist economies,* is utterly impractical and hence bound to be partial and haphazard.

This is where the academic supporters of socialism come in. "What is needed to achieve economic efficiency," they say, "is *a complete change in the system*, the jump into full-fledged socialism!" In this chapter, we examine that claim with another look at the Soviet-type economy.

TRADITIONAL PLANNING AND ECONOMIC INEFFICIENCY

We have already seen that Soviet-bloc economies are not guided by a price system. Now we must ask another question: Is there economic efficiency in the Soviet-bloc economies? At present, these economies are in a state of transition. Planners are discussing and experimenting with new ways of guiding the economy. Thus, it is somewhat difficult to decide what one is to mean by "the" Soviet-type economy. Actually, though, because the new type of Soviet planning, which we shall discuss later in this chapter, has not fully emerged, if it ever will, we have no choice but to discuss the traditional state of affairs. It was the only state of affairs up to the mid-1960's. To a large extent, as we shall see, it still describes present-day realities. In this traditional Soviet-bloc economy, just as in the United States, economic efficiency was achieved only by chance. We can easily see why.

Physical Planning

Consider the traditional Soviet planning of "important" goods via material balances. The only concerns of the central planners were in this case technical efficiency and internal consistency of the plan (for detail, see Chapters 16 and 17). Ultimately, each individual producer was given physical input and output targets. Tractor factory A was told to use 50 machines (and a variety of other inputs) to make 10,000 tractors a month. Tractor factory B was told to use 100 machines (and a variety of other inputs) to make 7,000 tractors a month, and so on. It was perfectly possible that shifting a dozen machines from one to the other would raise output of one producer more than it would decrease output of the other.

That is, the marginal physical product of machines in making tractors might have differed between A and B. Thus, economic efficiency might not have prevailed. Yet, no one would have been aware of this, and there would have been no incentive to do anything about it. Planners were perfectly content if every producer could produce what he was told to. The same went for managers. There was no mechanism to indicate the existence, nor to encourage the abolition, of economic inefficiency. There was no mechanism, to use our example, for one firm to give up machines in favor of another.

Monetary Planning

Not all planning, however, was done via material balances. Not all transactions were made in response to direct central commands. Managers have always made a number of decisions of their own *on the basis of prices*. This helped them to maximize profits, although this has traditionally been just one goal of many and certainly not the most important one. To the extent, however, that more important goals (as the quantity or value of gross output) were unaffected, managers always had an incentive to buy the cheapest inputs and produce the highest priced outputs. As long as the plan handed down to them allowed it, they would, therefore, make such decisions on the basis of existing prices. Yet, even in this case, economic efficiency only prevailed by chance. For one thing, consider how prices were set.

setting industrial wholesale prices   The wholesale prices for industrial goods, which were used to set certain input and output targets in monetary terms, were set by government such as to equal "planned, weighted-average, adjusted branch cost plus profit." This is quite a mouthful, but can be easily explained. Suppose there were three plants in a certain "branch" of an economy (as tractor production) and their average total costs were as shown in column (3) of Table 23.1.

Note one thing. Although one of these days all this may be changed, until the late 1960's, at least, total "costs" under Soviet-bloc conditions have diverged considerably from the concept used in the West and employed, for instance, in our calculation of GNP in Chapter 5. According to Marxian dogma, interest and rent serve no function, except (in capitalism) to exploit labor. Hence, socialists (who are out to abolish capitalist exploitation) are admonished not to charge such costs. Soviet-bloc economists trying to set prices on the basis of cost have traditionally ignored rent and interest, including under costs only wages, materials, and depreciation charges. Now consider Table 23.1.

Given such data, price setters would typically proceed by first "adjusting" the cost data by excluding "exceptionally" high-cost operations from consideration altogether. Let us say in this case the data of Plant 1 are eliminated (which is a completely arbitrary matter). Then they would calculate a "weighted" average cost for the remaining plants. Because Plants 2 and 3 do not produce equal output quantities, we cannot simply average their average cost data into $(1,500 + 2,100)/2 = 1,800$ rubles. The average cost figure of Plant 3, which produces twice as much as Plant 1, is much more important. There are twice as many tractors

Table 23.1   SOVIET TRACTOR PRODUCTION, HYPOTHETICAL DATA

	TOTAL COST (MILLION RUBLES) (1)	OUTPUT (TRACTORS) (2)	AVERAGE TOTAL COST (RUBLES) $(3) = \frac{(1)}{(2)}$
Plant 1	2	200	10,000
Plant 2	15	10,000	1,500
Plant 3	42	20,000	2,100
	59	30,200	

costing 2,100 rubles on the average than there are tractors costing 1,500 rubles on the average. The easiest way to find the weighted average is simply to calculate the total cost of all plants under consideration and divide by their combined output. The total cost is given in column (1). It amounts to 57 million rubles for Plants 2 and 3. Their combined output is 30,000 tractors. Hence, the "adjusted weighted-average total cost" is 57 million/30,000 = 1,900 rubles. The weighted average is not in the middle between 1,500 and 2,100 rubles, but closer to the latter figure, which applies to a greater share of physical output than the former.

This is not the end of the story. Price planners in the Soviet bloc have traditionally made two adjustments (both equally arbitrary). First, they would take the *actual* weighted-average adjusted branch cost of 1,900 rubles and turn it into a *planned* figure. If it was expected that costs could be or should be reduced, costs were taken not at 1,900 rubles, but at some lower figure, say 1,700 rubles. Second, a small percentage of such "planned" costs, say 5 percent, would be added as profit. The resultant, in our case 1,785 rubles, would be set as the legal price.

Economic Inefficiency in the Goods Market

It is unimportant in the present context to consider what financial procedures were employed if firms made losses under this arrangement. The question is rather whether use of industrial wholesale prices set in this way lent itself to the achievement of economic efficiency. A single example will suffice to show that the answer is no, except by accident.

an example from foreign trade   Take the typical problem encountered in foreign trade among Soviet-bloc countries. This is a problem that has only come to the fore since the mid-1950's. As long as Stalin was alive, Soviet-bloc countries each attempted to hold foreign trade to a minimum. This was the result of a general tendency to slavishly copy Stalinist policies. One of these policies was the "building of socialism in one country." Stalin had deliberately forgone for the Soviet Union the potential advantages of an international division of labor (as described in Chapter 21).

Quite understandably, he felt that the Soviet Union, from its inception being surrounded by a hostile world, should not become dependent for any product on other countries. He preferred to be safely poor rather than insecurely rich. Although there was foreign trade (especially imports of machinery needed for industrialization and paid by whatever was necessary to get them), it was never looked on as anything but a "safety valve" assuring economic development plans. It was seen as something temporary rather than permanent. The optimum foreign trade volume was zero.

In the mid-1950's, however, it dawned on Communist-bloc leaders that what might have been wise policy for the Soviet Union prior to 1945 was foolish in a world of many Communist countries. Being close political allies, no one such country had to fear, they argued, dependence on another. Maybe the "socialist camp" *as a whole* was still a beleaguered fortress (and should strive for economic independence from the capitalist world), but there was no reason why countries *within* the bloc could not organize the grandest of all international divisions of labor! There is nothing wrong, went the argument, with being dependent on *friends*. There is no reason why Poland could not produce all the tractors for the entire group of Communist nations, Czechoslovakia all the buses, and Hungary all the light bulbs if these were the areas in which their resources could do relatively best.

how to find comparative advantage   And this is where planners' troubles began.[1] Who *was* relatively best at producing what? If prices had been set on the basis of marginal costs of production, one could simply have compared relative prices in different countries. One could then have been sure of simultaneously also comparing any firm's relative marginal costs. In this way (as on pages 475–479) the most efficient pattern of production specialization could have been determined.

prices may be misleading   What happens if we use Soviet-bloc-type industrial wholesale prices for this purpose? The data confronting the planners may be as in Table 23.2.

Table 23.2   DETERMINING COMPARATIVE ADVANTAGE, HYPOTHETICAL DATA

PRICE	CZECHOSLOVAKIA	POLAND
Per bus	10,000 crowns	60,000 zlotys
Per tractor	1,000 crowns	30,000 zlotys

In Czechoslovakia one can exchange ten, in Poland two tractors for a bus. Thus, prices lead planners to believe that buses are cheaper, in terms of other goods forgone, in Poland. Poland should specialize in their production: As prices seem to indicate, planners could agree to produce a bus less in Czechoslovakia and a bus more in Poland, thereby having to sacrifice two tractors in Poland, while gaining ten in Czechoslovakia. The increased output of eight tractors could be shared and all could be better off than before.

---

[1] For a detailed discussion of the following points, see my *Economic Integration in the Soviet Bloc: With an East German Case Study* (New York: Praeger, 1965).

522   *efficient employment of resources*

A moment's reflection, however, will show that this may not happen at all. It is true, indeed, as we said above, that one can exchange in Czechoslovakia ten and in Poland two tractors for a bus. But "exchange" in this context means exchange *in the market*. These quantities happen to cost the same amount of *money*. After all, the data of Table 23.2 are *price* data. They only tell us that someone could get, by spending 10,000 crowns in Czechoslovakia, either a bus or ten tractors, or he could get, by spending 60,000 zlotys in Poland, either a bus or two tractors. Thus, it is legitimate to conclude that buses are cheaper in Poland (relative to tractors) *when traded in the market*. The Polish bus price is double that of a tractor. The Czech one is ten times as large. Yet this does in no way determine comparative advantage.

relative marginal costs have to be known   We *cannot* conclude that Poland should specialize in bus production unless buses can be traded for tractors at the rate implied by Table 23.2 also *in the process of production*. If it were also true that the same amount of *resources* could produce either one bus or ten tractors in Czechoslovakia and either one bus or two tractors in Poland, the above conclusions would hold. In this case relative prices would indicate relative marginal costs. As it stands, we cannot be sure of this. In fact, things may be (unknown to planners) as in Table 23.3.

Suppose it is possible to produce at the margin one bus or two tractors with the same resources in Czechoslovakia. In whatever way we wish to evaluate the resources used for an

Table 23.3   RELATIVE PRICES MAY NOT REFLECT RELATIVE MARGINAL COSTS

		CZECHOSLOVAKIA	POLAND
1 bus	Price	10,000 crowns	60,000 zlotys
	Marginal cost	8,000 crowns	30,000 zlotys
1 tractor	Price	1,000 crowns	30,000 zlotys
	Marginal cost	4,000 crowns	3,000 zlotys

extra bus, the resources used for an extra tractor must be half that amount. Thus, if the marginal cost of one bus is 8,000 crowns, that of one tractor must be 4,000 crowns.

Again, for Poland, suppose that, technically, at the margin one bus can be "transformed" in the factory into ten tractors. By not producing one bus, just enough resources could be freed to produce ten tractors instead. Suppose the value of whatever resources are used for one bus (which is the marginal cost of one bus) is 30,000 zlotys. This implies that the value of resources used for ten tractors is also 30,000 zlotys, or the marginal cost of *one* tractor is 3,000 zlotys.

Given *this* information, it turns out that relative prices do not reflect relative marginal cost. In Czechoslovakia, the price of a bus is ten times that of a tractor. Its marginal cost is only double. In Poland, the price of a bus is double that of a tractor. Its marginal cost is ten times higher. Anyone knowing the technical facts, that is, relative marginal costs, could tell immediately that not buses but tractors are cheaper in Poland. What counts are not money prices but real marginal resource costs! The former can indicate comparative advantage only if they reflect accurately marginal costs. In this case, were Poland to specialize in tractors, she could, by not producing one bus, release 30,000 zlotys of resources and produce ten more tractors. Czechoslovakia could make up for the lost bus production by shifting 8,000 crowns of resources from tractor making to bus production, thereby losing two tractors. Together, the two countries would have gained eight new tractors while using the same total of resources. Everyone could be better off.

specialization according to comparative disadvantage?   Now watch what happens if specialization were decided on the basis of relative prices which *misrepresent* relative marginal costs. Central planners decide that Poland should specialize in buses, Czechoslovakia in tractors. They think that they will gain eight tractors in the first step of reallocating production. The sad fact is, however, that Poland (unbeknownst to the planners) will have to give up ten tractors (not two) to make one more bus. (Relative marginal costs, not relative prices count!) Czechoslovakia (also contrary to planners' expectations) will be able to produce two more tractors (not ten more) with the resources released by not producing one bus. (Again, relative marginal costs, not relative prices, tell the true story.) Thus, instead of gaining, the two countries are losing eight tractors. They have mistakenly specialized according to comparative *dis*advantage. If, as is likely, the output of all goods is growing each year with the growth of the quantities of resources used, this may never be noticed. The rate of growth of output will simply be slowed down. Instead of gaining twenty new tractors (say, eight through increased economic efficiency and twelve through use of more resources), the two countries will gain only four (twelve through use of more resources, offset by the loss of eight through increased economic *in*efficiency).

the historical record   This story, furthermore, is more than hypothetical. Soviet-bloc planners have, indeed, made international specialization decisions on the basis of existing prices, and relative prices did indeed differ from relative marginal costs, except by accident. Just recall the above discussion of setting industrial wholesale prices.

Average vs. marginal costs.   First, the cost figures of Table 23.1 are average, not marginal costs. Thus, although a tractor may cost 40,000 zlotys on the average (and a bus 50,000), it may cost 80,000 zlotys at the margin (and a bus 160,000). This would mean that *another* bus can be made not by sacrificing 1.25 tractors (as relative average costs say) but by giving up 2 tractors (as relative marginal costs indicate).

Marxian ideology.   Second, as was pointed out already, Soviet-bloc economists have typically neglected rent and interest charges. Thus, even if they *did* look at marginal costs to determine comparative advantage, they were apt to come out wrong, because they refused to accept some costs as costs! Take the case just mentioned where the same inputs can make either one bus or two tractors at the margin. Soviet-bloc economists may not have come to this conclusion at all, even if they did (as they did not) look for marginal cost. They would put it this way: "To make another bus (or another tractor) how much extra labor, materials and depreciation cost must be incurred?" Suppose the answers are as simple as those given in Table 23.4.

Table 23.4   A MARXIAN RECKONING OF MARGINAL COST, POLAND, HYPOTHETICAL DATA IN ZLOTYS

EXTRA COST NEEDED TO PRODUCE	LABOR (1)	MATERIALS (2)	DEPRECIATION (3)	TOTAL (4)
1 Bus	100,000	20,000	30,000	150,000
1 Tractor	33,333	6,667	10,000	50,000

Then marginal cost Soviet-bloc style would be as in column (4), and it would be concluded that at the margin three tractors can be produced with the same value of inputs as one bus. Yet, this may not be true at all. Suppose bus production also requires the use of one unit of land, but tractor production does not. Suppose, further, ten times as much equipment and buildings are tied down in bus production as in tractor production, even though only three times as much capital is *used up* (depreciation). Then, it would *not* be true that not producing three tractors would release the inputs for making one bus. There would not be enough land and capital. A wise accountant would have put a value on the use of land (say 10,000 zlotys rent per unit). He would have put a value also on the use (in addition to the using up) of capital (say, 2 percent interest on the value of capital tied up in production). Suppose the value of capital (buildings and so on) needed at the margin is 10,000 zlotys per bus and 1,000 zlotys per tractor. Then, the wise accountant would have charged for bus production a rent of 10,000 zlotys and interest of $0.02 \times 10,000 = 200$ zlotys, or figured a marginal cost of 160,200 zlotys. Similarly, he would have added interest of $0.02 \times 1,000 = 20$ zlotys into the marginal tractor cost, making it 50,020 zlotys. Now it would have been quite clear that giving up three tractors would *not* make possible the production of one more bus. Three times 50,020 comes to less than 160,200.

Note how important interest and rent charges are. They indicate the amount of capital and land tied up in production. As such, they are indispensable for establishing correct marginal costs. This has always been recognized by academic socialists who would require interest and rent payments by socialist business managers for their use of society's scarce capital and land, as well as depreciation allowances for replacing used up capital. Note further that one can recognize this important function of interest and rent without having to be in favor of private income from the private ownership of capital and land. Academic supporters of socialism certainly are not in favor of this. Nor was Karl Marx. But the latter and many of his followers failed to see the important allocative function of interest and rent: helping to establish prices that can be used to achieve economic efficiency. Therefore, being against private rent and interest income, they throw out the baby with the bath water, admonishing price setters under socialism to forget about "exploitative" rent and interest altogether. Soviet-bloc economists have done just that. In following Marx's unwise precept, they have cut themselves off for many decades from the possibility of establishing correct prices that reflect marginal costs and making wise decisions for the sake of economic efficiency.

Other problems.   Third, Soviet-bloc industrial wholesale prices not only did not reflect (except by accident) true marginal costs, they did not reflect true average costs either. This was partly so because of the neglect of rent and interest, partly because of the arbitrary adjustments made: The substitution of planned for "actual" costs, the exclusion of "exceptionally" high costs, the addition of an arbitrary profit percentage. Of course, that made little difference, for marginal costs alone mattered anyhow.

Conclusions.   We can conclude, therefore, that any attempts to use traditional Soviet-bloc industrial wholesale prices to determine an economically efficient use of resources (whether within or among Soviet-bloc economies) was doomed to failure, except by accident. This also holds for agricultural and retail prices, established with a view to regulating the real income of peasants or of households, respectively. (See our discussion in Chapter 17.) There was nothing in the Soviet economy that would assure that the ratio of any two prices reflected that ratio of marginal costs of the two goods involved. Thus, any planner who decided on an "efficient" allocation of resources on the basis of these prices was practically sure to fail.

Economic Inefficiency in the Resource Market

In the same way, if for no other reason than the absence of rent and interest charges, economic efficiency in the resource markets was only accidental. Suppose firms were to strive after maximum profit (and remember, this was not necessarily their goal). Suppose they each *tried* to equate marginal revenue product with the official resource price. We saw in Chapter 20 how this would maximize profit. More importantly, we saw that it would maximize the economy's output if all producers are faced with the same resource price. By adjusting the volume of a resource used until its marginal revenue product equals the resource price, producers of a given good would all end up with the same marginal *physical* product for the resource. No reallocation of the resource could then increase output.

Yet, where some resource prices are zero, this cannot be achieved. As long as interest and rent, the prices for using capital and land, are zero, profit is only maximized when the marginal physical product of capital and land is also zero, when a firm has so much of it that another unit would add nothing to output. In the meantime, profit gets bigger every time more capital or land is added. Hence, all firms naturally want more capital and land.

In reality, only a few firms, if any, will succeed in getting so much of them, relative to labor, that another unit of either adds nothing to output. Therefore, most Soviet producers were always in some kind of disequilibrium with marginal revenue product above the zero resource price. But, there was no mechanism to make everyone's marginal revenue product (and by implication marginal physical product) end up above zero by the same amount. Different firms' marginal physical product of capital and land were equal only by the sheerest of coincidences.

More likely than not, one could have switched capital and land among firms and raised output. There were sure to be some firms where loss of a unit of capital would have cut output by less than it could have increased output somewhere else. The same goes for land. Thus, economic efficiency did not prevail.

AN OLD DREAM

Why then have academic socialists so long proclaimed the economic efficiency of socialism? Theirs was a dream of a different world! They envisioned a socialist world of *de*centralized planning. In fact, theirs was a world set up to *imitate* the invisible hand of perfect competition!

The Model

The idea is a fairly simple one. Oskar Lange expressed it brilliantly in a famous 1938 essay "On the Economic Theory of Socialism." Economic efficiency, he argued, was impossible to achieve by patching up an economically inefficient, privately run economy. But it could be easily achieved by letting *government* "run the show." What antitrust laws and the like could never do could be achieved by complete government ownership of the nonhuman means of production (capital and land).

Oskar Lange envisioned no violent revolution to establish his brand of socialism. He was thinking of a democratic country such as the United States, where socialism might be established by majority vote of the population without any change at all in the *political* system. Even in the economy, he thought, changes could be kept to a minimum after all capital and land had been transferred to public ownership. *As he saw it*, things would look as follows.

households   Households will, as always, freely dispose of their own labor in any way desired, including voluntary unemployment. Labor markets will be completely free. No unions, no government interference. Anyone may enter any occupation for which he is qualified and will get paid at "the going market rate." Unlike under capitalism, no household will have any income other than from labor, because all capital and land is publicly owned. No more *personal* income in the form of interest, rent, and profits! (An exception to this will be noted shortly.) In the goods market households may freely dispose of their money income in any way they wish at established market prices. Households, of course, can only buy consumer goods. They cannot buy any means of production, such as oil refineries, grocery stores, machine tools, or agricultural land.

enterprise managers   Production is carried on, as always, in a great variety of firms. Each firm is as large and operates as many plants as is technically desirable. It does not matted what the concentration of firms is in any one industry. There can be one firm, there can be one thousand. Engineers decide that. These firms are, of course, collectively owned by all the people. They are administered by *socialist enterprise managers* who are salaried state employees and differ in no way from the directors of modern capitalist corporations. The only difference is that they are now responsible not to a relatively small group of stockholders, but to the government, which is the trustee of the people as a whole. Every citizen is a "stockholder" in each socialist enterprise, be it the corner grocery or the giant maker of electronic machines.

As under capitalism, the socialist enterprise managers use inputs to produce and sell outputs. They use the capital and land held by the firm itself, they can buy outright or rent the services of capital and land from other firms, and they buy labor services from households. The market prices of all inputs (wages, rents, interest) are *given* to the firms by government price setters. Wage payments are obviously made directly to households. Rent and interest payments have to be made into the treasury for the use of land and capital by whichever firm holds these resources. The treasury also receives the firms' profits. Thus, the treasury, as a trustee of the people as a whole, receives the income from the use of publicly owned resources. It collects all the interest, rent, and profit income. Outputs of socialist firms are sold to households or other firms at the going market price. Enterprise managers are instructed to do three things:

1. They must make all decisions on the basis of input and output prices set by a central planning board, and *they are to regard these prices as constant when making decisions.*

2. They must produce any given level of output at the lowest possible total cost.

3. They must select that volume of output where the given output price equals rising marginal cost. They must buy that volume of any resource where the given resource price equals falling marginal revenue product. This amounts to maximizing profits or minimizing losses.

industrial managers   To establish a mechanism in the socialist economy by which the number of firms in any industry changes with the demands made on that industry, Oskar Lange's model also provides for a group of *industrial managers.* There is one for each industry. His task is to regulate the number of firms in such a way that the marginal cost *of the industry* equals output price. It means, briefly, that the cost anywhere in the industry of producing another unit of output, whether by expanding existing plants or by building new ones, should equal price.

central planning board   Finally, there will be a *central planning board.* It has three major functions.

Government demand.   First, the central planning board is to determine the extent of production of social goods (such as for defense, health, justice, and education) by placing appropriate purchase orders with socialist firms. Such expenditures can be financed from the profits of socialist enterprises or from their payments into the public treasury of rent and interest for their use of publicly owned land and capital. The expenditures can also be financed, of course, by additional money creation or through taxes on labor income. If, on the other hand, government demand for social goods is set below treasury receipts of profits, rents, and interest, the surplus revenue may be paid out to the "stockholders," that is, to the public at large as a "social dividend." This is the exception mentioned above to the households' receipt of nothing but labor income. If the government were to declare a social dividend of this type, every citizen would receive an equal share of the profit-rent-interest income earned by capital and land of which every citizen owns an equal share.

This first function of the central planning board is nothing new when compared to the role of present-day capitalist governments. However, Oskar Lange envisioned a much wider scope for government demand under socialism than under capitalism. He argued that *democratic* socialism must assure an equal opportunity to all citizens for material well-being. Therefore, not only must all equally own land and capital, but they must have an equal chance to supply labor. Hence, there should be publicly financed equal education and medical care for all.

Regulation of the size of investment demand.   The central planning board is also to determine the extent of production of new capital goods. Oskar Lange and, typically, other socialists argue that the public is apt to an irrational degree not only to prefer private consumption to collective consumption, but also to prefer present consumption to future consumption. Because of the former, we must have government demand. Because of the latter, we must have publicly determined investment demand. Sure, argue the socialists, there is *some* investment in any economy. But the private, voluntary addition to buildings, equipment, and inventories is apt to be smaller (from the national standpoint) than it should be. An economy may devote 15 percent of its resources to making new capital goods. As a result, its real GNP may grow at 3 percent a year. If it devoted 20 percent of resources to capital formation, its GNP may grow at 4 percent a year. By being so "piggish" and devoting 85 rather than 80 percent of resources to produce goods for *present* satisfaction, people are, in fact, reducing the potential well-being of future generations. People 100 years hence may have double the real GNP they would otherwise have if we decided to invest just a little bit more each year. Most people, argue the socialists, have a narrow short-run individualistic view. "What do I care how people live 100 years hence?" they say. "Why should I tighten my belt now? What has posterity ever done for me?" With this type of attitude, we will not do much for posterity, either. Yet, say the socialists, government should not only defend the social viewpoint (if people insist on private cars *and* on living together, they must be *forced* to pay for roads and policemen), but it should also defend the long-run viewpoint (if people insist on perpetuating the race, they must be *forced* to provide for future generations).

Obviously, it is a matter of judgment how much social consumption there should be as opposed to private consumption. So it is a matter of judgment how much capital formation (assuring higher future real GNP) there should be compared to present output use. But there can be no doubt, goes the argument, that a responsible government must make the decision on investment just as it does on government demand.

Price setting.   Finally, the central planning board is to determine all prices in the economy. In so doing, it is following a rule of its own. It may start out setting all prices at random. Then, it observes the consequences in all markets. As we saw, all enterprises are enjoined to buy and sell only at these prices and make all decisions only on that basis. Only by the sheerest of accidents, however, will the central planning board pick on the first round a complete set of equilibrium prices for all interdependent markets. More likely than not, many prices will be too high. Many will be too low. Yet, without knowing the shape of market demand and supply curves, without having solved millions of equations in giant computers, the central planning board will immediately be able to tell which prices should be lowered and which raised!

Wherever there is a shortage in any market, be it for labor, tractors, or red cabbages, price will have to be raised. Wherever there is a surplus, it will have to be lowered. This will, in turn, as under perfect competition, eliminate the shortage or the surplus.

More than that! As under perfect competition, the change in prices will be the only signal needed to tell all the relevant parties what action is required of them. There is no further need for central planning and allocation of inputs and outputs or for detailed directives for each firm. Suppose the government wants more highway equipment. The appropriate agency will simply put in the orders at socialist firms. If the demand can be met at current prices, everything will be fine. If it cannot, appropriate changes will automatically result. The central planning board's statistical section will report a shortage of highway equipment. The board will raise its price. Firms producing the equipment will automatically respond by producing more. Following the rule laid down for their behavior, socialist enterprise managers will increase production until marginal cost has risen sufficiently to meet the new and higher price.

Or suppose that there is a shortage of labor and unemployment of capital goods. Immediately, the central planning board would raise the price of labor and lower that for the use of capital. Enterprise managers, enjoined to minimize cost, would substitute, wherever possible, relatively abundant (and cheaper) capital for extra scarce (and more expensive) labor. As a result, the shortages and surpluses would disappear.

And most important of all is this. Because all firms continually adjust their output volumes until marginal cost equals the given price of the good, the marginal cost of production of a given good would be the same for all producers of this good. Because all firms continually adjust their input volumes until marginal revenue product equals the given price of the resource, the marginal *physical* product of a given resource would be the same for all users of it. Thus, efficiency prevails. There would be no possibility left unused for switching output or inputs among firms and thereby raising output. Whoever makes cars, the cost of making another car is the same for all. Whoever uses labor, the product derived from its use is the same everywhere. What capitalist market imperfections made impossible, argued

Lange (recall Chapters 18 and 20, for instance), a rational socialist economy achieves with ease.

Summary So Far

In summary, the central planning board in Oskar Lange's world is *not* setting up data and feeding them to computers to come up with input-output tables. Nor is it trying to guide economic activity by elaborately detailed instructions for all socialist enterprises (as in the model of Chapter 16). Rather, it sets out to guide economic activity through *nothing else but prices*. It alone has the right to set prices which all households and firms have to follow in their transactions with one another. Beyond that, households are free to do absolutely anything they like, and firms only have to follow the simple general rules laid down for their behavior. There is no unending maze of unpleasant bureaucratic intervention, as there might be in centrally directed physical input-output planning. This is a *decentralized* economy.

Thousands of enterprise managers decide for themselves what is the best resource combination, output scale and thus input quantity bought. Like perfect competitors, they must do so on the basis of prices *given* to them. Millions of households decide (as they would in perfect competition) how much labor to sell and what goods to buy. None can influence prices. Ultimately, just as in capitalism, households determine what kind of goods are produced. The only exceptions are the *public* determination (presumably by elected officials of the central planning board) of the size of collective consumption (as in capitalism), and of investment (which in capitalism is also strongly influenced by monetary policy). Suppose that 10 percent of resources are needed to satisfy normal government demand for goods. Suppose another 20 percent of resources are channeled into the production of capital goods. Then 70 percent of all resources are free to be disposed of by consumers. In this realm, their "sovereignty" is fully maintained. Matters stand even better than that. This economy, asserts Oskar Lange, would assure economic efficiency. As we have seen, the price of any output is the same for all parties buying or selling it. Even if there were only one or two giant firms in the industry, their socialist managers would *as a matter of rule* equate marginal cost with output price. Hence, efficiency would prevail, just as in perfect competition.

Similarly, the price of any resource is the same for all parties buying or selling it. Even if there were only one or two giant firms in the industry, their socialist managers would *as a matter of rule* equate marginal revenue product to resource price. Again, this would lead to efficiency, just as in perfect competition.

REALITY DIFFERS FROM BLUEPRINTS

Reality has the nasty habit of differing from blueprints. So it is, as we saw, with the Soviet-bloc economies. None has realized the Lange dream. Yet, Stalin's death has lifted many of the shackles with which minds were tied down during his lifetime. Instead of accepting his teachings with the former spirit of blind credulity and admiration, economists were urged by the Twentieth Soviet Party Congress in 1956 to think for themselves and to learn from others (including the West where economic analysis had proceeded far beyond the clumsy reasoning of Karl Marx). Before long, Soviet-bloc publications turned into a genuine forum for debate. This debate was widespread and frank, and it gave birth to a variety of proposals for reform. Economists were especially troubled by the obvious irrationality of prices. They began to realize, partly as a result of the above-mentioned problems with the international production specialization within the bloc, that the decisions of *any* planner or manager, if made on the basis of existing prices, were absolutely arbitrary. Whenever someone decided to use one input rather than another, to produce this output rather than that one, to use one kind of new capital equipment rather than another, he was kidding himself if he thought that prices could help him act in a rational fashion. He may buy a cheaper input so far as *money* expenditure is concerned, but he may actually use up more *resources*. L. V. Kantorovich, Director of the Laboratory for Economic Mathematical Methods of the Siberian Department of the U.S.S.R. Academy of Sciences, went so far as to argue that more rational methods of planning and management could increase Soviet industrial output by 50 percent without the use of new inputs. Probably, he was exaggerating to get people to listen. This kind of talk brought to the fore a number of proposals for reform.

Patching Up the Old System

We have already discussed the dreams of some mathematical economists who urged the full-scale introduction of input-output planning (as in Chapter 16). Others did not care to go that far, but proposed what amounted to patching up the weak spots of the actual system of planning.

As many saw it, the greatest weakness of all lay in the way incentives of managers were set up with bonuses paid on the basis of fulfilling the gross output target. As a result, as we saw in Chapter 17, managers tended to sabotage the very formulation of a feasible plan and ended up producing goods, especially "unimportant" goods, in incorrect assortments or of low quality, if they managed to produce them at all. As Premier Khrushchev lamented.[2]

It has become the tradition to produce not beautiful chandeliers to adorn homes, but the heaviest chandeliers possible. This is because the heavier the chandeliers produced, the more a factory gets since its output is calculated in tons. So the factories make chandeliers weighing hundreds of kilograms and fulfill the plan. But who needs such a plan? ... The plan for furniture factories is stated in rubles. Consequently the furniture factories find it more advantageous to make a massive armchair, since the heavier the chair the more expensive it is. Formally the plan is thus fulfilled since the furniture makers add this and that to the armchair and make it cost more money. But who needs such armchairs?

The major Soviet newspapare *Izvestia* echoed these thoughts:[3] "Our rockets fly farther

---

[2] *Pravda,* July 2, 1959.
[3] *Izvestia,* January 24, 1960.

than others, we circle the moon, but our clothes are poor and our footwear cannot stand inspection."

Then in 1962, Tabeyev, head of the Tatar Economic Council, disclosed "successful" experiments in his area of influence. Instead of rewarding managers on the basis of gross output, calculated in tons or rubles and including the value of materials taken over from other firms, they were rewarded on the basis of an entirely new index. This index was the NVP, or "normative value of processing," a concept more akin to value added, but by no means identical with it. It excluded the bulk of raw material inputs from the value of output recorded, thus hopefully removing the incentive of managers to use heavy or expensive raw materials, thereby producing goods no one wanted, yet fulfilling the plan. For a while it seemed as if the new index was to win general acceptance. The Council of the National Economy announced for 1964 the experimental conversion of a number of enterprises outside the Tatar Region to planning by NVP standards; but eventualy the idea was given up.

The defects of planning called for more than a new index by which to judge managers. It required, argued some, a complete reform of the relations between managers and planners in favor of more freedom for the former.

A Radical Change: Decentralization

Ever since Stalin's death a variety of steps had been taken to improve upon the central planning apparatus itself. During 1954–1956, the Council of Ministers and the Central Planning Board (Gosplan) had shed some of their powers in favor of the industrial ministries under them in the planning hierarchy. It was hoped that the ministries, in turn, would allow some of their new decision-making power to trickle down to the enterprise managers. This did not happen.

In 1957, therefore, the industrial ministries were abolished altogether. In their place, over a hundred regional economic councils were put. These were to be directly subordinate to Gosplan and superior to all the factories in their region. Again the hope of giving enterprise managers more flexibility in decision-making was not realized. If anything, the regional authorities were able to maintain closer contact with the enterprises than Moscow ministries had before, and they used this advantage to restrict them more than before.

In the early 1960's, the old question of how one can best plan centrally without excessively regulating managers was still unanswered. Oskar Lange's blueprint remained just that. Oskar Lange himself had participated in setting up the comprehensive Stalin-type centralized planning in Poland. He had argued that this was unavoidable in the early years of a socialist regime. The old managers were hostile to the regime. New ones had to be trained. So it was wise practice to concentrate the small numbers of loyal and experienced economic functionaries at the place where they were likely to be most effective: in the central government. But, said Oskar Lange, the methods necessary and useful in a period of social revolution become an obstacle when perpetuated beyond their time. As the socialist economy develops and matures, it becomes possible and necessary to introduce a large area of decentralized decision-making by managers at the enterprise level. The central authorities then must give up the detailed management of the economy by a flood of administrative orders. They can still determine the broad outlines of resource allocation. But they can do it by financial levers that induce people to act in the desired fashion. They need not do it by detailed direct command.

A growing number of other Soviet-bloc economists also proposed that widespread decentralization be introduced as a means of managing the economy. With the growth of any economy, they argued, the numbers of products, production processes, and firms multiply rapidly. Attempts at guiding every detail of economic life from a single center are increasingly doomed to failure. These would-be reformers proposed (very much in the spirit of Oskar Lange's model discussed earlier) that firms should be asked to follow the *profit motive*, while being guided from the center through meaningful prices.

the Liberman proposals   This type of proposal has been frequently associated with the name of Yevsei Liberman, Professor at Kharkov University and Director of the Economic Research Unit of the Kharkov Economic Council. His stirring articles have been repeatedly published since 1962 on the pages of *Pravda*, the major Soviet newspaper. He rapidly gained followers throughout Eastern Europe. Essentially, Liberman proposed that managers be given as few instructions as possible from central authorities and that prices be "rationalized."

1. Planning should occur, in contrast to the orthodox methods described in Chapter 17 above, "from the bottom up." Each firm should be asked to make (on the basis of governmentally set prices) a consistent and feasible proposal as to what, how, and when it wants to produce. It should ask its customers what they want and propose an output plan on that basis to higher authorities.

Central planners would have to approve the enterprise plans to make sure that the sum of individual plans stays within the national possibilities and within the "public interest." Planners were also expected in this way to continue to determine the major proportions of economic activity (such as the percentage of resources devoted to consumption, investment, and general government purposes). They were to channel investment into sectors desired by them, and to determine by direct command the output of "principal" products. Within these constraints, however, they would approve the output plans and input requirements submitted by the firms.

2. Managers should be judged not on the basis of gross output as so far, but on the basis of profit made in relation to the capital held by their firm. Relating profit to *capital held* was to discourage the hoarding by firms of idle capital goods (buildings, equipment, inventories). Judging on the basis of *profit* was to ensure the production of high quality output in exactly the proportions desired by customers. Customers were to be given the right to reject undesirable output (low quality, spare parts missing, the wrong goods, and the like). Thus, only output produced *and sold* (because acceptable to customers) was to be counted toward plan fulfillment. This was to encourage all-out efforts to maximize profits by (a) using inputs as frugally as possible and (b) increasing revenues by producing precisely what was wanted and when it was wanted by customers.

3. The bonus system (see pages 375–377) should be revised. Managers as well as workers should receive bonuses based not on output but on actual profit if the profit plan is fulfilled or underfulfilled, on less than actual profit if overfulfilled. This was designed to end another long-standing undesirable practice associated with attempts to overfulfill plans: hiding productive capacity. Thus, the new system was to encourage high voluntary output targets (there was to be no punishment for underfulfilling).

4. Plans were also supposed to be long term so as to encourage technical innovation. Under the old system, managers were typically opposed to the introduction of new technology because it was bound to upset the smooth fulfillment of the output plan. And continuous output plan fulfillment determined the bonus. In addition, managers opposed technical improvements because they were frequently moved around from one position to another (to upset any antistate "family relation" between the controllers and the controlled within the planning hierarchy). As a result, they had little interest in technological change that upsets the production process now (endangering their bonus) and boosts output later (when they might not be around).

the Liberman experiments   In May 1964, the Soviet Communist Party Central Committee made a major announcement. It had approved an *experiment* to test the Liberman-type proposal in two enterprises. The experiment involved two clothing producers, one in Gorky, the other in Moscow. It was to begin on July 1. The firms involved were given the right to gear their output to sales contracts. They could contract directly with retail stores, rather than the state wholesale organizations. They could negotiate higher prices for higher quality goods. They were to be judged by "profitability," the profit-to-capital ratio.

Khrushchev's subsequent fall did not lead to a reversal of this cautious policy of which he had highly approved. As of January 1965, 400 light industry enterprises in the garments, cotton, wool, silk, linen, and footwear industries were shifted over to the same system. For the first time since the 1920's, Soviet retail stores were allowed to contract directly with factories of their own choice (rather than wait for central commands). They were thus enabled to insist on the production of high quality goods of the type demanded by customers rather than being forced to take whatever someone else had decided on producing. Producers' output plans were in turn regarded as fulfilled only if their output was accepted by retailers.

This was exactly in line with the Liberman ideas. The experiment now spread from Gorky and Moscow to Lvov, Leningrad, Odessa, Kharkov, and Kiev. By mid-1965, 25 percent of clothing factories, 28 percent of footwear producers, and 18 percent of textile producers were under the new system. There was even talk of the film industry being brought under it, with box office receipts (minus costs) being divided among the films' casts.

the "new system of planning and management"   Apparently, the experiments went well. By September 1965, the Supreme Soviet approved what was called one of the most significant reforms since 1928. Entitled "On Improving the Management of Industry, Perfecting Planning, and Strengthening Economic Incentives in Industrial Production," the new act was to usher in a new era. The regional economic councils, introduced in 1957, were abolished. Industrial ministries reappeared. But there was a change. The central authorities were to give up all but eight of about forty key plan indicators in favor of enterprise managers. They were to use more financial inducements to guide managers, fewer direct commands. The powers of managers everywhere (whether operating under the new experiment or not) were to be increased for drafting the plan as well as for day-to-day operating decisions. Unlike before, wholesalers and retailers, for instance, could select their suppliers. Industrial enterprises could choose their own contractors and subcontractors. Managers could spend their total wage allowance freely: decide on the number of workers they needed and offer any type and amount of remuneration appropriate for any particular worker. They could also make independent decisions about how to use a large percentage of profits and depreciation allowances (previously paid in cash entirely into the state budget for centrally directed investments). A part of these funds could now go, at the discretion of managers, for investment to aid production or for the benefit of employees (for example, housing, bonuses for special work, year-end profit-sharing, and so on). Most "important" input and output quotas were to remain, but the detail involved was to be reduced.

Eventually, managers in the entire economy were supposed to have great freedom as to the determination of the composition of inputs and outputs. Managers were to be judged (as Liberman suggested) by the ratio of profit made (if also planned) to capital held (not any more by gross output). They were to be forced to finance investment themselves from profits or interest-bearing bank loans (instead of receiving, as in the past, grants from the state budget for this purpose, thereby having no incentive to economize on capital). The state bank was to make loans only to those able to repay, this decision being subject to social consideration of the desirable total of loans. Eventually, state subsidies were to end. All firms were to meet all their costs from their own revenues.

The new act also announced the introduction of a charge for the use of capital and the imminent completion of industrial price reforms long on the drawing board.

The general acceptance of the Liberman-type proposals and the transformation of Soviet economic planning into the type of world described by Oskar Lange in one sense has made great progress following the 1965 laws. In 1966, the experiment was extended to a great variety of transport and communications enterprises. In addition, 673 more industrial enterprises (producing 12 percent of industrial output) switched permanently to the new system.

This seemed to accelerate. By early 1967, 2,500 enterprises in many sectors of the economy were under the system. By mid-1967, it was reported that 4,600 industrial enterprises, producing over 30 percent of industrial output, had joined the new model. By the end of 1967, the numbers were 7,000 enterprises and 40 percent of industrial output. In addition, fifteen railroads, hauling 70 percent of traffic, were under the new system. During 1967, the transition was also prepared in public services, and the state farms. Of the latter, 390 of 12,000 farms producing 40 percent of agricultural output joined the new economic model.

By the end of 1968, it was reported that 30,700 industrial enterprises, producing 77 percent of industrial output were under the new system in the Soviet Union. Baibakov, chairman of Gosplan, announced that the reform was to be further extended during the 1971–1975 plan period. Yet another part of the reform so far has left much to be desired.

price reforms   As we noted above, Liberman and his followers (very much in the spirit of Oskar Lange) asked for more than greater freedom for managers. They also asked for a "rationalization" of the price-setting process. This made good sense. Producing the most valuable output and using the cheapest inputs makes no sense unless the prices of goods reflect something more basic—real resource cost. Only where this is true can one conclude, say, that the machine with the lower price can really be produced with fewer resources. For ideological reasons referred to above, however, many Soviet-bloc economists and party officials have found it extremely difficult to separate in their minds the use of rational prices for the sake of economic efficiency from the capitalist institutions with which market prices have been connected historically. Many argue, as Marx did, that charging rent and interest must imply exploitation of labor or that letting firms make input and output decisions on the basis of rational prices must spell the end of socialism. These people have resisted any attempts at price reform. On the other hand, those who realize, as Oskar Lange did, that use of rational prices to guide the economy is not synonymous with capitalism have advocated a complete overhaul of East European price-setting procedures.

The Soviet Union in fact instituted a first price reform as early as July 1, 1963. It was carried out, however, by the old-line economists and resulted, as one might expect, in a complete victory for the traditionalists, such as Maizenberg (Deputy Chief of the Gosplan Price Bureau) and Ostrovitianov (outstanding member of the U.S.S.R. Academy of Sciences). The goat having been appointed gardener, the so-called reform left completely unchanged the old principle of price setting. Agricultural and retail prices were not even touched at all. Industrial wholesale prices were only revised *on the basis of the old formula* discussed above (page 519). To take account of uneven changes in wage and material costs over the past years and of a revision of depreciation allowances, prices were changed to restore desired profit margins. Yet, the discussion on price reforms continued. More and more economists, for instance, advocated the charging, for the sake of promoting economic efficiency, of interest on capital held by a firm and of rent for its use of minerals, land, water, forests, and so on. In late 1965, Premier Kosygin announced another comprehensive price reform for 1966–1967. Prices at that time were supposed to include interest and rent charges. This reform took place, but when everything was done, prices were still based on average rather than marginal costs, thus remaining irrational.

conclusion   Because matters are in flux, it is hard to judge the outcome of all these changes. One thing, however, is certain: so far, the Soviet reforms have not been a vehicle for cataclysmic economic change. In the Soviet Union, each new step in the initial implementation of the reforms has been in the direction of making them less liberal. Although the press keeps treating the reforms as a big deal, many central planners stoutly maintain that their role has not diminished significantly. In fact, this may well be so. The eight planning indicators central planners have reserved to themselves are key indicators: the physical output of "principal" products (20,000 in 1967), sales, profits, wage fund, payments to the state budget, investment from centralized funds, material supplies, and the introduction of new technology. Enterprises have gotten powers of no vital concern to the center. There is little talk of direct contracting nowadays (as there was in 1964), managers have no latitude in setting prices (as they did in 1965), and their brief freedom to determine their wage fund has been removed. In addition, the new success indicator is more complex than the old one and often works at cross purposes. For instance, if a manager raises profitability by cutting capital held, he cuts his future profitability because the investment funds he gets are a percentage of his capital held. If he raises profit by cutting cost through using less labor, he will find his bonus and the funds for social-cultural purposes cut, for they are determined by the size of his labor force. Thus, managers are pulled in several directions simultaneously. They are still hemmed in on all sides by centrally determined "norms" and "targets." In fact, many traditionalists, as the news report introducing this chapter shows, reject summarily the whole idea of a profit-directed socialist economy. How about the rest of Eastern Europe?

new models in other countries in Eastern Europe   Other East European countries, including Bulgaria, Czechoslovakia, East Germany, Hungary, Poland, and Rumania, carried out major price reforms in the late 1960's. Price reforms in these countries also went hand in hand with the introduction of Liberman-type proposals for decentralized economic management. Some countries, notably Czechoslovakia and Hungary, went much further than the Soviet Union in dismantling centralized powers. All East European countries were originally contemplating the full introduction of "new systems of economic planning and management" by 1968. In 1967, there was much experimentation on this matter. All these experiments aimed at pruning the bureaucracy and hoped to encourage, via production for profit (a) the production of high quality goods of the types and in the proportions desired and (b) the speedy application of new technology.

Everywhere the traditional systems of planning (see Chapter 17) were in a state of flux. To give just one example, in Bulgaria a "new system" was tested in fifty enterprises starting in April 1964. In 1965, the experiment was extended covering industrial plants producing 44 percent of industrial output and employing a third of the industrial labor force, and including trade enterprises handling 30 percent of turnover. Further "tests" were scheduled for 1966. Beginning in 1967, the new model was scheduled for "application *on basic lines* in the whole national economy." Eventually, planners there envisaged a *three-price system: fixed* prices being set by the center for basic industrial and important consumer goods, *guided* prices set by firms for a number of other goods within centrally determined minima and maxima, and *free* prices set for the rest by supply and demand, such as illustrated by Figure 2.5 DEMAND AND SUPPLY CURVES SUPERIMPOSED. Guidelines published in December 1965 pointed out that future prices were to include a "tax" on the value of capital held by firms (that is, an interest charge) as well as a "tax" on agricultural, forestry, and extractive industry firms whose performance is influenced by varying natural conditions (that is, a rent charge). Firms were to set up their own annual and long-term plans (although subject to central correction).

On the other hand, the Central Planning Board in Bulgaria (as well as the other East European countries) planned to continue to determine "priority" inputs and outputs in physical terms, to fix the shares of investment and general government purchase of goods, to supervise technical progress, to regulate directly all foreign trade, and so on. This kind of reservation makes it impossible to judge how farreaching the reforms will really be in the end. On the one hand, planners insist on keeping direct control over a number of economic factors; on the other, they are playing with the thought of guiding the economy only indirectly through prices. There is much that reminds one of the market model of socialism proposed by Oskar Lange. Only time will tell how significant the change will be. More likely than not, the final outcome will be somewhere in between the orthodox type of planning (described in Chapter 17) and the pure market model (described earlier in this chapter). More recent events make it all the more likely that the Lange model (except, perhaps for Yugoslavia) will remain a dream.

Economic Liberalization in Eclipse?

There can be no doubt that new approaches to planning and management are being explored throughout the Soviet-bloc economies. The general idea is to find a "proper" combination of central direction of the economy with increased responsibility at the level of the enterprise managers. The public discussion of the problems of central planners who wish to increase economic efficiency without losing their grip on the economy has been widespread and frank. This is certainly a great improvement over the days of Stalin, an era characterized by a general deep-freeze of tongues if not of thought. *So far,* however, despite widespread "reforms," the new has not gone far enough to justify any belief that economic efficiency is likely to be achieved soon.

From the beginning, Soviet-bloc leaders were extremely sensitive to critics who talked of "bourgeois degeneration" of their economies, as if guidance by prices and reliance on the profit motive would automatically mean restoration of capitalism. Any reforms were termed a "long-range, complicated political process," and often completion was not contemplated until the mid-1970's. Then came the 1968 invasion of Czechoslovakia. In its wake, Czech Deputy Premier Ota Sik, prime mover of Czechoslovakia's "new economic model," resigned. He had been most popular in the Dubcek era among "progressives." He had wanted to tap the dormant initiative and superior knowledge about local conditions of enterprise managers by helping them escape from petty bureaucratic tutelage. Like Oskar Lange, he had hoped to make price signals compelling incentives for producers, thereby eliminating the need for detailed central planning. To save the energies pouring into planning and supervising a plan centrally, he had hoped to make use of the invisible administrative apparatus of the price system. Like Adam Smith and Oskar Lange, he had been fully aware of the price system's incredible capacity to spread vital information and generate quick response to it.

He had also been aware how bureaucratic insistence by a central government on deciding about every nut and bolt would imply widespread inefficiency in resource use. So he had worked vigorously for a downgrading of the powers of central planners. If socialist business managers find it more advantageous to cooperate with West German firms, why should Prague bureaucrats insist that they trade with Poles? Maybe Czechoslovakia would be better off trading more with the West, he had argued. Thus, he had elevated economic over political considerations.

He even had argued that the basic economic reforms stood no chance of ultimate success unless they were coupled with a revamping of the *political* system. If individual managers are to have greater responsibilities, they must have an enlarged sphere of freedom in which to operate. The authoritarian government must yield power for others to use it. Inevitably this leads toward political democracy. The occupying powers, however, thought otherwise.

In successive statements, they made it clear that economic reforms must not be allowed to erode Soviet-bloc solidarity as against the outside world. Nor must they eliminate continued ultimate control over economic affairs by the central governments. Ota Sik, especially, came under heavy attack by the occupying powers. They charged him with counterrevolution, trying to "restore capitalism under the vulgar economic slogan of confrontation between the enterprises and the market." The Soviet radio station in Czechoslovakia characterized his ideas as "devilishly resembling the capitalist wolves' law of the free play of market forces." He was pictured as engaged in a variety of "intrigues" against the people, including sponsorship of unemployment, elimination of central planning and the state monopoly on foreign trade, and even of the teaching of a course on the principles of capitalism to high economic functionaries. All this was alleged to have created "chaos" in the economy. It was predicted that the Czech economic reforms would "certainly be renounced."

In fact, in the other East European countries, too, economic reforms were being slowed. Everywhere new restrictions were imposed on managers, not because of any quarrel with the logic of the reforms but for fear of their noneconomic consequences. Going over to market relations among enterprises was pictured as undermining the power base of the Communist party. Bulgaria again can be used as a typical case. According to decisions made in late 1968, planning was to be no longer "from the bottom up." It was to be conducted largely at higher levels. The number of centralized plan indicators was to be sharply increased.

Thus, it remains to be seen whether or to what extent the future economies of Eastern Europe will look like the socialist world envisaged by Oskar Lange. At this point, the ultimate scope of the reforms has again become vague, their implementation more than cautious. In the Soviet bloc, as in the "Western" world of capitalist nations, economic efficiency does not now prevail, except by accident. There seems to be very little that can be done about it in either place, given present institutional realities.

SUMMARY

1 In the Soviet economy, just as in the United States, economic efficiency is achieved only by chance. This is particularly obvious when considering the traditional type of planning. The physical portion of the input-output plan was and is determined by

planners in complete ignorance of such matters as the relative marginal costs of different producers.

2 The same holds true to the extent that decisions are made on the basis of prices. This is so because prices are not rational. Relative prices of goods, for instance, do not correctly reflect relative marginal costs. Thus, only by chance will specialization according to comparative advantage (as it *appears* to be on the basis of prices) lead to higher output from given resources (which depends on marginal costs).

3 Using the example of Soviet industrial wholesale prices, we see that their irrationality was owing to the use of (planned, adjusted) average rather than (actual) marginal cost and use of the Marxian definition of cost. Soviet resource prices were irrational, too, largely because some (those of capital and land) have been set at zero for ideological reasons. Making decisions on their basis did not assure economic efficiency.

4 Socialist theoreticians have long advocated establishment of a socialist regime that differs substantially from traditional Soviet-bloc practice. Theirs is a model of decentralized planning. Proposed by Oskar Lange in the 1930's, it was especially hailed as a scheme that could achieve economic efficiency. Present Soviet-bloc leaders have been toying with the idea of moving their economies in the very direction indicated by Lange. Therefore, study of his scheme is of utmost importance for understanding the present and future economic reforms in the Soviet bloc.

5 The Lange model is an imitation of perfect competition. Households sell labor for money income. They buy goods with it, exactly as they would under perfectly competitive capitalism, at prices they are *unable* to influence by individual action. Socialist enterprise managers buy resource services for money (from households in the case of labor, from the treasury or other firms in the case of capital and land). They sell goods for money. Again, each enterprise or industrial manager acts on the basis of prices he is *not allowed* to influence and he is to assume as constant. In particular, enterprise managers are enjoined to produce such that marginal costs equal output price and to buy inputs such that marginal revenue product equals resource price.

6 A central planning board determines the size of the production of social goods (government demand) and of capital goods (investment demand) by demanding the appropriate amounts from producers. The board also sets and continually adjusts all prices by a procedure of trial and error until supply equals demand in all markets. All households and firms must make decisions on the basis of such governmentally set prices.

7 Following the rules of behavior laid down for socialist enterprise and industrial managers, socialist firms will produce exactly the types of goods demanded by households individually or collectively via government. Equality of output price and marginal cost and equality of resource price and marginal revenue product will also assure economic efficiency.

8 In the Soviet bloc since Stalin's death, imperfections of the traditional planning methods and economic inefficiency resulting therefrom have been openly debated. Many reform proposals have been made, ranging from full-scale mathematical planning to patching up the existing system to decentralization.

9 The latter proposals are in fact being carried out. Most important are the Liberman proposals asking for greater powers of managers, fewer central directives, and more rational prices. According to Liberman, most of the traditional defects of central planning would be eliminated by instituting planning "from the bottom up," judging managers by profit as a percent of capital held, changing the bonus system, and making plans long term.

10   Since early 1964, experiments have been conducted in the U.S.S.R. with the Liberman-type of planning and managing. By September 1965, the Supreme Soviet had approved a major new law, destined to introduce the "new system of planning and management" in the entire economy. By the end of 1968, industrial enterprises producing about 77 percent of industrial output were in fact operating under the new system of decentralized planning.

11   In conjunction with the new model's introduction, by 1968, price reforms were being undertaken in the Soviet Union and other East European countries, all of which were in the process of adopting the new. At present, it is doubtful that these prices will be rational as in the Lange model. Thus, it seems that economic efficiency will still be left up to chance, even though some of the major defects of old-style planning may well be overcome. Even that, however, is uncertain after the invasion of Czechoslovakia and a subsequent slowdown in the reform movement. There is no well-coordinated transition to a clearly outlined new system.

TERMS[4]

new system of planning and management	rational prices
normative value of processing	social dividend

SYMBOLS

NVP

QUESTIONS FOR REVIEW AND DISCUSSION

1   The text says that economic efficiency may not prevail under Soviet material balance planning. Explain.

2   Describe how Soviet industrial wholesale prices were traditionally set.

3   Show how Soviet-bloc planners, deciding on production specialization on the basis of such wholesale prices, may make a major mistake and *increase* scarcity. Why did the last sentence say "*may*"?

4   Show how free international trade in the West may lead to specialization according to comparative disadvantage and thus increase scarcity. (Hint: reread the discussion in Chapter 21.)

5   Consider your answers to questions 3 and 4. Which is likely to be more inefficient economically, the Soviet-type or the U.S.-type economy?

---

[4] Terms and symbols are defined in the Glossary at the end of the book.

6   Explain why Marx refused to count interest and rent as part of "cost." Show why this helps make Soviet prices irrational, that is, leads probably to a misuse of resources when decisions are based on such prices.

7   What is *wrong* with charging no rent, even when all land is collectively owned and utilized?

8   "The profit and loss system could even be used in the socialist economy." Explain.

9   The reading introducing this chapter says "My party conscience does not allow me to vote for profit." Explain.

10   "Households in Lange's model, as in perfect competition, cannot influence prices by individual action, but all households acting together can." Explain. Refer to the goods market and to the resource market.

11   "A firm in Lange's model must *pretend* that it cannot influence (governmentally set) price, as if it operated in perfect competition. Yet, it may in fact have the power to influence price." Explain.

12   "The power referred to in question 11 may breed economic inefficiency as in imperfect competition under capitalism." Explain.

13   Describe the role of the central planning board in Lange's model.

14   Why does Oskar Lange argue that government must determine the volume of capital formation? Does the U.S. government do so?

15   "If reality corresponded to the Lange blueprint, economic efficiency would tend to prevail." Discuss.

16   Why might an NVP index of judging managers help to reduce their disloyalty?

17   Describe the Liberman proposals.

18   Describe the *new economic system of Soviet planning and management.*

19   Why are the Soviets "going slow" on economic reform?

20   "Even though they are far apart politically, the economic systems of the United States and the Soviet Union are converging." Discuss. (Evaluate such terms as *creeping socialism* and *creeping capitalism* in your answer.)

epilogue

This ends our discussion in Part 2 of the economically efficient use of resources. As we have seen, economic efficiency is achieved neither in the U.S.-type economy (because of inevitable market imperfections), nor in the Soviet-type economy (because of the inevitable imperfections of the central plan). One could undoubtedly show the same for the underdeveloped nations of the world.

The conclusions we must derive from these truths, furthermore, are less comfortable than the ones derived from our study of full employment in Part 1. Although the macroeconomic policy recommendations derived for the capitalist economy often seemed to contradict the maxims of private finance, the message then was loud and clear: we can do something about unemployment.

Here it is different. Unlike the great macroeconomic problem of unemployment, the microeconomic problems of economic inefficiency are less easily dealt with. The policy message derived from their study is muffled and unclear. In both the developed economies of the capitalist and of the socialist world, the cure of economic inefficiency involves bitter pills. In fact, the institutional restraints are so formidable in both places that ideal solutions are out of reach.

Moreover, the cost of economic inefficiency cannot be measured even roughly as the cost of unemployment might be. Thus, people at least in the past, have been much more easily aroused about unemployment and inflation than about questions of antitrust action, agricultural surpluses, free trade, or air pollution. As we shall point out in the last chapter of this book, however, this may well be different in the future. Increasingly, questions of microeconomics, of what exactly we are doing with our resources, rather than whether we are doing anything with them at all, are becoming our foremost national concerns.

For the present, who is economically more efficient, the Soviets or the Americans? No one can possibly tell. We can only guess. As we have noted, irrational prices exist in both places. On that account, instances of economic inefficiency may well occur there as here. But the Soviets have one additional problem. By insisting on guiding the economy through many centrally planned norms, they have failed to avail themselves of the enormous organizing power of the market, even if it is bound to be an imperfect one. In the United States, the market does a great deal of allocating of resources that is accomplished in extremely cumbersome ways in the Soviet Union. The central planning apparatus and its mistakes must be a costly undertaking in terms of resources. Add that on top of all the wrong decisions made on the basis of misleading prices at decentralized planning levels and the Soviet economy should probably get the lower grade. But this is a guess, even though most experts support it.

We turn now, in Part 3, once again to completely different matters. Even if we could have full and economically efficient use of resources, the challenge of scarcity would not yet be met. There are other things still that might be done to reduce scarcity further. These matters are usually grouped under the heading of economic growth.

543

In this part of the book we shall discuss how
scarcity may be challenged through policy measures
deliberately designed to *enlarge* a country's capacity
to produce and the use of that capacity, rather than
only by full and efficient use of a *given* capacity.
This has become a key issue throughout the world
since the end of World War II. In most countries, population
is growing. Therefore, the full and efficient
use of given resources alone may not always
be able to prevent a decline in the
portion of GNP available per person.
As an introduction, we turn to the problem of
economic growth in the United States, but as on
earlier occasions, much of what is being said here is
equally applicable to other advanced capitalist
economies. In a second chapter, we discuss the sources
and extent of economic growth in the Soviet Union and
the types of policies used to achieve it. The same
policies are being used in the other Soviet-type
economies in Eastern Europe. Finally, we note that most
people on earth are living in societies that differ
markedly from any described so far. Although they also
differ in many ways among themselves, they are united
under the same mantle of poverty. Their economies are
backward, their living levels extremely low when
compared with those of, say, the United States or
the Soviet Union. In this third chapter, we turn
to the major problem of economic development
faced by the majority of mankind.

economic

growth

Attaining the Projected Economic Growth Rate

The U.S. economy has a potential for a rate of economic growth of between 4 and 4½ percent per year between 1965 and 1975. This is between one-third and one-half above the rate prevailing in the first two-thirds of this century, and is substantially above the 3.5 percent prevailing over the 17 years from 1948 to 1965. This higher rate of growth will not be achieved automatically, but will require improvements and adjustments in economic policies, both public and private, if it is to be achieved in a manner that does not generate undesirable inflationary byproducts. . . .

It has been pointed out, moreover, that the pace of economic expansion during 1962–65 has been considerably above the rate of increase that this Nation has been able to sustain over an extended period in peacetime, at least in the past. . . .

As a result of fiscal and monetary policies, structural measures to combat unemployment and other public and private efforts, the overall growth rate of the national economy has been accelerated during the past 5 years and the unemployment rate has been reduced substantially. However, not until the recent Vietnam military buildup did the rate of unemployment come down to the Council of Economic Advisers' "interim" target of 4 percent of the civilian labor force. . . .

Inability during the 1970–75 time period to maintain the current, historically high rate of economic growth would result in a substantial rise in the unemployment rate, assuming other factors do not change significantly.

But, other factors will be changing significantly. The Nation's labor force is projected to grow more rapidly in the next decade than in the past 10 years. Productivity (as measured by output per man-hour) is estimated to continue increasing, as a result of the large-scale investments in human and physical resources—business plant and equipment purchases, research and development, education, training, and so forth.

The accelerated expansion in the Nation's potential productive capacity can be responded to in a number of ways, and it may be helpful to examine some of them.

One level of choice involved in achieving a high and rising level of economic activity is the selection of emphasis among the major sectors of the national economy. . .

The choice of sector emphasis also implies decisions as to (1) whether the economy will become more or less oriented to private versus public needs and desires; (2) whether the major national concern is with the acceleration of the rise in the standard of living or with the enhancement of the Nation's productive capacity; and hence (3) whether the main thrust of the economic policies are of a relatively shortrun or longrun nature.

Joint Economic Committee, 1966

24

economic

growth

in the

united states

I N THE PRECEDING parts of this book we have been preoccupied with getting the most out of *given* resources. We considered what must be done to assure their full and efficient utilization, to avoid eternal ups and downs of real GNP below the level that could potentially be produced. We paid no particular attention to what exactly the GNP consisted of, whether of privately bought consumer goods, privately acquired investment goods, or goods purchased with public funds for collective use. Yet, the present *composition* of total output, among other factors, may influence strongly the potential future *size* of total output, and thus indirectly our own and our children's potential well-being in years to come. The implications of this fact are the main issue of this chapter.

THE MEANING AND SIGNIFICANCE OF GROWTH

Economic growth can mean a variety of things. Consider once more Figure 5.3 THE HISTORY OF U.S. GNP. It showed the growth over time of U.S. real GNP, that is, of the output of commodities and services evaluated at constant prices. Presumably one could take some kind of long-run average of these observed movements of real GNP and take this as a measure of economic growth. Or one could instead consider the movement of potential real GNP, also shown in Figure 5.3. This truly illustrates what has happened to our productive capacity. If actual real GNP was below it, owing to unemployment and inefficiencies, that is another matter. Finally, we might divide actual data on real GNP by the size of the population, thus defining economic growth as the *actual rise in real GNP per head*. We shall follow the latter procedure. Thus, our question will be essentially this: what if anything can we do to raise real GNP per head?

An Illustration

Consider Table 24.1 RECENT GROWTH OF U.S. GNP AND ITS COMPONENTS. As the data of Table 24.1 show, for instance, U.S. real GNP rose by $36.6 billion from 1967 to 1968, or by 5.4 percent. Yet, population grew at the same time by 2.0 million, or 1.0 percent. Thus, the rise in real GNP *per head* was smaller, or 4.3 percent. This is the kind of figure to which we shall refer when discussing economic growth.

Growth vs. Welfare

When real GNP per head is rising, everyone can potentially become better off at the same time. But remember: This is not to say that everyone does in fact become better off. Although everyone could become better off so far as the availability to him of goods is concerned, the increased output may be unequally distributed. Some people may become much better off, and others stay equally well off or become even worse off. Similarly, even if everyone shared equally in increased real GNP per head, we might want to know what kinds of additional goods have become available. They may consist of privately purchased consumer goods, C (refrigerators, cars, and ballet performances), of privately purchased investment goods, I

Table 24.1   RECENT GROWTH OF U.S. GNP AND ITS COMPONENTS*

| | TOTAL (BILLIONS OF DOLLARS) | | | | PER HEAD (DOLLARS) | | | |
| | 1967 | 1968 | CHANGE | | 1967 | 1968 | CHANGE | |
			ABSOLUTE	PERCENT			ABSOLUTE	PERCENT
GNP	681.8	718.4	+36.6	+5.4	3,411	3,558	+147	+4.3
C	434.1	455.4	+21.3	+4.9	2,171	2,255	+ 84	+3.9
I	104.7	113.1	+ 8.4	+8.0	524	560	+ 36	+6.9
G	142.0	151.2	+ 9.2	+6.5	711	749	+ 38	+5.3

* Figures do not add to total because of neglect of foreign trade data. Based on seasonally adjusted fourth quarter data at annual rates.
C = consumer expenditures, I = investment expenditures, and
G = government expenditures on commodities and services.
These recent U.S. data (measured in 1958 prices) show the growth of GNP and most of its major components, both in the aggregate and per head of population. Source: U.S. Department of Commerce.

(machine tools, factory buildings, and piles of coal), or of publicly purchased goods, G (highways, schools, and services of astronauts). There can be little doubt that a $147 increase in real GNP per head means a different thing if it consists entirely of consumer goods rather than investment or public goods. Only if it consists of consumer goods would most people consider themselves "really" better off. If it consists of investment or public goods, however, many people would only feel vaguely better off, if at all. It is much more exciting and personally satisfying to have bought a new record player than to have bought fuel for one's place of business or a piece of U.S. highway in the state of Utah. In the example of Table 24.1, the average American's share of real GNP rose by $147 from 1967 to 1968, yet consumer goods available to the average American rose by only $84, investment goods rose by $36 and public goods rose by $38. And remember: what was true for the *average* American was not necessarily true for *every* American. Can you figure out what happened to your parents, for example? (Hint: look at their gross income and its disposition in 1967 and 1968.) Furthermore, the standard of living does not consist entirely of material goods. We would certainly agree that a constant real GNP per head with increased leisure for all is an improvement. And that a small rise in real GNP per head with a greatly increased workload on all is not. Thus, some people prefer to define economic growth as an increase in real GNP per man-hour worked. In any case, we cannot conclude that economic growth, as we have agreed to use the term, does necessarily represent an increase in welfare, although it may and actually often does.

The Impact of Growth

At the moment let us concentrate on how output per head can be raised over time. Because

$$\text{real GNP per head} = \frac{\text{total real GNP}}{\text{population}},$$

total real GNP must rise *relative to* population for growth to occur. This can be accomplished in a variety of ways. (1) We might concentrate on raising total real GNP while keeping population unchanged. (2) We might accept a natural rise in population as inevitable and concentrate on raising total real GNP faster. (3) We might try to reduce population while keeping total real GNP the same, or raising it, or preventing it from falling as fast as population.

Let us take the case most realistic for the United States. There is no concerted effort to influence the size of the population and population grows over time. Thus, our goal to raise GNP per head will be accomplished depending on how fast we can raise total real GNP. Table 24.2 THE MYSTERY OF COMPOUND INTEREST illustrates dramatically how the difference of a percentage point or two in total real GNP growth can make all the difference in the world in a relatively short time. Suppose a U.S. population of about 200 million people were to grow at a rate of 1 percent per year, while a real GNP of $700 billion grows at alternative higher percentages to assure a rise in real GNP per head. You can take any GNP figure in Table 24.2 and divide by projected population to see what would happen to real

Table 24.2   THE MYSTERY OF COMPOUND INTEREST

YEAR	POPULATION (MILLIONS)	2%	3%	4%	5%	6%	7%
				REAL GNP (BILLIONS OF 1958 DOLLARS) GROWING AT ANNUAL RATE OF			
1970	200	700	700	700	700	700	700
1990	244	1,040	1,264	1,534	1,857	2,245	2,708
2010	298	1,546	2,283	3,361	4,928	7,200	10,478
2030	363	2,302	4,124	7,364	13,078	23,106	40,540
2050	443	3,413	7,448	16,135	34,697	74,115	156,870
2070	541	5,072	13,454	35,350	92,061	237,731	606,900
2170	1,462	36,736	258,883	1,782,941	12,110,000	80,739,474	526,166,666
2270	3,954	266,126	4,985,166	89,970,588	1,592,684,211	27,420,909,089	456,166,666,620

Someone once called compound interest the eighth wonder of the world. Economists have become acutely aware of its properties when it comes to enhancing the national well-being. This table shows what happens to the size of real GNP if it can be made to grow at various alternative rates. It is assumed that population will grow at 1 percent a year. Divide any GNP figure by the same row's projected population, and you will see the impact of growth in terms of real GNP per head.

GNP per head. If total real GNP were to rise at 3 percent per year, real GNP per head would rise from

$$\frac{\$700 \text{ billion}}{200 \text{ million}} = \$3,500 \text{ in 1970 to}$$

$$\frac{\$2,283 \text{ billion}}{298 \text{ million}} = \$7,661 \text{ in 2010 to}$$

$$\frac{\$13,454 \text{ billion}}{541 \text{ million}} = \$24,869 \text{ in 2070}$$

(all in 1958 prices). Yet the figures would be $3,500 to $16,537 to $170,168 if real GNP would rise at 5 percent per year. And they would be $3,500 to $35,161 to $1,121,811 if it rose at 7 percent per year.

If we could manage an annual rise of total real GNP by 7 percent, 20 years from now, when most of us will still be alive, the average American could enjoy a real GNP of $11,098, or 3.2 times as many commodities and services as in 1970! In 100 years, as has just been shown, the average American would have a real GNP share of over $1 million *per year*, in 200 years of over $350 million, in 300 years of well over $100 billion, all in 1958 prices! This defies the imagination, but such is the cumulative effect of growth and one is tempted to shout, "By all means, let the economy grow as fast as possible."

INGREDIENTS FOR GROWTH

The enthusiasm engendered when playing with compound interest, however, is easily tempered by a sobering thought: Growth does not materialize from thin air. True enough, we may get a spurt of growth in any one year by putting unemployed resources to work and raising total GNP fast. But how can we get real GNP to grow after that, assuming we continue to assure full employment? As we saw in Chapter 1, the total volume of output is limited by the quantities and qualities of resources available and strongly affected also by the environment in which they are put to use. Hence, total full employment real GNP can be expected to grow only if we increase the quantities or qualities of resources or improve on the environment in which they are put to use. Let us look at these in turn.

Natural Resources

A country that is able to increase the quantities of land, water, minerals, and similar gifts of nature available to its economy is lucky indeed. This can be done in the literal sense of expanding the territory utilized by man or by making technical improvements within a given territory, thereby also expanding the effective natural resource base of the economy. Until recently, with its open frontier to the west, the United States made use of the former method, but it has certainly not neglected the latter. To give one example, the last 100 years have seen spectacular changes in the use of nature's energy sources, and we can expect similar drastic changes in the next century. Although other potential sources of energy besides muscle power have been available all along (even long before the Pilgrims landed on these shores), they were not used. It has been estimated[1] that 65 percent of all energy used in the American economy was human or animal power as late as 1850. By 1960, these two provided less than 2 percent of the total, 98.7 percent being inanimate power sources, such as water, petroleum, natural gas, and coal. The importance of petroleum and natural gas, furthermore, has steadily increased in the first half of this century, but we should not be surprised if solar power or nuclear energy replace them in turn during its remaining decades.

[1] J. F. Dewhurst and Associates, *America's Needs and Resources* (New York: Twentieth Century Fund, 1955).

Any such increase in natural resources will significantly influence the potential size of total real GNP.

Yet, it must be clear that *existing* resources must be diverted from other potential uses to acquire such *new* natural resources. Labor and equipment, which might have produced a thousand different kinds of consumer goods, for instance, had to be channeled into years of research and the building of roads, dams, power stations, oil refineries, and the like before petroleum could become the major economic resource it now is. To be sure, as Table 24.2 reminds us so vividly, a small increase in the growth rate of total real GNP may make it all worthwhile in the end. But how many existing resources shall we now divert to the task of enlarging the pool of resources and of eventually increasing real GNP per head?

Capital

The identical question has to be asked when it comes to capital formation, the production of new buildings, equipment, and inventories usable for further production. The more we have of these, the greater can our total real GNP be each year.

Yet the more we produce of them now, the fewer resources have we left now to produce other goods, such as for current consumption. Figure 24.1 THE U.S. INVESTMENT EFFORT gives us an idea of what kind of decision Americans have made on this matter over the last century. Data prior to 1929 are 5-year averages and much rougher estimates than those since then. Although the annual dollar volume of private domestic investment has risen greatly over the last century (it was 106.9 billion in 1968 at 1958 prices, less than 6 percent of this 100 years ago), percentagewise its importance seems to have declined. From the end of the Civil War to World War I, Americans voluntarily took one quarter or more of their real GNP in the form of private domestic investment. The percentage was still above 20 until the onset of the Great Depression wherein it reached a low of 3.3 in 1932. During World War II, when the pressure was on to make goods for military consumption, capital formation dropped again to 3.8 percent of output in 1943. Since World War II it has clearly been close to about 15 percent of real GNP. Over the long haul, Americans seem to have been increasingly reluctant to devote as large a share of real GNP as in the past to the production of capital goods and thus to future growth of real GNP. We must realize, furthermore, that in the United States a significant percentage of annual investment only goes to *replace* the capital used up during the year in question and thus does not increase the size of the capital stock at all.

Nevertheless, to the extent that replacement of worn-out capital is made with new capital of a different technological character, even an "unchanged" capital stock may become more productive over time. In any case, the absolute size of the American capital stock is staggering (and some of it, such as highways, school buildings, and airports, is being created by public expenditures, excluded from Figure 24.1). In 1958, the total equaled $863 billion (in 1947–1949 prices). This was four times the capital stock at the turn of the century (see Table 24.3) and amounted to $20,000 per family. In addition to these man-made productive inputs, Americans held a total of $160 billion of consumer durables, such as automobiles and furniture.

Figure 24.1   THE U.S. INVESTMENT EFFORT

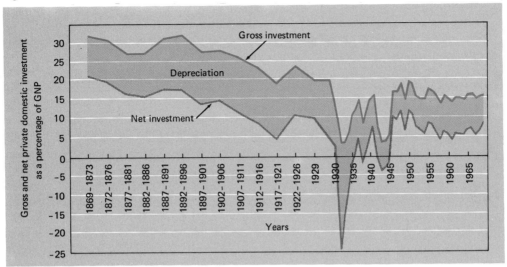

The percentage of GNP devoted by Americans to private domestic capital formation (top line) has varied greatly during the last 100 years. Notice the particularly small production of buildings, equipment and inventories during the Great Depression and World War II. Every year, a significant portion of the new capital produced, however, just offsets the annual wear and tear (shaded here) of the old capital stock. Deducting this depreciation from the gross addition to buildings, equipment, and inventories, we get net private domestic investment. This is the amount by which the privately owned capital stock actually changed. It is shown here also as a percentage of GNP. Note that gross investment in the Great Depression and during World War II was so small that it did not even offset depreciation. Thus, the actual private capital stock declined, in 1932 alone, by an amount almost equal to a quarter of the GNP. The percentages here are based on data in 1958 prices. Source: U.S. Department of Commerce.

Table 24.3   THE U.S. CAPITAL STOCK (BILLIONS OF 1947–1949 DOLLARS)

	1900	1925	1958
Buildings			
governmental	11.3	40.7	122.0
residential	78.2	177.5	288.4
farm	14.9	26.8	28.2
all others	56.3	113.8	154.2
Producers equipment	19.4	49.9	137.3
Inventories			
governmental	2.2	7.9	31.6
farm	18.5	20.1	25.5
all others	14.3	40.2	75.4
Total	215.1	476.9	862.6

Source: U.S. Department of Commerce.

Labor

Just as the increased availability of natural and capital resources can promote the growth of total real GNP, so can an increase in the labor force. Take another look at Figure 3.1 POPULATION, LABOR FORCE, AND UNEMPLOYMENT. The American labor force has indeed increased steadily during this century in conjunction with immigration and the natural growth of population. Moreover, although the work week has been halved since the turn of the century, total man-hours worked have increased together with more leisure per person. This has undoubtedly contributed to the observed growth of total real GNP. In principle, however, this must not necessarily produce economic growth as we have chosen to define it. If the increase in hours worked which raises GNP is brought about through the rise of population, both the numerator and the denominator in the fraction

$$\frac{\text{total real GNP}}{\text{population}} = \text{real GNP per head}$$

are being raised and the end result is uncertain. Only if real GNP rises faster than population (as has happened historically in the United States) will real GNP per head increase. Thus, any deliberate policy to promote economic growth through population increase (as was attempted by Hitler and Mussolini) may well be self-defeating. If real GNP rises less than population, it leads to more people being more miserable than before.

Education and Health

If we are interested in promoting economic growth, it would be much safer to concentrate on improving the *quality* of a given labor force, especially in the fields of health and education. To do this, however, again resources must be diverted from other uses for this purpose, just as for the acquisition of new natural resources and new capital goods. Historically, this has also happened increasingly in the United States. Just take a look at what has happened in education.

Gone are days when people were happy when they could just barely read, write, and do arithmetic. As late as 1870, only 57 percent of those aged 5 to 17 went to school, only 2 percent graduated from high school, and 20 percent of the American adult population was illiterate. In 1966, 95 percent of the age group 5 to 17 went to school. The high school graduates of 1967 constituted 72 percent of the group that had entered fifth grade together, and 55 percent of these graduates, or 40 percent of the original group, entered college. About 2 percent of the adult population was illiterate. Total expenditures on elementary and secondary schools alone have risen from $63.4 million in 1870 to $29.9 billion in 1966. In 1966, spending on institutions of higher learning added another $14.9 billion to the total. Even when corrected for price changes, a significant increase in total and per capita educational services remains. A similar picture emerges when studying the provision of health services to Americans.

There can be no doubt that education of the labor force adds greatly to the potential total real GNP. In a real sense, the trained human brain is the scarcest of all resources. Before we ran out of food, it discovered fertilizers, hormones, high yield crops and invented wonders of agricultural machinery, raising incredibly the yield per acre of land. Before we run out of conventional fuel, it will probably discover how to use nuclear and solar power on a large scale. Spending on education pays for itself over and over again in terms of increased real GNP.

This is also true in the monetary sense for the individual concerned. Taking American males, 25 years of age and over, the following held for 1966: Those having completed less than 8 years of school had an average annual income of $3,520. With 8 years completed, the average was $4,867; with 1 to 3 years of high school, $6,294, with 4 years of high school, $7,494; with 1 to 3 years of college, $8,783; and with 4 or more years of college, $11,739. Thus, someone dropping out of high school rather than completing college easily loses a quarter of a million dollars in lifetime income.

Technology

Not only can we devote resources to increasing the sheer quantities of natural, capital, and labor resources. We have just seen how qualitative improvement of labor may be just as important. This is similarly true for natural and capital resources and the very process in which they are used. This source of GNP growth comes from the systematic enlargement of the existing stock of knowledge. It is important here to stress the word "systematic," for this has become increasingly important during this century. Many of the great inventions and innovations of the past were the result of hard work by gifted individuals who, driven by curiosity, worked with little assistance and few resources. One thinks of the invention of the incandescent light bulb, the reaper, the telegraph, to name just a few. Yet, technological advance today can hardly be described accurately as the random results of efforts by a few independent tinkerers. It is better seen as a society-wide effort supported by fantastically expensive facilities and the high general level of education referred to above. The first industrial research laboratory in the United States was established, for example, as late as 1876 by Thomas Edison. In 1960, there were over 5,400 such laboratories. It may be useful to consider a number of stages leading to the discovery and use of new knowledge in the productive process.

basic research   Technological change first of all involves, in a stage far removed from production, *basic research*; that is, scientific inquiry not particularly directed toward any specific "useful" discovery. Biologists may want to know why cells proliferate. Chemists may study the property of fluids, and physicists, the laws of motion. Such pure scientific inquiry is carried on for its own sake, to enhance understanding, not necessarily with any application in mind.

Although science is in many ways a supranational phenomenon (its discoveries are frequently available to all), the performance of a given society in this field depends on many factors, such as a scientific tradition attracting people into scientific careers, the society's attitude toward free inquiry, experimentation, and testing of hypotheses, and the existence of research centers. In many capitalist countries, basic research often gets slighted unless government intervenes. It is apt to be very expensive. Its results are unpredictable. Its commercial profitability is low, because, characteristically, the benefits accrue to a large segment of the economy and not simply to the one undertaking such research. As a result, such research is carried on by universities and then often as a sideline to teaching. But one could clearly encourage such activity by the establishment or subsidization of research institutions. The U.S. government has in fact done just this, as we shall see below.

applied research   A further step in technological change is *applied research*, or the application to a particular problem of the knowledge gained in basic research. Basic research may have established general principles in such areas as physics, chemistry, or biology. It has to be followed by a long process of experimentation to gain the empirical knowledge required for practical application. Think of the application of physical principles to the design of electronic computers, electric power stations run by solar energy, ships propelled by nuclear energy, and communications via artificial satellites. Think of the application of chemical principles to the creation of new drugs or fertilizers. Think of the application of biological principles to the creation of specified varieties of plants and animals or the production of food from sea water or medical techniques inhibiting the growth of undesirable cells. Thus, applied research is distinguished from basic research essentially through the motivation of the researcher. Applied research, unlike basic research, is expected to have a payoff relatively soon.

product development   Finally, we move, so to speak, from the laboratory and drawing board to the factory bench, to *product development*. Here, at the level of the firm, the new is experimented with and actually adopted. Research findings are reduced to practice, are translated into new products, new qualities of old products, the use of new materials, new machines, new forms of organization. This is the kind of activity in which American business has long excelled. In 1960, for instance, 10 percent of sales of U.S. manufacturing firms were of products developed since 1956. Only 5 years earlier, they had not existed at all!

The development of a new product is a well-defined goal, its costs and benefits can be reasonably well foreseen. It is in this field that competition (even if not of the perfect variety) does much to promote progress. It is this kind of innovating activity by large, imperfectly competitive firms that is seen by some as so conducive to economic growth that all the economic inefficiency (discussed in Part 2 above) can be forgiven (see also our discussion at the close of Chapter 22).

Environmental Factors

Other factors, however immeasurable they may be, must certainly also contribute to growth of real GNP. The social-political climate in the United States is favorable to the pursuit of material rewards. Although there are exceptions (and we shall discuss them in Part 4), more often than not individual initiative and effort is correspondingly rewarded. Risk-taking by those who wish to venture into business is looked on with approval rather than discouraged. Government is stable. It can be relied on to protect property rights and to uphold the sanctity of contracts. Financial institutions are widely developed. There are at least no political barriers to the mobility of goods and resources over a large territory, making many markets potentially very large. Thus, the American labor force has become extremely adaptable to changes in the economy. American workers in large numbers move across the continent when changing conditions of demand or technology demand it. Similarly, American businesses have taken advantage of the technical possibilities offered by a large and unrestricted internal market. Such markets, as we saw earlier, enable them to be extremely efficient *technically*. Complex production processes can be divided into a series of simpler ones, the use of specialized equipment becomes possible at each stage, and the resultant "economies of scale" can be reaped. Cost per unit of product drops in mass production.

Thus, the scale of the national market alone can contribute to the size of GNP. If workers could not move beyond the boundaries of their states, the North American labor force undoubtedly would be allocated in an economically less efficient way and be much less productive than now. Workers in Massachusetts would be trying to produce steel and corn, though they could produce much more of each in Pennsylvania or Iowa, where the required natural resources are more abundant or more easily accessible. If firms could not hope to sell beyond the boundaries of their states, they could not be large enough to engage in mass production. As each state tried to produce its own cars, the quantities of resources needed per car would be higher everywhere than if production were arranged in fewer centers in technically more efficient ways.

THE U.S. RECORD

The distinction made so far about increases in real GNP caused by a variety of *separate* factors is somewhat artificial, however. It was used only for expository purposes. In reality, all these elements enter into the process of growth simultaneously and the sharp dividing lines become inevitably blurred. Technical progress, for instance, is impossible without widespread education. One cannot have scientific research without people trained in its techniques. One cannot have innovational activity in firms without people with enough knowledge, perseverance, and ingenuity to implement new ideas. One cannot do without large numbers of intelligent and trained production workers capable of using and perfecting the new. Nor can one have technical progress without embodying it through investment in new types of capital goods.

Past Sources of Growth

A recent study tried to separate out the various elements responsible for the American record of real GNP growth during this century. The data are reproduced in Table 24.4 THE SOURCES OF THE U.S. GROWTH OF REAL GNP.

Table 24.4   THE SOURCES OF THE U.S. GROWTH OF REAL GNP

	1909–1929 (PERCENT)	1929–1957 (PERCENT)
Increased quantity of labor	39	27
Increased quantity of capital	26	15
Increased education	13	27
Improved technology	12	20
Others	10	11

Source: E. Denison, The Sources of Economic Growth in the U.S. *(CED, 1962).*

They suggest that for the period 1909 to 1929, 65 percent of the increase of real GNP can be explained by additions during this time of sheer quantities of labor and capital. From 1929 to 1957, however, only 42 percent of the growth of real GNP can be thusly explained. Why did real GNP grow so much faster than increased *quantities* of resources would lead us to expect? From 1909 to 1929, why did every 6.5 percent increase in labor and capital lead to a 10 percent increase in output? From 1929 to 1957, why did every 4.2 percent increase in labor and capital lead to a 10 percent increase in output? Denison suggests the answer lies in *qualitative* changes, which, as a matter of fact, were more important in the later than in the former period. From 1909 to 1929 or 1929 to 1957, improved education and technical knowledge had the same effect on output as if the quantities of labor and capital inputs had been raised sufficiently (above what their actual increase was) to produce 25 or 47 percent, respectively, of the observed rise in output. Finally, such environmental factors as the growth of market size, allowing, for instance, a technically more efficient use of given resources owing to better means of transportation and communication, were found to explain about 10 percent of the observed increase in output.

U.S. Growth In Perspective

The rise in total real GNP produced by these factors, combined with the rise in population, produced during this century the kind of economic growth pictured by Figure 24.2 THE U.S. GROWTH RECORD. This U.S. record of economic growth has by no means been a smooth one.

From one year to the next, per capita real GNP has done everything from falling by 15 percent (in 1932) to rising by 15 percent (in 1941). Over the long haul, however, the record has been a pleasing one, showing from 1900 to 1968 an average annual rate of growth of about 3.5 percent. This has produced one of the highest standards of living in the world today with a real GNP per head of about $3,600 in 1968 and consumption per head of $2,255 (at 1958 prices). At present, Americans comprise 6 percent of the world's population; they produce a third of the world's total real GNP.

The U.S. record of economic growth is even more remarkable when viewed in proper perspective. Most of mankind's history is characterized by the very *absence* of economic

Figure 24.2   THE U.S. GROWTH RECORD

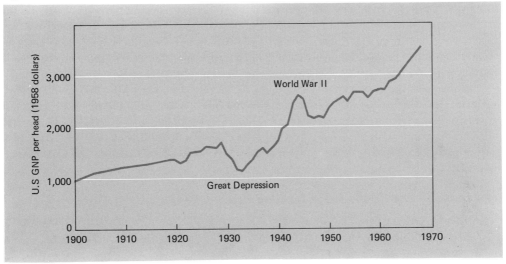

The U.S. record of economic growth (real GNP per head) is shown here since 1900. During this period, real GNP per person has more than tripled. But be careful: consumer goods received per head is only a portion of real GNP per head, and even then what is true for the average American is not true for every American. Source: U.S. Department of Commerce.

growth. In many countries, most of the time all of the existing resources had to be devoted to providing sufficient consumer goods barely to sustain life or just to replace whatever small quantities of capital goods were available. The increased requirements of consumer goods production owing to steadily increasing populations could defeat any attempt at economic growth. Take a history book and read about life even in the United States only 150 years ago. Poverty was perfectly normal. People lived simple lives, mostly on farms, laboriously producing the small quantities of goods they did manage to produce. Hardly anyone wore fancy clothes, ate a great variety of food, and was surrounded by beautiful furnishings. People had shorter lives, more work, more sickness and pain, and hardly anyone had hospital care. Naturally, no one had cars and television sets, and very few had annual vacation trips. If you compare your life with that of even the richest around 1800, you will realize what a wealth of material comforts you have of which our ancestors could only dream.

the Malthusian doctrine   In fact, many people firmly believed that mankind was doomed to misery. Take the dismal theory of Thomas R. Malthus. As he saw it in 1798, population had a "natural tendency" to double every generation (and this only requires each woman to bear two girls surviving to adulthood). Thus, population would grow as the series 1 2 4 8–16–32–64–and so on. Food supply, however, argued Malthus, could not be expected to grow as fast. Because there were no resources left over to produce significant amounts of capital goods or to promote education or technical improvements, more and more labor would essentially be applied to a fixed amount of natural resources. The result: diminishing returns (see also pages 409–412). Food output may grow, but by less and less for equal additions of labor, possibly like 1—2—3—4—5—6—7— and so on. Unless people practice "moral restraint," argued Malthus, their numbers will be cut down by famine, disease, and war, as the food available per man successively declines, eventually to and below the level required for physical subsistence. Luckily, for the United States at least, this dire prediction has not been realized. Again and again, massive increases in the capital stock, improvements in the quality of labor, and above all unprecedented technological advance have kept the Malthusian devil in check, allowing food supply to increase faster than population and in fact freeing great quantities of resources for use elsewhere. These forces are also our hope for the future.

Future Prospects

Yet, there is no assurance that the U.S. superiority *relative* to the rest of the world is assured for all ages. In recent years, the rates of economic growth of some countries (such as Italy, Japan, and West Germany) were larger than that of the United States. As Table 24.2 THE MYSTERY OF COMPOUND INTEREST reminds us, small differences in growth rates can quickly translate themselves into large differences in potential living standards. If the U.S. real GNP grows at 3 percent per year (and the population at 1 percent), the real GNP per head will reach about $25,000 in 100 years (at 1958 prices). If another country's real GNP were now half that of the United States, but growing at 6 percent (with populations equal and growing equally), its real GNP per head would reach $219,714 in 100 years (at 1958 prices). It would then be almost nine times as large as that of the United States. Thus, not only the future relative well-being of Americans, but also the American strength as a political power, can be decisively influenced by what may now look like a negligible difference in dynamic economic performance.

THE CASE FOR GOVERNMENTAL POLICY

To any individual, whose life is limited to a few decades, present differences in dynamic economic performance among economies will make little difference. He is likely to be interested in momentary gratification. Some people argue: "Whatever individuals as a group (through innumerable individual decisions) decide to sacrifice of potential current consumption, that is the sacrifice that should be made. This determines the correct rate of economic growth." Others object. "Individuals," they say, "do not realize what consequences follow from the sum of their individual decisions. The decision as to the proper rate of economic growth must be made collectively through government, which has the responsibility to plan for generations to come. Personal wants will have to be sacrificed to the aspirations of the nation as a whole."

You will recall from our discussion on page 528 that socialists have long made the identical argument. This argument can best be discussed by considering a country's production possibilities in any one year.

A Nation's Production Possibilities

In any one year, any country is faced with a great variety of choice as to the potential use of its resources. Let us consider the hypothetical major divisions of its GNP into private consumer goods, private capital goods, and public goods. These are the divisions symbolized by C, I, and G in our GNP accounts. Theoretically, the country could use all its resources to produce nothing but goods for private consumption: food, clothing, washing machines, and vacation trips. Suppose it did just that. By using all its resources fully, and by using them in economically and technically efficient ways, the country may be able to produce a maximum of $800 billion of consumer goods. Naturally, it then would produce no private investment and no public goods at all. There would be no new factories, machines, hospitals, schools, or roads.

Now consider something else. Suppose we sacrificed $200 billion of these potential consumer goods. Suppose we just produced $600 billion of them. This would imply that a certain percentage of our resources are freed for other purposes. Because using all our resources for consumer goods allowed us to produce $800 billion of them, making only $600 billion of such goods implies using less than all of our resources. Suppose we put those resources to work making private investment and public goods. We may be able to produce $320 billion of private investment and public goods. Thus, we have our first two production alternatives. Either we can produce $800 billion of consumer goods and no private investment and public goods at all or we can produce $600 billion of consumer goods and, in addition, $320 billion of private investment and public goods.

We might look at other possibilities. Suppose we sacrifice another $200 billion of potential consumer goods, producing only a total of $400 billion of them. This frees additional resources for other uses. We may now be able to produce, say, $560 billion of private investment and public goods. The combination of $400 billion of consumer goods and $560 billion of private investment and public goods is a third alternative.

There will be countless others. If we produce only $200 billion of consumer goods, we may be able to produce a total of $720 billion of private investment and public goods. If we produce no consumer goods at all, we may be able to produce a maximum of $800 billion of private investment and public goods.

Such production possibilities are summarized in Table 24.5 AN ORIGINAL PRODUCTION POSSIBILITIES SCHEDULE. A country must choose each year which of these combinations of goods, or of others not shown in the table, it actually wants to produce.

The Consequences of Choice

Does it matter which of these combinations are chosen? Of course, it does. Suppose a country chooses combination a, producing consumer goods only. For a short while, people will be able to "live it up." No other alternative offers them so many consumer goods.

Table 24.5   AN ORIGINAL PRODUCTION POSSIBILITIES SCHEDULE

ALTERNATIVE COMBINATIONS	QUANTITIES PRODUCIBLE PER YEAR BY FULLY AND EFFICIENTLY USING GIVEN RESOURCES (BILLIONS OF DOLLARS)	
	CONSUMER GOODS	INVESTMENT AND PUBLIC GOODS
a	800	0
b	600	320
c	400	560
d	200	720
e	0	800

An economy's production possibilities schedule shows alternative combinations of two groups of goods that can be produced in a given period with present technical knowledge by fully and efficiently using given resources.

People would eat well, wear beautiful clothes, fill their houses with gadgets. Yet, as their numbers grew from one year to the next, they would find that the goods available to each would become fewer. When $800 billion of consumer goods are shared by 200 million people, each can enjoy $4,000 of them. When, a few years later, $800 billion of consumer goods have to be shared by 210 million people, each can have only $3,810 of them. Living levels will decline!

Nor is this the whole problem. As the country fails to produce anything but consumer goods year after year, unless it exports some of them in exchange for investment and public goods, its capacity to produce will actually *shrink*. Buildings and machines will wear out. Roads will fall into disrepair. So will bridges and harbors, hospitals and schools. In fact, unless there are private efforts, a whole new generation will grow up without any education. It would not even know how to handle the remaining capital stock. Before long, the nation's production alternatives may be those pictured in Table 24.6 A SHRUNKEN PRODUCTION POSSIBILITIES SCHEDULE. There being less capital, a labor force of lower quality in education as well as health, and no technological change, the country will be only able to produce less of everything. After a while, even if it continues to devote all its resources to consumer goods production, it can make only $400 billion of them. Divide that by a higher population figure of, say, 210 million, and annual per capita consumption is seen to have dropped from the earlier high of $4,000 to $1,905. Thus, the first alternative depicted by Table 24.5 AN ORIGINAL PRODUCTION POSSIBILITIES SCHEDULE is a sure road to disaster.

By the same token, the other extreme, of producing only private investment and public goods (Table 24.5, alternative e) is also untenable. Unless some of these goods are exported in exchange for consumer goods, the population would literally starve to death in the midst of a growing productive capacity.

The less extreme alternatives (b through d of Table 24.5) will be better in the long run.

Take combination b of Table 24.5 AN ORIGINAL PRODUCTION POSSIBILITIES SCHEDULE. If the country produces annually $600 billion of consumer goods and $320 billion of investment and public goods, it may just maintain its present productive capacity. The annual increase of $320 billion of private investment and public goods may just replace whatever private and public capital wears out. The annual output of public schools and hospitals may just maintain a labor force of constant skill and health. As a result, each year the country may be faced again with the production possibilities shown by Table 24.5. Yet this may not be good enough. As long as there are 200 million people, they can each on the average have $3,000 of consumer goods annually. But levels of living will never rise. They may even fall, if population rises.

Thus, a country that desires economic growth will have to choose a combination such as c or d on its production possibilities schedule. By sacrificing even more of present consumer goods, the country can produce even more private investment and public goods. This will enable it to increase its stock of private and public capital over time or to increase the quality of its labor force or to accelerate the creation and use of new technical knowledge. Then, it may be able to raise its productive capacity and its output more than population. Living levels will rise over time. Table 24.7 AN EXPANDED PRODUCTION POSSIBILITIES SCHEDULE illustrates what may happen. A country that chooses combination c of Table 24.5 in one year, will end up with the enlarged menu of choice shown in Table 24.7 in another year. Suppose its population has risen in the meantime from 200 to 210 million people. If it continues to choose combination c, the average consumer will continually become better off. Sharing $400 billion of consumer goods among 200 million people yielded $2,000 worth for each. Sharing $440 billion among 210 million yields $2,095 for each.

Naturally, a greater sacrifice earlier would yield an even greater return now. People could have originally produced $200 billion of consumer goods only and $720 billion of in-

Table 24.6   A SHRUNKEN PRODUCTION POSSIBILITIES SCHEDULE

ALTERNATIVE COMBINATIONS	QUANTITIES PRODUCIBLE PER YEAR BY FULLY AND EFFICIENTLY USING GIVEN RESOURCES (BILLIONS OF DOLLARS)	
	CONSUMER GOODS	INVESTMENT AND PUBLIC GOODS
a	400	0
b	300	160
c	200	280
d	100	360
e	0	400

A country's production possibilities schedule can fall over time. Failure to produce investment and public goods (choosing combination a in Table 24.5) will eventually reduce a country's range of choice. Each entry in this table is lower than the corresponding one in Table 24.5 because the country now has fewer or lower-quality resources.

Table 24.7   AN EXPANDED PRODUCTION POSSIBILITIES SCHEDULE

ALTERNATIVE COMBINATIONS	QUANTITIES PRODUCIBLE PER YEAR BY FULLY AND EFFICIENTLY USING GIVEN RESOURCES (BILLIONS OF DOLLARS)	
	CONSUMER GOODS	INVESTMENT AND PUBLIC GOODS
a	880	0
b	660	352
c	440	616
d	220	792
e	0	880

A country's production possibilities schedule can rise over time. Producing more private investment and public goods than are wearing out each year (choosing combination c in Table 24.5) will enlarge a country's range of choice. Each entry in this table is higher than the corresponding one in Table 24.5 because the country now has more and higher quality resources as well as improved technical knowledge.

vestment and public goods (Table 24.5, combination d). In later years, their production possibilities would have been wider still than is shown in Table 24.7. The capital stock, private and public, would have grown faster. Education would have been more widespread still, and technical change more rapid. All the entries of Table 24.7 would have been larger. Choosing combination d over c might have yielded $233 billion instead of $220 billion of consumer goods (as well as $840 billion instead of $792 billion of other goods). Per capita consumption would have risen from $1,000 to $1,110 per year.

True enough, in the short run, consumers would be worse off. They would consume $1,000 rather than $2,000 in one year. They would consume $1,110 rather than $2,095 in the next. But the *rate* of improvement would be larger: 11 percent rather than 4.8 percent. And, eventually, the greater sacrifice that yields the greater rate of improvement would yield absolutely higher levels of living. No matter how many more dollars worth of goods you consume this year than I do, if you get 4.8 percent more each year, while I get 11 percent more, eventually I will be the richer.

Increasing Marginal Costs

Does the above mean that it is best to restrict current consumption as much as possible? There is no obvious answer to this question. Each society has to decide for itself. One thing certainly is clear: no society, in the absence of foreign trade, can ever choose a combination of output such as e in Table 24.5. But a society could restrict its consumption to the bare physiological minimum. It could produce nothing but bare necessities for households, using all other resources for the production of private investment and public goods. Nothing could produce faster economic growth for this country. Eventually, in 50 or 100 years, that society may well be able to consume more than any other in the world. Certainly, it will be able to consume more than it would have been able to had it pursued any other policy.

Each society must somehow decide whether it is worthwhile to make such current sacrifices for future bliss. It must note, furthermore, that there may well be diminishing returns to such sacrifices. Consider once more Table 24.5. Going successively from combination a to b to c and so on, consumption is always decreased by $200 billion. Yet, the gain in private investment and public goods purchased by that sacrifice becomes smaller and smaller. At first, $200 billion of consumer goods sacrificed yield $320 billion of other goods. Then another $200 billion of consumer goods given up (moving from combination b to c) yields only $240 billion of private investment and public goods ($560 billion minus $320 billion). Thereafter, the gains in private investment and public goods drop further to $160 billion ($720 billion minus $560 billion) and $80 billion ($800 billion minus $720 billion). Thus, we might say that the "marginal cost" of private investment and public goods in terms of consumer goods forgone is increasing the more we produce of the former. At first (moving from alternative a to b) $320 billion of private investment and public goods "cost" us $200 billion of consumer goods. If we want the former, we cannot have the latter. Each $1 billion of the former cost us $625 million of the latter (dividing $200 billion by $320 billion yields .625). Eventually (moving from alternative d to e), $80 billion of private investment and public goods still cost us $200 billion of consumer goods. Thus, each $1 billion of the former costs $2.5 billion of the latter.

The common sense of this is quite easily perceived. Even if all our resources were usable in the production of all types of goods, they may not be equally good at everything. Resources are not of uniform quality. Picture a country in the hypothetical state in which it only produces consumer goods. Clearly, there will be all kinds of resources now making butter and clothing and cameras that would be much better suited to making machine tools and railroad freight cars and highway bridges. Thus, we can first transfer those resources least suited for consumer goods production out of consumer goods production. This production will fall by, say, $200 billion. These very resources, best at making private investment and public goods, may then produce $320 billion of them. The man who awkwardly put together cameras and clothing excells at designing highway bridges. The machine that helped only slightly in building washing machines will hardly be missed, but it may be very productive in making other machines.

Now imagine that we continue on this path. Let us make fewer consumer goods still and more of other goods, Things are different now. We have to take resources that are pretty good in either field of production. Thus, for any given fall in consumer goods production, the production of other goods rises by less than before. What is the same thing, any given rise in the production of private investment and public goods will now entail a greater sacrifice of consumer goods.

Eventually, only the resources best suited to consumer goods production will be left in this field. Taking them out to make private investment and public goods will cost us plenty in consumer goods forgone, but will yield only little in private investment and public goods. In Table 24.5, only $80 billion of the latter can be had for sacrificing the last $200 billion of the former. At this point, the men and machines superb at making butter, clothing, and cameras are being awkwardly put to work to making machine tools and railroad freight cars and high-way bridges.

Thus, we can summarize in this way: a country can enlarge its production possibilities by sacrificing sufficient quantities of present consumption in favor of private investment and public goods. This will yield higher production possibilities later on. Indeed, it will yield opportunities otherwise unattainable. The costs of those future benefits, however, are likely to be the larger the more the composition of GNP has already been shifted away from consumption. That is, the greater the sacrifice of consumption already made, the less will an equal further sacrifice add to the rate of growth. Nevertheless, one can make a clear case for governmental policy to encourage economic growth. Although growth does not come without cost, eventually economic growth will enable a country to have more of all types of goods than would have been otherwise possible.

A Graphic Exposition

The above arguments can be brought out clearly with the help of a graphic device, the *production possibilities curve*. Figure 24.3 shows hypothetical production possibilities for the U.S. economy, considering only the major division of real GNP into consumer goods, on the

Figure 24.3   THE PRODUCTION POSSIBILITIES CURVE

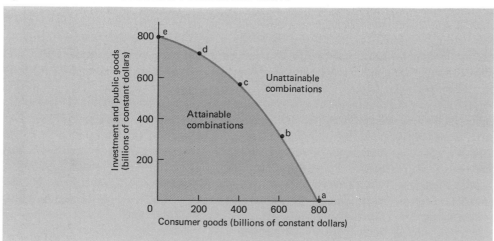

The production possibilities curve is a graph of a production possibilities schedule. By using its resources fully and efficiently, a country can produce with present technology any one of the output combinations shown by the curve. Failure to use resources fully and efficiently would amount to producing a combination to the left and below the curve. All output combinations to the right and above the curve are unattainable at present. Once on the curve, a country can produce more private investment and public goods only by sacrificing consumer goods (moving from a toward e). The concave curvature suggests that equal sacrifices of the latter will bring smaller and smaller increases of the former.

one hand, and all other goods, notably private investment and public goods, on the other. The curved line would give us, for instance, all alternative combinations of consumer goods and investment plus public goods that the U.S. economy is capable of producing in a given year by fully and efficiently using all its resources given present technical know-how.

In fact, Figure 24.3 THE PRODUCTION POSSIBILITIES CURVE is a graph of Table 24.5 AN ORIGINAL PRODUCTION POSSIBILITIES SCHEDULE.

Now suppose, as suggested earlier, we actually had full and efficient employment, that is, were *on* the curve rather than below it. Suppose we did produce combination a, $800 billion of consumer goods and no other goods at all. This would maximize present well-being. The average person in a 200 million population would have $4,000 of goods. Yet, as we saw, the day of reckoning would come. The country's production possibilities frontier would shrink toward the left. This is illustrated in Figure 24.4 HOW PRODUCTION POSSIBILITIES CAN SHRINK. It is a graph of Table 24.6 A SHRUNKEN PRODUCTION POSSIBILITIES SCHEDULE. Figure 24.3 THE PRODUCTION POSSIBILITIES CURVE is redrawn as the broken line for comparison.

Figure 24.4   HOW PRODUCTION POSSIBILITIES CAN SHRINK

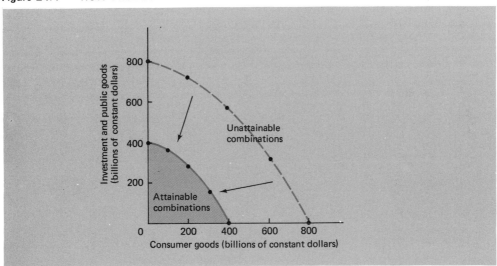

Failure to produce private investment and public goods will reduce a country's range of choice. Previously attainable output combinations will become unattainable as the decrease in the quantities and quality of resources shifts the production possibilities curve to the left.

Again, consider the alternatives suggested earlier. If we produce at point b of Figure 24.3, our production possibilities curve may remain exactly in the position illustrated there. Although we only get $600 billion of consumer goods each year, the $320 billion of investment and public goods produced at least prevent a decline in our productive capacity.

On the other hand, if we make greater current sacrifices, producing combination c or d of Figure 24.3, our fortunes will improve over time. The private production of new capital goods, plus certain governmental expenditures (such as for education, research and development, and public capital goods), together with a possible increase in the sheer size of the labor force, will then bring about an enlarged capacity to produce. Suppose present private investment and public expenditures at the rate of $560 billion per year (combination c) together with all other relevant factors, cause the economy's productive capacity to rise. Then, the production possibilities curve would shift outward each year, eventually reaching the heavy line of Figure 24.5 HOW PRODUCTION POSSIBILITIES CAN EXPAND. This heavy line is a graph of Table 24.7 AN EXPANDED PRODUCTION POSSIBILITIES SCHEDULE. Along that line, we can then choose output combinations previously unattainable. In fact, we may well succeed,

Figure 24.5   HOW PRODUCTION POSSIBILITIES CAN EXPAND

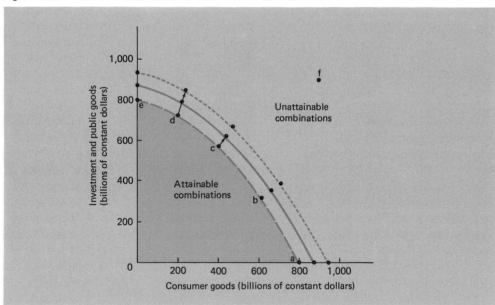

The more private investment and public goods a country produces, the greater will become its range of choice. Previously unattainable output combinations will become attainable as the increase in the quantities and quality of resources shifts the production possibilities curve to the right. If the country starts out by producing combination b on the broken line, the production possibilities curve may not shift at all. If it instead produced combination c, with greater I and less C, the curve may shift out to the solid line after a few years. If it, instead, produced combination d, with even greater I and still less C, the curve may shift to become the dotted line after the same number of years. Each higher line requires a greater present sacrifice: moving now from b toward d, or sacrificing more and more consumer goods now. Each higher line promises future benefits greater than those found on a lower one. Thus, each generation must ask itself how much present sacrifice future well-being is worth.

by continuing to enlarge our production possibilities, to one day produce at point f, containing more consumer goods than we could now produce if we placed *all* our resources into consumer goods production. Yet, point f, unlike point a, would not lead us into disaster. It not only contains $900 billion of consumer goods, but also $900 billion of investment and public goods!

And note something else. Had we made greater sacrifices of consumption in the past (gone from b to d rather than to c only), the dotted line would be our production possibilities line now. Thus, greater sacrifices will get us to point f faster.

THE U.S. GOVERNMENT AND GROWTH

Governments have on hand the means to influence the rate of growth within wide limits. Given what we have learned so far, it should be fairly clear what kinds of policies the U.S. government might pursue in this regard. If it dislikes the composition of real GNP between consumption and other goods because it is not conducive to growth, it can easily influence that composition. In fact, however, the U.S. government has never considered growth as one of its policy objectives until the administration of President Kennedy. He proclaimed the objective of raising total real GNP at a rate of 4.5 percent per year in the 1960's. Undoubtedly, this decision to add economic growth (in addition to full and efficient employment of resources) to the goals pursued by public policy has been influenced by the kind of considerations thrust on anyone who considers the implications of Table 24.2 THE MYSTERY OF COMPOUND INTEREST above. The name of the most powerful economy in the world has changed before, as from France to Great Britain to the United States. The launching of Sputnik in 1957 rudely awakened the world to the possibility that the lead may change hands again. Economists unanimously concurred that Soviet real GNP was smaller than that of the United States but growing much faster, and this immediately became a matter of great public concern. Khrushchev's threat that "we will bury you" was felt to be more than a boast. During the late 1950's, even the most optimistic analysis from the U.S. standpoint (assuming a U.S. growth rate of 5 percent and a Soviet growth rate of 6 percent, while the actual U.S. rate was lower and the actual Soviet rate higher) concluded that the Soviet total real GNP would equal that of the United States by the end of the century.

As our preceding analysis suggests (especially Table 24.4 THE SOURCES OF THE U.S. GROWTH OF REAL GNP), we can hope to accelerate our rate of growth in essentially three ways: by employing more resources in research, in education (and health), or in the production of physical capital goods.

Promoting Technical Progress

Technological change can be and is being accelerated by widespread government subsidization of research and development. This can be done through outright grants to private industry and nonprofit institutions. It can be done through direct government employment of scientists (as in increasingly the case: Department of Defense, Atomic Energy Commission, National Aeronautics and Space Administration). It could be accomplished indirectly, as by special tax treatment of private research and development expenditures (which are fully deductible from taxable income in the year in which they are incurred).

An estimate of the resources devoted in the United States to the "production" of technical progress is provided by statistics on the annual expenditures on research and development. This kind of spending has grown at an exceedingly rapid rate since World War II. In 1967, a total of $23.8 billion was spent in the United States, a sum just about equal to the total of all nonresidential structures erected in that year. Of this amount, 63 percent were financed by the federal government, 33 percent by private business, the rest by nonprofit institutions, such as universities. Again, 15 percent of the total went for basic research, the rest into applied research and development. In contrast, the further we go back in time, the smaller were such expenditures. In 1953, they amounted to little over $5 billion (with $2.8 billion of federal funds); in 1940, to well under $1 billion (with the federal government paying only $74 million). In fact, it has been estimated that half of all measured research performed in the entire U.S. history was performed in the last 10 years. This, furthermore, is a worldwide phenomenon. Half the scientists who ever lived on earth are still living!

In addition to monetary support, the government is encouraging technical progress through the patent system. An inventor is granted exclusive control for 17 years over his invention. In return, he must make the invention public knowledge. Naturally, this granting of a monopoly position is a strong incentive for private research. Furthermore, the early disclosure of inventions stimulates others and accelerates technical progress. The excessive secrecy of medieval guilds has been blamed, for instance, for the absence of technical advance over many centuries. How important early disclosure is has been shown again and again in the "fallout" effect of military and space research. The civilian economy is continually stimulated by governmental research results. Just consider the civilian benefits derived from the military and space effort in such areas as synthetic rubber, new power sources (solar cells), medical instrumentation, civil communications, weather prediction, electronic computers, and control systems. Present government research in other areas, such as water desalinization, pollution control, weather modification, and detection of natural resources may well have tremendous future impact on the economy, just as governmental research in agriculture has had in the past.

Promoting Education and Health

Government spending on education is particularly worthwhile as the estimates of Table 24.4 make so abundantly clear. This again could be and is being accomplished through direct public education or outright grants to private educational institutions or individuals or indirectly through special tax treatment of such expenditures or the making available for this purpose of low-interest or interest-free loans from the banking system. In the United States at present, about three quarters of expenditures for education are paid through government budgets. In fact, the United States has been one of the first countries to commit itself to free and compulsory elementary and secondary education. In addition, a number of federal and state student loan programs have been initiated since 1958. The 1965 Higher Education Act also provided for guaranteed student loans via private banks. As was shown on page 555 above, there is hardly anything in the U.S. economy that pays off so handsomely as a financial investment in education. This, of course, only reflects the tremendous impact education has on productivity. If human slavery were allowed, it would pay any financial investor to buy a share in a promising youngster rather than in the most profitable of American businesses. By paying, say, $10,000 for a high school graduate's college education using the above 1966 data, this person's annual earnings would on the average rise by $4,245 over what they would otherwise have been. This sum the investor might then appropriate, thus making a return of 42.45 percent *per year!* Because this form of slavery is not allowed, such profitable investment opportunity may remain unused in the case of poor families, unless government in one way or another helps disadvantaged individuals to "invest in themselves."

Over 6 percent of GNP is now being devoted annually to education. The percentage is about the same for health services, with governments contributing one quarter of this. As with education, the importance for productivity of adequate health care can hardly be overemphasized. And as with education, the poor can seldom afford all the care which might be given. Because society at large gains immeasurably, quite beyond the individual persons concerned, one can make a good case for government subsidies in this field, too. This is all the more true because no private individual would find it profitable to spend money on certain types of medical research or on such matters as the control of contagious diseases.

Until 1965, most of the poor and many of the aged were completely unprotected from health hazards. Since the enactment of Medicare, practically all the aged have hospital insurance and insurance covering part of the cost of doctors' bills. In addition, a Medicaid program is to aid the poor in meeting their health needs.

Yet, if we are to take advantage of new technical knowledge and great improvements in the quality of labor, we must simultaneously renew and enlarge our stock of physical capital goods.

Raising the Rate of Investment

Government can force households to spend less on consumer goods by pursuing a tight fiscal policy. By increasing household taxes, consumer spending can be effectively cut to any desired level, and thus society's rate of saving (nonuse of resources for consumer goods production) can be raised. This would just be the reverse of easy fiscal policy that we have seen to be so effective in increasing aggregate demand. In terms of Figure 24.5 HOW PRODUCTION POSSIBILITIES CAN EXPAND, this policy *by itself* would decrease aggregate demand or shift the economy from a point such as b to the left, leading to underutilization of resources. The equilibrium level of GNP would fall. As households buy less of output, and as yet nobody else buys more, businesses would find themselves with unwanted inventories and would decrease production and thus employment. Being interested in promoting economic growth, however, the government could *simultaneously* cut business taxes and engage in easy monetary policy to encourage business borrowing and spending for investment. The cut in business taxes, furthermore, could take a variety of forms. In the Kennedy administration, for instance, the U.S. government allowed business firms to write off depreciation on new machinery and equipment faster than normally on their income statements. This would increase reported costs and thus decrease taxable profit. The government hoped it would encourage business investment demand. Of course, the same could have been accomplished by reducing the business tax rate. Taxes paid by businesses are reduced equally whether the tax rate is 50 percent and reported profit reduced from $5,000 to $2,500, by raising depreciation by $2,500, or the rate is cut to 25 percent and reported profit remains at $5,000.

Apart from stimulating private investment, the government could, of course, increase its own purchases of public investment goods (schools, hospitals, communications satellites, and highways). In terms of Figure 24.5, this would shift the economy from a point to the left of b back to the production possibilities frontier at c or d, putting to use in the production of investment and public goods the very resources released from the production of consumer goods. The equilibrium level of GNP could thus be raised right back to its previous level. Only the *composition* of aggregate demand and real GNP would have been changed—changed, that is, in the direction conducive to faster economic growth.

As with most policies, however, this change may not be a painless process, nor may it be accomplished overnight. If resources are less than perfectly mobile, there may be a transitional period of varying length wherein some resources become frictionally unemployed. In terms of Figure 24.5, we may actually end up to the left and above b, but below c or d. Then some of the sacrifice of consumption would be wasted in unemployment rather than in employment for growth.

There can be little doubt that a deliberate policy to promote economic growth is possible. There can also be little doubt, if we want to perpetuate the U.S. economic leadership in the world, that such a policy is a necessity. Otherwise, this role will be lost to other countries just as accidentally as it was acquired.

SUMMARY

1   Although other definitions are possible, we define economic growth as a rise in real GNP per head. The occurrence of growth does not indicate, however, that everyone has become better off. The composition of output among private consumption, investment, and public goods must be considered. So must the distribution of output among persons and the conditions under which the output was produced.

2   Owing to the phenomenon of compound interest, a slight difference in the rate of GNP growth can over time lead to great differences in the absolute size of GNP.

3   When considering the reasons for the increase of total GNP over time, we can isolate changes in the quantities of natural resources, capital, and labor, as well as developments in education and health, technology, and environmental factors. During the last few decades, education and technological advance have contributed more to the rise of U.S. GNP than the sheer increase in the quantities of labor and capital combined.

4 U.S. economic growth in this century has been remarkable, real GNP per head having more than tripled. At least for the United States, the dire predictions of Malthus have not been fulfilled. Yet this good record does not assure that the economic position of the United States relative to that of other countries is impregnable.

5 If a country is interested in maintaining its position relative to other countries, or even in improving that position, it must pursue a well-thought-out policy for economic growth. In a fully employed economy, any increase in the rate growth, however, requires a present sacrifice of consumption.

6 The deliberate promotion of economic growth has been debated since the 1950's (especially in view of Soviet successes) and become part of official government policy since the Kennedy administration. The most promising areas of governmental activity for growth seem to be the stimulation of technical advance, education and health, and capital formation.

TERMS[2]

applied research   economic growth
basic research   Malthusian doctrine
                       production possibilities
                         curve (schedule)

QUESTIONS FOR REVIEW AND DISCUSSION

1 "Economic growth does not necessarily mean an increase in welfare." Explain.

2 "A slight difference in their rates of economic growth may completely change the relative economic strengths of two countries within a few decades." Explain.

3 What are the principal factors favoring a rise in real GNP over time? A rise in real GNP per head?

4 "Many potential students forgo education because they are unwilling or unable to wait, that is, to defer careers, marriage, and present earnings. But society can afford to wait more patiently than many of the young, especially the poor. Even if the persons involved were never made to repay them, scholarships for their education are a good investment for society." Discuss. (Hint: there are substantial external benefits from education that do not show up in the incomes of the educated.)

5 In many countries there has been concern over the "brain drain," the migration of scientists to the United States. What difference does it make?

6 "The best way to get economic growth is not by sacrificing consumption, but by sacrificing leisure. Work harder!" Discuss.

[2] Terms are defined in the Glossary at the end of the book.

7   "The formation of capital in the United States during the process of economic development has led to a great increase in unemployment. But we manage to hide the fact: Instead of working until they die, people retire at 65. Instead of working the moment they are able, young people go to school endlessly. And instead of working a 60-hour week or more, people work 40 hours or less. All this is equivalent to discharging half the labor force!" Discuss.

8   Explain the Malthusian doctrine and show that it is *correct*, given its assumptions. Do you think it could ever become relevant to the United States?

9   "The law of diminishing returns is disproved by the very fact that the United States has more food per person now than 100 years ago. All this in spite of a larger population and a fixity of land." Discuss.

10   "Faster growth comes not without cost." Explain.

11   Using the production possibilities curve of the chapter, show how it was possible during World War II for Americans to have more consumer goods *and* more public goods than before the war.

12   MR. A: "Every time a family decides to save, it is promoting economic growth."
        MR. B: "Every time a family spends money on the education of its children, it is promoting economic growth, but you, Mr. A, may be wrong."
        Evaluate.

13   "Research and development activity by government is dangerous, for public policy can easily become the captive of a scientific-military elite." Evaluate.

14   "The United States is doing too much research and development in military and space areas, too little elsewhere, as in transportation, housing, and pollution control." Evaluate. How could one possibly decide on the optimal allocation of research funds?

15   Each year, agencies of the U.S. government, such as the Department of Defense or the Atomic Energy Commission, spend billions of dollars on research. Much of this research concentrates on areas of engineering or the natural sciences. Would it not be better if they concentrated on social sciences?

16   Do you think it right that private patents are issued on results of research and development that was financed with government funds? Should not such results be treated as public property, belonging to everyone? Why should the contractor who happened to receive the government research subsidy be allowed to exploit it against his competitors whose tax money helped finance the research?

17   "Elimination of the business cycle and promotion of economic growth are incompatible with each other. The latter policy enlarges the investment component of GNP. That component, however, is the most unstable portion of aggregate demand, responsible for the fluctuations in GNP." Evaluate.

18   Over the long run, U.S. real GNP has grown impressively. Yet, from one year to the next growth is most unpredictable and irregular. Can you explain that?

19   If you had to decide on how fast the U.S. economy should grow, how would you decide? Why? Should government set the rate of economic growth?

20   Show how easy monetary policy, combined with tight fiscal policy, may stimulate the rate of economic growth.

Russia's Economy Thrives, but Its Growth Is Threatened by Cuts in Industrial Outlays

By RAY VICKER
Staff Reporter of
THE WALL STREET JOURNAL

MOSCOW — Grandfather Frost, Russia's Santa Claus, and his granddaughter Snow Maiden will deliver more toys than ever before to good children on New Year's Eve.

But if there is a Russian who doesn't believe in Grandfather Frost this year, it is the economic planner. The record supply of refrigerators and television sets for consumers and rockets and other weaponry for Soviet generals cheer him not. For Soviet cutbacks on industrial investment to pay for the current abundance of both guns and butter are stunting the growth of the economy.

Talk with Western observers here, or scan the charts, graphs and reports compiled elsewhere by Western students of the Soviet economy, and one conclusion emerges: "The Soviet Union," in the words of one diplomat, "is milling its seed corn to keep food on the table and a gun in the closet."

Badly needed construction and equipment for the oil, power, mining, chemical and other key industries are being sacrificed to keep current production high. These deprivations are causing industrial expansion to fall behind schedule.

Reading the Signs

To the Moscow visitor who ascends prayerfully to his hotel room in a 60-year-old elevator (when it works), or watches his bill being toted up on an abacus, some other conclusions arise. Among them:

—After spectacular gains in the economic race with the U.S. during the 1950s, the Soviet Union has been unable to narrow the U.S. lead throughout the 1960s. The Soviet gross national product, by U.S. calculations, has leveled at about 48% of the U.S. figure.

—The Soviet growth rate may continue only to parallel that of the U.S. through 1975 because of current investment cutbacks. Building on its broader base, the U.S. would thus be gaining in absolute dollar terms.

Soviet economists and analysts bitterly contest these statistics. But in the next breath, they aver that with a broadening base of its own, Soviet economic growth should be expected to slow somewhat.

Gross national product comparisons are perilous, of course, and subject to argument. The USSR doesn't include services in its count, and Soviet inflation or lack of it is hard to determine. The Soviets count some goods twice, moreover, and their quality is generally lower than in the U.S. Thus, while most Western economists calculate the Soviet GNP at 48% of the U.S. figure, other estimates range from 40% to the 63% claimed by the Russians themselves.

Industral Production to Rise

However, anybody who thinks that this is a puny economy merely because it isn't catching up with the U.S., knows little about Russia. For all its problems with prices frozen by executive fiat, industrial production in the Soviet Union wil rise by 8.3% this year from last. The nation is going forward in dozens of areas. It claims the world's largest atom smasher at Serpukhov near Moscow, it has a whole city dedicated to science and research near Novosibirsk, it has an Army that moved with clock-like precision into Czechoslovkia in a matter of hours.

With the U.S. economy booming in recent years, the Russians have done some powerful producing of their own just to stay even. At the giant GUM department store here, gleaming new refrigerators with freezer compartments are on display. Television sets stand nearby in abundance. A sporting goods section recently opened for skiers and ice skaters offers stylish ski costumes. This year, for the first time in Soviet history, the consumer goods sector of the economy has grown faster than the capital goods sector.

Soviet factories will deliver 5.7 million television sets, 3.2 million domestic refrigerators, and 4.7 million washing machines to consumers this year. That is a hefty boost from 1960's output of 1.5 million television sets, 518.000 refrigerators and 957,000 washers.

Consumer Goods Stay in Spotlight

Emphasis on consumer goods output will continue next year, too. Though total industrial production is scheduled to rise by 7.3% in 1969 from the 1968 level, output of "cultural utility and household goods" will increase by 12%. Refrigerator output is being expanded by 17%. TV production by almost 15.5% and plastic goods by almost 36%.

At the same time that Soviet industry is straining to turn out more consumer goods, the pressure is on for increased military production, too. Official Soviet defense expenditure for 1969 is set at $19.6 billion, 6% ahead of last year and up sharply from the $10 billion level of the years 1955-60. After soaring to $15 billion in 1961, the year of the Cuban missile crisis, the defense budget trended downward until Chairman Khrushchev was dismissed in 1964. Since then it has risen steadily.

The Soviets claim next year's defense spending will represent a lower percentage of the budget than did this year's military outlays. But Western sources aver that evidence of military spending is hidden in many ways (under atomic energy, for example) that the actual current military budget is closer to $50 billion annually.

Military Outlays

Military spending has been going to close the big missile gap held by the U.S., and also for a major buildup in the weapons of conventional warfare. An expanding Navy also draws increasing funds, as the Soviets try to become a major sea power.

"Our defense spending is up because the Soviet Army is being reorganized to fight on conventional as well as nuclear lines," says Vadim

Nekrasov, deputy chief editor of Pravda, the daily voice of the Communist Party.

With both defense and consumer goods spending on the rise, something has to give. Foreign aid for one thing, is being severely trimmed, but most of the defense and consumer goods increases are coming at the expense of capital equipment. Industry after industry has had its investment requests pared.

Rocket construction, atomic weapons and computers aren't suffering. But investment cutbacks are hitting the vital oil industry, hydroelectric power, ferrous metals, chemicals and other industries. Housing construction investments, though rising, aren't increasing at anywhere near the rate of favored industries.

Soviets also stretch available resources further, to minimize the investment squeeze. Lives of old machines and equipment are being extended to reduce requirements for new items. This comes when an economic publication, Voprosy Ekonomiki, estimates that "no less than 55% to 60%" of the total inventory of machinery and plant in the Soviet Union already is obsolete. The same source estimates "the amount of equipment requiring modernization is significantly greater, consisting of about 60% to 65% of all operating plants."

It remains for the government newspaper, Izvestia, however, to cite the height of antiquity in production. Earlier this year, it called attention to a Leningrad wallpaper factory. "Obsolete equipment is an understatement," said the paper. "Eighty percent of the machines date from the last century (1895). Here snort obsolete metal monsters which are mistakenly called machines."

The investment lag is already taking its toll of industrial production. In 1967, output increased by 10% from the preceding year; in 1968 it increased by 8.3%; and in 1969 it is scheduled to increase by 7.3%.

Long-term net effect is evidenced in growth trend studies. B. N. Mikhalevskii, a young Soviet mathematician, projects an average annual growth rate of 5.4% for the Soviet Union. The U.S. Congressional Economic Committee projects a U.S. growth rate to 1975 of 4% to 4.5% annually. Estimates are so close that they offer Soviets little hope of catching up with the U.S. in this century. Moreover, even the 5.4% Red growth estimate is based on maintenance of investments to industry, something not assured.

The Wall Street Journal, December 31, 1968

25

economic growth
in the
soviet union

THE SOVIET GOVERNMENT, just as that of the United States, is not pursuing any active policy to influence the size of the country's population. Except for the extraordinary events of World War II, the Soviet population also has been increasing.

Since 1950, this has occurred at an average annual rate of 1.6 percent. Thus economic growth in the Soviet Union, as in the United States, must involve an increase in total real GNP at a faster rate than population. As we have seen in Chapter 24, the U.S. government has shown explicit concern for economic growth only within the last decade. In the Soviet Union quite the contrary has been true. The Soviet government, from its inception in 1917, has been literally obsessed with the problem of achieving rapid economic growth. The implications of compound interest, which we noted in Table 24.2, have been quite clear to Soviet leaders and economic growth has consistently been policy goal number one. Naturally, this has tremendous implications for the rest of the world. This is the story we shall explore in this chapter.

THE HISTORICAL SETTING

Soviet propaganda tries at times to divide history into night and day, with light appearing on earth at the time of the Bolshevik Revolution in 1917. Especially when addressing themselves to the underdeveloped countries of the world today (whose problems we shall discuss in the following chapter), Soviet leaders like to compare prerevolutionary tsarist Russia with the most inaccessible and underdeveloped regions of the world today, thereby setting the stage for most glamorous and dramatic comparison with the present-day industrial might of the U.S.S.R. Soviet economic achievements are most impressive without a doubt. By 1969 Soviet GNP was about half that of the United States, but two and one-half times larger than that of West Germany, the third-ranking economy in the world. Yet the starting point of this amazing economic development was not, as the official myth has it, the year 1917.

Ever since Peter the Great, modernization had made its impact on Russian society. To be sure, the beginnings were gradual and the pace of change did not appreciably quicken until after 1861, the year in which the serfs were freed. Although power and property remained largely in the hands of small pleasure-loving aristocracy, the winds of change were blowing strong. More and more individuals attempted and succeeded in establishing industrial enterprises and in introducing modern industrial techniques into an economy backward by West European standards (but hardly by those of deepest Africa). It is estimated that industrial output grew at a rate of over 5 percent per year from the 1880's to World War I. By 1913, Imperial Russia was the sixth largest industrial power of the time, even though she probably produced only an eighth of U.S. GNP. Nevertheless, she did have a modest machine industry, moderate numbers of skilled technicians, and a tradition of excellence in mathematics and pure science. About 10 percent of her GNP consisted of capital goods. A substantial stock of "overhead" capital, such as housing, transportation and municipal facilities, had been accumulated. Population was not growing too fast so that GNP per head was rising. The prospects for further economic growth looked good.

THE SOVIET STRATEGY OF DEVELOPMENT

War and revolution seemed to end all that. In the wake of the revolution, the banks, transport enterprises, and large industry had been nationalized. Land had been distributed among millions of peasants. The first few years after 1917, the period of so-called War Communism, can only be characterized as a period of general confusion. They were filled with civil war. There was popular unrest about the widespread use of brutal force by the Soviet authorities, who ruthlessly requisitioned agricultural produce to feed the military and urban populations. Old methods of factory management were thrown out as so much bourgeois nonsense. And GNP declined considerably below its 1913 level. Inflation was widespread. Exchange deteriorated into barter. Economic progress came to a halt.

In 1921, in order to reverse this trend, Lenin proclaimed a *New Economic Policy*, giving official sanction to capitalist activities in agriculture and trade. He hoped that the peasants now owning the land would (in the context of free markets in which to buy and sell) have the incentive to produce a maximum of output. Whatever they did not need for their own family's consumption would presumably be offered for sale, providing both industrial raw materials and foodstuff for the urban population. With the income received, farmers would demand industrial goods needed as inputs in agriculture or for personal consumption, and this would set the wheels of industry into motion again. As before the war, Lenin speculated, the population was likely to refrain from consuming all its income, the aggregate saving allowing a corresponding use of some resources for capital formation stimulating economic growth. Directly, the government would only control the "commanding heights" of industry and finance.

In fact, the "natural" process of economic growth seemed to work. Until Lenin's death in 1924, industrial output grew at record rates (large-scale industrial output more than tripled between 1920 and 1924). Following his death, a serious debate arose within the Communist Party about the advisability of leaving up to accident (as under capitalism) the rate of economic growth.

The Arguments of the Right

The "right" wing of the party, under the leadership of Bukharin, proposed an indefinite continuation of Lenin's policy. Bukharin even proposed denationalization of small-scale industry so as to encourage production by it of consumer goods wanted by the peasants. The ready availability of industrial consumer goods, he asserted, would stimulate the peasants' efforts to the utmost. It would thus raise to a maximum the flow of agricultural produce to the industrial sector. In addition, government could levy a small tax in kind on the peasants, thus receiving materials needed to run the nationalized large-scale industries: food for the workers, raw materials to be processed, produce to be exported in exchange for foreign machinery, and the like. Bukharin strongly opposed any "monopolistic parasitism" of nationalized industry, by which he meant any attempt to speed up capital formation and industrialization at the expense of the peasants' standard of living.

This, however, was exactly what was proposed by the "left" wing of the party, notably by Trotsky and Preobrazhenskii. They pointed out (correctly) that the "success" of the new economic policy was by nature not sustainable. The reason for the rapid rise in industrial output up to 1925 was simply the fact that large reserves of labor and capital, *unemployed* in the confusion of War Communism, had finally been put to work again. The country was only regaining the level of economic activity which had already prevailed in 1913. Continuing the New Economic Policy, they argued, would probably *maintain* the new (and old) level of output. It might in fact, they asserted, reduce it because the existing capital stock was then very old and more and more of each year's investment was needed just to keep it from falling. Possibly investment was not even sufficient for this task. Even if it was, output could at best be raised only slowly. As the right wingers had pointed out themselves, capital formation could occur in two ways under their policy.

how to accumulate capital   First, people could save and invest voluntarily and by themselves. That is, having received income, people might voluntarily not spend it on consumer goods but instead on newly produced buildings, equipment, and inventories for private agricultural, trade, and small industry enterprises.

Second, people could be forced to save, and investment be carried out by the government. Government could make it impossible for people to spend all their income on consumer goods by (1) taxing some of it away and buying investment goods publicly or (2) creating and then spending new money on public investment goods, thereby driving up the price level after full employment is reached and making it impossible for people to get all the output produced even if they do spend all of their incomes.

In terms of Figure 24.5 HOW PRODUCTION POSSIBILITIES CAN EXPAND, both these policies would move the composition of output from a point such as b to one such as c on society's production possibilities curve. People (voluntarily or because they are being forced to) refrain from consuming $200 billion of goods. With the resources so released, they produce $240 billion of capital goods. As a result, society's production possibilities curve shifts out over time, as from the broken to the solid line in the figure.

Yet, as long as the level of income per head is relatively low (that is, not too much above subsistence), argued the leftwingers, resources released for growth via the first method will be few. As long as the government does not want to destroy private producers' incentive to work, it cannot be too forceful in pushing the second alternative either. If it did, Russia would slip back into War Communism and peasants would simply refuse to produce anything beyond subsistence for their own families. Why work if all the extra income is taxed away? Why work if prices of industrial goods are sky high so as to make them almost unavailable? Shall one toil half a year on the land just to buy a bicycle?

Thus, concluded the leftwingers, continued *rapid* growth of industrial output and GNP required more than the New Economic Policy could provide. This could only be achieved by *drastically* reducing consumption (maybe by cutting it from $600 billion to $200 billion in

Figure 24.5), while using the resources released for purposes conducive to growth. *Force* was seen as the only solution. Without it there would be no rapid growth. Without it there would be no catching up with the economic power of the advanced nations in the world.

Stalin's Decision

As it turned out, the Soviet leadership determined to follow the path of rapid growth *whatever the cost.* Stalin, who originally sided with Bukharin and was instrumental in exiling or "liquidating" the leaders of the party's left wing, eventually carried out the very program of the left. "Something like a tribute," he argued, had to be imposed on the peasantry in order to speed up economic growth. The device used was the collective farm.

collectivization of agriculture   Millions of independent peasants, who had received their land at the time of the revolution, found that land expropriated starting in 1930. Had they continued to own their land individually, they would have been impossible to control. They would have reacted to drastically increased taxes exactly as both the right and the left had said they would react: by cutting production and income to practically nil, thereby entirely crippling the urban economy. This reaction was to be forestalled by the creation of the collective farm wherein large groups of farmers own their land collectively. Such farms were to be managed by officials ostensibly elected by the members, but in fact loyal to the central government. And above all, such farmers were to deliver large percentages of their output to the state *at prices set by the state.* These prices were set so low (relative to industrial consumer goods) that peasants were effectively "selling without purchasing." If the device worked, argued Stalin, the state would ensure continued agricultural production at a high level, for the individual peasant was now reduced to the dependent status of a factory worker, supervised by loyal managers and threatened with severe punishments for "sabotage." The state would get most of agricultural output (in return for negligible quantities of industrial consumer goods). Finally, the state could use this agricultural surplus for export (to import foreign capital goods) or to feed the urban population (engaged in producing capital goods domestically and in other growth-producing activities). Industrial workers, in turn, could be prevented, reasoned Stalin, from demanding many industrial consumer goods by "mopping up" most of their money income as payments for food. This could be accomplished by letting state retail stores sell at extremely *high* prices to urban consumers the agricultural produce exacted at extremely *low* prices from the collective farms. (This difference between the two prices was and is officially called a turnover tax which corresponds exactly to the type of tax represented by a sales tax in the United States.)

In fact, Stalin's scheme did work. Agricultural output at first fell, agricultural *collections* by the state increased. In the case of grain, they rose from 12 million short tons in 1928 to 32 million in 1937. At the same time, industrial consumer goods became all but unavailable. Tensions mounted and social relations came to the point of explosion. Peasants, for instance, were never fooled for one minute by the official presentation to them of the collective farm as a "vehicle for the introduction of mass production methods into agriculture." In fact, rebellious peasants originally responded to collectivization with the wholesale slaughter of livestock. In millions of heads, the numbers of cattle were 60.1 in 1928 and 33.5 in 1933, of hogs 22.0 and 9.9, of sheep and goats 107.0 and 37.3, of horses 32.1 and 17.3, respectively. Stalin, characteristically, responded with the exiling or extermination of 5 million peasants. And peasants have been responding ever since with less than admirable eagerness to work! Industrial workers, guided by trade unions loyal to the state and intimidated by a totalitarian government, similarly "consented" to sacrifice present living standards for future bliss.

the justification   Stalin was absolutely pitiless in carrying out his policy. Though his people were groaning, his ears were deaf, but his eyes were fixed to the stars. As he put it,[1]

To slacken the tempo would mean falling behind. And those who fall behind get beaten. But we do not want to be beaten. No, we refuse to be beaten! One feature of the history of old Russia was the continual beatings she suffered for falling behind, for her backwardness. She was beaten by the Mongol khans. She was beaten by the Turkish beys. She was beaten by the Swedish feudal lords. She was beaten by the Polish and Lithuanian gentry. She was beaten by the British and French capitalists. She was beaten by the Japanese barons. All beat her— for her backwardness: for military backwardness, for cultural backwardness, for industrial backwardness, for political backwardness. . . . Do you want our socialist fatherland to be beaten and lose its independence? If you don't want this, you must liquidate our backwardness and develop a real Bolshevik tempo in building our socialist economy. There is no other road. . . . We lag behind the advanced countries by 50 to 100 years. *We must make good this distance in ten years.*

Whatever one may think of the means, the goal was achieved; even if not in 10 years. Through Stalin, the Soviet Union was on her way, "starving to glory." Having assured a source of food for the urban population as well as a means of payment for record-breaking imports of machinery from the West (then in the midst of the Great Depression and eager for business), it now became simply a matter of coordinated central planning to assure the production by the nonagricultural sector of the economy of the types of goods most conducive to economic growth.

THE RECORD

Such central planning, as described in Chapter 17, has been carried out, ever since 1929, in a series of five- and later seven-year plans. Planners have stressed the production of capital and public goods at the expense of consumer goods. Since World War II, roughly 45 percent of Soviet GNP has consisted of consumer goods, 25 to 30 percent of investment goods, and 10 to 15 percent each have been devoted to military and nonmilitary government activity. In contrast, for the United States in 1969, the percentages were consumption goods = 62; private investment goods = 15; and government goods = 23.

You might take another look at Table 16.1 THE INPUT-OUTPUT TABLE AS A HISTORICAL

[1] J. Stalin, *Voprosy Leninizma* (Moscow, 1952), pp. 362–363. Italics supplied by the author.

DOCUMENT. The Soviet policy just described amounts to minimizing entries in column (4), while maximizing those in columns (5) and (6), although, as we have seen (see pp. 372 ff), this has been done not in the form of input-output tables but via material balances. Investment and public goods were the ones treated as "important," consumer goods the ones categorized as "unimportant."

What were the results of this policy? Because the Soviets publish voluminous statistics on actual production, it is very tempting to make quick comparisons of the Soviet and U.S. levels or growth rates of GNP. This, however, cannot be done very easily, as we shall see presently.

GSP vs. GNP

As we noted in Chapter 5, the definition of output is necessarily an arbitrary one and we must expect that other countries define it differently from our GNP. This is in fact the case in the Soviet Union. Their concept of output, called the *Gross Social Product*, or GSP, differs from our GNP in at least three ways. (See also the news report introducing this chapter.)

product defined   First, following a distinction made by Adam Smith and later by Karl Marx, they differentiate "productive" from "unproductive" labor. Essentially, all human effort used in the industrial, agricultural, and construction sectors (including services of white collar and transportation workers in these fields) is termed productive. On the other hand, all other types of human effort, such as personal services (barbers, doctors, restaurants) or the provision through government of defense, education, research, municipal services, transportation done for households, and so on, are termed unproductive. This is not to imply any value judgment and has nothing to do with calling one type of work useful and the other useless. It only indicates that one kind of work ultimately brings forth something we can *see* (a product), the other does not. Based on this distinction, the Soviet measure of output is much *narrower* than that of the United States, counting only what has been produced by "productive" labor, but not what has been made by "unproductive" labor. To make their GSP and our GNP comparable, we would either have to add the services not counted in output to their GSP or have to deduct them from our GNP.

multiple counting not eliminated   Second, the Soviets do not eliminate multiple counting of production. If 100 rubles of wheat is produced by labor, land, and capital of firm A, it is counted as output. If this wheat is taken over by firm B to be transported to firm C and sold to it for 120 rubles, another 120 rubles of output is counted. If firm C holds the wheat for a year, finally selling it to firm D for 130 rubles, another 130 rubles of output is counted. If firm D turns the wheat into flour, selling it to firm E for 215 rubles, another 215 rubles of output is counted. And so it goes. At this point, we would have recorded an output (Soviet definition) of $100 + 120 + 130 + 215 = 565$ rubles, having counted the value added by A four times (100 rubles), the value added by B three times (20 rubles), the value added by C twice (10 rubles), and the value added by D once (85 rubles). The U.S. definition of output (value added) would have only yielded a total of $100 + 20 + 10 + 85 = 215$ rubles. In short, the Soviet measure of output is much *broader* in this sense.

Note that there is nothing *wrong* with such a procedure, as long as we are aware of what is being done, even though we might prefer to measure output one way or the other. But it would be wrong to compare the GSP and GNP without a second adjustment. To make them comparable, we would have to either take the multiple counting out of the GSP (here reduce 565 to 215) or put it into our GNP. Most American economists would undoubtedly prefer to eliminate the multiple counting because it tends more to measure through how many stages of production output has gone than what final output has been. If, for instance, in our above example firm D had sold the wheat back to C and C back to D for 130 rubles each time, the GSP would have become 825 rubles, yet the GNP remained at 215 rubles. As a slightly growing final output is handled by more and more firms (as is likely to happen in an expanding economy), a GSP measure would tend to grow much faster than a GNP measure. Yet such growth would not only measure the availability of more goods to final demanders but in addition the fact that more firms handled these goods. Thus, two countries' GNP's (availability of goods to final demanders) may grow equally, yet their GSP's unequally (if the number of production stages in one changes differently from the other).

prices not comparable   Third, the Soviet GSP, as the U.S. GNP, is measured at actual selling prices. However, prices can and do mean very different things. In the United States, prices are made up of wage, material, depreciation, tax, rent, and interest costs plus profit; but, in the Soviet Union, at least rent and interest cost until recently were not counted as cost at all. Thus, comparability of their output and ours would require a third adjustment, measuring output of both (in the GNP or GSP sense, whichever has been decided) at the prices of one or the other.

Western Estimates of Soviet GNP

Having made these adjustments, we could thus compare Soviet and U.S. outputs in four different ways, comparing (a) GSP's in Soviet prices, (b) GSP's in U.S. prices, (c) GNP's in Soviet prices, (d) GNP's in U.S. prices. As you might expect, not all of these will give the same result. According to (a) Soviet output may be 29 percent of ours. According to (b) it may be 44 percent, according to (c) 39 percent, and according to (d) 50 percent. There is *nothing* one can do to avoid such ambiguity. The best one can do is to compare what is comparable and to know what exactly it is one is comparing!

Western scholars have in fact spent a great deal of effort trying to compare United States and Soviet levels and growth rates of output in a meaningful way, usually via method (d) above.

Such *rough* estimates by western scholars (do not let the decimal points fool you) are the only meaningful guide we have for judging Soviet economic performance. These estimates suggest that Soviet total real GNP (defined in the United States sense) has grown very rapidly indeed by almost any standards of comparison. The average annual rate of growth of real GNP was certainly over 4 percent per year from 1928 to 1940, a little less than 10 percent per year in the early 1950's, 6 percent in the late 1950's, and 4 percent in the early 1960's. The average rate of Soviet real GNP growth for the entire 1928–1966 period was about 6 percent per year; in the United States, it was 3.3 percent. However, the Soviet rate of growth of industrial output, construction, and transportation has been higher, of agricultural output and services lower than the GNP rate throughout. Industrial output, for instance, has grown at an average annual rate of only 0.1 percent from 1913 to 1928 (reflecting the great output decline till 1921 and the rapid rise to the 1913 level thereafter), but at 9.8 percent from 1928 to 1940 (machinery output at 15.7 percent), at 11 percent in the early 1950's, 8 percent in the late 1950's, and 6 percent in the early 1960's. Agricultural output grew at 0.3 percent per year from 1928–1940, but at almost 5 percent in the 1950's and at probably 3 percent in the early 1960's. Real GNP per head seems to have grown at annual rates above 5 percent from 1950 to 1958, at 3.5 percent since. In 1950 Soviet GNP was probably little over 30 percent of that of the United States. By 1970, it was practically half.

The Record Explained

We have discussed above the overall strategy of the Soviet leadership which has resulted in rapid economic growth. At this point we may add some of the finer detail. Why was the Soviet strategy so staggeringly successful at first? Why does it seem to be less successful (but successful nevertheless) as of late?

the high rates of growth   The very high rates of growth of real GNP can be explained by favorable circumstances with respect to all the ingredients of growth discussed in the previous chapter.

Natural resources.   First of all, the Soviet Union is richly endowed with all types of natural resources. As men and equipment were channeled into discovering and developing them, their flow into the economy could be increased rapidly.

Capital.   Second, the drastic reduction of consumption levels to less than half of the GNP allowed great increases in investment. The Soviet leaders have seen to it that consistently about 25 percent of GNP was new capital goods. (For a contrast, take a look at Figure 24.1 THE U.S. INVESTMENT EFFORT.

Moreover, capital formation has been stressed in economic sectors most likely to produce the fastest growth of real GNP. Here is a simple example that will give you the idea. Suppose a country can produce $100 million of output, and its citizens choose to produce 25 percent, or $25 million of capital goods. If there are few old capital goods to replace, $24 million of this may be a net addition to the capital stock (gross investment = 25, depreciation = 1, net investment = 24). Next year, with a larger capital stock, other resources will be able to produce a higher output. But exactly how much higher will depend on the exact *form* the new capital goods have taken.

If they consisted of residential houses for 1,200 new families, and, as is customary, the output of residential houses is evaluated by what their services sell for (their rental value of say $1,500 per year each), the GNP might rise by 1,200 times $1,500, or $1.8 million. Then an investment of $25 million gross (or $24 million net) has raised the $100 million GNP to $101.8 million, or by 1.8 percent.

If the new capital goods instead consisted of $24 million of new and fully equipped chemical plants, the output of chemicals next year may rise by $13 million. Then an investment of $25 million gross (or $24 million net) has raised the $100 million GNP to $113 million, or by 13.0 percent.

This ratio of extra output producible with extra capital, or the *marginal output-to-capital ratio*, differs widely among economic sectors. In our example, it was $1.8/24 = 0.075$ in residential housing, but $13/24 = 0.542$ in the chemicals industry.

It just so happened that in the Soviet Union (1) a large percentage of GNP was invested, (2) a large percentage of that was net investment, and (3) investment was stressed in sectors with high marginal output-to-capital ratios. Much of Soviet investment went into industry or into agriculture, relatively little into housing, transportation, communication, and municipal services, which exhibit low marginal output-to-capital ratios. Luckily for the Soviets, they could afford to sidestep the latter type of investment because much of it had already been made prior to 1917, thus laying the foundation for the observed rapid growth of real GNP.

Labor.   Third, the pool of labor available to Soviet planners has been particularly large. Great numbers of people could be shifted from agricultural unemployment or underemployment into the urban economy. In 1925, 84 percent of the labor force were employed in agriculture. The percentage now is only 30. General unemployment was eliminated. Large numbers of women were drawn into the labor force (more than 50 percent of those of working age are employed).

Education.   At the same time, the quality of the labor force has been enhanced greatly. The general level of education has been raised remarkably. Between 1914 and 1964, for instance, the number of higher educational institutions has been raised from 105 to 742, their enrollment from 127,400 to 3.3 million. Enrollment in all types of schools has risen from 10.6 million to 65.1 million persons. Significantly, in 1939, only 12.3 percent of working inhabitants of the Soviet Union had any (complete or incomplete) higher or secondary education. In 1964, the percentage was 50.1. Experts, furthermore, have found the quality of Soviet education to be excellent, both with regard to the content of the curriculum and the level of achievement by students. The intellectual effort put forth astounds many visitors, but this is not really surprising if we remember how in the Soviet Union (much more so than in the United States) upward mobility in society depends on the level of education achieved. From the standpoint of economic growth, furthermore, the Soviets have done the right thing by closely integrating educational policies with economic objectives. This means training the type of people in the numbers needed for the economy, rather than letting people get just any education that suits their personal fancy. Hence, there are relatively large numbers of people trained in mathematics, engineering, and the sciences (rather than in the liberal arts), as such are the needs for trained manpower by the economy. As anywhere, such use of resources *from the purely economic standpoint* is a wise one and bound to explain a substantial part of each year's harvest of output.

Technology.   Rapid technological change, besides improvements in the quality of the labor force, has been a factor most stimulating to Soviet economic growth. Building, as they did, many new industries from the ground up and being, to begin with, in a state of economic backwardness (compared to Western Europe and the United States), the Soviet government organized the wholesale copying of the most advanced production techniques from the West. While ignoring international patent conventions, this skillfully executed policy enabled the Soviet economy to leap in a few decades over a long period of research and development that had preceded economic growth in the West. (Even today, the Soviets are running the most elaborate organization in the world, which systematically monitors all scientific and technical progress abroad.) Instead of simply producing on a large scale more capital of the same kind found in tsarist Russia of 1916, the Soviets installed on a large scale more capital *of a completely different kind,* embodying the latest scientifice discoveries and technical advances.

In addition, domestic technical advance has also been pushed hard. An extended system of scientific research institutions, culminating in the Academy of Sciences of the U.S.S.R., has been established. Soviet leaders have been most eager to supply them lavishly with resources and, with few exceptions, have provided scientists with all the perquisites conducive to creative thinking. Altogether the present Soviet establishment for the discovery, dissemination, and application of new knowledge is impressive indeed. As Soviet progress in rocket technology has shown, they are quite capable of making advances on their own.

Environmental factors.   How are we to judge the influence of the Soviet environment on growth? In a certain sense, we might argue that growth must have been stifled by the disasters in morale following the draconic measures of collectivization, the purges of the 1930's, and similar incidents of terror. Might Soviet peasants and workers not have produced more had they been given more of the carrot than of the stick, that is, positive incentives (such as more consumer goods) rather than negative ones (such as the threat of a bullet or exile in Siberia)? Might they not have produced more had they been given more responsibility instead of being pushed around by the ever-present clumsy hand of Gosplan? This is a moot question. Since 1950 at least, positive incentives have in fact increasingly replaced negative ones, and, as we have already seen in Part 2 of this book, attempts at decentralizing the planning apparatus are being made at present. This is being done for the very reason of speeding up growth.

Yet, the incredibly *rapid and large-scale* mobilization of resources (getting more labor, getting more capital, getting more natural resources) and their deployment for more capital formation still, plus crash programs of education and technological catching up—these things could hardly have been done *in such a short time* without the iron will and iron hand of the Stalinist government. Undoubtedly, not all the sacrifices made were necessary. Some must be ascribed to honest planning errors or sheer stupidity or fiendish brutality. Yet many sacrifices had to be made *if one insisted on "catching up in 10 years."* They were the genuine, unavoidable cost of growth. In this sense, the cruel and brutal environment of the totalitarian state was a positive factor stimulating and organizing the process of growth and compressing into a few decades the misery that also accompanied growth in the West (but where it was spread over a century and a half at least). This is not to say, of course, that such rapid growth and complete neglect of noneconomic factors, as human freedom and dignity, are to be recommended to anyone for imitation.

the decline in the growth rate   As we saw above, the extraordinarily high rates of growth achieved in the early 1950's have given way since the middle 1950's to a declining trend. As we go down our checklist of the ingredients of growth, a number of explanations come readily to mind.

Natural resources.   Many of the easiest fruits provided by nature have been picked. In the past, large increases in agricultural output were made possible by drawing new lands into cultivation. The practical limits of this policy have now been reached. Further increases in agricultural output (which accounts for a substantial portion of Soviet GNP) will require increases in yield per acre. And such increases are much more resource-absorbing. A given amount of machinery, labor, and chemicals will raise output by a lot more if applied to new land than if superimposed on land already cultivated. As the law of diminishing returns tells us, if a certain amount of resources added to an area of new land produces a certain amount of output, only a larger amount of resources will raise output equally on an equal area of old land already under cultivation. Thus, equal sacrifices in consumer goods (to make given amounts of machinery and chemicals, say) will now yield smaller increases in agricultural output.

One other factor plays a role—the weather. Much of Soviet agricultural land is subject to drought or short growing seasons. Lack of rainfall or an early winter can seriously affect agricultural output and, because of its importance in the economy, also the over-all growth rate.

So far as diminishing returns are concerned, they have also become a problem in the exploitation of minerals and fuels. The highest grade ones, and those nearest industrial centers, have been mined first. As the Soviets resort to lower grades, or mines farther away, more resources are needed to obtain identical results. The marginal cost of production is rising. If previously 10 machines mined 100 tons of iron ore per day (with 60 percent pure iron content) and 10 freight cars used for 1 day could transport them to the steel mill, the same amount of pure iron can be obtained now only if 20 machines mine 200 tons of ore (with 30 percent content) and 20 freight cars are used for 2 days to transport them a distance twice as long. Equal sacrifices in consumer goods (to make, say, mining machinery and freight cars) will now yield smaller increases in industrial output.

Capital.   Although the rate of investment has continued high (at least 25 percent of GNP), the Soviet capital stock is now so large that an increasing portion of gross investment just replaces what is being depreciated. Thus, equal sacrifices of consumption (to make capital goods) now yield smaller increases in the capital stock (less *net* investment). To make things worse, Soviet leaders have made the decision to channel more of the (relatively lower) net investment into uses with lower marginal output-to-capital ratios. This by itself would be enough to slow the rate of growth. As shown by the news report introducing this chapter, planners have been willing to satisfy consumer demand more than heretofore.

Labor.   Since the late 1950's, the wartime decrease in the birth rate has made itself felt by a remarkably slower annual increase in the labor force. In addition, opportunities to shift labor from agriculture to industry are becoming rarer (especially in view of the diminishing returns in agriculture just discussed). Opportunities to increase the labor force by raising the female participation rate in it have also been exhausted. To make things worse, the length of the work week has been reduced.

Technology.   Not only have opportunities to increase rapidly the sheer quantities of labor, capital, and natural resources become slim, those for making rapid technical advances have also become less abundant. At least in the economic sectors given priority by the Soviet planners, everything that could be copied from abroad has been copied. *Further* technical advance, therefore, has to await new breakthroughs abroad (which can then be copied) or it has to be made by the Soviets themselves. The former cannot be controlled by Gosplan, the latter (of which they are quite capable) is again more resource-absorbing than copying would be. It takes a lot more time and more research personnel and facilities to work out the new than just to borrow it from someone else and adapt or adopt it at home. Again equal sacrifices in consumption (to devote resources to, say, education, research, and development) are now apt to be less productive than earlier of economic growth.

Environmental factors.   Environmental factors are also responsible in part for the slow-down of growth. In a sense, the very type of planning that was so successful under Stalin (be-cause it uprooted established ways so thoroughly, forced on society sacrifices in consumption so successfully, and deployed resources for growth so skillfully) is becoming a drag on growth. The economy has outgrown the old planning mechanism. *Central* economic planning and administration of a rapidly growing and increasingly complex economy is bound to get increasingly difficult. As a result of plan errors, economic inefficiency abounds and fric-tional unemployment of resources mounts in importance (see our discussion in Chapters 17 and 23).

The dream of mathematical planning, with the whole country covered by a network of computers, receiving and processing economic data, passing them along to large computing centers, and finally to a giant electronic brain in Moscow where planners get a perfect pic-ture of feasible alternatives, is just that—a dream. To get rid of the central planning drag on economic growth, nothing short of a complete overhaul of the present system of planning and administration is likely to do. As we have already seen in Part 2, many of the institutions which were used so successfully since the 1920's are in fact now being subjected to severe scrutiny because they are less and less responsive to the political leadership's unrelenting efforts to promote growth. Stalin's forceful methods may have been ideal for increasing the sheer quantities of resources in the 1930's and 1940's and for using them to promote increased output of a *few* key products, as electric power, coal, steel, and machine tools. Now things are different. Planners are interested in a great variety of products, ranging from petroleum and chemicals to nonferrous metals, electronic control machines, space rockets, and even television sets. And they must rely primarily on technological improvements, education, and institutional changes to bring about growth. Hence, their increased concern with decentralization and the incentives of peasants, workers, and managers alike. Given their vested interest in the old, however, there is also the planners' extreme caution with implementing anything new.

FUTURE PROSPECTS

There is nothing inevitable about any continuation of the declining trend in Soviet growth rates. We can expect the deceleration in the growth of the labor force to be temporary. We can expect the massive establishment for education and research to generate the usual dividends of higher GNP, and Soviet leaders have already expressed their determination to alter the planning mechanism so as to be more conducive to good old economic goal number one.

Even if the Soviet GNP were to grow forevermore at the recent average rate of "only" 4 to 6 percent per year, take a minute to think what this means. In absolute terms, this means (in 1970) an annual addition of $18 to $27 billion of output. It is up to the Soviet leadership to determine what kind of form this addition shall take.

More Private Consumption (Case a)

They *could* take the increase entirely as consumer goods which would raise the annual quantity of consumer goods by 8.9 to 13.4 percent, a truly spectacular gain. In short, the Soviet Union could very quickly reach one of the highest living standards in the world which would certainly not be without political repercussions. On the other hand, the Soviets are most unlikely to do this, because such a policy (of taking the entire increase of GNP in the form of consumption) would gradually shift the composition of GNP toward consumption and thus reduce the rate of investment and of growth of GNP. (Again, note the discussion of this point in the previous chapter and the news report introducing this chapter.)

More likely, they may (as in the past) divide up the $18 to $27 billion annual *addition* to GNP like the original GNP itself, that is, give about 45 percent to consumption, or from $8.1 to $12.2 billion. Then total consumption would only rise as fast as GNP (and per capita consumption somewhat less). This would still assure steady, if less rapid, increases in living standards.

More Capital Formation (Case b)

They could take the increase entirely as capital goods which would raise (under present conditions) the annual quantity of investment by 15 to 24 percent. This would quickly raise the

rate of growth by enlarging net investment, and it would counter some of the growth-slow-
ing effects just discussed. The development of the living standard in this case would depend
on the rate of population change. Because the absolute amount of consumption would remain constant (and the percentage fall), a rising population would bring a fall in the living
standard (as measured by consumer goods available per person). This extreme policy is unlikely to be pursued, either, and the same goes, for the same reason, for the next two alternatives.

More Public Consumption (Case c)

They could take the increase entirely as collective consumer goods, be they of the civilian
or military category (hospitals or ICBM's). Given 1970 circumstances, this would raise their
annual quantities by 20 to 30 percent. If devoted to the military, the effect on the outside
world is obvious. The Soviet Union could annihilate everyone else even more thoroughly than
now! Yet this choice again is unlikely.

More Foreign Aid (Case d)

Finally, Soviet leaders could really make an impact on the world by devoting the entire increase in GNP to foreign aid, which now takes less than 0.1 percent of their GNP. (We will
discuss this further in the following chapter.)

The Likely Course of Events

In reality, the Soviet leadership is likely to make none of the decisions represented by cases
a to d above. But they will make some combination of them. If, as seems to be the case, they
want to continue to promote rapid growth until their GNP per head greatly surpasses that
of any other nation, they will tend toward solutions b and c. If they find it politically advantageous, they might reverse all established policies and pursue alternatives a or d. The
fact remains that rapid growth does not just happen. It is *chosen* as a goal and pursued re-
lentlessly. So it has been in the Soviet Union. Prospects are that it will continue to be so in
the future. More likely than not, as has been the case since 1950, policy a will be pursued to
the degree necessary in order to raise consumption levels per head gradually. Further increases in consumer well-being will, as in the past, come through increased public civilian
consumption (railroads rather than private cars). The minimum of resources, consistent with
the political situation, will be devoted to public military consumption and foreign aid. The
rest will be used to spur on growth through capital formation and the encouragement of
education, health and technological advance.

SUMMARY

1   For the Soviet government, the achievement of *rapid economic growth by whatever means necessary* has been for many decades the most important economic policy goal.

2   Economic growth began in Russia long before the Soviet Revolution, but it has been considerably accelerated since.

3   From the Soviet Revolution to the late 1920's, the exact strategy of development was a matter of debate. Lenin's New Economic Policy was followed by rightist arguments to continue it, and leftist arguments for economic development via widespread use of force. Eventually, the leftist policy was carried out by Stalin.

4   It involved forced collectivization of agriculture and use of the agricultural surplus for industrialization. The share of private consumer goods in GNP was depressed to less than half, with the rest devoted to capital formation and collective consumption.

5   It is tempting to check Soviet output statistics to assess the results of such policies. However, although such official measurements of actual output exist, the Soviet concept of national production differs greatly from that of the United States. It does not count as production at all the results of using "unproductive" labor. It does not exclude the multiple counting of the output of "productive" labor. Hence, any comparison of Soviet and U.S. national production is fraught with many problems. Not only must one agree on the concept of production to be used, but output (however delineated) must be evaluated at identical prices. As a result, any comparisons of U.S. vs. Soviet GNP or of the movements of Soviet GNP over time can *never* be more than rough estimates.

6   The Soviet growth rates of GNP and industrial output (based on independent western estimates, rather than official figures) have been high relative to other countries. On the average, real GNP grew by about 6 percent a year from 1928–1966: by over 4 percent per year from 1928 to 1940, by almost 10 percent a year in the early 1950's, 6 percent a year in the late 1950's, and 4 percent a year in the early 1960's. Industrial output, which had grown on the average only by 0.1 percent a year from 1913 to 1928, grew at over 8 percent from 1928 to 1940, at 11 percent in the early 1950's, at 8 percent in the late 1950's, and at 6 percent in the 1960's. By 1970, Soviet real GNP seemed to be half that of the United States, larger than that of any third country.

7   The high growth rates can be explained by:
    a. Favorable circumstances with respect to natural resource availability;
    b. Large increases in capital (one quarter of GNP going into investment, there being originally little depreciation, and investment going into sectors with high marginal output-to-capital ratios);
    c. Shifts of labor from involuntary or voluntary unemployment into employment, from agriculture into industry;
    d. A crash program in education;
    e. Large-scale copying of advanced technology, as well as a crash program for own technological advance;
    f. A determined and ruthless government pursuing the goal of growth singlemindedly (the mind being Stalin).

8   Recent declines in the growth rate can be explained by:
    a. Diminishing returns to natural resources (and bad weather);

b. Greater need to replace depreciating capital, and direction of investment into sectors with lower marginal output-to-capital ratios;

c. A slower increase in the labor force (an aftereffect of World War II) and exhaustion of possibilities to shift labor on a large scale out of agriculture or out of involuntary or voluntary unemployment;

d. Exhaustion of many, though not all, possibilities for copying foreign technology, own advances bringing naturally only slower fruits;

e. Increasing complexity of the economy, calling for a reform of old methods of planning and managing.

9 There is nothing inevitable about a continuation of the declining trend in Soviet growth rates. The same factors making for growth in the United States (capital formation, technical advance, education), together with decentralization of planning and management, may further stimulate growth. The dividend from growth (increased real GNP) can be used at the discretion of Soviet leaders in a great variety of ways.

TERMS[2]

gross social product
marginal output-to-capital ratio
New Economic Policy

productive labor
unproductive labor
War Communism

SYMBOLS

GSP

QUESTIONS FOR REVIEW AND DISCUSSION

1 "When the Soviet Union tells underdeveloped countries just to follow her example, she is misleading them seriously." Discuss.

2 In the late 1920's, there raged a debate in the Soviet Union over the correct strategy for economic development. State the two sides of this debate.

3 The text says that "Bukharin strongly opposed any 'monopolistic parasitism' of nationalized industry, by which he meant any attempt to speed up capital formation and industrialization at the expense of the peasants' standard of living." Can you illustrate this argument with the help of a production possibilities curve?

4 Illustrate with the aid of a production possibilities curve why the success of Lenin's New Economic Policy "was by nature not sustainable."

[2] Terms and symbols are defined in the Glossary at the end of the book.

5 As the text shows, Stalin's policies to create capital for growth was far from popular. Explain the rationale of forced collectivization. Do you think a policy to promote growth could *ever* be popular?

6 Why is it so difficult to compare a given year's GNP between the United States and the Soviet Union? Would the difficulties disappear if we were content with comparing rates of change only?

7 "The proportion of U.S. GNP consisting of services has been rising steadily for some time. Because services are no *real* goods at all, this is a clear sign of weakness. The Russians would never kid themselves in this way." Evaluate.

8 "The Soviet concept of national production excludes all services." Evaluate, explaining carefully the Soviet distinction between "productive" and "unproductive" labor.

9 "According to the Soviets, doctors, taxi drivers, professors, and prime ministers are 'unproductive' and such parasites should be liquidated." Discuss.

10 Explain the general and *inevitable* problems inherent in international GNP comparisons by using the United States–Soviet case as an illustration.

11 If Soviet real GNP is half that of the United States now, and if Soviet GNP grows at 6 percent a year, but that of the United States at 4 percent, when will Soviet GNP equal U.S. GNP? What about per capita GNP?

12 Explain *in detail* the high rates of growth of Soviet real GNP and industrial output observed in the past.

13 Explain *in detail* the recent decline in Soviet real GNP growth.

14 Find the latest data on the composition of U.S. GNP between consumption, investment, government, and net exports. (You might just look at last month's *Federal Reserve Bulletin*.) If U.S. real GNP were to grow at 4 percent over the next year, what kinds of things might we do with this "growth dividend"? In every case consider what would happen if we continued to do this in the long run.

15 "Given the way their GNP grows, the Soviets can do anything they want." Discuss.

16 What effect on Soviet growth might we expect from the introduction of the "new system of planning and management" discussed in Part 2?

17 "Lenin's *New Economic Policy* and Kosygin's *New System of Economic Planning and Management* are really the same thing." Discuss.

18 "For reasons that go beyond economics, it may be preferable to have slow rather than rapid economic growth." Discuss.

19 Do you think the United States could have growth as rapid as has been observed in the U.S.S.R.? Explain your answer.

20 Do you think that there has been in western countries anything equivalent to the sacrifices made by the Soviet population for the sake of economic growth?

Birth Rates Strain Developing Economies

By JUAN de ONIS

Special to The New York Times

UNITED NATIONS, N.Y., Sept. 30—President Arthur da Costa e Silva of Brazil, where the economy is growing at a strong 6 per cent this year, lamented recently to a diplomatic visitor that the benefits of this growth are being diluted by a soaring population.

"If we didn't have so many more new people each year, we would rapidly be approaching decent living standards for everyone," he said.

Brazil, with a population today of nearly 90 million, is growing at a rate of 3.5 per cent a year. This means a doubling of the population in 20 years.

Even with very strong economic growth performance, the increase in the size of the productive pie must be shared among so many new people that the benefits per capita are meager. Living standards remain low, and frustrations rise.

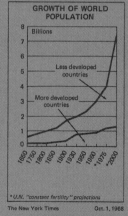

GROWTH OF WORLD POPULATION

Billions

Less developed countries

More developed countries

* U.N. "constant fertility" projections

The New York Times   Oct. 1, 1968

This is what Robert S. McNamara, President of the International Bank for Reconstruction and Development, called today a "crippling effect" on the growth aspirations of developing countries where population is growing rapidly.

In announcing that the bank, for the first time, was prepared to finance national family-planning programs, Mr. McNamara opened an important new front in the international campaign to assist developing countries

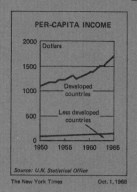

PER-CAPITA INCOME

Dollars

Developed countries

Less developed countries

Source: U.N. Statistical Office

The New York Times   Oct. 1, 1968

that want help in controlling their population growth.

There has been growing recognition in this decade that population growth represents a global problem of explosive potential. The present world population of 3.5 billion is expected to double by the end of this century.

Since the largest part of this increase by far will be in developing countries, which have per capita incomes of less than $300 a year, the population explosion threatens to aggravate the existing "poverty gap" between these countries and the wealthier, industrialized nations, where per capita income, as in the United States, exceeds 3,000 dollars a year.

The massive distribution of modern drugs, particularly antibiotics, combined with higher levels of nutrition and sanitary medicine, such as malaria control, have brought a dramatic decline in death rates in developing countries.

This has not been accompanied, as yet, by any significant decline in birth rates. In developing nations, births run from 40 to 50 per 1,000 persons, compared with 17 to 20 per 1,000 in industrialized countries.

As a result, the poorest nations must spend the most proportionately on schools or medical facilities, instead of factories, roads or agriculture.

If the rate of population growth could be halved in such countries as Pakistan, Brazil and Kenya, per cap-

ita income could be doubled in 15 years instead of 25.

The only way to effectively cut the population growth rate, in the opinion of demographers and medical men, is to intensify greatly the national family-planning programs, usually with Government support.

Experts consider the use of modern contraceptives, such as the "pill," essential to achieve as strong an effect on birth control as the "wonder drugs" had in reducing mortality.

The International Planned Parenthood Federation, a private group that has pioneered in this field, maintains voluntary family-planning programs in some 60 countries, but the scope of the problem and the financial requirements are so large that public programs are considered vital.

Since 1968, the United Nations has officially recognized the problem, and has set up a population division, but it lacks resources. But the World Bank, which announced today it would enter the field, does have large resources and international experience in development financing.

The United States Government's assistance in international population programs has grown sharply—from $2-million in 1966 to $35-million this year for programs in 25 countries, the Pan-American Health Organization and the United Nations, as well as the Planned Parenthood Federation and other organizations.

Congress has approved a $50-million authorization for next year, and has authorized the distribution of contraceptive materials under United States-financed programs and the employment of funds generated by the sale of United States food in developing countries for local population programs.

The biggest United States-supported program is in India, where $8-million in grants and $40-million from food sales are backing the national program.

The World Bank's program will supplement the United States international population efforts for countries that request family-planning assistance.

economic growth in the underdeveloped countries

I N THIS CHAPTER we examine the meaning of and reasons for economic underdevelopment. We discuss the kinds of policies that may bring about development. Such policies are urgently needed, because in most countries on earth real GNP per head is extremely low and in view of the relentless growth of population, it is in constant danger of falling below the level of subsistence. Under such circumstances, full and efficient employment of given resources is not enough to win the battle against scarcity. A country's capacity to produce must be increased. The United Nations General Assembly, following a 1961 proposal by President Kennedy, has underscored the urgency of the problem by designating the 1960's as the development decade. More recently, the 1970's were named as a second development decade during which a global development strategy is to be drafted.

IDENTIFYING UNDERDEVELOPMENT

When economists talk about underdeveloped countries, they are not making a moral judgment about two thirds of the world's population. They are not denying that some of these countries (such as China or India) contain advanced cultures, going back thousands of years, while others (such as the Congo or Papua) are practically untouched by civilization. The term underdeveloped as used by economists, and as used in this book, refers simply to the economic fact of *poverty*. However advanced, however diverse they may be in areas other than economic life, these countries have in common, compared to the standard of, say, North America, an *extremely low level of real GNP per head*. Table 26.1 THE RICH COUNTRIES AND THE POOR represents a most convenient way of identifying these areas of the world.

A Word of Caution

The data of Table 26.1, however, must be regarded as the roughest of estimates. We have discussed the problem of international GNP comparisons before in connection with U.S.-Soviet growth comparisons (see pages 584–586 above). These and similar problems are generally encountered. In addition, it is difficult for any country to gather even accurate raw data on aggregate economic activity. Even U.S. GNP statistics are subject to a wide margin of error. But remember: the United States has a most reliable statistical apparatus and an educated and cooperative population to facilitate data-gathering. There can be no doubt that data gathered by the governments of the underdeveloped countries are considerably rougher. This is not only so because their civil service is likely to be less developed, but also because the environment in which data must be gathered is a lot less conducive to this enterprise. Respondents may be illiterate or quite uninterested in giving information. Communications in the form of roads, telephones, and the mails may be imperfect or nonexistent. And the share of economic activity that does not go through the process of exchange for money is likely to be relatively much more substantial than in the United States. The latter requires a greater degree of conjecture by statisticians since it necessitates hazardous guesses. Furthermore, the U.S. definition of GNP refuses to count many types of "do-it-yourself" activities.

If you paint your own house, build your own hi fi set, or grow your own vegetables, this is not counted as production in the statistics of U.S. GNP.

If underdeveloped countries follow the same definition, this may seriously understate the level of their economic activity relative to that of the United States, because such activities may be a lot more important there than here. Counting or not counting them in the United States may make little difference to the over-all measure of economic activity, but it may make a substantial difference in a less developed and less market-oriented economy. A man in the tropics who grows his own food and needs no heating in winter needs fewer dollars than an American to achieve a comparable living level. Finally, there is the problem of converting GNP estimates in local currencies to a common currency unit as has been done by United Nations statisticians for data contained in Table 26.1. The problems involved in this have also been discussed in the previous chapter. Thus, it is extremely important, as we turn to inspect Table 26.1, to realize that the data presented there identify only roughly the stages of economic development achieved by the countries of the world.

What the Data Show

Possibly, as some scholars have suggested, some of the low entries in Table 26.1 (C) should be raised as much as threefold to make them truly comparable with the estimates for the developed countries. Yet, even if we did so, the enormous differences in the economic development among countries, which are real enough, would be clearly evident.

The data of Table 26.1 have been divided (quite arbitrarily) into three main groups. Countries with per capita GNP of probably $1,000 or more are termed "developed," those with a probable per capita GNP from $301 to $999 are classified as "intermediate," and those with a probable per capita GNP of $300 or less are called "underdeveloped." However arbitrary this division and however imperfect the data themselves, they, nevertheless, convey accurately a sad fact of life: At least two thirds of mankind are desperately poor. The table confirms exactly the impressions a traveler brings home from a trip around the world. Except for the small enclaves of North America, Western Europe, Australia, New Zealand, and most recently the Soviet Union and Japan, mankind shares the common lot of poverty. In its most extreme manifestation, poverty, with negligible exceptions, is king over all of Africa and Asia, as well as much of Latin America and Southeastern Europe. Try to visualize what it would be like to live, as the average Indian must, for less than $100 a year. How would you manage on $35 a year, if you were a *poor* Indian?

ELEMENTS OF UNDERDEVELOPMENT

No underdeveloped country is exactly like every other. Yet, on studying the economies of the poor countries of the world, one is likely to find certain features over and over again. We shall call them the "elements" of underdevelopment. One or several of them are likely to be present in every underdeveloped country.

Table 26.1   THE RICH COUNTRIES AND THE POOR

A. DEVELOPED COUNTRIES (840 MILLION PEOPLE)

United States	$3,200	Denmark	$1,800
Canada	2,200	United Kingdom	1,700
Switzerland	2,200	France	1,600
New Zealand	2,200	Netherlands	1,500
Sweden	2,100	Belgium	1,400
Norway	2,000	Soviet Union	1,400
Australia	2,000	Austria	1,000
Germany	1,900	Italy	1,000
Luxembourg	1,800	Japan	1,000

B. INTERMEDIATE COUNTRIES (240 MILLION PEOPLE)

Finland	$900	Chile	$500
Ireland	900	Greece	500
Puerto Rico	900	Hungary	500
Czechoslovakia	800	Jamaica	500
Venezuela	800	Panama	500
Israel	700	Spain	500
South Africa	700	Barbados	400
Cyprus	700	Cuba	400
Argentina	600	Malta	400
Poland	600	Mexico	400
Trinidad and Tobago	600	Portugal	400
Uruguay	600	Singapore	400

C. UNDERDEVELOPED COUNTRIES (2,220 MILLION PEOPLE)

British Guiana	$300	Yugoslavia	$300
Columbia	300	Zambia	300
Costa Rica	300	Albania	200
Gabon	300	Algeria	200
Guatemala	300	Brazil	200
Turkey	300	Bulgaria	200

Inadequate Natural Resources

Some underdeveloped countries are richly endowed with many kinds of readily accessible natural resources, even when viewed from a per capita basis. Others are the stepchildren of the earth in this regard. They may have the poorest of soil or climate, no water (or too much of it), no known or accessible mineral deposits and fuels, or a huge population pressing on the arable portion of the land.

Table 26.1   THE RICH COUNTRIES AND THE POOR (Continued)

Dominican Republic	$200	Paraguay	$100
Ecuador	200	Philippines	100
El Salvador	200	Senegal	100
Ethiopia	200	Tanzania	100
Ghana	200	Thailand	100
Honduras	200	Uganda	100
Iran	200	United Arab Republic	100
Iraq	200	BELOW $75:	
Jordan	200	Afghanistan	
Lebanon	200	Angola	
Libya	200	Bechuanaland	
Malaysia	200	Cambodia	
Morocco	200	Chad	
Nicaragua	200	China	
Peru	200	Dahomey	
Rumania	200	Guinea	
Syria	200	Indonesia	
Tunisia	200	Laos	
Bolivia	100	Malagasay Republic	
Burma	100	Malawi	
Central African Republic	100	Mali	
Ceylon	100	Mauretania	
Congo (Brazzaville)	100	Mozambique	
Formosa	100	Nepal	
Haiti	100	Niger	
Hong Kong	100	Nigeria	
India	100	Republic of the Congo	
Ivory Coast	100	Somalia	
Kenya	100	Sudan	
Korea	100	Togo	
Pakistan	100	Upper Volta	
		Vietnam	

Estimates of 1965 real GNP per head in 1958 United States dollars. Source: United Nations.

Insufficient Capital

Even when lack of natural resources is not the crucial impediment to growth, lack of high-quality capital, or any capital for that matter, very likely is. We have seen in the previous chapters how important the role of capital formation has been in the growth of the United States and Soviet economies. The same is true for all the rich countries in class A above. The poverty of most underdeveloped countries is reinforced by the fact that their population is large relative to their stocks of man-made productive inputs as well as relative to natural resources, In addition, their annual production of new buildings, equipment, and inventories is small also. This should not surprise us. If real GNP per head is extremely low, it may be necessary to devote almost all available resources to the production of basic consumer goods (food, clothing, shelter) just to keep the population alive. The poor nations, like low-income individuals, find it much harder to save than the rich ones. As we saw above, in recent decades the Soviet Union has devoted about one quarter of her GNP to the production of capital goods and the United States about 15 percent. In 1966, the U.S. share was 16 percent, the Soviet one 26. Other rich countries in class A have done the same or better. The percentages were, in 1966, above the U.S. share in all cases. They were above 19 but below the Soviet share for these countries in group A—Belgium, Denmark, France, Germany, Italy, Sweden, and the United Kingdom. For the remaining nine group A countries, the share was equal to or higher that the Soviet one, going to 34 in the case of Japan.

The share of GNP devoted to capital formation among class B nations has varied greatly in 1966, from as little as 13 percent (Uruguay) to as much as 29 percent (Finland). Of the B countries listed in Table 26.1, about one third invested less and two thirds more than 20 percent of GNP. Among the underdeveloped nations, fairly low percentages (around 15) were frequent, but there were a number of noticeable exceptions (above 30 percent for Bulgaria, Yugoslavia, and Zambia).

For many an underdeveloped country, this state of affairs can be seen as part of a vicious circle. Agricultural output is low because of the lack of capital goods employed in agriculture. The digging stick, the wooden plow, and the cart may be the only tools available to man. Industrial output is low because capital goods and agricultural raw materials are lacking, and most of the available labor has to be used in agriculture to wrest from the land the minimum of food required per man. Because of the low income, saving and investment are low, perpetuating the problem.

Low-Quality Labor Force

Few, if any, underdeveloped countries lack labor when it comes to sheer quantity. All of them, however, lack the kind of labor prerequisite for the establishment of an economy resembling those of the advanced nations. In the sense of quality, many have a serious "manpower gap."

Significant percentages of the labor force are likely to be employed on the land. They are likely to be indispensable at planting and harvest time, but partially unemployed much of the time. Smaller percentages of the work force are typically found in handicraft production (weaving, dyeing and cutting cloth, sewing garments, and making kitchen utensils), in petty retail trade (wherein a small volume of goods is moved about in a most time-consuming manner), or in the service sector (as barbers, messengers, porters, priests, and domestic servants). An even smaller percentage of the labor force is possibly employed in a "modern" sector of the economy: In factory industry, the export-import business, in banking and in government. If you look at the characteristics of such a labor force as a whole, you are likely to find that a very large percentage is illiterate, very few have any, let alone a higher, education. People are likely to have enough food, clothing, and shelter to sustain life, unlikely to have enough to fend off disease. The daily calorie intake is substantially lower per person in the underdeveloped countries than in the developed ones. The nutritionally desirable composition of the diet is seldom achieved. Diets are likely to be monotonous and protein-short. The availability of decent shelter and of medical attention is severely restricted. Life expectancy is low. (In 1966, life expectancy for an American boy or girl was 67 and 74 years, respectively. At the same time, the figures were 41 years in India, usually much lower throughout Africa.) As a result, physical and mental energy for sustained hard work is lacking as are skills.

Nature also plays its role. Look at the map and see how many of the underdeveloped nations are situated in the tropics. As we all experience at times even in the temperate zones, the desire to work declines markedly when the temperature goes above 90°F. and the humidity hovers close to 100 percent. Now add lack of skills and shelter, add hunger and sickness, and you have gone a long way toward explaining why some countries do not seem to be able to get started on the road to material wealth.

Lack of Modern Technical Know-How

Another aspect of the problems just discussed in the sections above is the fact that in many underdeveloped countries technical knowledge is very primitive. Even where there are natural resources, tools, and human energy to work, lack of knowledge may keep output below what it might otherwise be. Agricultural activities, for instance, may be carried on now in exactly the same way as in times immemorial. Even such simple pieces of knowledge as the value of crop rotation, of contour plowing, of raising storage bins off the ground to avoid spoilage may be unknown. Yet a few miles away, there may be a bustling modern oil refinery, copper mine, or rubber plantation. More often than not, however, the latter will be isolated outposts of some developed economy and more part of it than of the country on whose soil they have been placed. Frequently, modern technical know-how is embodied neither in the minds of men nor in machines. Tradition is likely to be the most powerful recipe used in the productive process.

Environmental Factors

A great number of environmental factors contribute in many countries to the perpetual state of poverty that exists. We shall consider some of them in turn. There are others. And certainly not all of the ones discussed here will be found in every country of the underdeveloped world.

the attitude toward change   For economic development to occur, there must be someone to engineer change, someone who is willing and able to depart from customary and traditional practices. The prospect for economic progress is bleak if no one exhibits initiative, uses foresight, takes risks, and introduces and organizes something new. Without such organizers of progress, without people willing, say, to introduce new crops to an area, to extend cultivation to new regions, to adopt novel techniques of production, to develop new trading connections and routes of transport—without them, progress will not occur. Frequently, such entrepreneurs are lacking. The social environment in most underdeveloped countries is inimical to experiment and innovation. To some extent this is understandable. Introducing a new type of seed and chemical fertilizers means introducing risk. To an American there seems nothing wrong with that. But what about the Arab farmer tilling a tiny patch of sandy soil? What about the Peruvian peasant villager working a rocky hillside? For them, failure of the seeds to germinate may mean certain starvation. Thus, the chance for higher output, no matter how slight the accompanying chance of failure, may be passed up for the certainty of lower output. Therefore, new ideas and the exercise of intellectual curiosity often are distrusted. Innovators, who interrupt the established order of things, are the object of suspicion, if not of persecution. Frequently, in fact, the force of custom, the unwillingness to learn and change, is simply overwhelming. Many primitive superstitions freeze people to their "proper" places in society. Thus, the ways in which people think and behave can become as important a hindrance to economic development as the physical unavailability of resources itself. (To take just two cases, think of the popular resistance in India to the slaughter of the sacred cows that eat the food desperately needed by people. Or consider the Burmese resistance to the extermination of rats and insects that are believed to harbor the souls of ancestors and annually eat one-fifth of the rice crop.)

the extended family   We have just noted how the social environment may contribute to the lack of economic development by discouraging innovation per se. It frequently also destroys incentives to put forth such effort even if it is not frowned on. In many parts of Africa, as well as in China and India, we find the institution of the entended family. In it each member has obligations to support, if he is able and when the necessity arises, a great number of even most distant relatives. It is expected that lavish hospitality is extended to scores of relatives and clansmen should the opportunity arise.

Actually, at a low stage of development this system is very much akin to social security in the United States. People often live off the land. There are often no markets in which to sell output which is not needed to maintain the immediate family. Hence, such surplus may just as well be used to support the "family at large." This giving up of the surplus (such as social security taxes) establishes the right of the donor to be supported in turn by the active members of the family when he is too old or too sick to support himself. (It establishes his right to receive social security benefits!) The larger the number of those in the "family," the more effective becomes the insurance, that is, the greater becomes the likelihood that someone will take care of you should that need arise.

Such treasured institutions as the extended family can easily be seen to discourage the initiative of any one member. If you go out and work harder, you will have to share the fruits not just with wife and children, but with 117 cousins and uncles as well. Thus the effective insurance system called the extended family becomes a drag on economic development. It is as if a tax were to eat up 99 percent of any addition to your income. Why should you bother to work harder or to take advantage of opportunities to innovate which promise higher output and income?

land tenure systems   In some places, land is owned collectively. It may be used collectively. It may be used individually for limited periods, followed by periodic redistribution by, say, a tribal authority. Either way, such a system prevents the energetic (who are not frightened off by the public frown or the extended family) from acquiring land privately and from experimenting with it. It also discourages methods of conservation. (A public pasture is nobody's pasture, and it will probably be overgrazed and become less productive.) It makes impossible the acquisition of capital by the methods of borrowing on the basis of land or selling part of it outright.

In other places, land is owned by relatively few, absentee landlords. Their interest in the land is often limited to getting from it a sufficient income for their accustomed standard of living (a house in the capital, an annual trip to Europe, an education for the children abroad, annual additions to the family stock of precious jewels, and the like). They are uninterested in making improvements on the land. Or they fear that improvements will be ruined by the tenants. The tenants, in turn, are uninterested, for they fear that they might be ejected from the land after having made improvements on it. Or they fear that the landlord would take all of extra output.

Even if innovation were not frowned on by society, even if the individual tenant does have the incentive to experiment (say, he is able to keep the extended family as well as the landlord from capturing the fruits of success), even if there are roads and trading connections so that higher output can be sold (and these are big ifs), the tenant's wealth may be nil and his ability to save too small to acquire capital goods by himself. He would have to become indebted first to the landlord or the local moneylender, and the cost of borrowing is likely to swallow up any increases in income. So the tenure system reinforces the general lack of incentives toward development.

The opposite extreme is just as bad and found just as often. If land is privately owned, but each man's ownership is split up into hundreds of tiny plots strewn over a large area, the application of modern equipment and techniques becomes technically impossible. Because of the ownership pattern alone, people may be condemned to stick to 2,000-year-old methods of cultivation (as plowing with ineffectual wooden plows and reaping with hand sickles, not even scythes). Thus they may be prevented from raising output per acre.

the narrowness of markets   In many countries of class C, a large portion of GNP consists of agricultural products and much of this output is produced within small, self-sufficient family units. Little, if anything, is sold in the market for money. Exchange and the use of money are thus peripheral to the countries' major economic acivity. Resources employed in manufacturing are few; money demand for manufactured products is small. Thus, the size of many national markets for agricultural as well as industrial goods is small relative to the volume that might be producible with the most efficient methods known to man. Hence, application of modern technical know-how to agriculture or industry, even if not prevented by other obstacles mentioned above, may in fact be sporadic, haphazard, or completely absent. Even if resources for investment in modern industry are available, the narrowness of the domestic market may reduce the incentive to do so. Who wants to build a technically efficient automobile plant with a capacity of 100,000 cars per year, if national demand will only be for 3,979 cars? On the other hand, if the establishment of one or a few technically efficient producing units is allowed by the size of the domestic market, we are still likely to find monopolistic tendencies on their part with resultant economic inefficiency (see Part 2 above). Production of manufactured goods for sale in the developed countries, furthermore, is likely to be out of the question.

bad government   It is extremely important for the realization of any type of national aspiration to have a government willing and capable of administering appropriate policies throughout the country. This condition is by no means always fulfilled with respect to the underdeveloped countries. For sustained economic development to occur, the existence of a stable government, pursuing policies that are generally accepted (be it with joy or grudgingly) and that are conducive to growth, is an absolute necessity. Some underdeveloped countries have known a settled government and the sway of law and order for a long time. Many others are subject to perpetual political instability, violence, and disorder. Tribal, racial, military, or other groups fight among each other for power with varying degrees of success. The local medicine man may well be more powerful than the national leaders. In such instances, even the most basic functions of government, such as the provision of a legal and judicial system and of basic overhead capital, are bound to get neglected. All policies are likely to be confused, contradictory, and abortive.

Worse yet, the group in power may have no interest whatever in economic development. Military leaders are likely to be interested in nation-building activities and to pursue policies aimed at impressing the world outside rather than eradicating poverty at home. They may use scarce resources lavishly for embassies abroad, presidential world tours, and new fleets of jet fighters, and they may well be supported in all this by their own countries' rich classes who have vested interests in warding off change. Why should the large landowners, the religious leaders, the tribal chieftains, whose personal wealth depends on guarding *tradition*, be instrumental in bringing about *change*?

Fortunately, not all underdeveloped nations are in irresponsible hands. Yet even where the group in power is interested in genuine economic advance, its efforts may be frustrated by lack of a reliable administrative machinery. There may be a few top administrators, educated abroad and as bright as the brightest, yet they can achieve little without an army of reasonably intelligent and honest civil servants. These in turn can achieve little in the short run if the populace (possibly tired of years of chaos) greets every governmental effort with cynicism, indifference, or even sabotage. Building a government machinery that can guide development efforts takes time, maybe more time than the subsequent replacement of footpaths and muletracks by superhighways and railroad tracks.

A typical symptom of this administrative problem is the unreliable tax collecting apparatus in many underdeveloped countries. Taxes on income and wealth are often avoided on a large scale without any adverse consequences. This is partly owing to the lack of a tradition of honesty (on the part of tax collectors as well as the taxed). It is partly owing to the absence of bookkeeping. In many underdeveloped countries, as a result, taxes on exports, imports, and foreign firms provide the only substantial amounts of governmental revenue. In many cases, total tax revenue is a great deal less than it could be with better administration. Very frequently, government spending is limited to tax revenue. Hence, we observe it to be, in most underdeveloped countries, equal to only about 15 percent of GNP, while the percentage is between 20 and 30 percent in the developed countries. Yet successful economic development requires a substantially larger effort on the part of government than this, especially given the lack of educational facilities and public capital goods.

The Population Explosion

Two thousand years ago, the world population was probably 250 million people. It took 1,650 years for this figure to double. It took only 200 years for it to double again, giving us 1 billion people by 1850. Then, it took fewer than 100 years to add the second billion and fewer than 25 years to add a third. By the end of this century, if the present trend continues, world population will have doubled once more. It will then rise at a rate of 1 billion every 8 years!

This population explosion is by no means evenly distributed over the face of the earth. Although there are exceptions, many underdeveloped countries (unlike both the United States and the Soviet Union) are experiencing since World War II extremely rapid increases in their populations. Thus, even if aggregate real GNP is rising, real GNP per head may fail to do so. These countries are in the position of a man trying to climb a downward moving escalator. He has to run just to stay where he is.

From 1960 to 1965, for instance, the entire world's population was rising at an average annual rate of 1.9 percent. Yet the rate per year for Africa was 2.3, for Latin America 2.8, for Southern Asia 2.5. Or taking the classification of Table 26.1, the population of countries in group A rose by 1.3 percent per year on the average, that of countries in group B by 1.8 percent per year and that of countries in group C by 2.1 percent per year. The countries that need economic growth most are saddled with the greatest obstacle thereto!

The crude birth rate, or the number of live births per 1,000 persons in the population, was 34 from 1960 to 1965 for the world as a whole. Yet, it was 47 for Africa, 41 for Latin America, 38 for Asia. In contrast, it was 23 for North America as well as the Soviet Union, 19 for Europe, 23 for Australia and New Zealand.

The crude death rate, or the number of nonfetal deaths per 1,000 persons in the population, was 15 from 1960 to 1965 for the world as a whole. For Africa it was 24, for Latin America 13, for Asia 20. The corresponding figure for North America was 9, for the Soviet Union 7, for Europe 10, and for Australia and New Zealand 9. If we look at history, we see that the death rates in underdeveloped countries, particularly infant mortality, used to be much higher, but have declined spectacularly with the introduction of western medical practices and the application of new knowledge (from insecticides to antibiotics) since World War II. The most spectacular case is Ceylon where DDT (and the eradication of malaria through it) decreased the death rate by 34 percent in a single year and by 70 percent in 10 years. Throughout the world, United Nations and other campaigns have completely eradicated diseases that affected millions, and the death rate has been smashed in an incredibly short time at an incredibly low cost. In addition, it has declined with the suppression of certain traditional practices, such as widow burning and infanticides.

Because the underdeveloped countries' birth rates typically did not decline similarly (old attitudes toward prolific childbearing, which made sense when death took most children before adulthood, are unchanged; women are healthier and have fewer miscarriages; they are less frequently widowed; and so on), their populations are rising as shown above. (The rate of population increase follows directly from the relation between the birth and death rates. As you can see, if per 1,000 persons in the world 34 are born and 15 die on the average per year, the net rise is 19 per 1,000 or 1.9 percent, as indicated above. Can you tell what must have been the 1960 to 1965 average annual rate of European population change? What about the Soviet Union's?)

POLICIES FOR DEVELOPMENT

A Sense of Urgency

We should note that the conditions of poverty that follow from the elements described above have been the common lot of *all* of mankind until maybe a hundred or so years ago. So far as man's life span on earth is concerned, it was only yesterday that he changed from a food gatherer to a food producer. Until 8,000 years ago, man, like the animals, took whatever nature provided by itself. During the last 8,000 years, man succeeded in wresting an existence from a reluctant and niggardly nature for greater and greater numbers of people, but man always continued to live close to starvation. If the rains failed to come, men had to die. It is only in this century that one third of mankind, those lucky inhabitants of class A countries above, have escaped from this lot. They have achieved not only much greater and more dependable levels of consumption, but they also enjoy significant periods of leisure.

For two thirds of mankind, neither of these achievements hold, but they see (or their governments do) that the historical lot of man is not inevitable, and they want change. At least this seems to be more true among the 2 billion sick and undernourished inhabitants of class C countries than is suggested by some books painting an idyllic picture of the South Sea islander, basking in the sun all day, eating what nature lavishly throws in his lap, and not having a single worry on earth. More likely, he is living in a mud hut, wearing crude articles of clothing, forever hungry and sick, his vitality and ambition being sapped by parasitic worms, anemia, and other diseases. In fact, the spread between the rich and the poor nations is increasing. The GNP per head of the former is rising much faster than that of the latter. And the poor nations, rather than being filled with a dull sense of hopelessness, are aroused by their nationalistic leaders to a state of acute discontent. They demand that someone do something and do it *now*. The sense of urgency they feel is real, and it is strong. For them economic growth is more than a luxury. It spells the difference between life and death.

The Need for Governmental Guidance

Just as for the United States or the Soviet Union, there is no reason to believe for the underdeveloped nations that growth "will just happen." The enterprising role of government is needed. Historically, governments have aided the process of economic growth in *all* the rich countries of class A above, although the methods used have varied widely. By deliberately failing to act, for instance, in the face of widespread exploitation of labor by the classes likely to save and invest (as in Great Britain) or by heavily taxing the peasants (as in Japan and the Soviet Union), governments have seen to it that consumers failed to share, or failed to share very much, for considerable periods of time in the increases in GNP per head. This made possible private and public capital formation as well as the promotion of education. The governments of underdeveloped nations must similarly act. In fact, many of them want development fast and have little sympathy for "letting private enterprise do the job."

The Grand Strategy of Development

Given the decision of the government of an underdeveloped country to promote economic development, the question of how it should be done arises immediately. Sometimes people put this question in terms of two alternatives. Shall they follow the U.S. "model" or shall they follow the trail to riches blazed by the Soviet Union? If you think about it, and if you have carefully followed the discussion of Part 3 to this point, you will realize that this is a foolish way of putting the question. The conditions facing most underdeveloped countries now are different than those having faced the United States or the Soviet Union at any time in the last 100 years. Neither "model" will do.

Most governments of the underdeveloped world are quite aware of this truth. They know that they have to forge new policies appropriate to *their* particular circumstances (which, however, does not have to prevent them from playing the United States against the Soviets to get aid from both!). They usually see the grand problem of development strategy in a different way. It is not a matter of following a socialist or capitalist "model," it is rather a question of "shall we promote growth (by whatever means are appropriate) of agriculture or of industry?"

industrialization vs. agricultural progress   Should economic growth be initiated by developing industry before all else, or through a transformation of the agricultural sector instead? The latter is oftentimes least palatable to the governments of underdeveloped countries, especially if they identify agricultural development with perpetuation of their former role of primary producers for colonial powers.

Industrial might is usually equated with high per capita incomes, and examples to the contrary (Denmark, New Zealand) are treated as negligible exceptions to the rule. *Rapid* industrialization is so strongly desired and so universally viewed as a panacea that it is often forgotten that *a prosperous agriculture was in all leading economies of the world the basis for industrialization.* The ability of a small part of the labor force to produce all the food the whole population needed was their solid foundation for growth. To some extent, the potential surplus food was actually produced and exported in return for industrial goods. In other cases, the potential surplus was not produced and resources were used directly for nonagricultural production.

Possibly, many underdeveloped countries that will not hear of agricultural development *first and foremost* are closing themselves off from the road to growth—a road, furthermore, that might be least painful in the way of social adjustments, being closest to the ways of the past. Quite possibly, the vigorous development of agriculture, by infusing it with modern knowledge and equipment, could turn out to be in some countries the best method yet to escape the trap of poverty (as New Zealand and Denmark have shown to be possible).

This does not, however, have to be true for all developing countries, nor does it mean that agricultural development should favor a single crop only. Such extremely *one-sided* development may, indeed, prove harmful to a country. Having all its "eggs in one basket," say coffee production, a country would be extremely dependent on world demand for this one product. The preceding remarks are only intended to point out that agricultural improvements are necessary in all underdeveloped countries.

All underdeveloped countries have to make some sort of decision on this issue. Some may do best to become developed agricultural economies. Others may be better off to improve their agriculture, but to stress industry eventually. In any case, these two sectors are not mutually exclusive, but mutually interdependent. Agriculture can play a crucial role in limiting the whole economy's pace of economic growth (and not just because it is the supplier of some industrial raw materials). In most underdeveloped countries, domestic food production has failed to keep pace with or has barely exceeded population growth. Hence, the imported food volume had to be increased, restricting the supply of foreign exchange for the importation of capital goods, and thereby slowing the pace of industrialization.

Certainly the insistence of some underdeveloped countries on conspicuous and spectacular investment (building a steel mill first and acquiring a modern airline second) may be utter folly and often it serves no other purpose but to create national "prestige." Having a national airline does not make a desert country automatically rich, even though all rich countries have national airlines!

Specific Policy Measures

Having decided to promote growth and having decided which economic sector is to receive the lion's share of its attention, the government must wrestle with the specifics. The elements of underdevelopment discussed above can provide us with a convenient checklist. It goes without saying that governments will concentrate on removing whichever obstacles to growth in this list are the most serious.

natural resource development   Wherever desirable, governmental efforts can also be directed toward improving the supply of natural resources. This must not necessarily mean discovery, exploitation, or making accessible of local resources. Some countries, as Switzerland, have overcome a very poor natural resource endowment through imports from abroad. Hence, a poor natural resource supply can be alleviated also in indirect ways (such as educating people to produce toys and watches for export!).

capital formation   Governments of underdeveloped countries are acutely aware of the need for capital accumulation. This is true, furthermore, both for the types of buildings, equipment, and inventories used directly in specific sectors (say, in agriculture and industry) and for the types used indirectly by all sectors of the economy. The latter, often referred to as "social overhead" capital, would involve the construction of roads, bridges, railroads, harbors, public utilities (electric power, gas, water, sewerage, communications facilities), hospitals, residential housing, schools, and so on. If you just look at the economic history of the United States or of Russia, you will note how important social overhead capital has been. The transcontinental railroad in the United States opened up development of the West and allowed large-scale commercial farming. The large agricultural productivity increases were the foundation for industrial development. The trans-Siberian railroad in Russia had similar consequences.

So far as the present underdeveloped countries are concerned, however, the *means* for achieving capital formation will probably have to differ markedly from both the United States and Soviet methods described above. One can hardly engage in monetary and fiscal policies (as described on pages 571–572) where the institutional environment necessary thereto is completely absent or in an utterly primitive state of development. Similarly, Soviet methods of planning and administration (even if the desire to use them existed) will in most underdeveloped countries be utterly out of place. Here are some of the policies which might be followed.

Cutting leisure or reducing underemployment.   In countries where the monetary sector of the economy is most rudimentary, governments may demand a "tax" in kind from the rural population, as in the form of so many days of labor during the off-season, in the form of building materials, and so on. By providing the proper leadership, resources that would be idle part of the time may be thus shifted during that time to the production of such capital goods as irrigation canals, wells, drainage ditches, schools, roads, and so on; or they may be used in the control of pests and diseases of man, animals, and plants—all without any loss of agricultural output. This may be the closest equivalent to the U.S. practice of stimulating investment by a levy of higher (money) taxes on households, which frees resources from the production of consumer goods and which resources are then used to build capital goods demanded by government or businesses.

Cutting consumption by taxes in kind.   Where agricultural output is more than sufficient to sustain life, governments may, of course, also follow the Bukharin-type policy of taxing away in kind some of the surplus output and using it for growth. This output can be used to feed workers engaged in building capital goods. It can be used to pay for imports of foreign capital goods. It can be used to support people engaged in teaching or research. Thus, the economy may gather strength slowly. Under some circumstances, governments could also follow the more forceful methods of Stalin, which may yield faster results, although at higher cost (see pages 582–583).

Cutting consumption by monetary taxes.   In economies where the use of money is widespread and some minimum level of reliable administrative machinery exists, government can, of course, follow the U.S.-type practice of cutting consumer spending (and hence the production of consumer goods) by levying taxes in money. This may be particularly effective if directed against consumption by the rich (of whom even the underdeveloped countries have their share) and against any significant *increases* in the level of living of the masses.

To elaborate on the latter, it is frequently alleged that the poor countries' propensity to save out of additional income is extremely low because everyone tries to emulate the consumption behavior of their North American fellow men. "The life of the American household, supported by all the gadgets of the mid-twentieth century," goes the argument, "is well known to the populations of the underdeveloped countries. Tourists, American troops, movies, and magazines have seen to that. Thus any increase in income is immediately spent on whatever desirable gadget can be acquired, and the incentive to save is missing just in the very countries where it is most necessary as a prerequisite for investment and economic growth." If this is true, taxes that expropriate whatever portion of new income should be saved (as the government sees it) could remedy the situation. Actually, however, one may doubt that the "international demonstration effect" is as serious as people make it out to be. Why should the masses in underdeveloped countries want to imitate the consumption habits of North Americans, while being totally unaffected by those of their own wealthy fellow citizens? Why should they at the same time be utterly unaffected by the saving and investment habits of the Americans? The effect may just as well work for the good of economic development, as when the desire for industrial consumer goods provides the incentive to try new techniques and raise new crops for the market to provide the necessary money income. This may enlarge the size of the money economy (and of potential government revenues for public investment) and whet the appetite for further experiments with the new. Quite possibly, *governments*, rather than masses of people, are the ones affected adversely by the demonstration effect, as when they are led to adopt policies of advanced countries that are inappropriate in their circumstances (the above steel mill and airline are cases in point).

In any event, where a money economy exists, monetary taxes can reduce consumption first and be used subsequently for public capital formation. Or private capital formation can be encouraged on the basis of resources released from consumer goods production.

Cutting consumption by inflation.   "Taxation" can also take the form of inflation. In countries with well-developed money economies but imperfect tax systems, governments frequently have resorted to the printing press to finance their spending on capital goods. The result for the fully employed economy, as we learned in Part 1, is inflation. People may spend their whole income and all of any additions to income, yet they will be unable to buy all the output. The government gets some of it. Whether this, on balance, promotes capital formation is, however, a moot question. It all depends on whether private investors are encouraged or discouraged by the inflation, and this may well vary with the degree of inflation experienced.

In some underdeveloped countries inflation has led to certain undesirable compositional changes in investment. Private investors have refrained from investment in factory buildings and machinery, but turned to the hoarding of inventories and the (excessive) building of luxury apartments. *Rapid* inflation, as recently found in Latin America, is likely to retard growth. Furthermore, in countries where it is still necessary to make the transition from a barter to a money economy, inflation is exceedingly bad, because it is bound to undermine confidence in money and thus the establishment of division of labor and exchange relations within society.

Cutting consumption by voluntary saving.   Governments might also try to get people to save voluntarily, as by buying government bonds. However, cutting consumer spending by selling bonds is often a hopeless undertaking in underdeveloped countries. High income classes frequently prefer to "save" in the form of precious metals or jewelry, or they prefer to buy foreign securities. Nevertheless, developing countries are trying to encourage the habit of voluntary saving by such institutions as savings banks, high sales taxes on "luxury" consumer goods, tax concessions when income is saved, and the like.

Foreign borrowing.   All the above solutions to capital formation assume that there *are* resources that can be diverted to investment (and away from idleness or consumer goods production). What if this is not the case at all because available resources must be used fully for consumer goods production just to maintain life? Or what if the investment possible in this fashion is so negligible that it is insufficient to raise GNP faster than population?

Then sufficient capital formation becomes impossible except through the medium of foreign aid. If other countries can be persuaded to give up (as a gift or as a loan) part of *their* GNP, an underdeveloped country may be enabled in the short run to get capital goods without reducing its own consumption. In terms of Figure 24.3 THE PRODUCTION POSSIBILITIES CURVE, the country may then use a combination of goods beyond or above its production possibilities curve. Instead of moving from a to b, it can move to a point vertically above a. It matters little how exactly this acquisition is accomplished. The country may physically import capital goods from abroad, but it could just as well import food and use its own labor force, previously needed for food production, to make capital goods. We will discuss foreign aid in further detail below.

improvements of the labor force   There is no underdeveloped country that can afford to be content with the quality of its labor force. Resources obtained by one of the five methods just described must also be channeled toward education and technical progress. Many underdeveloped economies could benefit immensely from the gradual adoption or adaption of modern technical know-how. This cannot be done without education. Illiterate natives, who do not even know how to use a plow, can hardly be expected to work along a modern industrial assembly line, even if it could be produced or imported. No modern economy can exist without great masses of people who can read, write, and perform simple calculations. That is the minimum.

Also in the realm of higher education, governmental efforts can attempt to provide the type of manpower needed for a growing economy, such as scientists, engineers, teachers, and managers. In many underdeveloped countries, such fields attract few and those few who do receive a higher education tend to go into areas with higher prestige (such as law). Unfortunately also, many who are educated abroad stay abroad.

Similarly, measures designed to improve the health of the population are a must. Without them no vigorous and sustained activity can be maintained.

environmental changes   As we saw above, inadequate quantities or qualities of resources are not the only obstacles to growth. Corrupt governments may have to be replaced, tax systems may have to be revised thoroughly, such treasured institutions as the extended family may have to be broken up to provide incentives. There is no easy recipe for accomplishing such a feat. In many underdeveloped countries, *land reform* is an absolute necessity for agricultural progress. In some cases, large landholdings have to be split. In other cases, too small landholdings have to be consolidated, either for reasons of incentive or so that plots can be efficiently utilized. Note that such reforms have occurred in many of the rich countries. The enclosure movement in the United Kingdom (from the thirteenth to the eighteenth centuries) is one example. The Soviet experience of revolution (breaking up too large holdings) and later collectivization (combining too small holdings) is another. Chinese reforms in the 1950's served the same purposes and were even quicker.

Another problem we noted above was the narrowness of markets discouraging technically efficient production units. This may often be mitigated by *cooperation among the developing country and other countries.* For instance, the commercial policies pursued by developed countries with regard to the trade with the underdeveloped ones are not less important than their foreign aid policies. You will recall from Chapter 21 that commercial policy refers to such measures as tariffs and quotas. A tariff is a tax on imports, a quota is a direct legal limit on import quantity. Both measures discourage imports (or prevent exports from the partner country). For a country faced with the need to import capital goods an increase in export earnings can contribute as much to the lessening of this constraint on growth as an increase in foreign aid.

There are many historical precedents. The elimination in the last century of the British corn laws, for example, allowed massive U.S. grain exports to Britain. This paid for the imports of capital goods. Yet today, developed countries are frequently pursuing contradictory polices of liberal aid, on the one hand, and simultaneous restrictive commercial policies, on the other. The latter is especially true if an underdeveloped country tries to sell processed products and manufactures that are also produced in the developed countries. Even trade in primary products is frequently restricted by tariffs or quotas to protect domestic agricultural, mineral, and fuel producers in the developed countries. Thus developing countries which are unable to produce capital goods themselves, but which could (following a land reform, say) produce more agricultural goods than are needed at home, may be unable to export them, hence be unable to pay for capital goods imports.

United Nations efforts may soon change this, however. According to an outline of a scheme approved by most of the developed countries, nonreciprocal tariff preferences might be granted to underdeveloped nations that desired access to the markets of developed countries.

Closer cooperation among the developing countries themselves can, of course, also contribute to the enlargement of markets. Such cooperation may include coordinated export policies to developed nations or trade within the underdeveloped group. The former is presently achieved in part by international "commodity agreements," but they cover only a limited range of commodities.

Such agreements create buffer stocks of certain primary products, such as coffee. The parties to the agreement buy or sell the commodity in question to stabilize its world market price. The purchase by the U.S. government of wheat to keep its price up domestically is the exact equivalent of this (see Chapter 19). In addition, just as the U.S. government arranges for monetary subsidies to farmers, the International Monetary Fund's "supplementary finance" program allows underdeveloped countries to borrow whenever their exports fall below the trend owing to reasons beyond human control.

Recently regional trade cooperation among developing countries themselves has aroused much interest as an instrument of fostering industrial growth and efficiency. Faced with the difficulties of finding export outlets for manufactures in developed countries, developing countries have looked to regional trade agreements among themselves. Their aim is to create protected markets to promote both technical and economic efficiency within the region. This tendency has also been furthered by the General Agreement on Tariffs and Trade according to which developing countries may not discriminate in favor of each other's products except within such formal groupings.

A number of such groupings have been established. They usually involve the gradual elimination of tariffs within the group, a common tariff to the outside world, a number of cooperative ventures in such areas as transportation, communication, education, research, as well as the coordination of development policies. Examples of such groupings are the East African Customs and Currency Union (among Kenya, Uganda, and Tanzania), the Maghreb Economic Union (among Algeria, Libya, Morocco, and Tunisia), the Central African Economic and Customs Union (among members of the Equatorial Customs Union and Cameroon), the Central American Customs Union (among six Central American Republics), and the Latin American Free Trade Association. At the time of this writing, in 1969, six Latin American countries (Bolivia, Chile, Columbia, Ecuador, Peru, and Venezuela) were in the process of establishing an Andean Common Market.

population control   Take another look at page 549. Real GNP per head can clearly be raised not only through measures raising GNP, but also by a control of population. As we mentioned above, the long-run effect of western medical aid has not always been for the good. It has led to skyrocketing population growth in the underdeveloped world. Thus, ironically, the compassion for the poor and the sick that brings medical missionaries to the underdeveloped countries often results in more people starving in adulthood, rather than dying of infectious diseases during infancy! Because real GNP can often not be raised substantially faster than population, efforts to achieve economic growth will remain frustrated unless population growth can be restricted.

Responsible governments cannot take an ostrich attitude with respect to this problem. They only ignore it at their peril. They must do more than vaguely hope for a drop in fertility in some distant future, when people are more educated, urbanized (with many alternatives for leisure), and when the social status of women has improved. They must stop the population avalanche *now,* lest economic development is obstructed forever. An example of such action is Japan. In 1963, it had a population density of 259 persons per square kilometer (as opposed to 20 in the United States). In 1948 its birth rate had been 34, its death rate 12. In that year, the government took action. It legalized abortion and sterilization. It initiated a nationwide campaign for family planning, employed tens of thousands of birth control guidance officers, and opened marriage advice centers. The results were spectacular. In 1966, its birth rate was down to 13.7, the death rate 6.8. Hence, population growth was cut from 2.2 percent per year to 0.7 percent.

If they are serious about economic development, the underdeveloped countries will have to take similar measures, even if it means offending religious elements and other guardians of traditional values. Theirs is not a choice between something ideal and undesirable. It is a choice between the undesirable and disaster. Unless births are cut humanely and now, the cruel forces of famine and war will do it with certainty before this century is over. Will the danger signals of the present be heeded?

FUTURE PROSPECTS

As always, one can only guess about the future. Since 1950, most underdeveloped countries have undertaken the formulation of medium- and long-term plans to assess requirements and guide policies for their economic development. This process has been spurred by the newly achieved independence of many African countries, as well as by the Alliance for Progress in Latin America. The success so far has been variable and in no case spectacular. The United Nations has pronounced as a minimum goal a growth of the underdeveloped countries' real GNP at a rate of 5 percent a year by 1970 and of 6 percent during the 1970's. For this the prospects are bleak. According to United Nations estimates, the aggregate real GNP of these countries grew at an average annual rate of 4.9 percent from 1950 to 1955, at 4.5 percent from 1955 to 1960, and at 4.0 percent from 1960 to 1964. Hence, real GNP per head grew considerably less.

The future performance will depend essentially on how vigorously wise policies are pursued. But there can be little doubt about one thing: *Even the most rapidly growing underdeveloped country does not have a chance to catch up with the per capita GNP of, say, the United States in the foreseeable future.* Make the most pessimistic assumption for the United

States and assume that its real GNP per head only rises at 2 percent per year. At 2 percent annual rise of the above $3,200 figure (see Table 26.1) would mean an absolute annual *increase* of $64. This is almost equal to the *total* present GNP per head of mainland China! Or take Venezuela, with a GNP per head of $800, the "richest" country in South America. Even if its GNP per head were to rise at 8 percent a year (a most unlikely story), it would (with the U.S. per capita GNP still rising only at 2 percent) take almost 25 years for the two figures to become equal. As you can see from Table 26.1, most countries are presently in a much worse position (in relation to the United States) than is Venezuela. Relative growth rates are considerably more unfavorable for the underdeveloped world than in our example. Hence, the poor are going to be with us for a long time to come.

This, brings us to one more point. Can we expect this situation to be changed by the process of the rich helping the poor?

The Role of Private Foreign Investment

After all, many a presently developed country got started on the road to economic development with substantial doses of foreign aid (loans or grants). Such aid was traditionally of a private nature with foreign entrepreneurs seizing available opportunities to build up profitable enterprises in the developing country with imported equipment and imported skilled personnel. Examples are British foreign investment in Australia, Canada, Latin America, and the United States; German investment in Eastern Europe; French investment in tsarist Russia; United States investment in Canada. The amounts involved were often huge. British citizens, for instance, invested abroad 7.5 percent of national income in the nineteenth century. The "import" of foreign entrepreneurs was frequently, however, just as important as the capital they brought along. More likely than not, it was the most enterprising and ambitious who emigrated. They were stimulated by the new environment and not inhibited by local customs. They were freed from the restraints of the "old country." And their industry, endurance, and frugality, which brought success, stimulated imitation by latent entrepreneurship in their adopted country.

It is unlikely, however, that such private foreign investment will aid the presently underdeveloped countries to any large degree. Since World War II, the governments of the underdeveloped countries, possessed by a spirit of extreme nationalism, have discouraged foreign private investors by all possible means, such as discriminatory taxes, red tape, prohibition to use profits freely, and outright confiscation of property. To them there is little difference between the old colonial administrator and the official of the Standard Oil Company of New Jersey. Thus, many measures aimed at reducing "dependence" on foreigners and taken by governments that have recently won independence from colonial powers may be understandable. But it is doubtful that they were in the true interests of the nations involved. Capital formation on their soil is the one thing they could least afford to discourage.

This is not to deny that the governments of underdeveloped countries might have a legitimate interest in regulating the direction foreign investment takes. Often foreigners were only interested in building up a country's export sector (such as rubber in Liberia and Malaya, sugar in the Philippines, oil in Iraq and Venezuela, copper in Chile and Zambia, bananas in Central America, cocoa in Ghana, cotton in Egypt and the Sudan, coffee in Colombia, rice in Burma). If governments disliked such one-sided economic development, they could have easily discouraged it without discouraging private foreign investment in general.

The way things have happened, much U.S. private investment abroad has been diverted from the underdeveloped countries to politically stable areas of Canada and Western Europe. Data for 1967 are typical of the recent trend. Direct U.S. private investment abroad equaled $4.5 billion, but only 18 percent of this went to underdeveloped countries. To counter this trend, President Nixon's advisers have recommended an expansion of government guarantees for private investments in the underdeveloped world. Such investment would be insured against inconvertibility of currencies, revolution, insurrection, and expropriation. Backed up by formal agreements between the United States and seventy-five underdeveloped countries, about half a billion dollars of U.S. private investment a year has been covered recently by such political risk insurance.

The Role of Public Foreign Aid

As a result of the nationalistic policies since World War II, foreign aid today involves primarily public funds. Hence, it has been a matter of *public* concern that these funds be used most effectively. (In the case of private foreign investment, the *private* investor usually supervises the project and does whatever is necessary to ensure its success.) Donor countries have encouraged developing countries to adopt well-thought-out "self-help" policies simultaneously with the receipt of foreign assistance. Yet, such conditions often prove to be politically embarrassing and are resented by the recipient.

If the U.S. government, as a condition of giving economic aid, demands that the recipient country weed out corrupt government officials, tax the rich more and distribute their land to the peasants, cease discrimination against certain social classes, and stop wasting resources in wars against its neighbors, you can well imagine the diplomatic problems this creates. More likely than not, it is just the people in power who stand in the way of economic progress. Will they voluntarily change their behavior, make the necessary sacrifices, and give up the inherited privileges to promote economic development? One can doubt it. Consider how *violent* upheavals preceded economic development in France, Germany, Russia, and the United States. Everywhere power had to be redistributed before change could proceed. The U.S. government can only be frustrated if it tries to bring this about by moral suasion.

Similarly, a U.S. government is in no position to change attitudes of the people at large. Can the U.S. government really tell the Indians to stop treating cows as sacred and to use them in agriculture and as food? What if foreigners told us to stop treating churches as sacred and to use them as factory buildings instead?

Yet, if the U.S. government fails to make demands for reform, chances are great that much of the aid will have no effect on growth. One cannot have economic development and avoid social tensions at the same time.

U.S aid programs   The major types of public aid originating in the United States are the following. (1) So-called "hard" loans, made in dollars and repayable in dollars, at interest rates of 4 to 6 percent per year, are made on a "strictly business" basis by the Washington, D.C., Export-Import Bank and the Inter-American Development Bank, both U.S. government agencies. (2) So-called "soft" loans, made in dollars, but repayable in the recipient's currency, at lower interest rates, are made by the Agency for International Development (AID). (3) There are a variety of U.S. government grants, ranging from monetary grants to technical assistance (including the Peace Corps) to surplus food shipments. The total value of U.S. economic aid to countries other than in class A above has been $31 billion from 1948 to 1967, or on the average $1.6 billion per year, a fraction of 1 percent of U.S. GNP. (Note: total U.S. aid in the form of loans or grants has been higher, but much of it went to developed countries or was of military nature. According to the London Institute for Strategic Studies, the underdeveloped countries spent $1 billion on armament imports in 1964. They are said to spend considerably more now, buying "surplus" weapons mainly from the United States, Soviet Union, France, the United Kingdom, and other European countries.)

Soviet aid programs   After years of denouncing western aid as an ill-disguised instrument of imperialism, the Soviet Union initiated an aid program of her own in 1954 to project her presence into the underdeveloped world. The Soviet foreign aid program consists entirely of "soft," long-term (10 to 30 year) loans at low rates of interest (1 to 2.5 percent per year). This, as well as the features described below, has been politically advantageous to the U.S.S.R. Unlike U.S. aid, Soviet aid can be used for whatever project the *borrower* decides. The Soviet Union has been most willing to go along with the whims of the borrowing countries and provided for the construction of many a heavy industry showpiece without regard to the appropriateness of such use. U.S. aid has, in contrast, concentrated on less spectacular needs, such as agricultural development, sanitation facilities, education, and the like. Also, U.S. aid was until recently thinly spread over about a hundred nations (with no significant results anywhere), while Soviet aid was from the beginning heavily concentrated on a few selected countries: in order of importance, India, the United Arab Republic, Afghanistan, Indonesia, and Iran had by 1965 received $3.3 billion of the $5 billion of total Soviet aid given. Thus, Soviet aid has provided on the average $0.4 billion per year, also a tiny fraction of 1 percent of Soviet GNP.

international aid programs   *A proposal.* Some people, such as Senator Fulbright in the United States, have argued that all foreign aid given by the rich countries should be channeled through international organizations. This would effectively counter some of the difficulties any national aid program is certain to encounter. Just as the blacks in our city ghettos rightly resent the arrogant assumption of some whites that they know what is best for the ghetto dweller, so the underdeveloped countries resent the strings attached to aid by another government. Similarly, Americans have expressed the fear that we will be pushed into political alliances and all kinds of commitments through the medium of foreign aid. They have pointed to South Vietnam as an example.

But suppose, as Senator Fulbright and others have proposed, we internationalized all foreign aid. Suppose all countries, rich and poor, agreed to contribute to a common pool a certain percentage of their GNPs. Just as all families in the United States contribute to the U.S. Treasury in accordance with their income, the rich countries may contribute most, the poor only modest amounts. In turn, these funds can then be distributed to the poor nations in a continuous, predictable fashion. Just as poor families can count on government transfer payments, the poor countries can *as a matter of right,* count on development aid. It could be dispensed according to need, through a corps of international civil servants, free from any stigma of charity. This would only recognize internationally what is recognized by every system of ethics: the obligation of the rich to help the poor. Gratuity by national governments would be replaced by a worldwide community responsibility.

In this framework, developing countries may well accept advice that they now reject. What they cannot hear from American or Russian experts, they may hear when told by an international official. Then the U.S. and Soviet aid programs may cease to be competitive Cold War instruments, as they become a *cooperative* venture. In fact, this could become a vehicle for disarmament. Without hurting their relative positions of power, the big nations could simultaneously and equally divert military expenditures into this development fund. By de-escalating the arms race and promoting economic development, this would doubly serve the goal of world peace.

The World Bank.   The above is nothing more than a proposal. Yet, there are already a few international agencies dispensing economic aid. The International Bank for Reconstruction and Development (the *World Bank*) is an international agency with 110 member nations. It has a net worth of $21 billion. Of this 20 percent have been paid in; 2 percent in gold and U.S. dollars, 18 percent in member currencies. The rest is on call. The United States is liable for one third of this amount. The bank also sells its own bonds in the rich countries to acquire funds for lending to the poor and it guarantees private loans. Between 1947 and mid-1968, the World Bank had made $12 billion of loans. They were "hard" loans for particular (usually revenue-yielding) projects, repayable in 15 to 25 years at 4.5 and 5.0 percent interest per year, and in the currency borrowed. Loans are made only to governments or for government-guaranteed projects. Thus, the World Bank has provided on the average $0.6 billion in aid per year.

Possibly these efforts will become larger in the future. Mr. McNamara, the new bank president, announced in 1968 that the World Bank would "during the next 5 years" lend as much as in the past 22 years. Also the emphasis was to be shifted away from steel mills, factories, and dams to less spectacular, but in the long run much more promising projects: development of education, agriculture, and methods to curb population growth. Particular focus is to be on Africa and Latin America. Note the news report introducing this chapter.

The World Bank has two affiliates. The International Finance Corporation, established in 1956 with a net worth of $100 million, makes loans to private enterprises. The International Development Association, with a net worth of $1 billion, was established in 1960. It makes "soft" loans for up to 50 years at very low interest (.75 percent). It has favored the financing of social overhead capital, such as highways, education, sanitation facilities.

The United Nations.   In addition to the monetary aid of the World Bank, technical assistance is provided by two United Nations agencies. The Special United Nations Fund for Economic Development (SUNFED) and the United Nations Expanded Program for Technical Assistance (UNEPTA) are financed by voluntary contributions by members. About $80 million a year are spent by these agencies to make a variety of surveys. These have included, for instance, surveys on mineral, soil, and water resources, and locust migration patterns. Often, such surveys become the basis for subsequent World Bank financing.

conclusions   Combining the three major sources of public development aid (U.S., Soviet, international), underdeveloped countries have received on the average about $2.6 billion of *economic* grants or loans per year in the 1950's and 1960's. Augment this by the amounts of public aid from other rich countries and of private investment from all sources and the total rises to perhaps double that. Yet, this is still a negligible figure so far as the rich countries' GNP is concerned. (If the United States were to make in 1970 an effort equivalent to that made by private British investors during the nineteenth century, she alone would have to make foreign loans and grants of over $50 billion each year!) Thus aid to the underdeveloped nations comes to the staggering figure of at most $3 per inhabitant per year. The aid received by them amounts probably to 1 percent of the combined GNP of the underdeveloped world. To them in the aggregate, aid is, therefore, negligible also. Thus, it is most doubtful that foreign aid will appreciably brighten the sad prospects for the underdeveloped world. In fact, the United Nations has estimated that the underdeveloped countries, should current trends continue, will by 1975 need all the aid they get just to pay interest and principal on past loans from abroad.

CHINA AND INDIA—A BRIEF CASE STUDY

In conclusion let us take a closer look at two specific cases of economic underdevelopment, China and India. Almost 60 percent of the people of the underdeveloped world live in China and India. Thus, events in these two countries are of more than passing interest. This interest is heightened by the fact that China is a Communist and totalitarian country, whereas India is a democracy, and the eyes of the world are on them to see which of the two forms of government will be more successful in dealing with the problem of scarcity. In fact, scarcity in both countries is at its most intense compared with the rest of the world. Per capita GNP in India is perhaps $80, in China, somewhat less.

The two countries' natural resource endowments are vast (yet often in an underdeveloped state), but populations are huge also. In 1969, there were 850 million people in China, over 530 million in India. In the early 1970's, China's population will pass the 1 billion mark;

India's will do the same before the end of this century. As of 1969, in China, there are 230 people per square mile, in India 423 (in the United States, there are 56). Energy consumption per person in India was in 1966 only 189 kilograms of coal equivalent. (It was 10,283 kilograms in the United States.)

The capital stock per person in China and India is a small fraction of that figure for the United States. An impressionistic view of this is given by the following data (referring to the mid-1960's). The crude steel used annually per head was 735 kilograms in the United States, but 19 kilograms in China and 16 kilograms in India. In the United States 5,291 ton-kilometers of freight were transported by rail annually per head; in China 345; in India 200. The United States had 471 motor vehicles per 1,000 persons; India had 1.7 vehicles. The United States had 502 telephones per 1,000 persons; India had 1.9.

The quality of the labor force in the two countries is incredibly low compared to the United States. In 1961, 72 percent of the Indian population above 15 years of age were illiterate (and 69 percent of the active population were employed in agriculture). India had 24 engineers and scientists per 100,000 people, the United States had about 550. Hopes for rapid improvements of the educational level in India are dim. In 1960, only 22 percent of those aged 15 to 19 went to school in India. University (and equivalent) enrollment around 1960 was 335 for every 100,000 persons in both China and India (as opposed to 2,014 per 100,000 persons in the United States). The absolute numbers of those engaged in higher education in the United States equaled that of those similarly engaged in China and India combined.

In 1964, the average Chinese and Indian received 2,000 calories per day (compared with 3,100 for the average American), an Indian received 49 grams of protein per day (as opposed to 92 for an American). The average Indian dwelling had two rooms (and 77 percent of all dwellings had one or two rooms), whereas the average American dwelling had five rooms (with 61 percent of all dwellings having at least five rooms). On top of having inadequate food and shelter to fend off disease, there was one physician for 5,800 Indians (as opposed to one for every 700 persons in the United States and 490 persons in Russia). Life expectancy in India was 41 years.

Yet, both China and India have stable governments that exhibit the strong determination to promote economic development. They both have undertaken since World War II vigorous programs of economic development, but their approaches to the problem differ drastically.

China

Similar to the Soviet Union, the Chinese have concentrated much economic power in the hands of government and have carried out a determined program of planned economic development. As in the Soviet Union, their strategy involved large-scale mobilization of resources for capital formation (directed especially into heavy industry), as well as for universal education, for the widespread improvement of health services, and for scientific research. The period from 1949 to 1952 (and probably beyond) was a period of recovery from the disruptions of the Sino-Japanese war and the civil war that followed. During this period, production levels regained what had already been attained in China proper in the 1930's and in Manchuria in the 1940's. At the same time, the ground was being laid, by a number of institutional reforms, for Soviet-style industrialization. By 1952, the Chinese investment component of GNP was raised to 20 percent, a remarkable feat for a country with such a low per capita GNP. Apparently, the percentage has never been lower since.

Together with capital formation, education has been pushed. During the period since 1949, the number of young people going to full-time educational institutions has multiplied rapidly. All urban and the majority of rural children now go to primary schools. Attendance in primary schools has risen to over 100 million by the mid-1960's, compared to 25 million in 1949. Secondary school enrollment rose from 1 to 10 million in this period and that in institutions of higher education from a mere handful to 1 million. In addition, educational efforts are made in many study groups on a part-time or spare-time basis, particularly in the communes, the factories, and the army. Education, furthermore, is directed to more than basic skills, such as learning to read and write. Scientific and engineering education has been greatly favored, partly to dispel myths and superstitions that may stand in the way of the new, partly to train the type of manpower required by a modern economy.

China's remarkable gains in the field of health have recently also been attested to by a number of expert visitors. Most startling is the prevention and control of infectious and parasitic diseases that had ravaged China for centuries. Through intensive radio propaganda the general environmental sanitation in cities and rural areas has also been phenomenally improved.

Finally, although most underdeveloped countries seem to devote less than 0.2 percent of GNP to research and development, the Chinese figure seems to be well above 1 percent, about equal to the West German percentage, but considerably below that of the United States or Soviet Union. This relatively strong showing reflects the determination of the Chinese government to achieve great power status and self-reliance. It has also made China the only country among the economically underdeveloped ones that possesses The Bomb.

As a result of all these efforts, Chinese real GNP, from 1952 to 1966, grew at an estimated average annual rate of 4 to 5 percent. Growth of per capita real GNP was, of course, smaller (given the rise in population): from 2 to 3 percent annually. Industrial output seems to have grown, from 1949 to 1965, at a rate of 11 percent per year on the average. The Chinese economic performance, remarkable as it may seem, has, however, been highly uneven. The above averages are by no means representative of reality in any one year. This fact needs special emphasis, for without it no realistic appraisal can be made of the future prospects of Chinese economic development.

the first 5-year plan, 1952–1957   The first 5-year plan was a consistent program of Soviet-style industrialization. We cannot be absolutely sure about its results. Worse even than with data for the Soviet Union, reliable statistics on the Chinese economy are hard to come by. Western experts have, however, become convinced that Chinese economic progress in the 1950's was more than remarkable. After centuries of stagnation, and despite a population increase from 583 million in 1953 to 647 million in 1958, per capita GNP probably rose 3 to 4 percent per year at least, while aggregate GNP grew at a steady pace from 6 to 7 percent per year. Industrial output seems to have risen at the unprecedented rate of 20 percent per year!

Much of this was made possible by the above-mentioned programs of capital formation, education, health, and research, which were carried out in an atmosphere strongly resembling the Soviet industrialization model. Peasants were collectivized and made to work harder and for less. Labor was shifted on a large scale from agriculture to industry. The agricultural surplus collected by the state from the collectives was used to free young people for education and to accumulate capital by feeding the urban population while providing them with domestic raw materials and imports of equipment for industrial pursuits. This was further aided by friendly relations with the Soviets and the import of capital goods on credit. Soviet aid alone erected 156 projects in such areas as steel and iron manufacture, automobiles, aircraft, chemicals, power plants, and mining. In fact, up to 40 percent of China's annual capital formation consisted of imported goods. During this period, the Chinese themselves also produced their first power-generating equipment and their first motor vehicles. Altogether, throughout the first plan period, capital formation equaled between 19 and 23 percent of GNP, a solid, even though painful, achievement, for per capita consumption rose by less than 2 percent per year.

Apparently, this was enough to keep effort coming and produce the good results shown above. Workers and peasants alike, as in the Soviet Union, worked on the basis of material self-interest within the framework established by the state. Wages, bonus payments, and the like were stressed for industrial workers and managers, while private plots of land, together with some private animal holdings and sale of the product in free markets, kept peasant incentives up. Although the full range of nonmaterial incentives (medals, awards, emulation contests) was developed, they were deemphasized. Professional managers and engineers were running the show during the first five-year plan. They fashioned the kind of incentives that make human self-interest work for the programs of the state.

the "great leap forward," 1957–1962   Strangely enough, the Chinese leaders considered the remarkable results of the first five-year plan unsatisfactory. They were also unhappy with the (selfish) ways in which people had been motivated to work. So impatient were they with the growth rate attained that they drew up a radically different program for the second five-year plan, from 1957 to 1962. Industrialization was to make a "great leap forward." Output throughout the economy was to increase 100 percent in one year. Counting on such breakneck speed of industrialization, the Chinese leaders announced their intention to surpass the United Kingdom in industrial output within 15 years.

This could never be achieved, argued Mao Tse-tung, by relying on people's material self-interest, on such capitalist devices as piecework rates and bonuses. People's motives must be *pure,* they must be filled with revolutionary enthusiasm, be altruistic about working for the good of their society.

Correspondingly, the Chinese government initiated the second five-year plan by putting on the pressure to increase output at unrealistically high rates. Mao, confident in his ability to motivate the masses, as he did his guerilla fighters earlier, by revolutionary fervor alone, abolished many material incentives. The new policies were pursued with a ruthlessness and a disregard of the individual that would have put even Stalin to shame: In agriculture, an army of 100 million peasants was organized on "mass irrigation projects," building canals, dikes, and reservoirs in ceaseless day and night shifts under unbelievably harsh conditions. The irrigated area was doubled, and the land was worked under a new "deep-plowing and close-planting policy." Ninety-nine percent of all peasants were forced into "communes." They lost title to their private family plots and with it the age-old hope for independence. The free private farm markets (which had previously provided significant percentages of vegetables, milk, butter, eggs, and meat) were closed. Peasants were made to work more and harder on the collective land, and for less, and they were virtually treated like draft animals. The individual family unit was practically abolished. Women were forced to work at all jobs as equals with men. All private property was abolished. Children were raised in government nurseries, people ate in common mess halls, slept in common barracks. Wages were mostly received in kind and in no way related to the amount of work performed: "From each according to his ability, to each according to his need." For the sake of development, "need" was defined as physical subsistence.

Outside agriculture, the same principle of mass mobilization of labor was used. Organized by military principles, and driven to the limit of endurance, 60 million students and women were to supplement the new modern industrial complexes by producing steel in "backyard furnaces." They, too, worked in night and day shifts.

The new efforts were apparently successful during the first 2 years. While the share of investment was raised to an unbelievable one third of GNP during 1958 and 1959, and the campaign to use "masses of labor without capital" progressed, real GNP spurted ahead, possibly at 13 percent a year or more, with industrial output growing much faster. Possibly, industrial output doubled between 1957 and 1960. Yet the seeds of disaster had also been sown. The utopian neglect of labor incentives, the exhausting pace of work, the excessive regimentation of all of life (imposing, among other things, unrealistic farming practices), and two years of thoroughly bad weather combined to take their toll. Agricultural output began to fall in 1959, accelerating as time passed. This, in turn, caused a fall in industrial output after 1960. The continuation of the downturn can in addition be blamed on the withdrawal of Russian aid as political tension between the two nations began to mount. On top of this, resources were diverted from investment to military pursuits. (Some people argue that the Chinese leaders deliberately manufacture international tensions, as with India, the United States, and Russia, in order to keep the country continually on a war footing, which makes it easier to justify the harsh measures used for the economic revolution at home.)

The "Great Leap Forward" turned into the "Great Crisis." In 1959, the Chinese ceased to release data on economic development, they retreated substantially from their communes policy (some land was even returned to private ownership), the "backyard furnaces" died, and industrialization plans were scaled down. But it was too late. By 1963, industrial output was possibly 40 percent below its previous 1960 peak level. Real GNP was estimated in 1961 at 15 percent below 1958, while per capita GNP probably dropped back to its 1955 level. The latter point is particularly serious.

With a rapidly rising population, any fall in output in China can spell national disaster on a scale unheard of in human history. Interestingly, the Chinese, as early as 1953, had recognized this and reversed their previous stand against birth control. Previously, they had argued that overpopulation is a "vicious figment of the bourgeois mind." The census of 1953 changed all that. It gave mainland China a population of 583 million, over 100 million more than some experts had been estimating. To "improve maternal and child welfare," the government initiated a campaign to spread the idea of birth control, and began to offer contraceptive supplies for sale in government stores. In the late 1950's (with the birth rate still at 34 and the death rate at 11), this campaign was intensified.

the "period of consolidation and readjustment," 1962–1965
Starting in 1962, rationality came back into its own. As revolutionary fervor was restrained, the economy gradually recovered. "Selfishness" once more replaced Mao's "purism" in the realm of incentives. Investment was pushed less, though not necessarily by choice. Massive crop failures and the disruptions of the "Great Leap," which continued to be felt, forced massive food imports at the expense of capital goods imports. Though they had taken only 2 percent of total imports during the first five-year plan, food imports now took up to 40 percent annually.

By 1965, real GNP reached once more its previous 1958 peak. Thus China lost 7 full years of economic growth. Worse still, industrial output is not expected to reach its 1960 level until 1970. Food consumption in 1965 was still below the 1957 level. (A second birth control drive had begun in 1962, encouraging contraception, sterilization, postponement of marriage, abortion, and the three-child family. It never held high priority, however, and lost its impetus by 1964.)

the "great proletarian cultural revolution," 1966–1970
With the inception of the third five-year plan in 1966, the same set of attitudes that brought on the "Great Leap Forward" came to the fore again. There was nothing new in the thoughts of Chairman Mao, whose Red Guards were trying to spread the "Great Proletarian Cultural Revolution." What Mao and his Red Guards were saying was that spectacular and rapid economic achievements require guidance of the economy by politicians, not professional managers. They saw growth born in altruism, revolutionary idealism, and nothing else. To them economic development required transforming *people,* not as certain pragmatic managers and engineers would have it, transforming inputs into outputs by whatever means seem appropriate. These thoughts were carried by the Red Guards throughout the country, and especially onto the factory floors where production stood still, as political indoctrination proceeded. As Mao saw it, the masses of China must be filled with "purity of motive," ready to work not for grimy pay, but the good of society. As he saw it, China could achieve this (and ultimately grow faster than *any* country in the world) if she held on fast to the Communist ideal ("betrayed" by the Soviets) of a *classless society.* Thus, the Red Guards pushed to eliminate all class distinctions. There were to be no differences any more between leaders and followers, between experts and

laymen, between the skilled and the unskilled, between mental and physical labor, between worker and manager, between urban and agricultural labor, between rich and poor. Thus, Mao and his followers abolished differences in pay, they forced managers to do two days a week of physical labor on the production line, and they allowed workers to make management decisions.

Yet, as everyone crammed the writings of Chairman Mao, there were those practical-minded technicians who agreed with the "revisionist" Russians and their acceptance of human selfishness. They proposed to work through human nature, as was done in the first five-year plan, not to change human nature. They argued that Mao's ideological extremism was conducive to economic crisis, not to economic development. They recalled with horror the disastrous "Great Leap." They did not care to repeat it. They called off the sessions on the factory floors and reintroduced the good old piecework rates.

The struggle between the Maoists and the anti-Mao forces was intense. Their confrontation was more than verbal. Large groups of people, even troops, moved within and between the cities and around the countryside, to emphasize the importance of their beliefs. As they struggled over public buildings, the news media, transport facilities, and water supply, agricultural and industrial outputs again began to fall in 1967.

In 1968, China's head of state, Liu Shao-chi, leader of the anti-Mao forces, was stripped of his party rank. Yet simultaneously, the power of the unruly and fanatical Red Guards was reduced, too. "Mao Tse-tung thought propaganda teams" were formed, consisting of urban workers and soldiers. They invaded the schools and "haunts of intellectuals," teaching them instead of the other way around. As the slogan went "The lowly are the most intelligent. The elite are most ignorant." Red Guards and party members became the object of a giant purge, being turned into manual laborers for "re-education." Mao announced that he would completely reconstruct the party organization, filling it with "new blood," that is, members of the propaganda teams and the revolutionary committees governing the provinces that had previously fought the Red Guards! Significantly, the 1968 industrial production report made no mention of any figures at all. An exhaustive study by the Japanese foreign ministry released in 1969, however, reported Chinese GNP in 1968 only slightly above its 1965 level. As we noted earlier, the 1965 level was equal to that of 1958. Thus, it seems that the rejection of rational judgment in favor of the "nobility of the spirit" has cost the Chinese 10 full years of growth. But 1969 was pronounced "the year of economic upsurge" in which industry would again "walk on two legs." Indeed, the Japanese researchers concluded that the resumption of normal economic activity in 1969 may allow a GNP growth of 4 percent, but no more, in the foreseeable future.

conclusion   When seen in this light of perpetual oscillation between authoritarian pragmatism (1949–1957, 1962–1965) and revolutionary utopianism (1958–1961, since 1966), the good over-all performance of the Chinese economy since 1949 cannot be considered as a sure thing on which one can count. Unless the expert economists and engineers can keep Mao's revolutionary zeal under control, the Red Guards, the "proletarian story tellers," or whoever replaces them, are likely to impose their political magic, which so far has been a disaster for economic growth. We cannot be sure that Mao and whoever follows him will realize that there is a fundamental difference between running an economy and running a guerilla war. The driving force of the latter may well be idealism. No economy has yet been run on that principle.

India

In a way, the task of the Indian leaders is more than difficult. It is next to impossible. To achieve growth, they must, as the Chinese, get their poverty-stricken people to restrict consumption, to save, and to invest. But they have decided to persuade people to do this on a *voluntary* basis, without violence and dictatorship. Can it be done? India will give one answer to the question of whether a huge free nation can escape the trap of poverty in the framework of democratic planning or whether human freedom and dignity have to be traded in as a price for material progress.

balanced growth   India has so far gone through three 5-year plans (covering the period 1951 to 1966), relying on private enterprise guided by general governmental planning. A fourth five-year plan was abandoned as unrealistic in 1967, and a new version of it was brought before parliament in 1969. India so far has stressed the importance of "balanced" growth, that is, the simultaneous development of all sectors of the economy.

The government has hardly raised taxes, and it purchases only about 10 percent of GNP. It concentrates its efforts on the accumulation of social overhead capital (irrigation, transportation, educational facilities) and on improving technology (especially in agriculture). Even this relatively small governmental effort is in danger of being seriously crippled owing to the intermittent Chinese aggression along India's frontiers. This forces the diversion into military channels of substantial shares of the resources at the government's disposal. Apart from governmental efforts, about 5 percent of GNP has been privately invested, and it has been directed toward both agriculture and industry. Industrial development has been concentrated in coal, electric power, fertilizers, and heavy industry, but there has also occurred development of small-scale industry (as textiles).

birth control   The Indian government has also been active to control the growth of population. In fact, among all the countries of class C, India has the boldest population policy. It was initiated by Nehru and began with the first plan in 1951. As in Japan, the policy involves the establishment, throughout the nation, of "health centers" providing family planning services. In addition to the national program, there are state and city programs concerned with birth control, and many influential citizens are leading strong movements for birth control. This policy seems to have had only limited success. The birth rate has been falling, but so has the death rate, and population growth still is around 2 percent per year. Since 1967, the government has intensified its birth control campaign. It planned to spend ten times as much on family planning during 1966–1971 as during the previous five years. Although emphasis is on contraception and voluntary sterilization, the questions of legalizing abortion and raising the legal marriage age are also being considered. The government hopes to reduce the annual population increase to below 1 percent by 1975, but given its communications problem with the illiterate rural masses, who speak hundreds of different languages, the prospects do not look bright. Reports for 1969 indicated that the birth control drive was losing momentum. Only 6,800 family planning clinics were operating for half a million villages.

over-all results   The over-all results have not been spectacular. From 1950 to 1955, real GNP seems to have risen at 3.9 percent per year, from 1955 to 1960 at 4.4 percent per year, and from 1960 to 1966 at 3.5 percent per year. Manufacturing output has risen faster than agricultural output, at an annual average from 1949 to 1965 of 6.5 percent. Per capita GNP has risen, the estimates tell us, at 2.1 percent a year from 1950 to 1955, at 2.3 percent from 1955 to 1960, and at 1.1 percent from 1960 to 1966. The rise in living levels has been negligible. In 1969, as in 1950, the 200 million poorest Indians had an annual income of $35. By 1981, if development plans succeed, this figure is to reach $42.

Even the small achievements that have occurred have been heavily reliant on foreign aid (and could thus easily be reversed). From 1948 to 1966, the Indians received $2.8 billion of U.S. economic aid, or 10 percent of U.S. economic aid to the underdeveloped countries. Although small in absolute amount per year, in India's third 5-year plan, a quarter of investment was scheduled to be financed through foreign aid, nearly half of this through U.S. aid. From the Soviet Union India has received, between 1954 and 1965, a total of $1 billion of aid, or 20 percent of Soviet aid to the underdeveloped world. In view of this dependence, the fourth 5-year plan puts great stress on self-reliance. In fact, the plan expects that foreign aid is going to be cut in half.

An Evaluation

It is difficult to evaluate the case of China vs. India. Over all, looking at the entire period from 1949 to the mid-1960's, China seems to be the winner. Its real GNP grew faster on the average (4 to 5 versus 3.5 to 4.5 percent), its industrial output spectacularly faster (11 vs. 6.5 percent). Chinese per capita real GNP grew somewhat faster also. Chinese per capita consumption grew somewhat, India's not at all.

The case for China can be made even stronger: First, China achieved what she did with only modest foreign aid (after 1955 her repayments of previous loans exceeded new credit extensions). India relied much more heavily on foreign aid. Second, the income distribution in China is probably the most equal in the world (owing to the Maoist insistence on purity of heart and stress on a classless society); it is very unequal in India. This means that some growth in per capita consumption in China corresponds to some improvement in practically everyone's level of living. It also means that the same or lesser growth in per capita consumption in India is quite likely associated with increasing misery for many millions.

On the other side of the ledger, there is, of course, the question of stability. Indian growth may have been disappointingly slow, but it was steady, always near 3 or 4 percent per year for real GNP. In China, on the other hand, a corresponding figure jumped around from maybe 6 to 13 percent, down to negative numbers and up again.

Also for India may count the fact that the costs of growth to the Chinese people, as the loss of freedom, may have been higher. But this is a very moot question, indeed. Although one cannot help but admire the humanistic bias of the Indian leaders, possibly India must have a firmer and seemingly less compassionate leadership to force on the country true economic progress. Maybe there is too much indecision and too much bureaucracy to achieve *rapid* economic growth, and the costs may only be postponed till disaster strikes a generation from now. In the end, these costs may not be avoided at all. Even within India the debate about this point continues. In 1969, when the fourth 5-year plan was being discussed in parliament, there was much less of the earlier confidence that "socialist" India could combine the discipline of Soviet-style planning with liberal political life. Because it could not be done, central planning was in fact downgraded significantly. Private initiative was stressed more than ever before. But others would have preferred to move in the opposite direction. They scoffed at India's pretention to be socialist. The Communist chief minister of Kerala, Namboodiripad, put it succinctly when he compared India with "the man who begins the week with one day of prayers, only to end it with six days of sin."

Finally, one may argue that all the data used in this section are estimates anyhow. Maybe they are wrong. Maybe these data are not comparable. Hence, maybe India and China have done equally "well" after all. This is, of course, a possibility.

However, there seems little doubt about the Chinese superiority in economic performance in the 1950's. Their failure in the "great leap forward," which Mao seems so anxious to repeat in the "Great Proletarian Cultural Revolution," badly tarnished this favorable record. It must also have badly tarnished the image of China in the eyes of the "uncommitted" leaders of the world and reduced the chances for imitation of the Chinese model. The big question remaining is whether the Chinese achievements of the 1950's can and will be repeated. We know that it *can* be done. We do not know that it *will* be done. That would probably require something unlikely as long as Mao is in power: Trading in ideology for pragmatism and, given present Chinese conditions, placing agricultural development foremost as a basis for industrialization.

SUMMARY

1   A country is economically underdeveloped if it has an extremely low level of real GNP per head compared to such areas as the United States or Western Europe. It is an arbitrary matter where one places the dividing line between the "rich" countries and the "poor."

2   If we call countries with a probable per capita GNP of $1,000 or more "developed," and those with a probable per capita GNP of $300 or less "underdeveloped," we find two thirds of mankind in the latter category. Thus, underdevelopment means desperate poverty.

3   Among the features most commonly found in underdeveloped areas are the following:

    a. Inadequate natural resources;

    b. Lack of capital;

    c. Low quality labor force (little education, lack of health);

    d. Lack of modern technical know-how;

    e. Unfavorable environmental factors (a hostile attitude toward change, the extended family or land tenure systems discouraging effort, the narrowness of markets discouraging application of modern techniques, bad government);

    f. Rapid population growth.

4   Most underdeveloped countries show urgent concern with economic development. For any rapid development, governmental action is absolutely necessary. Because the conditions facing these countries are so different from those ever faced by the United States or Russia, it is silly, furthermore, to expect them to copy either the American or the Soviet road to riches. Forgetting that in all leading economies a prosperous agriculture preceded industrialization, many underdeveloped countries are anxious for industrialization at once. Quite possibly a more balanced policy would be wiser.

5   Naturally, any government anxious to lead development efforts is going to concentrate on removing the major obstacles encountered thereto (see the list in point 3 above). Especially important for all underdeveloped countries are capital formation, a qualitative improvement of the labor force, and reforms with respect to government, attitudes, and land tenure. Possibly freer trade with all other countries can help. In addition, population control is a must.

6   Since 1950, most underdeveloped countries have formulated plans to assess the requirements for and guide policies of economic development. Even so, no underdeveloped country has a chance to catch up with the GNP per head of the United States in the forseeable future.

7   There is little hope that foreign aid will improve on this outlook. Private foreign investment has been pretty much discouraged. U.S. economic aid to underdeveloped countries has been only a fraction of 1 percent of her GNP since World War II. The same is true for Soviet aid. Aid by international agencies, such as the World Bank, has also not been staggering. In fact, in recent years, the combined economic aid from all sources amounted to at most $3 per year per inhabitant of the underdeveloped world.

8   It is especially illuminating to discuss the recent history of economic development of India and China, comprising 60 percent of the people of the underdeveloped world. Both countries have stable governments determined to promote economic development. Their approaches, however, differ strongly. Whereas the Chinese favor development by brutal force, neglecting human freedom and dignity, the Indians have preferred a much gentler road. During the 1950's China's total GNP rose twice as fast as India's, industrial output four times faster. During the 1950's Chinese per capita GNP seems to have risen at 3 to 4 percent per year, India's at 2 percent. In view of events since 1959, it is by no means certain, however, that the Chinese economy performs better than the Indian in the long run.

TERMS[1]

balanced growth   extended family system
crude birth rate   international demonstration effect
crude death rate   social overhead capital
                 underdevelopment

SYMBOLS

SUNFED
UNEPTA

QUESTIONS FOR REVIEW AND DISCUSSION

1 "Economic development is not something that has or has not happened, it is a continuing process. Any dividing line between developed and underdeveloped countries is arbitrary." Discuss. Can you explain the order of countries found in Table 26.1 THE RICH COUNTRIES AND THE POOR?

2 What, do you think, would life be like in the United States if we had a per capita income of $500 a year, as do people in Greece? How do the Greeks manage? How do Chinese and Indians manage with one sixth of that? Why did Marco Polo wonder at the wealth of China, and Vasco da Gama marvel at that of India? Were they richer in the past?

3 During the early 1960's, GNP rose per year by 2.2 percent in Ceylon, by 5.7 percent in Italy. The birth rates were 35 per 1,000 in Ceylon, 18.9 per 1,000 in Italy. The death rates were 8.5 per 1,000 in Ceylon, 9.8 per 1,000 in Italy. What happened to GNP per head in the two countries?

4 Consider the following data on the rate of growth of per capita real GNP in various countries for the period 1955–1966:

Argentina	15.5 percent	Ecuador	12.9 percent
Belgium	37.0 percent	Germany (West)	58.6 percent
Brazil	24.4 percent	Israel	66.2 percent
Canada	29.2 percent	Japan	149.0 percent
Chile	32.5 percent	Paraguay	7.4 percent
China (Taiwan)	70.7 percent	Puerto Rico	106.9 percent
Dominican Republic	3.3 percent	Zambia	40.0 percent

Can you explain the differences observed? (Hint: from your knowledge of economics make a list of *possible* reasons, then try to find statistics to back up your hypothesis.)

---

[1] Terms and symbols are defined in the Glossary at the end of the book.

5   Explain each of the most commonly found elements of underdevelopment. (Hint: use point 3 of the summary as a guide.)

6   "Many an underdeveloped country finds itself in a vicious circle of poverty." Explain.

7   "The real trouble in underdeveloped areas of the world is income distribution. Everyone would have more than enough without the rich landlords, oil sheiks, princes, and foreign tycoons who live in magnificent splendor." Discuss.

8   Suppose you are an economic planner in the Congo. How would you develop entrepreneurship in the country? How would you increase capital formation? Would your answer differ for Venezuela?

9   "A population that refuses or is unable to save cannot have economic development." "An underdeveloped country can accumulate capital in a great variety of ways." Evaluate both statements.

10   "In some underdeveloped countries, public investment projects are made possible because they are financed with newly created money, and this results in *forced saving* of the population." Can you figure out the exact meaning of "forced saving?" (Hint: read pages 612–613.)

11   Suppose you were to advise an underdeveloped country to undertake a development project. If there were only enough resources for *one* of them, which of the following would you recommend and why: better schools, more housing, better transportation facilities, an airline, a steel mill, a fertilizer plant, an irrigation or drainage system.

12   Suppose the marginal output-to-captial ratio in an underdeveloped country is 1 to 3. How much investment would be needed to raise real GNP per head by 3 percent if population grows at 1 percent a year? Must your answer refer to net or gross investment?

13   Analyze the role of foreign aid in economic development. Contrast the U.S. and Soviet foreign aid programs.

14   "The United States should convert all its military expenditures to foreign economic aid." Discuss.

15   MR. A: "The United States should never give economic aid to underdeveloped countries ruled by dictators, because that would enhance the prestige and power of nondemocratic forces."

MR. B: "Then what should the United States do? It can hardly foster revolution, for that would lead to political instability stifling economic development. Only a totalitarian, ruthless government can bring about economic development."
Evaluate. Who is right? Why?

16   The text says that it matters little in what form foreign aid is given. If an underdeveloped country wants capital goods, it can import them directly, or "it could just as well import food and use its own labor force, previously needed for food production, to make capital goods."

Does that sentence suggest something to you with respect to the common argument that "it is all right to loan wheat to a Communist country, but it is dangerous to send them strategic ball bearings"?

17   "One of the things an underdeveloped country does *not* want is borrowing abroad. Such external debt, as we learned in Chapter 13, imposes a burden on future generations when interest and principal have to be repaid. Thus, the present generation can only gain at the expense of its grandchildren, and that's a lowdown thing to do." Evaluate.

18   "Underdeveloped countries should be helped by trade not aid." Discuss.

19   "The best way for Malayans to get private cars is not to build automobile plants, but to produce more tin and rubber for export." Evaluate.

20   MR. A: "The best thing a country can do to encourage its economic development is to erect high tariff walls around it."

MR. B: "Nonsense. A country should help its industry by taxing agriculture, as the Soviets did, not by taxing imports."

Evaluate.

epilogue

We have reached the end of Part 3, which dealth with the important question of economic growth. The conclusion we can now derive is quite clear. Neither capitalism nor socialism has a monopoly on the ability to achieve rapid increases in total or in per capita real GNP. Some capitalist market economies have done extremely well in this regard. Consider the outstanding examples of Japan and West Germany. Others have been plagued by sluggish or uneven growth. Some socialist economies, notably the Soviet Union, have given spectacular performances of their own. Others have not done so well at all.

But we have also noted one other thing. Wherever rapid economic growth was achieved, governmental action played an important role. This has been true not just in socialist countries, but in capitalist ones as well. This governmental action, of course, can take and has taken a great variety of forms. Interestingly, in all successful cases of economic growth it has relied, however, on a substantial degree of economic incentives for the individual. No society that abolished economic self-interest as the driving force has yet achieved rapid economic growth. China and Cuba are examples of the unsuccessful attempt to motivate people by appeal to their altruism and social conscience alone.

We turn now in Part 4 to different matters. Undoubtedly, these matters are of greater importance than anything we have studied so far. We turn to questions that lie in part beyond economics, although economists have a great deal to say about them. These questions deal with more than the quantity of goods we manage to procure. They are questions about the quality of our life. We may be producing the largest possible GNP, and all the while destroying ourselves. This may be so because we are sharing our riches very unequally. Social tensions may be building up that tear apart our society. Or this may be so because we neglect the consequences of our actions on the physical environment in which we live. By insisting on private satisfactions and by ignoring the wider consequences of our actions on the rest of nature of which we are but a part, we may be destroying the very planet on which we live. This again is a matter of sharing the riches we command. Just as some families might be called on to forgo some private gain for the sake of other families, so mankind as a whole might have to give up some private gain for the sake of the rest of nature, without which future generations will not be able to live at all.

In this final part of the book, we turn to a number of questions that reach, at least in part, beyond economics. Still, the economist has a great deal to say about them. As will be shown, all we have learned so far can be put to good use at this point. The problem we shall be dealing with is simply this: We may have succeeded in reducing scarcity to the barest minimum by having organized the full and efficient utilization of resources in a country. We may have taken measures assuring rapid economic growth. Nevertheless, even though total income, and indeed income per head, may be high and growing, deep problems may beset society. The total, for instance, may be distributed very unequally. Not every citizen receives an average income. We must determine exactly how we ought to share our riches. Domestic peace and tranquility may well depend on how this problem is solved.

Similarly, production of a large GNP, however it is distributed among persons, has certain side effects. A society may become urbanized. Its air and water may become polluted. The whole of nature may be affected, and adversely so. In the long run, this process may threaten the very survival of man on this planet. So again a question of sharing arises: should we not, as individuals, give up some of our riches to be able, as groups, to deal with the side effects of our actions? Questions such as these will make the newspaper headlines for the remainder of this century.

sharing the output

NEGATIVE TAXES TESTED IN JERSEY

80 Families Are Being Paid Guaranteed Income

By RONALD SULLIVAN
Special to The New York Times

TRENTON, Oct. 24—Eighty poor families here are taking part in the country's first practical experiment with a negative income tax, the controversial proposal that would guarantee the poor an annual income.

For nearly three months the families have been receiving checks twice a month with no strings attached—no advice, no restrictions, just money to spend. All they have to do is submit a report of the family's total income each month.

The three-year experiment, in which the first check was delivered here on Aug. 1, to incredulous slum dwellers, is being financed by $4-million in Federal antipoverty funds. By next spring, approximately 1,000 families in New Jersey's six largest cities will be included in the project designed to test the social, economic and political impact of a guaranteed income on poverty-stricken families.

Under a negative income tax, the Federal Government would pay taxes to the poor in much the same way that it now collects taxes from the more affluent. In the experiment here, 80 families were selected in a controlled sampling from six slum areas of the city and from two other neighborhoods that were slightly better off.

The families—many of whom at first could not believe they were getting something for nothing—were chosen by the Council for Grants to Families, an organization established jointly by the University of Wisconsin's Institute for Research on Poverty, and Mathematica, a private research and consulting company in Princeton, under a mandate of the United States Office of Economic Opportunity.

Schemes Tested

Seven schemes are being tested based on the amount of income and dependents the families now have. They will receive the payments for the next three years, even if they move.

For example, a Negro family of five —the 35-year-old father is a $96-a-week machine operator—is receiving $10.75 a week from the council. If his regular income falls to $50 a week, the council will increase its payment to $43. If, for any reason, the man's income falls to zero, he will receive a maximum of $78 a week from the council.

The family is better off if the father continues to work, even though the payments are reduced as his income rises. The total income the family receives is always greatest when its own income is the greatest.

Among other recipients, a white cook with a family of six who earns $100 a week is receiving $28.50 a week. If he loses his job, the council will increase its payment to $58.50 a week.

Least-Generous Plan

Another white family—the husband is an $85-a-week gardener—has 12 members, but it gets only $6.75 a week. This is because the council is using this family to test its least-generous income plan.

According to David Kershaw, the project's 26-year-old director and a former director of admissions at the Woodrow Wilson School of Public and International Affairs at Princeton, seven different combinations are being tested. The most important one involves a 50 per cent negative income tax—that is, that with every increasing dollar the recipient earns he will receive 50 cents less from the council.

Under most existing welfare systems, the money earned by recipients is deducted in full from their welfare benefits, thus often reducing the incentive to work.

For instance, a family of four persons enrolled here may be eligible for a payment of $3,300 a year if it had no other income. This is the annual income level that the Social Security Administration has set as the poverty level in the United States, and it is estimated that 30 million Americans live at or below this level. If the family earns $2,600 in one year, its $3.300 payment from the council will be cut by $1,300. Thus it ends the year with a total income of $4,600—the $2,600 it earned and the $2,000 it received as a negative tax.

If the family next year earns $6,600 it will receive nothing from the council.

The identities of all the families are being kept confidential by the council to preserve the integrity of the experiment. However, the council reported that two-thirds of the families were Negro, with the remaining third evenly divided between Puerto Ricans and other whites.

Younger families were generally selected rather than older ones so that the project's impact on the job market could be measured. In addition, no families were included in that were receiving aid to dependent children.

27

*income
distribution
and poverty
in the
united states*

IN THE PREVIOUS chapter we have seen how exceedingly rich (in terms of income) Americans are when compared to the overwhelming majority of mankind. This picture is easily misleading. Not *every* American is an *average* American. Not every Americans enjoys an equal money income that would enable him to buy an equal share of our large real GNP. In fact, whether we look at Americans individually or by family groupings, the income of many is below average, and they are poor. Many others are even better off than the average suggests. This unequal distribution of income among persons in the United States will be the main concern of this chapter.

We shall not discuss the personal distribution of income in the Soviet Union nor in the underdeveloped countries, because sufficiently detailed and reliable data are missing. All the data that do exist, however, suggest strongly that the income distribution in the Soviet Union as well as most underdeveloped countries today is at least as unequal as in the United States. The incomes earned by Soviet government officials, scientists, and artists, for instance, are much higher, relative to those earned by the millions of workers and peasants, than are the high incomes in the United States relative to the lower ones. Note also that many of the world's richest as well as poorest families live in the underdeveloped countries. The same seems to have been true, furthermore, throughout the history of mankind, whether we think of ancient Egypt, Greece, or Rome or of Brazil, Ethiopia, or India today.

THE LORENZ CURVE

A simple device, the *Lorenz curve*, gives us an immediate picture of the extent of income inequality. We draw a square, as in Figure 27.1, measuring percent of total personal income received on the vertical axis and the percent of families (arranged from the one with the lowest to the one with the highest income) on the horizontal axis.

Perfect Equality

Now imagine drawing a straight line from the bottom left corner at 0 to the top right corner at e. This line could be called the "line of perfect income equality." You can easily see why. If all families in a country shared total income equally, it must be true that 20 percent of the families share 20 percent of total income (we are at a), that 40 percent of all families share 40 percent of total income (we are at b), and so on, until 100 percent of all families share 100 percent of total income (at e).

Perfect Inequality

At the other extreme, imagine that one family received all the income, whereas all the others received none of it. If we arranged the families on the horizontal axis as before on the basis of income, we would find that the poorest 20 percent of all families receive 0 percent of total

Figure 27.1   THE LORENZ CURVE

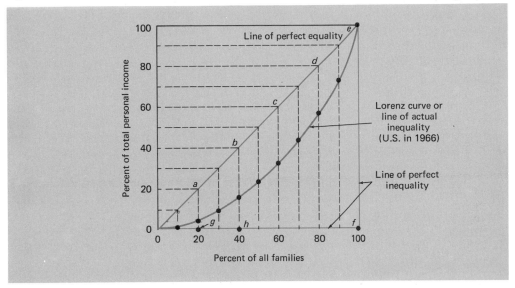

The Lorenz curve is a graphical picture of the extent of income inequality in a country. If all shared personal income equally, any given percentage of families would share the same percentage of total personal income. If inequality exists, the 10, 20, 30, 40, etc. percent lowest income families will share less than 10, 20, 30, 40, etc. percent of income. Source: Table 27.1, columns (4) and (5).

income (we are at g rather than a), that the poorest 40 percent of all families similarly share 0 percent of total income (we are at h rather than b), and so on. Even 99 percent of all families would still share 0 percent of total income (we are just a little bit to the left of f rather than the left and below e). Yet, when we consider *all* families, including the one having all the income, we find that 100 percent of families have 100 percent of income (we are at e). Thus, we could call the line 0fe a "line of perfect inequality."

Actual Inequality

As you might expect, reality is somewhere in between these two extremes. Money income in the United States is distributed neither perfectly equally (as would be pictured by line 0e) nor perfectly unequally (as shown by line 0fe). If we arrange all families (including throughout this chapter unattached individuals) in ascending order starting with the one with the lowest and going to the one with the highest annual money income, we get Table 27.1 THE DISTRIBUTION OF PERSONAL INCOME IN THE UNITED STATES, 1966. In 1966, there were 60.6 million families in the United States, receiving a total of $584 billion of personal income (this refers to wages, rents, interest, dividends, unincorporated business profits, and transfer payments, all before federal personal income taxes). The 10 percent of the poorest families (income-wise), as column (2) tells us, received only 1 percent of total income—column (3). Under perfect equality, they should have received 10 percent of the total. They all received less than $1,810 in that year. Next come families receiving between $1,810 and $3,009 annually. They comprised another 10 percent of the total number of families and received only 3 percent of total income. And so it goes. You can easily interpret the remainder of columns (1) to (3).

We can, however, also calculate from this information the data needed to draw the "line of actual income inequality" for the United States in 1966. For this purpose, we have added cumulatively in columns (4) and (5), respectively, the data of columns (2) and (3). If the 10 percent poorest families received 1 percent of total income—row 1, columns (2) and (3)—and if the 10 percent next poorest received 3 percent—row 2, columns (2) and (3)—then 10 + 10 = 20 percent of poorest families must have received 1 + 3 = 4 percent of total income. This is shown in row 2, columns (4) and (5). Thus, the data of columns (4) and (5) are exactly the ones needed to draw the Lorenz curve. These data are plotted as the heavy curve in Figure 27.1 THE LORENZ CURVE. Like a loose string fastened to points 0 and e, this line hanging below 0e and above 0fe provides a visual picture of income inequality in the United States. Any increase in equality would shift it toward 0e, any decrease toward 0fe. In fact, federal personal income taxes in the United States have the effect of reducing after-tax income inequality somewhat, although not appreciably so.

Table 27.1   THE DISTRIBUTION OF PERSONAL INCOME IN THE UNITED STATES, 1966

INCOME CLASS	PERCENT OF ALL FAMILIES IN CLASS*	PERCENT OF TOTAL INCOME RECEIVED BY FAMILIES IN CLASS	PERCENT OF FAMILIES IN CLASS OR LOWER ONES	PERCENT OF TOTAL INCOME RECEIVED BY FAMILIES IN CLASS OR LOWER ONES
(1)	(2)	(3)	(4)	(5)
under $1,810	10	1	10	1
$1,810–3,009	10	3	20	4
$3,010–4,359	10	5	30	9
$4,360–5,609	10	6	40	15
$5,610–6,949	10	8	50	23
$6,950–8,039	10	9	60	32
$8,040–9,519	10	11	70	43
$9,520–11,029	10	13	80	56
$11,030–14,129	10	15	90	71
$14,130 and over	10	29	100	100

* A family is two or more persons living in the same dwelling unit and related to one another by blood, marriage, or adoption. A single person unrelated to the other occupants in the dwelling unit or living alone is treated as a separate family.
Source: The University of Michigan, Survey Research Center, Survey of Consumer Finances.

INCOME INEQUALITY VS. POVERTY

Incomes can be very unequal, yet there may not be any poverty. If under present price conditions, and given the size of American families today, the American family with the lowest income received $10,000 a year, but many other families many times that amount, we could hardly call anybody poor, although there would be inequality. Column (1) of Table 27.1 shows us, however, that 10 percent of all American families (not only individuals)—more than 6 million—received less than $1,810 in 1966. Most people would agree that these families (unless they owned large assets on which to live) were poor. Many people would go further and argue that "one should do something about poverty." In fact, in his 1964 State of the Union Message, President Johnson committed the nation to a war on poverty.

Counting the Poor

It is difficult to define what is to be meant by poverty, and not everybody will agree with any definition chosen. Yet, such a definition is needed if we are to measure the extent of poverty as a prerequisite for abolishing it. One way of going about the task might be to figure out the annual dollar expenditures needed by a family and to compare such a figure with the dollars available to that family. However, this is easier said than done.

the meaning of "need"   What is one to consider a family's "needs?" Is one to include all its wants? Then the total of needs could never be satisfied. So maybe we might classify some wants as "true needs" and others as "luxuries." We might go about it "scientifically," establishing first a minimum adequate diet required to keep a person alive. For a moderately active man, such diet may involve the annual consumption of the following:[1]

370 pounds of wheat flour
57 cans of evaporated milk
111 pounds of cabbage
23 pounds of spinach
285 pounds of dried navy beans

We might then proceed to evaluate this minimum adequate diet. At Amherst, Massachusetts, in May 1969, it cost $133.75 to purchase the above quantities. The average American family—three to four persons—might, therefore, "need" $500 for food annually. Experience shows that poor families typically have to devote twice as much money to other purchases besides food (for clothing and shelter). Thus, we might triple the figure, giving us minimum necessary spending of $1,500 per year per average family. Any family of average size having this dollar amount or less available may then be called poor. Over time, of course,

---

[1] This interesting piece of information is taken from George J. Stigler, "The Cost of Subsistence," *Journal of Farm Economics,* May 1945, pp. 303–314. This diet contains the optimum amounts of calories, protein, minerals, and vitamins established by the National Research Council. Thus it is a *physiological* minimum and leaves out of account such "luxuries" as variety and palatability of diet.

this meaning of need is bound to change. Luxuries of today have a habit of becoming the needs of tomorrow.

available means   The dollars available to a family will, however, also be a difficult figure to establish. Surely, this figure should include earned money income, such as wages, rent, interest, and profits. It should also include money transfers, such as pensions, unemployment relief, and welfare payments, which are not received in return for services currently rendered. But what about a family's access to credit? What about assets in its possession? A family with no money income at all, but a million dollars of bank accounts, stocks, bonds, and real estate and ample opportunity to borrow can hardly be called poor compared to one with an annual income of $1,000 and none of the former's advantages. Unfortunately, data on assets and credit availability are hard to come by, and most estimates of poverty in the United States are in fact based on comparisons of family *money income alone*. During the early 1960's, such money income figures typically have been compared with a minimum needs figure of $3,000 per family, or twice what we calculated above.

the U.S. definition and count   The U.S. government, at first, listed all families with a money income below $3,000 per year as poor, all others as above the poverty line. The $3,000 figure was calculated to assure a family's minimum need in the way of food, clothing, medical care, and shelter, the latter including such "luxuries" as heat, a refrigerator, cold and hot water, an indoor flush toilet, a bed for every person, electric lighting, and enough furnishings to have a common meal. The government's argument was similar to ours. In 1959, argued the Department of Agriculture, a minimum nutritional meal cost 22.8 cents per person. Given the average family size of 3.65 persons per family, a bare daily minimum of food was considered to cost about $2.50, or somewhat below $1,000 per year per average family. This figure was then tripled.

According to Table 27.1 THE DISTRIBUTION OF PERSONAL INCOME IN THE UNITED STATES, 1966, this definition of poverty would place almost exactly 20 percent of American families, or 12 million families, below the poverty line in 1966. These are the families who together shared 4 percent of total income. Notice, however, how inadequate this kind of figure is bound to be.

First, as we have already pointed out, family asset holdings are neglected. To the extent that some of these families have large assets, they should not be classified as poor. This may be especially true for some of the older people. It has been estimated that the measured incidence of poverty among the old would fall by a third were we to count their ability to draw on their assets. But the incidence of measured poverty among all people may fall by only 3 percent when we take assets into account.

Second, concentration on annual income alone may cause distortions if incomes fluctuate. A family having a temporary $1,000 income will be classified as poor, even though it had $25,000 for years before (and has similar prospects for the future) and may have easy credit access. There is, in fact, considerable turnover among the poor. Only 69 percent of the poor in 1963 were poor in 1962. In fact, the U.S. Department of Commerce has suggested for this reason that the average income over 2 years be used for the purposes of establishing the incidence of poverty.

Third, much income in kind is left out of consideration. Some families may grow large amounts of fruits and vegetables on their own land, receive milk, butter, cheese, and eggs from their animals, and live in a house to which they hold clear title. Their cash needs are lessened by the value of such income in kind. If they receive cash income of $2,900 in addition to income in kind, we might not want to classify such families as poor along with others less fortunate. This is especially important for urban vs. rural comparisons, but also for regional comparisons (any family in southern California needs less cash for heating than any family in Maine).

Fourth, the $3,000 criterion doesn't account for the actual circumstances of different families. Old people may need less food (hence cash) than young ones; sick people may need more cash (for drugs) than others; and a family of twelve has greater needs than a family of three. The latter point is likely to lead to especially bizarre cases. A single couple with $2,900 a year of money income will be poor, but a family with *any* number of children and $3,100 a year will be above the poverty line. Unless other factors mentioned above make up for it, this would hardly satisfy our sense of reasonableness.

To overcome these difficulties, in recent years, the government has used a more sophisticated definition of poverty. The Social Security Administration (SSA) now counts the poor on the basis of over 100 family types with different required cash needs for each. This accounts for differences in income in kind, family size, and age composition, but not yet for asset holdings and temporary income fluctuations.

The SSA also has defined a somewhat higher income line for the near-poor. It is on the average about one-third higher than the poverty line. That is, if you are at or below the poverty income line; you are classified as poor. If you are above it, but at or below the near-poverty line, you are near-poor. Table 27.2 POVERTY AND NEAR-POVERTY INCOME LINES, 1967, shows the definitional limits used in 1967.

Who Are the Poor?

The U.S. constitution requires that a population census be taken every ten years to allocate among the states the seats in the House of Representatives in proportion to the states' populations. The census takers attempt to reach every American during the census. The census yields detailed information as to who is poor by the official definition and how many poor there are. In between, other methods are used to estimate the numbers involved. Figure 27.2 NUMBER OF POOR PERSONS AND INCIDENCE OF POVERTY gives the available postwar data for the United States. The top line shows the number of poor persons (*not* of families); refer to the left-hand scale. As you can see, the number has declined from 43 million in 1947 to 22 million in 1968. The broken lower line refers to the percentage of poor persons in the population; refer to the right-hand scale. This percentage has also declined, from 30 in 1947 to 12 in 1968. Clearly, percentage figures are much more revealing of the seriousness of the problem than are absolute numbers.

Table 27.2   POVERTY AND NEAR-POVERTY INCOME LINES, 1967

HOUSEHOLD CHARACTERISTICS*	POVERTY INCOME LINE		NEAR-POVERTY INCOME LINE	
	NONFARM RESIDENCE	FARM RESIDENCE	NONFARM RESIDENCE	FARM RESIDENCE
1 member	$1,635	$1,145	$1,985	$1,390
65 years and over	1,565	1,095	1,890	1,330
Under 65 years	1,685	1,195	2,045	1,450
2 members	2,115	1,475	2,855	1,990
Head 65 years and over	1,970	1,380	2,655	1,870
Head under 65 years	2,185	1,535	2.945	2,075
3 members	2,600	1,815	3,425	2,400
4 members	3,335	2,345	4,345	3,060
5 members	3,930	2,755	5,080	3,565
6 members	4,410	3,090	5,700	3,995
7 members or more	5,430	3,790	6,945	4,850

* Households are defined here as the total of families and unrelated individuals.
Source: Economic Report of the President, *January 1969, p. 152.*

Census data give us more than totals, however. If you looked at the poor families in 1967 (still including unrelated individuals), you would find that 37 percent of them were headed by a person over 65 years of age. Another 28 percent were headed by a woman under 65. The rest, naturally, were headed by men under 65, but the important thing to note is that most of these had little education, were under 25 years of age, or both.

More interesting still are data on the incidence of poverty within particular groups. We can see from Figure 27.2 that in 1967 about 14 percent of all Americans (outside institutions) were poor. It is also true that 16 percent of all American families were poor. But if you looked at all families headed by people over 65, you would find not 16 percent, but 36 percent of them poor. Only 12 percent of the families headed by people below 65 were poor. Now look at groups within this category. Of the families headed by a white man under 65, only 5 percent were poor. Of the families headed by a nonwhite man under 65, 21 percent were poor. Of the families headed by a white woman under 65, 25 percent were poor. And of the families headed by a nonwhite woman under 65, 55 percent were poor.

In short, poverty disproportionately hits the aged and families headed by nonwhite men or by women of all colors. Most nonwhite poor were blacks (96 percent); the rest were American Indians and Eskimos. Although only 29 percent of all poor families were nonwhite in 1967, proportionately they carried a much greater burden of poverty than their white fellow citizens. Even among the white poor, there was a high concentration of minority groups (Mexican Americans and Puerto Ricans).

To sum up, if you want to find the poor, look at old people, at broken families headed

Figure 27.2   NUMBER OF POOR PERSONS AND INCIDENCE OF POVERTY

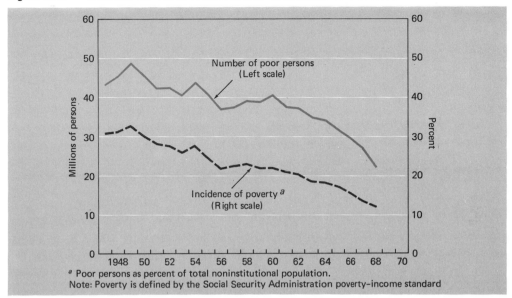

a Poor persons as percent of total noninstitutional population.
Note: Poverty is defined by the Social Security Administration poverty–income standard

---

Except for periods of recession (1954, the late 1950's), poverty in the United States has been declining since 1949.
Source: Economic Report of the President, *January 1969, p. 154.*

---

by women, and at families headed by young or uneducated men. Because among the minorities (the American Indians, the blacks, the Eskimos, the Mexican Americans, and the Puerto Ricans) relatively many families are headed by women or by uneducated men, a greater percentage of families in these population groups are poor than in other groups.

THE ROOTS OF POVERTY

Why are the poor poor? Some existing poverty is easily explained. Many of the poor within the United States are in a position very much like that of the underdeveloped countries in the world at large.

Unequal Ownership of Property

The poor own few, if any, natural resources and capital goods to bring them money income. The ownership of such income-producing wealth is even more unevenly distributed in the United States than is annual income. (A Lorenz curve with *wealth* on the vertical axis would hang down further toward the line of perfect inequality than the one in Figure 27.1.) The top 5 percent of income recipients, as a result, get more than two thirds of all dividends, half all other property income, and still 10 percent of all wages.

Low-Quality Labor

Some of the poor have not even labor services to sell. They may be the victims of physical infirmities, mental breakdown, or accidents. They may be mothers with many children to be cared for. Typically, the remaining poor do have their labor to sell (and nothing else), and typically it is of low quality. Here we have people who enjoy only a bare minimum of food, shelter, and medical care, and, most importantly, who have only a minimum of education and training.

At the time of the 1960 Census, 31 percent of the poor families were headed by a man between 25 and 65 years of age who had fewer than 9 years of education. If we include high school dropouts, the percentage is 38. Clearly, when you are poorly educated in an economy wherein the demand for educated labor is relatively higher, your chances of being unemployed (fully or in part) or employed at low pay are excellent. These factors go a long way to explain why certain people remain poor in the midst of a prosperous economy. But *why* are so many of the poor insufficiently educated?

inherited intelligence   There are some who will give you a simple answer. "It is all a matter of heredity," they say. "Some people are simply *born* with inferior intelligence and endowed by nature with a generous dose of laziness in addition." As if to prove their point, they point out simultaneously how lack of education and poverty are more frequent among nonwhites than among whites. There is no evidence, however, to support such racist "explanations" of poverty. For one thing, although poverty hits a greater percentage of nonwhite than of white families, in 1967, 71 percent of all poor families were white. In addition, no one has yet devised a way of measuring a person's genetic intellectual potential. If one were to prove racial differences in inborn intelligence, such a test would have to be made *at the time of conception,* and it is very hard even to conceive of doing this. Thereafter, environmental factors begin to play a role. Potential native intelligence can, so to speak, become eroded during pregnancy by the mother's malnutrition, emotional stress, and lack of medical care all of which *could* be the result of society's discriminatory treatment of the mother. Interestingly, in the United States in 1963 only 0.4 percent of all white mothers went through pregnancy and birth entirely without medical help, but the figure was 10 percent for nonwhites. In 1966, nonwhite infant mortality was almost twice that of whites. Maternal deaths were almost four times as frequent. Life expectancy was 7 years shorter for nonwhites.

It is also a well-established fact that without adequate prenatal health care the likelihood of brain damage in the newborn is much greater. In fact, American psychiatrists find the incidence among children of mental deficiency and neuropsychiatric disorders *resulting from inferior medical care of expectant mothers* to be significantly larger among blacks than whites. Hence, tests in later life which purport to show lower intelligence for blacks than whites may well be a measure of discrimination that started before birth rather than of any genetic differences. Furthermore, scientists distinguish two meanings of "intelligence." One is intellectual potential. It is determined at conception by the genes you inherit. It cannot be measured. The other is the development of this potential after conception. It is determined by the environment: the mother's before birth, the child's afterward. We can attempt to measure the degree of actual intellectual development later in life with the help of intelligence tests testing comprehension and performance. Clearly there *are* inherited physical differences among people. That is why not all girls become movie stars and not all boys become famous athletes. More likely than not, there are inherited mental differences also. But we can never look at a black boy's IQ score of 80 and a white boy's score of 100 and conclude anything about their genes, about where both might have gone had both been equally nourished by a friendly environment. Indeed, unless physical damage to his brain has occurred since conception, the black boy may yet end up with an IQ of 140. IQ can only measure the degree of development of the potential, but not the potential itself; it is not an unchanging figure.

One other thing should be noted. Even where the development of intelligence has proceeded equally for all, many IQ tests still score higher for whites than for blacks. This is because some tests are "culturally biased." One intelligence test for children aged 5, for instance, contains sketches of two women. Both are white. But one is the Hollywood stereotype, straight-nosed, thin-lipped. The other is flat-nosed and thick-lipped. The child is asked to choose the prettier face. The child is not supposed to choose the (white) face with Negroid features. But which will be picked by black children? Another question asks children to distinguish maples, oaks, and pines. How well are you likely to do, if you have never seen anything but hot pavement? As a result, IQ test scores do not necessarily indicate either intellectual potential or actual intellectual development!

the culture of poverty   We have shown that we cannot blame the lack of education of the poor on their genetic inferiority. But we also saw that the development of intellectual potential may well be stunted. This deserves a few additional comments. There is a vicious circle about poverty. Many of the poor are poor not because they were born "naturally dumb," but because their parents were poor. And this childhood environment predisposes them to becoming poor in turn.[2] Often the poor of today grew up in densely packed, dirty, and dreary neighborhoods. Houses were dilapidated and structurally unsafe; even basic plumbing was lacking. The father may have been the victim of discrimination in his job. (In the United States, the income of black men, for example, is, on the average, 52 percent of that for white men with the same level of education and the same area of residence.) The father's job is likely to have been of low status as well as low paying. (In the case of black people, this reflects a long history of injustices and brutality going back to slavery.) Or the father may have been unemployed. There was, perhaps, lots of friction in the home. There was little hope and much despair. Maybe the father just took off one day and never came

---

[2] For a detailed discussion of this tragic point, you are urged to read Daniel Patrick Moynihan's, *The Negro Family: The Case for National Action* (Washington, D.C.: U.S. Department of Labor, 1965).

back. (Only a minority of black children reach 18 having lived with both parents all along.) Then the mother was working. Either way, the child was neglected, perhaps ill-treated. There was no intellectual stimulation: no adult conversation, no books, no crayons. The authority of the father was undermined by his inability to provide or was nonexistent owing to his absence. For long periods, the family probably scraped by on welfare. (A minority of black children have not been on welfare at some point during their childhood.) The child had no one to look up to. It grew up without discipline. It picked up socially disapproved behavior. It grew up without aims and ambitions for itself.

It is in early childhood that we learn characteristic patterns of behavior. We learn to feel in certain ways about the world and ourselves. Children from such destitute homes enter school not only with little developed intelligence, but also with an attitude of indifference, or even hostility, not conducive to intellectual achievement. Their unstable home environment, itself the result of poverty, becomes the prime determinant of their own future. The attitudes, beliefs, customs, habits, and morals pervading such an environment are referred to as the *culture of poverty. This culture of poverty cripples those who come in contact with it because it shapes their behavior in such a way as to program them in turn for a lifetime of poverty.*

Shall we believe the racists and call the children of today's poor "naturally lazy and shiftless"? That would be grossly unfair. But people *are* this unfair. That is why we must again issue a word of warning. The above material, as the unthinking comparison of IQ test scores, can easily be twisted to substantiate a (mistaken) view of inferiority of the poor. A discussion of the family instability of the poor can easily be used to justify prejudices. But we must take this risk of being misunderstood. We must look at the culture of poverty with all its ugliness of family disruption, lack of love, and deprivation. We must not hide it, for we are here uncovering an important mechanism that helps us explain what causes poverty. This is a first and necessary step for abolishing it. Describing how people live is not the same thing as pointing an accusing finger at them. We should not hold people responsible for conditions clearly beyond their control.

discrimination in schooling   The above problems feed on themselves. Imagine now what happens when a child from the culture of poverty enters school. He may be apathetic or wildly undisciplined. He may make a bad showing on IQ tests because he was never stimulated intellectually. He may be inattentive—perhaps because he gets little sleep at home with seven people in one room, perhaps because he is sick and has no medical care, perhaps because he is hungry and cannot afford to pay even 10 cents for the school lunch. He may, finally, be dressed shabbily and even dirtily most of the time. In short, he may not be particularly *lovable,* especially when compared with those well-behaved, bright, attentive, well-dressed, and clean middle class children in the other school down the street! Many teachers, perhaps unconsciously, will make that comparison. And they will expect that little can be achieved by "the slum kids." This prophecy on the part of the teacher is likely to be self-fulfilling. Psychologists tell us that people have a vested interest in being right. They hate to be wrong. And teachers are people. The teacher, expecting nothing, will (perhaps unconsciously) make sure that nothing occurs! He will pay little attention to the child, will challenge it little. And the child's intelligence will continue to be stunted rather than developed.[3]

This is made all the worse by the fact that the children of the poor are being educated in school facilities and by teachers incredibly inferior to those used by the children of their more fortunate fellow citizens. This is, in part, the result of the long-standing U.S. tradition of "separate but equal" education for the races (read: separate and extremely unequal). This is only slowly being overcome.

Is it any wonder that even motivation to learn fails to get instilled? The bad school perpetuates what has started in the home. It further *stunts* intellectual development. It becomes a place of defeat, of humiliation, a place to drop out of. And so they drop out. The dropout rate among the poor is vastly greater than among the nonpoor. So are the rates of illegitimate pregnancies and delinquency.

discrimination in job training   By giving up on education prematurely, the poor, in effect, give up on escaping poverty. Job training is unlikely to make up where the schools have failed them. Formalized hiring procedures of businesses discriminate against people with little education, no work experience, and arrest records. Union rules discriminate against young people and assure jobs first to older and experienced union members. Add to this informal outright discrimination against women and racial minorities, and you can figure out the chances of a high school dropout from the culture of poverty ever learning a decent skill on the job.

And again be careful. Don't say: "It was all his own fault." Was it his fault that his mother was malnourished during his prenatal life? Was it his fault that no one cared for him when he was very young? Was it his fault that he never knew a real home, but life taught him all too well the meaning of unanswered hunger and untreated sickness? Was it his fault that he was so "unlovable" in first grade that teachers and fellow students turned on him and made school a place of permanent humiliation? Was it his fault, finally, that he became "tough" and sought solace in drugs and sex and riots and just dropping out?

conclusion   Not all the poor, of course, are victims of the culture of poverty or of direct discrimination with respect to race, sex, or age. Other factors also play a role. Some people may be healthy and well educated, although in skills that have become obsolete. Think of the victims of chronic unemployment discussed in Part 1. They may well join the ranks of the poor for prolonged periods. In all cases, though, the root of poverty is the inability to sell resources. This may be because no property is owned. It may be because people are in no position to offer even their skills (as in the case of the aged or disabled or mothers with young children). It may be because no labor skills have been acquired. Or because those skills that have been acquired and are offered are not in sufficient demand. As we have seen, the lack of education and training is often caused and strongly reinforced by a variety of forms of discrimination.

---

[3] For a moving account of this situation, read Jonathan Kozol, *Death at an Early Age: The Destruction of the Hearts and Minds of Negro Children in the Boston Public Schools* (Boston: Houghton Mifflin, 1967).

ATTACKING POVERTY

Is Poverty Inevitable?

It has been said that " the poor are always with us," from which is often concluded that it is useless to try to do anything about it. Throughout history, some people have considered certain groups in the population as "doomed" to poverty, as if by inborn traits of inferiority. More often than not, history has proved them wrong. In the United States as least, the laborers of one decade became the bank presidents of the next, and even for the population as a whole the incidence of poverty has declined remarkably. This was illustrated above by the broken line in Figure 27.2 NUMBER OF POOR PERSONS AND INCIDENCE OF POVERTY. Poverty is not inevitable, and this true in the United States for particular groups of people, as well as for the population as a whole. Poverty in the United States *could* be eliminated if we cared to do so. This happens to be a lucky circumstance, and it is certainly not a statement one could make about every country in the world. If the total income of China or India were distributed with absolute equality, poverty could *not* be eliminated. As proved by the data in the last chapter, even if all of their GNP consisted of consumer goods, an absolutely equal distribution would give less than $100 worth to each person per year. Quite the contrary holds for the United States. Take 1969. Even if we left the major divisions of GNP untouched (23 percent for government, 15 percent for investment, 62 percent for consumption), we would be left with $558.4 billion of consumer goods, or $2,757 worth per person (based on first quarter data). For the average family, there were almost $9,000 of consumer goods available. Thus, it would have been easy to redistribute consumer goods from the rich to the poor so that no family remained below the poverty line.

Something *can* be done about poverty. Whether it *should* be done is another question you must decide for yourself. However, we can narrow down the choices by considering a number of alternative ways to attack the problem of poverty.

Redistribution of Wealth

Some people put great emphasis on redistributing income-producing property. "What we need," they say, "is socialism. Everyone should share equally in the ownership of capital and land. Because poverty is obviously the result of exploitation of some people by other people (the property owners), socialism would put a quick end to poverty." We have already noted how fallacious this argument is in most countries of the world. Socialism has not made the Chinese rich simply because they do not have enough capital and land to produce a large per capita GNP. Their poverty was not owing to private ownership of property.

the possibilities   But what about the United States? One way to assess the possibilities is to look at the functional distribution of income in the United States. We already have briefly discussed in Chapter 5 (pages 102–104). The functional distribution of income shows how much of our gross national income is payment to labor, how much payment for the use of capital and land. This was shown in column (2) of Table 5.1 MEASURING THE GNP. Depreciation and indirect business taxes can be ignored for our purposes. The reason is simple: even if everyone shared equally in the ownership of capital and land, capital would continue to wear out. Thus, even under socialism part of output would have to be used to replace capital; otherwise, the capital stock would disappear through wear and tear, and income from it would become zero. This would defeat the entire purpose of having introduced socialism in the first place. Hence, the amount shown by depreciation could not become available for general consumption.

Government would continue to exist also. It would continue to levy indirect taxes as one way of preventing households from commanding all the resources for consumer goods production. Thus, using the data of Table 5.1, we could only hope to gain for general distribution the sum of rents, interest, and profits—or $180.5 billion in 1967. But not even this is true. As we also noted in Chapter 5, these apparent returns to property ownership include a great deal of labor income. The incomes of unincorporated businessmen, professionals (as doctors or lawyers), and farmers are counted under "profit." They made up 43 percent of the profit total in 1967. But much of the income earned by small businessmen, professional people, and farmers is not a return on the property they own and use, but simply a salary they earn for working in their own business. Let us assume that two thirds of their profit is really labor income (that is, two thirds of those 43 percent). Then, the total of 1967 property income shrinks to $140.7 billion.

But not all of this would be available for distribution either. The government levies direct or income taxes also. In 1967, it took $33.5 billion of corporate profits alone. Thus, at most, $107.2 billion could have been distributed. Divide this among the population and you get $538 per person. But further income taxes (those now levied on rents, interest, unincorporated business profit, and dividends) would be levied on this figure. Whatever is left, perhaps $400 per person is the amount by which poor people might have become richer through socialism in 1967.

the dangers   We should note three things, however. First, the amount involved, although hardly negligible, is much smaller than most proponents of socialism would expect. Looking at *billions* of corporate profits, they are typically dreaming of thousands of dollars coming to each person. They would be bitterly disappointed.

Second, we must not ignore further consequences. Interest, rent, and profit, after all, serve a *function*. They are in many cases the reward for risk-taking and enterprise. Property owners take risks, and they innovate in the hope of getting some margin of income beyond what other people get. Sometimes they do. At other times they even lose. In addition, property owners save a large part of their income. Instead of buying consumer goods and just replacing their existing capital stock as it wears out, they expand the capital stock. In 1967, corporations alone retained and invested over half their net profits. Unincorporated businesses, professional people, and farmers often do likewise with their net income from property. But what do you think will happen if everyone in the country gets an equal and, as we noted, relatively small share of this net property income? The private incentive—and the means—to take risks, to innovate, to be thrifty would be gone. Why take risks, innovate, and be thrifty if in any case my income will be the same as anybody else's? As a result, the growth of our capital stock and the rate of technical advance will slow down. Our production possibilities will cease to expand! As population grows, but real GNP does not, real GNP per head will fall. Those nice $400 per person in 1967 will become $380 per person in 1968, $360 per person in 1969, and eventually will disappear altogether. As children fighting over a pie, and ending up with less than they could have had (as they spill a third of it on the floor), our insistence on getting a certain share of GNP may lower what we can get!

Nor have we considered the entire problem. Not only may absolute property income equality affect GNP growth by discouraging effort, innovation, and investment; it will do so also by interfering with efficiency. Business income differences in a market economy are needed as a signal to channel resources in the direction demanded by consumers. If consumers want more cars and fewer buggies, businesses would ordinarily begin to earn more if they use resources in the production of the former than in the latter. This would cause resources to shift until the right kinds of goods are being produced. There is no reason, however, for any private or public manager of resources to shift resources in response to shifts in demand if his firm's income will be like every other's.

Of course, one can and will have to do something about this. Government can take over the role of private entrepreneurs, of private savers and investors, and of the price system, too. Government can levy *extra* taxes on the $400 property income everyone received. It can use the proceeds to finance new capital formation and technological advance. It can use them to set up an elaborate central planning mechanism to take over the work of the price system of channeling resources in the right directions. In this way, perhaps, production possibilities would continue to expand. As population grows, per capita GNP may be prevented from falling. It may even rise. But we cannot be certain that government succeeds where private property owners did. Consider the East European and Chinese experience discussed in Chapters 16, 17, 23, and 26.

In the short run, therefore, the gain to the poor of establishing socialism would be absolutely negligible. Unless we want to court disaster, they could not even keep those $400 per person discussed above. In the long run, everyone may lose if socialism is a failure. There is no reason to expect that it would do better than capitalism. Eradicating poverty by socialism is a most inefficient way of going about it.

Third, in the United States, this method is, of course, totally impractical. The poor after all (unlike in many countries) are a minority. The majority of the American electorate would never buy this approach. A violent revolution on this issue has, in turn, no chance of success.[4]

Black Capitalism: An Alternative?

Some people have suggested an alternative. Instead of taking property from those who now have it, they propose giving the racial minorities in this country, who are bearing such a dis-

---

[4] If you would like to pursue this subject, you are urged to read Barrington Moore, Jr., "Revolution in America?" *The New York Review,* January 30, 1969.

proportionate burden of poverty, a chance to acquire their own property. Let us have lots of black-owned businesses, employing blacks, buying from and selling to blacks, for example, and poverty among the blacks will become a thing of the past. Instead of having socialism for all, let us have capitalism not just for whites, but also for American blacks, Puerto Ricans, Indians, and so on. As we noted above (page 313), President Nixon has shown interest in this possibility. Let us evaluate the chances of black capitalism. A brief look at history will help. Except for history, what is said here about the chances of black businesses in the future can be said about other minorities as well.

Some blacks have been in business for a long time.[5] Ever since emancipation, blacks have had free access to commodities. If they had the money, they could buy any commodity that was for sale (with the noticeable exception of houses). But blacks have not enjoyed open access to services. Whites simply would not sell certain services to blacks. Others they would sell only at exorbitant rates. Life insurance companies would charge blacks triple the rate charged whites (although such discrepancy was not justified by differences in mortality rates). Whites in fact, opened up a fertile field for black businessmen. Late last century, hundreds of black-owned insurance companies were formed. And blacks opened barber shops, beauty parlors, hotels, restaurants, and undertaking businesses. They had no competition from whites. And they had a captive market: other blacks. Segregation also provided specialized advantages to some black manufacturing firms. They supplied the above-mentioned service establishments. And, also owing to segregation, there arose a group of black professionals (doctors, lawyers, teachers) who served a black market only. Given the small income of the black community, all these businesses remained relatively small. In 1960, there were 50,000 of them. And the 1960 Census revealed an interesting fact. The average income of all blacks in the United States was about 50 percent that of whites. But the income of black businesses and professionals serving the captive black market was 80 percent that of whites in similar jobs.

But during the 1960's, the effects of the 1954 Supreme Court decision against segregation began to be felt. For the black business and professional class the effect was disastrous. They had operated behind a protective wall, free from competition of white-owned businesses. The Supreme Court decision and the changing mood of the country toppled that wall. Large national corporations began to look at the black market. They began to compete with the small black businesses. Of 200 black-owned insurance companies, more than three quarters died. Black-owned cosmetics companies went out of business as national cosmetics firms began to offer special cosmetics for the black market. Other white-owned companies introduced African motif garments and even "soul food" preparations. Black-owned restaurants and hotels closed as blacks began to use white facilities.

It is against this background that we must judge the chances for black capitalism. We cannot reverse the trend of established white-owned national corporations competing with black-owned small businesses. Is this the time to create more of the latter? Is this the time,

---

[5] The remainder of this section is based in part on an April 1969 lecture at Amherst College by Andrew F. Brimmer, a governor of the Federal Reserve System. See also his "The Trouble with Black Capitalism," *Nation's Business,* May 1969, pp. 78–79.

as some blacks urge, to create an entire spectrum of black-owned industries serving the black market?

The answer is no. Consider the technological realities. As we move from service businesses to retailers to wholesalers and to manufacturers, the optimum size of the firm rapidly increases. Should we urge blacks to set up more service and small retail establishments? It certainly is *possible*, for these firms require relatively little capital. But these firms also have the lowest profit margin (maybe 3 percent) throughout the economy. Are we going to cure black poverty by pulling blacks into the most marginal of businesses? This is like creating an urban equivalent of subsistence agriculture!

Well, some people say, blacks should establish large shopping centers, in the city ghettos perhaps. In fact, they have. Consider the much publicized case of a 1968 Los Angeles "ghetto conglomerate," Action Industries, Inc. It is tightly controlled by area residents, mostly black and Mexican American. It features, or plans to feature, a supermarket, two service stations, a home and commercial maintenance company, subcontracting of bench assembly work, a catering service, a doughnut shop, a "soul food" restaurant, an auto diagnostic center, an arts and craft shop, an employment agency, and a real estate development. Yet, in late 1968, it was only employing 200 persons.

Another black-owned shopping center opened in Philadelphia in 1968, partly financed by a Ford Foundation grant. It rented space to the A&P, the Bell Telephone Company, and the old black-owned North Carolina Mutual Insurance Company. It established a number of small black businesses: a dry cleaning shop, pharmacy, book store, card and gift shop, hardware store, furniture store, and apparel shops. It sounds great.

But what has been the experience of this type of venture in a dozen cities studied? Uniformly, the experience was this: sales volume rose significantly in the early months of operation and then fell precipitously. The reason: operating costs were higher than in established businesses, so prices had to be higher. Customers went to chainstores. Alternatives being available, these new black-owned businesses did not have a captive market. Why, finally, were operating costs higher? Partly because of lack of entrepreneurial experience, higher land prices and taxes, higher insurance rates, smaller average purchases, slower turnover of perishable items, increased pilferage; mostly because employees were recruited from the culture of poverty. Their absentee rate was exceedingly high. Three people might have to be hired to ensure two on the job.

How about the chances of black-owned manufacturing plants? Again we must look beyond proud dreams and face realities of financing, costs, and profits. First, truly large plants cost hundreds of millions of dollars. It can be doubted that such financing can be obtained. Second, many manufacturing operations are not suitable for the areas where blacks live. One cannot put up an oil refinery in the midst of an urban ghetto. After all, it is a residential area. Third, the possibilities of establishing medium-sized and smaller plants are clearly limited. From 1958 to 1963, the annual rate of all new manufacturing plant formation in the United States was 3,500. Of these, only 2,600 were suitable for the areas where poor blacks live. But only 500 of these employed more than twenty people. In addition of course, there is no reason to believe that all new manufacturing plants in the country can be owned and operated by blacks and located near black residential areas. The chances of blacks to establish an entire spectrum of black-owned industries are truly negligible.

What about white-owned plants coming to black neighborhoods and sharing ownership or management with local residents? To some extent, this has already happened (see also page 313). There has been federal government encouragement. The Congress of Racial Equality (CORE) has promoted the idea. The record so far has not been a pleasing one.

The Aerojet Corporation in Watts, Los Angeles, for example, received a federal subsidy of $1,300 per employee for training area poor. Its actual training costs turned out to be $5,000 per employee. It planned to hire 500 poor people. It had to hire 1,200 in order to have an average of 500 present. Many could not handle the training program. Employment dropped to 300.

Should the government give a richer set of incentives for this type of operation? Senator Robert Kennedy introduced a bill in the Ninetieth Congress designed to lure firms to poverty areas. It had the most generous set of tax incentives ever devised: a firm locating in the area and employing more than fifty poor people would be able to deduct from its tax bill 7 percent of plant construction costs, 10 percent of machinery costs, and 25 percent of wages paid to the poor. The Department of Commerce estimated that this would save firms $91,000 on a $1 million investment. It also estimated that the types of firms likely to take advantage of the incentive program would be found exactly in those industries already found in poverty areas (textiles and leather, for example). These industries then were paying an average wage of $3,000 per year. In short, the richest set of incentives ever devised would bring to the poor the kind of firms paying poverty wages! Over a 10-year period, estimated the Department of Commerce, $770 million in wages might be generated (from 250,000 new jobs). The cost to the government: $500 million. Surely, there must be better ways of doing things.

But "black capitalism" is fashionable. Private foundations have also entered the picture. In a major policy shift, the Ford Foundation announced in 1968 that it would engage in ventures aiding the poor and minority groups, looking only for "high *social* yield." Traditionally, the foundation had looked for high money yield, using the income from its financial investments for charitable purposes. In a shift away from safe philanthropy, the foundation has supported bold projects designed to calm social tensions. Among the first of these were a black business development (already mentioned above), racially integrated and low-income housing, grants to test community control of schools and promote voter registration, and the purchase of land for aesthetic, recreational, and scientific purposes.

A 1968 study by the Brookings Institution confirmed, however, that the possibilities of developing "ghetto industry" and thereby eliminating inner-city unemployment and poverty "were strongly limited." In addition to the factors mentioned above, great transportation difficulties put all ghetto plants at a marked competitive disadvantage. The study showed that much publicized moves by big companies to set up ghetto plants (see pages 312–313 above) were giving jobs to only a handful. And to suggest that black entrepreneurship can produce much more than a token number of new jobs, even for a long time to come, was called "pure romanticism."

General Economic Policies Encouraging Growth

Let us now consider an alternative. Suppose we relied on policies known to be practical. Suppose we looked at our arsenal of monetary and fiscal policies and set out to give poor people *jobs*. As a matter of fact, public opinion surveys show that this is the path out of poverty that most of the poor, as well as most other Americans, would prefer to any other alternative.

We have discussed in Chapters 10, 12, and 24 what would be required for an all-out effort to promote full employment and economic growth. The maintenance of a fully employed and growing economy can by itself be a powerful force in the reduction of poverty. In a market in which demand for labor is strong relative to the supply, the chances of the poor unemployed, partially employed, and low skilled are enhanced as employers have greater incentive to seek out and train workers. The methods used to promote full employment and growth could, furthermore, pay special attention to the lot of the poor.

If, for instance, it is necessary to raise aggregate demand to reach full employment, this may be done by providing additional income *to the poor* rather than to the rich. An unemployed steelworker can be put to work just as well by increasing the demand for steel to make refrigerators for the poor as by increasing it to make yachts for the rich. A tax cut could, for instance, easily discriminate in favor of the poor. In fact, there is nothing to prevent us from cutting taxes of the poor below zero by giving them tax refunds for taxes they have never paid.

The 1969 *Economic Report of the President* reviewed the issues involved here. It showed that all the progress in reducing the number of poor persons was made in periods of prosperity. From 1949 to 1953, 1954 to 1956, and since 1961, the number of poor persons has declined on the average by well over 2 million per year. On the other hand, the short recession of 1954 wiped out half the gain of the preceding 4 years. Similarly, the sluggish economic growth of the late 1950's set back the fight against poverty by 7 years. (You can verify all this by studying the top line in Figure 27.2 NUMBER OF POOR PERSONS AND INCIDENCE OF POVERTY.)

who was helped   Who were the poor people helped most? They were male family heads of working age. The number of poor people in this category changed not at all from 1959 to 1961. It declined by 400,000 per year from 1964 to 1966. The tight labor market increased their wages if they were employed. It reduced the incidence of unemployment and part-time work. Businessmen who could not find skilled workers to hire increasingly turned to the chronically unemployed and the poorly educated, and they trained them on the job.

Interestingly, the prosperity of the 1960's did not help poor families headed by females of working age. Why? They are less likely to look for work. Many have children to take care of, and there are no day care centers. Or they are hired last, because of sex discrimination or because they have even less prior job experience on the average than men do. And even when hired, they are paid lower wages and have less steady employment than men (hence they are less likely to escape poverty).

Another group of poor people helped by prosperity in the 1960's was the aged. The in-

cidence of poverty among them declined substantially. In part, this was owing to a 21 percent increase in social security benefits (which would probably not have been voted in a recession). In part, it was owing to the fact that old people were allowed to work beyond normal
retirement age, again because of the great demand for labor. To the extent that these people
would have had poverty incomes otherwise, this is reflected in less poverty among those aged
65 and over. A period of prolonged prosperity can, furthermore, reduce the number of poor
in this group by giving people a greater chance to accumulate higher pension rights.

The percentage of poor ill and disabled also fell in the 1960's. As people with low education and no work experience, they are more likely to find good paying jobs when labor is
hard to get.

Finally, the 1960's brought a substantial decline in the number of near-poor. Most of
these are employed, but employed at low wages. The decline in this category is significant.
Because most of the poor who ceased to be poor became near-poor, it means that more
people moved out of the near-poor category than entered it.

an evaluation   Is this then the way to end poverty? The President's Council of
Economic Advisers estimated that a continuation of the 1961–1968 trend of poverty elimination would end all poverty within 10 years. But it also warned not to expect this. The reason:
there are diminishing returns to this route. You can help many able-bodied men, some old
people, and some disabled. But you cannot help poor female family heads with children. You
cannot help all the elderly, ill, and disabled. (Significantly, by 1967, 59 percent of the remaining poor were in one of these categories.) Finally, you may not be able to help the most
disadvantaged, the uneducated and unmotivated victims of prolonged unemployment and
discrimination, who are most deeply steeped in the culture of poverty. They may not even
have the strength to take advantage of the opportunities offered them.

In short, this approach is not perfect. It does not solve the whole problem. But it solves
some of it. It is well worth pursuing. This should particularly be stressed in view of those
critics who argue that a little bit of recession is a good thing because it prevents inflation.
And inflation, we are told, hurts the poor more than anyone else. The poor have relatively
fixed incomes: low hourly wages, fixed pensions, fixed welfare payments. As inflation proceeds, they can buy less and less with their money. Not so with the nonpoor, we are told.
Middle-class auto workers force up wages. Doctors raise fees. If the price of oranges goes up,
the middle-class housewife just switches to strawberries. The poor cannot do that; they are
stuck with buying beans.

This is, of course, a serious argument. Does it stand up to analysis? It is quite true that
a policy that continually pushes aggregate demand to the limit of our productive potential
will accelerate inflation. (On the trade-off between unemployment and inflation see Chapter
14.) But a careful study by investigators at the Institute for Research on Poverty revealed
this: during inflation, the prices paid by the poor rise less rapidly than the prices paid by the
nonpoor. In other words, the price of beans may rise less than that of oranges or strawberries.
But more importantly, the money income of the poor rises much *faster* during inflation than
that of the nonpoor: Social security benefits are, in fact, not fixed. They are continually

raised by deliberate policy decision. And above all, as we have seen, the poor get more income from work during prosperity. They have higher wages, more steady work, and full-time work instead of low wages, part-time work, and no work at all. The harm done to the poor by inflation during prosperity is more than offset by the gains that prosperity brings for them. In other words, it is better to earn $3,000 a year when prices rise at 5 percent than to earn $500 with prices rising at 1 percent.

As Figure 27.2 NUMBER OF POOR PERSONS AND INCIDENCE OF POVERTY so vividly shows, recessions and sluggish growth raise the number of the poor. As was shown in Chapter 14, more unemployment is a remedy for inflation. But so far as the poor are concerned, this would hurt them more than inflation itself.

Improving the Labor Resources of the Poor

As we saw above, we cannot hope to help the poor by redistributing capital and land. Most income earned in this country is income from labor. It is silly to suppose that it could be otherwise for those now poor. What we can change, however, is poor people's chances to earn an above-poverty level of labor income. We can do this, furthermore, not just by raising the demand for labor in general. This we discussed in the previous section. We can do it also by improving the kind of labor the poor have to offer. We can help them to become healthier, more educated, and more highly trained.

education and health   Some progress has already been made. Seventy-five percent of poor youngsters aged 16–21 are either in school or have graduated from high school. In contrast, more than half of their parents have had no high school education.

But this is not good enough. Ninety percent of nonpoor youngsters aged 16–21 are either in school or have graduated from high school. In addition, as we have noted, the poor are stuck with inferior facilities and less-qualified teachers. This lowers the value of education to the poor. As we noted also, when they get to school, the poor are already handicapped and continue to be handicapped by the culture of poverty. Their health and nutrition is bad, as is their mental development. They are behind the nonpoor when they get to school. The school does not help them catch up. (In fact, studies show that the intellectual difference between racial minority children and others is greater at the end than at the beginning of schooling.)

Some psychologists think segregation itself has an adverse effect on performance. They find that fellow students have a greater effect on a pupil's academic achievement than the quality of his teacher or the physical facilities of his school. In recent years, more than 60 percent of black first graders entered schools that were more than 90 percent black.

There is clearly much that can be done. It simply is not enough to provide all youngsters with free access to *some* school and then to tell them that it is their own responsibility to achieve. Many children are much too crippled by the culture of poverty to take advantage of whatever opportunities (if any) are offered them.

Superior facilities. One can in fact make a good case for reversing the present tradition and giving the poor not inferior, but superior facilities and teachers. This would recognize that the school, not the child, has responsibility for assuring educational achievement. The successful school would then be the one that reduces the child's dependence on his social origin, that allows it, in the end, to compete on an equal basis with others. Equal access to schools is irrelevant. We must assure not just a right to compete. We must give to all an honest chance to win. As some have put it, "Equal *outcome* is what matters."[6]

Head Start. Poor children could be helped even before they enter school. The Head Start program serves the purpose of counteracting the culture of poverty. It is to give poor youngsters a better start on education. It provides for better child nutrition, health care, and parent involvement as well as an academic program. This recognizes the importance of the home environment. In 1969, however, the worthwhileness of the program was being questioned. A study by the Westinghouse Learning Corporation of Ohio (contracted by the Office of Economic Opportunity) had tested 2,000 disadvantaged children nationwide in the first three grades of school. It found that summer Head Start programs had left no noticeable impact on the children's linguistic abilities, mathematical skills, or attitudes. Year-round programs had made a marginal difference only between Head Start participants and equally disadvantaged children not in the program. Congress and the President, however, were determined to push the program. They criticized the report for having presented nationwide figures. (Possibly, the averages covered up superb results in some places with failures in others.) They argued that possibly good results had been frittered away afterward by bad teaching. They figured that in any case the severe damage done to the children of the poor from early infancy on cannot be expected to be erased in one summer or even a single year of part-time attention. Over time, effects would show, both on children and parents. Therefore, they urged that the program should start earlier and continue longer (that Follow Through programs be instituted). President Nixon reduced the 1969 participants in the summer program from 417,000 to 217,000, but raised enrollees in the year-round program from 220,000 to 275,000.

Aid to teenagers. Special attention and monetary aid even might be given to teenagers. Financial aid may be given to ensure their staying in school. Many poor teenagers face a bitter choice: drop out and help provide for the family or stay in school and starve. To tell them that "free" schooling is theirs for the taking is a cruel hoax. Helping them financially is a good investment for society. It reduces the social costs of drug addiction, delinquency, crime, and continued poverty. One may go even further than this.

Professor James Tobin of Yale has proposed the creation of a federal government endowment to encourage education *beyond* high school. This would pay everyone $5,000 at age 19 if used for higher education or training. The amount would be repaid in full or in part after age 28 from the higher income realized. As we noted above, the monetary returns to educa-

[6] You are urged to read James S. Coleman, "Equal Schools or Equal Students?" *The Public Interest,* no. 4 (Summer 1966), 70–75, and "The Concept of Equality of Educational Opportunity," *Harvard Educational Review,* Winter 1968, pp. 7-22.

tion are truly staggering (see page 555). Furthermore, such a program would be only fair. At present, the states, for instance, subsidize the education of many "rich" children at state universities. Why not help all? Why not also subsidize the education of those poor not interested in university training, but who could benefit from vocational counseling and training?

Birth control.   As in underdeveloped countries, one cause contributing to poverty of American families is a high birth rate.[7] In 1965, among all families with children, the poor had 3.23 children on the average, others only 2.30. If we count the number of children under 22 per 1,000 persons of prime working age (22–64) we find this for 1966: the nonpoor had 79, the poor 148. In the central cities, the nonpoor had 71, the poor 168. The figures were substantially higher for nonwhites, reaching 211 for central-city poor.

A larger number of children contributes to poverty in a number of ways. There is less income per head. Thus, per capita expenditures on good food, health care, and education drop. The more children, the less attention each receives. Their mental development is held back. In fact, the incidence of mental retardation is higher after the third child. In addition, children from large families leave school earlier. (The percentage of youngsters who complete high school falls sharply with a rise in the number of siblings. In 1965, considering children under 18, 11 percent of American families with one or two children were poor. Of those with three children, 15 percent were poor; with four children, 21 percent; with five children, 33 percent; with six or more children, 43 percent. Thus one can make a good case for birth control as a device to improve the chances of the poor. And, studies show, the poor want fewer children. In 1966, found the Department of Health, Education, and Welfare, the poor had 450,000 unwanted babies.

Until very recently, however, the poor in the United States were denied by government any assistance as to birth control. Strong religious opposition to the idea is to blame. This is beginning to change. By 1965, there were 689 public birth control clinics in twenty-one states. President Nixon promised in 1969 that the government would reach all the poor with birth control information within five years. But the moral issues remain. Should birth control devices be made available to all who request them, including the unmarried? Should government be passive or actively encourage family planning?

It is by no means easy to give answers. On occasion emphasis on use of birth control in poverty programs has added further tension to race relations. Some blacks tend to see the suggestion of whites that blacks as well as whites ease poverty by limiting their families as a perhaps unconscious attempt of the whites to eliminate black people. This may seem unduly paranoid, but is it really? In 1968, a Delaware state senate committee recommended legislation that would provide for sterilization of women who use welfare funds to support more than two illegitimate children. The dangers involved here are obvious.

Furthermore, as psychiatrists tell us, people who are poor and unskilled often find that bearing and raising children gives them a feeling of creative accomplishment. It is the only

---

[7] You might wish to consult Harold L. Sheppard, *Effects of Family Planning on Poverty in the United States* (Kalamazoo: The Upjohn Institute for Employment Research, 1967). Some of the data below are based on this source.

time they really feel alive and worthwhile. Does anyone have the right to take away the only joy a woman may experience? Do economists have the right to decide for others what is best for them?

job training and employment experience   Besides formal schooling, on-the-job training can help the poor acquire important skills also. This may require an all-out effort attacking discriminatory hiring procedures. Discrimination can frustrate the efforts of those who have been educated to realize full returns from their schooling. (A greater percentage of white male high school *dropouts* end up getting skilled and semiskilled jobs than of nonwhite male high school *graduates*.) As an antidote to private discrimination against the poor, governmental hiring and licensing procedures could discriminate in their favor.

Discrimination can also prevent certain groups in the population from acquiring skills in informal ways. To compensate for past mistakes, a variety of programs are designed specifically to train the poor or to give them employment experience. Slightly more than half the trainees under the Manpower Development and Training Act came from poor families, in late 1968. Other disadvantaged persons are being trained in a variety of ways, as in the Job Corps, in neighborhood youth corps centers, and under the Jobs program. (These and others have been described in detail on pages 310–314 above.)

black power   Many programs designed to improve the labor resources of the poor may be substantially aided by increased political power in the hands of the poor. The black power movement is an example of this approach.[8] To be sure, to some extent this movement is substituting rhetoric for analysis. The fond dreams of black capitalism (or black socialism) as a panacea for poverty are an example. (See our discussion above.) To some extent, black power advocates confuse defiant gestures with political action. But there is much reason to welcome the movement. A group cannot cooperate on an equal basis with others without having first developed a sense of its own distinctiveness and of its own worth. In the process, the blacks may escape the culture of poverty that holds them back. Just consider the effect of the strict rules of behavior laid down by the Black Muslims. Followers are encouraged to hold on to their jobs and their families, to forgo "loose" living. Women are told to be subservient to their husbands. If you know anything about the history of blacks, you can see the importance of this. White slave masters in North America never showed any respect for the integrity of slave families. Fathers were separated from their wives and children. As a result, children tended to grow up in a mother-centered household. After emancipation, this tendency continued. Given society's cruel treatment, the black male was of little use for the family. He was a bad provider. This has continued to the present with black men being unemployed, underemployed, or employed at low wages disproportionately to their numbers. This has contributed to continued dominance of black female-headed households, doomed to poverty and dooming children to the same. The Muslim creed may reverse this tendency, mainly by changing *attitudes* so as to make black families more stable units, units that have

[8] You are urged to read Stokely Carmichael, "What We Want," *New York Review of Books,* September 22, 1966.

aspiration and hope. In a way, this can get at the roots of poverty from the inside, while government programs of promoting prosperity, education, and training do so from the outside.

Such government programs can, in turn, be strengthened if blacks have a voice in government. Black power can help channel funds to better schools of the poor. (At present, per student expenditures in the mostly white suburban schools greatly exceed those in typically nonwhite inner-city schools.) It can enforce antidiscrimination laws in education, training, employment, and housing. It can, through bussing or neighborhood control of schools, enforce higher quality education.

Income Maintenance

We have noted that prosperity by itself does not reach all the poor. Measures to improve the labor resources of the poor are, in turn, bound to take a fairly long time. They also cannot help all the poor. This leads to a third alternative for attacking poverty. We can make outright income transfers to all the poor as long as their poverty is not eliminated in other ways.

We can essentially follow the splendid example of Robin Hood and attempt to redistribute the existing total of income by robbing rich Peter to help poor Paul. A great many of such transfers occur voluntarily within families, as between the productive family members, on the one hand, and the children, the elderly, and the sick, on the other. We are not concerned with such voluntary intrafamily transfers here.

There are also a number of voluntary interfamily transfers (via the churches, Red Cross, and the like), but these are not of great significance in alleviating poverty. They involve altogether a tiny fraction of 1 percent of GNP. To quote some figures, in 1966, all thirty-three Christian churches in the United States contributed together $676 million in benevolences, or 0.09 percent of GNP. However, they spent almost twice this amount on new construction, just about four times this amount on all congregational expenses. In the same year, the United Fund Campaigns raised almost the identical amount of $626 million. Not all of these amounts, however, went to Americans (church benevolences include foreign missions), nor to American poor families. Even if they had, this would only have equaled 6 percent of their aggregate income.

What we really must talk about, if we are serious about income redistribution, is a system of *involuntary* transfers through governmental taxation and spending. This is bound to be resented and, partly at least, for good reasons. Some families may have higher incomes than others because they work harder or have been thriftier or worked harder in the past. Most of us would consider it unfair if they got penalized by higher taxes designed to equalize incomes. Others may have the good fortune to inherit a great deal of income-producing property, or they may be the lucky owners of a skill that just happens to have come into great demand. Should they be asked to subsidize their less fortunate fellow citizens? If so, how far shall we carry the equalization of incomes?

desirable extent of transfers   Should we go so far as to create absolute income equality? Some people, such as the (academic) socialists, frequently argue for a *complete* equalization of money income by government. Failure to do so, they fear, will allow some rich people (with large money demand) to commandeer resources toward the production of such luxuries as private airplanes and summer houses by the sea, while there are still poor people (with lower money demand) in need of such necessities as refrigerators and children's furniture. "Everybody," they say, "should have an equal number of *dollar votes* in the market, and then we can be sure that the whims of some do not get satisfied before the crying needs of their brothers."

This argument is attractive to many, especially to those who favor political democracy, a system that (ideally) also gives an equal vote to each man. It is equally attractive to others for religious reasons, because they believe that every man is equally precious in the eyes of God. Yet, an equal distribution of income may seriously affect incentives (and has for this reason not been introduced in any actual socialist country). We have already discussed the problem involved in the section on redistributing wealth above. Thus one can make a good case for not carrying income equalization too far. Poverty, in fact, can be eliminated easily with only minor redistributions of income while retaining substantial inequality. For instance, we might look at the difference between the actual income of the poor and the income needed to place them above the poverty line. In 1967, this difference was $9.7 billion. It has been called the "poverty income deficit," and one might set out to tax the "rich" only to the extent required to fill this gap.

There is even a less painful way. As the President's Council of Economic Advisers noted in 1969, on the average, the real per capita income of Americans grows at about 3 percent per year. We could simply redistribute this growth dividend. Suppose we taxed the nonpoor (of whom there are so many) just enough to cut their annual real income increase to 2.5 percent. If we give this to the poor (of whom there are fewer), their real income could rise at 12 percent per year. As a result, the poverty gap would be closed in 4 to 8 years.

existing transfer programs   As a matter of fact, the various levels of government in the United States are already engaged in a great number of programs designed to alleviate poverty. Let us look at the payments side first. Table 27.3 MAJOR POVERTY-REDUCING GOVERNMENT TRANSFERS IN THE UNITED STATES lists the major programs in effect.

The programs listed in Table 27.3 alone add to $58.7 billion for fiscal 1969, or 7 percent of GNP. Of course, not all of these expenditures, as the last column indicates, were direct payments to the poor. Many, however, helped to alleviate poverty associated with old age, ill health and nutrition, disability and youth. However, the amounts shown in Table 27.3, even when adjusted downward to exclude payments to the nonpoor, may greatly exaggerate the net gain to the poor.

financing transfers   The net gain to the poor is exaggerated by the data of Table 27.3, because the poor as well as the rich pay taxes that provide the funds for government transfers. They may not benefit at all or much less than the data seem to imply. How much in

Table 27.3 MAJOR POVERTY-REDUCING GOVERNMENT TRANSFERS IN THE UNITED STATES, FISCAL YEAR 1969

PROGRAM	TOTAL OUTLAYS (MILLIONS)	NUMBER OF BENEFI- CIARIES (THOU- SANDS)	AVERAGE OUTLAY PER RE- CIPIENT PER YEAR	PERCENT OF RECIPIENT HOUSEHOLDS WITH INCOME LESS THAN $3,300 PER YEAR
	(1)	(2)	(3)	(4)
1. Assistance to those 65 years and over	$34,812		n.a.	
a. Social security retirement and survivors benefits	24,681	21,931	$1,125	31
b. Old age assistance	1,833	2,123	863	100
c. Retirement (military, civil service, railroad)	6,171	2,568	2,403	n.a.
d. Veterans' pensions	2,127	2,252	944	80
2. Disability programs	$ 7,940			
a. Workmen's compensation	1,686	n.a.	n.a.	n.a.
b. Veterans' compensation	2,611	2,390	$1,092	24
c. Social security	2,691	2,278	1,181	39
d. Aid to the blind	92	84	1,095	100
e. Aid to the permanently and totally disabled	726	721	1,007	100
f. Others (federal employees, railroad)	134	81	1,654	n.a.
3. Aid to families with dependent children	$ 3,206	6,146	$ 522	100
4. Unemployment insurance	$ 2,463	5,777	$ 426	19
5. General assistance	$ 32	700	$ 46	100
6. Assistance-in-kind	$10,226		n.a.	
a. Food stamps	273	3,600	$ 76	100
b. Child nutrition	128	3,900	33	100
c. Direct food distribution	264	3,800	69	100
d. Public housing	456	2,800	163	57
e. Rent supplements	28	100	280	67
f. Medicare	6,222	9,500	655	36
g. Medicaid	2,384	9,500	251	75
h. Maternity and infant care	193	3,200	60	70
i. Public health service medical programs (Indians, seamen, neighborhood centers)	278	1,400	199	66

Note: n.a.—not available.
Source: Economic Report of the President, *January 1969, pp. 164 and 167.*

taxes do the poor pay? To answer this intelligently we cannot just look at the federal income tax. But, we must consider federal excise and corporate taxes as well as state and local levies.

The federal income tax is often used to illustrate how the tax system may reduce the extent of income inequality, a fact we observed in passing above as we noted that the Lorenz curve for the United States after federal income taxes lies slightly closer to the line of perfect equality than before taxes are figured. The federal income tax is a *progressive* tax, which means that it takes a larger *percentage* of higher than of lower incomes. (A tax taking the same percentage of all incomes is called *proportional*; a tax taking a smaller percentage of higher than of lower incomes is termed *regressive*.) The effect of a progressive income tax on income distribution can easily be illustrated as follows in Table 27.4 THE PROGRESSIVE INCOME TAX. Take three families with annual incomes as in column (1) below. They receive a total before-tax income of $16,000. Thus, to calculate data equivalent to Table 27.1 THE DISTRIBUTION OF PERSONAL INCOME IN THE UNITED STATES, we would say that the poorest one third of all families (here family A) receive ($1,000/$16,000) × 100 = 6.25 percent of total income, the poorest two thirds of families (here A plus B) receive ($6,000/$16,000 × 100 = 37.5 percent of the total, and all families (A plus B plus C) receive 100 percent. From this we could draw a Lorenz curve analogous to the curved heavy line in Figure 27.1.

Table 27.4 THE PROGRESSIVE INCOME TAX

	INCOME BEFORE TAX (1)	TAX RATE (PERCENT) (2)	TAX AMOUNT (3)	INCOME AFTER TAX (4)
Family A	$ 1,000	0	0	$ 1,000
Family B	$ 5,000	10	$ 500	$ 4,500
Family C	$10,000	20	$2,000	$ 8,000
	$16,000		$2,500	$13,500

The effect of a progressive income tax is to reduce after-tax income inequality.

Now we introduce a progressive tax as evidenced by column (2), yielding amounts shown in column (3). Using after-tax data of column (4), it turns out that the poorest one third of families now receive ($1,000/$13,500 × 100 = 7.4 percent of total income, the poorest two thirds receive ($5,500/$13,500 × 100 = 40.74 percent and, as always, all families receive 100 percent. The Lorenz curve has shifted toward the line of absolute equality.

This shift would be even more pronounced if the government now transferred its $2,500 tax revenue to poor family A, giving it an income of $3,500. The Lorenz curve percentages would become 21.9, 50.0, and 100, respectively, for the one third, two thirds, or total of families. Income inequality would persist; poverty, official definition, might not.

You can see now why it is important not to look at transfers by themselves, *unless* the tax system is such that the poor in no way (as in our example) finance the transfers. If the poor through taxes, had financed all or part of the transfers, the net benefit to them would have been much smaller.

In reality, it turns out that in 1968 only 30 percent of *all* governments' tax receipts came from the federal personal income tax. Another 38 percent came from other federal taxes (corporate taxes 15 percent, social security taxes 16 percent, indirect business taxes 7 percent). The final 32 percent were levied by state and local governments (property and sales taxes bringing in 22 percent and corporate and personal income taxes the remainder of the grand total).

tax incidence   A great number of studies have been made to determine the over-all incidence of all taxes. Who, in the last analysis, really pays them? What is the percentage of *all* taxes paid by various income groups? The answer is surprising. The poorest income recipients (under $2,000 a year) pay over 40 percent of their income (before transfers) in taxes. The richest (over $15,000 a year) pay slightly *less* (percentage-wise). Everyone else pays close to 30 percent. This is illustrated in the top portion of Figure 27.3 TAXES AND TRANSFER PAYMENTS AS PERCENT OF INCOME (EXCLUDING TRANSFERS), BY INCOME CLASS, 1965. How is this possible?

The progressiveness of the federal personal income tax and its impact on income inequality is negated by other taxes that are typically *regressive*. For example, low-income families pay a much larger percentage of their incomes than high-income families in property, sales, gasoline and local and state income taxes. This is not surprising because they tend to have less insurance or savings (untouched by sales taxes), they pay a larger percentage of their incomes on housing (subject to property tax), and so on.

The same regressive impact has been found to hold for the combined total of social security taxes, corporate profits taxes, and other federal taxes (estate, gift, excise, customs). Social security taxes have this effect because they only touch the first $7,800 of income, and, if paid by employers, they may be shifted to consumers by higher prices or lower wages. The poor end up paying them because their income is mostly wage income and most of it is consumed. Corporate income taxes might have this effect by being passed along to the consumer via higher prices.

Even the redistributive effect of the federal personal income tax is less than the progressive tax rates seem to imply. High-income families frequently are able to avoid high tax rates and can do so quite legally. (For instance, if all of the annual income of a rich man comes from public school bonds, he pays *no* federal income tax.)

To sum up, transfers from the rich to the poor through government do occur, but the net effect is considerably lower than the dollar amount of transfers implies. About 40 percent of the poorest people's income is taken in taxes which help in part to finance transfers to the poor. As is indicated in the bottom portion of Figure 27.3, only those with incomes below $2,000 per year end up with any net gain at all.

reforming welfare?   The very fact that poverty persists is proof that existing welfare programs have not been able to abolish poverty. In part, this is so because they were not exclusively designed for that purpose. In part, as we saw, this is so because they are financed by taxes that partially or wholly offset the intended effect. Still, in 1965, welfare programs reduced the number of poor by 30 percent below what it would have been otherwise. Yet 31 percent of welfare recipients remained poor despite help. And 54 percent of the poor received no welfare payments at all. Should we reform welfare to make it do a better job?

To judge the chances, we must realize that in the United States, as in other countries, much welfare legislation has been influenced by the Puritan ethic. According to this, the poor themselves are responsible for their condition: "They are shiftless and lazy (why else

Figure 27.3   TAXES AND TRANSFER PAYMENTS AS PERCENT OF INCOME (EXCLUDING TRANSFERS), BY INCOME CLASS, 1965

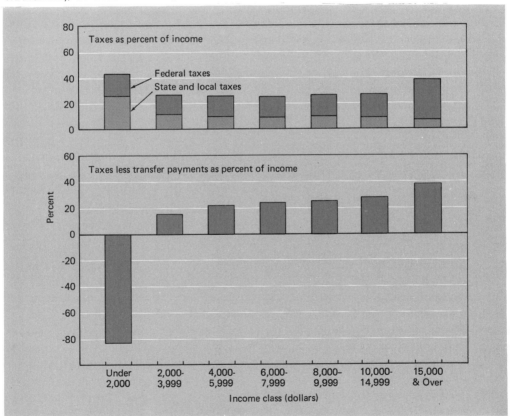

Because the poor receive not only transfers but also pay taxes, the net gain to them of transfer payments is reduced. In fact, only those with incomes under $2,000 per year have any net gain at all. Source: Economic Report of the President, *January 1969, p. 161.*

would they have so little education?). They are short-sighted (why else would they have saved so little, have such large families, and be so stubborn about moving away from their depressing environment?). Therefore, poverty is well deserved. Help them we may, but we should help as few as possible as little as possible lest we reward their undesirable behavior," went the argument.

Nowadays, we are more inclined to see poverty as a result of social deficiencies (lack of aggregate demand, technological change, discrimination). Hence, we tend to believe that society should remove what it has created. Thus, we might argue for expanded coverage and benefits.

Enlarge coverage.   As noted, many of the poor are not reached by welfare programs. Workmen's compensation and unemployment insurance is an example. It excludes 11 million domestics, agricultural workers, and small business employees. Even those "covered" are usually not paid for more than 26 weeks in any 1 year. More than a fifth of recipients thusly exhaust their benefits. States also set residency requirements. Poor families are denied all public assistance unless they have been residents of the state for a minimum period. (Some of these requirements have now been overturned by the courts.) There is much room for action.

Increase benefits.   Look at column (3) of Table 27.3 MAJOR-POVERTY REDUCING GOVERNMENT TRANSFERS IN THE UNITED STATES, FISCAL YEAR 1969. In spite of the total welfare expenditures of close to $60 *billion*, the average monthly benefits (items 1c and 2f excluded) never exceed $100 per recipient (just divide the annual column (3) entries by twelve). Benefits often are substantially lower than that. Mothers with dependent children get on the average $43.50 per month. (In 1969, this ranged from a monthly $8.50 in Mississippi to $71.50 in New York.) Child nutrition aid is as low as $2.75 per month. All this reflects the Puritan ethic. These programs are often designed to save money, not to save people. But we could save more money in the long run by spending more now.

Less humiliation.   Many welfare programs subject recipients to a great deal of humiliation. Their affairs are investigated meticulously and continually. Their homes are searched. They are continually treated as untrustworthy, promiscuous, and lazy. They are "pushed around" in a hundred different ways, and they better be quiet, "or else." In fact, bureaucratic supervision has helped to enhance the breakdown of the family among the poor. Families with an able-bodied man present (be he the legal father or not) were denied aid for dependent children. But aid was granted to the mother in the absence of a man. An unemployed father, or one who could not earn enough even if working, had a choice: desert the family to put them on welfare or stay home seeing them starve.

Such insane pieces of legislation can and must be changed. In addition, supervision is costly, taking on the average 10 percent of welfare funds.

Hunger in America.[9]   If we are to take the route of reforming existing programs, one is of the greatest urgency. Some people in America are starving to death. Helping them cannot

---

[9] This section is based in part on a series of articles by Homer Bigart, "Hunger in America," *The New York Times,* February 16–20, 1969.

wait. In 1968, the Department of Agriculture estimated that 5 million Americans were chronically hungry. Ten million more were undernourished. The Senate Select Committee on Nutrition and Human Needs made a similar estimate in 1969.

Who are these people? You will not find them in the all-white suburbs. You find them living in tarpaper shacks in eastern Kentucky, the migrant labor camps in Florida, the Mississippi delta, the Mexican-American slums of San Antonio, the Indian reservations throughout the country. There you find conditions resembling those of the worst spots in the underdeveloped world. People have marasmus (calorie starvation: loose flesh hangs on spindly arms and legs). People have kwashiorkor (protein deficiency leading to irreversible brain damage). People have rickets (vitamin D deficiency, leading to soft and deformed bones). People are plagued with intestinal parasites. And people die.

As evidenced by items 6a through c in Table 27.3 MAJOR POVERTY-REDUCING GOVERN-MENT TRANSFERS IN THE UNITED STATES, FISCAL YEAR 1969, there are already programs dealing with this problem. But the aid is woefully inadequate. (See also column (3); it shows average *annual* outlays per recipient.) At first, the government instituted a program of free commodity distribution (6c). It failed to meet nutritional requirements (no vitamin D fortified milk, for instance). Some people suspected a simple reason: it was a program to get rid of particular farm surpluses and to shore up farm prices more than to help the poor (see our discussion in Chapter 19). More recently the food stamp program was instituted (6a). People would either buy or receive "free" (for a 50-cent fee) so-called food stamps allowing them to exchange the stamps for a variety of food items in regular stores. People who bought stamps would receive, perhaps, double the money value in stamps. To qualify for free stamps, in May 1969, a family of three or less had to be certified at a monthly income of less than $20, a family of four or more at less than $30. As a result, the bulk of poor people had to buy their stamps.

All over the country, however, recipients have criticized the stamp program. First, it forces the values of the nonpoor administrators onto the poor. The poor are not allowed, for instance, to buy foreign grown food (excepting coffee, tea, cocoa, and bananas). As a result, some people could not buy hamburger, because it contained some Argentine beef. Food stamps cannot be used for diaper soap, mops, or crayons, and similar items sold in grocery stores.

Second, participants are unanimous that the monthly allotment runs out in 2 or 3 weeks. Third, they charge outright abuses in administration. In many a county, the political machine dominates the administration of the program. Local officials do not always follow the spirit of the federal law. Poor people may be rejected illegally (but they do not know their rights of appeal). Or poor people are invited to buy stamps, but for a minimum of $50 only (and they never have that much cash). Hundreds of families in one Mississippi county did not even have 50 cents to get the "free" stamps. Some poor people cannot afford transportation to the county seat where stamps have to be claimed in person. Or they are physically unable to go. In one Georgia county (Glascock), the sheriff even ran the welfare representatives out of the county, declaring that a food program would "just mean a lot of niggers lined up." Or take Collier County, Florida. Officials rejected the program (for migrants), stating that they could take care of their own "worthy" poor. Direct federal intervention (which is authorized by law in low income areas) was impossible however, because the county's *average* income (swelled by a booming tourist business) was high.

conclusion   Here we are, handing out almost $60 billion in transfers annually (with a poverty income deficit of only $10 billion) and still 12 percent of the population remains poor! This, argue some, is owing to a number of factors. As we have seen, the programs are in part financed by the poor. They are also costly to administer. They were enacted at many different times, without any master plan. One may have been enacted in response to the exigencies of the Great Depression, another to mitigate dissent and unrest fed by slum living and discrimination. Given the many deficiencies of present welfare programs and the multitude of uncoordinated programs, one can make a good case for abolishing the existing patchwork in favor of radically new approaches to income maintenance. Two of these new approaches are discussed now.

New Approaches

the negative income tax   Suppose we said instead something like this. Every American, every year, files an income tax return. He sums up all his income, which quite possibly is zero. He then, as the tax law provides, subtracts any exemptions and deductions. If the resultant figure is negative, as it would be with a zero or very low income, the individual gets a check *from* the government. He "pays" a *negative* income tax.

Such a program would automatically reach all the poor, even the working poor. It would make unnecessary the present crazy patchwork of welfare programs. There would be no necessity to establish "need." The poor would receive help as a matter of right. To be sure, it would be a radical innovation and a politically difficult one. But, as it has been said so often, "people will act wisely only after all other alternatives have been exhausted." Many people believe this time has come.

The negative tax could be set at such a rate as to bring *every* American family's income above the poverty level. It could abolish poverty over night. In addition, there is no reason why a negative income tax must discourage the poor from seeking income-earning activities as present welfare programs do. (Present programs often discourage the poor from seeking income-earning activities by reducing welfare payments by a dollar or almost that for every dollar of earned income received.) As long as the negative tax is reduced by a lot less than earned income rises, the poor person can increase his income by working rather than being idle. Note the proposal made in the news report introducing the chapter.

What would be the *extra* cost of a negative income tax package? Would it just cost another $10 billion (in addition to making up for present welfare payments), as indicated by the poverty income deficit? No, it would cost substantially more than this.

For simplicity assume we wanted to give every family an annual income of $4,000. A family earning nothing would receive a negative tax of $4,000. Suppose the father finds a job and earns $2,000. Should we reduce the negative tax by $2,000, leaving his total income unchanged? Of course not. This is exactly what many present welfare programs do. As a result, people lose all incentive to work. Why work for a year if your income remains the same as if you had not worked at all? Reducing welfare or negative tax payments by a dollar for every dollar earned is equivalent to slapping a 100 percent tax on earned income. It is the last thing we want to do to the poor. We want to encourage them to become educated and trained and to work.

We must tax their own earnings less. Suppose we reduce negative taxes by 30 cents for every $1 earned. Then our man will find this: If he earns $2,000, he loses $600 in negative taxes. His total income rises from $4,000 to $5,400. It pays him to work!

How much will our man have to earn before he loses all his negative tax revenue? Four thousand dollars divided by 30 cents, of course, or $13,333. If he earns $13,333, he is taxed (at 30 cents on the dollar) exactly $4,000. At this point, his negative taxes disappear. They are offset by the positive taxes he has to pay on his earned income.

The formula is simple. Divide the official poverty income level (our assumed $4,000) by the tax rate on earned income (our 30 cents per dollar), and you find the exact income level at which net taxes paid are zero. People below this income level will get more taxes than they pay. People above it will pay more taxes than they get.

But note what this implies. It implies (in our case) that everyone who earns less than $13,333 receives a net amount of money *from* the government. This is hardly the case at present. Thus, the government will not only lose a great amount of tax revenue, but it will also have to pay large sums *to* people who are not even poor! It must do this, we noted, in order not to discourage the recipients of negative taxes from working at all. For this reason, the negative income tax would cost a great deal more than $10 billion. It may well cost $30 billion or even more. It is up to each of us to decide whether abolishing poverty is worth this price.

Note also that there is no real way out of this incentive-cost dilemma. Consider once more our formula

$$\frac{\text{Desired minimum family income level}}{\text{Tax rate on earned income}} = \begin{array}{l}\text{Family income level at which} \\ \text{net positive tax payments begin}\end{array}$$

Reducing the income level at which net positive tax payments begin (and thus reducing the over-all cost of the program) can be achieved in two ways: (1) We can lower the desired minimum family income level. But then there is more poverty. (2) We can raise the tax rate on earned income. But then we ruin people's incentive to work. (By the way, a presidential commission on income maintenance was to study this very problem and report on it by the end of 1969.)

Children's Allowances

Another equally radical departure from the traditional American welfare system is often suggested: a system of children's allowances. These are systematic payments by government to all families with children. This would be a birthright, independent of family income.

In fact, the United States is the only western industrialized nation that does not have such a program. The proposal rests on the knowledge that three quarters of poor youths come from fatherless families or families with five or more children. These allowances might greatly enhance family stability and cut into the vicious circle of poverty breeding poverty. It has been found abroad, furthermore, that such allowances do *not* encourage more births (as some critics fear) and that they *are* spent on the better health and education of children. Unlike the negative income tax, this plan is politically attractive. Public opinion hesitates to support "the lazy poor," but is enthusiastic about "investing in the future of children."

There are two major drawbacks to this system. It would require substantial payments to families now not poor. Hence, it would be a costly and highly inefficient way of helping the poor. Almost certainly the cost of such a program would exceed even the cost of the negative income tax. Also, childless adult poor would not be helped at all.

CONCLUSIONS

Poverty is costly, not only to the poor. There are many by-products of poverty that also affect the rich: ignorance, despair, disease, delinquency, crime, indifference, to mention just a few.

As has happened in many societies before, these are powerful forces that can affect the nation's future as thoroughly as a major international war. Thus, poverty is more than of private concern. It is a social problem far beyond the individuals concerned who are deprived of material comfort, human dignity, and lives of fulfillment. In a very real sense, it is everybody's problem. And we know how to deal with it. The most promising approaches seem to be general economic policies encouraging growth, policies improving the labor resources of the poor, and additional income maintenance programs, especially the negative income tax. Economic analysis shows other approaches to be less efficient in attacking poverty. Because we can act, we must act. As James Tobin has put it:[10]

The war on poverty is too crucial to be relegated to the status of a residual claimant for funds that peace in Asia and the normal growth of tax revenues may painlessly and gradually make available. When asked to make sacrifices for the defense of their nation, the American people have always responded. Perhaps some day a national administration will muster the courage to ask the American people to tax themselves for social justice and domestic tranquility. The time is short.

Quite possibly, the first step in this direction was taken in 1969. President Nixon announced plans to abolish, by 1971, aid to families with dependent children in favor of a new Family Security System. Regardless of its residence, an American family of four would be guaranteed annually a minimum federal payment to bring its income to $1,600. Other earnings of recipients would be taxed after they exceed $720 a year, at a rate of 50 cents on the

[10] James Tobin, "Raising the Incomes of the Poor," in Kermit Gordon, ed., *Agenda For the Nation* (Washington, D.C.: Brookings Institution, 1968), p. 116.

dollar. Thus, the negative tax is to be eliminated when regular earnings reach $3,920 a year. The program is expected to cover over 22 million persons and cost $4 billion in the first year. In return, the recipients (except the disabled and mothers with preschool children) will be required to register with the employment service. If capable, they will have to work in or train for a "suitable" job. Additional training allowances and day care centers for half a million children are also planned.

SUMMARY

1 Although the average American is rich compared to most people in other countries, not every American is an average American. Incomes in the United States are unequally distributed.

2 The extent of inequality can be measured by the Lorenz curve. In recent years in the United States, the 10 percent lowest income families received only 1 percent of total income, but the 10 percent highest income families received 29 percent of total income.

3 Income inequality does not necessarily imply poverty. It is difficult to agree on the meaning of poverty, because it involves a comparison of two slippery concepts, "needs" and "means." The U.S. government originally used a family income of $3,0000 a year as the "poverty threshold." In recent years, a more sophisticated definition has been in use taking account of different cash needs for different family types. This definition placed 22 million Americans (12 percent of the population) below the poverty line in 1968.

4 Over the long run (since 1949) poverty in the United States has declined. A detailed look at the data shows that poverty is closely associated with old age, broken families headed by a woman with children, and with families headed by men of very young age or little education. Within these categories, it is more frequent (percentagewise) among the nonwhite.

5 The most common causes of poverty are lack of income-producing property (capital or land) and lack of high quality labor that can be sold at a reasonably high income. Some people are physically unable to work (the aged, disabled, mothers tied down with small children). Others do not have any salable skills. This lack of education and training is explainable by a complex set of factors. These include intellectual inheritance, the debilitating effect of the culture of poverty itself, discrimination in schooling, in job training, or the obsolescence of skills owing to technical progress.

6 In the United States, at least, poverty is not inevitable. This is so because per capita GNP is so high. In principle, poverty can be attacked in a variety of ways:
   a. by redistributing wealth or by creating income-producing wealth for poor minorities
   b. by general economic policies encouraging growth
   c. by improving the labor resources of the poor
   d. by income maintenance programs

7 Method a, contrary to general opinion, would not eliminate poverty. All-out socialism in fact, would have a number of highly undesirable consequences. The reported advantages of black capitalism and similar ventures by minority groups are pure folklore.

Method b is particularly likely to help male family heads of working age. It even helps old and disabled people. Less likely to be helped are female family heads. For the poor in the aggregate, this approach is very helpful, even if it should accelerate inflation.

Method c may involve providing superior schooling facilities to the poor. It may involve Head Start and Follow Through programs. It may involve financial aid to poor teenagers or young people after high school. It may also involve birth control programs, on-the-job training and attempts to change attitudes and political power (as by the black power movement).

Method d may involve expanding present welfare programs or replacing them by new approaches. A program that needs expanding most urgently is the one designed to fight hunger in America. New approaches may include a negative income tax system or a system of children's allowances.

8 When using method d, one has to debate the extent of transfer desired and then note that the net gain to the poor of any transfer payments may be smaller than the payments made if the poor, together with others, are taxed to pay for the transfers. It is extremely difficult, however, to establish what is the tax burden on anyone, because taxes paid by one party may be shifted onto others and may ultimately come to rest on parties other than the taxpayer (tax incidence). This may happen if the taxed party can charge others higher prices than before for what it sells or pay others lower prices than before for what it buys. In any case, one can make a good case for not relying on improvements in the present welfare system. But we must note that the alternatives (negative income tax or children's allowances) are costly propositions.

9 Methods b, c, and the negative income tax seem to hold the greatest promise.

TERMS[11]

black capitalism	near-poverty line
black power	negative income tax
children's allowances	poverty income deficit
culture of poverty	poverty threshold
functional vs. personal income distribution	self-fulfilling prophecy
Lorenz curve	tax incidence

QUESTIONS FOR REVIEW AND DISCUSSION

1 "If we were to draw a Lorenz curve as in Figure 27.1 for different occupations, we would find the curve for lawyers out further from the line of perfect equality than

[11] Terms are defined in the Glossary at the end of the book.

that for doctors. That for doctors, in turn, would be out further than that for college teachers, and that for college teachers out further than that for army officers."
Try to explain.

2 Explain why it is so difficult to establish the extent of poverty and why possibly some of the "poor" are not poor. Define "poverty." Would you have defined it the same way in 1920? Why or why not?

3 Take the following data for 1935–1936 U.S. families and draw a Lorenz curve in the graph below.

INCOME BEFORE TAXES	PERCENT OF ALL FAMILIES IN CLASS	PERCENT OF TOTAL PERSONAL INCOME RECEIVED BY FAMILIES IN CLASS
under $2,000	77.7	45.4
$2,000–2,999	13.1	19.5
$3,000–3,999	4.4	9.2
$4,000–4,999	1.7	4.5
$5,000–7,499	1.6	5.8
$7,500–9,999	0.6	3.2
$10,000 and over	0.9	12.4

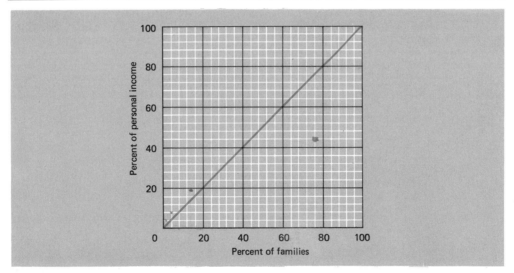

Was personal income distribution more or less unequal in 1935–1936 than in 1966? (Hint: redraw the 1966 line on the same graph, using the data of Table 27.1.)

4 Take a look at text Table 27.2 POVERTY AND NEAR-POVERTY INCOME LINES, 1967. Using the definitions shown there, consider your family and all your acquaintances. Are any of them poor? On that basis, do you consider the definition reasonable? Why or why not?

5 Consider the kinds of incomes earned by people in different occupations: by movie stars, famous athletes, doctors, college teachers, electricians, pilots, retail clerks, dope peddlers. How would you explain the differences in their incomes?

6 If you were interested in maximizing your lifetime income, which occupation would you choose? Justify your answer.

7 In 1968, people in Mississippi had personal incomes of $2,081 per head, people in Connecticut $4,256. (All other states were in-between.) Can you explain this?

8 There used to be a great controversy over whether intelligence was determined by "nature or nurture." In light of what you have read in the text, what do you say?

9 Roy Wilkins, executive secretary of the NAACP has argued against black capitalism because it perpetuates black ghettos. What do you think?

10 Some have argued that private initiative, not government, should be relied on to eliminate poverty. The Ford Motor Company, for instance, initiated a program of hiring and training poor people who are completely unskilled. This program was initiated in 1967, only 3 months after a Detroit riot that resulted in the loss of forty-three lives and $50 million in property. Within a year, Ford hired 5,000 such hard-core "unemployables." What do you think?

11 "The real problem of the poor is not that they are important to the economy and are being exploited. The problem is they are not important, in fact dispensable." Evaluate.

12 In 1968, the American Public Health Association urged that, as in Japan and the Soviet Union, safe, legal abortions be made available to all women as a matter of right. In the same year, the Pope issued an encyclical "On Birth Control." He said: "We must once again declare that the direct interruption of the generative process already begun, and, above all, directly willed and procured abortion, even if for thera-peutic reasons, are to be absolutely excluded as licit means of regulating birth. Equally to be excluded . . . is direct sterilization. . . . Similarly excluded is every action which . . . proposes . . . to render procreation impossible." What do you think?

13 "The U.S. experience shows clearly that poverty in this world can be eliminated by nothing else but a proper redistribution of income." Discuss.

14 MR. A: "An equal distribution of income is only fair."
MR. B: "It would be a catastrophe. Nor would it be fair."
Discuss.

15 If you think that our country's income distribution is unjust, what would you sug-gest to improve it? Suppose a distribution of income considered fair by most resulted in no economic growth, whereas a distribution of income considered grossly unfair led to rapid economic growth. Which of the two would you choose?

16 The text says that "the amounts shown in Table 27.3, even when adjusted downward to exclude payments to the nonpoor, still may greatly exaggerate the net gain to the poor." Explain.

17 Using a demand and supply diagram as in Figure 2.5 DEMAND AND SUPPLY CURVES SUPERIMPOSED, what would happen if buyers of the good suddenly were taxed $1 per pound? Who ultimately bears the burden of the tax? (Hint: You can assume that curve D still shows the amount per unit buyers are willing to pay for each quantity, yet having to pay $1 per unit to the government, they are willing to pay $1 per pound less *to the firms*. Thus it *appears* to the firms that D has shifted down vertically by $1. Now read off new equilibrium price and quantity traded. Note that sellers get less per unit than buyers pay according to old line D, government gets the difference. Note also that sellers get less per unit than they used to. Thus, buyers have *shifted* some of the burden to sellers!) Now redo the problem assuming the tax per unit is levied on *sellers*.

18 "Residential property with high market value in the United States tends to be under-valued by tax assessors relatively more than property of low market value." Do you think this tends to make property taxes progressive or regressive?

19 "Unless we have negative income taxes, a tax cut to stimulate aggregate demand would never stimulate the demand of the poor, only that of the relatively well-to-do." Discuss.

20 In eighteen states, in a recent year, the standards set for public assistance presumed that a family of four could manage for a month on $180. They also reduced public assistance dollar for dollar of earnings by the recipients. Evaluate both these policies.

Nixon Diverts 200-Million To Fix Up Riot-Torn Areas

By JOHN HERBERS
Special to The New York Times

WASHINGTON, April 8—President Nixon earmarked $200-million today for a special effort to begin cleaning and refurbishing riot-damaged areas in 20 cities. The money was taken from funds appropriated by Congress last year for various urban programs.

"The neighborhoods of our cities torn by the disturbances of last spring and before still bear the marks of violence and destruction," the President said in a statement. "Little rehabilitation or reconstruction has taken place.

"Months, and in some cases years, have passed—months of planning, argument and frustration—but the wreckage of the riots remains: fire-scarred, boarded-up buildings, vacant retail stores and rubble-strewn vacant lots," he said.

This, he added, shows the "impotence of modern government at all levels.

"No wonder our citizens are beginning to question government's ability to perform," he said.

George Romney, Secretary of Housing and Urban Development, will send officials from his department to the cities involved to see that rehabilitation begins.

The cities are Akron, Ohio; Baltimore; Boston; Cleveland; Chicago; Detroit; Kansas City, Kan.; Los Angeles; Louisville, Ky.; Memphis; Nashville; Newark; New Haven; New York; Pittsburgh; Providence, R. I.; Rochester; Tampa, Fla.; Washington, and Wilmington, Del.

Riot Areas Pictured

The President's plan was announced in the Fish Room of the White House by Daniel Patrick Moynihan, special assistant for urban affairs, and Richard C. Van Dusen, Under Secretary of Housing and Urban Development. They showed pictures of the riot areas taken during a recent survey. . . .

Of the pictures, Mr. Nixon said, "There could be no more searing symbol of governmental inability to act than those rubble-strewn lots and desolate, decaying buildings, once a vital part of a community's life and now left to rot."

"Little has changed," he added, "and not always, or even chiefly, for lack of Federal aid as such. The survey shows that many of the riot-scarred, burnt-out areas are included within designated and planned Model Cities and neighborhood development program areas. Much of the damaged property is privately owned. But almost all sectors of the community seem paralyzed by a combination of obstacles, some federally imposed, which forestall action."

In response to questions, Mr. Moynihan said, "I don't know what's wrong, I don't think any one does."

Technology and Environment: Senators Hear Gloomy Appraisals

By ROBERT H. PHELPS
Special to The New York Times

WASHINGTON, April 27—Is the United States set on an irreversible course that will destroy the natural base on which it has built the highest standard of living in the world?

This is one of the questions that the Senate Subcommittee on Intergovernmental Affairs, headed by Senator Edmund S. Muskie, has been looking into for months. While at least another round of hearings is scheduled, the answers so far are pessimistic. .

The gloomiest appraisals of all came last week from Barry Commoner, director of the Center for the Biology of Natural Systems, at Washington University in St. Louis, and W. H. Ferry, vice president of the Center for the Study of Democratic Institutions, Santa Barbara, Calif.

Both witnesses said that nothing less than a change in the political and social system, including revision of the Constitution, was necessary to save the country from destroying its natural environment.

Both agreed, too, that the peril came from uncontrolled technology. In the process of creating new goods and services, they said, technology is destroying the country's "capital" of land, water and other resources as well as injuring people.

Dr. Commoner said, "Our present system of technology is not merely consuming this capital, but threatening—probably within the next 50 years—to destroy it irreparably." . . .

Dr. Commoner cited the success of inorganic fertilizers, high-compression automobile engines and insecticides as examples of "progress" that damages the environment.

The massive use of inorganic nitrogen fertilizers greatly increases crop yields for a few years, he said, but damages the soil by altering its physical character. The unusued nitrogen fertilizer, he went on, drains out of the soil into rivers and lakes, where it stimulates overgrowth of green plants and causes organic pollution.

"The drainage of nitrogen from fertilizer has already destroyed the self-purifying capability of nearly every river in Illinois," Dr. Commoner said, and in the Middle West and California "has raised the nitrate level of drinking water supplies above the safe limits recommended by public health authorities."

Referring to Dr. Commoner's testimony, Mr. Ferry asked:

"What good will color television in every room and outposts on the moon be to the grandchildren, if their air is unbreathable, their water undrinkable and their dwellings half buried in their own débris?"

The basic problem, Mr. Ferry said, is that no one can be held responsible for the perils of the environment. "No one is to blame if everyone is to blame," he said.

28

the united states: crisis of an urban society

W̲E HAVE NOTED in Chapter 19 how the story of U.S. agriculture, in a technical sense, is one of unbelievable and unmatched success. When this nation was founded, almost everyone lived and worked on farms. This was not really a matter of choice. People had to, otherwise there would not have been enough food. In 1790, for instance, 95 percent of Americans worked and lived in rural areas. But things have changed. Agricultural advances have made it possible for a smaller and smaller percentage of the labor force to produce all the agricultural products needed by all of the people. And people have been moving away from rural areas to areas urban and constantly growing in number and size. The release of labor from agriculture, which has made possible the development of industry, has, in turn, stimulated further agricultural advances and has accelerated the urbanization of our society.

In 1850, for instance, about two thirds of the American labor force was still engaged in agriculture. Fifteen percent of the population was living in urban areas. By 1900, just over a third of the labor force remained in agriculture. Forty percent of all people lived in urban areas (14 percent in cities with over a quarter million inhabitants). By the late 1960's, less than 5 percent of the labor force was engaged in agriculture. Over 70 percent of all people were urbanized, with over 22 percent living in cities with over a quarter million inhabitants. By 1985, it is estimated, at least 75 percent of all Americans will live in cities. Quite possibly, the great migration of people from the country to the city is about over. From 1968 to 1969, for the first time, there was no change in the adult farm population.

But as the news reports introducing this chapter show, there is another side to all this progress. The very production and use of all these wonders of the industrial age, which have increased farm productivity so vastly and have driven so many millions to the cities, have serious side effects. The technical advances that have brought us electric milking machines, mechanical harvesters, tractors, fertilizers, and herbicides have also brought us something else: a hitherto undreamed-of destruction of our natural environment through all kinds of pollution. This problem is becoming so serious that the survival of mankind is in question at the very time that our success in conquering scarcity appears to be the greatest.

Similarly, consider the *social* consequences of agricultural progress. Although the country-to-city migration has been nationwide, as of late it has involved disproportionately the movement of nonwhite people. During the 1950's and 1960's, from half to two thirds of this migration has involved blacks from the southeast going to northeastern cities. (At a rate of 400,000 per year during the 1950's, 50,000 per year during the 1960's.) In addition, it has involved blacks from Mississippi going to Chicago, Mexican Americans from Louisiana and Texas going to California, and, of course, poor whites from Appalachia mostly going to Ohio. Why did they and are they migrating? They are pushed out of agriculture and pulled into cities. No one wants them in agriculture anymore, and the relatively high wages (or welfare payments) in the cities are a constant lure.

As you can well imagine, however, these people are not particularly prepared for urban life. In urban jobs, there is much less of a premium on physical strength, for instance, or on manual dexterity. Instead, literacy, technical and professional knowledge, count. As a result, few migrants are ready for the demands made on them by an industrialized urban economy. So they join the ranks of the city poor. In 1966, 9.6 percent of metropolitan area families were poor; 7.4 percent of white, but 26.3 percent of nonwhite families; 6.7 percent of male-headed, but 31.3 percent of female-headed families. Is it much wonder that the century-old neglect of black education in the South explodes in the streets of our northern cities?

This migration of poor people, many of them black, to the cities has had further consequences. Earlier in this century, cities were inhabited by whites. Over 90 percent of all blacks lived in the rural South. Now the twelve largest cities alone account for one third of the black population in the country. As the blacks and other poor began to move in, the whites abandoned the cities, fleeing to newly built suburbs. The racial minorities, and the poor in general, were barred from these new areas. Eventually, giant pieces of countryside were swallowed up by the "urban sprawl." Large parts of the former cities became "ghettos," areas characterized by acute poverty and inhabited by members of racial or ethnic groups under conditions of involuntary segregation. The government even had to change its earlier definition of urban area. The former city has become the "central city" (if it has at least 50,000 inhabitants), the entire conglomeration of central city and its noose of white suburbs has become the "standard metropolitan statistical area," or SMSA. (There were 233 of these in mid-1968.) Interestingly, from 1960 to 1966, 98 percent of all black population growth occurred in central cities, 78 percent of all white population growth in suburbs.

These new metropolitan areas have unending problems. Housing is one. Traffic congestion is another. Garbage, sewage, water, and noise are more. And crime and riots, fed by poverty and segregation, are others still.

It is not saying too much, therefore, that ours is an urban society in crisis. It is a crisis involving both our natural environment and our social arrangements. Exactly what the problems are, what has been done about them so far, and what might be done in the future is discussed in this chapter. As was the case with income distribution and poverty, the economist has a great deal to say here also. Yet, in many ways, the problems go beyond economics. Again, there is the overwhelming importance of justice. How are we going to share the riches that might be ours? If we insist on maximizing personal satisfaction, while ignoring the effects of our action on others living now or as yet unborn, we may do so to our sorrow. Unless we face the external repercussions of our actions and willingly share part of what might be ours with society at large, including future generations, we may kill the goose that lays the golden eggs! After a flash in the pan, so to speak, wherein a tiny minority of all men on earth reached unprecedented living levels, all mankind may sink back into abject poverty. It may even cease to exist.

THE PROBLEMS CITIES MUST FACE

Let us begin with a survey of how the major problems arose that now confront our cities.

Land Use Patterns

Some city problems, such as dilapidated housing, a welfare-dependent population, increased crime, health and traffice problems, stem from the particular ways in which their land has been utilized. We shall consider industrial and commercial uses first, residential uses later.

industrial and commercial uses   Cities arose as centers of manufacturing and trade. For both these activities, good transportation routes were vital. Raw materials, including food, had to be brought in. Finished products had to be shipped out. No wonder then that the first cities were founded near water, the most ancient means of easy transportation being ships. You will find many cities along the coast or along major rivers. After the railroads were invented and built, railroad lines began to rival rivers in importance for the location of urban growth. Where railroad lines met or where the railroad met rivers, large cities arose because business firms sought out such places. They attracted other businesses, such as their suppliers and customers. And all of them attracted people. Businesses and residential areas tended to cluster around the nodal points of the transportation system.

The invention and large-scale introduction of the automobile earlier in this century changed all this. As roads were built and trucks became generally available. manufacturing activities began to spread out, away from the center of cities. A change in production methods accelerated this tendency. Continuous-flow methods of mass production required single-story plants, rather than the multistory ones built in the cities at the turn of this century. Firms left the city center for more space near its periphery or in smaller towns throughout the country.

The above trends, however, are being somewhat counteracted in recent years. As jet transport takes on greater importance, it pays firms to be located in or near large cities, which alone can support major airports. Similarly, "piggyback" transport (carrying truck trailers on railroad flat cars specially designed for this purpose) is available in large urban centers only. So are many specialized business services (computer centers, legal advice, advertising, research activities). These new developments have slowed the decentralization trend of manufacturing activities—but they have only slowed it. The movement of business out of the city is mirrored in the budget of city governments: they find their tax base shrinking. Where there was a bustling manufacturing plant one year, there is an empty building the next. The city's tax revenues drop as a result.

residential uses   We have already noted how the white population of the central cities has been fleeing the city, insulating itself from "contamination" with the poor. They do not only flee, however, to get away from something. They are also after something. They are after the (as yet) cheap lots to be bought out in the country, fresh air, open space. But note the consequences. Because the suburbs have typically different governments, the central city again loses part of its former tax revenue. Where there was a white family earning $10,000 a year, now lives a black one barely subsisting at $1,800. Thus, levying income taxes is out of the question. Sales taxes bring in less revenues. In fact, more likely than not, the new residents will end up on welfare, swelling the central city's *expenditures*. The effects on property tax collections are equally bad. Where riots have replaced former businesses and apartment houses with block after block of burned ruins, the effect on the property tax base is most obvious. Where there is less property left, you cannot tax as much as before. But this is by no means the crux of the problem. Even the property left standing in the central cities (and that is most of it) has been undergoing steady physical deterioration. This is so because owners of rental housing in the central city have found it profitable to allow this to happen. They have had a captive market. The typical apartment occupant is a relatively new migrant from the country. There are many others like him and more coming. They all are poor. They are uninformed about housing alternatives. They are too poor or uneducated to seek out such information. In any case, they are apt to be self-conscious about their being different from other people. They prefer to live with their own group. Even where this is not the case, discrimination effectively closes other areas to them. Being ignorant about their civil rights, or too poor to fight for them, they are likely to settle for central-city housing. Landlords are faced wih a strong and rising demand that has no other place to go.

Now consider this: what is the *cheapest* way to meet this demand? It certainly is not by making improvements in existing housing or by building new housing. The cheapest way to increase the supply is to convert existing housing into smaller units. Take a six-room apartment and cut it in half. You have two apartments. Cut the size of each room in half, and you have two more. In addition, don't spend a dime on maintenance or repair. (The new occupants are likely to be ignorant of housing codes, anyway.) As long as demand keeps rising faster than supply (assuming no rent controls), rents may even rise. This is illustrated in Figure 28.1 THE CENTRAL-CITY HOUSING MARKET.

As the average apartment size shrinks, overcrowding develops. Together with insuffi-

Figure 28.1   THE CENTRAL-CITY HOUSING MARKET

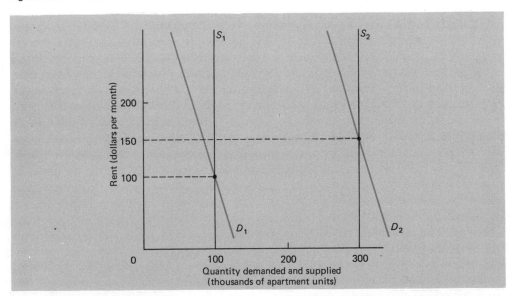

Over time, the demand for apartments may rise from D_1 to D_2. If supply rises to S_2 only, pressure develops for rents to rise. Landlords' monthly revenue in this example rises from 100,000 units times $100, or $10 million, to 300,000 units times $150, or $45 million.

cient maintenance, a host of problems arise, all tending to worsen the financial position of the city government:

Buildings turn into firetraps, and insurance rates go up. The city must spend more on fire protection and the water department. Its revenue base is hurt further as higher taxes and insurance rates drive businesses away. So it raises the *rate* of taxation on the remaining base.

Overcrowding in dilapidated housing decreases privacy and raises the level of frustration of the occupants. There is more crime and delinquency. The incidence of serious crimes (assault, robbery, murder, rape) is up to thirty-five times higher in some central cities than elsewhere. Again, insurance rates for businesses go up. So do tax rates, as the police budget must rise.

Living closer together under such undesirable conditions also becomes a health menace. People use multiple toilets and water facilities, often dirty ones. They sleep in vermin-infested, badly ventilated quarters. (Of 14,000 rat bites in the United States, in 1965, most occurred in city ghettos.) People eat ill-preserved food. Colds, food poisoning, lead poisoning (as children eat peeling paint), children's diseases, digestive diseases, skin diseases, tuberculosis multiply. Poor wiring and lighting cause more accidents in the home. These call for more public health expenditures.

This is likely to feed on itself. (See also our discussion of the culture of poverty in the previous chapter.) Once a neighborhood begins to deteriorate, it pays all the owners to undermaintain their buildings, for instance. If any one improves his property, its market value is not increased proportionately because of the bad condition of neighboring houses. But he will get the attention of the tax assessors who will raise his property taxes!

Worse still, suburbanites continue to cost the central city plenty. They commute to the city. Many still have jobs there. Their wives go shopping. They visit the city for recreation. *And they come in their own cars.* The more the limits of the city expand, the more serious becomes the traffic of people coming back into the center for relatively short periods of time. There is a definite rhythm to traffic. More than half of urban transport, for example, involves moving to and from work. (In 1969, the Department of Transportation estimated that auto commuters in large cities spend 13 percent of their waking hours in traffic.) Before you know it, traffic congestion develops. Thus, the facilities must be large enough to meet the demands of *rush hour* traffic. Even for other occasions, traffic demand peaks at certain hours or seasons, as at the time of ball games or special shows or during the tourist season. This gets particularly bad where various types of traffic meet, as at airports. As a result, more and better traffic control, new roads, airports, and parking facilities are constantly demanded. Once more, the central city's expenditures jump. At the same time, its tax base shrinks once again. Every new parking lot and every new freeway removes land from the tax rolls.

The other side of all this is, of course, the financial happiness of the suburban governments. They have all the money they need from industry and higher income families living in expensive homes. They can and do provide superb services: good roads, good lighting, good schools, good fire and police protection.

Living Means Polluting

The problems discussed above are bad enough by themselves. Unfortunately, cities face other, equally serious ones. All of life can be pictured as a continuous flow. Life takes mineral, vegetable, or animal materials from its environment, uses them, and discards other materials into the environment. This is inevitable. People are no exception. But where there are many people living closely together, as they do in an urban society, this becomes suddenly very noticeable.

In fact, the law of the conservation of mass reminds us that the quantities of materials taken in by living beings *equal* the quantities retained or discarded in one form or another. The average city dweller uses 150 gallons of water per day, 4 pounds of food, and 19 pounds of fossil fuels (coal, motor fuel, natural gas, oil). He releases 120 gallons of sewage, 4 pounds of refuse, and about 2 pounds of air pollutants. As population grows, so does its total intake and its discard of wastes. These wastes, deposited on the land, in water, or released into the air, are polluting our environment.

In principle, this need not cause any problem. There are, happily, counterforces at work. Animal and vegetable matter can be degraded by bacteriological action in the soil or in water. In a matter of a few weeks or months, it can disappear. Unless the level of such new pollution exceeds the capacity to "take care of things" of the body into which it is discharged, such pollution need cause no concern. But it is different with inorganic wastes. They are not self-purifying. Metal wastes are broken down gradually by rusting. Glass and plastics stay with us forever in their original form. So do many chemicals. The phosphates from our detergents, the hydrocarbons and nitrogen oxides emitted from our cars, just accumulate in ever-increasing quantities in soil and water forever. Sometimes these inorganic matters interact. This can make things worse. During temperature inversions in Los Angeles, a stinging smog develops from an interaction of sunlight with hydrocarbons and nitrogen oxide. This produces irritating nitrogen dioxide (plus ozone).

Thus our cities are facing increasing problems of air, water, and soil pollution.

air pollution   The two major sources of air pollution in the cities are (in this order) the automobile and industry. Los Angeles has the dubious honor of having been called "the city where one is awakened by the sound of birds coughing." In 1968, sixty faculty members of UCLA medical school recommended that "anyone not compelled to remain in Los Angeles should leave immediately for the sake of his health." But don't think the problem is confined to Los Angeles. Look at any large city (especially the next time you fly in an airplane). You will find a yellow-brown dome of hydrocarbons and carbon monoxide, soot, fly ash, and sulfur dioxide covering the city, reaching perhaps as high as 10,000 feet. Above that is the crisp blue sky, hidden to any observer on the ground by thousands of tons of particles suspended in the air. Industrial smokestacks, auto exhausts, city dumps, and private incinerators continually add to the supply. Once in a while, a rainstorm will bring it all to the ground (causing water or soil pollution instead). Or strong winds will push the materials over hundreds of miles of countryside. (Persistent southwest winds during the summer push New York air pollution right up to Vermont, blanketing much of rural New England.)

The trouble with all this goes beyond eyes that burn, dirt in the city home, greater commuting costs (for those fleeing to the suburbs), and inability to see the blue sky. Quite possibly, it costs human lives. The possible linkage between cigarette smoking and lung cancer is a warning sign. High incidence of chronic bronchitis has been traced to air pollution in Great Britain. In California, the death rate from pulmonary emphysema has quadrupled, possibly because of air pollution. Why don't the offenders prevent this? Because it would be expensive business, of course. Well-designed electric power plants can remove more than 90 percent of all particles from stack gases. They could also switch to fuels emitting fewer undesirable combustion products in the first place. That is, they could switch from bituminous coal to oil or, better still, to natural gas. They could even give up fossil fuels entirely, going over to atomic power. (That, however, might involve radioactive by-products instead.) All this would be terribly expensive.

It would be even more expensive to install antipollution devices in every single residence, auto, bus, and truck. But it would not be impossible. In fact, California has required a (partially effective) system since 1966.

A General Motors executive estimated in 1969 that devices on 1970 model cars to reduce hydrocarbon emissions cost up to $100 per car. Another $200 per car might be needed to eliminate all air pollution by cars. Another possibility exists also. Automakers (understandably) have blamed gasoline producers for car-caused air pollution. They say gas contains too much tetraethyl lead (which makes gas burn more evenly) and too much butane (which facilitates the evaporation of gas in the carburetor). Should we convert the refineries? Conversion to nonlead gas production in 1969 was estimated to cost $4.25 billion initially, raising production costs by 2 cents per gallon thereafter. Cutting out butane was said to raise cost by another 2 cents per gallon.

But air pollution can be avoided. New York Citly's requirement that ships use low-sulfur content fuel in the harbor serves the same purpose. (New York City's sulfur dioxide level was twice that of other cities.)

water pollution   One of the perpetual concerns of cities is a sufficient supply of clean water. In New York City, 150 gallons are needed per person per day. The city is often short of clean water. In the summer, its lawns must die, its pools remain empty. All the while, of course, billions of gallons of fresh water flow past the city each day into the sea. As it is, this polluted water is unusable. New York City now must get its clean water from reservoirs at the headwaters of the Delaware River. There are plans to extend the conduits into the Adirondack Mountains. Boston gets its water from western Massachusetts. Los Angeles had to build a 440-mile aqueduct to the Sacramento River. Santee, southern California, even reclaims sewage (which is 99 percent water) for drinking purposes. This idea is repugnant to many. They do not think one should do anything with sewage except get rid of it. Many cities do just that.

In early 1969, the sewage of 32 million urban Americans got no treatment at all. It was dumped raw into the ocean, rivers, or lakes. However, many cities give sewage *first stage* treatment. This involves, prior to dumping, the settling out of the coarser solids. Nothing more. Many other cities have more costly *second stage* treatment. Benign bacteria break down 80 percent of the pollutants into (for people) innocuous chemical compounds. The resultant liquid is often used for irrigation. At an additional cost of $29 billion, it is hoped that cities throughout the United States will have such second stage treatment by 1974. When chlorinated, the resultant liquid is even drinkable. However, when dumped into rivers or lakes, severe problems arise. The "innocuous" chemicals (mostly nitrogen and phosphorus) act as a fertilizer. They stimulate the growth of moss-like and seaweed-like algae. These strangle boat traffic and use up the dissolved oxygen supply in the water, killing off the fish. In fact, algae use eighteen times as much oxygen as an equal quantity of organic raw sewage. And algae end up as stinking piles on the banks of beaches, ruining waterfront property.

Relatively few cities have *third stage* treatment facilities. By chemical and mechanical processes (such as precipitation, coagulation, filtration), further impurities are removed. But it has been estimated that introducing this throughout the United States would cost more than the annual federal budget.

The dying lake.[1]   An example of what water pollution can do is given by Lake Erie, the fourth largest and shallowest of the Great Lakes. Lake Erie receives the wastes of parts of Indiana, Michigan, Ohio, Pennsylvania, New York, and Ontario. The 300-mile industrial complex from Detroit to Buffalo is the worst offender. Detroit auto plants, Cleveland steel mills, Erie paper companies, and even Akron rubber plants—these and others dump 11 million pounds of chlorides, cyanide, acids, oil, and the like every day. Besides industrial wastes, treated and partially treated municipal sewage enters the lake directly, or indirectly via rivers. While its main sewer line was under repair, Cleveland has on many occasions for many months dumped some 30 million gallons of raw sewage per day. Also entering the lake are pesticides and fertilizers from the countryside that enter the rivers as a result of normal runoff. The materials thus entering the lake upset the normal plant-animal life cycle. For reasons given above, algae in Lake Erie have been growing faster than Jack's beanstalk, choking all else. They cover hundreds of square miles. The lake degenerates into a swamp. Northern pike, blue pike, and sturgeon have given way to suckers and carp. The number of wild ducks has sharply declined. Once beautiful beaches and the voices of happy children have been replaced by mounds of decaying algae and "no swimming" signs. A once flourishing fishing industry has died.

Another factor killing off fish and stimulating the growth of algae is a slight warming of the water temperature by *thermal* pollution, the hot water emissions from power plants. (In 1969, such plants were using 100 billion gallons of water per day in the United States for cooling. This figure is expected to quadruple in 50 years.) The Federal Water Resources

[1] This section is based in part on Kenneth G. Slocum, "The Dying Lake," *The Wall Street Journal,* February 10, 1969, pp. 1 and 24.

Council sees thermal pollution as the most serious long-range water problem. Avoiding it is also costly business, though possible. It would involve the construction of holding lagoons or cooling towers. For the presently existing industries this would cost $400 million a year.

The beautiful Ohio.[2]   Many of America's rivers are in the same sad shape as Lake Erie. Take the Ohio. Ever since 1948, it has been the target of the broadest clean-up effort in the nation. Indeed, it is cleaner now than during the 1930's. But in many places, the bacteria count still matches pure sewage. Imagine yourself taking a boat trip along the river's 981-mile course from Pittsburgh (where it is formed) to Cairo (where it flows into the Mississippi). While still in Pennsylvania, you would see its water turn a bright poisonous green near the Crucible Steel Company. An oil discharge from Jones and Laughlin Steel would create miles of irridescent splotches—green, blue, and red. (A similar oil slick on the Cuyahoga River in Cleveland catches fire periodically, making it "the only body of water ever classified as a fire hazard.") Near a blast furnace in Steubenville, Ohio, the river turns red brown from iron oxide. A company in Wheeling, West Virginia, fills the river with a bluish black goo. Union Carbide in Riverside, Ohio, dumps phenol (which you cannot see), and 300 communities add raw sewage. In some places, you can see chocolate brown water bubbling like a witch's brew from fermenting at the river bottom. In the winter, parts of the river always remain free of ice because of heat pollution by power plants and acid drainage from thousands of abandoned mines. This also shows by dark yellow-brown stains on the river's banks and rocks. In some places, algae clog city water intakes. Drinking water tastes unbearable. The costs of getting drinking water are greatly increased. (In 1969, the U.S. Department of Agriculture estimated that over $1 billion are spent each year in the United States to get rid of aquatic weeds.)

Why all this in spite of the valiant work by the Ohio River Valley Water Sanitation Commission? Again, because pollution avoidance is expensive for the polluter. The commission has set up standards and tried to *talk* people into complying. As a result, $1 billion have been spent so far, but at least another $2 billion are needed to finish the job. To stop the Western Pennsylvania acid drainage from coal mines alone would cost $400 million. To add water pollution control to an old steel mill might cost over 13 percent of its construction cost!

San Francisco Bay.   San Francisco Bay stinks. Each day 600 million gallons of sewage are released into a stagnant bay. Only a tiny portion of it has received (rudimentary) treatment. In 1969, a $1 billion plan by twelve counties called for shifting the emission farther out into the ocean where it could be "flushed out by the tides."

soil pollution   Wastes that are not dumped into air or water remain with us on the land. One single statistic can illustrate the size of the problem: A year's rubbish of one million people now covers 100 acres of ground, seven feet deep.

---

[2] This section is based in part on Michael K. Drapkin and Thomas L. Ehrich, "The Dirty Ohio," *The Wall Street Journal,* March 17, 1969, pp. 1 and 14.

Conclusion

There is one inevitable conclusion we can reach from our discussion. *Our cities face enormous problems. And these problems arise essentially from one simple fact. Cities are called on to bear costs of private consumption and private production that millions of private decision-makers manage to avoid. City governments are the victims of external repercussions!* (See also our earlier discussion of externalities on pages 505–508.) A steel plant that freely pumps pollutants into lakes, rivers, and atmosphere forces untold millions of people to pay for it. Fishermen lose their jobs. Beaches close. City water taxes go up. People die earlier than otherwise.

In fact, if you have read carefully the above, you will see that mounting city expenditures for freeways, traffic control, police, health, and welfare are nothing else but the price we now have to pay for the centuries-old system of slavery and segregation. Even man's inhumanity to man has a cost in dollars and cents! It is silly to think that cities alone can bear that cost.

SOLVING CITY PROBLEMS

From what we have learned so far, it is quite clear that cities need cooperation from other governmental units, especially financial and legal help from their suburbs, the states, and the federal government. To some extent, this has already been forthcoming. Real solutions, however, have to involve more than this. They require more imaginative actions than those taken so far, in particular *a pushing back onto the private offenders of the external costs of their actions.*

What Has Been Done

overcoming political fragmentation   One problem hampering city action is purely organizational. It derives from the fact that a metropolitan area contains a number of independent political units. Somehow, their actions must be coordinated. A central city, for instance, cannot impose a sales tax successfully if people can easily shop in the suburbs to avoid it. Coordination has been attempted in a number of ways: The city can annex the surrounding territory (Knoxville). The surrounding territory can annex the city (Dade County, Florida). Two governments can be consolidated (Nashville and Davidson County). Municipalities can form a federation (Toronto). Regional authorities can be formed to deal with a particular area-wide problem (Port of New York Authority). There can be direct state or federal action.

securing finances   The second problem prior to action is finances. As we have seen, the needs of cities are virtually limitless. Their revenue sources are not. Such sources have often been shrinking. Figure 28.2 THE MAKE-UP OF CITY GOVERNMENT SPENDING shows budget

Figure 28.2   THE MAKE-UP OF CITY GOVERNMENT SPENDING

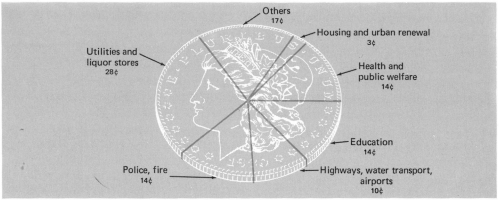

City government spending in 1966 amounted to $22.4 billion in the United States. Here we see the purposes to which each dollar was put. Source: U.S. Department of Commerce.

allocations for a recent year. Note how the greatest chunk went for utilities. Almost 9 cents of each dollar went for pure water, 8 cents for sewage, 7 cents for electric power and gas, 3 cents for mass transit, the rest for liquor stores. General administration, listed under other expenditures, was next in importance. Police and fire protection, education, and health and public welfare had equal shares of 14 cents per dollar each. It is interesting to compare this breakdown with Figure 11.2 THE MAKE-UP OF STATE AND LOCAL GOVERNMENT SPENDING, which includes the cities. The cities spend relatively much more on police and fire protection and welfare than do all state and local governments combined. They spend relatively much less on education. This reflects the special problems they face. In 1968, over two thirds of all old age, dependent children, and disabled welfare recipients lived in standard metropolitan statistical areas. In face of this and the urgent demands for pure water, sewage removal, crime control, and transportation, the school budgets get slighted. Figure 28.3 THE MAKE-UP OF CITY GOVERNMENT REVENUE reflects the bad revenue situation.

Almost a third of each revenue dollar comes from the property tax. Licenses and charges (as parking fees) provide 21 cents of each dollar. Charges for water provide 8 cents, for electricity and gas the same, for mass transit 2 cents (liquor store revenue is negligible). The sales tax brings in 8 cents per dollar, and intergovernmental aid, 19 cents. Insurance trust revenue include such things as city employee retirement contributions. Income taxes are completely negligible over all. They play a role only in a few places, such as New York, Philadelphia, St. Louis, and a number of Ohio cities. The effect of reliance on nonincome taxes is this: each 1 percent rise in the GNP raises federal revenues by 1.5 percent, but city revenues by only 0.5 percent. So the cities have the problems, but not the money.

Again you might wish to look at Figure 11.5 THE MAKE-UP OF STATE AND LOCAL GOVERNMENT REVENUE. The property tax for cities by themselves is much more important, sales

Figure 28.3 THE MAKE-UP OF CITY GOVERNMENT REVENUE

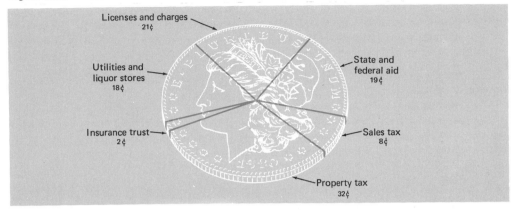

City government revenue in 1966 amounted to $21.9 billion in the United States. The typical revenue dollar shows clearly the relative importance of the various types of revenues. Source: U.S. Department of Commerce.

taxes are less important. Aid from other governments is more significant. In the future, as the plight of the cities is recognized as of national origin, the aid category may rise even further. In 1969, Daniel P. Moynihan, President Nixon's leading adviser on urban affairs, urged a doubling (after the end of the Vietnam War) of federal assistance to state and local governments to supply a third of their revenues on a permanent basis. President Nixon announced a plan to share federal revenue with the states providing for a mandatory pass-through to local governments. It is to go into effect in 1971. The shared revenue is to rise to one percent of the federal income tax base by 1976.

As important as political coordination and financing is, of course, the method of attack once the above have been procured.

housing and urban renewal   Much attention has been given to urban renewal. It was initiated with the 1949 National Housing Act, amended many times since (example: the Model Cities Act of 1966). Under the program, the city is asked to set up a comprehensive "workable program" involving plans for the rehabilitation of buildings, outright clearance of others, and the substitution of new residential, commercial, industrial, or educational structures. (In early 1969, 150 cities had received grants to prepare such plans.) This plan goes for certification to the Renewal Assistance Administration in the U.S. Department of Housing and Urban Development (created in 1965). Subsequently, a local urban renewal agency is established. It may declare a blighted area a redevelopment area. It can acquire all real property therein, either by negotiation or eminent domain. An independently appraised fair market value is paid. Any tenants must be relocated to "decent, safe, sanitary" housing or federal aid is withheld. The federal government pays up to two thirds of the net project cost. It also gives rent supplements to households and cash grants to small businesses relocated. Federal government expenditures on this have risen from half a billion dollars in 1949 to well over $6 billion in 1968.

Typically, after site clearing, improvements are added (streets, sewers, and so forth). Land is then sold to private redevelopers. Typically, they have built high-rise upper and middle income housing or commercial buildings. On occasion, city governments develop the land for public housing, parks, or schools.

Has the program worked well? Not really. In 1969, we had not even constructed the public housing units planned to be built under the act by 1955. In fact, more low cost housing was *demolished* by public action than has been built through all federally aided programs. We still had 11 million substandard and overcrowded housing units in 1969. The construction of upper- and middle-income housing has helped the higher-income people by depressing their rents. The destruction of low-income housing has hurt the low-income people by raising their rents.

Prospects look bleak. To give every family a decent home would require construction or rehabilitation of 26 million units during the next 10 years, said President Johnson in a 1968 message on housing and cities. Yet, at present, fewer than 1.5 million new units are started each year. In fact, because of high interest rates, no progress was made at all during the first year after the Johnson message for low-income housing. Not that good hopes are missing. Secretary Romney announced Operation Breakthrough in 1969. It called for mass production of low-cost housing. What happens remains to be seen.

Many have criticized the approach taken by urban renewal for other reasons. The highest density slum buildings were condemned first. They command the highest price per acre. Landlords had to be paid dearly. The people evicted move into nearby neighborhoods raising density and landlord income there, by the same process illustrated in Figure 28.1. THE CENTRAL-CITY HOUSING MARKET. They will be the next targets of urban renewal. It is like playing a game of "musical houses." It turns the slum dwellers into a kind of urban gypsy.

It would be much cheaper to build housing first on vacant lots, unload the slum dwellers, and thereby reduce density and profitability of slum housing. (Consider again Figure 28.1. Imagine what would happen if, supply being given, demand fell.) This would reduce slum housing rents and hence property values, and *then* the city should buy it. In addition, there may be serious social consequences of "human bulldozing." The people uprooted from their neighborhoods, often against their will, end up paying higher rents for hardly better housing. They may react with destructive force.

solving the traffic problem   The Urban Mass Transport acts of 1964 and 1966 were designed to channel federal aid to cities trying to cope with traffic congestion. The idea is to lure people away from the private automobile by making public transport faster and more convenient. During the next 20 years, urban traffic is expected to double. Can you imagine the horrors this entails? President Nixon's secretary of transportation, Volpe, has also urged priority attention to mass transit rather than to more highways. The construction of freeways in and around cities has never yet solved the problem of congestion. The moment a highway appears, it lures people to live even farther out in the countryside. The demand for highway use rises as much as the supply. However, so far, federal aid has favored highways. The federal government pays 90 percent of interstate highway costs and spends $5 billion a year on this. States have loved this aid, but they stop building highways at city limits. So cities get stuck with building access roads. (In 1961, the forty-three largest cities ended up spending twice as much on motor vehicle facilities as they received in tolls or grants for this purpose.) In contrast to its highway aid, the federal government only pays 66 percent of mass transit construction and *hopes* to spend about $1 billion on this by 1974.

cleaning up air and water   Federal aid is also available for pollution control: the Water Pollution Control Act of 1954, the Clean Air Act of 1963, the Water Quality and the Solid Waste Disposal acts of 1965, the Clean Water Restoration Act of 1966, and the Air Quality Act of 1967 are examples. In many cases, the federal government can call a conference, hold hearings, and sue offenders. Hearings have been a strong weapon. They spotlight offenders and stimulate public pressure. In a widely criticized move, however, the new secretary of the interior, Hickel, in 1969 announced his intention to rely less on or even to abandon water pollution hearings (as a "yelling and screaming" process) in favor of behind-the-scene negotiations. President Nixon, recognizing that "we have become victims of our own technological genius," established a Cabinet-level Environmental Quality Council. It is to guide the pollution fight. It consists of the President, his science adviser, the vice president, and the secretaries of agriculture; commerce; health, education, and welfare; housing and urban development; the interior; and transportation. A Citizens' Advisory Committee is attached to the council. In one of its first meetings the council agreed to fund research that might lead to the production of a low-pollution automobile for the 1990's.

What Is Being Talked About

Some people suggest that more imaginative and more radical steps be taken to solve urban problems. The Department of Transportation is experimenting with steam-powered buses in San Francisco to halt pollution of the air. Others hope to get water from atomic desalination plants. City planners dream of "gravitrains," propelled by their own weight through underground tunnels, then rolling up on their own momentum at speeds of 300 miles an hour. They dream of land and water vehicles riding on cushions of air. (Such an air cushion test is in fact slated for 1972 between Miami and its new airport in the Everglades.) The Department of Transportation is studying moving sidewalks for Boston. Some are contemplating automatically controlled freeways with electric cars. Milwaukee hopes to create a two-lane "mini-freeway" for buses only, moving at 70 miles an hour between the suburbs and downtown. And new high-speed trains are being introduced for the Northeast metropolitan corridor from Washington to Boston. Everyone is experimenting: Detroit with a monorail from Pontiac, Ithaca with free bus service, Newark by paving subways to make them usable for buses. Perhaps the most elaborate try is being made in San Francisco. It is building the first wholly new mass transit system in the United States in 50 years. It hopes to operate, by 1971, an electric rail system running at an average speed of 45 miles per hour. It involves the largest bond issue ever voted for mass transit—and voted by auto owners! In general, however, there is little indication that Americans are willing to forgo the comfort, convenience, guaranteed seating, independence of schedule, privacy, and storage capacity of private cars.

This is why the real solution to city problems must lie in pushing the external costs of the offenders right back onto the guilty parties. This is where the economist comes in.

What Might Be Done

Suppose we make use, as a matter of principle, of the disciplinary force of price. Suppose we force every individual to bear financial responsibility for his actions. Suppose we internalize the costs that must now be borne by society at large.

governmental charges   We have already learned in earlier chapters how charging too low or too high a price can cause all kinds of trouble. In this case, where we have slum development, traffic congestion, and pollution, we are charging wrong prices. Landlords who own empty lots in city centers are taxed less on them than their neighbors who build or improve apartment houses. This reflects attitudes that might have been appropriate when we were a nation of farmers. We are not now. Suppose we taxed unused land *double* the rate charged for built-up land (Pittsburgh is the rare city doing this). Before you know it, unused land would be built up. The supply of apartments in city centers, for example, would rise. The upward pressure on rents would ease. (Again, use Figure 28.1 THE CENTRAL-CITY HOUS- ING MARKET.) People would be less likely to flee to the suburbs. The poor could spend less of their budget on housing. They would be less likely applicants for public assistance.

All this can be reinforced. Suppose improved or new houses are taxed *less* than dilapi- dated or old ones. (This has in fact been tried with great success in Southfield, Michigan.) Landlords would find it advantageous to improve rather than to run down their buildings. Again the lot of the poor would be improved. City spending on crime control and health could be cut in favor of more or better schools. Fewer people would flee the city. Urban renewal money could be saved.

More than that! People who do move to the suburbs, by causing traffic congestion, push terrible costs onto the residents of the city that must provide roads and policemen and deal with air pollution. Let them pay the full costs of their actions. If a city charges too low a price for its public services, it should not be surprised if people make profligate use of its offerings. A correct system of user charges would solve the problem. *Wherever there is too much traffic, the charge is incorrect.*

Just charging a flat toll for every car entering the city, for instance, would be wrong. During rush hours or in generally congested areas, the charge should be higher. This would keep shoppers and sightseers off the road at that time or in that area. During off-peak hours or in lightly traveled areas, the charge should be *lower* to encourage housewives and delivery trucks and tourists to use facilities then and there. (Such variation is often encountered in parking meters.) And charges should *not* be subsidized by city, state, or national taxpayers. If people want to live in the suburbs, they should be made as fully aware as possible of the *full* costs of their action. If they hurt society, they should pay for it.

Many cities do have tolls for the use of roads and parking facilities. But they are all wrong as the persistence of the problem indicates. Peak traffic users, such as commuters, for instance, are given quantity discounts on bridge tickets. This encourages people to move out of town or to travel more often. It is a subsidy to traffic congestion and air pollution! No matter how people react to the charges, the problem is solved. If they abandon their cars for mass transit, congestion is relieved. If they do not abandon their cars, the city has the funds to expand facilities and traffic control. And note how nicely this approach overcomes the political fragmentation problem referred to above.

The same principle of user charges can be applied generally. People who use airport facilities should pay for them, be it through parking fees, landing fees, gasoline taxes, ticket taxes, or whatever. They should be made aware of the *full* costs of their actions.

Pollution could be attacked in the same way. A superb proposal has been made by J. H. Dales.[3] He proposed that we create a market for pollution rights. It would work something like this.

The government determines the maximum amount of pollution that can be engaged in without harmful long-run effects. It may determine, for instance, that 100,000 tons of raw sewage per year can safely be dumped into Lake Erie. This may be the amount that would be degraded by natural biologic processes and thus "disappear" without causing any noticeable side effects. The government can offer for sale 100,000 "raw sewage pollution rights." Each "right" would entitle the owner to dump one ton of raw sewage per year into Lake Erie. (Similar rights could be set for other types of pollutants and for other bodies of water, for the soil, and the air, of course.) This supply of pollution rights may be illustrated by the vertical supply line in Figure 28.4 THE MARKET FOR POLLUTION RIGHTS.

Demand, however, can be expected to have the regular characteristics we have met so often before. Consider the demand for 1970, or D_{1970} in the graph. At a zero price, people naturally pollute (as they do now) as much as they like (in our case, just over 110,000 tons per year). "Let others worry about the consequences," they say. At some positive price, however, if government forced them to pay, say, $200 a year for each ton of raw sewage dumped, some polluters may think twice. They may find it cheaper to avoid pollution altogether. So the quantity of pollution rights demanded is less. At successively higher prices, quantity demanded drops further and further. At some very high price, perhaps $1,800 per right, no one wants to buy pollution rights. Thus, in 1970, supply and demand would establish a price of $200 per right. People who bought the rights would dump 100,000 tons of raw sewage into Lake Erie. Others (who would have added to this at a zero price) prefer to avoid the pollution in other ways.

Over time, we can expect demand to rise. Population grows. There are more cities. Each has more sewage. In 1980, demand may equal D_{1980}. At a zero price, people would now dump

[3] In his *Pollution, Property, and Prices* (Toronto: University of Toronto Press, 1968).

Figure 28.4   THE MARKET FOR POLLUTION RIGHTS

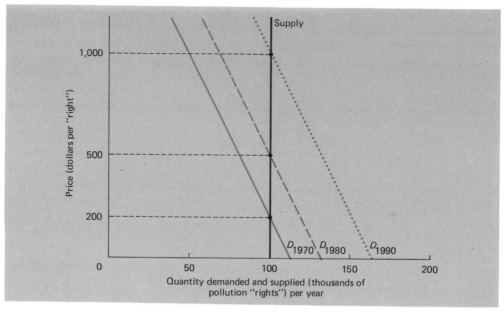

Demand for and supply of pollution rights might determine their equilibrium price. Although the quantity supplied never rises, the price can be expected to rise over time. Only those polluters who find it cheaper to purchase pollution rights than to engage in pollution prevention on their own will buy the rights and pollute. (Each "right" allows the owner to dump one ton per year.)

over 130,000 tons. Instead, price rises to $500 per right. The purchasers continue to dump 100,000 tons into the lake. All others find it cheaper to avoid pollution.

By 1990, demand may be like D_{1990}. Without our system, people would dump over 160,000 tons (where the demand curve cuts the horizontal axis). Instead, price rises to $1,000 per right. Still only 100,000 tons are dumped The rest is avoided. The price system has helped us to save the lake. The very people who might have ruined it were forced to change their behavior!

The revenues received for the "bearable amount" of pollution, as you will note, are rising every year. They can be used to police the system or for other purposes. It is also possible for conservationists to buy up the pollution rights thereby preventing even the amount of pollution the government has considered allowable.

The same system can, of course, be used throughout. Farmers who burn smudgepots in their orchards, power plants that pump soot and sulfur into the atmosphere, automobile drivers whose cars spill hydrocarbons—all can be forced to buy pollution rights in the air. Unless they do, they must prevent the consequences of their actions in other ways or abstain from so acting entirely. (Don't think it can't be done. Just consider how people have to buy rights to certain transmitting frequencies nowadays. In the 1920's, they were everybody's property.) Naturally, relative prices throughout the economy would look very different. Pears may cost twice as much per pound as steak. Refrigerators may cost as much as half a car. A ride to the city in your own car may cost ten times as much as a subway trip. But all this is for the good. We would all suddenly wake up and realize what it *really* costs to do what we have been doing! Only with this knowledge can we be expected to use resources efficiently, to shape our lives rationally.

private ownership rights   There is another way to solve some of the problems. The reason people pollute lakes and rivers, for instance, is that no one really *owns* those bodies of water and the fish therein. Suppose now we changed our laws and allowed private individuals to own, say, the fish in Lake Erie. The moment pollution threatened these fish, the owner could sue the offenders, just as I could sue you if you came on my property and started cutting down my trees! This would force the offenders to avoid the pollution. Or a court would force them to pay damages (which revenues the owners might use to abate the effects). In either case, as before, the offenders are made aware of what they are doing to society. The prices they charge for their products would come to reflect correctly the true social cost of their products. (By the way, this system has worked exceedingly well in Great Britain and in Germany.)

A First Step

People don't always listen to economists. Just suppose they don't. Is there anything left economists can do to help our cities? Decidedly, yes.

marginal benefits vs. marginal costs   Even if we continue the *present* approaches to city problems, economists can help cities make the most effective decisions. At present, cities are not really using any systematic approach to pinpoint the best ways of spending their money. As we learned in Part 2, the trick is to compare systematically marginal benefits and marginal costs. (We have noted earlier that the federal government is beginning to make use of this technique. (See page 250.)

Suppose a city has $100 million to spend. What shall it do? Build more freeways? Build a rapid transit system? Build houses for the poor? Give them better schools, or birth control devices? Strengthen its police force? Raise welfare payments? Build a sewage treatment plant? It cannot do all. It clearly wants to do what is best.

The city may proceed as follows. Suppose it breaks down its $100 million budget into ten $10 million chunks. Let us call the first $10 million the *marginal cost of a project*. What would be the extra or marginal benefit gained from spending $10 million on any of the above? The results may be as shown in Table 28.1. Having more freeways, for instance, may reduce the city's police and health expenditures (owing to fewer accidents) by $1 million. It may save commuters $1 million worth of time previously lost in delays. It may decrease

Table 28.1 BENEFIT-COST ANALYSIS

ASSUMED MARGINAL BENEFITS (IN MILLION DOLLARS) OF A $10 MILLION INCREASE IN SPENDING ON.

	FREEWAYS	MASS TRANSIT	HOUSING	SCHOOLS	BIRTH CONTROL	POLICE	WELFARE	SEWAGE PLANTS
1. Expense avoided	police and health 1, delays 1, welfare 10	pollution 4, police 2, welfare 2	health 50, police 30	welfare 100, police 50, health 10	welfare 1,000, police 500, fire 50, schools 100	insurance 10	health 99, police 31	welfare 100
2. New expense caused	pollution 2, police 10	population removal 6, pollution 1	water 15, pollution 40, fire 1	pollution 10		riots 1, pollution 1	pollution 1	
3. Net (1–2)	0	1	24	150	1,650	8	129	100
4. Direct benefits	jobs 50	jobs 49	jobs 64	jobs 90	jobs 850	jobs 10	jobs 500	jobs 300, health 100
5. Marginal benefit (3 + 4)	50	50	88	240	2,500	18	629	500
6. Discounted benefit	30	40	80	200	700	10	500	400
7. Marginal benefit to marginal cost ratio	3:1	4:1	8:1	20:1	70:1	1:1	50:1	40:1

In this hypothetical case, the city's money is most effectively spent on birth control, least effectively on police.

welfare expenditures by $10 million, because some poor people can now reach jobs formerly not accessible. But more traffic means more pollution. Hence, costs to others on that account rise by $2 million. It also means more traffic control. So costs rise by $10 million. Net, we have a zero gain so far. Add $50 million of new income earned by the poor now having jobs, and you get a marginal benefit from the whole project of $50 million.

But some of this benefit occurs in the future, whereas the cost is incurred now. To compare, we must make the two comparable. How much is $50 million—occurring at various future times—worth now? We can estimate the figure by using the current rate of interest. If it is 5 percent, we know that a present dollar becomes $1.05 in 1 year, $1.1025 in 2 years, and so on. Or we know that $1.1025 in 2 years is worth $1 now. This procedure, of converting future dollars into (a smaller amount of) present dollars is called "discounting." Suppose our $50 million of future benefits are worth $30 million now. This is shown in row (6). And this figure we can compare with our $10 million marginal cost. Row (7) shows the marginal benefit to marginal cost ratio (of 30 to 10) as 3 to 1. For each dollar spent on freeways, we gain $3 of net benefits.

The same procedure can be followed for the other alternatives. No attempt has been made to include all possible entries in this illustration. In addition, as you must well realize, this is a difficult task. Clearly, some of this information is easily available, especially when one goes after it. Other information can never be more than a guess. Exactly what are all the costs caused by another 100 tons of air pollutants owing to increased auto traffic? If everyone has to paint his house twice as often, we could calculate the figure. But how should we evaluate the life of even a single person who died from pollution? How should we evaluate the cost of sickness?

Guesses may be better than making no attempt at all to evaluate our actions. In our illustration, the answer is crystal clear. The best way to spend our first $10 million is to disseminate birth control information and devices. Possibly, for reasons discussed in the previous chapter (pages 662–663), no other program is so beneficial to society. Here we get the most for our money. (Note that an actual study by the Office of Economic Opportunity calculated an actual 70:1 ratio for planned parenthood programs.)

This is not to say that the *next* $10 million should be spent in the same direction. There may well be diminishing returns to this route. If we set up another table such as Table 28.1 (assuming that the best program just found has been carried out), we may find it best to spend the next $10 million on schools. We can proceed in the same fashion until the entire budget has been allocated. Subject to the inevitable guesses involved in all human decision-making, this technique would then assure the greatest benefit from a given total expenditure.

SUMMARY

1 The United States has gone through a long process of urbanization. Close to three quarters of the population now lives in urban areas. Less than 5 percent of the labor force feeds all of us.

2   The enormous technical advances in agriculture and industry, however, have had serious side effects on our natural environment as well as on social relations.

3   The country-to-city migration has been disproportionately a nonwhite migration, a migration of people unprepared for urban life and modern jobs. It has converted the central cities into socially explosive ghettos inhabited by poor people. Yet the city is unable to help them much. It faces a serious disparity between financial needs and its revenues. Its tax base is often shrinking, owing to outmigration from the cities of industry and white population to the suburbs and because city landlords have a strong incentive to let housing deteriorate.

4   Demands on city finances are large. Suburbanites commute to the city and require traffic facilities. The city must take care of water, sewage, police, and so forth. Little is then left for good schools and welfare assistance for the poor.

5   An inevitable by-product of all life is pollution. However, in a growing and urban society its effects are more noticeable. In American cities, air and water pollution have reached serious proportions. This adds to the financial demands made on city governments. Essentially, city governments are the victims of external repercussions from the actions of millions of private decision-makers.

6   Solving city problems requires more than what has been done so far. So far action has involved intergovernmental cooperation, legally and financially, in an attempt to make up for the external consequences of other people's actions. But urban renewal has not solved and cannot be expected to solve the slum problem. Past and present actions in the transport field will not solve city traffic problems. And antipollution measures taken so far have even less of a chance of success.

7   Real solutions require the pushing back onto the offenders of the external costs of their actions. A system of governmental user charges or taxes could internalize these costs and make people aware of the social consequences of their actions. Such user charges may include a market for pollution rights. Another approach involves the extension of private ownership rights.

8   Even barring such radically new approaches to city problems, the introduction of benefit-cost analysis may improve present-day city decision-making. It may lead to a more efficient use of resources.

TERMS[4]

benefit-cost analysis	"piggyback" transport
discounted benefit	pollution
ghetto	slum
gravitrain	standard metropolitan statistical area
	urban renewal

[4] Terms are defined in the Glossary at the end of the book.

QUESTIONS FOR REVIEW AND DISCUSSION

1 "Urbanization is a new worldwide phenomenon. To be sure, there were cities 5,500 years ago, but they were small, surrounded by a rural majority of people. Before 1850, *no* society on earth was urbanized. Even by 1900, only one was (the United Kingdom). Today, *all* industrial nations are urbanized. In 1960, a third of the world population lived in cities. In 1990, over half of it will." Explain this trend. Do you think it is a desirable one? Explain.

2 Kenneth B Clark testified before the Kerner Commission: "I read that report . . . of the 1919 riot in Chicago, and it is as if I were reading the report of the investigating committee on the Harlem riot of '35, the report of the investigating committee of the Harlem riot of '43, the report of the McCone Commission on the Watts riot.

"I must again in candor say to you members of this commission—it is a kind of Alice in Wonderland—with the same moving picture reshown over and over again, the same analysis, the same recommendations and the same inaction." Can you ex-explain this analysis of city conditions?

3 Under the 1965 Water Quality Act, the fifty states have submitted to the Department of the Interior proposals for cleaning up interstate waterways. Iowa was the only state that refused to require secondary treatment of sewage (dumped into the Missouri and Mississippi Rivers). What would you do about this?

4 "Lake Ontario is less polluted than Lake Erie because the algae-fertilizing salts which enter the lake are counteracted by acids put into the lake with steel mill wastes. Thus the solution to algae pollution is clear: dump in acids with the salts." Comment.

5 In early 1969, the Reserve Mining Company of Duluth was dumping 60,000 tons of ore wastes per day into Lake Superior. It is (so far) the cleanest of the Great Lakes. What would you suggest be done about this?

Wellsburg, West Virginia, with a population of 5,000, spills raw sewage into the Ohio River. They cannot afford a sewage treatment plant that would cost $1.8 million. What do you suggest they do?

6 We can't stop pollution, for it would put people out of work.
EXAMPLE 1: PPG Industries, Inc., said that meeting Ohio's limit on discharge of calcium chloride into the Tuscarawas River (an Ohio River tributary) would force it to close its Barberton, Ohio, soda ash plant. Two thousand six hundred workers would lose their jobs.
EXAMPLE 2: State governments are keenly aware that differences among states of antipollution laws affect industrial location. A few years ago, Union Carbide decided against building a chemical plant in West Virginia and built it in Louisiana instead for this reason.
Discuss.

7 In 1969, when unmanageable piles of garbage had accumulated, New York City reverted to incineration, a method partially abandoned earlier. What would you have done as mayor of New York?

8 In 1969, construction was halted on a nuclear power plant at Cayuga Lake, New York, because people protested the thermal pollution danger. How would you handle the problem? Why?

9 MR. A: "The way to solve the pollution problem is to shoot all pollutants into outer space."

   MR. B: "You are silly. Technology right here on earth will solve the pollution problem. It is already busily doing so. Consider how sawdust, which used to be a waste, is now pressed into boards. Consider how smelter gases are turned into fertilizer, how cinders become building materials, scrap turns into new steel." Discuss.

10 One argument that crops up regularly whenever any type of pollution control is discussed is this: "We do not yet have enough scientific knowledge about the effects of pollution. Therefore, further study is indicated before action is taken." What do you think about this?

11 In 1969, the National Committee on Urban Growth (consisting of senators, representatives, governors, mayors, and county commissioners) proposed the building of 100 new cities for 100,000 people each and of 10 new cities for 1 million people each. It referred to the creation of twenty-eight "new towns" in Great Britain since 1945. It asked for long-term federal loans and grants to engage in similar *planned* endeavors. What do you think of this?

12 "Not all is bad about the urban ghetto. The poor living in it are better off than they were before. Surely it is better to move into a formerly middle class white house in the city than to keep living in a tarpaper shack in the Mississippi delta. It's like used cars. The rich discard their cars each year for the latest model. As a result, wealth filters down to the poor. They get perfectly good cars that have hardly been used for a great deal less money." Discuss.

13 Consider the following "pay-off" matrix. The lower left corner of each cell shows the

		CHOICES OPEN TO OTHER LANDLORDS	
		MAINTAIN HOUSES WELL	POORLY MAINTAIN HOUSES
Choices open to landlord A	maintain houses well	$300,000 / $300,000	$350,000 / $150,000
	poorly maintain houses	$150,000 / $350,000	$200,000 / $200,000

value of apartment houses of landlord A if he makes the choice indicated on the left and other landlords make the choice indicated on top. (For instance, if A maintains his houses well and others do, too, his houses are worth $300,000. But if he maintains his houses well and others do not, his houses are worth only $150,000.) Given uncertainty about the behavior of others, where would everybody end up? Why? What if people got together and agreed on a *joint* strategy of behavior? Why don't people get together in this way?

14 "If necessary, we should *pay* people to use mass transit facilities instead of private cars." Discuss. Show why it may well be *cheaper* for a city government to do this than to charge a positive price.

15 Transportation Secretary Volpe said: "We ought to get rid of the idea once and for all that public transportation must make a profit. Public transportation is so important that we must look at its financing much like any other public service. We don't expect the Army to make a profit" (*The Wall Street Journal*, May 21, 1969, p. 19). Evaluate.

16 "We should not ban cars from city streets. Nor noisy airplanes from airports. We should simply force those who hurt others to pay fully for all the consequences of their actions." Explain.

17 Why are some wild animals extinct, but no domesticated ones? (Hint: if people *owned* kangaroos and whales, might they survive?)

18 "The doctrine of 'freedom of the seas' is pernicious. It leads to an inefficient use of the ocean's resources. What we should do is extend each country's territorial waters to the middle of the ocean it borders." Discuss.

19 In biological warfare laboratories, we are developing virulent strains of viruses and drug resistant bacteria. What external repercussions may develop from this?

20 Suppose you build a new house surrounded by lovely orchards. One spring morning, you wake up coughing. Tar smudge pots are being burned throughout the orchards to prevent the frost from killing the crop. Your house, and 25 square miles around it up to 1,000 feet, are filled with heavy black smoke. You see birds dying. Everything in your house is filthy (presumably, including your lungs). What would you do about it?

epilogue

Economists who are out to reduce scarcity to the minimum are often tempted to equate the measurable with the desirable. More GNP is what we want, isn't it? In this fourth part of the book we have seen that another question is equally important: How is GNP shared? If some people get too large a portion of income, or if some people selfishly refuse to pay for the consequences of their actions, serious social and environmental problems can result.

The problems, furthermore, go beyond the cities. Scientists tell us that air pollution may eventually shut out the sun rays sufficiently to cause a permanent cooling of the earth. This would take much of present agricultural land out of production and cause worldwide starvation. Others believe that instead sun rays that reach the earth will be trapped by the layer of polluted air, causing a warming trend that would melt the ice caps. This would flood all the major cities on earth. It would certainly provide a unique way of solving our urban ills!

Or consider the use of DDT. As with radioactive wastes, we do not really know its ultimate effect on life on earth. It could kill us all. When it was discovered, it was hailed as a great miracle. Its developer received the Nobel Prize for Medicine: Before DDT, India had 100 million cases of malaria, with 750,000 deaths per year. Now it has 15,000 cases and 1,500 deaths per year. DDT, by killing the malaria mosquito, did it. Can one quarrel with that?

Now consider this: DDT (and its relatives) have been widely used in agriculture as pesticides. In a process of "biological magnification," DDT has entered higher life forms in large quantities. Through runoff from the fields, minute quantities enter algae. Smaller water organisms feeding on algae take in larger quantities. Little fish that eat these water organisms take in more. Large doses of DDT are found in larger fish that feed on the little fish. And the American eagle, which eats the larger fish, is dying out. DDT affects its calcium metabolism. As a result, it lays eggs with thin or no shell. The embryos die. In plants, DDT slows the rate of photosynthesis, the source of a large fraction of the world's oxygen. In laboratory animals, DDT attacks sex hormones, and the central nervous system. It incites cancer. But by now DDT is spread all over the world. It has been found in such unlikely places as the petrels living on rocky islets off Bermuda and in the fat of antarctic penguins. It is in you.

Soviet scientists report that workers exposed to DDT for 10 years show stomach and liver trouble. The University of Miami medical school reports that persons dying of liver cancer, leukemia, high blood pressure, and carcinoma (an early cancer form) have two to three times more DDT in their bodies than persons dying accidental deaths. Nevertheless, breast-fed infants throughout the world in 1969 were ingesting double the quantities of DDT recommended as the maximum daily intake by the World Health Organization.

So maybe in the end mankind will die because it *thoughtlessly* pursued the goal of abundance. Still, as the chapters of Part 4 show, we can act now to prevent catastrophe, if only we have the will. But this involves changing our basic outlook. The world has not been put here for man's sole benefit, to be despoiled at his pleasure. Man cannot forever evade the truth that he is only part of nature. He must strive to live in harmony with nature.

glossary

This glossary contains brief definitions of the most important terms used throughout this book. It may be used, therefore, as a convenient study guide for the terms found at the end of each chapter.

The definitions found in this glossary are those with which most economists would agree. Yet definitions are by nature arbitrary, and some people may at times prefer to use a term in a way slightly different from the one given here. This glossary only shows the sense in which terms have been used in this book. This will help you understand what this book is trying to say. If then you should prefer to use different terms than employed here, you can always do so.

Finally, note that oftentimes new terms have been defined with the help of other terms newly learned in this book. Then you might also want to look at their definitions.

ability-to-pay principle a principle of taxation requiring everyone to contribute to general government revenues according to his financial ability

absolute advantage a situation in which one producer can produce a good at absolutely less cost than another

accelerator the marginal capital-to-output ratio, or the change in capital divided by the change in output requiring it

accelerator theory a theory postulating that the *level* of (at least a portion of total) investment demand depends on *changes* of other variables, such as the GNP

acceptance method a Soviet method of transferring bank balances which is initiated by the payee, rather than the payer, as in the case of checking accounts

actual labor force potential labor force minus the voluntarily unemployed

actual reserves *see* reserves

administrative budget one of several budget concepts used by the United States federal government, including only expenditures requiring congressional appropriations and receipts that enter the general account of the Treasury

administrative lag the lag between the time the need for economic policy is recognized and the time such policy is executed

advances Federal Reserve System holdings of member banks' IOU's (mostly) secured by interest-bearing government securities owned by the member banks

aggregate demand the amount of money people in the aggregate are able and willing to spend on new output in a period

aggregate demand schedule a listing of a series of total demand–GNP combinations showing the dollar amounts people in the aggregate are able and willing to spend on new output in a period at alternative levels of GNP, graphed as the aggregate demand line

aggregate supply *see* gross national product

aggregate supply line a graph showing the value of new output available for sale at each conceivable level of GNP

antitrust laws a series of laws designed to foster competition and restrain monopoly, such as the Sherman Act (1890), the Clayton and Federal Trade Commission acts (1914), the Robinson-Patman Act (1936), the Wheeler-Lea Act (1938), the Celler-Kefauver Act (1950)

applied research application to a particular problem of the knowledge gained in basic research

asset anything of value held by someone

automatic monetary pilot a proposal according to which monetary authorities annually would increase the money supply at a predetermined rate regardless of economic circumstances

automatic stabilizers vs. discretionary stabilization elements intervening between gross national income and disposable personal income (depreciation, taxes, undistributed corporate profits, and transfers) are called automatic stabilizers; their automatic change, when gross national product changes, may make disposable personal income, hence spending, change by less, ultimately limiting any GNP change; discretionary stabilization instead refers to deliberate changes in tax rates and government spending to change GNP to any desired level (*see* fiscal policy)

automation the automatic handling of the entire production process by self-regulating equipment, not reliant on human strength or guidance

autonomous vs. induced demands demands that do not vary with income vs. demands that vary with the level or rate of change of income

average productivity real GNP per person employed

---

balanced growth the simultaneous development of all sectors of the economy

balance of capital the value of titles exported minus the value of titles imported, or capital imports minus capital exports of a period

balance of current account the value of current account exports minus current account imports in a period

balance of gold the value of gold exported minus the value of gold imported in a period

balance of payments a systematic record of all economic transactions during a specified period between two parties, usually referring to a year and one country vs. the rest of the world

balance-of-payments deficit or surplus a measure of the seriousness of balance-of-payments disequilibrium, equals, *for instance*, all credits minus debits, *excluding* short-term capital and monetary gold; called deficit if negative, surplus if positive

balance-of-payments disequilibrium a balance-of-payments situation that cannot be maintained because of imbalance in individual accounts

balance of services the value of service exports minus service imports of a period

balance of trade the value of commodity exports minus commodity imports of a period

balance of unilateral transfers the value of gifts imported minus the value of gifts exported in a period

balance sheet a still picture of someone's wealth at a moment of time, showing assets equaling liabilities and net worth

base year in the construction of price indices the year whose price level is arbitrarily called 100 and to which the price levels of all other years are compared

basic research scientific inquiry, not directed toward any specific useful discovery

benefit-cost analysis *see* cost-benefit analysis

benefit principle a principle of taxation requiring that people be taxed in proportion to the benefit they receive from governmental activity

black capitalism a scheme to create a whole spectrum of black-owned and black-run businesses to eliminate the poverty of black people

black market all contact points between buyers and sellers trading illegally

black power a movement to change the attitudes, habits, and political power of black people as a way to make them fully accepted as first class citizens

board of directors the elected representatives of the stockholders of a corporation who appoint the corporate management

Board of Governors the seven governors of the Federal Reserve System

bond a corporate or governmental promissory note (IOU) often marketable, paying interest at regular intervals plus a stated face value at maturity (a stated date)

boom a situation in which real GNP and resource use are close to or at potential

bottleneck inflation inflation in a bottleneck sector of the economy, where demand exceeds supply, though this situation is not yet generalized

business cycle the irregular movements of real GNP around its trend, together with the concomitant phenomena of changing levels of employment and prices

capital the total of manmade resources existing at a moment in time; includes all buildings, all types of equipment, and all inventories of producers (raw materials, semifinished, and finished goods)

capital export in the balance of payments, the import of a title

capital gains income derived from the appreciation of property held for more than 6 months

capital import in the balance of payments, the export of a title

capitalism in its pure form, a society wherein all resources are privately owned and utilized

capital stock *see* capital

cartel a formal agreement among firms to restrain competition

cash coins and paper bills

central economic planning the planning of all economic activity by a central agency, usually the government

Central Planning Board in a socialist country, a group of people in charge of planning and supervising economic activity for the country

ceteris paribus clause an assumption that "everything else is held equal," allowing us to study the effect caused by the change of a single factor

check a written order to his commercial bank by the owner of a demand deposit to transfer the deposit to someone else

check clearing the transfer of demand deposits between different owners

checking account *see* demand deposit

children's allowances a system of government payments for children designed to eliminate poverty associated with youth

chronic unemployment a type of (probably) long-run unemployment caused by discrimination requiring for its elimination basic changes in attitude on the part of employers, or caused by change in tastes or technical change requiring for its elimination massive relocation and retraining on the part of workers

circular flow a simplified picture of the capitalist economy, showing households as owners of resources supplying resources to firms, which demand them to produce goods that are in turn supplied to and demanded by households (flow of real goods and resources); also showing firms incurring costs that (together with profits) become the incomes of households, which are spent on goods bought from firms that take in revenue (counterflow of dollars)

citizens' sovereignty a state of affairs in an economy in which the desires of citizens for goods are realized through the political process, such as the election of government officials who then buy the goods desired

civilian employment U.S. definition: all members of the civilian labor force who worked even 1 hour for pay or profit during the survey week (in which statistics are gathered), including those having jobs or businesses but not working because of illness, vacation, labor-management dispute, bad weather, or personal reasons (such as hunting for another job) and including family members working at least 15 hours a week in a family enterprise without pay

civilian labor force all members of the actual labor force not in the armed forces

classical economics the economic doctrines taught prior to 1936 that were based on the validity of Say's Law

closed shop a firm operating under a collective bargaining agreement forbidding the hiring of nonunion members; illegal since 1947

collective farm in the Soviet Union, a farm owned by a group of farmers operating it

collective farm market a market in the Soviet Union in which collective farmers may sell privately produced goods at unregulated prices to anyone

collective goods goods that provide benefit to groups of people collectively, regardless of who pays for them, such as national defense or police protection

command economy an economy in which all or most economic transactions are guided by a central human authority

commercial bank a private bank having demand deposit liabilities

commercial policy the setting of tariffs and import quotas and similar barriers to trade

commodity any material object, solid, liquid, or gaseous

Common Market a customs union formed in 1957 by Belgium, France, Italy, Luxemburg, the Netherlands, and West Germany, also known as the European Economic Community (EEC)

common stock a transferable share of ownership in a corporation entitling the owner to a voice in corporate management, a share of corporate profits (which may or may not be paid out as dividends), and to a residual claim on corporate assets (after all creditors)

comparative advantage a situation in which one producer, although not absolutely lower cost than another, is less high cost in the production of one good than in another; hence, he is "comparatively" lower cost; or if he is absolutely lower cost, he is more lower cost in one good than in another

competitive economy a capitalist economy in which private resource owners and firms compete with each other and among one another for the best "deal" in the markets for goods or resources

conglomerate merger the merger of firms dealing in completely different lines of business, such as a tire manufacturer with a cattle ranch and a hotel chain

consolidated cash budget one of the several budget concepts used by the U.S. federal government, covering not only funds wholly owned by the federal government (and counted in the administrative budget), but also trust fund transactions (social security, highways, and so on)

conspiracy doctrine a doctrine held originally by the courts according to which workers "conspiring" through unions to raise wages were common criminals

consumer credit the amount of loan money made available to households

consumer good any good after entering into the possession of a household (excepting, by U.S. Department of Commerce definition, residential houses)

consumer price index an index measuring the movement of prices paid by "typical" wage earners and clerical workers' families

consumer sovereignty the state of affairs in an economy in which the desires of consumers for goods are realized through their "dollar votes" in the market, as the dollars spent set up the appropriate incentives for private producers to produce the goods in demand and not to use resources for other goods

consumption demand the amount households are able and willing to spend on goods (excluding residential houses) in a period, equal to the amount they actually do spend, or personal consumption expenditures

consumption demand schedule a listing of a series of household demand-income combinations, showing the dollar amounts one household is, or all households as a group are, able and willing to spend on goods in a period at alternative levels of income, graphed as the consumption demand line

contractionary gap the gap between actual GNP and lower aggregate demand

control figures in the Soviet Union, the original material and monetary plan targets set up by Gosplan in the process of plan construction

corporation an artificial person, established by law through a corporate charter, owned by stockholders, usually engaged in some sort of profit-making business

cost-benefit analysis the systematic comparison of costs and benefits of alternative means of achieving a certain end in order to find the most desirable way of achieving the end; used for evaluating government projects under the PPBS, or programming-planning-budgeting system

cost-push inflation inflation caused by the wielding of monopoly power of sellers of resources and output, who push up prices regardless of demand, trying (as a group) to get more than 100 percent of the economy's maximum real income

Council of Economic Advisers a group of three economic experts in the Executive Office of the President

coupon interest rate the rate of interest on bonds implied by the annual dollar amount of interest paid and the bond's face value; if the face value is $100 and the annual interest paid is $6, the implied rate is 6 percent

craft unions organizations of skilled craftsmen only, such as of electricians or plumbers

credit in the balance of payment, anything of value given up

creditor someone to whom debts are owed

creeping inflation an inflation in which the price rise is slow per unit of time

crude birth rate the annual number of live births per 1,000 persons

crude death rate the annual number of nonfoetal deaths per 1,000 persons

culture of poverty the set of beliefs, customs, habits, morals, and so forth shaping the life of many poor people

cumulative preferred stock a preferred stock on which any dividend payments omitted in past years must be paid before any dividends can ever be paid on common stock

currency reform a reform of the domestic monetary system, wherein usually all existing money is declared worthless and new money is issued to the holders of old money according to a given formula

current account in the balance of payment, the commodity, service, and unilateral transfer accounts combined

customs duty a tax on the importation of foreign goods

cycle amplitude the maximum deviation of real GNP above or below its trend

cycle length the time between analogous positions of real GNP, as from the time it rises above its trend once until it does so again

---

debit in the balance of payment, anything of value received

deficient reserves negative excess reserves

deflating GNP a method of calculating real GNP by dividing any year's GNP at current prices by that year's price index and multiplying by 100; differences in real GNP data can then only result from differences in physical output

deflation a general fall in prices

demand desire backed up with purchasing power; for a single good or resource: a series of price-quantity combinations, showing the amounts of a good or resource people are able and willing to buy at alternative prices (*see also* quantity demanded); for groups of goods: a series of hypothetical spending-income combinations, showing the amounts of money people are able and willing to spend at alternative income levels

demand curve a demand schedule graphed

demand deposit a noninterest-bearing liability of a bank, evidenced by nothing else but an entry in the bank's books, transferable by check at the owner's request, also called checking account

demand-pull inflation a general rise in prices caused by aggregate demand exceeding the economy's maximum output evaluated at current prices, as demanders have enough money to buy more than 100 percent of maximum output

demand schedule for a single good or resource: a list showing alternative quantities demanded at alternative hypothetical prices, given all other factors; for groups of goods: a list showing alternative sums people are willing to spend at alternative income levels, given all other factors

depreciation a dollar estimate of the wear and tear of capital used in production

depression a situation in which national output (real GNP) and resource use are significantly below potential

devaluation under the gold standard type of international monetary arrangement, a governmental act raising the domestic money price at which the government buys gold and sells gold (to "legitimate" users); as a result, each unit of domestic money is worth less in gold and foreign monies

direct intermediate good coefficient the amount of an intermediate good needed directly as an input per unit of gross output of a good, neglecting indirect effects (for example, 100 pounds aluminum per car)

direct resource coefficient the amount of a resource service needed directly as an input per unit of gross output of a good, neglecting indirect effects (for example, 51 labor hours per car)

direct tax any tax on income

discounted benefit a future dollar benefit that has been reduced to a lower present dollar figure such that the lower figure, if invested at the current interest rate, would yield the original larger figure at the future date

discount rate the rate at which member banks can borrow at the Fed via discounts or advances

discounts Federal Reserve System holdings of member banks' IOU's secured by IOU's of the member banks' customers

discretionary stabilization any deliberately brought about change (as in the supply of money, interest rates, tax rates, government spending), with the aim of stabilizing GNP at a desired level

disposable personal income the after-tax income, from all sources, of natural persons (as opposed to fictitious ones, such as corporations), consisting of a period's net wages, net rents, net interest, net dividends, net profits of unincorporated private firms and transfers

dissaving spending beyond income through reducing past savings or by incurring new debt

dividend the portion of corporate profits paid out to stockholders

doctrine of mutual agency the legal doctrine according to which any partner in a partnership can commit the whole partnership by his actions

dollar glut a situation in which foreigners hold more dollars than they care to keep

dollar shortage a situation in which foreigners hold fewer dollars than they would like to have

dollar votes the expenditures by buyers of goods that ultimately determine, in a capitalist free-enterprise economy, which goods continue to be produced

draft plan the final material and monetary balances set up by Gosplan after "discussions" with enterprises and subordinate planning agencies

dynamic efficiency the ability of an economy to ensure rapid economic growth through technical progress and raising the quantities of resources

---

econometric model a set of relationships describing the behavior of people in an economic system with the help of variables that have actually been measured

economic good a good (commodity or service) that man can make and that is not a free good; has a positive price

economic growth a rise in real GNP per head

economic wants those that can be satisfied by the provision of economic goods

economies of scale a situation in which a 1 percent increase in all inputs leads to a more than 1 percent increase in output

employment civilian employment plus membership in the armed forces

Employment Act of 1946 a 1946 act of congress establishing the federal government's responsibility to promote "maximum" employment, production, and purchasing power

endogenous theory a theory of the business cycle postulating that cycles are caused by forces internal to the economy, for example, the operation of the accelerator

entrepreneur the supplier of a special type of labor that organizes the production process; for his innovating, organizing, and risk-taking activities, the entrepreneur receives the firm's residual income (revenue minus wage, interest, and rent payments to hired resources); this can be positive (profit) or negative (loss)

equilibrium a condition that has no innate tendency to change

equilibrium GNP a level from which the GNP has no innate tendency to move because aggregate demand equals the GNP

escalator clause a contract clause specifying that nominal dollar payments (for example, of wages) are to be adjusted upward with any fall in the dollar's purchasing power (as shown, for example, by a rise in the consumer price index), thereby preserving the real purchasing power of the payments involved

escape clause a clause of the U.S. Reciprocal Trade Agreements Act allowing the revocation of tariff concessions to foreigners if domestic industry is "seriously" hurt as a result

estate tax a tax on the net worth of deceased persons

European Economic Community *see* Common Market

European Free Trade Association a customs union founded in 1960 by Austria, Denmark, Norway, Portugal, Sweden, Switzerland, and the United Kingdom; also called the "outer seven"

excess demand (or supply) a situation in which aggregate demand exceeds (or falls short of) the GNP

excess reserves actual reserves minus required reserves

exchange controls strict government control of all purchases and sales of foreign monies

exchange rate the dollar price per one unit of foreign money

exchange stabilization fund a government agency that buys or sells dollars and foreign monies in whatever quantities are needed to keep the exchange rate within narrow predetermined limits

excise tax a tax on the purchase of specific domestically made goods

exclusive contract a contract according to which a firm leases or sells commodities to another only under the condition that the other firm does not use or deal in the commodity of a competitor

exogenous theory a theory of the business cycle postulating that cycles are caused by forces beyond the control or predictive power of the economist, for example, by natural catastrophes, political upheavals

expansionary gap the gap between aggregate demand and lower actual GNP

free good a good that is provided by nature when and where needed in a quantity greater than is desired by all people; a good with a zero price

free monopoly a monopoly not regulated by government

free reserves the difference, if positive, between banks' excess reserves and their indebtedness to the Fed (*see also* net borrowed reserves)

frictional unemployment jobs and men are mismatched, yet the number of job openings and job seekers roughly coincides

full-bodied money a good used as money that has equal value in monetary as in nonmonetary use

full employment a situation in which between 96 and 99 percent of the members of the actual labor force have found employment

full employment budget a gauge of the impact of the federal government's operations on the economy, equals tax receipts (on the assumption that full employment exists and present tax rates hold) minus government expenditures on goods and transfers

functional vs. personal income distribution the distribution of income according to the "function" for which income was paid (how much was payment for labor, how much payment for land, how much for capital) vs. the distribution by persons (how much each person received, regardless of whether it was for selling labor, land, or capital or a transfer payment in return for nothing)

General Agreement on Tariffs and Trade an agreement among some forty governments to have at intervals multilateral discussions concerning a reduction in world trade barriers

general equilibrium analysis the simultaneous study of all interdependent markets

general government a producer using publicly owned land and capital and providing output without direct charges to the public, while financing its activity by other means, as general taxation, for example, the defense department

general price level a hypothetical concept of an average of all prices, can only be approximated by constructing specific price indexes (*see* consumer price index *or* wholesale price index)

general unemployment a situation in which the number of job seekers in all or most fields exceeds that of job openings owing to a lack of general demand

ghetto a city area characterized by acute poverty and inhabited by members of racial or ethnic minority groups under conditions of involuntary segregation

gift tax a tax on gifts made by a deceased person within 3 years of death

GNP deflator a price index for all goods counted in the GNP, obtained by dividing a series of GNP data at current prices by a series of GNP data at constant prices

gold certificates a warehouse receipt of gold, the only form of representative full-bodied "money" in existence in the United States (because most gold certificates are held by the Federal Reserve System, they do not count as part of the U.S. money supply)

gold parity rate the exchange rate between two currencies implied by the currency units' respective gold contents

gold standard an international monetary arrangement wherein each government defines its currency unit in terms of gold, stands ready to buy and sell unlimited amounts of gold at this price, allows free trading in gold, and pursues all required policies to preserve the system's functioning

good a commodity or service capable of satisfying human wants

goods market a market in which output is traded

Gosplan the Central Planning Board of the U.S.S.R.

government demand the amount general government is able and willing to spend on goods in a period including government enterprise expenditures on buildings and equipment, plus changes in their inventories, equal to the amount actually spent, or to government expenditures on goods

government demand schedule a listing of a series of government demand-GNP combinations, showing the dollar amounts all levels of government as a group are able and willing to spend on goods in a period at alternative levels of GNP, graphed as the government demand line

government enterprise a producer using publicly owned land and capital and charging customers directly for output attempting to cover costs at least roughly, for example, the post office

government expenditures on goods total expenditures on goods (commodities and services) by general government, plus government enterprise expenditures on new buildings and equipment, plus the change in their inventories

gravitrains a futuristic means of urban transport, propelled by its own weight through underground tunnels and pulled up by its own momentum

greenback *see* U.S. Note

grievance procedure an important point settled in union-management contracts specifying by what procedure grievances of workers (say, about safety rules) or of employers (say, about "goofing" on the job) are settled

gross national expenditure the gross expenditures on final goods in a period or the sum of personal consumption expenditures, gross private domestic investment, government expenditures on commodities and services, and net exports, equal to the GNP

gross national income the gross incomes earned in a period in the process of production, or the sum of wages, rents, interest, indirect taxes, depreciation, and profits earned by U.S. resources in a period; equal to GNP

gross national product the total of national production in a period, measured either as the value of all final goods or via the value-added approach; the value of final goods legally produced by the nation's resources in a period, measured by the prices actually paid for the goods; the sum of all producers' value added at current prices

gross private domestic investment household expenditures on new residential houses, plus private business expenditures on new buildings and equipment, plus the change in private business inventories

employment civilian employment plus membership in the armed forces

Employment Act of 1946 a 1946 act of congress establishing the federal government's responsibility to promote "maximum" employment, production, and purchasing power

endogenous theory a theory of the business cycle postulating that cycles are caused by forces internal to the economy, for example, the operation of the accelerator

entrepreneur the supplier of a special type of labor that organizes the production process; for his innovating, organizing, and risk-taking activities, the entrepreneur receives the firm's residual income (revenue minus wage, interest, and rent payments to hired resources); this can be positive (profit) or negative (loss)

equilibrium a condition that has no innate tendency to change

equilibrium GNP a level from which the GNP has no innate tendency to move because aggregate demand equals the GNP

escalator clause a contract clause specifying that nominal dollar payments (for example, of wages) are to be adjusted upward with any fall in the dollar's purchasing power (as shown, for example, by a rise in the consumer price index), thereby preserving the real purchasing power of the payments involved

escape clause a clause of the U.S. Reciprocal Trade Agreements Act allowing the revocation of tariff concessions to foreigners if domestic industry is "seriously" hurt as a result

estate tax a tax on the net worth of deceased persons

European Economic Community *see* Common Market

European Free Trade Association a customs union founded in 1960 by Austria, Denmark, Norway, Portugal, Sweden, Switzerland, and the United Kingdom; also called the "outer seven"

excess demand (or supply) a situation in which aggregate demand exceeds (or falls short of) the GNP

excess reserves actual reserves minus required reserves

exchange controls strict government control of all purchases and sales of foreign monies

exchange rate the dollar price per one unit of foreign money

exchange stabilization fund a government agency that buys or sells dollars and foreign monies in whatever quantities are needed to keep the exchange rate within narrow predetermined limits

excise tax a tax on the purchase of specific domestically made goods

exclusive contract a contract according to which a firm leases or sells commodities to another only under the condition that the other firm does not use or deal in the commodity of a competitor

exogenous theory a theory of the business cycle postulating that cycles are caused by forces beyond the control or predictive power of the economist, for example, by natural catastrophes, political upheavals

expansionary gap the gap between aggregate demand and lower actual GNP

employment civilian employment plus membership in the armed forces

Employment Act of 1946 a 1946 act of congress establishing the federal government's responsibility to promote "maximum" employment, production, and purchasing power

endogenous theory a theory of the business cycle postulating that cycles are caused by forces internal to the economy, for example, the operation of the accelerator

entrepreneur the supplier of a special type of labor that organizes the production process; for his innovating, organizing, and risk-taking activities, the entrepreneur receives the firm's residual income (revenue minus wage, interest, and rent payments to hired resources); this can be positive (profit) or negative (loss)

equilibrium a condition that has no innate tendency to change

equilibrium GNP a level from which the GNP has no innate tendency to move because aggregate demand equals the GNP

escalator clause a contract clause specifying that nominal dollar payments (for example, of wages) are to be adjusted upward with any fall in the dollar's purchasing power (as shown, for example, by a rise in the consumer price index), thereby preserving the real purchasing power of the payments involved

escape clause a clause of the U.S. Reciprocal Trade Agreements Act allowing the revocation of tariff concessions to foreigners if domestic industry is "seriously" hurt as a result

estate tax a tax on the net worth of deceased persons

European Economic Community *see* Common Market

European Free Trade Association a customs union founded in 1960 by Austria, Denmark, Norway, Portugal, Sweden, Switzerland, and the United Kingdom; also called the "outer seven"

excess demand (or supply) a situation in which aggregate demand exceeds (or falls short of) the GNP

excess reserves actual reserves minus required reserves

exchange controls strict government control of all purchases and sales of foreign monies

exchange rate the dollar price per one unit of foreign money

exchange stabilization fund a government agency that buys or sells dollars and foreign monies in whatever quantities are needed to keep the exchange rate within narrow predetermined limits

excise tax a tax on the purchase of specific domestically made goods

exclusive contract a contract according to which a firm leases or sells commodities to another only under the condition that the other firm does not use or deal in the commodity of a competitor

exogenous theory a theory of the business cycle postulating that cycles are caused by forces beyond the control or predictive power of the economist, for example, by natural catastrophes, political upheavals

expansionary gap the gap between aggregate demand and lower actual GNP

employment civilian employment plus membership in the armed forces

Employment Act of 1946 a 1946 act of congress establishing the federal government's responsibility to promote "maximum" employment, production, and purchasing power

endogenous theory a theory of the business cycle postulating that cycles are caused by forces internal to the economy, for example, the operation of the accelerator

entrepreneur the supplier of a special type of labor that organizes the production process; for his innovating, organizing, and risk-taking activities, the entrepreneur receives the firm's residual income (revenue minus wage, interest, and rent payments to hired resources); this can be positive (profit) or negative (loss)

equilibrium a condition that has no innate tendency to change

equilibrium GNP a level from which the GNP has no innate tendency to move because aggregate demand equals the GNP

escalator clause a contract clause specifying that nominal dollar payments (for example, of wages) are to be adjusted upward with any fall in the dollar's purchasing power (as shown, for example, by a rise in the consumer price index), thereby preserving the real purchasing power of the payments involved

escape clause a clause of the U.S. Reciprocal Trade Agreements Act allowing the revocation of tariff concessions to foreigners if domestic industry is "seriously" hurt as a result

estate tax a tax on the net worth of deceased persons

European Economic Community *see* Common Market

European Free Trade Association a customs union founded in 1960 by Austria, Denmark, Norway, Portugal, Sweden, Switzerland, and the United Kingdom; also called the "outer seven"

excess demand (or supply) a situation in which aggregate demand exceeds (or falls short of) the GNP

excess reserves actual reserves minus required reserves

exchange controls strict government control of all purchases and sales of foreign monies

exchange rate the dollar price per one unit of foreign money

exchange stabilization fund a government agency that buys or sells dollars and foreign monies in whatever quantities are needed to keep the exchange rate within narrow predetermined limits

excise tax a tax on the purchase of specific domestically made goods

exclusive contract a contract according to which a firm leases or sells commodities to another only under the condition that the other firm does not use or deal in the commodity of a competitor

exogenous theory a theory of the business cycle postulating that cycles are caused by forces beyond the control or predictive power of the economist, for example, by natural catastrophes, political upheavals

expansionary gap the gap between aggregate demand and lower actual GNP

exploitation a situation in which workers are paid a wage below their marginal revenue product

extended family system in many countries, the obligation of each person to support (when he is able) even most distant relatives

external effects *see* external repercussions of consumption *and* external repercussions of production

external repercussions of consumption the burden or benefit imposed on parties other than the consumer of a good because of and for no other reason than his consumption of this good

external repercussions of production the cost or benefit imposed on parties other than the producer of a good because of and for no other reason than his production of this good

---

featherbedding requiring payment for work not done or not needing to be done

federal budget one of several budget concepts used by the U.S. federal government, including federally owned and trust funds, distinguishing between expenditures proper and loans, and separating receipts arising from the government's compulsory powers from others stemming from its business-type activities

Federal Deposit Insurance Corporation a U.S. agency insuring most deposits up to $15,000

federal funds market a market in which banks trade excess reserves among one another

Federal Reserve Note a paper bill issued by a Federal Reserve Bank

Federal Reserve System the twelve Federal Reserve Banks in the United States, the U.S. Central Bank

final demand sector in input-output analysis, the sectors in the economy that receive final goods

final goods goods produced during a period and not sold to another producer in that period (and in that sense not "used up" in the making of other goods)

financial intermediary an institution that cannot create money, but helps to transfer it between parties, as savings banks from saver to investor

firm *see* producer

fiscal drag a situation in which the full employment budget is in surplus indicating that tax rates are too high; as a result, the GNP remains below full employment, because any rise in GNP raises tax collections and thereby dampens aggregate demand so much that the GNP rise is stopped prior to full employment

fiscal policy the deliberate exercise by the federal government of its power to tax and spend in order to influence the levels of GNP, employment, and prices

fixed costs the costs of inputs held constant in the period under consideration, costs that would occur even at zero output

foreign exchange foreign monies or claims thereon

free-enterprise economy a capitalist economy in which everyone is free to engage in any economic activity he likes and use his resources for whatever purposes seem best

gross social product the Soviet concept of national production, excluding the output of non-productive labor and including multiple counting of all other outputs

gross vs. net investment the annual addition to the capital stock through new production of buildings and equipment and inventory change vs. the same figure reduced by the same year's depreciation

---

horizontal merger the merger of competitive firms dealing in the same line of business, such as two book publishers or two oil companies

household one or more persons; in the latter case, typically living under one roof, making joint financial decisions

hyperinflation an inflation in which the price rise is extremely rapid per unit of time

---

imperfect competition a situation wherein one or all the conditions of perfect competition do not hold

imperfect competitor any buyer or seller not operating under perfect competition

import quota a maximum limit on imports

income velocity of money the ratio of a period's income (GNP) over that period's average money supply

index of concentration a crude measure of the market power of firms, such as the percentage of industry shipments made by the largest four firms

indirect business tax any tax not levied on business income, for example, a sales or property tax

industrial unions unions that allow all workers of the industry to become members regardless of their specific skill or job

infant industry a relatively young industry

infinity of wants the fact that the variety and number of human wants are presently, and can be expected to remain in the foreseeable future, beyond any recognizable limit

inflation a general rise in prices affecting all or most goods and resources at the same time

inheritance tax a tax levied on individuals inheriting an estate or portion thereof

injunction a cease-and-desist order by a court enforceable by arrest and jail

input *see* resource *and* intermediate goods

input-output table a table illustrating the interdependence of economic sectors, listing the distribution of output and resources among their users

input quota a command by a Central Planning Board to use a certain amount of input (intermediate good or resource service) and to produce with it a certain output (for example, use 100 tons of aluminum and 5,000 manhours to produce cars)

interest in economic theory, a payment for the use of capital; in practice, a payment for the use of money

intermediate goods goods that were produced during a period and also sold to another producer in that period (and in that sense completely used up in the making of other goods adding their value to that of those other goods)

internal vs. external national debt the portion of the national debt held by Americans vs. the portion held by foreigners

international demonstration effect the attempted emulation of the consumption levels of advanced countries by the populations of the poor countries

international liquidity the quantities of gold, convertible currencies and special drawing rights held by countries that can be used as international means of payments

International Monetary Fund an international organization founded in 1946 that tries to promote free international trade and lending by providing for sufficient international liquidity and normally stable exchange rates or orderly agreed-on changes therein

investment demand the amount private businesses are able and willing to spend in a period on buildings and equipment, plus the desired change in their inventories (including household expenditures on new residences), not necessarily equal to the amount they actually do spend (not necessarily equal to gross private domestic investment)

investment demand schedule a listing of a series of investment demand-GNP combinations, showing the dollar amounts private businesses as a group are able and willing to spend on goods in a period at alternative levels of GNP, graphed as the investment demand line

investment expenditures *see* gross private domestic investment

invisible hand the price system in a capitalist free-enterprise economy that coordinates (as if it were an invisible hand) the actions of self-seeking households and firms

involuntary unemployment U.S. definition: all members of the civilian labor force not working *at all* during the survey week (in which statistics are gathered) if they are currently available for work (even if, perhaps, temporarily ill), and if they (1) have looked for work in the preceding 4 weeks or (2) have not looked for work because they are (a) temporarily laid off subject to recall or (b) scheduled to begin a new job within 30 days

---

Joint Economic Committee a group of seven senators and seven representatives of the Congress

Juglar cycle intermediate 10-year cycles of business activity observed by Juglar

jurisdictional strike a strike arising not from a fight between union and management, but from a conflict between two or more competing unions all of which claim to be representatives of the workers

---

Kitchin cycle minor 4-year cycles of business activity observed by Kitchin

Kondratieff wave long 60-year cycles of business activity observed by Kondratieff

---

labor all types of human effort put forth in the process of production, physical as well as mental

labor books in the Soviet Union, a worker's passport giving a record of his work experience, introduced in 1938

laissez faire the doctrine that a capitalist economy works best with an absolute minimum of government intervention in economic life, such as protecting private property and upholding contracts

land natural resources in their natural state, or nonhuman gifts of nature

law of demand the observed tendency of quantity demanded to rise with a fall in price

law of diminishing returns the technical fact that, given at least one input fixed, and given technical know-how, *eventually* equal increases in one or more other inputs will add less and less to output, that is, yield declining marginal physical products

law of supply the observed tendency of quantity supplied to rise with a rise in price

legal tender money that must be accepted by law for the payment of debts (in the United States: coins and paper bills)

liability anything of value owed by someone

limited liability the liability of a corporate stockholder, which is limited to the price paid when purchasing the stock

long-run frictional unemployment *see* chronic unemployment

long-term capital movement in the balance of payments mainly the export or import of titles other than money

Lorenz curve a graphical device measuring the extent of inequality among persons of income or wealth

---

macroeconomics economic analysis dealing with the entire economy or large parts of it, an example being the theory of income or output determination

Malthusian doctrine a theory showing that man is doomed to misery if population grows at a steady rate and attempts to wrest more and more food from fixed land, given capital and technology

marginal capital-output ratio the change in the capital stock (required to produce extra output) divided by the change in output (requiring the aforementioned change in the capital stock)

marginal cost the change in total cost associated with a unit change in output. This marginal cost can be measured in a variety of ways, as by the change in the quantity or value of resources involved in producing the unit of output or by the change in the output of other goods that is made possible when producing a unit less of the good in question or that is required when producing a unit more

marginal external cost the change in total cost incurred by parties other than the producer of a good when the producer changes output of it by one unit

marginal outlay the change in expenditure to the buyer of an input when changing the input quantity bought by one unit

marginal output-capital ratio the reciprocal of the marginal capital-output ratio

marginal physical product the physical change in output caused by a unit change in the use of one input, given all other inputs and technical know-how

marginal private cost the change in total cost incurred by the producer of a good when the producer changes output of it by one unit; usually just called marginal cost

marginal propensity to consume disposable personal income the ratio of change in consumption demand over change in disposable personal income causing it

marginal propensity to consume GNP (or gross national income) the ratio of change in consumption demand over change in GNP (or gross national income) causing it

marginal revenue the change in total revenue associated with a unit change in output sold

marginal revenue product the value of the marginal physical product

marginal social cost the change in total cost incurred by society as a whole, including others as well as the producer, when changing output by one unit; equals the sum of marginal private and marginal external cost

margin requirements the requirement for a minimum down payment for stock purchases on credit

market all contact points between buyers and sellers of a good or resource, such as personal meetings, telephone calls, newspaper ads

market basket a collection of quantities of consumer goods that certain families typically buy, used to calculate the consumer price index

market economy an economy in which private owners of resources sell services for money to private firms in *resource markets* with firms producing the kinds and quantities of goods recipients of money income demand in *goods markets.*

material balance a Gosplan planning tool, listing and balancing in physical units all the sources and uses of a given commodity (material), equivalent to a processing sector row of an input-output table

mercantilism a doctrine according to which a nation gets rich by bringing about an excess of commodity and service exports over corresponding imports and importing gold for the difference

microeconomics economic analysis dealing with individual units in the economy, such as particular persons, firms, or markets, an example being the theory of profit maximization of the single firm

minimum wage the minimum wage that can legally be paid to certain groups of the labor force, as defined by the Fair Labor Standards Act

mixed economy the actual U.S. economy in which economic power is shared among private individuals and firms and various levels of government; thus resources are partly allocated through the "invisible hand," partly through conscious central decision

monetary balance same as a material balance, but in value terms instead of physical units

monetary policy regulation of the supply and cost of money in the United States by the Federal Reserve System in order to influence the levels of GNP, employment, and prices

money supply U.S. definition: the total of coins, paper bills, and demand deposits owned by the public (that is, by anyone other than the U.S. Treasury, the Federal Reserve System, or the commercial banks)

money vs. real income the actual number of dollars received (money income) vs. the quantity of goods they can buy (real income)

monopolistic competition a situation in which many sellers sell differentiated, but close substitute goods or resources

monopoly the only seller of a good or resource having no close substitutes

moral suasion an economic policy that relies solely on persuasion aimed at making people change their behavior voluntarily

multiplier an expression (usually containing marginal propensities) by which autonomous demands have to be multiplied to find mathematically the equilibrium level of GNP; in this book equal to

$$\frac{1}{1 - \text{mpc}}$$

national debt the total of U.S. government securities issued

national debt refunding paying off individual maturing government securities with funds obtained by the issue of new securities, leaving unchanged the total of securities issued

national income budget one of several budget concepts used by the U.S. federal government; a refinement of the consolidated cash budget used to measure the impact of the federal government on the economy

near-money any asset that can easily be exchanged for money, such as a savings account

near-poverty line an income level about one third above the poverty threshold

negative income tax a scheme according to which persons with low or zero income receive payment from, rather than make payment to, the government

net borrowed reserves the difference, if negative, between banks' excess reserves and their indebtedness to the Fed (*see also* free reserves)

net export demand the difference between the amount foreigners are able and willing to spend in a period on American goods and the amount Americans are able and willing to spend on foreign goods; equal to the difference between the amounts actually spent, or net exports; also equal to the balance of current account

net export demand schedule a listing of a series of net export demand-GNP combinations, showing the net dollar amounts foreigners as a group are able and willing to spend on American goods in a period at alternative levels of U.S. GNP, graphed as the net export demand line

net exports exports minus imports of goods, excluding gifts

net national income or product gross national product minus depreciation

net worth the difference between someone's assets and liabilities

New Economic Policy Lenin's policy beginning in 1921, allowing the operation of free markets in several sectors of the economy

new system of planning and management a system of decentralized planning being introduced in Eastern European economies since 1964

noneconomic wants wants that can be satisfied with goods that do not exist and cannot be made, or with free goods

nonprofit organizations private businesses serving households and businesses at cost, for example, certain athletic clubs, labor unions, schools, colleges, hospitals, churches, trade and welfare associations

nonrecourse loan the particular device used to support farm prices, whereby a farmer "pawns" his crop to the government and gets paid the support price value

nontariff barriers quotas and "red tape" restrictions on international trade

normative value of processing an experimental Soviet method of calculating output, similar to value-added

---

oligopoly one of few sellers of identical or differentiated, but substitute goods or resources

open-market operations the buying or selling of domestic securities by the Fed

operational lag the lag between the time economic policy is executed and the time the desired consequences appear

optimum firm the technically and economically best size of firm; may contain several plants

optimum plant the technically best size of plant

Orgnabor in the Soviet Union, a nationwide network to redistribute the labor force, as from farms to cities, among regions, and so on

output quota a command by a Central Planning Board to produce a certain amount of output and to deliver it to specified users

---

paper bills noninterest-bearing IOU's of the U.S. Treasury or the Federal Reserve Banks

parity price an agricultural support price set in such a way that a given quantity of a farm commodity can buy the same quantity of nonfarm commodities as in a specified earlier period

partial vs. general equilibrium analysis studying the behavior of one market at a time, assuming the equilibrium prices and quantities of all other markets are known (partial) vs. studying the behavior of all markets simultaneously, realizing that changes in one affect all others, that all are interdependent

partnership a private unincorporated business owned by two or more co-owners

party directives directives to Gosplan from the presidium of the Central Committee of the U.S.S.R. Communist party, specifying in broad terms the desired composition of next year's GNP

perfect competition a hypothetical economy that fulfills certain strict conditions: there are so numerous buyers and sellers that no single buyer or seller can by his own actions influence the market price; there is free entry into all markets; all market participants are fully informed, they consider all units of a good or resource as alike

perfect competitor any buyer or seller operating under the conditions of perfect competition

peril point a limit set by law below which tariffs cannot be set through administrative actions

personal consumption expenditures total expenditures on goods by households, except on residential houses

personal saving disposable personal income minus consumption demand

personal saving schedule a listing of a series of household saving-income combinations, showing the dollar amounts a household is able and willing to save in a period at alternative levels of income, graphed as the personal saving line

Phillips curve a graphical device illustrating the trade-off between unemployment and inflation

piggyback transport carrying truck trailers on railroad flat cars specially designed for this purpose

plan law in the Soviet Union, the parliamentary-approved draft plan of a period's economic activity

plant the physical production facility

pollution the dumping into the environment of something without value that nobody would pay for or accept as a gift; the wastes so dumped

pools business combinations designed to restrict competition by dividing up markets, sharing profits, and so on

potential GNP the value (at current prices) of the maximum quantity of goods that can be newly produced by fully employing our resources

potential labor force U.S. Bureau of the Census definition: everyone 16 or above, outside institutions

poverty income deficit the difference between the actual aggregate personal income of the poor and the total income required to give each family the poverty threshold income

poverty threshold the income level below which a family is counted as poor by the government

preferred stock as common stock, except that a claim on dividends prior to the common stockholder exists, but dividends are usually limited to a maximum percentage of the stock's face value

price controls governmental determination of prices, usually at levels above or below what would normally prevail

price leadership a phenomenon in oligopolistic markets in which all firms imitate the price changes of one firm, the "price leader"

price system in a capitalist economy the totality of interdependent prices in goods and resource markets to which self-seeking households and businessmen respond and which, in turn, change with their combined actions; the governor, or "invisible hand," of the free-enterprise economy

processing sector in input-output analysis the sector of the economy in which output is produced and in which intermediate goods are used up

process of consumption the process within a household of using and using up economic goods; direct want satisfaction, such as eating a cake or driving a car

process of production any activity outside a household that helps make available to people economic goods where and when they are wanted, such as manufacturing, transporting, storing, and selling a cake or car

producer the legal and administrative entity in charge of the process of production

production possibilities curve a graphical exposition of a production possibilities schedule

production possibilities schedule a listing of all the alternative combinations of two goods or groups of goods a producer is capable of producing in a given period by fully using a given total of resources with present technical know-how (the "producer" can also refer to a nation)

productive labor in the Soviet Union, all types of human effort contributing *eventually* to the production of a material object, such as labor in agriculture, industry, construction, and services serving these fields

profit the value of sales (after rebates and discounts) minus costs attributable to goods sold (such as wages, rent, and interest paid to hired resources, depreciation charged, indirect business taxes incurred, raw materials purchased)

progressive tax a tax that takes a larger *percentage* of higher than of lower incomes

proportional tax a tax that takes the same *percentage* of everyone's income

proxy a stockholder's permission for someone to vote in his stead at the stockholder's meeting

---

quantity demanded the physical amount of a good or resource that people are able and willing to buy at a given price

quantity supplied the physical amount of a good or resource that firms are able and willing to sell at a given price

quota *see* import quota, input quota, *and* output quota

---

rational prices the system of prices emerging in perfectly competitive equilibrium, wherein, for example, relative goods prices reflect every producer's relative marginal costs or relative resource prices reflect their relative marginal physical productivities

raw material any commodity bought or manufactured by a producer that is destined to be used up (physically or through resale) in the process of production, typically within a year

real capital *see* capital

real GNP looking at real GNP involves a comparison of the GNP's of different years, or countries, evaluating all data at the prices of any given year or country (*see also* deflating GNP)

recession a small depression

recognition lag the lag between the time economic policy becomes necessary and the time this is recognized

regressive tax a tax that takes a larger *percentage* of lower than of higher incomes

regulated monopoly a monopoly created and supervised by government for reasons of technical efficiency or public safety

rent in economic theory, a payment for the use of land; in practice, a payment for the use of land or capital

representative full-bodied money money that is exchangeable into an equal amount of full-bodied money

required reserves the reserve requirement (in percent) multiplied by the dollar amount of liabilities subject to the requirement

reserve requirement a requirement that a bank hold a dollar amount of designated assets (reserves) equal to at least a stated percentage of the dollar amount of certain liabilities

reserves the dollar amount of designated assets of a bank; for commercial member banks of the Federal Reserve System cash in vault plus demand deposits at the Fed

resource labor, land, or capital (also called factors of production and primary resources as opposed to intermediate goods); any ingredient used in the process of production

resource market a market in which resource services are traded, such as labor, land, capital

right-to-work law a state law outlawing the union shop

Rule of Reason a 1911 U.S. Supreme Court interpretation of the Sherman Act, making only deliberate and unreasonable "restraint of trade" illegal, not bigness as such

---

sales tax a tax on the sale of broad groups of commodities and services

sampling error the inevitable error resulting from the gathering of statistical data via sample surveys which makes the data only correct within a certain range (as $\pm$ 10 percent of a stated figure) and for a stated probability (such as nine out of ten cases)

saving the part of income not spent on consumer goods

savings account an interest-bearing liability of a bank, evidenced by nothing else but an entry in the bank's books, redeemable in money on demand or after due notice, not transferable by check; also called time deposit

Say's Law the classical economists' idea that *any* level of output is maintainable because incomes of equal value are generated in the process of production (correct) and all of income (no more, nor less) will voluntarily be spent (doubtful): "supply creates its own demand"

scarcity the fact that people's desire for economic goods in general exceeds their availability

scientific tariff a tariff set such that all domestic and foreign price differences disappear; would end all foreign trade

selective monetary controls Federal Reserve controls designed to affect particular borrowers and spenders rather than borrowers in general, such as consumer credit controls, stock market credit controls

self-fulfilling prophecy the fact that believing in something (perhaps because this belief shapes action) leads to its happening; for instance, if you believe you are inferior, you are likely to turn out inferior because you will not try hard enough to prove otherwise

seniority a rule according to which a person employed longer has to get preferential treatment over others, such as in pay, vacation, layoffs, rehiring, promotion

service the use of labor, land, or capital

shortage a situation in which quantity demanded exceeds quantity supplied at the given price

short-run frictional unemployment a type of (probably) short-run unemployment, caused by new entry into the labor force, seasonal factors, and regular labor turnover between different employers and locations

short-term capital movement in the balance of payments, mainly the export or import of money

Silver Certificate a type of paper bill issued by the U.S. Treasury and in process of retirement, redeemable in token "silver coins"

single proprietorship a private unincorporated business owned by a single person

slum any area where dwellings predominate which, by reason of dilapidation, overcrowding, faulty management or design, lack of ventilation, light or sanitation facilities, or any combination of these factors, are detrimental to safety, health, and morals (from the 1937 Housing Act)

social dividend in socialism, a payment of money income to every citizen derived from the use of publicly owned land and capital

socialism in its pure form, a society wherein land and capital are collectively owned and utilized

social overhead capital capital outside agriculture and industry, as transportation, communication, educational and health facilities

Soil Bank land taken out of production in order to restrict agricultural output and raise agricultural prices and income, as well as preserve land for nonagricultural purposes

solvency a situation in which net worth is positive

special drawing right an artificially created international means of payments established by agreement under the International Monetary Fund; "paper gold"

standard metropolitan statistical area an urban conglomeration consisting of at least one central city (with at least 50,000 inhabitants) and contiguous urban areas

state farm in the Soviet Union, a farm owned by the people as a whole

static efficiency the ability of an economy to maximize output from given resources and with given technical know-how

stock exchange an organized trading place where corporate stock certificates are bought and sold regularly

structural unemployment a category of chronic unemployment caused by changes in tastes or technology requiring for its elimination massive relocation and retraining of workers

supply a series of price-quantity combinations, showing the amounts of a good or resource people are able and willing to sell at alternative prices (*see also* quantity supplied *and* aggregate supply)

supply curve a supply schedule graphed

supply schedule for a single good or resource: a list showing alternative quantities supplied at alternative hypothetical prices, given all other factors

suppressed inflation inflation that is avoided only because of direct government price fixing, not by eliminating the causes for it

surplus a situation in which quantity supplied exceeds quantity demanded at the given price

---

tariff *see* customs duty

tax (amount) a compulsory payment to government without return of any special benefit to the taxpayer, equals tax rate times tax base

tax base the thing that is taxed, such as income, property value, purchase value

tax incidence where the burden of a tax ultimately rests

tax rate percentage of tax applied to the tax base

technostructure the group of experts managing large modern corporations

theory of income (or output) determination an explanation of the actual level of real GNP and employment and of changes therein

time deposit *see* savings account

title a certificate of ownership (deeds, stocks) or indebtedness (bonds, money, personal IOU's), including potential "certificates" (as an oral promise to pay)

token coins noninterest-bearing IOU's of the U.S. Treasury minted on metal with a monetary value exceeding the value of the metal contained

transfers income payments to households other than for their current contribution of labor or property services; examples are pensions, social security benefits, unemployment benefits, and (somewhat inconsistently) government bond interest

trend the average deviation of real GNP from its potential

trust the combination of several corporations under the trusteeship of a single board of directors, which manages their affairs jointly

trust certificate the equivalent of a share of common stock designating an ownership share in a trust, but usually nonvoting

trust fund in the case of government, a fund into which payments are made for unemployment insurance, life insurance, social security programs, and so on, and from which benefits are paid

turnover tax a Soviet sales tax

tying contracts a contract according to which a seller agrees to sell one good, but only if the buyer also buys another good from him; similarly, a buyer may agree to buy one good, but only if the seller sells him another good also

underdevelopment an extremely low level of real GNP per head

unemployment equilibrium an equilibrium level of GNP that coincides with unemployment of resources; because at full employment aggregate demand would fall short of the value of output (GNP), full employment cannot be maintained

unilateral transfer an entry in the balance of payments indicating the export (or import) of a "thank-you note" assumed equal in value to the gift imported (or exported)

union shop a situation in which all employees, within 30 days after hiring, have to become union members or at least pay union dues as a condition of continued employment

U.S. Note a type of paper bill issued by the U.S. Treasury, in process of retirement

unlimited liability the liability of an owner of a single proprietorship or partnership with almost all of his personal belongings for all debts of the business

unproductive labor in the Soviet Union, all types of human effort not resulting ultimately in a material object, such as labor in government administration, education, personal services

urban renewal a systematic program of slum eradication by tearing down or rehabilitating buildings

---

value added the value added by a given producer to the total of economic goods emerging from the productive process, that is, his production excluding the value of purchases from other firms incorporated in his production

velocity of money the rate at which money circulates, for example, income velocity that equals GNP divided by average money supply, or transactions velocity that equals total monetary transactions divided by average money supply

vertical merger the merger of a firm with its suppliers and customers, such as of an oil refiner with crude oil producers, railroads transporting crude and refined oil, and gasoline stations

voluntary unemployment all members of the potential labor force who do not want to work at the wage presently paid for the skill and experience they have to offer (as evidenced by the fact that they are neither working nor looking for work, hence the category includes discouraged workers)

---

wage a payment for the use of labor

wage-price guideposts rules of wage and price setting recommended by the President's Council of Economic Advisers to avoid cost-push inflation

War Communism the period in Soviet history immediately following the 1917 revolution

wholesale price index an index measuring the movement of prices paid by firms for goods they buy

workable competition imperfect competition among oligopolies that allegedly promotes progress at the cost of economic efficiency

---

young economy an economy with a relatively underdeveloped industrial sector

SYMBOLS

The following list gives the meaning of all symbols and abbreviations used in this book. If you wish, you can turn to the Glossary for more exact definitions.

AD	aggregate demand
AFL	American Federation of Labor
AS	aggregate supply, equals the GNP
C	personal consumption expenditures
CIO	Congress of Industrial Organizations
D	demand
EEC	European Economic Community
EFTA	European Free Trade Association
G	government expenditures on goods
GATT	General Agreement on Tariffs and Trade
GNP	gross national product
GSP	gross social product
I	gross private domestic investment
IMF	International Monetary Fund
IOU	"I owe you," a promissory note or certificate of indebtedness
MPC	marginal propensity to consume disposable personal income
mpc	marginal propensity to consume GNP (or gross national income)
NVP	normative value of processing
NX	net exports, or exports minus imports of goods, excluding gifts
P	price
Q	quantity demanded or supplied
S	supply
SDR	special drawing right
SUNFED	Special United Nations Fund for Economic Development
UNEPTA	United Nations Expanded Program for Technical Assistance
X	commercial exports of goods
Y	gross national income, gross national expenditure, gross national product

index